AUTISM AND AUTISTIC-LIKE CONDITIONS
IN MENTAL RETARDATION

AUTISM AND AUTISTIC-LIKE CONDITIONS IN MENTAL RETARDATION

Dirk Kraijer

SWETS & ZEITLINGER PUBLISHERS

| LISSE | ABINGDON | EXTON(PA) | TOKYO |

Library of Congress Cataloging-in-Publication Data

Kraijer, Dirk W., 1936-
    [Zwakzinnigheid, autisme en aan autisme verwante stoornissen.
    Dutch, 2th ed.]
    Autism and autistic-like conditions in mental retardation / Dirk
Kraijer
        p.   cm.
    Includes bibliographical references and index.
    ISBN 9026514638
    1. Mental retardation.   2. Autism in children.   3. Autism.
    4. Autism in mental retardation--Psychological aspects.
    5. Developmental disablities--Psychological aspects.   I. Title.
    RJ506.M4K6813 1997
    616.85'88--dc21   97-29573
                                                                    CIP

Translation: Ellie van Saane-Hijner, assisted by Phil Brammer

On the inside pages: 'The world is too much for me', the portrait of a four-teen-year-old severely mentally retarded boy with an Autistic Disorder. This boy had his own favourite spot on a settee upon which he would sit whilst hiding beneath a blanket.

Cover design and inside page illustration: Juul Kraijer
Printed in the Netherlands by Grafisch productiebedrijf Gorter, Steenwijk

Copyright © 1997, Swets & Zeitlinger B.V., PO Box 825, 2160 SZ, Lisse,
The Netherlands

ISBN 90 265 1463 8
NUGI 758

FOREWORD

The way in which the present volume came into being is rather complicated. The study was originally written in Dutch. Shortly after its first edition in 1991, a grant was awarded for an English translation. Preparations for a second revised Dutch edition were made as soon as it became clear that the first edition would sell out. This second Dutch edition was published in 1994.

Arranging for the translation and the translation itself took much more time than I, at least, had anticipated. Meanwhile a third Dutch revised edition was called for. This edition was also to include the manual to and the rationale of the PDD-MR scale, an instrument devised for the identification of a PDD in mentally retarded persons. This scale had been published in Dutch in 1990; a slightly revised version was issued in 1992. The additions and amendments made in the second and third Dutch editions of the book, time-consuming in themselves, also found their way into the translation. Consequently, the translated version of the book may be regarded as the most complete and up-to-date possible.

Writing a book such as this and the research upon which it is based leans heavily on the collaboration, support and guidance of a great many people. I feel obliged to name some in particular, but at the same time fear that I may fail to mention some persons whose contributions were nonetheless very important.

Chronologically, the first person to whom I feel greatly indebted is Eddy Hoejenbos, child psychiatrist and for many years head of the Hendrik van Boeijen-Oord (Assen, the Netherlands). Hoejenbos was without a doubt the first person to arouse my interest in the intriguing, arresting and saddening phenomenon of 'retraction.' In 1960 the staff of the Hendrik van Boeijen-Oord had been won over to the view that autism and related disorders occur quite frequently in mentally retarded people, but this insight still had to gain general acceptance in the outside world. Even nowadays the extent and nature of the problems resulting from autism in mentally retarded people are insufficiently understood. This is indeed my main reason for writing this book.

5

The clinical psychologist Ron van Raalte, a colleague from the very beginning of my career, certainly also deserves to be mentioned. His then pioneering approach to profoundly mentally retarded people was particularly inspiring to me.

When the collection of research data began in 1968, this coincided with the opening of the Eekwal Observation Home, an extension of the Hendrik van Boeijen-Oord. At this observation home a team of experts from various disciplines collaborates in the diagnosis, treatment and the framing of recommendations concerning people with developmental deficits and concurrent disabilities. Mentioning all team members who in the course of my research project made important contributions would certainly make too long a list. Suffice it to name but a few. Frits Haaksema and his successor Jan Willem Postma, heads of the nursing staff, represent the group of attendants. The psychiatrist and neurologist Wim Kronenberg, a perceptive diagnostician, greatly enriched my views. My long collaboration with child psychiatrist Henk Jan Boevé and neurologist Joke Weits was an invaluable experience. Hans Kleve, physiotherapist-kinesitherapist, Janny Ezinga, speech therapist-audiologist, the special-education teachers Dout Schut and Alie Punt, the paediatrician Gottlieb Nelck, and Fenna van der Meulen, social worker, apart from contributing much from their own fields of expertise, should also be thanked for their long and dedicated service.

I appealed many times and never in vain to many psychologists and educational-psychologists working at the Hendrik van Boeijen-Oord, if only to provide me with classifications, PDD-MRS assessments and diagnoses of persons under their care. Of these I want to mention Marian Blom, Geert Kuiper, Piet Meerse, Alice Miener, Gerharda de Munnik, Gerrit van Osch and Netty Witmer. Staff members, psychologists and educational psychologists of twenty institutions and child day-care centres have also been very helpful in this respect.

At a much later date I was deeply impressed by lectures given by Ruud Minderaa, now professor of Child and Adolescent Psychiatry at the University of Groningen. I shared his view that it is vitally important to specify the discriminating features which differentiate autism and especially related disorders from many other conditions, among them what the DSM-IV has labelled attention-deficit and disruptive behaviour disorders. We also agreed that all of these disorders occur much more frequently than is generally assumed.

Molle Eijer, former professor of Child and Adolescent Psychiatry at the University of Groningen, spent many hours reading the manuscript and discussing it with me.

At the Hendrik van Boeijen-Oord I was now not only given free rein, but also the facilities needed to organize research and examine data. Additional financial support was given, if necessary, by a foundation for the promotion of health care (Stichting Dienstbetoon Gezondheidszorg, Soesterberg), for which I am also very grateful.

Our library provided essential services; Paul Verheugt in particular did a great deal in his unassuming manner to trace the many publications needed for a book of this sort.

The translation of the book was for the largest part financed by the Netherlands Organisation for Scientific Research (Nederlandse Organisatie voor Wetenschappelijk Onderzoek, The Hague). Ellie van Saane-Hijner fulfilled her translation task conscientiously; she involved me in the entire process much more than I would have thought possible. On more than one occasion she even forced me to improve the wording of my Dutch manuscript. Thus she did more than merely translate, and I consider the text to have benefitted from our many discussions. Ellie also secured the assistance of an English native speaker for the final stages of translation. Phil Brammer, an experienced editor of scientific publications, collaborated with Ellie in polishing the English.

I have saved my last words of gratitude for Trui van der Veen. With the commitment and accuracy which she has already brought to bear in the preparation of manuscripts for many other publications, she has prepared the present text and its numerous tables. An indispensable contribution!

CONTENTS

14

15

PART I

UNDERLYING PRINCIPLES

CHAPTER I.1

INTRODUCTION

The subject of the present study is autism. In contrast to previous studies, this book looks at autism from the perspective of a professional in the field of mental retardation. Although it is primarily intended for mental retardation professionals, a considerable number of findings and conclusions will apply to the entire population of persons with autism and related contactual disorders, as a very high percentage of autistic persons are functioning at retarded levels.

My work as a clinical psychologist and educationalist within a large residential institution for the mentally retarded and in a clinical setting for observation, diagnosis and treatment of children and adults with developmental deficits and additional disorders, provided the material for the present study.

This book discusses in broad outline a number of aspects of *autism and related disorders within the population of the mentally retarded*. There are good reasons indeed to single out this group of autistic persons from the entire population of autistic individuals. In the behavioural respect alone, mentally retarded autistic persons and autistic persons of normal intelligence, while having many characteristics in common, also display considerable differences, as Bartak and Rutter (1976), among others, have pointed out. According to these authors, "Mentally retarded autistic children more often show self-injury, finger stereotypies, deviant social responses, and delayed social development. [...] The present findings demonstrate that mentally retarded autistic children are much more likely [...] to have a worse outcome in terms of educational attainment and employment." Of no less importance is the fact that within the entire population of the mentally retarded it is possible to discriminate between autistic and non-autistic children, adolescents and adults, on the basis of behavioural differences (Jacobson & Ackerman, 1990; Kraijer, 1987a, 1990, 1991).

Although autism in mental retardation has received some attention since the early Sixties, albeit only incidental in the earlier years, I think that almost everywhere in the world knowledge and understanding of the size, nature and gravity of the problems concerning the group of mentally retarded individuals with autism and related disorders is still highly inadequate. A good illustration of this is to be found in the *Annotated bibliography of recent research on dual diagnosis* drawn up by Sturmey and Sevin (1993). Their bibliography contains titles of studies which, on the basis of the DSM-III-R classification system, focussed on mental health needs in persons with intellectual disabilities. Under the heading: 'Disorders usually evident in infancy, childhood or adolescence' a general category which includes autism and related disorders, only three articles are mentioned. One deals with anorexia nervosa, another one with anorexia nervosa and depression and only one with pervasive developmental disorders and psychoses. None of the titles of studies mentioned under the other headings, covering a total of 178 articles, makes reference to autism or pervasive developmental disorders. Similarly, the most recent edition of *Mental Retardation, Definition, Classification and Systems of Supports*, published in 1992 by the American Association on Mental Retardation, contains no information about the prevalence of autism or pervasive developmental disorders, although the concurrence of mental retardation with psychiatric disorders and personality disorders is considered at length. Crews et al. (1994), studying inhabitants of a large residential facility for individuals with mental retardation, found that only 1.81% of the 1273 persons investigated displayed one of the additional Disorders Usually First Evident in Infancy, Childhood or Adolescence.

Two examples taken from the situation in the Netherlands may also serve to illustrate my point.

- In 1990 a fact-finding survey was carried out in the Netherlands to explore the need for specialized training in the field of autism. One of the questions put to residential institutions for the mentally retarded was: "How many cases of autism and autistic-like conditions are found among the mentally retarded young, adolescent and adult residents of your institution at this moment?" Usable returns were obtained from 67 institutions, jointly in charge of 19,453 mentally retarded residents, constituting about two-thirds of the total population of mentally retarded persons in residential care. Eleven of these institutions, together representing 1,243 residential places, reported that they had no autistic residents at all. The remaining 56 institutions reported a total number of 1,053 autistic residents. This would mean that 5.4% of all residents of these institutions are individuals with autism or related disorders.
- Another fact-finding survey carried out in the same year in this country was concerned with the prevalence of severe behavioural problems in residential institutions for the mentally retarded (Schuring et al., 1990). Additionally, more detailed information was gathered from a sample of 211 residents with severe behavioural problems. With respect to their diagnoses, the writers reported that contactual disorders had been observed in nearly thirty residents, many of them having been labelled autistic or autistic-like, but that only a minority of cases had firmly been diagnosed as autistic. If 'nearly thirty' is understood to mean 29, it must be inferred that, of this sample of persons with highly disruptive beha-

viour, some 13.7% were suffering from autism or related contactual disorders.

However, even if allowance is made for the fact that in the three instances only samples were studied, the real percentages cannot possibly be as low as has been suggested above, as I intend to demonstrate in various ways.

Before elaborating on this point, a terminological question should be discussed first. Until now the terms *autism, related (contactual) disorders* and *autistic-like conditions* have been employed. However, in the two most important international classification systems, DSM-III-R/-IV (1987, 1994) and ICD-10 (1992), the entire spectrum of autism and autistic-like conditions is collectively termed Pervasive Developmental Disorders (PDD); this is a term which has provoked valid criticism (from, among others, Gillberg, 1991; Happé & Frith, 1991), but has also been defended with equally reasonable arguments (Volkmar & Cohen, 1991). As this study uses the DSM-III-R classification system, the present work will conform to the same terminology. Personally I have in fact come to prefer the term pervasive developmental disorder (or, more briefly, pervasive disorder). The condition differs substantially from pure mental retardation. A mentally retarded person shows a rather consistent delay in all aspects of development, a delay which has to a large extent been quantified and is therefore fairly well identifiable. Given the limits set by this delay, a person may function *in a reasonably sound and harmonious way.* By contrast, many persons with PDD, notably those with a fair level of functioning, are at first sight not very disabled. Moreover, the nature and extent of the disability may be disguised by good or even excellent performance in small and very specific domains. Actually, however, the disability is a great handicap, especially in *social* and *emotional* areas. As a consequence, many a person with a PDD lives a *disharmonious or even unhappy existence,* his specific skills, if present, constituting islets of ability.

To summarize, mental retardation is in my view a disability which mainly stems from a more or less quantifiable developmental *deficit*, whereas a PDD is a disability which mainly stems from a specific developmental *disturbance* or *distortion* which can only be described qualitatively and which insidiously pervades all aspects of functioning.

I would now like to indicate more explicitly what I hope to demonstrate:

1 classification and diagnosis of all forms of PDD in mentally retarded individuals is possible, in spite of the many difficulties involved;
2 the behaviour profile of mentally retarded PDD persons is clearly distinguishable from that of otherwise comparable non-PDD persons;
3 pervasive developmental disorders occur much more frequently in mentally retarded people than is generally assumed;
4 management and treatment of mentally retarded PDD children is in many respects a difficult task, requiring a specific approach;

5   mentally retarded PDD persons show significantly more behavioural problems than otherwise comparable non-PDD persons;
6   prognoses as to future developments are significantly more unfavourable for mentally retarded PDD persons than for otherwise comparable non-PDD persons.

To find evidence research within various types of facilities has been carried out. A preliminary study was done among a group of mentally retarded children who were clinically observed and (tentatively) treated in an observation home. On the one hand this study should be seen as a blueprint for future research into the prevalence of pervasive developmental disorders in a population of mentally retarded people. On the other hand it is still only an exploratory study, as the group in question is in all probability not representative for the entire population of mentally retarded children. A subsequent study focussed on two types of facilities which have much experience with and thorough understanding of mentally retarded PDD persons: residential institutions for the mentally retarded and day-care centres for mentally retarded children.

As one of my primary concerns was that the results of my studies should be as well founded as possible, the residential institution selected was a large one and both this setting and the day-care centres were known to possess a comparatively high degree of knowledge and expertise in the field of PDD.

In the second place I wanted my conclusions to be based not only on a clinical classification (according to successively the DSM-III-R and DSM-IV manuals), but on a diagnosis which leaned on a valid and reliable measuring instrument. To this end the PDD-MR Scale (original Dutch version: Kraijer, 1990) was developed.

The present book is divided into three parts. The first part deals with general issues. The next chapter will deal with the history of changing views on the dual disability of mental retardation and PDD, and recapitulates some research findings concerning this dually diagnosed group, taken both from relevant literature and from the present writer's own research.

In Part II the results are presented of my study amongst a group of 393 children who had been admitted for observation in the observation clinic 'Eekwal', Assen, The Netherlands, of whom 137 were suffering from autism or related disorders. They all stayed for at least a few months in the home. Chapter II.1 gives a general description of the sample studied. In Chapter II.2, the behavioural problems of PDD and non-PDD children in the observation home are compared. Chapter II.3 focusses on the thorny problems encountered in everyday clinical practice with the classification (and diagnosis) of pervasive disorders. Chapter II.4 discusses some aspects of treatment and management of mentally retarded PDD children. Finally, Chapter II.5 follows the later career of PDD individuals after their stay in the observation home.

In Part III, other categories of mentally retarded persons are considered. First a description is given of the PDD-MRS (Scale of Pervasive Developmental Disorder in Mentally Retarded Persons), and its place in the diagnostic process is pointed out. The scale is a valid and reliable measuring instrument, specially devised to detect pervasive developmental disorders in mentally retarded persons of all levels of functioning. Chapter III.2 gives a description of my research concerning the prevalence of pervasive disorders in the total population of the mentally retarded. This is the most extensive study to date, particularly as far as the group of profoundly, severely and moderately mentally retarded persons is concerned. Moreover, the diagnostics were partly based on the application of the PDD-MRS. In Chapters III.3 and III.4 some crucial idiosyncrasies of mentally retarded PDD individuals are examined in greater detail. Special attention is given to their self-isolation, the characteristics of their temperament, and their high chance of displaying difficulties in behaviour, as demonstrated by a comparative study. In Chapters III.5 and III.6 the prevalence of pervasive developmental disorders in two special groups of mentally retarded people, respectively those with Down syndrome and those with fragile-X syndrome, are considered.

In the concluding chapter the views and findings presented in Parts II and III are evaluated and possible future developments discussed.

Additionally, Appendix A provides a detailed report of the problems encountered when classifying mentally retarded people for the presence of a PDD in terms of the DSM-IV (1994), and Appendix B presents complete directions for the use of the PDD-MRS along with a sample of the scale form.

THE RELATIONSHIP BETWEEN MENTAL RETARDATION, AUTISM AND AUTISTIC-LIKE CONDITIONS

I.2.1 Early concepts of autism and mental retardation

'Autism' and mental retardation are nowadays regarded as two basically independent conditions. In other words, mentally retarded persons can be either autistic or not, and conversely, autistic persons can either be mentally retarded or not. However, before this became a widely accepted view, noticeable changes took place in the views held with regard to the two concepts. The first scholar to be mentioned here is Leo Kanner. In his famous article, written in 1943, he said, concerning features of the autistic condition he had found: "These characteristics form a unique 'syndrome', not heretofore reported, which seems to be rare enough, yet is probably more frequent than is indicated by the paucity of observed cases. It is quite possible that some such children have been viewed as feeble-minded or schizophrenic. In fact, several children of our group were introduced to us as idiots or imbeciles ..." Kanner, for his part, was convinced that his young patients were in fact intellectually quite normal. But he did admit that, if a general intelligence test was administered (which in this case was the Binet test), an average intelligence was generally not demonstrable. Only on the Seguin form board, which is, even within the domain of testing performance, a very limited test, these children did well. But it was on these partial test results that Kanner based his opinion, pointing furthermore to their intelligent physiognomies, their astounding vocabulary (especially on the reproductive level), their phenomenal rote memory, the absence of physical and motor defects, and, finally, to the fact that they had highly intelligent parents. Later evidence showed that he had unintentionally chosen a sample of young patients which had been strongly biased with respect to educational opportunities and parental intellectual level (see, for instance, Schopler et al., 1979b).

Only an outline of the history of subsequent changes in professional views on the relationship between autism (broadly defined by some authors, narrowly by others) and mental retardation can be given here, leaving many ideas and contributions unconsidered.

Tredgold, in the *Textbook of Mental Deficiency*, writes absolutely nothing about autism, not even in its eighth edition of 1952, although, quite remarkably, his index does include the name Leo Kanner. Kanner is quoted here only because of his study, published in 1938, which related to the family histories of mentally defective delinquents.

On the other hand, in Sarason's handbook *Psychological Problems in Mental Deficiency* (1953), much space is devoted to a discussion of Kanner's descriptions of 'inborn autistic disturbance of affective contact.' Autism is, in Sarason's view, "one of the clinical syndromes sometimes mistaken for mental deficiency." On the one hand this is a step forward, but on the other hand the author fails to recognize that (many of) these children are actually mentally deficient. He believes that, in so far as some of these children may seem mentally deficient, their condition is merely transitory, provided proper treatment is given. A similar view can be found in Baker's handbook *Exceptional Children* (1959), when dealing with "... the autistic child who is a pseudodefective type, incorrectly diagnosed as mentally retarded."

Even as recently as 1956 no suggestion whatsoever that mentally retarded children might be autistic could be found in the third edition of a Dutch short monograph on mental retardation (written by Herderschêe, then a very influential Dutch authority in the field).

Van Krevelen wrote in 1959 that autistic persons, rather than being intelligent, were actually suffering from intellectual malfunctioning. According to him, autistic children are not open-minded towards the wealth of experiences which the world offers. They don't explore their surroundings. Their fascination for particular elements of reality, their disposition to obsessiveness, in other words, points to limited capacities and flaws in intelligence. This is still a sound line of reasoning.

In *Infantile Autism* (1964), an authoritative study at the time, Rimland writes "... autism is a rare and unique form of oligophrenia", and (elsewhere in the same book): "autism tends strongly to occur under conditions which also predispose toward other forms of mental retardation."

A quite different approach is used in the research of Lotter. In his two extensive epidemiological studies of 1966 and 1967 he comes to the conclusion that 84.4% of autistic children in the age-group of eight to ten years (chronological age) had a performance IQ level of 79 or below. In other words, there is evidence available to suggest that autistic persons can be either mentally retarded or not.

Asperger (1968), however, who studied a group of patients with a syndrome he termed 'autistic psychopathy', persisted in describing them as highly intelligent; but, as has been pointed out by Van Krevelen (1963), Asperger (1968), and Rutter and Schopler (1987), these patients are (still) not quite comparable with autistic persons in general.

An illustrative example of the confusion and lack of clarity in this field can be found in a 1968 study by Frye, whose work in Nijmegen (The Netherlands) undoubtedly made her a pioneer in the treatment of autism. Opposing Rimland, she stated that the seven autistic children she observed functioned initially on an idiotic level. But should this term idiotic be understood in the broad and dated sense of the word? Might not just a casual remark of, say, a general practitioner have been reported here? It is a fact, in any case, that one of her well-known patients, Siem L., said, even before his first birthday, "tick-tock" when standing with his father in front of a clock, that he walked alone between his first and his second birthdays, and that, when it was about meal-time, he would fetch a pillow and, laying his head down upon it, wait to be given his bottle (being bottle-fed until he was two years old). He had, however, developmental lags in the areas of speaking, bowel and bladder control, and play interests. When he was admitted to the clinic on 26-10-1936, at the age of almost four, he obtained a Bühler-DQ of 80. The Stanford-Binet-IQ scores of six other children, later admitted, and similarly tested when about four years old, were respectively: 60, 62, 'between 70 and 100', 98, 75 and 65. I omit their often (much) higher Merrill-Palmer scores, because of the test's heavy emphasis on performance skills. From the biographies of these seven children, too, no impression of an idiotic level of functioning emerges. In fact, viewed from a present-day perspective, Frye studied comparatively intelligent PDD children, some of them not even mentally retarded. Thus considered, it is quite understandable that Frye refused to recognize that autism can be (and quite often is) accompanied by mental retardation. Clearly, Frye used a lopsided method. Only successful treatments are reported and she herself declares (on page 29) that, in addition to the seven cases described in her book, she had seen other autistic children or children with autistic-like behaviour, but that these children could not be treated as successfully because they suffered from serious demonstrable brain-damages, due to such causes as birth trauma, tuberculosis and meningitis. Was it not only due to their demonstrable brain damage and (strong likelihood of) mental retardation that Frye regarded these children not to be bona fide cases of autism?

In 1968, Wassing and Van Krevelen argued that splinter skills in autistic persons need not be indicative of high intelligence. According to these authors intelligence should not be regarded as a simple, homogeneous attribute, but as a system consisting of quite a number of specific skills and processes. Consequently, performance rates which are based on only one or few cognitive processes should never be used as indicators of 'the' intelligence.

Four years later, in 1972, Van Krevelen elaborated on this view by stating that he believed infantile autism to be primarily a contactual disorder, with intellectual impairment or in many cases mental retardation as a secondary consequence. Autism should be seen as *a separate syndrome,* to be diagnosed as such, since etiological factors other than mental retardation may be responsible for it.

Meanwhile, the observations of another expert, Hoejenbos, were not receiving the attention they deserved. As early as 1960 he had written an article about the relationship between autism and mental retardation, and was the first author, as far as I know, to do so from the viewpoint of the mental retardation field. He introduced the term *retraction syndrome,* which resembles PDD-Autistic-Disorder (DSM-III-R), its key features being: withdrawal from human contact, self-absorbtion, occasionally accompanied by a tendency to use human beings impersonally. It is this syndrome in its most extreme form which Hoejenbos labels infantile autism. Other conditions, many of them less pronounced in character, such as schizophrenic-like conditions in childhood and Mahler's symbiotic psychosis, are also subsumed within the same clinical group. Hoejenbos points out that the causes of these disorders are often unknown, but that in some cases there is evidence of brain damage, and in others social-environmental factors might be held responsible. The question of etiology is therefore left open by Hoejenbos, as it still is by present-day classification systems. His research study, published in 1963, covered 280 residents of a residential institution for the mentally retarded, aged under twenty years and most of whom were functioning at a severe or moderate level of mental retardation. Hoejenbos found that forty residents (i.e., around 15%) fitted into the picture of retraction syndrome, a syndrome which, according to him, is *a disorder which is very common in mentally retarded persons, but at the same time fundamentally unrelated to mental retardation.* It took quite some time before this view found a broader acceptance in the mental retardation field. Even in the late Sixties I personally knew of institutions where the staff sincerely believed that there were no autistic persons at all among their residents.

The Seventies saw a gradually increasing interest in the dual disability of mental retardation and autism, especially narrowly defined autism. DeMyer et al. (1974) reported that 97% of a group of autistic children of a mean age of 5.5 years had verbal IQs below 67, while 79% had performance IQs in the same range; follow-up tests of these same children at a mean age of 11.5 years yielded percentages of 84% and 76%, respectively. Wing (1976) came to the conclusion that only one in five autistic children obtain normal average scores on intelligence tests. According to Klijn (1978), 90% of the scores obtained by autistic children on intelligence tests were indicative of 'feeble-minded, imbecile, or idiotic levels.' DeMyer (1979), presenting figures for general intelligence in autistic adults, concluded that "only about 11% at later ages have a general (combined verbal and perceptual-motor) IQ in the normal range, about 11% achieve borderline normal general intellectual skills." The remainder (78%) was found to have a general IQ in the mentally retarded range.

I.2.2 Differential diagnostics of autism and mental retardation

From the Seventies on, the differential diagnostics of autism and mental retardation began to attract professional attention. By now the problem had become abundantly clear: a great number of autistic persons are also mentally retarded. However, the autistic and non-autistic retarded individuals not only display differences, but also similarities in behavioural characteristics and defects, such as retarded speech and stereotypic motions and actions (e.g., see Kraijer, 1990). Clearly, differential diagnostics can be a great help, and clinical observation alone will not always suffice to find final answers.

As might be expected, there have been efforts to develop special instruments to this end, and to the more general objective of detecting and delineating autism within the realm of normality and that of the other psychiatric conditions. The first full-fledged scale was developed by Rimland in 1968 (first version), and is known as the Diagnostic Checklist for Behavior Disturbed Children. Current scales most frequently used are: CARS (Childhood Autism Rating Scale, developed by Schopler et al., 1980) and ABC (Autism Behavior Checklist, developed by Krug et al., 1980). In the Netherlands the AUTI-scale has been issued (Van Berckelaer-Onnes et al., 1981); a revised version of this scale, covering an age-range up to and including twelve and based on a larger norm group, was completed ten years later (Van Berckelaer-Onnes & Hoekman, 1991). Most scales are able to distinguish autistic and non-autistic retarded persons, especially as far as differences in group averages are concerned (Van Berckelaer-Onnes & Snijders-Oomen, 1982; Teal & Wiebe, 1986; Rutter & Schopler, 1987; Volkmar et al., 1988). However, they are not always suitable to the same degree for all age-ranges and all levels of functioning. Moreover, these instruments are for the most part primarily devised to test narrowly defined autism, not the whole spectrum of pervasive developmental disorders. Chapter III.1 comes back to this issue.

Recently, another scale was published, the AVZ, followed by a slightly revised version, the AVZ-R (Kraijer, 1990, 1992). The scale is quick and easy to administer instrument of classification, in which the concept Pervasive Developmental Disorder, according to the DSM (and to the ICD-10) have been operationalized specifically for mentally retarded persons. The scale is suitable for subjects in the profound, severe, moderate and mild ranges of mental retardation, covering the chronological age-range 2-55 years. An English version of the AVZ-R scale has been published under the name PDD-MRS, Scale of Pervasive Developmental Disorder in Mentally Retarded Persons. The scale is a valid and reliable measuring instrument within the limits of what it intends to measure. For further details the reader is referred to Chapter III.1 and to Appendix B in which directions for the use of the scale are presented as well as a sample form.

Apart from the specially designed scales, differential diagnostic research has also applied intelligence tests. Time and again the findings indicate that autistic persons have serious additional speech and language problems.

On this subject, I would like first to discuss some important research studies which have been done outside the Netherlands and which are based on clearly delineated samples.

In the first place, two studies by DeMyer et al. (1972, 1974) should be mentioned.

In the 1972 study, one of the objectives of DeMyer and her colleagues was to compare 54 autistic and 29 non-autistic subnormal children, whose group means of chronological age ranged from 56.1 to 71.8 months; the researchers developed a special test battery to fill the gap between the Bayley and WPPSI tests. On all points the autistic children were less advanced than the non-autistic retarded children; the aspects measured were: motor, perceptual-motor, perceptual and verbal performance. It was in verbal performance, however, that the difference was greatest, and also significant.

In the 1974 study of DeMyer et al., the WISC scores of 115 autistic children, nearly all of them mentally retarded, were compared with those of non-autistic retarded children. As far as the full-scale IQ was concerned, the autistic children obtained scores which were significantly - even up to 20 points! - below those of the non-autistic children. In both the autistic and non-autistic retarded children, verbal IQ (VIQ) was below performance IQ (PIQ). However, the VIQ/PIQ discrepancy was widest in the autistic children, averaging up to as many as 30 points in the subgroup of moderately retarded children. Further, the authors claimed that their findings were very reliable. Follow-up measurements six years later produced stability coefficients for VIQ, PIQ and full-scale IQ of .58, .63 and .70, respectively.

Two research studies of Ando and Yoshimura (1979) and Ando et al. (1980) should be mentioned as well. They compared 47 autistic and 128 non-autistic mentally retarded children in the age-range 6-14 years, all of them attending a special school. These children functioned intellectually at severely and moderately retarded levels. With respect to receptive and expressive language skills the autistic children were significantly less advanced than the non-autistic group. The autistic children also displayed considerably more maladaptive behaviour, notably: self-injury, aggression, destruction, hyperactivity, withdrawal, avoidance of eye contact, and stereotypy. In a number of social skills, too, such as toilet training, participation in group activities, initiative, and 'self-control', these children had significantly lower levels of performance, although they did perform better with respect to eating skills. Finally, non-autistic retarded children had better results with respect to reading and writing skills, and numerical concepts. Over the years, the autistic children of the age category studied showed a slight improvement with respect to academic skills and a significant improvement with respect to adaptive behaviours. In general, however, the difference with the non-autistic retarded children continued to be significant. Similar results were obtained by Jacobson and Ackerman (1990); they report: "... developmental patterns of children and adolescents with autism and mental retardation were more similar for basic activities of daily living and self-care skills than for more academic or social skills..."

Only a limited number of studies dealing with autistic retarded persons employ (social functioning) scales specially devised to test retarded subjects. No such procedure was followed, for instance, in the extensive study by Bartak and Rutter (1973a,b), nor in any of the studies included in the handbooks of Schopler and Reichler (1976) and Schopler and Mesibov (1983). In the research studies of Ando et al. mentioned above, only an abridged and adapted form of the Adaptive Behavior Scale was employed, which is again not a full-scale examination tool.

Before reviewing Dutch studies based on general intelligence tests and on scales developed in the field of mental retardation, I would like to mention some research findings obtained by means of social functioning scales which are also suitable for samples of average-normal subjects. Gould (1977), using the Vineland Social Maturity Scale (Doll, 1953) and the Reynell Developmental Language Scales, found that with regard to social maturity the scores of autistic mentally retarded persons were only just significantly lower than those of non-autistic Down syndrome persons, and with regard to language skills highly significantly lower. Volkmar et al. (1987), using a new version of the VSMS, the Vineland Adaptive Behavior Scales (Sparrow et al., 1984), found that autistic children functioned significantly lower on the subscales Communication and Socialization, whereas no difference could be demonstrated on the subscales Daily Living Skills and Motor Skills. In addition, the autistic children displayed more maladaptive behaviour. Loveland and Kelley (1988), again using the VABS, found exactly the same profile in mentally retarded adolescents and young adults with autism with regard to the subscales Communication, Socialization and Daily Living Skills as Volkmar et al. (1987). Loveland and Kelley (1991), Rodrigue et al. (1991), Fombonne (1992), and Volkmar et al (1993), again using the VABS, found in young autistic children and adolescents only delays in Socialization. However, it may be important to point out that in the studies of Fombonne and Volkmar et al. the control groups partly consisted of children with language disorders.

Finally, I would like to consider a number of important research findings reported in publications of Baron-Cohen (e.g., 1992, 1993) and of Leslie and Frith (e.g., 1990). Although in these studies no explicit comparison was made between mentally retarded autistic children and mentally retarded non-autistic children, their findings show clearly that, with respect to 'Theory of mind', significantly better results were obtained by non-autistic mentally retarded children, even those of a somewhat lower mental age, than by autistic children. This means that mentally retarded children are not specifically impaired in their ability to understand mental states (such as beliefs, desires, intentions etc.), either of themselves or of others. On these - not directly observable - mental states predictions concerning other people's behaviour are based.

To summarize, the following conclusions may be drawn: autistic retarded persons compare unfavourably with non-autistic retarded persons with regard to social skills (doing things together, consideration for others, ability to understand and predict other people's behaviour), communicative language, and reading and writing skills. With regard to the rather technical aspects of social functioning or 'daily skills', such as the ability to dress and undress and do household chores, the level of performance of autistic retarded persons often equals that of non-autistic retarded persons. This seems also to apply to motor skills. Not surprisingly therefore, Loveland and Kelley (1988) conclude: "Our results show that domains of adaptive behaviour should be assessed separately." Exactly the same thing could be said with regard to the findings of the Dutch research studies which will be the subject of the next paragraph.

I.2.3 Differential diagnostic research done in the 'Hendrik van Boeijen-Oord'

In the period between 1976 and 1980, a working group of psychology students at the State University of Groningen, with the present author acting as one of its supervisors, was involved in a research project at the Hendrik van Boeijen-Oord, a large residential institution for mentally retarded persons in Assen, the Netherlands. The project concerned differences in levels of functioning between autistic and non-autistic retarded persons.

In the initial stages of the research the SRZ was used; this is a modified version of the Cain-Levine Social Competency Scale, adapted to Dutch norms (Kraijer & Kema, 1972, 1994). While leaving the principle of four subscales unchanged, their content and corresponding descriptions were slightly modified on the basis of a factor analysis. (For more information about the SRZ, and also about the still to be discussed SGZ and SMZ, see Appendix C) Three research studies were carried out: one by Brakenhoff-Splinter et al. (1977), a second by Altena et al. (1980), and a third, supplementary study carried out by the present writer (Kraijer, 1986, 1987a). The project covered a total of 296 moderately-to-severely retarded persons in the age-range 3 to 35 years, most of whom lived in residential homes. The samples were subdivided into two categories: contact-disordered subjects (C) and non-contact-disordered subjects (NC). Both categories were matched on their level of functioning. To evaluate this level, I selected an area of behaviour which was as neutral for both groups as possible. In my opinion both the verbal and the performance parts of the full-scale IQ were (and are) less suitable to this end, especially when testing mentally retarded subjects. From results of an unpublished pilot study it appeared that a more appropriate choice would be either the SRZ subscale Self Help (SH), or gross motor ability, this latter notably to test children and profoundly retarded persons. However, a reliable test to evaluate motor performance was not available at the time. Consequently, matching was done on SH, a subscale which is comparable with the VABS subscale Daily Living Skills.

In all, the three research studies reported the following significantly lower performance levels achieved by subjects of the C category:

- a lower score with respect to the subscale Social Skills;
- a lower score with respect to the subscale Communication;
- a lower full-scale score, which means a lower general level of social competence; yet both groups had been matched on the SH subscale, and did not differ with respect to the fourth subscale Persistence.

In conclusion, autistic and autistic-like mentally retarded persons may be said to be surpassed by non-autistic mentally retarded persons with respect to adaptive behaviour, in particular the social and communicative aspects of adaptive behaviour. These findings almost completely fit in with those of the aforementioned studies of Gould (1977), Ando et al. (1980), Volkmar et al. (1987), and Loveland and Kelley (1988).

In the second set of studies the SGZ scale was employed; this is a Maladaptive Behaviour Scale for the Mentally Retarded, which has been developed in the Netherlands (Kraijer & Kema, 1977, 1994). The set consisted of two studies: one by Brakenhoff-Splinter et al. (1977) and another by Altena et al. (1980). These two studies covered 256 moderately-to-severely retarded persons in the age-range of 6 to 35 years. Again, the C and NC categories were matched on performance on the SRZ subscale SH.

All in all, the two studies yielded the following results:

- the C category displayed significantly less Verbal Maladaptive Behaviour (including such things as abusive language, nasty remarks and the like);
- the C category displayed significantly more Mixed Maladaptive Behaviour;
- the C and NC categories did not differ regarding Aggressive Maladaptive Behaviour;
- the C category displayed a significantly higher frequency of general maladaptive behaviour, as indicated by the full-scale score of the SGZ;
- with respect to separate items, the C category had significantly more problems in the area of pinching food, pica, hyperactivity, masturbation and stereotyped behaviour; these items all fall under the SGZ subscale Mixed Maladaptive Behaviour.

These findings fit in well with those of Ando and Yoshimura (1979).

Other research done used the SMZ - a Gross Motor Skills Scale for the Mentally Retarded, developed in the Netherlands (Kraijer & Kema, 1981, 1994) - and the subtest 'Locomotor' - from the Griffiths Mental Development Scales. A number of 162 moderately-to-severely mentally retarded subjects were examined; no differences between the categories C and NC were found with respect to the level of spontaneous gross motor skills in children of a chronological age of eight years or under and in severely retarded persons (Mulder et al., 1977; Kraijer, 1986, 1987a). This finding is in complete agreement with that of Volkmar et al. (1987), who had used the VABS subscale 'Motor skills.'

Finally, I would like to mention a study carried out by a working party and the present writer, in which the same two categories were compared with respect to results from a number of tests. It might be useful here to clarify the fact that *scales* are understood to mean those instruments which measure *spontaneous behaviour* in everyday circumstances and environments within the person's own family, peer group, or class, whereas *tests* are administered under more or less *artificial circumstances*, with place, time, the instructions given and the material presented standardized as much as possible (Kraijer, 1978).

Brakenhoff-Splinter et al. (1980) used the WISC in a tentative Dutch translation. What they found in C and NC categories, again matched on SH, may be summarized by saying that their findings are similar to those of DeMyer et al. (1972, 1974). Mulder et al. (1979) and Kraijer (1986, 1987a) employed the Griffiths scale. Their sample covered 120 moderately to severely retarded persons in the chronological age-range of 3 to 35 years. Matching was successively done on the SRZ subscale SH and the Griffiths subtest Locomotor. The two procedures produced virtually no differences. The findings were:

- in the subtests Personal-social and Hearing & speech the scores of category C were significantly lower (p <.005 and <.001);
- in the subtest Eye & Hand Co-ordination the scores of category C were significantly lower (p <.05 and <.01);
- neither in the subtest Performance nor in the subtest Locomotor were the scores of category C lower than those of category NC;
- the Griffiths-General Quotient shows a tendency towards a lower value within the category C.

Again, these findings fit in with the scores of tests and scales mentioned in Section I.2.2 and in this Section, with the exception of those concerning Eye & Hand Coordination. A strikingly similar Griffiths profile emerged in an investigation involving seventy children with a PDD-Autistic disorder, most of them mentally retarded, which was carried out by Sandberg et al. (1993). The scores in the subtest Locomotor were significantly higher than the scores for the other subtests, those obtained in the subtest Hearing & Speech being significantly lower; the next highest scores were obtained in the subtest Performance.

I.2.4 Research on the prevalence of autism in mentally retarded persons

Subsequent to the survey done by Hoejenbos (1963) mentioned in Section I.2.1, three other important studies on the prevalence of autism in mentally retarded persons have been carried out.

The first one to mention in this connection is a doctoral thesis by Assink (1976), which has long escaped the notice of professionals, including that of the present writer. Assink, using a questionnaire based on relevant literature, gathered data about four hundred mentally retarded residents from three different institutions. However, as the questionnaire's validity and reliability lack a sound quantitative basis, the findings of this study must be treated with caution. In this sample of four hundred residents, some 158 subjects, or 39.5% of the residents, were classified as decidedly autistic. These percentages did not differ when taken individually for each setting.

An important prevalence study was done by Wing and Gould (1979) and Wing (1981a). They carried out a survey in the former southeast London borough of Camberwell, covering all children aged under fifteen who were functioning at a retarded level. The aim was to find the prevalence of the following triad of behavioural variables: impairment of social interaction, impairment of verbal and nonverbal communication, and impairment of imaginative activities. The children involved were living at home or in residential care. A classification according to level of intelligence was based on verbal and non-verbal skills combined. The figures extracted from these studies are presented in Table I.2.1; the table also includes figures for non-mobile children.

Table I.2.1 Prevalence of the Triad of Social Impairment at different levels of intelligence (Wing & Gould, 1979; Wing, 1981a)

Intelligence quotient	All children (number)	All with triad (%)
0 - 19	45	82.2
20 - 34	38	47.4
35 - 49	50	40.0
50 - 69	700*	1.8

* estimate.

Wing and Gould suggest that the close association between level of intelligence and the items investigated may be due mainly to the higher prevalence of organic brain damage in children in the low intelligence ranges. Of very great interest is their conclusion that there were also severely or profoundly mentally retarded children whose communicative potential was entirely consonant with their developmental or mental age.

The most recent prevalence study in this area was that by Gillberg et al. (1986). The population they studied consisted of a group of mentally retarded children of specified age-ranges living in Göteborg, Sweden. This group was subdivided into a category of severely mentally retarded (IQ 0-49) children and a category of mildly mentally retarded (IQ 50-70) children. In these two categories they found percentages of autistic and autistic-like disorders of 48.5% and 13.3%, respectively. In addition, the authors reported that assessments were difficult to make regarding a considerable number of profoundly mentally retarded children, but also that some of these children definitely did not display any autistic disorders.

I.2.5   The etiology of autism and mental retardation

I would like to present also some views on the etiology of autism, particularly because the disorder often occurs in combination with mental retardation.

Wing (1977), noting that autism was frequently found together with other disturbances, estimated that probably only 20% of autistic children having

IQs within the normal range should be considered to represent cases of autism in its pure form. She assumes that the remainder have *additional disabilities* caused by other forms of organic brain damage.

Rutter and Schopler (1987) give two reasons why a clear distinction should be made between autism and other disabilities, such as mental retardation. In the first place they state that, from a clinical viewpoint, "there is no doubt that autism constitutes a valid and meaningfully different psychiatric syndrome; indeed, the evidence on its validity is stronger than for any other psychiatric condition in childhood." The second reason they give has to do with differences in etiology. Notably there are boundaries which should be drawn between autism and mental retardation, in view of such facts as:

- autism is in general not associated with gross abnormalities of brain structure or histology, but severe mental retardation is;
- some specific impairments which give rise to mental retardation, such as Down syndrome, only rarely give rise to autism;
- although in both autistic and mentally retarded persons epileptic seizures are a comparatively common condition, the age of onset differs: early childhood in mental retardation, but adolescence in autism;
- autism is much more common in boys than in girls, at a ratio of 3 or 4 to 1 (for mental retardation these figures are 1.5 to 1).

Evidence for different etiologies was also found in a study which I did in collaboration with a paediatrician (Kraijer & Nelck, 1989), in which mentally retarded subjects with and without pervasive developmental disorders were compared with each other. (For further details see Chapters II.1 and II.3.) This study of a sample of 393 mentally retarded subjects in the chronological age-range of 3-14 years who had previously been carefully examined, yielded the following results:

- General conclusions applying to the sample as a whole:
  - evidence of a purely somatic etiology was more often found in moderately, severely and profoundly mentally retarded individuals than in mildly retarded individuals: 56.1% versus 35.1% (p <.001);
  - a family history of mental retardation was more frequent in mildly retarded than in moderately, severely and profoundly mentally retarded individuals: 17.6% versus 11.5% (p <.05).
- Comparison of children with and without PDD:
  - evidence of a somatic etiology was more often found in children without PDD than in children with PDD: 56.3% versus 35.8% (p <.001);
  - a family history of mental retardation was equally more frequent in children without PDD than in children with PDD: 16.8% versus 7.3% (p <.01).

- Conclusions pertaining to PDD children divided into different levels of functioning:
  - evidence of a somatic etiology was found more often in moderately, severely and profoundly retarded PDD children than in mildly retarded PDD children: 45.7% versus 14.0% (p <.001);
  - evidence of a somatic etiology was more often found in mildly retarded non-PDD children than in mildly retarded PDD children: 45.5% versus 14.0% (p <.001);
  - a family history of mental retardation, too, was more frequent in mildly retarded non-PDD children than in mildly retarded PDD children: 26.1% versus 0.0% (p <.001);
  - in moderately, severely and profoundly retarded children only evidence of a somatic etiology was found more often in non-PDD children than in PDD children: 61.9% versus 45.7% (p <.02).
- Finally:
  - no difference was found between boys and girls with pervasive disorders with respect to demonstrability of etiology;
  - the subgroup classified on the basis of DSM-III (1980) as Infantile Autism was in no respect distinguishable from the subgroup classified on the basis of DSM-III as Atypical PDD.

The general conclusions in this study correspond closely with what for many years has been reported in relevant literature. The specific conclusions correspond with the views held by Rutter and Schopler (1987), mentioned above. They comment that "there must be something particular about the pathological processes that give rise to autism." Evidently, there is sufficient reason that mental retardation and pervasive developmental disorders should not simply be lumped together!

On the other hand, mental retardation and PDD are not infrequently co-existing on the basis of the same etiology. Notably Gillberg has repeatedly drawn attention to this fact (e.g., Gillberg, 1990b). At the same time, however, neither PDD nor mental retardation are necessarily bound up with any specific defect. Gillberg and Steffenburg (1989) found, for instance, that of the Moebius syndrome cases in their study 40% displayed autistic behaviour (so 60% did not), whereas 45% of these cases were (in addition) mentally retarded (so 55% were not). Thus, persons with this syndrome can be either autistic or mentally retarded or both or neither.

A special problem is the association of epilepsy with mental retardation and with PDD. Although epilepsy in itself does not constitute a somatic etiology for these two disorders, it is in many cases an important symptom. The prevalence rate for epilepsy in the general population is 0.5-1%. However, epilepsy occurs much more frequently in the mentally retarded population, as Branford and Collacott (1994), among others, were able to demonstrate, as well as in the autistic population, as demonstrated by Gillberg and Coleman (1992).

Data available until recently suggested that in about half of the autistic persons with epilepsy this later disorder manifests itself between the third and sixth years of age, and in many other persons at puberty (Gillberg & Steffenburg, 1987; Volkmar & Nelson, 1990). Moreover, a specific association seemed to exist between epilepsy on the one hand and autism and autistic-like conditions on the other. However, a different picture emerges from a study by Kraijer et al. (1996) which involved eight hundred adult and non-adult persons living at home and in institutions. In this study it was found that:

- There are no significant differences in prevalence rates of epilepsy in mentally retarded people with and without a PDD. (The prevalence figures were respectively about 22% and 27%, corrected for the variables chronological age and level of functioning.)
- There are no significant differences in age of onset of epilepsy between mentally retarded people with and without a PDD; in about 80% of the cases of both categories epilepsy had become manifest in the first ten years of life, and in the remaining 20% the disorder manifested itself later in life and then only occasionally.

As the prevalence rates of epilepsy and mean age of onset are very much alike in mentally retarded people with and without a PDD, there is good reason to assume that mental retardation, PDD and epilepsy have a common cause or background.

I.2.6   Some concluding remarks

It may be helpful, if only for diagnostic reasons, to summarize now some of the main issues concerning the simultaneous occurrence of autism and mental retardation and to present my own vision on the subject.

- I agree with DeMyer (1976) that the intelligence of autistic persons can be measured validly and reliably. On the basis of a large number of research findings it must be assumed that 80% of autistic persons are mentally retarded as well, and to my mind this estimate is more likely to be too low than too high. The first thing to consider here is that intelligence should be measured with a general intelligence test; too often the common practice is to use non-verbal or performance (parts of) tests, producing a rosier picture of the autistic subjects than is warranted. Moreover, not only the level of intelligence should be considered; social functioning is at least as important an aspect. After all, social functioning is one of the criteria used when diagnosing mental deficiency (Grossman, 1983; Luckasson et al., 1992). In particular, in the group Borderline Intellectual Functioning (DSM-IV V62.89; IQ in the 71-84 range), covering, according to DeMyer (1979), 11% of all autistic adults, deficits in social competence will be the deciding diagnostic criterion for mental retardation. On the basis of the percentage given by DeMyer, the conclusion must be that 89% of the autistic adults are functioning at a retarded level. Similarly, in a population study carried out in Göteborg (Sweden) by Steffenburg and Gillberg (1986) 88% of the children identified as autistic or autistic-like (in other words, belonging to the entire spectrum of pervasive developmental disorders) had IQs below 70 and were therefore identified as also mentally retarded. It is my opinion that these percentages are more realistic estimates than the oft-quoted figure of 75%.

No such information can as yet be given with respect to the whole spectrum of pervasive disorders.

- Evidently, a considerable number of mentally retarded persons are also cases of autism in one form or another. A comparison of the percentages reported by Hoejenbos (1963), Assink (1976), Wing and Gould (1979, 1981a), and Gillberg et al. (1986), widely divergent as they are, would be most interesting, but could be misleading, as the definitions of autism on which these four studies are based are not simply interchangeable. Moreover, Hoejenbos and Assink studied only retarded persons in residential care, whereas Wing and Gould and Gillberg et al. studied all (registered) mentally retarded persons, including those living at home.

- Although both autism and mental retardation (leaving out, at least partially, mild retardation) are determined by organic brain damage or dysfunctioning in the broadest sense of the word, the etiological differences give some reason to discern two separate medical conditions, or, if so preferred, consequences of a disease, but convincing evidence is still lacking. However, from the viewpoint of clinical description, the difference between mental retardation on the one hand and autism or PDD on the other is indeed much more prominent; obviously, both cannot be put into one diagnostic category. It is not very helpful, I think, and it may even be inaccurate, to look upon mental retardation as a disability existing concurrently with autism (Wing, 1977). Just as rightly autism might be looked upon as sometimes occurring concurrently with mental retardation (in much the same way as faulty eyesight or cerebral palsy). Statistically, this would even be a more justified way of putting it, as by all appearances the proportion of autistic persons in the mentally retarded population is much lower than that of mentally retarded persons in the population of autistic persons.

- In spite of the fundamental differences which, in my opinion as stated above, exist between mental retardation and autism, the two conditions are also undeniably interconnected in some ways. Both DeMyer (1976) and Wing and Gould (1979, 1981a) have reported that the socially most isolated autistic children are also those with the lowest IQs. Almost inevitably the question arises whether "the withdrawal caused the low IQs or the low IQs were the cause of the withdrawal." Like DeMyer, I am unable to provide an answer. Nevertheless, it seems to me rather self-evident that the serious and all-pervading cognitive and social-emotional deficits in autism, which are present from an early age, must affect the general mental condition very unfavourably, making the person more retarded than he would have been, had he not been autistic.

PART II

RESEARCH ON THE POPULATION OF A CLINIC FOR THE MENTALLY RETARDED

GENERAL PROFILE OF THE ENTIRE GROUP OF CHILDREN ADMITTED TO THE OBSERVATION HOME

II.1.1   General features of the entire group examined

The present chapter concerns the *entire* group of children examined. This is the initial group from which the sample of *mentally retarded children with autism and autistic-like conditions,* who formed the special focus of my study, was drawn. There is no doubt indeed that the only way to approach the specific problems of these children is by considering them against a background of the characteristics of mentally retarded children in general. However, I would like to point out right now that retarded children who have been admitted to an observation home are very unlikely to constitute a representative sample of the entire population of the mentally retarded. Two things follow from that. In the first place, it makes it even more compelling to describe the entire group examined. Secondly, should any differences be found between autistic and non-autistic children admitted to the observation home, these will call for special interpretations. This last point will be discussed in more detail in Chapter II.2. Nevertheless, I believe that the methods used in this study to identify specific and concurrent problems in mentally retarded people and the ways in which to tackle them may be used as a blueprint for studies in facilities elsewhere, such as clinics, institutions and group homes.

This study involves 393 children of chronological age 0-14 years, all of whom were eventually diagnosed as mentally retarded. They make up the entire group of children who, during a twenty-year period, from August 1968 to August 1988, were clinically observed and given tentative treatment in 'Eekwal', an observation home in Assen, the Netherlands. Their average length of stay was 4.8 months. For a better insight into the group of children concerned, it is essential to know something about the methods used in 'Eekwal' and about what kind of facility it is. This information is presented in Section II.1.1.1. The sources of information regarding these children and the way they were used are dealt with in Section II.1.1.2.

II.1.1.1   The observation home 'Eekwal'

This clinical observation home has an admission capacity of twenty, and specializes in giving help to children, adolescents, and adults with developmental disabilities. In what follows, however, only the children will be considered.

The following represents the criteria for admission:

a   *Children with mental retardation or with a developmental disability combined with suspected mental retardation.*
b   *All sorts of (combinations of) disabilities* such as: motor disabilities, auditory and visual deficits, epilepsy, psychiatric disorders, and behaviour disorders.
c   *Children who have psychological, physical and behavioural problems which are difficult to diagnose and to treat, and who are living either at home or in community-based group homes.* Therefore, children with such problems who are in the residential care of large institutions are not admitted.

   Only problems which require a comprehensive, multidisciplinary approach come up for consideration. Accordingly, the regular staff is made up of an educationalist, a neurologist, a psychiatrist, a clinical psychologist, a paediatrician, a speech therapist-audiologist, a physiotherapist-kinesitherapist, a dentist (Van Grunsven, 1977), specially trained nurses, and special-education teachers, all of whom are very familiar with the field of mental retardation.

Throughout the period of observation and treatment, a high standard of diagnostics is of basic importance with respect to both physical condition and behavioural aspects. Every kind of intervention or treatment can under certain conditions be pointless and even contraindicated; consequently, a careful examination of the causes and background of the problems in question is a prerequisite. The following procedures are used to obtain the most complete picture of the child as possible:

■   gathering as much medical, paramedical and psychological data as possible, as well as collecting information about the way the child was functioning at home or in the group home, and at school or day centre; in addition, making a detailed case history;
■   an extensive physical examination, in which the following procedures have become routine: general physical examination, neurological examination, dental examination, an electroencephalogram, a number of laboratory tests (including tests to check up on disturbances of metabolism and chromosomal defects), and an examination of the functioning of the sense organs and of posture and locomotion. In addition, all sorts of investigations by other specialists are possible, if they seem appropriate, to which

end the observation home has established liaisons with various specialists and university institutions;

- examination of the level of cognitive, emotional and social development by means of the following procedures: intelligence tests, projective techniques, special tests, (mal)adaptive behaviour scales, clinical observation scales, psychological and psychiatric observation, and contact-making combined with (participant) observation by the child's attendants, the special education teacher, and the educationalist.

However, not only the child's present condition is considered; due attention is paid to another key aspect, the etiology of the disorder. The clinic must therefore seek answers to the following questions: which physical, psychological and social factors are impairing or limiting the child's development or have done so in the past and to what extent? In this connection, we also need to ask where and when, exactly, did things actually go wrong?

As for treatment, the first basic principle is to try to optimize the child's physical functioning and well-being. Appropriate measures to be taken in this respect include bringing such conditions as epilepsy and diabetes under control, and reducing visual and hearing deficits by prescribing glasses and hearing aids, etc. In other words, every physical condition which might, directly or indirectly, give rise to behavioural problems should, as far as possible, be remedied.

The second basic principle in treatment is to create, from the very first day of admission, a supportive climate for therapy. The basic guidelines are:

- The general atmosphere should not be clinical, but rather warm, sociable and informal; the daily program should include a variety of (adapted) household chores, games, sports and recreational activities, special education based on a highly individualized approach, and frequent personal contacts of a more or less therapeutic nature with nurses and staff members.
- Adjustments are made for the specific developmental deficiencies of each individual child, and these indeed form the main focus of attention. Being mentally retarded, these children inevitably call for concessions to be made with respect to the level of cognitive and performance abilities which might reasonably be expected or demanded of them. The children have to be accepted as they are, to be provided with a clear-cut and well-marked structuring of their environment and social contacts, and to be protected against any situation which may be confusing or upsetting.
- Finally, in order to offer a maximum of opportunities within the therapeutic milieu, the strategy is to gradually discontinue all previously prescribed psychotropic drugs. This policy has the additional advantage that it helps a better insight into the child's character and behaviour to be

obtained, although occasionally this idea has to be abandoned, particularly when serious and long-standing behavioural disturbances are likely to ensue.

If the procedures outlined above need to be supplemented by additional measures, *more specific forms of approach* can be applied, such as: behaviour-modification techniques, various forms of individual (play) therapy, kinesitherapy, etc.

Not until the methods outlined above have proven to produce no results or hardly any, i.e., not even a tolerable condition, is the prescription of psychotropic drugs considered as a means to make the child more receptive to treatment.

The whole process of diagnosis, (tentative) treatment, assessment and making readjustments, generally covers a period of 4-5 months, after which recommendations concerning management at home, proper treatment facilities, appropriate residential care, etc. are drawn up. As far as possible, all measures recommended will have previously been tried out by the observation team.

II.1.1.2   *The sources of information and the way they were used*

Two main sources of information have been used to categorize, classify, diagnose, and describe the children admitted to the observation home (both in the present chapter and in those that follow):

- For all 393 children, complete case files were available. As already mentioned, the children were examined by specialists in the fields of neuropsychiatry, clinical psychology and educational treatment. From the case files, diagnostic considerations noted at the end of the hospitalization period were used. (This is actually a type of long-term diagnosis based on cumulative records, a system which will be discussed in more detail later.) Further information was found in case histories, in assessments of social environment written by the social worker, in résumés of reports from attendants and psychiatric nurses, and in reports from the speech therapist-audiologist, physiotherapist-kinesitherapist, the paediatrician, and the special-education teachers. The present writer was coordinator of the observation team from 1968 onwards, and personally examined, monitored and treated all of the children in his capacity as clinical and developmental psychologist and educationalist.

  Considering the theme of this book, it is important to point out that from the outset the observation team paid much attention to a problem for which Hoejenbos, as early as 1960, had introduced the term retraction (see I.2.1). Hoejenbos, a specialist in child psychiatry, was from 1955 to 1984 head of the mental retardation institute of which the observation home involved in the present study is but one department. During this period he had a very positive and stimulating influence on the approach adopted by the home.

- Detailed reports were made at the end of each observation period by the present author in collaboration with the specialist in neuropsychiatry. These reports were designed to determine the skills, impairments, disabilities and handicaps of each child; collating this information produced profiles of the children which were as precise and comprehensive as possible. This exercise meant that what may have been tacit assumptions and considerations of members of the observation team now had to be clarified and made more explicit. In this way parents and professional helpers could be given clear and reliable advice concerning such issues as child-rearing and the choice of an appropriate school or day-care centre, for both present and future considerations.

In fact, these two sources sufficed for the purpose of classification alone, but in the 1960s and 1970s no international system of classification in mental retardation was as yet employed. Furthermore, during the period of the present study, the DSM-III (1980) was gradually being substituted by DSM-III-R (1987). However, for the sake of comparability of results within the sample, the use of a single classification system is a prerequisite, and to be in step with current research the best system is the most recent one. Consequently, the entire sample had to be assessed or reassessed in order to classify the children by means of a system which was either not yet available or not being applied during our period of observation. Such a problem is neither new nor uncommon, as can be seen in the research study of Szatmari et al. (1989), to which I will briefly return in Chapter II.5.

Classification and reclassification was carried out by the present author using the DSM-III-R system. In view of the subject of the present study, obviously the most important distinctive feature was the presence or absence of a Pervasive Developmental Disorder (DSM-III-R 299.00 Autistic Disorder or 299.80 PDD Not Otherwise Specified). Although the members of the observation team had committed themselves to producing unequivocal conclusions and the records of observations from which these conclusions were derived were generally quite satisfactory, in some cases a final decision was still difficult to make, which is hardly surprising in such an area bristling with pitfalls. Bias on the part of the author might interfere. To prevent this, the help of a highly competent specialist in neuropsychiatry, Joke Weits-Binnerts, was called in to make a fresh additional classification of a random sample of 113 children, all of whom had been diagnosed before the DSM-III system was applied. The figure of agreement for the three categories PDD, Doubtful PDD, and non-PDD, was 86.7%; Cohen's kappa coefficient of agreement value 0.78 (see Siegel & Castellan, 1988). This is 'excellent' according to the criteria given by Cicchetti and Sparrow (1981). Doubts with respect to other classification items and questions as to whether or not a given feature should be labelled a handicap were discussed with the paediatrician of the observation team, Gottlieb Nelck, and with Joke Weits-Binnerts. When no agreement on a given item could be reached, the matter was left undecided. It may be apposite here to inform the reader that I use the terms 'handicap' and 'disability' according to the definition given in the ICIDH (WHO, 1980).

In my opinion, any classification in the field of mental retardation is bound to be a tricky affair. I will come back to this issue in Chapter II.3 and also in Appendix A, which especially deals with the use of the DSM-IV.

II.1.2   Specific features of the entire group examined

A better idea of the profile of the group of mentally retarded children involved in this study will emerge, I think, by presenting some of their basic personal data and the prevalence rates of their problems and additional disabilities. Moreover, the problems which are possibly due to faulty child-rearing practices will be enumerated. There seems to be no denying that the group is not representative of the entire population of mentally retarded children, as the number of complex cases and children with severe forms of behavioural difficulties is extremely high. This could hardly be otherwise, in fact, as the severity of the problems is one of the criteria for admission to this observation home. However, little can be said about the degree of divergence, since nothing is known about the prevalence of the features concerned within the entire population of mentally retarded children.

In the following paragraphs each feature will be discussed separately.

II.1.2.1   *Age distribution*

The age classification given in Table II.1.1 is based on the child's age in completed years at the date of admission.

Table II.1.1 Chronological age of the research subjects

Age at admission date	Number	Percentage
0 - 2	30	7.4
3 - 4	93	23.7
5 - 6	94	23.9
7 - 8	71	18.3
9 - 10	47	12.0
11 - 12	27	6.9
13 - 14	31	7.9
Total	393	100.0

All age groups cover an interval of two years, with the exception of the first category which covers the age-range of zero up to and including two years. The majority of the children (65.9%) belong to the age group of 3-8 years. This may be explained by the fact that children of this group have attained school age and are now expected to meet certain levels of development and social adaptation; any failings can no longer be ignored. Soothing remarks, such as "he'll soon grow out of it" have become pointless. Furthermore, these children have now become more mobile and are physically less easy to manage, which is especially the case in children whose chaotic or aggressive behaviour is an important factor.

II.1.2.2   *Level of functioning*

Quite naturally, all levels of mental retardation are represented, as in this respect, just as with chronological age, the observation home does not apply any restrictive admission criteria. Table II.1.2 shows the distribution of levels of functioning. Assessments are based on the criteria intelligence and social functioning, as defined in DSM-III-R and DSM-IV.

Table II.1.2 Level of functioning of the research subjects

Level of functioning	Number	Percentage
Profound	31	7.9
Severe	117	29.8
Moderat	136	34.6
Mild	109	27.7
Total	393	100.0

This table shows that most of the subjects are categorized as severely, moderately and mildly retarded, with IQs roughly in the 20-70 range. Taken together, they constitute 92.1% of the total number of subjects. What the table does not show is that there is a considerable number of children who are somewhere on the borderline between moderately and mildly mentally retarded.

Comparing this finding with DSM-IV ratings of the entire population of the mentally retarded (1 to 2% profoundly retarded, 3 to 4% severely retarded, 10% moderately retarded, and 85% mildly retarded), the conclusion must be that in the children of the present study the group of severely retarded children is the most heavily over-represented group, while the group of mildly retarded children is an extremely under-represented group.

II.1.2.3   *Sex distribution*

Almost all studies of children with problems - and mental retardation should be seen as falling within this category - report a higher proportion of handicapped or difficult boys than girls (see Robinson & Robinson, 1976; Verbraak, 1979). Among all the disorders which the DSM-III-R manual lists under Disorders usually first evident in infancy, childhood or adolescence, it is only anorexia nervosa and bulimia - rare in childhood - which are indicated as showing a significant female preponderance. The children in the present study fit into this general picture: there are 248 boys against 145 girls, i.e., 63.1% and 36.9%, respectively, or a boy/girl ratio of 1.71:1. This figure lies between that given by DSM-III (about 2:1) and by DSM-IV (about 1.5:1).

II.1.2.4   Indications for admission

The indications for admission are formulated by both the child's parents and other parties concerned, such as the staff of the day-care centre or school, the medical specialist, the Mental Retardation Service, the Mental Health Service or the Early Detection Team. Invariably, worries about the child's development are more or less prominent. The issues often mentioned are: developmental lags in speech, language, motor ability, daily living skills, play interests, and taking initiative. Additional complaints are not so easy to categorize. First, there are such miscellaneous problems as sleeping problems, chaotic behaviour and disobedience. Although frequently two or more behavioural problems of the child in question are reported, on admission it often becomes evident that these are in fact only the principal complaints. In line with the nature of the information as originally obtained, in Table II.1.3 the list of behavioural problems as formulated by parents and/or other parties involved in the referral preceding admission are presented in an unsystematic way. The problems are just arranged according to frequency. Obviously, some overlapping is to be found in the descriptions, for example: fearful/extremely scared vs. screaming tantrums; or: short-tempered/temper tantrums vs. irritability.

Table II.1.3 Frequencies of behaviour disorders, as indicated upon application for admission into the observation home

Type of behaviour disorder	Number of times mentioned*
Hyperactive/chaotic/attention deficit	128
Strange/elusive/unpredictable/'psychotic'	78
Short-tempered/temper tantrums	75
Not easily accessible	75
Beating/kicking/pinching/biting	58
Eating problems	36
Restiveness/waywardness/obstinacy	32
Hurting oneself/self-injury	23
Destructive acts	20
Dictatorial behaviour	20
Fearful/extremely scared	18
Sleeping problems	15
Excessive claims	14
Rigid/compulsive	11
Noncompliance	9
Irritability	9
Sad/unhappy	8
Screaming tantrums	7

Some other reported disorders with still lower frequencies were: defiant behaviour, problems with elimination, vomiting, apathy, smearing of stools, sweet tooth and pinching food, lying, stealing, sex play activities.

* Per child more than one of the disorders may have been reported.

In many cases indications for admission consist only of one or more of the behavioural problems mentioned in Table II.1.3. However, the complaints in question being extremely serious or protracted or intractable, admission is highly desirable indeed. In many instances parents are at the end of their tether, another telling sign that admission is urgently required. Obviously, those who are bringing these children to professional attention also hope to be advised on such matters as appropriate child-rearing methods, housing facilities and/or day centres, or medication as an adjunct to treatment.

In almost half of the applications, additional disabilities and suspected socio-cultural or emotional neglect play a very important or even crucial role. Other recurrent questions, which in some cases are actually the main reason for applying, are those having to do with choice of a proper school, prognosis with regard to future development, etiology of the mental retardation (and of associated disabilities), control of epileptic attacks, need for closer examination for reasons of arrested development or even degenerative overall functioning.

II.1.2.5 *Organic Personality Syndrome and Dementia*

Of the 393 children studied, 93 (23.7%) display the Organic Personality Syndrome (DSM-III-R, 310.10, q.v.). Usually, the sub-criterion A(4): "marked apathy and indifference", is the overriding feature in the condition. Only incidentally, A(1): "affective instability, e.g., marked shifts from normal mood to depression, irritability, or anxiety" is present. Those cases which are tending towards sub-criterion A(1) will generally be better fitted into the category Attention-deficit Hyperactivity Disorder (DSM-III-R., 314.01, q.v.).

The condition discussed in this section is a real handicap, as the child, lacking in energy and liveliness, is restricted in taking an active part in everyday life.

Separately, I mention Dementia (DSM-III-R, 294.10), found in seven cases. These children are not categorized as OPS, although they do display some of its features; however, disintegration is their major characteristic. I will come back to this issue, in particular because four of these children also display a Pervasive Developmental Disorder (DSM-III-R, 299.00 or 299.80).

II.1.2.6 *Motor handicaps*

Again, the criteria employed are as unequivocal as possible. The term motor handicap is used only when there is an unmistakable paralysis or paresis of one or more extremities, and when the defect restricts movement to such a degree that it is evidently handicapping the child in his daily functioning. Especially with respect to such disturbances as athetosis, chorea, and ataxia, controversies are apt to arise among clinicians about whether or not the condition is present and whether or not it is restricting movement.

Of the 393 children in the present study, 39 (9.9%) display a paralysis or paresis as defined above.

II.1.2.7   *Visual and auditory handicaps*

Under this category fall those deficits which, in spite of the use of appliances (spectacles, a hearing aid), are restricting to such a degree that they must be regarded as handicaps. Of the children in the present study, 25 (6.4%) display this handicap.

II.1.2.8   *Pervasive Developmental Disorders*

For the moment, I will limit myself to saying that some 137 children (34.9%) in the group studied met the criteria to be labelled as PDD-AD (Pervasive Developmental Disorder Autistic Disorder) or PDD-NOS (Pervasive Developmental Disorder Not Otherwise Specified), the numbers in the DSM-III-R being respectively 299.00 and 299.80. In mentally retarded children too, PDD is in my view an extremely serious disability. The question of which disability 'came first' I leave unconsidered. After all, the primary criterion for admission into the observation home is mental retardation or suspected mental retardation, rather than PDD. Or, to put it another way, the observation home focusses primarily on mental retardation.

Table II.1.4 The main additional disorders (as listed in DSM-III-R) and further handicaps found in the children studied (n = 393), arranged according to frequency

Disorder	Number[*]	Percentage
Pervasive Developmental Disorder	137	34.9
Organic Personality Syndrome	93	23.7
Motor handicap	39	9.9
Visual and auditory handicap	25	6.4

[*] There were children with more than one disorder.

II.1.3   Other additional classes of disorders and problems due to faulty child-rearing practices in the non-PDD children

Before the additional classes of disorders and also - and not to be overlooked! - the problems due to faulty child-rearing practices can be explored in more detail, a separate analysis of the non-PDD children in the group studied has to be made. The reasons for this are twofold.

First, the rules of the system being what they are, the presence of PDD preempts classification in several of the DSM-III-R disorders. As examples could be mentioned Developmental Language Disorders, Separation Anxiety Disorder and Overanxious Disorder. After all, language problems and anxiety are indeed an intrinsic part of PDD.

Secondly, experience shows that diagnosing problems due to faulty child-rearing practices is far more difficult with the group of mentally retarded PDD children than with the mentally retarded non-PDD children. This issue will be treated in more detail in the next chapter. What matters for the moment is that problems of child rearing are better discussed separately for each group. As noted above, only the non-PDD children, a group of 256 children (393 minus 137), will be considered in this section.

Faulty child-rearing practices have been categorized according to the definitions given by Kobi (1975). However, one qualification seems to be pertinent. The term neglect is used by Kobi when the child's needs for proper guidance are disregarded due to indifference and lack of concern with respect to the child's lot; this author places neglect in a context of guilt on the part of those who are responsible for the child's upbringing, but I would certainly not go as far as that. From my own observation I know that there are a considerable number of parents, in particular those who are functioning at a borderline intellectual level or who are even mentally retarded, whose shortcomings in child rearing should be regarded as sheer incapacity for which they cannot be blamed.

Grossman's (1983) description of faulty child-rearing is more neutral: "insufficient quantity, variability, or discriminability of stimulation in the environment."

Two forms of neglect can be distinguished. The first one is primarily a *sociocultural form of neglect* which, in line with Kobi, can be defined as a failure to make the most of the child's natural developmental potential through insufficient stimulation and discipline. The second form is primarily an *emotional form of neglect* which, again on the basis of the study by Kobi, can be defined as a failure on the part of those responsible for the child's upbringing to offer him, by means of intimate personal contact, models for relationships.

Aside from neglect, two other types of faulty child-rearing practices found in the present study are (a) *overloading* and (b) *pampering*. The problem with faulty child-rearing is, as Kobi put it, that, in spite of a serious willingness and commitment to bring up the child, the practices used are inappropriate and not geared to the child's needs.

Finally, it should be emphasized that both neglect and faulty child-rearing practices will only have a damaging effect when they occur as a continuous and structural process rather than only occasionally. Ultimately, the consequences may be so limiting that the child in question must be regarded as handicapped.

II.1.3.1   *Other additional classes of disorders in non-PDD children*

II.1.3.1.1   *Developmental Language Disorder*
Developmental Language Disorder (DSM-III-R, 315.31) is found as an additional disability in twenty of the 256 non-PDD children, or 7.8%. Of these,
nine are cases of Developmental Expressive Language Disorder, while the
remaining eleven children show a combination of Developmental Expressive
and Receptive Language Disorder. I know of no cases of a receptive language disorder occurring singly, that is to say, not combined with expressive
disorders, at least not in mental retardation. These findings are entirely in
keeping with the conclusions drawn by Cohen et al. (1987).

II.1.3.1.2   *Attention-deficit/Hyperactivity Disorder*
Attention-deficit Hyperactivity Disorder (DSM-III-R, 314.01) is found in 74 of
the 256 non-PDD children, or 28.9%. Again, the presence of PDD preempts
classification in Attention-deficit Hyperactivity Disorder (without/a rather
tautological designation, by the way, as the word deficit itself implies a disorder). As already stated in an earlier publication (Kraijer, 1988a), the single
classification in the DSM-III-R manual of what DSM-III categorized as two
separate Attention-deficit Disorders (respectively with and without hyperactivity), seems to be an improvement. Attention-deficit of the type discussed
here is certainly - at least in the mentally retarded - almost always accompanied by hyperactivity. Invariably, an Attention-deficit/Hyperactivity Disorder constitutes a (either or not additional) handicap.

II.1.3.1.3   *Other DSM-III-R classes of disorders*
Oppositional Defiant Disorder (DSM-III-R, 313.81) either with or without
AD/HD, is found in nine non-PDD children. Conduct Disorder - solitary aggressive type (DSM-III-R, 312.00) - is found in four children. There are two
children with late onset true psychosis, with onset at about the age of 10,
one with manic-depressive features, the other with schizophrenic features.
There was one eleven-year-old boy who entirely met the criteria for Borderline Personality Disorder (DSM-III-R, 301.83). All sixteen children mentioned
in this paragraph were either mildly mentally retarded (ten cases) or moderately mentally retarded (six cases).
    Furthermore, there is a small number of cases of the following disorders:
Avoidant Disorder of Childhood (DSM-III-R, 313.21); Tourette's Disorder
(307.23); Chronic Motor Tic Disorder (307.22); Separation Anxiety Disorder
(309.21); Overanxious Disorder (313.00); Obsessive Compulsive Disorder
(300.30); Reactive Attachment Disorder (313.89); and Organic Mood Disorder
(293.83).
    All these classes of disorders should be regarded as thoroughly handicap-
ping daily functioning.
    The label Stereotypy/Habit Disorder (DSM-III-R, 307.30) proved to be
rather inapplicable. The criterion mentioned under B, "causes physical injury", is clear enough, but the criterion "markedly interferes with normal activ-

ities" is somewhat puzzling. In young children with a low level of functioning, it is not always clear whether other activities are indeed interfered with. After all, as soon as stereotyped behaviour is ruled out, these children often have no other choice than to do nothing at all or experience feelings of displeasure. In investigating adolescent and adult mentally retarded individuals, the label seems easier to apply (see also II.3.2.2).

Finally, more or less isolated symptoms such as pica, rumination, encopresis and stuttering were not classified separately.

Table II.1.5 The main additional classes of disorders in the non-PDD children (n = 256), arranged according to frequency

Disorder	Number*	Percentage
Attention-deficit/Hyperactivity Disorder	74	28.9
Developmental Expressive/Receptive Language Disorder	20	7.8
Oppositional Defiant Disorder	9	3.5
Conduct Disorder	4	1.6

* There were children with more than one disorder.

II.1.3.2 *Problems due to faulty child-rearing practices in non-PDD children*

II.1.3.2.1 Overloading
Experience teaches that bringing up a mentally retarded child almost always means overloading the child to some extent. Normal or almost-normal expectations need to be reconsidered again and again in the light of the continuous disappointments the life of a retarded child presents to his or her parents. Bringing up a mentally retarded child is rather like fighting a rearguard action. For many years, often until the child has reached adulthood and sometimes for even longer, the parents and their child are living in a field of forces, the poles being formed on the one hand by standard expectations and on the other hand by the limitations caused by the child's retardation. Prospects become less hopeful over the years, and at the same time achievement of those aims which do seem feasible require more time and effort than with normal children.

Overloading plays and important role in producing behaviour disorders. A previous study demonstrated that overloading had been the cause, or at least one of the causes, of behaviour disorders in 75 out of 116 cases (64.5%) of mildly or moderately mentally retarded adolescents and adults admitted for observation (Kraijer, 1985). A research study of 1988 (Kraijer, 1988b) came to the conclusion that, in 34.9% of the cases, overloading was the main cause of behaviour disorders found in 63 adolescents coming from community-based group homes who had been admitted for observation, while in 31.7% of the cases it played certainly a secondary role in originating these disorders.

In the present study, the term overloading is only applied to those children whose behaviour disorders are more or less *primarily* caused by overloading. These disorders fall into two categories. First, there are the clearly perceptible, overt forms, such as aggressive and destructive behaviour. Secondly, there are the more intrapersonal, inward or implosive problems, such as apathy, sadness, and so on. The term overloading is considered to be applicable whenever the behavioural problems show a substantial improvement or even vanish when the child is released from the emotional pressure of excessive achievement-oriented demands and expectations, so that he no longer feels the need to *be* better and to *perform* better than his limited potential will allow. To find evidence of this problem, clinical observation for several months is a very apt method, notably in children. In adolescents and adults, however, this form of faulty child-rearing may have exerted its influence over such a long period and may have left such deep traces that this criterion is often inappropriate. Be that as it may, the percentages given here - in this case only pertaining to children - will certainly represent minimum values.

To turn now to the present research findings, in 54 of the 256 children in the study (21.1%), overloading was the only faulty child-rearing method found. In eleven cases both overloading and pampering were found, a curious combination discussed in an earlier study (Kraijer, 1985). On the one hand the child is too much excused, especially with respect to demands concerning self-care skills, conformity to rules, and willingness to accept frustrations; on the other hand, demands in the verbal/cognitive areas, especially those having to do with linguistic competence and school performance, are constantly too high. Whether the four other children in the study who had been both overloaded and socially and emotionally neglected should also be included in the present list may be a matter of dispute. Anyhow, if all cases of overloading are counted they number 69, representing 27.0% of the children studied.

Two earlier studies, aforementioned, provide strong evidence to suggest that overloading plays a more important role in adolescent and adult cases who are mildly retarded or on the borderline between moderately and mildly retarded. Gresnigt and Gresnigt-Strengers (1973), who investigated a group of profoundly, severely and moderately retarded children, found similar evidence: they were under the impression that the less profound the child's mental retardation, the more he ran the risk of being overloaded. In order to find out whether this problem was also present in my study, the group of 256 children was divided into subgroups of severely retarded and mildly retarded children. The first subgroup, S, covers profoundly, severely and moderately retarded children; the second subgroup, M, includes children on the borderline between moderate and mild retardation plus mildly retarded cases. Table II.1.6 shows the incidence of overloading in both subgroups.

Table II.1.6 Incidence of overloading in severely retarded (S) and mildly re-tarded (M) non-PDD children, either occurring singly or in combination with pampering or with emotional and social neglect

Kind of approach	Absolute numbers			Percentages		
	S+M	S	M	S+M	S	M
Overloading only	54	24	30	21.1	14.3	34.1
Overloading + other faulty practices	69	33	36	27.0	19.6	40.9
Total	256	168	88	100.0	56.6	34.4

Overloading, whether occurring singly or in combination with other faulty practices, has a significantly higher incidence in the mildly retarded sub-group (p <.001, two-tailed test, Chi-square test). Mildly retarded children generally hardly look like being retarded; often, in fact, they appear quite normal. Their functioning level comes very close to the normal-average level. As a result, there is a tendency to make 'normal' demands of them, which in their case will actually mean overloading. Frequently, in counselling inter-views with parents, the complaint is heard: "It would have been better if our child had been a mongol." Parents feel that if their child had looked like a mentally retarded child, he would have been better protected against their excessive demands.

II.1.3.2.2 Pampering
A child who has been spared too much and/or who is treated below his age, has been denied the opportunity to reach the levels of emotional and social development and of self-care skills which the observation home has found him or her to be capable of reaching. Clear evidence of pampering was found in eight of the 256 children, or 3.1%. Of particular note is that four of these children have motor defects, while two others are epileptic, all six of these children being severely handicapped through their respective disor-ders; this makes it quite easy to understand that their parents should become overprotective. If the eleven children who were found to have been both overloaded and pampered are included, the total number of cases of pam-pering amounts to nineteen, or 7.4%. Distribution over the two categories se-verely and mildly retarded is very proportional, with thirteen and six chil-dren, or 7.7% and 6.8%, respectively, this being in contrast to the findings presented in Table II.1.6.

II.1.3.2.3 Socio-cultural and emotional-social neglect
The children categorized as socio-culturally neglected are in the majority of cases from disadvantaged homes, and some of their families are, additional-ly, functioning at a borderline intellectual level or are actually mentally re-tarded. The main forms of neglect involved here are inadequate stimulation of language and speech development, deficient attention to training in daily

living skills and self-care skills, and a limited supply of play and pastime activities. The diagnosis was considered to be warranted when the child, during his stay at the observation home, made perceptible progress in cognitive, verbal and self-care skills. Or, in other words, the child in question went through an accelerated development and the developmental lags turned out to be partly due to socio-cultural factors rather than to mental retardation. Twenty children of the 256, or 7.8%, were found to be cases of only this form of neglect. In emotional and social respects their upbringing lacked a certain degree of refinement and clarity, but was not devoid of affection and involvement. Eleven children were found to be cases of both socio-cultural neglect and emotional-social neglect; many of the parents concerned had personality disorders, combined with additional problems, such as alcoholism, prostitution or criminality. Child-rearing was in these cases marked by a lack of affection and consistency. Only rarely were cases found of exclusively emotional-social neglect, without socio-cultural neglect. Conclusive evidence of the presence or absence of emotional-social neglect is, for that matter, not so easy to provide. Given the length of stay in the observation home, its effects are in some cases amenable to treatment (e.g., with fear of mistreatment or battering), but in other cases only partly or not at all (e.g., with making only superficial and fleeting contacts; lack of consideration; sadness). Apart from these eleven children, four children were found to be cases of both overloading and emotional-social neglect. Thus, the total number of emotionally and socially neglected children is fifteen, or 5.9%.

Findings regarding both forms of neglect are summarized in Tables II.1.7 and II.1.8, again with the proportions for severely retarded children (S) and mildly retarded children (M) also included.

Table II.1.7 Incidence of socio-cultural neglect in severely retarded (S) and mildly retarded (M) non-PDD children, occurring singly or in combination with emotional-social neglect

Kind of neglect	Absolute numbers			Percentages		
	S+M	S	M	S+M	S	M
Socio-cultural neglect only	20	7	13	7.8	4.2	14.8
Socio-cultural neglect + other forms of neglect	31	10	21	12.1	6.0	23.9
Total	256	168	88	100.0	65.6	34.4

Socio-cultural neglect occurring singly is significantly ($p < .01$) more frequent in the subgroup mildly retarded. Socio-cultural neglect in combination with other forms of neglect is even more significantly ($p < .001$) more frequent.

Table II.1.8 Incidence of emotional-social neglect (occurring singly or combined) in severely retarded (S) and mildly retarded (M) non-PDD children

Kind of neglect	Absolute numbers			Percentages		
	S+M	S	M	S+M	S	M
Emotional-social neglect, either singly or combined	15	6	9	5.9	3.6	10.2
Total	256	168	88	100.0	65.6	34.4

Emotional-social neglect seems significantly (p <.05) more likely to occur with mildly retarded children. However, with regard to this finding I am in doubt as to whether the diagnostic tools available allow any reliable judgement at all. Obviously, a lower level of functioning makes it more difficult to recognize and ascertain unfavourable social-emotional circumstances. These children express themselves so poorly and also so deviantly that diagnosing them is a very laborious, subjective and inconclusive process.

II.1.4   Summary and conclusions

As already stated in II.1.2, there seems to be no denying that, in comparison with the entire population of mentally retarded children, the behavioural difficulties of the children in this study are more severe and the group contains a disproportionate number of complex cases. However, figures to support this statement are hard to give, due to the simple fact that there are no figures on the incidence of behavioural difficulties, classes of disorders, and disabilities for the entire population of mentally retarded children.

The percentages found in this study, such as: 34.9% for pervasive disorders; 23.7% for Organic Personality Syndrome; 16.3% for motor and sensory handicaps, are far from low indeed. The same thing can be said regarding the incidence and types of behavioural problems reported at admission (see Table II.1.3). Finally, I would like to stress the high percentages of 28.9% non-PDD children with Attention-deficit/Hyperactivity Disorder, and 37.9% of these children evidently having problems due to faulty child-rearing practices.

The importance of all this for comparisons to be made between the PDD-children and non-PDD children within the group studied will be discussed in more detail in the next chapter.

There is another aspect - directly pertinent to the subject of the present book - which is also worthy of attention. Even when due allowance is made for the fact that this study covers children with exceptionally serious problems, an incidence of 34.9% pervasive developmental disorders still seems extremely high; even more so when this finding is compared with the estimated figure given by the DSM-III-R manual of the overall PDD prevalence in children: 10-15 per 10,000, or 0.1 to 0.15%. The highest prevalence found in the entire population thus far is, according to Gillberg (1990a), 21 per 10,000, or 0.21%. In fact, when reconsidering the results of an earlier study by Wing and Gould (1979), and now including non-ambulatory mentally retarded children in the profound, severe and moderate ranges of retardation, Wing (1981a) herself concluded that the Triad of Social impairment was found in ninety children, or 0.26%. The percentages presented in Table I.2.1 are based on this most recent computation. It is remarkable how much the percentage found in the present study lies above this figure too. More causes must have played a role than the sheer fact that the group of children in the present study is obviously far from representative of the entire population. I shall come back to this issue in Chapter III.2.

CHAPTER II.2

COMPARISON OF THE CHILDREN IN THE STUDY WITH AND WITHOUT A PERVASIVE DEVELOPMENTAL DISORDER

II.2.1   Introduction

The foregoing chapter mainly concerned the entire group of children in the study. As my aim is to compare mentally retarded children with and without a pervasive disorder, the present chapter will consistently consider this group as being composed of two distinct subgroups:

- a subgroup of 137 children (or 34.9% of all children in the study) who, apart form being mentally retarded, had at any rate a Pervasive Developmental Disorder (PDD) as a concurrent disability;
- the remaining 256 children (or 65.1%), possibly having concurrent impairments or disabilities, but no PDD.

Both subgroups will be compared with respect to the same features which were discussed in Chapter II.1, following the same order.

First, however, a question of a more general nature has to be considered. As early as 1968, some of the first children admitted to the observation home were found to suffer from severe pervasive developmental disorders. The impression was that over the years these children steadily kept coming to the clinic in comparatively high numbers. There has been some speculation that possibly recent years have seen an increase in the number of children with this disorder. It would therefore be relevant to find out whether such a tendency could in fact be demonstrated for the period covered by the present study: from 1968 to 1988. Unfortunately, from the data available no evidence on this issue can be derived. Yet it is possible to ascertain whether or not an increase in the number of referrals of PDD children to the observation home has taken place in that twenty-year period. As a uniform classification system was employed for the whole period, it must be feasible to discover such a trend. This can be done by dividing the children in the study into four subgroups, corresponding with four periods in which their admission took place, each period covering five years. Numbers, percentages and the statistical test are presented in Table II.2.1.

Table II.2.1 Incidence of PDD during successive periods of admission ($n_{total} = 393$)

	1968-73	1973-78	1978-83	1983-88
PDD	46	39	28	24
Non-PDD	82	79	58	37
% PDD*	35.9	33.1	32.6	39.3

* Percentage of PDD per period
Chi-square = 0.98; df = 3; ns

As the table shows, the percentages are very evenly distributed. Accordingly, testing does not confirm the hypothesis of an increasing number of children with PDD. It seems very likely that the problem was just as serious twenty years ago as it is today. For the sake of completeness, it may be convenient to add that the decrease in absolute numbers of referrals is largely due to demographic factors (see Kraijer, 1988b). It is probable that the origin of this often heard speculation should rather be sought in an increased awareness of the problem among both parents and professional helpers.

II.2.2 The children with and without PDD compared separately for each feature

In the following sections the PDD and non-PDD children admitted for observation will be compared with respect to the same features as discussed in Chapter II.1. In a few instances frequencies were too low to allow statistical testing, making a comparison pointless.

II.2.2.1 *Age distribution*

The question to be answered here is whether, at least for the children in the present study, the incidence of PDD is correlated with chronological age. Table II.2.2 shows the number of PDD and non-PDD children in the various age-ranges.

Table II.2.2 Chronological age and incidence of PDD ($n_{total} = 393$)

	0-2	3-4	5-6	7-8	9-10	11-12	13-14
PDD	5	40	43	22	10	8	9
Non-PDD	24	53	51	50	37	19	22
% PDD*	17.2	43.0	45.7	30.6	21.3	29.6	29.0

* Percentage PDD per age-range
Chi-square = 16.78; df = 6; p = .01

Apparently PDD is significantly correlated with chronological age. When adjacent age-ranges are joined together, the correlation becomes even more pronounced.

Table II.2.3 Chronological age and incidence of PDD, compared for broad-range age categories (n $_{total}$ = 393)

	0-2	3-6	7-14
PDD	5	83	49
Non-PDD	24	103	129
% PDD*	17.2	44.6	27.5

* Percentage PDD per age-range
Chi-square = 15.99; df = 2; p = <.001.

Through this procedure the level of significance has increased. What does this finding mean? With respect to the low percentage in the age-range 0-2, the only plausible explanation, given the low number of cases, is that at such an early stage the problems (and their origins) were not yet fully recognized. An argument in favour of this hypothesis could be that, unlike the non-PDD children, all five PDD children in this age-range are two (some almost three) years old. Or, to put it another way, the age of this group of very young PDD children for whom admission was necessary comes very close to that of the next age category.

In view of the fact that PDD never 'wears off', at any rate not in children of an age within the range covered by the present study, the decreasing percentage of PDD children older than six years can only be explained by assuming that by that time the majority of these often very severely disturbed children had already been clinically observed in the Eekwal observation home or one of the other observation/treatment settings. A further indication that this might indeed be the case is to be found in the comparatively high number of children in the narrow age-range of 3-6 against that in the broader age-range of 7-14: 83 against only 49, respectively.

II.2.2.2   *Level of functioning*

A not unimportant question is whether PDD is associated with level of mental retardation. Research studies done by Assink (1976), Wing and Gould (1979) and Gillberg et al. (1986) all found an association between the prevalence of autism and level of functioning. The findings of the present study are presented in Tables II.2.4 and II.2.5, and the conclusions concerning this problem are based on these figures. It may be worth reminding the reader that children who are intermediate between moderately and mildly retarded have been categorized as mildly retarded, as was previously the case.

Table II.2.4 Level of functioning and prevalence of PDD (n_{total} = 393)

	Profound	Severe	Moderate	Mild
PDD	9	47	45	36
Non-PDD	22	70	91	73
% PDD*	29.0	40.2	33.1	33.0

* Percentage of PDD per age-range
Chi-square = 2.27; df = 3; ns

Table II.2.5 Level of functioning and prevalence of PDD, compared for broad ranges of levels of retardation (n_{total} = 393)

	Severely mentally retarded	Mildly mentally retarded
PDD	94	43
Non-PDD	168	88
% PDD*	35.9	32.8

* Percentage PDD per age-range
Chi-square = 0.36; ns

As can be seen from the tables, the distribution of PDD children over the various degrees of mental retardation unmistakably runs parallel to that of the non-PDD children. In at least one respect these findings are not completely comparable with those of the other studies mentioned above: the children in this study are far from representative of the entire population of mentally retarded children or of mentally retarded children in residential care. The children involved are almost invariably children with very serious problems. This is actually a weak point in all studies which derive their data from clinics and hospitals. In Chapter III.2 we will return to this issue.

The present findings are felt to highlight the fact that pervasive disorders are very common in mentally retarded children of all levels of retardation, and this should certainly be born in mind, at any rate.

II.2.2.3   *Sex distribution*

A very obvious question to ask is whether pervasive disorders also have a tendency to occur more often in male than in female mentally retarded children. As already mentioned in Chapter II.1.2.3, the children in the study are, as a matter of fact, predominantly male. As for the 137 PDD children in this group, 91 children, or 66.4%, are boys, against 46, or 33.6% girls, which on the face of it does not seem to point to an over-representation of boys in the present study. Table II.2.6 presents the results of statistical testing.

Table II.2.6 Sex distribution and prevalence of PDD ($n_{total} = 393$)

	Boys	Girls
PDD	91	46
Non-PDD	157	99
% PDD*	36.7	31.7

* Percentage PDD per sex
  Chi-square = 1.00; ns

Evidently PDD is very evenly distributed amongst boys and girls. The conclusion seems warranted that PDD is about as common in mentally retarded boys as it is in mentally retarded girls. It is only because mentally retarded boys outnumber mentally retarded girls that the ratio is 1.98:1. The ratio which the DSM-III-R manual gives on the basis of available research data is between 2:1 and 5:1, a figure to which the present findings come very close indeed. In Chapter III.2 we will return to this issue as well.

II.2.2.4 *Indications for admission*

The present section will deal with a comparison of PDD and non-PDD children with regard to behavioural problems and complaints as reported by parents and/or other parties involved. But two points should be discussed first.

- As stated in II.1.2.4, the standard procedure was to use the reports of behavioural problems or complaints as given in the application for admission. Clinical experience has shown that this is the moment when parents in particular tend to emphasize only a few outstanding problems, and mostly just the one. When the anamnesis is examined and further details are discussed during the interview on admission, a broader gamut of worries about annoying or deviant behaviours will generally emerge. Thus, with respect to the complaints and behavioural problems reported on application, it has to be kept in mind that:
  - the complaint in question is a rather inarticulate formulation of the child's problems and further questioning is required in order to find out their full extent;
  - whenever a complaint is reported, the child will in fact display the behaviour referred to, while conversely, not reporting certain behaviour should not be interpreted indiscriminately as signifying the absence of that behaviour, as this problem may have been overgrown with worries about the other forms of strange or maladjusted behaviour.
- It has to be emphasized once more that *all* children who entered the Eekwal observation home were, certainly on admission, *children with problems*. As noted before, in a great number of applications behavioural

difficulties were prominent in both PDD and non-PDD children. Therefore, when children within this group of already extremely difficult children are found to display additional behavioural difficulties or an extremely great number of such difficulties, the reader should realize that their condition must be far more worse than when this had been observed in only a random sample of mentally retarded children.

II.2.2.4.1   Insufficient contact

Obviously, when dealing with autism and related contact disorders, a comparison of both groups with respect to complaints about poor contact is apropos. Table II.2.7 shows the data and statistical test.

Table II.2.7 Prevalence of the complaint: poor contact in PDD and non-PDD children (n $_{total}$ = 393)

	Non-PDD children	PDD children
Complaint voiced	22	53
Complaint not voiced	234	84
% Complaint voiced*	8.6	38.7

* Percentage complaint voiced in each group
  Chi-square = 52.33; p <.001

Not surprisingly, the complaint 'poor contact' is indeed highly significantly more frequent in those children who were eventually categorized as PDD children. Nevertheless, the fact that 8.6% of the non-PDD children displayed contact problems should not be ignored either. The next chapter will come back to this issue.

II.2.2.4.2   Strange/elusive

As may be expected, PDD children are described as strange, elusive, unpredictable or 'psychotic.' After all, in addition to showing developmental lags, these children are also 'different', 'faraway', displaying enigmatic or even incomprehensible behaviour. Table II.2.8 shows the figures and statistical test.

Table II.2.8 Prevalence of.the complaint: strange/elusive in PDD and non-PDD children (n $_{total}$ = 393)

	Non-PDD children	PDD children
Complaint voiced	20	58
Complaint not voiced	236	79
% Complaint voiced*	7.8	42.3

* Percentage complaint voiced in each group
  Chi-square = 66.86; p <.001

The data fully come up to expectations, but here, too, the 7.8% non-PDD children reported to be strange, elusive, unpredictable or psychotic should not be ignored, especially in view of the fact that only a small number of non-PDD children were diagnosed as displaying psychotic or psychotic-like behaviour (see II.1.3.1.3).

II.2.2.4.3   Hyperactive/attention-deficit

According to the DSM-III-R manual, children diagnosed as PDD cannot be placed in the Attention-deficit/Hyperactivity Disorder category as well. Or, as the manual puts it: "Symptoms characteristic of ADHD are often observed in Pervasive Developmental Disorders; in these cases a diagnosis of ADHD is preempted." Whether this assertion also holds true for mentally retarded PDD children when compared with an exceptional group of mentally retarded non-PDD children can be seen in Table II.2.9.

Table II.2.9 Prevalence of the complaint: hyperactive, chaotic, attention-deficit in PDD children and non-PDD children (n_{total} = 393)

	Non-PDD children	PDD children
Complaint voiced	91	37
Complaint not voiced	165	100
% Complaint voiced*	35.6	27.0

* Percentage complaint voiced in each group
  Chi-square = 2.96; ns

The complaint 'hyperactive, chaotic, attention-deficit' does not occur less frequently in PDD children than in 'difficult' mentally retarded non-PDD children. However, in both groups the percentages are far from insignificant. Consequently, it may be assumed that AD/HD is less frequent in 'normal' mentally retarded children, i.e., those not displaying behavioural difficulties and who are therefore not in need of clinical observation. Furthermore, in view of the gravity of the complaints mentioned in II.2.2.4.1 and II.2.2.4.2, not only the hyperactive PDD children, but nearly all PDD children are likely to be brought to the attention of the clinicians. If these assumptions are correct, this will mean additional support for the principle followed by the DSM-III-R (and the DSM-IV) manual, which is in my view a sound principle.

II.2.2.4.4   Further complaints

Table II.2.10 presents the proportion of children from both categories with regard to the complaints which were less frequently reported, together with the (two-tailed) test results. Complaints which for reasons of low frequency could not be tested have been omitted.

Table II.2.10 Incidence of further complaints reported in non-PDD children (n = 256) and PDD children (n = 137)

Complaint	Non-PDD	PDD	Level of significance
Short-tempered/temper tantrums	46	29	ns[*]
Physical aggression[**]	42	16	ns
Eating problems	24	12	ns
Restiveness/waywardness	24	8	ns
Self-injury	15	8	ns
Destructive acts	17	3	ns
Fearful/extremely scared	9	9	ns
Sleeping problems	5	10	<.01

* Chi-square test
** Beating/kicking/pinching/biting

The only complaint with a significantly higher incidence in PDD children is that of sleeping problems. Yet, according to Swaak (1977), sleeping problems are already more common in the group of mentally retarded children in general. When comparing mentally retarded infants with normal infants in particular, he found a significantly higher frequency of difficulties in falling asleep (continued wakefulness, head banging, talking to oneself, or crying), and a higher frequency of prescription of sedatives for the sleeping problems of these children. Unfortunately, the studies of mentally retarded children by Clements et al. (1986) and Quine (1991) report only isolated instances of those behavioural problems which are known to be closely associated with sleeping difficulties. Consequently, they do not present complete profiles on the basis of a clear-cut classification or diagnosis. However, there does seem to be a close association between the behavioural problems mentioned and PDD, of which later chapters will give evidence. Clements et al. report self-injury, non-socially directed difficult behaviour and attachment to routines as concomitants of sleeping problems. (Incidentally, no such association was found for echolalia, stereotyped movements or quality of social interaction.) Quine found that poor communication skills in particular - a crucial deficit in individuals with pervasive disorders - were very common in children with night settling problems and night waking problems.

As for the relationship between, on the one hand, reporting a given complaint or problematic behaviour and, on the other, the child's actual problems, the reader is referred to Section II.2.2.4.

II.2.2.5   *Additional handicaps determined by organic brain damage*

As already stated in II.1.3, according to the classificatory principles of DSM-III-R, the number of categories applicable to children with pervasive developmental disorders is limited. Even a child with PDD who is overactive and has a short attention span cannot be placed in the category Attention-deficit/Hyperactivity Disorder. This also applies to Developmental Language Disorders, Overanxious Disorder and Separation Anxiety Disorder. This might leave one with the impression that PDD children compare favourably with non-PDD children with respect to frequency of additional behavioural problems and handicaps. However, given the classification system as it is and considering the purport of the concept pervasive, this drawback may be accepted.

For the present study this means that the two subgroups of mentally retarded children can only be compared with respect to handicaps determined by organic brain damage. This will be done in the next three sections.

II.2.2.5.1   Organic Personality Syndrome and Dementia

In Table II.2.11, the number of children with Organic Personality Syndrome (OPS) in each subgroup is presented, giving within parentheses the number of those children who have Organic Personality Syndrome combined with Dementia (four PDD children and three non-PDD children). The statistical test is also given.

Table II.2.11 Incidence of Organic Personality Syndrome (and Dementia) in PDD children and non-PDD children (n_{total} = 393)

	Non-PDD children		PDD children	
OPS (+ Dementia)	77	(80)*	10	(14)
No OPS (+ Dementia)	179	(176)	127	(123)
% OPS (+ Dementia)**	30.1	(31.3)	7.3	(10.2)

* In parentheses: OPS + Dementia
** Percentages of children with OPS and OPS + Dementia in each category
Chi-square = 26.86 (21.69); p <.001 (p <.001)

Organic Personality Syndrome, with and without Dementia, occurs significantly more frequently in mentally retarded children without PDD.

II.2.2.5.2   Motor handicaps

Table II.2.12 presents the proportions of children with Motor handicaps, as defined in II.1.2.6, in each category.

Table II.2.12 Incidence of motor handicap in PDD children and non-PDD children (n_{total} = 393)

	Non-PDD children	PDD children
Motor handicap	35	4
No motor handicap	221	133
% Motor handicap*	13.3	2.9

* Percentages of children with motor handicaps in each category
Chi-square = 10.97; p <.001

Motor handicaps, too, occur significantly more frequently in mentally retarded children without PDD.

II.2.2.5.3 Visual and auditory handicaps

Visual and auditory handicaps are, as Table II.2.13 shows, very evenly distributed between the two categories.

Table II.2.13 Incidence of visual and auditory handicaps in PDD children and non-PDD children (n_{total} = 393)

	Non-PDD children	PDD children
Vis. and aud. handicap	16	9
No vis. and aud. handicap	240	128
% Vis. and aud. handicap*	6.3	6.9

* Percentages children with visual and auditory handicaps in each category
Chi-square = 0.02; ns

II.2.2.6 Problems due to faulty child-rearing methods

Comparing mentally retarded PDD children with more or less 'normal' mentally retarded children, i.e., those without a PDD, with respect to the effects of child rearing, would in the context of the present study actually mean trying to find out whether or not there is any difference between PDD children and non-PDD children with respect to overloading, pampering, neglect, and pampering combined with neglect. However, such a comparison is not feasible for two interrelated reasons. In the first place, while overloading, pampering and neglect have almost the same meaning whether applied to 'normal' mentally retarded children or to average/normal children without handicaps, with PDD children the situation is completely different. The exact nature of the difference, however, is not so easy to indicate. In the second place - and this is in fact the main point - parents of children with autism and related contactual disorders face child-rearing problems which differ fundamentally from those faced by parents of mentally retarded children.

The problems of bringing up a mentally retarded child have been briefly discussed in Section II.1.3.2.1. As Gresnigt and Gresnigt-Strengers (1973), among others, have pointed out, it is a painful and distressing experience to have a mentally retarded child. Upbringing and day-to-day care present considerable difficulties indeed. However, contacts with many parents of children of both categories have convinced me that the problems with which parents of a child with autism or related contactual disorders are confronted are even much more serious.

A 'normal' mentally retarded child is capable of making contact, even very enjoyable and heartwarming contact. True, it is a kind of contact that betrays a developmental lag, but, given the limitations posed, the contact can still be a fully harmonious one for both parties. Parents who have learned to adapt themselves to their child's developmental failure may feel very happy with him; the child himself is aware of all the love and attention given to him and is able to respond in his own way. A natural and spontaneous intimacy may develop. This interaction, which is the social environment framing the child's upbringing (Langeveld, 1955), is of vital importance to the whole process. Or, adopting the imagery of another author, the parents are in a position to *recognize* their child's 'demand' for upbringing, and to respond with a 'supply' of upbringing, possibly with some professional help (Kok, 1987). It may well be that both the supply and the demand deviate somewhat from those familiar to parents of normal children, but there is still much correspondence with what is normal. Thus, there is room left for the development of an interaction process between parents and child, which is stimulating for both parties involved.

When dealing with the relationship between parents and children with autism and related contactual disorders, I shall concentrate on the problems of the children, which are as a matter of fact the primary problems, whereas those of the parents are by and large secondary. Consequently, the issue will be approached with an eye to the management problems presented by PDD children, leaving aside the complex child-rearing situation of homes with PDD children and the parental role in particular. A similar approach is adopted by Van Berckelaer-Onnes (1979). In this connection I would also like to make reference to a critical comment made by Rispens (1989), that the time spent in analyzing parental feelings equals that spent in analyzing the problem or complaint in question. Too often have I seen parents 'treated' when a proper diagnosis of their PDD child and practical advice concerning the management of this child were in fact the things they primarily needed.

In an article written by Baartman (1982), in which the subtitle speaks of bewildering/bewildered children and perplexed parents, the author argues that with all the attention literature has given to the cognitive and perceptual components of autistic behaviour, a far more relevant aspect has been neglected: the disruption of the naturalness of the mutual commitment between parents and child. As a result, parents are losing their self-confidence and become confused. Goldfarb (1961) speaks in this connection of *parental perplexity*.

Finally, I present a quotation, taken from a study by Berckelaer-Onnes and Kwakkel-Scheffer (1988), in which the problems of parents with an autistic child are delineated in a concise and lucid way; these authors, too, point out that children with communication disorders in particular constitute an extremely distressing experience for their parents:

Parents of an autistic child are faced with an arduous task. At an early stage they discover that their child is different. The difference is not primarily caused by a developmental lag, or a hearing defect, or a motor disability, but rather by a lack of contact, interaction, and communication. The relationship between parents and child seems to have been nipped in the bud. This deeply affects parental emotions. 'It is as if your child rejects you ...' Moreover, the child's behaviour evokes so many questions, so much bewilderment, that you are constantly at a loss what to do. The contact loses its naturalness, bringing up is no longer a spontaneous process: what on earth can you do?

Coming back to the point at issue, the question to be dealt with is: how do we deal with the concepts overloading, pampering and neglect with respect to this group of children? As for pampering and neglect, these two seem virtually irrelevant, which possibly can best be demonstrated by analyzing what the concept overloading means when considering PDD children. If overloading is already inherent in the upbringing of and care for 'normal' mentally retarded children, this holds even more true for mentally retarded children with a pervasive developmental disorder, and with them the overloading is very intrusive to boot. Unlike the mentally retarded child, who shares with us one common world, the PDD child is faced with two worlds: our world and his world, although actually to speak of his 'world' is certainly an overstatement. After all, a PDD child is a contorted, seclusive, fearful, and confused being, who - above all - lives a bleak existence full of incomprehension and insecurity. In many situations the autistic child (and the autistic adult as well) has to cope with a poorness of fit between the two worlds, which means that even dealing with the most simple elements of our world may in his case mean overloading in one form or another. However, it is possible to tailor our world a bit more to his, making it somewhat less threatening, as the observation clinic has been able to demonstrate. But in a family setting this is far more difficult to realise than in a residential setting. Moreover, many families had received little or no professional help before their child was admitted to the observation clinic. In view of this fact, and on the basis of observations made in the clinic, the conclusion seems warranted that overloading in at least 70% of the 137 PDD children in the study had surpassed the unavoidable amount. This percentage is at any rate much higher than the 27% found in the group of non-PDD children. Again, in the PDD children overloading tended to be more frequent in children of higher levels of functioning.

II.2.3   Summary and conclusions

First let me emphasize that mentally retarded children with a PDD are not merely dually disabled, but suffer from two disabilities of a *fundamental* nature, or from disorders which result in two *basic disabilities*, mental retardation representing a *deficit*, and a PDD representing a *disorder*. Basic disabilities create more handicaps and handicap more severely than what I would call *peripheral disabilities*, such as impaired vision, impaired hearing and motor disabilities. As I stated in an earlier publication (Kraijer, 1971), due to these two basic disabilities, i.e., mental retardation and autism, the possibilities of management and education are limited and for these children the way to full adulthood is blocked off for good. Moreover, the coexistence of two disabilities is as a rule not an addition but rather a *multiplication* of problems.

74

Thus, a combination of two basic deficits involves a very serious condition indeed.

To summarize, the most important conclusions of this chapter are:

- As for the eleven complaints considered, three of them occur significantly more frequently in the PDD children than in the otherwise problematical non-PDD children, while none of them occurs more frequently in the non-PDD children. The conclusion is therefore warranted that PDD children constitute a very distinct problem group in the mental retardation field.
- Of the 393 children in the study, 137 could be placed into one subclass of disorders, Pervasive Developmental Disorder, as defined by DSM-III-R. This may be seen as an indication that the profile of these children has at least some homogeneity. Additional support for this assumption can be found in the fact that the differences are all falling into one pattern, but above all in the kind of differences, notably: Poor Contact, and Strange/Elusive/Unpredictable or Psychotic (highly significantly more frequent; the exact figure was in fact: $p < .00001$).
- A significant difference of incidence in PDD and non-PDD children was found for two of the three additional handicaps caused by organic brain damage:
  - Organic Personality Syndrome (with and without Dementia) was found to have a much higher incidence in non-PDD children. The actual level of significance is in the neighbourhood of .00001;
  - Motor handicaps were found to have a significant higher incidence in non-PDD children.

  These two differences are very substantial.

  Visual and auditory handicaps, in general less frequent for that matter, are evenly distributed between both groups of children.

  As far as the incidence of some gross and atypical brain damage disorders is concerned, there is, I think, sufficient ground to conclude that these findings, even though they pertain to a very specific group of problem children, prove once again that, so far as Pervasive Developmental Disorders are concerned, the DSM-III-R manual is right in regarding them as a fairly homogeneous subclass. Etiologically, these findings fit in with those of Rutter and Schopler (1987) and of Kraijer and Nelck (1989). The reader is also referred to I.2.5. For the sake of completeness, it may be worth adding that in a general article Gillberg (1990a), on the other hand, stresses the similarities between autism and mental retardation. The fact that they are often found together is felt by him to be an indication of a common neurobiological basis.
- When dealing with children with autism and related contact disorders, the concept of faulty child-rearing methods should not be applied off-hand. Nevertheless, there is no denying that these children, compared with 'normal' mentally retarded children, constitute a problem group in

terms of education and management as well. Overloading, in particular, is found to be an omnipresent and almost unavoidable pitfall.

PROBLEMS WITH CLASSIFICATION AND DIAGNOSIS IN EVERYDAY CLINICAL PRACTICE

II.3.1   Introduction

In Chapter II.1 the group of children admitted to the Eekwal observation home who served as subjects for this study was analyzed in terms of the DSM-III-R classification system. Before going into the practical problems encountered in classifying and diagnosing these children, I would like to make clear how educational intervention can benefit from such classification. Three years after completion of the Eekwal-home investigation the DSM-IV was published (APA, 1994). Some time was needed before I had gained sufficient experience with the modifications made in this new version. In 1996 I carried out a study on the basis of the DSM-IV. This investigation is actually outside the scope of the Eekwal-home study and it involves moreover not only *children*, but also *adolescents* and *adults*. Consequently, the findings should be regarded as a distinct contribution and are presented separately in Appendix A of the present book.

In my view, *classification* is a very useful procedure in the mental retardation field; it provides a broad and general framework for individual diagnosis, and allows a general overview of the symptoms and features of disorders and conditions. *Diagnostics*, however, mainly concern the specific shape and colour of symptoms and features found in a given individual. Therefore, within the context of individual treatment, it is the diagnostic approach which is needed. As has been pointed out in a textbook on diagnostic models (Rispens, 1988), diagnostics play a key role when courses of treatment are planned by professional helpers. The diagnostician should found his conclusions on the sound and objective basis of substantiated knowledge and clearly defined concepts in which behavioural problems and the ways of properly managing them are delineated in a more or less standardized way. A classification should give such a basis, although present classification systems (as yet) do not give directions for treatment. Anyhow, granted that people with a given disorder have similar needs for help - and I am convinced that in general this does apply to children and adults with pervasive developmental disorders - the first thing to do is to identify the disorder in question and to describe it properly. To find out which kind of help is needed by trial and error would mean a heavy loss of time and energy, while causing unnecessary suffering for those who are in need of it. A given complex of symptoms is recognized as forming an entity and given a name. On the level of the individual, this is a diagnosis, which at any rate should indicate a certain need or type of needs (Kok, 1987), and from which, ideally, it would be possible to derive a certain type of intervention. Thus, classification and diagnostics are procedures which are subservient to educational intervention and special educational treatment. They must be regarded as the first crucial steps to be taken, even when present systems are often unable to give indications for treatment.

In actual practice, the classification procedure is far from being easy, as the following discussion of some of the classification problems regarding the children in the present study will demonstrate. As has been noted above, classifying is preliminary to making diagnoses. It follows that conditions which are difficult to classify will as a matter of course also be difficult to diagnose. To highlight the classification problems found in this study, two of the most striking subtypes within the entire group of mentally retarded children with pervasive developmental disorders will be examined in Section II.3.2.1. Thereafter, Sections II.3.2.2 to II.3.2.9 will discuss those disabilities and categories of disorders in mentally retarded individuals which will often be hard to differentiate from pervasive developmental disorders.

II.3.2 Problems in delineating a PDD

II.3.2.1 *Two subtypes of mentally retarded PDD children*

The DSM-III, DSM-III-R and DSM-IV systems present pervasive developmental disorders as a continuum, ranging from classic childhood autism or PDD-AD, the severest form, to the least severe form, termed by the manual as Atypical or Not Otherwise Specified (NOS). However, several other investigators, such as Wing and Attwood (1987), prefer to speak of a spectrum of disorders, rather than of a continuum. Although the disorders in question all belong to one category, several very characteristic forms may be distinguished. As early as 1979, Wing and Gould subdidived the group of children exhibiting a triad of social and verbal impairments into the aloof group, the passive group and the active-but-odd group. Other suggestions for subdivisions can be found in publications of such authors as Siegel et al. (1986), Cohen et al. (1987), and Rescorla (1988). The present writer, too, gave some consideration to this issue, especially as far as the mentally retarded is concerned (Kraijer, 1988a,b). On the basis of differences in the clinical picture, two major subtypes of mentally retarded PDD children, adolescents, and adults can be distinguished: a *rigid* group and an *erratic* group. Using an earlier version of the PDD-MR Scale (see Chapter III.1), two groups of 23 children, each group as far as possible representative of their respective subgroups, were compared (Kraijer, 1991; see also II.4.4.1). Both groups were matched on chronological age, and functioned at severe, moderate, and mild levels of mental retardation. These two groups, which correspond closely to the aloof group and the active-but-odd group as distinguished by Wing and Gould, showed the following characteristics:

- Common characteristics:
  - Poor contact with peers
  - Unusual and obsessive interests
  - Stereotyped way of handling objects and own body
  - Strong attachment to patterns, routines and/or rituals

- Specific characteristics:

Rigid group
- Predominantly severely mentally retarded or slightly above that level
- Social response towards adults very poor

- Expressive language skills in many cases absent

Erratic group
- Predominantly mildly mentally retarded or slightly below that level
- Although there is social response towards adults, it is deviant (e.g., contact is fleeting, lacks growth, is bizarre, extremely 'shy,' predominantly defiant/ trying or overdemanding, or too unreserved towards strangers)
- Although expressive language skills are predominantly present, there are deviations with respect to content and/or ways of producing language
- Many cases of self-injury
- Erratic, unpredictable behaviour
- Unusual and excessive anxiety and/or panic reactions.

By making a distinction between the rigid and erratic forms of PDD I do not aim to discard the notion of a passive type of PDD, which was introduced by Wing and Gould. As a matter of fact, the passive type is clinically observable. However, I was unable to find sufficient evidence that it represents a separate type with its own distinctive features.

The fact that the disturbances constitute at least as much a spectrum as a continuum adds to the classificatory (and consequently diagnostic) problems.

In the following sections those disabilities or categories of disorders which are likely to present special problems of delineation with respect to PDD will be discussed separately.

Generally, there is no doubt that the lower the level of functioning, the more difficult will it be to make a classification and a diagnosis. As far as mildly retarded children and adults are concerned, their behaviour has still much in common with that of the average-normal population; only the skills in language and abstraction tend to be comparatively underdeveloped. Individuals who are severely or indeed profoundly mentally retarded, however, have an extremely limited repertoire in the cognitive, emotional and social areas of behaviour. Many of them have hardly any verbal skills or none whatsoever. As for the non- verbal aspects of their behaviour, lack of differentiation is the predominant feature. Therefore, the question may arise of whether classifying and diagnosing, notably with respect to pervasive disorders, is possible at all with these categories of mentally retarded persons. Concerning this question, it is very important to repeat a statement made in the original Dutch companion manual to the PDD-MR Scale (1990) that, especially in individuals below the level of moderate mental retardation, fearful aloofness and stereotyped behaviour are easily liable to be taken for symptoms of a contact disorder. Hoejenbos, realizing that profoundly mentally retarded persons are highly vulnerable to environmental factors, made, as early as 1967, an attempt to differentiate between what he called 'purely idiotic behaviour' and the 'psychotic behaviour displayed by an idiot.' He pointed out that:

The behavior is not in itself the symptom of sickness but the manner in which the subnormal, undeveloped mind copes with reality at a certain stage of development. [...] The 'idiotic' behavior is the way in which subnormality reacts on reality. It is necessary to find out the background of the behavior in the individual. It may be that only some changes in the surroundings will diminish the disturbances. We can find these possibilities by communicating with the idiot in his way, on the floor and slowly moving and touching him, and not in our way with words and standing upright. An attitude of soothing. An attitude of handling, moving, sucking, sniffling and touching on his level, factually too. The so-called psychotic traits in some idiots may be normal reactions to inconvenient surroundings. In other cases they may be signals of a psychotic state.

More recently, similar views have been put forward by Velthausz (1987), who states that profoundly retarded individuals have very idiosyncratic, but not necessarily disturbed, ways of making contact. The DSM-III-R manual makes a similar point when referring to stereotyped behaviours in severely and profoundly mentally retarded people. With regard to the category Stereotypy/Habit Disorder, the manual states:

The essential features of this disorder are intentional and repetitive behaviors that are nonfunctional, i.e., serve no constructive, socially acceptable purpose. The behaviors may include: body-rocking, head-banging, hitting or biting parts of one's own body (e.g., face slapping, hand-biting), skin-picking or scratching, teeth-grinding (bruxism), bodily manipulations (e.g., incessant nose-picking, hair-pulling, eye- and anus-poking), non-communicative, repetitive vocalizations, breath-holding, hyperventilation, and swallowing air (aerophagia). Frequently the behaviors are performed in a rhythmic fashion.

The diagnosis is given only when the disturbance either causes physical injury to the child or markedly interferes with normal activities. *The diagnosis is not given when a Pervasive Developmental Disorder or a Tic Disorder is present.*

Anyhow, the profoundly mentally retarded person in particular may present types of behaviour which suggest a pervasive disturbance without, however, having such a disturbance. Frequently, the behaviour in question is caused by a serious lack of coping abilities, which is indeed an inherent and almost irreversible feature of this level of functioning. Clinicians who want to identify pervasive disorders in individuals in the profound range of mental retardation - and I believe this is possible - should have a thorough knowledge of both conditions, i.e., of autism and related contact disorders as well as of profound mental retardation in all its manifestations.

The only exception which has to be made regards the category of seriously multiply disabled, non-ambulatory mentally retarded persons who are functioning at the very profound levels of retardation. This group presents serious and sometimes insurmountable problems of classification and diagnosis, as both experience in the Eekwal observation home and the PDD-MR Scale study have made clear. Wing and Attwood (1987) also found that below a certain level of development - a mental age below twenty months - diagnosis becomes increasingly difficult.

II.3.2.3   Hearing defects

As clinical experience demonstrated, congenital or early onset deafness does not necessarily rule out the possibility of establishing the presence or absence of a pervasive disorder, even in mentally retarded children. Mentally retarded children who are deaf should in principle be perfectly able to make normal social contact and to take part in social life in an almost normal way. Nevertheless, some deaf mentally retarded children are in fact shy and withdrawn, and in those cases it may take somewhat more time to arrive at a proper diagnosis.

However, the combination of autism and a hearing defect does occur, as was indicated in Section II.2.2.5.3. In practice, the main diagnostic problem is to establish the hearing defect. In such cases brain-stem audiometry can be helpful.

II.3.2.4   Visual impairments

A considerable number of blind or almost blind children develop forms of stereotyped behaviours, including the so-called blindisms. Obviously these children cannot look straight into the eyes of other people and lack an animated facial expression. However, the social skills and language skills of these children should in principle be fully consonant with their mental age. Hence, a pervasive developmental disorder can reliably be diagnosed in these children.

II.3.2.5   *Language disorders*

As mentioned in II.1.3.1.1, mentally retarded persons may present Developmental Expressive Language Disorder singly (DELD) or combined with Receptive Language Disorder (DELD/DRLD), but receptive language disorder was not found to occur singly in the present study.

At least as far as mentally retarded children are concerned, language disorders seem seldom to occur separately. Often they are associated with overactivity and poor concentration. Or to put it differently, children with language disorders often also fit perfectly into the category Attention-deficit/Hyperactivity Disorder. As a result, the situation is rather complex, and it may take quite some time before enough insight has been gained to classify and diagnose a given child with a fair degree of reliability. This also applies to the disorder discussed in the next section.

II.3.2.6   *Attention-deficit/Hyperactivity Disorder*

As mentioned in Section II.1.3.1.2, a comparatively large number of mentally retarded children, both with and without a PDD, present problems of attention span and overactivity. And it is particularly with disorders of this type that the number and variety of problems make it extremely difficult to decide on the presence or absence of autism and autistic-like conditions. Many children with AD/HD make only superficial and fleeting contacts with adults and peers alike. Other frequently found features are a short attention span and insufficient interest in the surrounding world. The question to which the diagnostician has to find an answer is: does the child's hyperactivity and orderlessness simply leave him no time for better contact-making, more attentiveness, and deeper involvement, or is there really something wrong with his ability to communicate and socialize? The importance of this problem of differential diagnostics is, I think, underrated by both Wing and Attwood (1987) and Cohen et al. (1987), while Gillberg et al. (1990) did give at least some consideration to it. But the only expert who has repeatedly and emphatically given attention to this problem is Minderaa (Minderaa, 1989; Minderaa & Uleman-Vleeschdrager, 1989). There can only be a fair chance that such children are properly categorized and diagnosed if they are clinically observed and (tentatively) treated for many weeks, and in some cases even months. Although the exact number of puzzling cases in the present study cannot be given, there were at least twenty children about whom the observation team was in doubt for quite some time as to whether they should be categorized as AD/HD or as PDD. (Evidently, the children to whom I refer here are not those with PDD-Autistic Disorder, but those who fall under PDD-NOS as well as under the erratic form of PDD.) However, there will always remain a rather strong likelihood that sometimes classifying and diagnosing cannot be done with a hundred per cent certainty, which is acceptable as long as all considerations and difficulties in making a decision are clarified. Neither can wrong decisions be fully precluded. As an

illustrative example of this may serve a diagnosis made at the Eekwal observation home of a nine-year-old boy. After a long period of indecision, he
was finally labelled as an excessively overtaxed case of AD/HD. This
seemed a plausible diagnosis, as he calmed down a great deal during his
stay in the clinic and became much more 'normal', although his attention
span remained poor and he was still liable to become highly agitated by
minor incidents. In order to protect him against excessive demands and to
relieve the other members of his family, the boy in question was admitted to
a residential institution for mentally retarded persons. However, the present
writer, applying the criteria of the PDD-MR Scale to his case file, arrived at
a score of 10, PDD-MR Scale classification PDD. Not long afterwards -
twelve years after having been discharged from the Eekwal observation
home - this same boy was examined by an educationalist of the institution
and then scored 11, again the PDD-MR Scale PDD classification. The general
feeling of the institution's experts concerning this boy is also that he completely fits into this category.

II.3.2.7   *Organic Personality Syndrome and Dementia*

Although OPS and Dementia occur significantly more frequently with mentally retarded children without PDD, as stated above in Section II.2.5.1, difficulties of classification with respect to OPS/Dementia and the presence or
absence of PDD have to be anticipated, in any case in the mental retardation
field. Of at least fifteen children who had been labelled OPS or Dementia,
the observation clinic was in doubt as to whether or not they should be regarded as PDD cases as well (once again PDD-NOS). The outstanding features of these children were: little or only perfunctory interest in the surrounding world; often rigidity and adherence to fixed patterns; inflexibility;
and - in a few cases - a high degree of irritability and unpredictable reactions. These are all symptoms which, when found together, suggest a pervasive developmental disorder. At the same time, these children seem to represent a notable atypical form of autism or related contactual disorder when
compared with the AD/HD group. This is especially the case with Dementia. As mentioned in Section II.1.2.5, four Dementia children were classified
as PDD-NOS. Three of them, two boys of five and three years and a girl of
seven, were severe cases of Bourneville disease. The fourth was a four-year-
old boy with the Sanfilippo syndrome. In these four children the early onset
of degenerative processes had led to autistiform behaviour. Assessments
based on the observation records yielded PDD-MR Scale scores of respectively 6, 4, 8, and 11; PDD-MR Scale classifications: non-PDD, non-PDD, doubtful PDD/non-PDD, and PDD. Recent follow-up PDD-MR Scale measurements yielded for the first three children scores of 7, 6, and 8; PDD-MR Scale
classifications: doubtful, non-PDD, doubtful. The fourth child was no longer
alive by then.
    With respect to PDD children who in addition fall into one of these two
categories, a subclassification seems apposite, as has also been recommended

with almost identical arguments by Corbett (1987). In this connection, an interesting subclassification within the general group of pervasive developmental disorders made by the ICD-10 (WHO, 1992) should be mentioned: Rett's Disorder (F84.2), and Other childhood disintegrative disorder (F84.3). In fact, the first condition occupies an exceptional position - as the somatic factor plays a crucial role here - and therefore a separate label seems to me to be a rather peculiar overreaction to the (re)discovery of this disorder. However, it certainly makes sense to distinguish the disintegrative disorder, which in my view should include the Rett's Disorder, as a separate disorder. As such can be classified those children who, after an initial period of normal development until their second birthday, subsequently show an evident loss of skills in almost all areas. The exact nature and cause of the disorder are in many instances unclear. In some cases the condition is progressive, but often a stabilization is seen after an initial disintegration. Whether or not this difference in the pathological process calls for a further subdivision (Corbett, 1987) is, as far as I am concerned, still an open question. Two of the four aforementioned children completely or almost completely met the criteria for Other childhood disintegrative disorder, one of them being the boy with the metabolic disorder. One of the remaining two children was only eighteen months old when she showed an unmistakable regression, but her development was in all likelihood slightly lagging behind even before then. The other child's signs of developmental lags showed clearly from the outset, and gradually grew worse.

The examples given above illustrate that these subcategories, which by now have been adopted by the DSM-IV (1994), also create classification difficulties, at least in the mental retardation field. Nevertheless, as has been argued by Gillberg et al. (1990), Rutter (1989), Rutter et al. (1992) and Volkmar (1992), this subdivision should certainly be given a fair try. At the same time, however, it must be kept in mind that mentally retarded children may show *in addition* - due to whatever condition or cause - an unmistakable disintegration.

II.3.2.8   *Other overlapping or complicating (diagnostic) categories*

In addition, some of the DSM-III-R categories discussed in Section II.1.3.1.3 were occasionally found in clinical practice to be difficult to differentiate from PDD, notably the erratic form of PDD.

Let us consider schizophrenia first. At least in the field of mental retardation, there is no need in my view for the diagnostic category Childhood Schizophrenia. Although Cantor (1988) strongly recommends the reintroduction of this category, both Carr (1989) and Volkmar (1989), in their respective reviews of Cantor's study, comment that his suggestion lacks a solid basis and seems inexpedient.

Similarly, the category Childhood Borderline Personality Disorder seems to me of little use in this field. There is, after all, reason to believe that there is some overlap between autism and borderline personality. One of the researchers who recommends the introduction of Borderline Child Syndrome is Gunning (1989). He argues that this label should be applied to children who have difficulties in every aspect of their lives and in all areas of functioning, but who differ from genuinely autistic children in the following respects: less predictable behaviour; less insistence on sameness; less serious contact disorder; more affect; and more imagination. Their problems become more acute when they are under emotional pressure. The Eekwal observation home saw children with contact disorders - who therefore fit into the PDD category - who displayed some of these symptoms when confronted with too many stress factors. However, the symptoms described by Gunning are certainly also found as a primary condition, more specifically as the erratic form of PDD, within the group of the mentally retarded.

All in all, I recommend the categorization of all children who belong to the spectrum of autism and autistic-like conditions as cases of Pervasive Developmental Disorders, with, if possible, three subcategories: a rigid type, roughly corresponding with the classic form of autism; a somewhat borderline erratic type; and finally an unspecified residual category, which should also include the passive type distinguished by Wing and Gould (1979). Should the children thus classified develop a genuine Borderline Personality Disorder in later life, they may still be reclassified. In fact, the Eekwal observation home saw a number of mentally retarded adolescents with a Borderline Personality disorder who, judging by the available case histories, in childhood would most likely have been classified as at least PDD-NOS. An analogous situation was found with respect to the childhood and adolescent types of schizophrenia. Watkins et al. (1988) also came to the conclusion that many of these cases met completely the criteria for PDD in early childhood. The question of whether a common etiology should be taken as existing for autism, related contact disorders, (childhood) schizophrenia, and borderline conditions remains topical.

Again, there were only occasional doubts with respect to children who were eventually placed in such categories as Chronic Motor Tic Disorder, Separation Anxiety Disorder, and Overanxious Disorder (see II.1.3.1.3), and at any rate the doubts did not arise frequently enough to call for modifications in the classification system.

As other instances of overlapping disorders, Tourette's Disorder and Obsessive Compulsive Disorder have been mentioned (Minderaa, 1989; Minderaa & Uleman-Vleeschdrager, 1989). Only a few cases of the first condition were seen in the present study (see II.1.3.1.3). The symptoms of one case, a twelve-year-old boy with PDD-AD, had been described in detail by the observation team, but only in terms of 'tics.' The proper diagnosis, Tourette's Disorder, was made only later on. Problems of differential diagnosis did not arise frequently. Such problems were more often present with Obsessive-compulsive behaviour, but still not frequent enough to warrant further discussion.

On admission, a large proportion of the entire group of 393 children in the study was unsettled, psychotically disintegrated, and sometimes positively psychotic, in *response* to environmental factors. The diagnosis of a reactive psychosis on top of a (previously diagnosed or not) PDD was made for a number of these children, while being aware that overloading is a tricky concept, especially when applied to PDD children (see the preceding chapter). However, these children can also become confused by circumstances which are simply an intrinsic part of their situation, notably with respect to the number of stimuli. For instance, even the plain fact of being successively at home, in the schoolbus, at the day-care centre, again in the schoolbus, and at the end of the day back home again, may be more than such a child can cope with. Likewise, a comparatively large and vivacious family setting may be an exhausting experience. The differential-diagnostic problems posed by all these factors may be clarified by a stay within a setting such as the Eekwal observation home. Here an evaluation is possible of the effects of a controllable number of stimuli and/or demands which, if need be, can be geared to the individual case.

Finally, there seems to be no doubt that a PDD child, adolescent or adult may also develop an *endogenous* psychosis. With regard to this matter, Wing and Attwood (1987) in particular have advanced clear views. Giving an overview of the differentiation problems likely to emerge when diagnosing the psychotic disorder of schizophrenia, they remind us that such a predominantly endogenous psychiatric condition can be superimposed on the original autistic disorder. In many instances, no final diagnosis can be made as to the primary disorder until the most acute problems have been cured. Or, adopting the DSM-III-R terminology, the Axis-I problem has to be cured before the Axis-II problem can be identified properly. (In this connection, I would like to express my disappointment that the DSM-IV ranged the Pervasive Developmental Disorders under Axis-I instead of under Axis-II.) In actual clinical practice, however, these acute problems in persons with PDD in particular are often hard to treat in children, adolescents and adults alike, and then the diagnostician is left with a rather complicated picture. In the Eekwal observation home this was most clearly seen in adolescents and adults with PDD, and as a result many diagnoses had to be put into such vague terms as: 'autist (PDD-AD?) with catatonic and depressive episodes', or: 'PDD-NOS with psychotic disintegration with cyclic erethism and mania?' and the like. At any rate, a proper classification and diagnosis of these patients cannot be made without a solid case history, and often still cannot be made when one is available.

II.3.3   Short-term diagnostics versus long-term diagnostics

In clinical psychology, educational treatment and psychiatry, classification and diagnosis are usually short-term operations. Examinations, possibly spread over several meetings, more often than not take only one or a few hours in total. Clinical information thus obtained is normally supplemented with information given by parents, teachers, and/or previous examiners. On the basis of these comparatively meagre data, the case in question must be classified and diagnosed, and sensible recommendations provided. Feedback frequently does not occur, and as a result examiners, particularly those who are not directly involved in further treatment and guidance, are up in the air about the correctness of their statements. At the very most, such *short-term diagnostics* might be regarded as being passable for rather uncomplicated cases. However, I am convinced that in the vast majority of cases *long-term diagnostics* should be highly preferred. In an earlier publication (Kraijer, 1983), I recommended the use of long-term diagnostics even when ascertaining 'merely' mental retardation. With young children in particular, final conclusions concerning their exact level of mental retardation should not be drawn until these children have undergone at least one reexamination at a later date, while for the period between the two examinations a special development scheme is desirable. A short-term diagnosis can generally only give a satisfactory answer regarding the presence or absence of PDD in a given mentally retarded child when the mental retardation has already been firmly established, when the autistic features are outstanding, and when no other additional disabilities or problems are obscuring the picture. However, short-term diagnostics would have been totally insufficient for about one hundred of the close upon four hundred children in the present study, in the differential diagnostic respect alone. Of these children, fifty could only be classified and diagnosed after a quite considerable period of hospitalization and (tentative) treatment. In these considerations I have still left aside questions concerning the effects of conditions such as deafness, mental retardation or contact disorder (or their combination) on the general level of functioning. If answers to these questions could be given at all, they would require even more time.

Arguing cleverly, one could maintain that with a classification system such as the DSM, problems of etiology and genesis fall completely outside of its scope. This would mean that a mentally retarded child who is extremely unhappy, having been heavily overdemanded and pushed around, could be classified as AD/HD, as the child is evidently manifesting this behaviour. The stand I take on this issue is that in such a case the first thing to do is to test the hypothesis, by way of treatment, that the AD/HD behaviour has been caused by overdemanding. Both the proper formulation of such a hypothesis and designing a treatment strategy to test the hypothesis are time-consuming affairs. The final diagnosis in the given example may then be that the child in question is a 'simple' case of severe mental retardation, liable to AD/HD behaviour when overdemanded.

II.3.4 Summary

Problems of differential diagnostics with respect to the presence or absence of a pervasive developmental disorder occur mainly with the following groups of children: very profoundly mentally retarded children who are also multiply disabled; children with AD/HD; children with OPS or Dementia; and psychotically disintegrated children. As mentioned in Section II.1.1.2, the operations of classifying and diagnosing the 393 children in the study were without exception not finished before the end of their hospitalization periods. Obviously therefore, long-term diagnostics has been applied, and is indeed the procedure to be recommended.

CHAPTER II.4

ASPECTS OF MANAGEMENT AND TREATMENT OF MENTALLY RETARDED CHILDREN WITH A PDD

II.4.1   Introduction

The present chapter is not intended to be a general overview of the entire field of management, special educational intervention and treatment of children with a pervasive developmental disorder. For this the reader is referred to other studies, such as Rutter (1985), Howlin and Rutter (1987), Jordan and Powel (1995), Schopler and Mesibov (1995) and Siegel (1996). However, up until now hardly any special attention has been given in the literature in the field to the broad category of mentally retarded children with PDD, and least of all to the group of children in the more profound ranges of mental retardation. Moreover, in general the main emphasis has been on the familiar forms of autism rather than on the autistic-like disorders with their special features. The following paragraphs will hopefully fill these gaps. Another central theme in the present chapter is the - frequently behaviouristically inspired - approach used in the *clinical* management and treatment of the behavioural problems of children with pervasive developmental disorders. Some examples of this approach will be presented.

First of all, I want to state unequivocally that for children with a PDD there is no better place in which to grow up than *home*, and this holds true for mentally retarded children with a PDD as well. However, to bring up a child with these two disabilities is such an exceptional and extremely heavy undertaking that outside help on a professional basis is indispensable. Of primary importance are a reliable diagnosis and professional advice regarding practical management problems at home which is based on this diagnosis. Another crucial point is a good collaboration with the day-care centre or school. But even if these conditions are fulfilled, the burden may be so heavy for a given family that there is no alternative but to place the problem child in residential care. Understandably, this is an extremely difficult decision for parents to make. In a number of such cases, however, an interim solution is feasible, namely temporary observation and treatment in a clinical setting such as that at the Eekwal home. In such an environment it is possible to determine whether a different style of management may bring about an improvement in the child's behaviour and whether this approach is also viable within the family setting. Temporary hospitalization has other advantages as well:

- Parents will have a chance to summon up new strengths, and the entire family, including other children, may regain some peace of mind.
- Probably for the first time in many years, parents are in a position to view their child and his problems in a somewhat more detached way. Never before could it have been so plain to them that everything in the family has gradually come to revolve around this particular child: no visits to or from other people, the tiptoeing about the house after eight o'clock, the constant alertness while this child is around, the poor achievements at school of an elder child (now suddenly improving), the never ending troubles at meal-times, the clashes between the children, and so on and so forth.
- If placement in permanent residential care does eventually turn out to be necessary, the child's parents may by now have come to recognize that the new situation has not exclusively negative consequences, neither for themselves nor as a rule for the child in question. Parents may even feel hurt - although relieved at the same time - when noticing at visiting time or after a probationary weekend home that their child is clearly happy to be at the other place.

What I intend to contribute to the field in the present chapter is an account of some clinical experiences within the realm of special educational intervention and treatment of mentally retarded children with pervasive developmental disorders.

First, however, some general information has to be provided. All children staying in the Eekwal observation home were cared for exclusively within the clinical setting. In general, the length of stay was two to five months, which only in exceptional cases was extended to a longer or much longer period. Most treatments were given *within the child's own small group*, consisting of four to six children, and was administered by the day-to-day care staff. This staff was advised by a team of experts, with the present author acting as coordinator in his capacity of educational and clinical psychologist. In addition, *treatment and care on a purely individual basis* was provided. This was given by the following specialists (in increasing order of the time they spent): the psychiatrist; the physiotherapist-psychomotor therapist; the speech therapist-audiologist; the educational psychologist; the day-to-day care staff; qualified teachers who are also specialized in testing educability and in giving all sorts of more or less playful therapies for difficulties in the areas of social contact, language, social competence and perception. Each child was given a fair amount of personal attention, as will be clear from the following figures. On average, for each child about ninety minutes per working day were set aside for individual treatment. Thus, at the end of a hospitalization period of an average length, the time spent on individual care, given by whatever staff member, amounted to 130 to 160 hours. However, this does not come anywhere near to the number of hours of individual treatment reportedly given by the three therapists who are known to have applied the most intensive and almost completely individualized approaches. I am referring here to the following projects: the many years' clinical treatment given to seven autistic children by Frye (1968; see also I.2.1); the treatment given to the same number of autistic children by Van Soest (1989); the treatment given to nineteen autistic children by Lovaas (1987). The last two projects were of a non-clinical nature.

Although the study by Van Soest leaves many questions unanswered, it does report that the average amount of individual treatment given was one thousand hours (with a maximum of 1 433 hours). The children treated by Lovaas received, during a period of at least two years, more than forty hours of individual treatment per week. Moreover, Lovaas also called in the help of "all significant persons in all significant environments to maximize behavioral treatment gains by treating autistic children during most of their waking hours for many years." All three therapists claim that the autistic features of the children had been subdued considerably and that their intellectual development had been accelerated. However, in evaluating these results we should bear in mind that both Frye and Lovaas were dealing with a group of comparatively bright autistic children and that for Van Soest it was comparatively easy to achieve results because he treated children who had apparently escaped previous professional attention. Incidentally, none of the three authors claims complete cures. Even autistic children who have the privilege of intensive high-level professional attention will still have serious social integration problems in adulthood. And this holds true even for autistic persons who are not or are no longer functioning on a mental retardation level.

Better suited for making comparisons with the approach followed by the Eekwal observation home is the carefully planned programme of Howlin and Rutter (1987); both the methods used and the results obtained are very similar. Being a home-training project, it nevertheless applied a strategy which comes close to that adopted by the Eekwal observation home. Howlin and Rutter report an improvement, after a six-month period of treatment, in the areas of social competence, usage of language, and behavioural difficulties. However, the children's IQ's showed no increase. In the second follow-up treatment programme, there were clear signs that progress was levelling off. In this project the intellectual level of the children was also skewed towards the more fortunate ranges, as only children with an IQ above 60 were included. The mean IQ was, at the very start of the project, even as high as 86.8 (s.d. 17.9). However, this score was partly based on the Merrill-Palmer Scale which is known to place too much emphasis on performance skills and to give a flattering picture. Furthermore, physically disabled children, such as those with hearing or visual defects or epilepsy, were left out of the project.

As noted in Section II.1.2.4, the children in the present study displayed a great many problems of great diversity. The findings presented in Sections II.2.2.4.1 to II.2.2.4.4 indicate that the children with PDD were just as hyperactive/chaotic, short-tempered, aggressive, fearful, and wayward as the children without PDD (their behavioural problems in many of these cases having indeed been the very reason for application). Neither were there differences between the two groups with respect to eating problems and self-injury/self-mutilation. A significantly greater number of PDD children displayed the following problems: inaccessibility, strange/elusive behaviour, and sleeping problems. When developing the PDD-MR Scale (see Section III.1.3 and Appendix B), in which children and adults living in residential care and mentally retarded children visiting day-care centres were involved, the following problems were found to occur more frequently in mentally retarded persons with PDD than in those without PDD: insufficient contact; language and speech problems; obsessive, stereotyped, erratic, fearful, and rigid behaviours; self-injury/self-mutilation (Kraijer, 1990, 1992, 1996b). In an earlier study (Kraijer, 1991) I demonstrated that in mentally retarded persons living in residential institutions the incidence of disturbances of behaviour and hyperactive/chaotic behaviour is higher in those with a PDD than in those without a PDD. Finally, in Section III.1.3 and Chapter III.4, I will demonstrate that the following behaviours have a higher incidence in mentally retarded persons with a PDD than in those without a PDD: stereotyped behaviour; self-injurious behaviour; masturbation; rumination. (The higher incidence of stereotyped behaviour and self-injurious behaviour was also found, as noted before, when developing the PDD-MR Scale.) All in all, this is a collection of heterogeneous and in fact incoherent problems. For that reason, Rutter (1985) has tried to bring order into the broad area of behaviour problems displayed by autistic persons. He differentiates between (comparatively) *specific* and *non-specific* problems of autistic children. The specific problems more or less inhere in autism. They can be subdivided into two main types of problems:

- *developmental deviance and retardation* in the domains of cognition, language and socialization;
- rigid, stereotyped and inflexible *style of functioning*.

The non-specific type of problems is additional to and not necessarily bound up with autism. Among these Rutter mentions overactive behaviour, temper tantrums, aggression, self-destructive behaviour, fears and phobias, sleeping problems and problems with toilet-training.

In connection with the distinctions made by Rutter, I would like to make some additional remarks.

In the first place, the problems which Rutter has termed specific are not all of the same gravity. Developmental deviance and retardation in cognition, language and socialization - which in this context refers, as far as I can see, to social behaviour - are, unlike style of functioning, in all likelihood direct indications of the presence of crucial functioning deficits. (See also the findings of Baron-Cohen, Frith and Leslie, who were mentioned before in Section I.2.2.) Style of functioning, for its part, can in my view be more easily and more correctly understood as a response to these problems; therefore it comes rather close to the non-specific type of problems. As a matter of fact, rigidity and over-precision are not exclusively found in autism. These features may also be present in persons with other disabilities, such as organic psychosyndrome or epilepsy. Stereotyped behaviours also occur in mentally retarded persons without a PDD, albeit more frequently in mentally retarded persons with a PDD. Obsessive and compulsive behaviour is seen in persons with tics, and - as a distinctive feature even - in persons with Obsessive-Compulsive Disorder (DSM-IV, 300.3). In sum, it seems not to be such a good idea to consider style of functioning as a specific type of problem. However, since style of functioning does represent a typical feature in the entire profile, more so than the non-specific problems, the best solution will probably be to place them in an intermediate category of *half-specific problems*.

In the second place, experience shows that *all* mentally retarded persons with pervasive developmental disorders display a retarded or disturbed *emotional functioning*. Emotionally, even mildly retarded adults with PDD are seldom found to have a level above that of an infant. This deficiency, too, is in my view an indication of the presence of the above mentioned crucial functioning deficits. In view of this, I have decided to mention it separately as a specific problem, if only for pragmatic reasons. I shall come back to this issue in Section II.4.2.

The distinctions made by Rutter, combined with the qualifications given above and with my own research findings, have been summarized in Scheme II.4.1. This scheme, which on the one hand is restricted to mentally retarded persons but on the other hand covers the entire domain of pervasive developmental disorders of that group, implicitly denotes a third consideration which can be made with regard to Rutter's distinctions. This concerns the use of the term compulsive in the context of autism, as employed by Rutter and many other researchers. As has been rightly argued by Van Osch (1981), the term compulsive is only applicable to traits which are ego-dystonic. This means that persons with these traits labour under an incompatibility between what they are urged to do and what they want to do. There is a feeling of estrangement from the self, and of involuntariness, together with an inclination to suppress the ideas or impulses concerned. Contrariwise, many of the seemingly 'compulsive' behaviours observed in mentally retarded persons, and in my view certainly also in those with a PDD, are in fact ego-syntonic. An example of this is self-stimulatory behaviour (see Chapter III.4), which is in fact often experienced as lustful. In those cases, more neutral designations, such as *over-precision, ritualism or formalism*, should be preferred.

Scheme II.4.1 Specificity of problem behaviour in mentally retarded persons with a pervasive developmental disorder

Specific problems	Half-specific problems	Non-specific problems
Retarded/deviant LANGUAGE COGNITIVE SOCIAL EMOTIONAL development	RIGID STEREOTYPED OBSESSIVE RITUALISTIC HYPERACTIVE FEARS/PHOBIAS ERRATIC SELF-INJURY MASTURBATION (RUMINATION*) (SLEEPING PROBLEMS*)	SHORT-TEMPERED AGGRESSIVE DESTRUCTIVE EATING PROBLEMS CONSTIPATION NOT TOILET TRAINED

* Rumination and sleeping problems were in the present study in general more frequently found in mentally retarded children with PDD than in mentally retarded children without PDD; however, classification was made on the basis of a comparatively small sample and some of the scores were conflicting.

Treatment of autism should, according to Rutter (1985), be aimed at achieving the following goals:

- promotion of a normal development in the areas of cognition, language and social behaviour;
- reduction of rigidity and stereotypy;
- elimination of non-specific disruptive behaviours.

The scheme given above will be used in Sections II.4.5, II.4.6 and II.4.7 when discussing some of the experiences gained at the Eekwal observation home in treating problem behaviour with regard to, respectively: the specific problems of cognition, language, social behaviour and emotional development; the half-specific problems of self-injurious behaviour, stereotyped behaviour, hyperactivity, and sleeping problems; and the non-specific problems of short-temperedness and aggression, eating problems, constipation, and problems with toilet training.

First, however, some issues of a more general nature have to be considered.

In the first place, I will give special attention to the *high degree of disharmonious functioning* of mentally retarded persons with pervasive developmental disorders. To begin with, this problem makes a diagnosis more difficult. As for management and treatment, the central question here is: *how much can be demanded?* When too much is demanded of a person with a pervasive disorder in the cognitive, social or emotional areas, this means *overloading*. If too little is demanded - which in general occurs only rarely and within the family setting even less often - this would mean pampering or underloading.

For a further discussion see Section II.4.2.

Secondly, I want to underline the fundamental importance of structure in the management of mentally retarded children with PDD (although this also applies to PDD children who are not mentally retarded). As for the demands made on children, the central question here is: *How are things to be demanded?* And the possible mistakes are those of overstimulation and understimulation.

Although the answers to these two questions will frequently yield only differences in emphasis (and thus, as an example, overloading generally implies overstimulation), I nevertheless regard the distinction to be of fundamental importance for the practical management problems posed by these children. For a further discussion see II.4.3.4.

Finally, in Section 2.4.4 an attempt will be made to find out whether the distinction made in Section II.3.2.1 between an *erratic* and *rigid* group of mentally retarded persons with PDD has any consequences for their management. Furthermore, the *passive* type, distinguished in the studies by Wing and Gould (1979) and Wing and Attwood (1987) will be dealt with.

II.4.2   Profiles of disharmonious functioning

II.4.2.1   *Introduction*

Many mentally retarded persons, even those with no additional disabilities, are found to function disharmoniously. Their verbal skills in particular are comparatively poor (Van Osch, 1968; Reynolds & Reynolds, 1979; Kraijer, 1986). However, in mentally retarded persons with a PDD this disharmony is much broader and far more serious. The relevant research findings will be summarized below.

In Scheme II.4.1 the specific problems of autistic persons are indicated as retarded/deviant *cognitive, language, social, and emotional development*. However, an explanatory note is pertinent here. As has been shown in Sections I.2.2 and I.2.3, research findings based on the application of scales and tests have made it clear that developmental deficits may well be absent in some aspects of cognition, notably performance intelligence. Deviation and relative retardation were found in the following areas:

- development of the merely technical aspects of speech and language;
- verbal intelligence;
- verbal and non-verbal communication;
- social skills/socialization;
- academic skills;
- the entire domain of social maturity or competence/general adaptive behaviour.

Nothing really substantial can be said about emotional development; assessment of this level, already a complicated issue in general, is virtually impossible in mentally retarded persons.

II.4.2.2 *Problems of diagnosis, management and treatment*

In common clinical practice, disharmonious functioning gives rise to three major problems.

The first problem has to do with an inadequate use of diagnostic tools, both quantitatively and qualitatively, with the following effects:

- the general level of functioning either remains unclear or is overrated, which generally results in a far too optimistic assessment of the mental retardation level;
- the disharmonious style of functioning is ignored, i.e., weak points are more or less glossed over.

Inadequacies in the use of diagnostic tools may involve:

- No tests or scales being applied. This is justified by saying either that children and adults with a PDD are untestable, or that, even if the subjects are cooperative, no reliable assessment can be made of their intelligence or other domains of functioning.
- Tests being applied which are obsolete, too narrow, or which, like the Merrill-Palmer test, yield far too flattering results. As a matter of fact, for want of something better, the Merrill-Palmer test was used by the Eekwal observation home until 1970.
- Bypassing those abilities on which subjects with pervasive disorders tend to perform rather poorly. Unidimensional non-verbal tests are applied, such as the Raven Coloured Progressive Matrices, the Leiter International Performance Scale or the SON 2½-7 Nonverbal Intelligence Scale for Young Children (Snijders & Oomen, 1975).
- The standard instructions often being ignored when applying such trustworthy tools as the Wechsler tests; such practices seriously diminish the value of the outcomes.
- The use of the Psychoeducational Profile, PEP (Schopler & Reichler, 1979), which also more or less fits into this list. For the sake of completeness I would add that there is another version of this test, the AAPEP, intended to be used for adolescents and adults (Mesibov et al., 1988); however, the Eekwal observation home has had no practical experience with this latter version.

Due to ambivalences in the companion manual to the revised version of the PEP, the PEP-R (Schopler et al., 1990), this test is equally susceptible to misapplication. The authors claim that in practice the standardized observation scheme has proved to be a useful tool on behalf of "effective educational and home programming." This would not give rise to any objections if the test's aim was indeed to give concrete and practical suggestions. However, it is evidently considered to be able to do more than that, as we read on page 67 of the manual: "The DQ can be useful as an alternative or supplement to standardized IQ." Against such a claim I object that, as a measuring instrument, the PEP(-R) is far inferior to the renowned and specially devised general tests of intelligence and development; the proof of this assertion can be seen in Part 5 of this very manual, under the heading Test Construction and Validation. Furthermore, when the authors pretend that the Developmental Ages they arrived at are accurate to the month, and they even go as far as to leave it to the user to work out a Developmental Quotient, their claims must definitely be regarded as overstatements. Admittedly, compared with the Bayley Scales of Infant Development, in which verbal skills are of minor importance, its concurrent validity, expressed as r, is 0.77, which is fairly high. However, when compared with the WPPSI and WISC-R, the figure is only 0.47. Moreover, these figures do not tell anything at all about the absolute value of the scores, which, in my experience, often give far too rosy a picture. The conclusion must be, as has been rightly argued by Van Berckelaer-Onnes and Van Duyn (1993), that the PEP/PEP-R should only be used in combination with the appropriate standardized tools for measuring psychological characteristics. Unfortunately, however, in the Netherlands as well as elsewhere, actual practice tends to be different. Sloan and Marcus (1981), for instance, regard the PEP as a unique intellectual assessment instrument for a population of autistic children. Lam and Rao (1993) also seem to be in favour of substituting the PEP in place of the intelligence test.

A further objection to the PEP is that the very profile, on which the name of the test is based, completely lacks a sound statistical basis. The scales, or areas, as they are alternatively called (seven in number!), which together make up the profile, have been grouped according to their face value. In essence, this means that their validity and consequently their practical applicability must be poor. Thus, after a factor analysis of the five subtests of the Griffiths which had been formed in the same way, only three remained (Munro, 1968). As will be indicated in Section III.1.2.2, factor analysis also failed to substantiate a subdivision into five scales made on a subjective basis in the Autism Behavior Checklist (Wadden et al., 1991). Even after a first item-analysis, I am convinced that in the PEP and PEP-R ultimately only three or four areas, after much drastic rearranging, will prove to be valid.

Finally, apart from the rating categories 'passing' and 'failing', the PEP/PEP-R also employ a category 'emerging', which is doomed to be unworkable. After all, it is difficult enough even now to make predictions which are limited to the development of specific skills in normal children (Lutje Spelberg, 1987; Hamers et al., 1989).

All in all, the only conclusion can be that the PEP/PEP-R outcomes, too often miscalled test results, have nothing reliable to say about the general level, the profile, or the prognosis of children with a PDD.

The second problem is directly related to the first one. If there are particular favourable details in a general profile, these are often taken to indicate *the child's true level*, not only by parents (which is quite understandable), but also by many professional workers. Accordingly, management and treatment are geared to this small number of brighter aspects. For instance, the better results obtained on the performance part of a test or even the results of a subtest (such as the Block design) may faultily be taken as indicators of the real level. Likewise, and just as wrongly, are the distinct areas of social competence too often taken to be indications of the general level. Social competence cannot be determined by such subscales as Daily Living Skills or Self-Help, let alone Motor Skills. On the other hand, there is also a limited number of children with a PDD, mostly of the erratic group (see II.3.2.1), whose verbal intelligence is higher than their performance intelligence. In my experience and that of Schoonbeek and De Boer (1989), these children generally present a very disharmonious profile in their verbal and performance test results. Additionally, their comparatively high scores for verbal intelligence are in line with the frequently encountered better performance on the SRZ-Subscale Communication, which tests the more technical aspects of verbal skills. Again, this might lead to an overestimation of these children, the reason being this time that a predominantly senseless language, which is made up of automatisms and associations, is taken as an indication for a fair level of intelligence.

The third problem is that the level of emotional functioning receives too little professional attention. As a matter of fact, this level has undoubtedly a far more profound effect on the general level of functioning than socialization, although it is closely related to it. A differentiation between these two concepts is therefore imperative. Knowledge of the level of emotional functioning of a given child or adult is essential in deciding on the kind of approach to be preferred. However, if persons show outstanding special skills or are delivering an impressive-sounding treasure of information, their emotional limitations are liable to escape notice. An aforementioned additional problem, which applies in particular to the group of mentally retarded persons, is that there are hardly any tools available to make an adequate assessment of emotional level. Face-to-face contact in commonplace situations and observations of behaviour made both in everyday life and in the observation playroom are better ways of reaching a sound clinical judgement. Such observations may yield revealing information about children with a PDD (but also adolescents and adults!): their preference for the most simple stories, games and television programmes; their childish behaviour, such as an inability to wait their turn or to be a good loser; their strong need for predictability and stability; their infant-like deep absorption in tactile and haptic experiences; their great enjoyment when they are sitting comfortably in a bath, playing with a plastic duck and bucket, or driving around in a go-cart (even in an outsize one!). Assessments of emotional level cannot be otherwise than very subjective, but are nevertheless to my mind of fundamental and crucial importance. After all, the emotional level is the substratum lying beneath the general functioning. Thus, for example, the specific meaning and content of the cognitive and social aspects of general functioning are determined by the emotional level.

The three diagnostic and managemental problems outlined above may in the long run result in an accumulation of excessive demands made on the child's cognitive, social and emotional potential, probably for many years, producing a variety of non-specific or half-specific behavioural problems such as resistance, stubbornness, negativism, tantrums, aggression, etc. A decision to examine such problems in more detail and to consider a change in strategy may well have been postponed until the signals of overloading became patently obvious. Such behavioural problems, which possibly by now have become fixed patterns, are often hard to push back, in particular in mentally retarded persons with pervasive developmental disorders, an issue to which I shall have to come back several times. Perhaps it is nowhere more true than in this area that prevention is better than cure.

II.4.2.3   *What can be done?*

For many years I have advocated a number of measures:

- The use of *well standardized general development and intelligence tests*, applied according to standard procedures. Experience shows that such tests can also be employed with those mentally retarded persons with pervasive developmental disorders who present with behavioural problems (see also Chapter I.2; DeMyer, 1976; Gould, 1977). However, only those tests should be used which are able to draw up *a profile of cognitive functioning*. Thus, good options are: the Bayley-SID; the Kaufman-ABC; the WPPSI-R; the WISC-III; and the WAIS-R. Until recently, Dutch professionals had to make shift with the Griffiths, for lack of anything better, but the original norms of this test must be considered to have become obsolete by now. When, however, an experienced professional investigator concludes that a given child or adult is, in spite of his or her apparent fair level of functioning, 'untestable', this in itself is already a significant observation. Evidently, the child's cognitive faculties remain largely dormant, due to insufficient concentration and/or compliance. Consequently, the primary focus of treatment should be to promote concentration or social adjustment.
- Sufficient attention should in fact be paid to precisely those weak aspects of cognition and social competence, or, more generally speaking, to the disharmonious elements in the profile. If an attempt is made to do something about the weak points, it must be realized that they are not infrequently an intrinsic part of the pervasive disorder and will therefore as a rule fail to draw level with the strong points. A discriminate approach,

geared to the disharmonious profile, seems to be the best answer, as will be elaborated in the next point.

- Allowance should be made for the extreme degree of emotional immaturity, vulnerability and deviancy, which features are characteristic of people with pervasive disorders. This limits the possibilities for improvement and for applying a differentiated approach. The upper limit of a given person can only be determined gropingly and cautiously. Transgression of this limit should be avoided, as this may give rise to severe unsettlement, while undoing previously achieved successes for quite some time, occasionally even permanently. In general, it has been my experience that there is a greater risk of rendering the precarious existence of mentally retarded persons with pervasive disorders more difficult, and of causing behavioural problems and other negative effects, when even just a little too much is demanded in their treatment and management than when too little is demanded. In setting the aims for management, treatment and training, the saying has to be kept in mind that a chain is as strong as its weakest link.

II.4.3   Offering structure

II.4.3.1   *Introduction*

In this field the literature generally gives much emphasis to the necessity of offering children and adults with pervasive developmental disorders a clear-cut *structure*. Without a doubt this is sound advice. However, in recent years the principle seems to have fallen somewhat into disrepute, possibly because it is often employed in and out of season. One of the misconceptions of structure has been that it implies surly strictness, inflexibility and firm adherence to rules and regulations. Another, that offering structure is equal to creating a mirthless existence with a minimum of variation and very few things to enjoy. These misconceptions need to be put right.

All human beings need structure. Biological processes, such as the rhythm of sleeping and waking, follow patterns; culturally defined behaviour, too, is patterned by written or unwritten laws, by customs and habits, social conventions and routines. Structure enables us to gain an overall view of the situation and to create peace and quiet by means of planning and organization. Mentally retarded people, who are characterized by diminished coping abilities, as their cognitive, social and emotional potential is limited, need even *more structure* in order to be able to function adequately. And this principle holds even more true for mentally retarded persons with pervasive developmental disorders, as will be explained in the present chapter.

II.4.3.2   The concept of structure

The concept of structure in the context of the mental retardation field always means *extra structure,* compared with what is needed in society in general. By offering disabled persons this (extra) structure, external stability is created with the aim of compensating their inability to hold themselves upright in human society and their lack of inner steadiness (Moor, 1951, 1958). Disabled persons must perceive the world to be a chaotic, confusing, overwhelming or threatening state of affairs, and it is therefore our task to make it a place which is more livable and manageable for them. For children with a PDD in particular, the world is in fact a scene of ever changing and incomprehensible clusters of stimuli. Consequently, these stimuli should be tackled. Three interconnected aspects of these stimuli can be distinguished:

- *a material aspect:* the physical and spatial aspects of the home, the garden, the school, the workplace, the holiday home, etc.; the different ways in which things are arranged in these places; modifications in arrangements; the travelling between these places; the experience of being alternately in different places;
- *a serial aspect:* the way things are done at home, at school or at work, i.e., either routinely and according to fixed patterns or in a loose way;
- *a relational aspect:* the different contacts with all those people involved in the child's upbringing and with others who are interacting with him; their constantly changing numbers; their different ways of approaching the child (for instance, lively or calmly); their varying degrees of being consistent and the many other differences in their approaches.

In order to offer the child a less confusing world, a coherent body of measures are necessary. The general principle underlying these measures is that the *child's own poor ability to create structure* should, as far a possible, be compensated by an *external structuring* of his environment, which means: *a carefully balanced supply of stimuli.*

II.4.3.3   Five forms of structuring

The present section will describe in more detail the five forms of external structuring and indicate the differences in emphasis between them. The three different aspects of the stimuli, distinguished in the foregoing section, are in actual fact interrelated, as will be clear from the examples given.

Stimulus reduction. Experience shows that mentally retarded persons with pervasive developmental disorders are very liable to become overexcited, and as a consequence will become more aloof, more fearful, more chaotic or more agitated. As an example may serve the celebration of a birthday which for an average child is a red-letter day because of all the things that go with it: friends from school or from the neighbourhood who have been invited, a birthday cake with candles, games and festive decorations. However, these very things can cause a child with a PDD to go completely mad, possibly leaving him disconcerted for days afterwards. Similar effects may be produced by theme parks, fairs, and television programmes, and even by situations of a primary nature, such as family and group functioning. No hard and fast rules can be given as to where the line should be drawn. How much a given child can take must be determined individually, and, moreover, this threshold level may vary in time. So much is clear: external reduction of the number of stimuli is needed to prevent the child from becoming overexcited because of the burden. Notably the material and relational aspects of the stimuli are at stake here. Reduction of stimuli means that choices must be made. This brings me to the next point.

Stimulus selection. The question here is, which stimuli are acceptable and which are not? Several aspects can be distinguished. Let us take again the example of the birthday party. There is certainly no objection to a cake and a decorated room, but the number of visiting friends should be limited to one only, and Grandpa and Grandma can better wait until next week. However, in everyday situations selection of stimuli is also necessary. As an example, again involving both reduction and selection of stimuli, may serve the question: "What filling do you want inside your sandwich?" For many a PDD child this question will always remain too general and too complicated. There may be a choice of five kinds of fillings on the table, which he first has to count and then compare, before he can make a decision. If such a child is able to choose at all, he should rather be asked: "What do you prefer, cheese or meat?" By making a pre-selection, the problem has been structured in advance, and the child is helped to find an answer.

However, reduction and selection of stimuli are not always feasible. Some situations which are bound to give rise to fierce reactions are simply unavoidable. Examples of these are a haircut, or clipping of nails, or a visit to the doctor or dentist.

On the other hand, there is also the risk of narrowing down stimuli too much. The Eekwal observation home found that this applies especially to adolescent and adult mentally retarded persons with PDD who are living in residential settings, but also to adult persons with these disabilities who are still living at home. When their reactions of fear and panic to slightly unfamiliar situations and activities are invariably interpreted as indications that the number of stimuli has to be reduced still further, these people will end up leading an unacceptably bleak existence. Stimulus regularization, the issue of the next paragraph, should therefore contain elements to prevent this.

Stimulus regularization. When due care is taken that stimuli are patterned, so that, for instance, events take place at fixed times, in fixed sequences and in familiar contexts, more stimuli can be tolerated than without such a structuring. It is obviously the serial aspect of the stimuli which is at stake here. Regularity and patterning are means by which these vulnerable PDD children can be protected against being suddenly overwhelmed by incentives.

Examples of such means include a fixed day programme, a regular bedtime routine, and a standard repertoire of activities, games and jokes. While for normal children such patterning would soon turn life into merely a grind, it gives mentally retarded persons with a PDD the support they desperately need in a world which they find so confusing.

Stimulus regularization is obviously a very helpful strategy, and will often be a necessity. But again, there is a risk. Even for a mentally retarded person with a PDD, the day programme can become too dull and monotonous, and this will lead to behavioural problems of another nature, such as increased stereotypy. This might explain why, as the Eekwal-home team observed, mentally retarded persons with a PDD in particular show an inclination to step up the pace of the various items in a scheduled day programme. As soon as there are intervals between the items - as inevitably happens - they urgently want to move on, and in fact cannot bear to wait. Their impatience may be so prevailing that every day brings just another uninterrupted succession of frustrations. This may lead to serious behavioural problems, such as aggression and self-injurious behaviour. In my view, plain guidelines for tackling this problem cannot be furnished. By all means should the programme provide an ample amount of interesting and meaningful activities. First and foremost, gross-motor activities, such as walking, swimming, etc., have to be included in such a programme; other suitable exercises are, for instance, laying the table, washing the dishes and doing simple work. Moreover, it is at least as important to give the persons concerned ample space to follow and develop the interests which they themselves evince more or less spontaneously, and which are not part of a planned programme. Some such pursuits may seem to be rather futile, but the important thing is that the person concerned displays a personal initiative to do or to take an interest in something which apparently matters to him, despite the fact that others may fail to understand why. To give an example, during a walk a child or adult may like to stop at each tree along the road, absorbed in touching or sniffing at it, or to gaze at a flag flying on a flagpole or at smoke curling from a chimney; why urge him to walk on when it is also possible simply to set more time aside for walking?

To summarize, the daily programme has to go on steadily with the smallest possible number of intervals lasting the shortest possible length of time. Care has to be taken also that the programme is not too inflexible - stimulus regularization should not mean that there is hardly any variation left. After all, one of the outstanding problems of mentally retarded persons with a PDD is precisely that their need for concrete forms of safety, the presence of which they want to feel here and now, is so urgent that they are hardly able or even unable to tolerate any delay. In a number of cases it may be helpful to use special devices, such as a kitchen timer, or a series of movable photos, pictographs or short phrases which adhere to a flannel board or mount on a wooden board. Such devices, of which many more examples can be found in the well-known TEACCH-programme (Schopler & Mesibov, 1995), make the situation predictable and understandable. An additional advantage is that they are impersonal and hence unimposing; it is not the attendant who says what is going to be done or which activity still has to wait, but rather the kitchen timer or the pictograph. However, the inclination to step up the pace, which is typical for mentally retarded persons with a PDD, cannot always be checked.

Stimulus strengthening implies that more emphasis should be placed on those stimuli which are thought to benefit a particular child but which he is apt to disregard. Many persons with pervasive developmental disorders are found to display what has been termed *stimulus overselectivity* (Lovaas et al., 1979). For instance, a child may pay exclusive attention to the glasses worn by his father or mother, but almost completely ignore the face. Another child may only want to make sounds with a toy by tapping on it or throwing it on the floor, regardless of whether it is a doll, a toy car, or a building block. This deprives him of many things which might enrich his world, and what is worse that he will often do nothing whatsoever to extend his own interests. Special educational intervention is needed to change this. In the first example given above, a tactic which the adult might adopt is to take off his glasses and draw attention to other parts of his face by making facial movements. In the second example, other possible attractions and uses of playthings should emphatically and frequently be brought to the child's attention: aspects such as colour, form, texture, and above all, the purposes for which they were intended. A doll is meant to be fondled, a toy car to be pushed on its wheels, and building blocks are intended to be used in such a way as to build things. Sometimes it is better to begin by joining the child in his own way of using things, as the child may then be gradually enticed into playing with a toy in the more usual manner: both child and adult first tap with a block, then the child is taught to tap two blocks against each other and finally to build his first simple tower of two blocks.

Stimulus extension, the last one in this series, is not in fact a way of structuring in the proper sense of the word. Bringing up children and promoting their development always involves offering them fresh experiences. However, with PDD children special skills are needed to accomplish this. These children largely or completely lack a natural urge to explore the world. Two examples of stimulus extension may help to illustrate the point, the first of which concerns stereotypy. Again, the best thing to start with may be to join the child in question in his stereotyped movements, such as body rocking or hand flapping, to be followed by taking hold of the child and slightly adjusting his movements, and then gradually including new elements, probably even objects, into this activity. The second example concerns the offering of a cluster of entirely new stimuli: teaching a child to eat bread instead of porridge. In examples such as this, rather rigorous enforcement may be called for, not only to save the time and inventiveness required for gradual change (also referred to as successive approximation), but also to spare the person concerned a prolonged period of having to adapt to an extensive series of minor changes which are often actually not so gradual. An abrupt change of tack, preferably pertaining not only to the problem behaviour but also to other areas, may produce a break from routinized behaviour patterns, thus enhancing receptiveness to new experiences. This strategy may notably be called for in the management of sleep disturbances and eating problems (see II.4.7.4 and II.4.8.2).

As will be clear from the examples given above, stimulus extension with PDD children generally implies a certain amount of compulsion. Sometimes a question of health, such as eating problems, is at stake. More often, however, the aim is to enlarge the child's horizon. As long as the number of stimuli is kept low, there is a fair chance that the attempt will be successful. But some resistance will almost always be met, which may be a signal that too much is being asked of the child. As a given child has possibly been over-demanded consistently and for many years (see II.4.2.2), it is of crucial importance to stick to the principle that the five forms of structuring, i.e., reduction, selection, regularization, strengthening and extension of stimuli, are *integrated into a treatment plan which covers all measures in the areas of child rearing, educational intervention, and special educational treatment.* As matter of fact, for children with a PDD such treatment plans usually have to be made tentatively and by trial and error. These children present even very experienced professional workers with extremely complicated and sometimes insoluble problems.

II.4.3.4   *The distinction between overloading and overstimulation and their interrelatedness*

As *overloading* and *overstimulation* are two concepts which are by no means synonymous, they are certainly interrelated, and it may be apposite to explain how they differ.

As previously indicated (in Section II.1.3.2.1 and Section II.4.2.2), the term overloading refers to excessive demands made in the cognitive, emotional and/or social areas. In other words, the actual developmental level of the child or adult is below the level which he or she is supposed to have. *Active* overloading implies that a person (generally this concerns children) has to do more than he is capable of. This evokes tensions which often result in behavioural problems and/or mental problems. *Passive* overloading implies over-indulgence (generally this concerns adolescent and adult mentally retarded persons): this means, for instance, that a person is left alone to roam the streets, to watch television and videotapes, to go to the discotheque, or to spend money, without adequate adult support and supervision. Passive overloading gives rise to behavioural problems rather than to mental problems. If this, as often happens, induces the person concerned to overestimate his own capacities, then he also risks demanding too much of himself, which adds to the behavioural problems.

In terms of level of functioning, overloading was found to occur more frequently in moderately (significantly) and mildly (highly significantly) retarded children than in severely and profoundly mentally retarded persons. The association is more pronounced with passive overloading than with active overloading.

Overstimulation, on the other hand, affects elementary processes which are more or less of a physiological nature. An overstimulated person is unable to cope with the stimuli to which he is exposed; the exposure may be intended or unintended. Important factors are on the one hand the intensity and number of the stimuli and their sequence, and on the other hand, the threshold of responsiveness and the intensity of reacting in a given person. There seems to be only a very weak association with level of functioning. However, due to the fact that people in the lower ranges of mental retardation are in general less overloaded than people in the mild and moderate levels, they are in actual practice more likely to be affected by overstimulation than by overloading.

As for the links between overloading and overstimulation, experience indicates that stimulus regularization is of little avail when a person is overloaded, i.e., when demands are not geared to his coping ability. In such a situation non-specific or half-specific behavioural problems are generally bound to turn up. However, the same applies when the demands are consonant with a person's capacities but regularization and patterning of stimuli is inadequate. Thus, the two aspects may well be distinguished, but are also interdependent, implying that the boundary line for overloading may shift when stimulus regularization is improved.

To sum up, overloading and overstimulation partly overlap. In each case behavioural problems can be expected. Generally speaking, in daily practice it is easier to check overloading than overstimulation.

As will be understood, special treatment of behavioural problems, for example through behavioural therapy or medication, is only meaningful if stimuli and demands are geared to the coping ability of the person concerned. This principle should be the foundation upon which management and care firmly rest. Only if non-specific and half-specific problems persist in spite of this solid foundation are special treatment approaches worth considering.

The policy outlined above is summarized in Scheme II.4.2.

II.4.4 Differentiation of two groups of mentally retarded PDD children on the basis of the approach required

II.4.4.1 *Introduction*

In Section II.3.2.1 I discriminated two subtypes of children with pervasive developmental disorders on the basis of differences in the clinical picture: a *rigid* and an *erratic* subtype. When these two subtypes are matched for chronological age and level of functioning, they are found to display marked differences in the following respects: level of social response towards adults; level of expressive language skills; and the degree of non-predictable/erratic

106

behaviour. However, if the two subtypes are only matched for chronological age, the differences become much more pronounced. Evidently, level of functioning is a very discriminating factor (Kraijer, 1991).

Scheme II.4.2 Care and management of mentally retarded PDD persons according to the fundamental principles of adequate structuring and appropriate demands; the place of special treatment therein

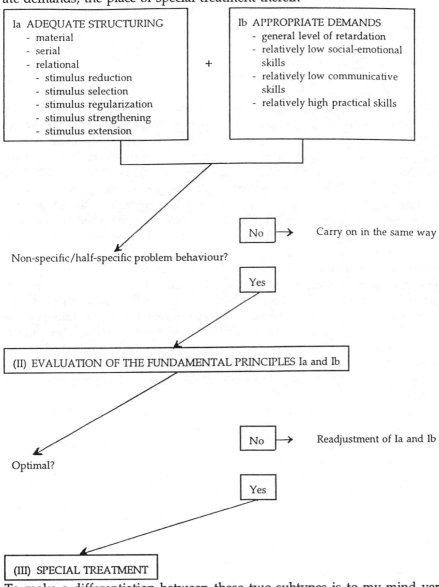

To make a differentiation between these two subtypes is to my mind very important because both groups are found to differ in the kind of educational intervention required. Although *both groups need structure,* each group needs

quite a different kind of structure. Until recently, literature in the field disregarded these differences in treatment needs. Wing and Gould (1979), however, did make a highly important general differentiation by subdividing children with pervasive developmental disorders into an aloof group and active-but-odd group. This differentiation comes close to the differentiation I suggest, as the two groups correspond clearly with the rigid and erratic types (see Section II.3.2.1). Similarly, some Dutch and Belgian experts (De Boer et al., 1989; De Vriendt & Vandenbussche, 1990; Minderaa, 1990) have emphasized the DSM-III-R differentiation between PDD-AD and PDD-NOS. The terms 'autism' and 'atypical pervasive developmental disorder' are also used in this connection. De Vriendt (1990) and Vandenbussche (1990) were also the first experts, as far as I know, to point out that each of the two subtypes of children has a different impact on parents and others involved in their upbringing, and that each subtype needs a specific kind of educational intervention. However, I am not quite so happy with the use of the DSM-III or DSM-III-R terminology to designate these two subtypes. My experience is that almost all moderately and mildly mentally retarded children with the rigid form of PDD can be classified under PDD-Autistic Disorder (DSM-III-R). But the same holds true for almost all moderately and mildly mentally retarded children with the erratic form of PDD. Only two of the 23 children who were very representative cases of the erratic subtype could be classified under PDD-NOS. The DSM-III-R category PDD-AD is indeed a very broad one (Kraijer, 1988a; Volkmar et al., 1988; Factor et al., 1989), whereas the category PDD-NOS is in fact a residual one. Apart from the children with the erratic form of PDD, the following other categories in my opinion should also be classified as PDD-NOS (DSM-III-R): profoundly and severely mentally retarded children with a pervasive developmental disorder; uncomplicated, mildly autistic children (possibly those designated by Wing and Gould as the passive type); many children with Childhood Disintegrative Disorder (DSM-IV 299.10); and, finally, the non-retarded children with the Asperger syndrome (DSM-IV, 299.80). Although PDD children of normal intelligence are largely outside my scope, it seems highly unlikely to me that the diversity of disorders found in the DSM-III-R category PDD-NOS would be a phenomenon limited to only the mentally retarded group.

However, in spite of my objections regarding the designations used, the aforementioned studies by De Vriendt, Vandenbussche and Minderaa deserve to be discussed in two separate sections. The studies of De Vriendt and Vandenbussche, although mainly focussing on PDD children of normal intelligence, are also of relevance to the mental retardation field. Minderaa describes the behavioural characteristics of a hitherto disregarded type of children who have much in common with children with the erratic form of PDD.

II.4.4.2   *The studies by Vandenbussche and De Vriendt*

Adopting a distinction which runs parallel to that between PDD-AD and

PDD-NOS children as made by the DSM-III-R, Vandenbussche (1990) describes the impact children with a PDD have on parents and the family as a whole, on attendants and on the peer group. The group of children with PDD-AD (notably those with classic childhood autism) is, according to Vandenbussche, felt by attendants to have a clearly defined disability requiring clearly defined management and treatment. These children do not disconcert the staff excessively, nor do they have much influence on the staff's internal relations. Staff meetings at which the special needs and abilities of each individual child are discussed and information is exchanged run smoothly. The autistic children's negative responses to their attendants' attempts to establish a social and emotional relationship are not taken personally. When children with 'atypical PDD' are admitted, however, Vandenbussche has observed that staff members anticipate that they are in for trouble, both on a personal level and as a group. She infers that these children must be more perceptive of individual and collective fears and underlying problems. They respond in a chaotic way, which is also frightening to themselves. As a result, the entire system of staff and children becomes unsettled, and the treatment milieu threatens to lose much of what is essential to the adequate functioning of these children: reassurance, security, structure, and the demarcation of clear boundaries. This author also states that many children with atypical PDD, while generally comparing favourably to PDD children in command of language and therefore appearing - and possibly even being - more intelligent, are certainly not less problematic, but seem, on the contrary, to present more problems of management. In their case a final diagnosis is often difficult to reach, due to unfamiliarity with the clinical picture; the impact they have on parents and other persons involved in their care is deeper; and in addition they are prone to overreact to disharmonious relations within the family or peergroup, with a vicious circle of unhappy interaction patterns as a possible consequence. The author concludes that children with atypical PDD and their parents need a special approach, which differs somewhat from that needed by autistic children and their parents.

The article written by De Vriendt (1990) states that while in general all children with pervasive developmental disorders need an approach in which structure is one of the basic elements, treatment and management of children with an atypical PDD should involve something specific on top of that. According to this author, these children rely less heavily upon structure than autistic children. On the other hand, they rely more on making contact, notably with adults. However, their contact-making is very possessive. As a result, the person who is in care of such a child may feel very needed, with over-engagement as a possible outcome. Contrary to autistic children, whose contact-making should be stimulated, children with atypical PDD need rather to be guided and restricted in this respect. Adults, for their part, should be very cautious in establishing a relationship with these children. De Vriendt also warns that much of the child's bizarre behaviour and speech is a distinguishing feature of atypical pervasive developmental disorder, and should not be taken too readily as a response to the attitude of the adult or as resulting from his or her relationship with the child. In fact, adults should maintain a considerable degree of detachment.

Another important observation made by De Vriendt is that children with atypical PDD are liable to be overrated because of their seemingly good language skills. Talking with these children should aim at reassuring them.

This can be done by simplifying, clarifying and demarcating their reality and by rectifying the erroneous notions these children tend to have. The adult should not aim at exploring and interpreting emotions. The author rightly warns against using the classical forms of free therapy and free play therapy, which may put too much pressure on the verbal and emotional potentials of these children, and are therefore unsettling, possibly even causing disintegration instead of mental development.

Finally, De Vriendt states that in dealing with a child with atypical PDD, the chief aims of structuring should be: to reduce anxiety; to give general support and reassurance; to prevent - as far as possible - the child from becoming a captive of his own delusive notions. With an autistic child, on the other hand, structuring is much more focussed on developmental aspects.

II.4.4.3   *The study by Minderaa*

Minderaa (1990) focusses on a category of children with autistic-like contact disorders. According to his description, these children are overactive, restless, too communicative, and show too little restraint in social contact. They are incapable of interpreting the social context, as they lack the cognitive faculty to see the interrelations between persons and events and to place them in a proper perspective. They are unable to assess the relative importance of things. Something is missing in their mental make-up and as a result they will never embed themselves firmly into time, place and situation. In their own social environment they remain very isolated. Thus are they seriously handicapped in controlling their own actions and in responding adequately to their experiences. They lack self-control and are inflexible, and follow mainly their own inclinations, without heeding other people's concerns. Furthermore they are overactive, constantly meddling and in a blind haste. Regulating mechanisms fail in conditions of changed inputs, leading to agitation or fear. These, in their turn, may produce short-lived reactions of verbal aggression. If these children are, in addition, mentally retarded, they are, according to Minderaa, comparatively inaccessible, unable to comprehend social signals, and their behaviour is strongly determined by internally generated incentives. The resulting patterns of behaviour may be either chaotic or rigid and compulsive. Since these children do not reject or ignore social overtures, but are on the contrary constantly interfering, they often fail to be identified as autistic or autistiform. Some of these children are overactive and always demanding attention from adults.

Although Minderaa hardly mentions non-predictable behaviour and reactions of anxiety and panic, the characteristics he enumerates are also on the whole features typical of children with the erratic form of PDD. Clearly, all these features strongly affect the child-rearing process.

II.4.4.4 *Some additional remarks concerning specific aspects of the management needs of mentally retarded children with the rigid form of PDD and those with the erratic form of PDD*

The statements made by De Vriendt with respect to what he calls the autistic and the atypical categories correspond closely with the management experiences gained at the Eekwal observation home with respect to children with the rigid form of PDD and to those with the erratic form. In the first place, both categories are liable to be overdemanded. In the second place, both categories need structure. However, as noted earlier, each one needs a somewhat different kind of structure. In the following paragraphs, the observations made and strategies followed by the team at the Eekwal home will be discussed separately for each of the two categories. The problems of persons with the passive type of PDD may seem to be milder than those with the rigid form of PDD, but in actual practice the managemental needs of both groups are very much the same. Therefore, the policy outlined here with respect to persons with the rigid form of PDD applies also to persons with the passive type.

Children with the *rigid* form of PDD remain aloof and avoid contact. For those in their environment this is obviously a painful experience, but at any rate these children stick to this behaviour, usually failing to perceive signs of affection. Their behaviourial repertoire is restricted, as well as being rigid.

The general approach towards these children should be marked by its tranquillity, predictability, and security. The five forms of structuring should all be provided, but preferably in a steady, smooth and what by common standards would be felt to be a monotonous rhythm. The forms of structuring should alternate and succeed each other in accordance with a fixed and clearly defined scheme. It may be very important to plan moments of rest between the various activities, which in practice more or less implies that there are gaps in the treatment programme. Many of these children draw much benefit, for example, from being allowed to retire to their own niche; as such a quiet corner in the room will suffice, or a private nook behind a bank or under a table, possibly screened off by means of a blanket or piece of cloth. Under such conditions, tensions which may have arisen can ebb away, but care should be taken to ensure that the periods of withdrawal are restricted in order to prevent excessive seclusion. Joy and relaxation, and a release from tension and overstimulation, may also be derived from daily playing in a bath with squeeze-bottles and toy animals, or from playing in a sandbox. The essential thing is that these children must not continually be exposed to more or less taxing situations which are aimed at promoting their development, and that they are also accepted as they are. If this aspect is ignored, even children with the rigid form of PDD tend to become highly overagitated or depressed, with behavioural problems as a frequent outcome. I shall return to this matter several times in the following sections of the present chapter.

Children with the *erratic* form of PDD are either alternately withdrawn and intrusive, or continually demanding, clinging, defying, putting people's patience to the test, and some have an almost diabolical sense of other people's weak spots. The kind of appeals they make to other people is much misapprehended. Although there is seemingly a call for affection, the emotional component is largely absent. As soon as affection is given to them, many of these children seem to be insatiable. Others respond by becoming confused, which in their case generally results in unsettlement and sometimes in being even more demanding. In other words, none of these children is in fact able to respond adequately to affection, and giving them affection from the fullness of one's heart has either no result at all or even negative results. Persons who are responsible for the child's upbringing should be protected against themselves to prevent them from burning themselves out. The most prudent and effective approach to this type of children is to keep the personal relationship with them as dispassionate as possible; although they certainly need warm involvement, the affections shown towards them should remain subdued and restrained. Experienced professional helpers may be able to combine these different attitudes, but parents - quite understandably - have a lot of difficulty in finding the right balance.

Children with the erratic type of PDD will also time and again throw us off the track in several other ways. Often their shifts of mood and sudden fads (embracing all sorts of habits, manners, obsessive notions and actions) are unaccountable, let alone how best to respond to them. These features, too, necessitate an approach which is at the same time engaged and detached, if for no other reason than to further a flexible and alert application of the principle of structuring. Again, all five forms of structuring are important when dealing with these children, although sometimes rather a deft manoeuvring of those forms is required for them, far more so than for children with the rigid form of PDD. In some situations all five forms of structuring have to be applied almost simultaneously, albeit with varying emphasis. The extreme unpredictability and capriciousness of children with the erratic form of PDD necessitate a structuring process which is on the one hand more flexible, but on the other hand often more stringent and thorough-going as well. Working according to routine is hardly ever possible. Moreover, opportunities to take a break are also scarce, as moments of rest in the structuring process, rather than benefitting these children, may even be conducive to the development of new problems, such as sudden derailment or unsettlement.

Talking things through is even less helpful with mentally retarded children with the erratic form of PDD than with the children described by De

112

Vriendt. Talking to these children is certainly important and even essential, but the words used should be pithy, providing them with clear guidelines. However, other treatment approaches are more crucial and effective for their therapeutic needs, such as: being constantly aware of the child's varying need to feel another person's presence; offering models for conduct and behaviour; preventing troublesome situations; and, last but not least, transmitting a spirit of tranquillity and security. As for this last element, PDD children really seem to be endowed with a sixth sense to perceive moods, and this, when placed besides other features, such as their lack of social empathy (see Minderaa's observations discussed in the foregoing section), is one of the enigmas surrounding these children.

On the basis of my own clinical experience I can fully endorse the statement made by De Vriendt that the application of time-out procedures according to the principles of operant condition - and indeed separation - may have a detrimental effect (certainly unintended) on this type of children. Instead of creating clarity and order, these procedures often cause bewilderment, panic and even complete unsettlement. Great caution is therefore required in applying such measures.

Two final remarks have still to be made concerning the management of children with PDD in its various manifestations. In the first place, as the erratic and rigid forms of PDD are in fact parts of a continuum and also of a spectrum, which implies that the differences between them are differences in degree and also in nature, the approaches made toward these children should likewise vary. In the second place, the approach towards PDD children who are unsettled and disintegrated, and also towards some psychotic PDD children, including those children who were previously considered to have the rigid form of PDD, should come very close to - and sometimes even be almost identical with - the approach which is appropriate for children with the erratic form of PDD.

II.4.5   A practical rule of the thumb

On the basis of the statements made in Sections II.4.1 to II.4.4, a general principle can be formulated regarding the upbringing, treatment and management of mentally retarded children, adolescents and adults with pervasive developmental disorders.

With respect to mentally retarded persons of all ages, the Eekwal observation home has over the years followed the principle, based on experience, that whenever in doubt as to which of two treatment situations or facilities is the most suitable, invariably the one should be chosen which is going to make the least heavy demands on the person in question. In this connection, demands are considered to be, on the one hand, all that is asked of the individual in the cognitive, social and emotional areas, and on the other hand the number and kind of stimuli involved. Thus, to give some examples, a school for trainable mentally retarded children may be preferred to a school for educable mentally retarded children; an adult day-centre may be preferred to a sheltered workshop; concrete guidelines and directions, which do not presuppose any self-knowledge, may be preferred to play therapy or psychotherapy; placement into a peaceful intimate group may be preferred to one into a busy and dynamic group; an institution may be preferred to a group home. Actually, such an approach is not very popular, but as I am convinced that it must be regarded as an absolute necessity, I was indeed happy to find exactly the same ideas, albeit somewhat differently worded, in a model presented by Siegel (1991) entitled *Clinical Model for Relationship between Degree of Mental Retardation and Later Adaptive Functioning.* On the basis of this clinical model and on the basis of the clinical experience in the Eekwal observation home, the following rule of the thumb can be given: on account of their limited social-emotional and cognitive potential, a large number of individuals with pervasive disorders who are predominantly or exclusively functioning below an average-normal level of intelligence benefit most from an approach which is tailored to a retardation level which is directly below their actual level. Thus, a mildly retarded person with PDD can generally best be approached as if he or she was moderately retarded. Consequently, even many persons with a PDD who are functioning on a borderline intellectual level (IQ 71-84; DSM-IV, V62-89) are nonetheless better helped by provisions from the mental retardation field. As for persons of normal intelligence with a PDD, however, I deem myself not competent to judge.

In view of the fundamental importance of this issue, the principle outlined above is summarized in Scheme II.4.3.

Scheme II.4.3 Best way of approaching mentally retarded persons with PDD

Level of mental retardation	Level of approach
Borderline Intellectual Functioning	Mild retardation
Mild retardation	Moderate retardation
Moderate retardation	Severe retardation
Severe retardation	Profound retardation

II.4.6 Special educational intervention and treatment of mentally retarded children with PDD: specific problems

II.4.6.1 *Cognition*

Treatment of cognitive deficits and disabilities will be discussed briefly. Children admitted to the Eekwal observation home are given lessons individually or in small groups of two to three children at the utmost in a special classroom. There are two special-education teachers.

Problems with the cognitive development of PDD children in the study were treated almost always on an individual basis. Some profoundly retard-

114

ed children could tolerate no more than twenty minutes of educational intervention per working day; only occasionally could a comparatively able child with some stamina stomach over two hours per working day.

In general, training of cognitive skills proves to be possible with mentally retarded children with PDD. However, much more time, patience, ingenuity, and individual attention is needed than with mentally retarded children without a PDD. The special problems are:

- *poor motivation* and lack of joy in doing new things;
- poor *concentration;*
- *overselectivity* (see II.4.3.3);
- *poor ability to bear frustration;* the best way to meet this problem is to raise the complexity of tasks very gradually, and to capitalize on successful performance;
- *rigid adherence* to a limited repertoire of favourite items and activities; too frequent and too rapid changes in the programme may provoke resistance, anger and similar reactions; on the other hand, care should be taken that the programme does not become merely a routine;
- *poor ability to generalize;* often explicit training is needed to teach children to use their newly learned skills in different settings.

An integral application of the five forms of structuring discussed in II.4.3.3, i.e., reduction, selection, regularization, strengthening, and extension of stimuli, is also of crucial importance in the educational programme. The special-education teachers were counselled weekly by the home's psychologist-educationalist, and were also in close contact with the attendants of their pupils. Very often, the teachers had to adjust radically the demands they made on their pupils. Learning difficulties, which obviously were the immediate focus of the educational treatment, were in fact but one of the reasons necessitating such readjustments. Another major reason was problem behaviour displayed during the lessons and/or out of class, signalling that the cognitive and/or emotional-social demands were too high. Significant increases in measured intelligence were achieved rarely, and only with those children who were very young and who on admission were functioning at mild and moderate levels of retardation. With some children, a less disharmonious test profile was the only effect of treatment. Generally speaking, however, advances in academic skills were minor.

To illustrate the principles outlined above, two examples from clinical experience will be presented. Both children stayed for a comparatively long period at the Eekwal observation home. A description will be given of the outstanding features in their case histories, the major findings obtained from examination, and the main treatment results. The report opens with a list of the basic personal data of the child in question, i.e., the number of the subject (allotted by the author and only known to him); sex; chronological age in completed years at the date of admission; level of mental retardation; DSM-III-R category of PDD; further concurrent disabilities if present.

Subject No. 093: girl; age 6 years; mildly retarded; PDD-AD

The child was the first born of three children. Her mother's pregnancy and delivery were normal, except for a period of overstrain (treated with a minor tranquillizer). The infant fed well, but had frequent and lengthy crying spells. Some concern was felt about the fact that she liked to look into the lamplight and avoided eye-to-eye contact. She began babbling in her ninth month, but a few months later gave up again. From the parents' account of her behaviour which they gave upon her admission, I will quote a few observations. "She is able to eat by herself, but she is an extremely slow eater with a very small appetite; sometimes she has to be fed. She is dry in the daytime, but by night she is wet and dirty, and often smears her stools. She is not aware of dangers and does not learn by her own unpleasant mistakes. She is a bad sleeper (she sleeps fastened in a harness). She is attached to an extensive set of patterns and rituals: everything has to be arranged in stacks; doors must be shut; before going to sleep, she insists that her toys are placed in a fixed order in the corner of her bed. She sniffs at things. She has talked since she was five, but tends to twist words in a curious way. She can draw figures, animals and cars, but crosses out her drawings as soon as they are completed. When wayward, she has sudden screaming tantrums." Her parents were almost at the end of their tether and her admission into the observation home came as a great relief to them.

Detailed examination failed to provide any clear indications as to why the girl was like she was. Not long before admission she had been tested with the Griffiths. On this test, generally yielding scores of approx. 10% above the actual level, she obtained a GQ of 57 (based on only four subtests, as the subtest Locomotor was not administered). Three weeks after admission, she was assessed by means of the SRZ scale, which measures social functioning in mentally retarded persons (see Appendix C). Her scores are presented in the tables below (under I), together with later scores (under II).

This girl stayed at the observation home for eighteen months. Her eating problems had gone in just a few weeks. From the very start of her stay in the observation home she was not fastened in her bed at night, but the door of her bedroom was locked. She did not wear a nappy; she was picked up once per night, initially at 11 p.m. After a period of less than four weeks, falling asleep was no longer a problem, and during the night she rarely got out of bed. Eventually she learned to stay dry throughout the night, but it took a while before her best time for being picked up and best means of reward were discovered. Five months after admission, she was usually not wet or dirty when picked up at 10.30 p.m; by this time she was spending her weekends at home, where the same strategy was followed with equal success. The screaming tantrums diminished from several times a day to only a few times a week, and were, moreover, less violent and less prolonged. As she had sudden impulses to slip away, when playing outside she was initially tied down with a long piece of string (as a matter of principle the playground at the Eekwal home is not fenced off); however, four months later this measure was no longer necessary.

Seventeen months after admission, her social competence was reassessed by means of the SRZ scale. The results of the first and second assessments are given below. (Standard marks based on the norm laid down for day-care centres.)

(Sub)scale	I	II
Self help	7L	8H
Communication	8H	9
Persistence	7L	7L
Social skills	4	6L
SRZ-Total	7H	9

The table shows an advance in Social skills (significantly at a level of 5%) and a rise in the SRZ-Total (significantly at a 1% level). I stress her improvement in the behavioural areas (concerning which more information will be given in the following sections), because they present a sharp

116

contrast to her comparatively small improvement in the cognitive areas. Nine months after her admission, the girl was tested for the second time with the Griffiths (and also, for the first time, with the WISC, about which later). The two sets of quotients on the subtests and the GQ (without Locomotor) are listed below.

(Sub)test	I	II
Personal-social	53	59
Hearing & speech	39	56
Eye & hand co-ordination	75	76
Performance	61	76
GQ (four subtests)	57	67

Nothing can be said as to whether or not the 10-point difference in GQ is significant, as the companion manual fails to provide guidelines for its calculation. My feeling is that there is at best only a slight chance that the improvement is a significant one. However, as the results show, the profile became less disharmonious with a decrease in the difference between the highest and lowest quotients from 36-20 points.

Sixteen months after her admission, the WISC was applied again, this time together with the Griffiths language subtest. The two sets of quotients are listed below.

(Sub)test	I	II
Verbal IQ	56	56
Performance IQ	94	97
IQ	72	73
Hearing & speech (Griffiths)	56	56

As the results show, the girl's development increased with chronological age, but no more than that. The V-P difference remained considerable; differences of respectively 38 and 41 points are very significant indeed. A noteworthy finding was that the girl started to make drawings consonant with her chronological level. She did not, however, give up fully the habit of destroying her own drawings by crossing them over, crumpling them up or throwing them away. None of the efforts made by the staff, such as praising her for a drawing, putting one up on the wall of her room, or asking her to wrap one up as a fine present for her relatives, succeeded in preventing her from destroying her work.

On the PDD-MR Scale the girl's score at the time of her discharge was 11 (classification: PDD) and she was diagnosed as PDD (determined on the basis of the data from her file). After discharge, she returned home and was placed (though over-age) into a special preschool-class for children with developmental problems. Thereafter she attended successively primary and secondary schools for educable mentally retarded children, and finally, ten years later, was placed in out-of-home care.

Subject No. 100: boy; age 4 years; mildly retarded; PDD-AD

This boy will be discussed in more detail in Section II.5.4.2. He stayed in the observation home for about eighteen months, during which time he received about two hours per day of individual education.

As in the previous example, the development of his cognitive skills was tested by means of the Griffiths. The two sets of quotients obtained on the subtests and GQ (without Locomotor) at the first and third testings are listed below. (The first test was administered a few weeks after his admission, and the third was seventeen months after the first test).

(Sub)test	I	III
Personal-social	54	68
Hearing & speech	59	68
Eye & hand co-ordination	84	76
Performance	91	68
GQ (four subtests)	72	70

The rate of his development did not change, nor was there any catching up. However, the profile became considerably less disharmonious; the difference between the highest and the lowest quotients reduced from 37 points to a normal figure of 8 points.

For the sake of completeness, I also present the SRZ results, measured with an interval of eighteen months (in standard marks based on the norm laid down for day-care centres).

(Sub)scale	I	II
Self help	7L	8L
Communication	8H	8L
Persistence	6H	7L
Social skills	4	6L
SRZ-Total	7L	7H

Again, these results confirm that his development increased with chronological age, without any real progress taking place. However, the profile became less disharmonious with a reduction of the difference between the highest and lowest subscale standard mark from 4.25 points to 2.00 points.

II.4.6.2   *Language*

Speech and language intervention with mentally retarded children with a PDD runs the risk of tending too much towards *deliberate training* (which also holds true for intervention in the area of social skills, the subject of the next section).

Normally, the living situation of a mentally and physically non-disabled child contains many intrinsic elements which benefit his developmental process in a natural way. These elements have been called by Langeveld (1955) *educational factors*. Play, for example, is such an educational factor. However, a child with a pervasive developmental disorder is less able or even unable to respond spontaneously to these educational factors. When offered new experiences he may turn them into fixed rituals which only serve to bring further development to a stop. In such a situation, educational intervention has no other choice, as Langeveld has argued, than to use the educational factors as *educational means*, i.e., to transform the accidental, playful and spontaneous moments which are entirely natural occurrences in the lives of children without disabilities into explicit learning experiences for PDD children. This may have a very unfavourable effect, however, on spontaneous processes in the adult-child interaction, as well as on the acceptance of the child as he is. Children with PDD are apt to be regarded as cases needing special strategies and treatment procedures. Such an approach will put a child under constant pressure, which may lead to passive resistance, rebellion, tensions, or even serious forms of unsettlement and behavioural problems. On the other hand, though, management of a PDD child is not possible without at least some degree of deliberateness in the educational process. The use of operant techniques, too, may be a prerequisite, although these will sometimes be felt to be rather chilly. In general, however, there is no doubt that the behaviouristic approach has made highly valuable contributions, such as highlighting the importance of making a meticulous functional analysis before treatment is started and of a systematic programming and evaluation of treatment. It is therefore in the light of an overall appreciation of the contributions of the behaviouristic school that the following critical remarks should be understood.

Many European experts, including the present writer, were very impressed by the film *Behavior Modification: Teaching Language to Psychotic Children*, made in 1969 by Lovaas, the American psychologist who pioneered the application of the behaviour-modification system in the field of autism and mental retardation. The film reported good results and conveyed an overall spirit of enthusiasm and optimism. The Lovaas language training programme is characterized by the following strategies (Klijn, 1978):

- *stimuli in the learning environment are kept to a minimum;* usually the room is unadorned;
- *disruptive behaviours are ignored;* this involves the use of such procedures as time-out;
- *conditions are created which necessitate attention and eye-to-eye contact;*
- *vocal imitation is taught as a sequel to motor imitation;*
- *an appropriate use of language is promoted;* this involves such procedures as: selection of vocal responses; curtailment of echolalia; - in more advanced stages - stimulation in the naming of things, in answering questions and forming sentences; and, finally, training in generalization for everyday situations.

The Eekwal observation home did employ Lovaas' methods of training language and social skills, but the results proved to be far from impressive. Newly acquired language skills remained too limited in scope and were insufficiently integrated into daily life interaction. As has been pointed out by Konstantareas (1986), Lovaas seems to have been overrated in the merits of his system, notably its long-term effectiveness; according to Konstantareas the only result achieved is a printer-like rattling off of texts. With respect to the behaviouristic approach in general, J.K. Wing (1966) had earlier reported that it hardly yields any improvement of language skills, although it is helpful in diminishing behavioural problems, while Newson (1986) states, "We are forced to look beyond the simplistic tool of the behavioural model. Useful though that tool may be, it is no longer enough as a total treatment programme."

Finding that the system developed by Lovaas produced rather disappointing results in the domain of language skills, the team at the Eekwal observation home formulated, on the basis of their own clinical experience, the following set of general principles:

- giving speech therapy on a purely technical level is pointless;
- not only the language and the cognitive levels (regardless of chronological age) have to be taken into account, but decidedly also the emotional and social levels;
- treatment is geared to existing assets of skills and interests;
- language skills have to be trained in concrete everyday situations, such as at meal-times, during bathing, dressing and undressing, while the child is being brought to the toilet or put to bed, during social interaction with peers, while the child is playing in the garden and during a game or walk, etc.;
- especially during the initial phase of the learning process, making gestures and actually doing things help much to clarify spoken words, and vice versa;
- not until a child has made fair progress does it make sense to teach language skills through the use of pictures (picture books and colourful large-format scrapbooks specially compiled for each individual child come in handy then as do miniature copies of common-or-garden things).

The general idea is to train the child in the use of meaningful gestures, sounds, words and sentences in everyday situations, which in this context means the day programme. Training should be step-by-step, and repetition is very important. In the initial phase, very young children and severely retarded children are often found to enjoy songs and rhymes accompanying infant amusements, finger-games and the like. Thus, by training language skills in a context of real experiences and with a note of playfulness, it is possible to come a bit closer to the way in which the educational factors, as defined above, operate. Thus may we avoid the whole process becoming too artificial and deliberate.

However, in setting treatment goals it must always be realized that the emotional-social deficits in children with pervasive developmental disorders seriously hamper their communicative potential. Consequently, the content of their speech and language will virtually always be out of keeping with their cognitive levels, and the technical and formal qualities very often.

Finally, one illustrative example is given of the principles outlined above. (More details of this case are presented in Section II.5.3.2.4.)

Subject No. 045: boy; age 2 years; mildly retarded; PDD-AD

On admission, this boy could say just three words (Mum, Dad, and Hello), but rarely did so. Repeated audiological examinations had ruled out the existence of a hearing loss that might have affected his development. His receptive language skills had reached the mental level of a one-year-old child. He had a very idiosyncratic way of babbling, once in a while using a clear intonation or even producing something like a melody.

A few weeks after his admission, he was tested with the Griffiths subtest Hearing & speech; a subtest age of 1-2 was the result, and the subtest quotient, computed separately, was 44. He had two serious problems: he tended to ignore being spoken to completely, and did not use his own limited vocal utterances to communicate.

His language skills were trained in the standard way, i.e., mainly through the use of a fixed vocabulary referring to everyday experiences, a set repertory of songs and games, and - at a later stage - through the use of picture books and small play objects. Training was given by both the attendants and the special-education teacher, under the joint supervision of the speech therapist-audiologist and the educationalist. After four months of training the results were still rather poor, so it was decided to switch over to language training on the basis of the Lovaas programme (1969) which would be carried out by the present author. This chap learned to produce small sequential series of words (not real sentences), such as "apple, eat, mmmh, nice", with the reinforcement of grated apple. However, being very rigid, the child could only be trained to say other words or another series of words if a different reinforcer was used, to prevent him from "learning" to become indifferent to previously successful reinforcers. A very unwelcome side-effect of this treatment programme was that it led to violent temper tantrums, which obviously also needed intervention. My tactic was to turn my back to him ostentatiously, which proved to work surprisingly well; this strategy could also be followed by attendants when the boy was in the group. After several months of daily training in sessions of about ten minutes, the boy was capable of using about twenty elementary words. Spontaneously he used them only rarely; if prompted, he produced them in a robotic manner. On finding that the boy started to become more talkative in the group (using predominantly words and sentences other than those he had learned in the training programme), the training sessions were discontinued. There were in fact strong reasons to believe that the improvement was due to factors other than the language training. Additional support for this impression was found in the fact that the boy's language skills continued to develop after the language training had stopped.

Nine months after the Griffiths test had been administered for the first time, the boy was tested again on the Griffiths subtest Hearing & speech. The subtest age found was 1-8, and the subtest General Quotient was 49. In all likelihood this does not represent a significant rise, but again, as in the foregoing case, no exact figure can be presented.

Another way of estimating his progress is by considering his language skills. Speaking on admission only three words and doing so rarely, on discharge his vocabulary consisted of 55 words used in frequencies of fifty to ninety times a day. Moreover, he now used these words meaningfully and in a communicative way most of the time. The boy clearly had even some understanding of the use of verb forms. Nevertheless, considering all the efforts made, the conclusion must be that for a mildly retarded child aged 3-5 (his age at discharge) his language development had not been very impressive.

With moderately retarded children with a PDD similar results were only occasionally obtainable. As for the category of severely retarded children, in their case the adequate use of a couple of gestures and words, i.e., above the level of mere echopraxia and echolalia, were regarded as a major advance indeed. The category of profoundly retarded children never even made a start with the acquisition of expressive language.

II.4.6.3   Social behaviour

Like language, social development of children with a PDD tends to be trained in too formal and deliberate a manner. Care should be taken to ensure that contact between the child and the professional helper includes moments of joy and relaxation for both; otherwise, social training will at best only generate yet another meaningless set of rituals. Although an emotionally deep-going contact with a mentally retarded child with a PDD will never come about, quite a few of these children proved nevertheless to be able to do more than just mechanically carry out a programme. With respect to specific goals in the treatment plan, the use of operant techniques may be required.

In my view, training social behaviour is not possible before sufficient eye-to-eye contact has been established. The child's attention to the face of the therapist may be drawn by pulling faces and making shapes with the mouth (just as with young infants, except for the fact that accompanying these with sounds is less advisable with pervasively disordered children). Another technique is to invite a child to look at his own face and that of the helper, whilst both are sitting in front of a mirror; initially, various parts of the child's face and those of the adult are touched or taken hold of; at a later stage these parts are pointed to and named; and perhaps the child may even eventually be ready to join the helper in drawing a human face.

Games such as peekaboo and hide-and-seek may be very instrumental in establishing contact, as they force the child to notice another. Frolicking and tickling, on the other hand, are less suitable to this end; although many children with pervasive disorders do in fact find much enjoyment in such games, they may become over-absorbed in the haptic and kinaesthetic aspects involved.

Some children are more willing to respond positively to overtures at moments when they feel comparatively safe, for example, when just tucked in, or when hidden in their own nook. Later contact-making may draw upon such first positive experiences.

Sometimes contact can also be established by first mimicking the child, in the way he is rocking forwards and backwards, for instance; subsequently, one can make one's presence felt by introducing minor changes into the child's own way of doing things.

Simple exchange games, such as running a toy car or rolling a ball between the child and adult, may also be a first step to communication. Initially, the adult and the child sit opposite one another with their legs wide apart and feet touching; in this way the child can neither miss nor ignore the car or ball moving towards him. After many play sessions, throwing the ball over may eventually become possible.

The adult may show the child extensively how to play with a doll or teddy bear: to cuddle and kiss it, to dress and undress it, to put it to bed, etc.; subsequently the child may join the adult in these activities. The adult may also invite a child to share in the babying of another child.

A child of a higher developmental level and one who has made some progress can be taught to cooperate and await their turns; while jointly playing with building blocks, for example. At a still further stage, playing such simple games as 'Colour Towers' or 'Lottino', possibly with more than two players, can serve the same ends.

Another activity which the Eekwal observation home has found to be helpful is to give children pictures of human figures from which they are asked to cut out the parts of the body; these have to be glued onto paper, fastened to a flannel board, or drawn around, may be even drawn; while busy with it, the children are also asked to point out the various parts on each other's bodies. The underlying thought is that making a child more aware of himself will help him to become more aware of other people.

Children who have a habit of hurting other children, by pulling at their hair, for instance, may be put through the same experience (but certainly not in a punishing way); hopefully this method will stir at least some consideration for other persons. However, there is only a slight chance that genuine empathy will ever develop, as will become evident in the next section.

The measures discussed above are in fact mainly suitable for mildly retarded children, the category with the best prospects for making improvements - although far from spectacular ones - in the domain of specific problems.

When social behaviour is considered within the larger context of *social competence*, the clinical practice at the Eekwal observation home with mentally retarded children with a PDD confirms the picture of the general profile of these children emerging from earlier research (see I.2.2 and I.2.3). The outcome may be summed up by saying that Self help and Daily living skills, i.e., the predominantly practical and technical skills in the domains of respectively social competence (SRZ scale) and adaptive behaviour (VABS), are trainable. Illustrative examples are presented in Sections II.4.6.1, II.4.8.2.2, and II.4.8.4.

II.4.6.4   Emotional development

In spite of the unmistakable emotional deficits displayed by children, adolescents and adults with pervasive disorders, it would be incorrect to speak of regressive or childish behaviour. In fact, the course of emotional development is seriously blocked right from the start, in all likelihood by the fundamental deficits and disorders identified by several investigators (such as Baron-Cohen, Frith and Leslie; see I.2.2). In other words, the behaviour of these people is not less mature or more infantile than could be anticipated on the basis of objective assessments.

The comparatively low level of emotional development is especially noticeable in mildly and more or less also in moderately retarded persons with a PDD. Notably the children falling in these categories have features which contrast unfavourably with some of their cognitive, linguistic and social skills:

- They show a preference for very simple games, stories, books, and television programmes.
- They are almost completely unable to tell something about their own feelings and experiences; their answers to simple questions (such as: whether

they did enjoy something or not; whether they consider themselves good or a bad; whether they feel lonely or bored; which people they like and dislike), if given at all, are often humdrum and of little substance. More emotive subjects, such as anxiety, pain, illness, and death, may even confuse them. Pressing for an answer may elicit uneasiness, stress or resistance, sometimes even explosive, aggressive and/or destructive reactions. Some children restrict themselves to a more or less mechanical echoing of phrases picked up from others, without expressing any genuinely felt personal emotion.

- They misinterpret or fail to understand even simple jokes and innocent teasing.

Severely and profoundly retarded persons with a PDD are even less capable of self-reflection. They communicate and interact with the surrounding world by responding to what their bodies and their senses tell them, which to all appearances is the only way they can feel and think.

A number of people with a PDD of all levels of mental retardation continuously claim attention and cling to parents and attendants, reminding us of a toddler tied to his mother's apron strings; in essence, this is possibly also a sign of severe emotional immaturity. Although claiming attention, these people are actually only capable of a very stereotyped and sterile form of interaction. More often than not interventions even in the long run fail to bring about the slightest emotional development.

As a matter of fact, clinical experience at the Eekwal observation home showed that management and treatment achieve no noticeable catching-up in the emotional development of this group of dually disabled people. Accordingly, the strategy became increasingly to switch over from treatment to just *taking into account*. Some measures proved to be effective in helping to make life easier for mentally retarded persons with a PDD. This was primarily noticeable in the emotional area, but problems in other areas, including behaviour, might be alleviated as a result. The distinctive features of the strategy are:

- as a general principle, management has to be geared to the numerous manifestations of an infantile level of behavioural and emotional development;
- care and management must offer clarity, consistency and very concrete forms of security. This applies to the physical and social environment as well as to sequence of items in the daily programme. It means moreover that it must be made absolutely clear which things are allowed and which are not. Often this will imply a rather black-and-white approach. Directions have to be given through simple words, gestures and facial expressions, while pictogrammes are also very helpful; the primary aim is that a given message is understood;

- tensions in children have to be handled with extreme cautiousness. When at such moments children are asked such (undoubtedly well-intended) questions as, "What made you so angry?", or, "Just tell me what is worrying you", they may feel that they should come up with an answer, but are in fact generally unable to give one. Such an approach can therefore be counterproductive, provoking even more anger, resistance, confusion or other similar reactions. This may even apply to the mildly retarded category of children with a PDD;
- the children have to be guarded against matters with which they are unable to cope; they cannot, for instance, come to terms with the emotions provoked by scenes of sex and violence in books, films and television programmes; such emotions tend to keep stirring through their minds and may suddenly crop up at quite inconvenient moments; this can be embarrassing for themselves as well as for people in their environment and may lead to other adverse consequences;
- in connection with the two foregoing principles, I wish to emphasize my view, which was put forward in Section II.4.4, that it is a misconception to think that the emotional development of children with pervasive developmental disorders might be promoted by giving them spontaneous warm-hearted affection. On the contrary, such an approach tends to make them - as well as adolescents and adults - confused and nonplussed, thus increasing their inclination to withdraw and avoid contact. An approach which is involved but at the same time detached, well-balanced, subdued and consistent, is far more effective. Although such a style of management may seem rather cold and unfeeling to us, it does help them by making things clear and unambiguous.

The preceding discussion has hopefully made it clear that, as far as emotional development is concerned, making the best of the existing state of affairs is the only feasible option. The emotional deficits have to be accepted as they are, and thoughts of remedying them have to be abandoned. Unmistakably the delays and distortions in emotional development are highly specific features of pervasive developmental disorders.

II.4.7 Special educational intervention and treatment of mentally retarded children with PDD: semi-specific problems

II.4.7.1 *Self-injurious behaviour*

The discussion of semi-specific problems opens with self-injurious behaviour (SIB) because it offers a good opportunity to highlight some theoretical considerations which are also relevant to issues to be dealt with in subsequent sections.

II.4.7.1.1 Some general remarks

SIB or self-injurious behaviour is undoubtedly one of the major and most serious behavioural disorders in the mental retardation field. Its incidence in mentally retarded persons with PDD in particular is very high (see below and Chapter III.4). There is therefore every reason to consider this behavioural problem extensively.

In fact, the term self-injurious behaviour (or self-mutilation) is somewhat misleading, as these behaviours are not necessarily injurious. However, to my knowledge the existing literature has so far failed to provide us with a more appropriate and generally accepted term, so I adhere to the term self-injurious behaviour herein.

When developing the SGZ scale for maladaptive behaviour (Kraijer & Kema, 1976, 1994), the criterion employed for SIB was that *the action caused pain, at least in the observer's assessment*. When devising the PDD-MR Scale (Kraijer, 1990, 1992), I followed the same principle.

SIB may occur only incidentally, but it may also be a daily recurring problem. The term covers a wide range of types of behaviour in various degrees of severity. Almost all parts of the body can be involved, although the predominant targets of such actions seem to be the head, arms and hands. The ways of hurting oneself range from rather harmless actions (scratching; pinching; beating; making the skin raw by rubbing; keeping sores open) to more harmful actions (banging the head against a wall; biting; eye-poking). In some cases SIB causes negligible physical damage (a scratch; a callosity), but sometimes the consequences are serious (blindness; severe wounds, notably around the mouth and on the forehead and fingers).

Estimates of the prevalence of this behaviour differ widely. According to Duker (1989), SIB occurs in 10-15% of persons in the severe and profound ranges of retardation. Hyman et al. (1990), basing themselves on various sources, state that 5 to 37% of the population in residential facilities for mentally retarded persons display this kind of behaviour, against less than 2% of the mentally retarded persons not living in such facilities. Repp et al. (1990) give prevalence rates for institutionalized psychotic and mentally retarded persons ranging between 5% and 23%. In all likelihood, these differences in prevalence rates are at least partly due to differences in the kind of populations investigated. Different definitions of the problem may also account for the varying outcomes. Hyman et al., for instance, included in their definition of SIB such behaviours as pica, air-swallowing and rumination.

When devising the PDD-MR Scale (Kraijer, 1990, 1992), I found the following prevalence rates of SIB (according to the criterion given above):

- 30.8% of 718 residents living in institutions for mentally retarded persons (all age-ranges);
- 11.2% of 305 visitors of day-care centres for mentally retarded children (age-range 3-15);
- 31.5% of 73 mentally retarded persons staying in an observation clinic (all age-ranges).

More details will be presented in Chapter III.4.

Data from other studies give added weight to the impression that SIB is a serious problem. Dutch researchers (Schuring et al., 1990) found that 14% of a sample of people with problem behaviour living in residential care displayed self-injurious behaviour, in the narrow sense of the word. Subdividing this group in terms of the seriousness of their problems revealed that SIB occurred in 20.5% of those with serious problem behaviours and in 30.7% of those with extremely serious problem behaviours.

Causes and conditioning factors for SIB have received comparatively wide attention in the literature in the field. For more than two decades SIB has been linked with the Lesch-Nyhan syndrome, which is itself associated with mental retardation. Scriver et al. (1989) state that 85% of children with this syndrome will sooner or later display this kind of behaviour, some even starting during their first year, although some do not start before the age of sixteen. On average, these children begin to engage in this behaviour at an early age, i.e., between their third and fourth birthdays. Often SIB is found to occur only during particular periods, but as yet no specific biochemical variables have been identified which might be held accountable for the onset and ending of these episodes.

Two critical remarks can be made with respect to the line of thought delineated above. In the first place, the association with a physical disorder can at best only indirectly provide an answer to the question where this particular kind of problem behaviour originates in. In the second place, the Lesch-Nyhan syndrome occurs rarely, whereas SIB is very common. A small number of other uncommon syndromes are also known to be associated with SIB, i.e., the Cornelia de Lange syndrome and some pain syndromes (inborn disorders which are coupled with pain indifference). In this connection, mention should also be made of the Prader-Willi syndrome (a neglected field of inquiry in the literature about SIB); persons with this syndrome feel a strong urge to scratch themselves and to keep their sores open. All in all, the conclusion must be that these rarely occurring syndromes are not likely to furnish a clue about the nature of the very frequently occurring SIB. Finally, as has been pointed out by Gillberg (1992b), SIB is also concurrent with the far more common fragile-X syndrome. Here, however, SIB may in fact be primarily associated with mental retardation or, indeed, with the symptoms of a pervasive disorder (see also Chapter III.6).

As yet no conclusive evidence has been found that there is a relationship between, on the one hand, SIB in mentally retarded persons and, on the other hand, abnormalities in the metabolism of dopamine, serotonin or endorphin (Verhoeven, 1992).

The various factors which have been considered to have had a bearing on SIB in the literature and the different approaches followed are very perceptively outlined in a study by Repp et al. (1990). The authors grouped current hypotheses into three types. These were presented in chronological order (but probably their relative practical relevance has also something to do with it). Briefly summarized, the authors differentiate the following groups of hypotheses:

- The *hypothesis of self-stimulation*. This hypothesis is based on the idea that persons engaging in such behaviour are in a condition of *hypoarousal*. According to this view, an organism needs a certain level of stimulation; notably the tactile, vestibular and kinaesthetic stimuli are especially important. When such stimulation is not forthcoming, the organism may engage in repetitive behaviours, such as stereotypies and SIB. As a matter of fact, since the early sixties a growing body of evidence has been accumulated in the field of mental retardation to demonstrate that a sharp reduction of various kinds of stereotyped behaviour is possible by counteracting this lack of stimulation. It is a problem mainly found in understaffed institutions for severely and profoundly retarded people where residents are offered no day programme and groups are large. (See, for instance, Berkson et al., 1963.)

  However, self-stimulation may also take place in conditions of *hyperarousal*. In this case it seems to be an attempt to stop or to reduce overstimulation. Perhaps in the future a more detailed analysis can clarify the mechanisms involved.
- The *positive-reinforcement hypothesis*. This hypothesis implies that SIB is a learned operant, maintained by contingent positive reinforcement. The idea is that by engaging in SIB a person may, for instance, acquire more individual attention: he is soothed, reprimanded, hugged, etc.
- The *negative-reinforcement hypothesis*. This hypothesis implies that SIB is a learned operant used to avoid or terminate an aversive stimulus. The idea is that by engaging in SIB a person may, for instance, escape demands made on him.

There is indeed no doubt that SIB does take place in the way described in the types of hypotheses presented above. However, there are more aspects involved. In the first place, there is also a communicative aspect to SIB, to which no explicit reference is made in the hypotheses mentioned. Groundwork in this area has been done, in particular, by a team of experts led by Duker (1989). According to these investigators, mentally retarded persons who lack effective means of communicating with other people will display more problem behaviour, such as SIB and aggression, than those who have such means. Therefore a special vocabulary of gestures was devised for a target group of mentally retarded persons to serve as substitutes for spoken words. Subsequently, a sample of mentally retarded persons was trained in the use of this sign language. It was found that a significant increase in the use of sign language led to a significant *decrease* in - but not a complete elimination of - SIB. Thus, SIB may at least partly be regarded as a - rather inadequate - form of communication, a conclusion which is in line with the second and third groups of hypotheses listed above.

There is another aspect of SIB to which I would like to draw attention, which is that the behaviour tends to be self-enclosed. In this respect SIB is similar to stereotyped movements, stereotyped handling of objects, masturbation and rumination. I will come back to this issue in Chapter III.4.

Using a slightly different approach to the problem I made my own division into types of SIB, on the basis of my clinical experience, and present them below. Similarities and dissimilarities with the views discussed above will be indicated for each individual type of SIB.

- *Instrumental SIB.* This type of SIB is primarily a means to attain something that stands in no relation to the action (self-stimulation) proper. There is clearly an attempt to communicate via an idiosyncratic - and hence inadequate - 'language.' In the system drawn up by Repp et al., this behaviour is seen as being based mostly on positive reinforcement and occasionally on negative reinforcement. Instrumental SIB is comparatively more common in young children. Incidence tends to drop with increasing age. In my view, SIB, especially in adolescents and adults, is too often interpreted as instrumental behaviour, notably by parents and attendants. This may be explained by the fact that many a self-injurious person is often observed to glance at other persons present with what seems to be a defying or expectant look. However, his looks probably express not so much that he wants to know whether he is going to have things his way, but rather that he anticipates hearing the familiar warnings or commands (such as: "Stop it! You are not going to hurt yourself!").
- *Reactive SIB.* This type of SIB is a more or less vital response to such things as discomfort, stress, panic and fear. Even a very small increase in demands, a slight change or a minor disruption may provoke strong reactions, including SIB. Negative reinforcement seems to be hardly at stake here. The behaviour is obviously enclosed in itself. This type of SIB can in fact not be regarded as an attempt to convey or express feelings. Above all, the behaviour has a strong resemblance to what Goldstein has termed the 'catastrophic reaction', characteristic of children and adults with brain injury when faced with a task which is beyond their capacities. Strauss and Lehtinen (1960) give the following description of this 'inadequate' way of responding: "a strong reaction of rage, despair, anxiety, or extreme depression, with all the accompanying body reactions of crying, changing color, trembling and so on." As the coping abilities and communication skills of mentally retarded persons are even more restricted, they will all the more easily lapse into self-injurious behaviour. In the Eekwal observation home, reactive SIB was frequently found in the group of extremely fragile mentally retarded children and adults, i.e., persons who are functioning at the severe and profound levels of mental retardation and have a concurrent pervasive disorder. Often there are overt signs of organic brain damage or brain dysfunction. There are strong indications

that this type of SIB is related to the kind of self-stimulation which stems from hyperarousal. In fact, both types of behaviour probably have a common background.

- *Self-stimulatory SIB.* This type of SIB tends to develop or to increase in conditions of hypoarousal or lack of stimuli (Repp et al., 1990), or, in more conventional language, in times of idleness and/or boredom. The behaviour is found in adults and children in the profound, severe and moderate ranges of mental retardation. Compared with 25 years ago, the prevalence of self-stimulatory behaviours, including SIB, has decreased considerably, in particular in residential institutions. This advance has been realized through staffing-up, reduction of the size of groups, and providing residents with a much broader range of activities, strategies which all have given these settings a radically different appearance.
- *Structural SIB.* Structural (or patterned) SIB is in all likelihood connected either with obsessive-compulsive SIB in some cases emerging at a very early age, or with transmuted or degenerated forms of instrumental or self-stimulatory SIB (and occasionally of reactive SIB). Whatever its origin, the behaviour looks as if it is almost completely autonomous and has compulsive or obsessive traits. Even in young children SIB may in my view be structural, but its likelihood increases in adolescents and adults. The behaviour tends to occur periodically, but often no external determinants can be identified.

The division given above calls for some further comment.

- A functional analysis of the self-injurious behaviour is necessary before proper categorization can be made. The instrumental, reactive and self-stimulatory forms are comparatively easily identified, whereas structural SIB is more or less a residual category.
- Both pure and mixed types of SIB are found.
- As indicated, prevalence rates of the various types differ per age group.
- There is some correlation between SIB (of all types) and level of functioning; SIB clearly occurs more frequently in severely and profoundly retarded persons. (See also Chapter III.4.)
- The distinction between types of SIB is helpful in predicting success in treatment. Structural SIB has a particularly poor prognosis, whereas self-stimulatory SIB has the most favourable prognosis. The rank order of the four types of SIB from fair to poor prognosis is as follows:
  - self-stimulatory SIB;
  - instrumental SIB;
  - reactive SIB;
  - structural SIB.
- All four types of SIB are found to be more amenable to treatment in higher-functioning individuals.

  Profoundly retarded individuals and those who are intermediate between profoundly and severely retarded display the largest number of problems.

- SIB is more amenable to treatment in individuals without a concurrent pervasive developmental disorder; this applies notably to the first three types of SIB.
- Treatment should start *at the earliest possible stage;* this applies notably to the first three types of SIB which are liable to grow into a habit, or in other words, to become structural (or patterned).
- The distinction between the four types of SIB is essential in deciding on the most appropriate type of treatment. Taking the aforementioned research project of Duker as an example, the measure of offering another communication system will be especially expedient in the treatment of instrumental SIB.
- Finally, similar distinctions may also be helpful with other forms of problem behaviour, such as: sleep disturbances; eating problems; short-tempered or aggressive behaviour; and constipation. However, the impact of the four underlying systems on these kinds of behaviour is different; self-stimulation in particular seldom plays a role of any significance.

II.4.7.1.2   Aspects of the treatment of SIB

The treatment strategies applied at the Eekwal observation home for the four types of SIB will be discussed separately. However, simple - though often effective - measures will not be considered (for example, children who are in the habit of scratching themselves should have their nails kept short by filing them daily). The present section will be concluded with some illustrative examples of treatment interventions.

In the following paragraphs a description will be given of the reasoning on which the various strategies are based.

In the treatment of *instrumental SIB*, two principles are essential:

- The *need* supposedly expressed through this kind of SIB must be met, either directly or indirectly.
- While, on the one hand, the inappropriate way of communicating the need has to be discouraged by withholding *at that moment* any reinforcement (the relevant techniques are discussed in detail in Duker & Seys, 1977), more appropriate ways of communicating have also to be offered (see Duker, 1989).

Treatment of *reactive SIB* calls for reduction, selection and regularization of stimuli (see II.4.3.3). Often an overall reduction of demands will be necessary in order to diminish overstimulation or overloading. The person concerned needs an approach with a high degree of *predictability, clarity* and *stability*. Furthermore, the programme must include daily recurring moments of relaxation and rest, such as: playing with sand and water; short moments of withdrawal in a screened-off nook; an afternoon nap; an occasional short walk; a restful hot bath. However, as noted in Section II.4.3.3, stimuli should not be narrowed down too much either, as this may lead to the development of other behavioural problems, including self-stimulatory SIB (which will then just take the place of reactive SIB). In some cases medication aimed at lowering sensitivity to stimuli may be helpful as an adjunct to treatment.

Treatment of *self-stimulatory SIB* calls firstly for extension of stimuli, and secondly for strengthening of stimuli; in other words, both the quality and the quantity of stimuli have to be enhanced (again, see II.4.3.3). An overall reconsideration of the demands made on the person may also be necessary. With this type of SIB, too little may have been demanded, which would mean *underloading*. For the sake of completeness, I would like to add that in my experience understimulation or underloading occurs rarely in children living at home or in group homes; furthermore, that children in the lower levels of functioning are more likely to be under-demanded. Self-stimulation and SIB can be reduced in the following ways: by providing more activities (preferably including gross motor activities) and by introducing more variation in these activities; by giving more personal attention; - in some cases - by imposing greater personal responsibility and making higher demands.

Treatment of *structural SIB* poses the most problems. Persons displaying this behaviour, for the most part adolescents and adults, are often inextricably enmeshed in it. If SIB has ego-dystonic traits, it is definitely compulsive. As compulsive behaviour in mentally retarded persons in general is known to be very resistant to intervention, this holds all the more true for severely and profoundly retarded persons with pervasive developmental disorders.

The policy followed at the Eekwal observation home was to stimulate an adult or child with structural SIB in an unimposing way to come out of his shell and to develop more agreeable and socially acceptable behaviour; helpers tried to remain physically nearby and in touch; as far as possible, SIB was curbed or prevented. This approach is comparable with the method which McGee et al. (1987) have named 'gentle teaching', involving the technique of 'interrupt-ignore-redirect-reward.' However, whereas reportedly their method represents 'a posture that strives to human solidarity', at the Eekwal observation home the close proximity of another human being was primarily aimed at creating a sense of rest and security. Positive results were obtained by providing a day programme in which high emphasis was placed on gross motor activities, such as walking, running, cycling, and swimming (or just water play). However, it should certainly not be expected that all SIB can be checked by this kind of intervention alone; the physical exercises have to be incorporated into a comprehensive treatment programme. Aversive techniques were sparingly employed at the Eekwal home, and aversive electric shocks not at all. In principle, aversive techniques were only employed in blind-alley situations; a similar stand has been taken by Jol and Duker (1984). The effects of psychotropic drugs, i.e., neuroleptics, antidepressants, and even drugs specially intended for obsessive-compulsive behaviour, were on the whole disappointing. All in all, in many cases it proved not to be possible to reduce structural SIB to an acceptable level.

For easy reference, the main types of SIB and the appropriate treatment procedures are summarized in Scheme II.4.4.

Scheme II.4.4 The main types of SIB and the appropriate treatment strategies

---

INSTRUMENTAL   SIB with the intention of either (a) obtaining something or (b) avoiding something

Treatment:
- fulfilment of the need in question in a direct or indirect way;
- curtailment of this form of communication by behaviour-modification techniques, such as positive reinforcement and extinction;
- if possible, the introduction of a more adequate form of communication.

REACTIVE   SIB which is a more or less vital response of a person to a feeling of being overloaded or overstimulated

Treatment:
- reduction, selection and regularization of stimuli;
- easing the burden of demands;
- medication to lower sensitivity to stimuli;
- if possible, introduction of a more adequate form of communication.

SELF-STIMULATORY self-enclosed behaviour aimed at counterpoising a situation of understimulation or underloading

Treatment:
- extension and strengthening of stimuli with the aim of widening the field of experience;
- providing more (gross) motor activities;
- making higher demands and giving more personal responsibility;
- giving more personal attention.

STRUCTURAL   either (a) compulsory or obsessive SIB or (b) SIB which is a degenerated form of instrumental or self-stimulatory SIB

Treatment:
- extension and strengthening of stimuli with the aim of widening the field of experience;
- providing more (gross) motor activities;
- application of behaviour-modification techniques, including aversive stimuli;
- medication as an adjunct to treatment.

The following four cases serve to illustrate the various treatment strategies aimed at tackling instrumental, reactive and structural forms of SIB, presenting either singly or combined. In actual practice, the outcomes of treatments are certainly not always successful, as the examples given will also make clear. (For the interpretation of test results on the SRZ, SGZ and SMZ scales, the reader is referred to Appendix C.)

Subject No. 029: girl; age 4 years; severely retarded; PDD-NOS and epilepsy

This girl was the second of three children. The mother's pregnancy was normal. However, the child was born eight weeks early and remained several weeks in an incubator. She was discharged in good health, although she did seem too "quiet." Her development was extremely slow: rolling over at eighteen months; learning to sit at two years; standing at 2.5 years; walking at three years. From the outset, contact-making was very insufficient and there was no eye-to-eye contact at all. On admission, she could speak just a word or two, but did so uncommunicatively. Switching over from liquid food to solid food had given much difficulty; she was still fastidious and had to be fed. She was not toilet-trained and wore nappies.

133

At the age of three, she began to show increasingly dysphoric states and SIB involving banging her head, hitting and pinching herself, tearing her hair and biting herself (mostly her hands and wrists, occasionally her knees and shoulders, and also her lips since the time she had had blisters in and around her mouth). SIB and dysphoria seemed to be linked together. At the time of the onset of her problems the girl possibly had received insufficient attention from her mother who was for the third time pregnant and had to rest regularly. At least, this was the only plausible explanation her parents could find. On the other hand, giving the child love and attention actually proved, both now and on previous occasions, only to make matters worse. Medication - for a year she used imipramine, first as the only drug, later supplemented with an anticonvulsant - had had no effect.

Detailed examination failed to reveal any etiology for the girl's mental retardation. She seemed to have a mild ataxia and hypotonia affecting particularly her gait. The EEG record revealed an occasional paroxysm. There was a family history of mental retardation (unaccounted for) and of Hurler's disease.

The girl proved hardly testable. On the Griffiths (generally yielding scores of approx. 10% above the actual level) she obtained a GQ of about 35. She was an extremely vulnerable child. Minor events such as a buzzing fly or the switching on of a light might provoke a complete breakdown, resulting in dysphoria, strain, restlessness and above all SIB. Strikingly, she might well ignore exactly the same event only a few moments later, and there was no predicting whether she was going to react or not.

The treatment strategy contained the following elements:

- She was helped to understand and predict events in her life through reduction and regularization of stimuli; however, not all unpleasant stimuli were cut out. She remained in the same room with the other children of her group, but was allowed to retire to her own mattress in her own nook.
- When an attendant had to leave the room for a short moment, she first played peekaboo with the girl in the doorway or behind a glass-panelled dividing wall; this measure proved to contribute much to diminishing the girl's SIB and other dysphoric reactions to being left alone for a while.
- She was trained (through modelling) to vent her dysphoria and 'self-aggression' on a tambourine (or - if this was out of reach - on something else, such as the hand of the attendant who might happen to be washing her at the time). If she refused to beat the tambourine she was ostentatiously given the cold shoulder, by way of an extinction procedure.
- Rapport-building through play activities and training of speech and language. (However, an operant language training programme was discontinued on finding that it produced an unacceptable amount of tension and discomfort.)
- The child's area of interest and world of experience was broadened by various activities and games such as: walking, helping to lay the table, playing ninepin bowls and ball games, etc.
- Her self-help skills were promoted so as to diminish her self-absorbtion. She was, for instance, trained to eat unaided (she even learned to eat bread-crusts, but in general remained very fastidious), and to remain dry in the daytime (she was set on a potty every ninety minutes; although still soiling herself frequently, she now began to dislike it).
- Some of her fixed routines and repetitive behaviours were granted her; thus, she was allowed to carry around a favourite object (a toy dog or a piece from a jigsaw puzzle) and to have a band of sticking plaster on the knuckles of her hand (which was regularly replaced by a clean one); on discharge, these mannerisms had not disappeared.
- She was given daily hydrotherapy for relaxation.
- She received drugs as adjuncts to treatment: no perceivable effects were obtained with benperidol, pimozide and a minor tranquillizer; eventually her vulnerability could be reduced by prescribing her a combination of haloperidol and the anti-convulsant valproic acid.
- During the first fourteen weeks her self-injurious behaviour could only be limited by regularly placing her arms in tube restraints; however, at the end of that period, so much gain had been made that the tubes could be removed permanently and she did not show the slightest relapse.

At the end of her ten months' stay in the observation home, she was able to tolerate a routine psychological examination. This time her conduct in the test situation was unmistakably better: she was more approachable and less irritable. The contact disorder, however, was still serious. The overall positive impression was not reflected in the test results: the Griffiths GQ was now 36. Her social competence was assessed by means of the SRZ scale; the results are given below (in standard marks based on the norm laid down for day-care centres).

(Sub)scale	
Self help	5L
Communication	6H
Persistence	6L
Social skills	4
SRZ-Total	5L

Her score was 17 (classification: PDD) on the PDD-MR Scale and she was diagnosed as PDD (determined on the basis of the data from her file).

According to the Eekwal-home team, this girl displayed some instrumental SIB, but most of all a typical picture of the reactive form of SIB as well as incipient structural SIB. In this respect she improved considerably. In the first place, the incidence of the behaviour decreased; its occurrence, which initially was ten to twenty times a day (occasionally going on for a long time), now fell to only one to two times a day (lasting much shorter periods). In the second place, the violence of the SIB decreased: the banging, etc., was done with far less force and in general did not cause physical damage. In the third place, she totally stopped pinching, hair-tearing and even biting. Team members as well as her parents were well aware that these improvements had been achieved mainly because at the Eekwal she was offered a well-organized environment and a professional approach marked by tolerance and stamina.

After her discharge, the girl was placed in an institution for mentally retarded people where she still lives, eighteen years later. On follow-up assessment (see Chapter II.5) she obtained a PDD-MRS score of 10 (classification: PDD) and was diagnosed as PDD. Her contact-making is still very insufficient and her speech largely uncommunicative. Her self-injurious behaviour has not disappeared, but its frequency is tolerable. Her behavioural problems and the ways of dealing with them call for quite a few staff discussions. She needs more tact and heedfulness than average to prevent behavioural problems. She displays many disruptive behaviours, as can be seen from the results of assessment by means of the SGZ scale made at the follow-up examination which are presented below (in standard marks based on the norm laid down for day-care centres).

(Sub)scale	
Aggressive maladaptive behaviour	5H
Verbal maladaptive behaviour	7L
Miscellaneous maladaptive behaviour	3
SGZ-Total	4

The girl still uses haloperidol.

Subject No. 033: girl; age 2 years; moderately retarded; PDD(-AD?)

This girl is a first-born child. The mother's pregnancy was normal, except for anaemia. Delivery was on time and without problems. At birth the child looked fine, but she soon began to display deviant behaviour. Oral reflexes proved to be mainly absent and she had difficulties being suckled. Not until she was two years old did she start to eat better. She showed no interest in light and sound, nor in the attention her parents gave her; at any rate, she hardly responded to these stimuli. Her overall development was delayed. A very striking feature was that she used her hands only to push things away; she explored things by touching them with her forehead. She also did not use her mouth very much; she only began to put her fingers into her mouth after her second birthday. At the age of one-and-a-half years she started head-banging. She seemed increasingly more keen to find hard and pointed objects to bang against. Initially she cried when the banging hurt, but at the same time she seemed unable to stop it. She also began hitting herself increasingly on her head with her hands.

On admission, her parents described her mood as generally good, but shaky. She was very rigidly adhered to familiar patterns; minor deviations from these immediately evoked dysphoric states. Some social response was felt to have developed by now. She spoke a few isolated words.

Examination failed to reveal any clear indications for the underlying disorder. The only observations which might be relevant were the girl's comparatively large head and a general state of dullness and apathy. She made insufficient social contact. On the Griffiths (generally yielding scores of approx. 10% above the actual level) she obtained a GQ of 44. The profile was flat; she had no special skills to draw upon for the treatment of her developmental lags. On admission she used thioridazine, which seemed to have no effect whatsoever; as a matter of fact, neither did discontinuation lead to a change for the worse. Banging was a very frequent occurrence from the outset. It was not felt to express panic, frustration, dysphoria or an attempt to have it all her own way, but seemed to be caused by an autonomous force which the child simply had to obey: when sitting on the floor, she banged her head on the floor, in the bathtub she banged it against its rim, and at meal-times against the tabletop. The remarkable observation was that the child became dysphoric after the banging. It seemed as if she tried to avoid its occurrence but could not. As far as the team at the observation home could see, the SIB was neither instrumental, reactive nor self-stimulatory; it was structural and without a doubt had typically compulsive traits.

The entire armamentarium of treatments, including drug treatment (first pimozide, later haloperidol), was tried successively, but all to no avail. Only an anti-convulsant prescribed for a suspected hyperaesthetic-emotional syndrome seemed to ease her dysphoric reactions slightly. All in all, little gain was made during the five months of her hospitalization period. The child seemed to feel most comfortable in situations where banging was not possible, such as while sitting on a high chair with a table-flap which was upholstered with a thick pillow, or while in bed in a harness.

After her discharge she returned home for some time, and was subsequently placed in an institution for mentally retarded persons. Her development over the next nineteen years was actually rather surprising. The institution placed her in a day school for trainable mentally retarded children; there she remained until she was twenty. Thereafter she attended a workshop within the grounds of the institution. She is currently living in a group home of the same institute. Her social competence was assessed by means of the SRZ scale; the results are given below (in standard marks based on the norm laid down for institutions for the mentally retarded).

(Sub)scale	
Self help	9
Communication	9
Persistence	9
Social skills	7H
SRZ-Total	8H

She still has the following problems: she makes very insufficient contact; she is a loner in the group; she has a stereotyped way of handling objects; she is rigid and ritualistic; her behaviour is erratic and unpredictable; she displays SIB, but no longer inflicts physical harm to herself. Her behavioural problems and the ways to deal with them call for an average amount of time in staff discussions, but she does need more than an average amount of tact and heedfulness to prevent behavioural problems. She does not use drugs. Her score on the PDD-MR Scale was 8 (classification D: presence of a PDD doubtful) and she was diagnosed as PDD (determined on the basis of the data from her file). Her current score on the PDD-MR Scale is 10 (classification: PDD) and she has been diagnosed as PDD.

Subject No. 115: boy; age 5 years; severely retarded; PDD-AD and OPS

This boy is a first-born and single child. The mother's pregnancy was normal, but the child had a forceps delivery. He cried well and looked like a normal infant. Somewhere between his twelfth and sixteenth months, when he was already able to speak a few words, his development seemed to stagnate and there was even some regression. He stopped talking, became less responsive and even seemed deaf. A special autism team provided home help. At the age of three he was placed in a day-care centre. Changes tended to upset him. He would respond to certain noises (washing machine, radio) by putting his hands to his ears. He was extremely interested in switches and plug sockets. He did not resume talking. He could not be toilet-trained. The most urgent problems of management were SIB, which started before his third birthday and involved violent head-banging and hitting himself, and his temper tantrums.

Detailed examination only revealed some hypotonia and a haziness which suggested brain damage. No EEG abnormalities were found. On the Griffiths (generally yielding scores of approx. 10% above the actual level) he obtained a GQ of 35, with a considerable dip on the language subtest. His score on the AUTI-scale was 49 and he was classified as autistic. On the PDD-MR Scale his score was 14 (classification: PDD) and he was diagnosed as PDD (determined on the basis of the data from his file).

The well-organized and predictable environment of the Eekwal home, as well as being relieved from his daily journey to the day-care centre and the return home with the need to accommodate to different places in between, evidently contributed to the easing of his self-injurious behaviour. In a matter of just a few weeks its occurrence dropped to half the original frequency. Apparently the SIB had been partly reactive. Meanwhile, it became more and more clear that the behaviour was also instrumental; one of his aims was obviously to have it his own way straightaway. A loud and clear, "No, Jan", followed by ostentatiously giving him the cold shoulder, was immediately effective. In addition, his social skills were trained, and pimozide was given as an adjuvant. He came to like a variety of social games, including simple exchange games, but showed a tendency to transform them into rigid patterns. Many unwelcome habits remained, such as: smearing of stools; eating inedible things; throwing and overturning things. Toilet-training did not catch on with him, at least not within the space of time available. However, SIB, occurring at least once a day prior to admission, completely disappeared in the last month of his four-month stay.

His parents were quite understandably hesitant about having him back at home. He was first placed in a short-stay home where he stayed for six months, and subsequently in an institution for mentally retarded persons, where he has lived for six years. At follow-up, his score on the PDD-MR Scale was 15 (classification: PDD) and he was diagnosed as PDD. He no longer receives medication. His behavioural problems and the ways of dealing with them do not call for much time in staff discussions, but he does need a more than average amount of tact and heedfulness to prevent behavioural problems. SIB has become a rare occurrence (less than once a month).

Subject No. 135: boy; age 12 years; severely retarded; PDD(-AD?) and blind

His mother was confined to bed from the fifth month to the end of her pregnancy. She was given a drip to prevent a premature parturition. The child was born seven weeks early. From the outset, his condition was a source of concern; for fourteen days he was given oxygen (initially 75%) and for five weeks gavage feedings. He was discharged from the hospital about two months after his birth. His development was very slow. He was an extremely quiet infant who slept most of the time. His blindness (retrolental fibroplasia) was discovered only after some time. He did not start walking until he was about four years old. At six he began to be very restless. His first few words were at ten years. At four, he went to a therapeutic nursery and two years later to a day-care centre for mentally retarded children, where he received speech therapy for a couple of years. At eight he started to have screaming tantrums coupled with violent SIB, often for no apparent reason, but also at times in an attempt to have his own way. While perspiring profusely, he screeched, hit and scratched himself, banged his head on the floor, and sometimes also hit others. Eventually these tantrums were daily occurrences, occasionally lasting an hour, while practically nobody and nothing was able to calm him down. Medication had no effect (three kinds of drugs were successively tried).

Detailed examination failed to reveal any demonstrable etiology for his problems other than the adverse prenatal circumstances and the boy's premature birth. Tested with some Griffiths subtests, the boy was found to have a developmental age between 2-0 and 3-0. His social competence was assessed by means of the SRZ scale, yielding an SRZ-Total of 4; his motor skills were assessed by means of the SMZ scale, yielding an SMZ-Total of 6L (both in standard marks based on the norm laid down for institutions for mentally retarded persons). On the PDD-MR Scale his score was 16 (classification: PDD) and he was diagnosed as PDD (determined on the basis of the data from his file).

The Eekwal-home team considered him to be a clear case of overtaxation and overstimulation. The strategy followed at the clinic was to keep him all day in the ward or its immediate vicinity, with the same attendants and the same group; he was given a predictable and simple day programme with limited demands. Daily he sat in the bath for a long time. Now and then a nice romp and twice a day a stiff walk were his favourite pleasures. His tantrums became significantly less protracted (five minutes at the most), less frequent (a few times a week) and less violent (mostly without SIB). This gain was achieved after two months of hospitalization and was not due to his medication (first pimozide and subsequently thioridazine), as far as the observation team could make out. The feeling was that in a suitable environment all medication could be discontinued. However, his restlessness and irritability persisted and his contact disorder remained very serious.

Shortly after his discharge, he was placed in an institution for mentally retarded persons where he still lives after two years. At follow-up, his score on the PDD-MR Scale was 16 (classification: PDD) and he was diagnosed as PDD. He does not receive any psychopharmacological medication, but does need more than an average amount of tact and heedfulness. SIB is virtually non-existent.

In the opinion of the Eekwal-home team, this boy was a clear case of the reactive form of SIB. The problems could largely be eliminated by adequately controlling exposure to stimuli.

II.4.7.2   Stereotyped behaviour

As noted in Section II.4.1, stereotyped behaviours (with or without the use of objects), have been found to occur more frequently in mentally retarded persons with a PDD than in those without a PDD. (Fore more detailed information the reader is referred to Chapter III.4.) Drawing on the theoretical considerations discussed in Section II.4.7.1.1 with respect to SIB, a brief review will be given of the clinical experience at the Eekwal home with stereotyped behaviour.

In children with a PDD, stereotyped behaviour was found to be associated with several conditions.

In the first place, a correlation was found with the degree of *discomfort and strain*. This applies notably to the reactive form of stereotyped behaviour, which is often found in children who are living at home and are overloaded.

Although complete elimination of the behaviour proved in many cases not to be feasible, a rapid improvement was often obtained - in some cases in just a few weeks - through such measures as reducing stimuli, alleviating the burden of demands made on a child (especially those pertaining to the cognitive and emotional areas), and creating a more relaxed atmosphere.

In the second place, a correlation was found with *understimulation and boredom*. This applies notably to the self-stimulatory form of stereotyped behaviour. The best strategies here are to give more personal attention, to provide more pastime activities (preferably including gross motor activities), to encourage independent task performance, and, if possible, to enlarge the field of interest. These strategies help to produce physical weariness and inner contentment, which may lead to a considerable decrease in the need for self-stimulation. Earlier findings reported in a study by Berkson and Mason (1963) support this view, but see also Repp et al. (1992).

In the third place, a correlation was found with *poor social skills*. This applies notably to the self-enclosed kind of stereotyped behaviour. The best approach here is to promote not only communication but above all the use of more adequate forms of communication and expression so as to improve social interaction. However, with mentally retarded children with a PDD this is extremely difficult to realize; at best success is only partial. (See also II.4.6.2 and II.4.6.4.)

Finally, I would like to point out that those stereotyped behaviours which are neither harmful to the mentally retarded person with a PDD himself nor annoying to others are best to be tolerated. As an illustrative example may serve the stereotyped behaviour of a 16-year-old severely mentally retarded boy with a PDD. He liked to busy himself with a piece of elastic throughout the day, which he did so fanatically that it frazzled under his very hands. He was quite happy when engaged in this activity, whereas he was peevish and unhappy if denied this pleasure. Intervention and medication had failed to cure him of this mannerism. Therefore, the Eekwal observation home rather perplexed the institution into which he was placed on his discharge by recommending to furnish the boy twice a day with a half-meter length of elastic.

II.4.7.3   *Hyperactivity*

Presumably, hyperactive behaviour in mentally retarded persons with a PDD must be regarded as a semi-specific problem. In several investigations, these persons were found to display significantly more hyperactive behaviour than mentally retarded persons without a PDD (e.g., Brakenhoff-Splinter et al., 1977; Ando & Yoshimura, 1979; Altena et al., 1980; see also Section I.2.2). In Chapter III.4, more research findings will be presented which bear out this view. Furthermore, I would like to remind the reader that the manuals to both the DSM-III-R and the DSM-IV specify that the presence of PDD preempts classification in Attention-deficit/Hyperactivity Disorder. In other words, hyperactive behaviour is so common in persons with a PDD that it is in fact a typical feature of pervasive developmental disorders.

There are no clear indications as to which deficit or which disorder might be held directly responsible for the comparatively high incidence of hyperactive behaviour in mentally retarded persons with a PDD. In the clinical practice at the Eekwal observation home, even cases with extreme hyperactivity often showed no overt signs of brain dysfunction, let alone specific organic brain damages.

The problem, although semi-specific, is occasionally so structural that all forms of intervention or treatment are to no avail. An example of this is presented in II.4.7.4.2 (Subject No. 1yy, not included in the sample of 137 children). However, in a larger proportion of children at least a *relative* improvement is feasible. And one thing is sure, a hyperactive child will inevitably become even more hyperactive when people in his environment are themselves very active and constantly activating him. Reduction, selection and regularization of stimuli may even be of crucial importance. An undue increase in hyperactive behaviour may also be the result of tensions created by excessive demands. For an example of reactive hyperactivity the reader is referred to Section II.4.7.4.2 (Subject No. 133).

II.4.7.4   Sleep disturbances

II.4.7.4.1   Some general remarks
The term sleep disturbance is applicable when for at least three months in succession a child has trouble going to sleep or is regularly awake at night, and after bedtime forces his parents - through calling, crying, screaming, hurting himself, getting out of bed, making noises, etc. - to give him attention.

In all likelihood, sleep disturbances occur comparatively frequently in mentally retarded children and even more frequently in children with a PDD (see II.2.2.4.4). A study carried out by Clements et al. (1986) came to a similar, though somewhat more equivocal conclusion. In their sample they found a higher incidence of sleeping problems in children who displayed self-injury, attachment to routines and non-socially directed difficult behaviour; however, no association was found with either the presence of echolalia or with poor quality of social interaction. Sleeping problems are, according to these authors, "in some ways typical of children with social and language impairments (autistic features)."

Sleeping problems can have far-reaching repercussions on family life. Some parents may struggle for hours in the evening or at night to calm their child down and to get him to sleep. Some parents decide to take the child to their own room, or to sleep in his room. Sooner or later they will become moody and overtired, and some will eventually be completely exhausted. When the little fidget is at last asleep, everybody in the house has to be as quiet as a mouse so as not to awake him. The domestic problems may well extend beyond the home to strained relations with neighbours and to problems at work.

In a number of cases some relief may be offered by agencies for outpatient mental-health care, including the special autism teams, but it is difficult to find out how often they succeed therein. At any rate, experience shows that, in spite of their efforts, sleep disturbances may be so intractable and unsettling that families are faced with an utterly unbearable situation; then there is no option other than to have the child admitted to a clinic at the earliest possible convenience.

Just as with SIB, sleep disturbances can roughly be subdivided into four types on the basis of their background or origin.

- *Instrumental sleep disturbances*. Typically a child with this type of sleep disturbance demands - through crying, calling, hammering on the door or SIB - the attention or nearby presence of his parents or other persons who are taking care of him. Invariably there are difficulties in falling asleep; many children also have one or more wakeful periods at night during which they cry or present themselves in other ways.
- *Reactive sleep disturbances*. With this type of sleep disturbance, tensions and/or unpleasant experiences gained during the course of the day undermine the child's ability to sleep, notably to fall asleep. It may take hours before the tensions have subsided sufficiently for the child to be ready to be overcome by sleep.
- *Self-stimulatory sleep disturbances*. This type of sleep disturbance is clearly the result of boredom. It was in fact very rarely found in the present sample of children. However, it did occur in a previously observed group of profoundly retarded children and adults who were used to being held in bed for too long in the residential institutions from which they came. Being not yet or no longer sleepy, they spent their waking hours in body rocking, bouncing up and down, SIB, roaming about or destroying things.
- *Structural sleep disturbances*. Unlike structural SIB, this type of sleep disturbance is the least common one. Two subtypes may be distinguished:
  - a sheer habit which has grown out of an instrumental, reactive or self-stimulatory sleep disturbance;
  - a manifestation of a fundamental and almost autonomous restlessness stemming from severe brain dysfunction which in a small number of cases is suggestive of a fundamentally disturbed periodicity of sleep and wakefulness; the brain dysfunction presents itself in profoundly retarded persons mainly as Organic Personality Syndrome, and also in higher functioning individuals as the Attention-deficit/Hyperactivity Disorder.

The division given above calls for some further comment.

- Just as with SIB, it is of crucial importance that a functional analysis of the sleep disturbance in question takes place before it is labelled and treated. If possible, this may be done prior to admission, by gaining information from parents and other persons involved in the child's care.

- Experience teaches that, by comparison with SIB, it is easier to label a sleep disturbance; accordingly, the procedure takes less time.
- Instrumental sleep-disturbance is mainly found in children (at all levels of mental retardation). The three other types are found in all age categories; its incidence is slightly higher in persons functioning at the profound and severe levels of mental retardation.
- The prognostic rank order of the four types of sleep disturbances, ranging from fair to poor prospects, is as follows:
  - instrumental sleep disturbances;
  - (self-stimulatory sleep disturbances);
  - reactive sleep disturbances;
  - structural sleep disturbances.

  I have placed self-stimulatory sleep disturbances between parentheses, as here prognostic assessment is mainly based on information provided by other experts.
- Sleep disturbances are more amenable to treatment in individuals without a concurrent pervasive developmental disorder; this applies in particular to the instrumental, self-stimulatory and reactive forms.
- Sleep disturbances should preferably be treated at the earliest possible stage, as they may become patterned (although this is actually less likely to occur than with SIB).

II.4.7.4.2   Aspects of treatment of sleep disturbances
Again the treatment strategies for the four types of sleep disturbance will be discussed separately. The instrumental type will be considered last, because it calls for a comparatively complex treatment plan. At the end of this section, some examples of treatment interventions will be presented.

Reactive sleep disturbances call for reduction, selection and regularization of stimuli (see II.4.3.3). In many cases children with this type of sleeping problem prove to have been both overtaxed and overstimulated. As a result, their feelings of tension, restlessness and discomfort would accumulate throughout the day. At bedtime they needed quite some time to digest the experiences of the day and to relax from the excessive strain. Not until this stage had been reached, they were able to fall asleep. Therefore the approach should be to gear demands to the child's capacities and to offer him a well-organized and predictable situation in order to prevent an accumulation of tensions during the day.

Self-stimulatory sleep disturbances, on the contrary, call for more and stronger stimuli to be provided. Those affected should stay up longer and be offered a larger number and wider variety of activities. If they spend fewer hours in bed during the day and find gratification in the things they do, they will feel drowsier and more contented at the end of the day. Thus, it will be easier for them to fall asleep and to sleep through the night.

Structural sleep disturbances, like structural SIB, are least amenable to treatment. To quell restlessness during the night (which is often paralleled by restlessness during the day), prescription of neuroleptics - not hypnotics - will in many cases be unavoidable, although success is certainly not guaranteed (but hypnotics are definitely without any effect).

Instrumental sleep disturbances. According to western standards, children are not supposed to share their parents' bed or bedroom. Therefore, if in our culture a child nevertheless tries to have it that way, it cannot be granted to him. In so far as a child's sleep disturbances express a need for safety and security, this need has to be met during the hours that the child is up. At bedtime, the child should be put to bed quietly and cheerfully. Thereafter, any form of undesirable seeking or claiming of attention should be firmly curtailed. The best way to do this is by extinction, a method which has proven to be very effective without inflicting any psychological damage.

The treatment package used at the Eekwal observation home in the management of instrumental sleep disturbances contains the following elements:

- Treatment starts right from the first night of hospitalization. Therefore the treatment plan must be prepared in advance. Attendants are thoroughly acquainted with the procedures used, and are experienced in applying them. For the child, however, the observation home constitutes a completely new environment; on the one hand, this is certainly a reason for him to feel fearful, but on the other hand he is also less likely to maintain all of the annoying patterns of behaviour which he has developed in the course of time, as now his familiar routine is completely disrupted.
- The child is given a single room which is located in such a way that crying and other ways of drawing attention cannot cause great inconvenience to the other children of his group.
- Good care is taken that the child cannot harm himself in any way. If a child has the habit of getting out of bed, his room is appropriately heated.
- In principle, the child is not fastened to his bed in a sleeping bag or by any other device, even if this was usually done at home. In a small number of cases, however, fastening may eventually prove to be an unavoidable measure. The bed should be safe, i.e., for a young child the customary cot with barred sides is provided, and for an older child a low couch with, if need be, mattresses placed on the floor around the bed. For a violently head-banging child the edges of the bed and the adjacent wall are padded. If a child has the habit of scratching himself, his nails are trimmed short (and filed daily thereafter); if need be, his hands are placed in flannels which are fastened around his wrists with Velcro or clips. If necessary, the door is locked. A child who is toilet-trained is provided with a potty in his room which is brought expressly to his attention before he goes to sleep.
- The child is put to bed and awakened at the usual times.

- The child is not allowed to sleep during the day. Only a very young child may, if necessary, have a short nap according to a fixed schedule. No opportunity is given to catch up on missed hours of night's rest. Enough daytime activities, including motor activities, are provided.
- During the night, the staff on duty can keep an eye on the child without the child noticing, as there is a night-light in the room and a glass panel in the door.
- The child is put to bed in a kind and pleasant manner, but the whole ceremony should not take too much time. Experience shows that the duration of the child's crying or other signs of protest is often commensurate with the length of the bedtime ritual.
- Except when there is a really imperative necessity, it is crucial never to re-enter the child's room, no matter whether he is crying, getting out of bed, destroying things, hurting himself, etc. Reinforcement of such behaviour should be avoided at all costs.
- There is no reason to be alarmed when initially the sleep disturbances grow worse. After all, almost all behaviour-modification techniques through extinction must go through this stage. Many parents who were advised to ignore the child's protests gave up precisely because of this deterioration; they were able to apply the extinction method for a couple of nights, but then decided to stop, either because they could not find it in their hearts to be "so hard on him", or because they had qualms about the nuisance they were causing for other children or neighbours, and because they felt, moreover, that "it didn't work." However, if the policy is stopped at this moment, this will amount to intermittent reinforcement, even giving an extra boost to the unwanted behaviour, which in this case is the sleep disturbance.
- As soon as the treatment has caught on, i.e., nights are passing without trouble, this result has to be consolidated. The rule of the thumb adopted at the Eekwal observation home is that a child should have slept for at least a month with no or only minor problems before the treatment can be considered a success. Not until the child himself has become accustomed to his newly acquired behaviour will he be ready to stick to it in his parental home as well.

In what follows, the principles outlined above will be illustrated by a selection of five individual case histories and interventions which are taken from the clinical practice at the Eekwal observation home. (For interpretation of the assessments by means of the SRZ, SGZ and SMZ scales presented in the examples, see Appendix C.) The first example is a very clear case of a serious instrumental sleep disturbance.

Subject No. 130: girl; age 4 years; mildly retarded; PDD(-AD?)

When admitted, this girl was to be five in a few weeks. She was a second child. Her mother had had five miscarriages preceding the birth of this child. No foetal examination was carried out; medical examination of the mother failed to reveal any abnormalities. During her pregnancy, the

mother was three times admitted to hospital: in the third month of her pregnancy for prophylac-
tic reasons, in the fifth month because of an infection of the urinary passages, and in the seventh
month because of hypertension. At the end of term, labour was induced by means of a drip; the
delivery was satisfactory and the baby was normal. However, after just a few weeks it struck the
parents that the child, compared with other infants, gave inadequate responses to personal
attention. Her psychomotor development was slow; she learned to walk at around her second
birthday. Her behaviour became more and more deviant: her reactions were highly erratic and
volatile; she displayed extreme panic in response to high-pitched tones and the sound of a
saxophone; she was very attached to routines; her speech was echolalic; at times she had peculiar fads, such as taking an umbrella to bed with her; she made strong claims on adults, demanding their continuous presence. An extensive physical examination carried out by a
paediatrician and an additional examination at the university clinic did not reveal any abnormalities.

When the girl was four, her parents obtained help from a guidance agency specialized in
giving advice for practical managemental problems. On a tentative basis, she attended a special
class for children with developmental problems twice a week for just a few hours. This proved
to be an outright failure; being away from home was unbearable for her and put her in a flurry.
It was at about this time that falling asleep and sleeping uninterruptedly became problematical.
When left alone she would start to scream and bang her head and go completely berserk. Trying
to prevent these fits, her parents let her stay up longer; when putting her to bed, they sat at her
bedside until she dropped off. However, she often awoke in the middle of the night and had to
be calmed down again. The problem was not eased by keeping her home from school, neither
did the continued counselling from the guidance agency (the parents were sound, solid and very
cooperative people) nor the night sedatives prescribed by the GP bring any relief. The girl was
sent to a child day-care centre, but if anything at all this served only to make matters worse.
Both her mother and father were at the end of their resources and eventually the father was no
longer able to do his work (he was a bus driver). Finally, the girl was admitted to the Eekwal
observation home as a very urgent case.

The team at the observation home saw a seriously disordered girl who fully met the criteria
for the DSM-III category Childhood Onset Pervasive Developmental Disorder (COPDD), except
for the criterion of onset after age 2-5. Her score on the AUTI-scale was 18 and she was classified as non-autistic; on the Childhood Autism Rating Scale (CARS) her score was 32,5, and she
was classified as doubtful mildly autistic or non-autistic; on the PDD-MR Scale her score was 14
(classification: PDD) and she was diagnosed as PDD (determined on the basis of the data from
her file). On the Griffiths (generally yielding scores of approx. 10% above the actual level) she
obtained a GQ of 61. The results of assessments made by means of the SRZ scale, the SGZ scale
and the SMZ scale are given below (in standard marks based on the norm laid down for day-
care centres).

(Sub)scale	
Self help	6H
Communication	8H
Persistence	6H
Social skills	5H
SRZ-Total	7L

(Sub)scale	
Aggressive maladaptive behaviour	6H
Verbal maladaptive behaviour	7L
Miscellaneous maladaptive behaviour	5L
SGZ-Total	5H

Her SMZ-Total was 6H.

On the very first day of her stay at the Eekwal home, the girl started to cry (without tears) as soon as an attendant moved more than four metres away from her, howling and bellowing like a siren. The crying stopped abruptly - as if a switch had been turned - when the attendant was again in her proximity. The nightly crying-fits had probably begun as a sign of separation anxiety. However, it now seemed to be an almost automatic and impersonal response, certainly as far the daytime fits were concerned. On the first night of her stay at the Eekwal home things went definitely not according to plan. From 7 until 9 p.m. she cried and screamed almost continuously and so loudly that none of the other children of her group could sleep, although the girl's bedroom was at the other end of the corridor. The attendant on duty saw no other solution than to enter the room suddenly, and to put a stopper on her tantrum by giving her one good spank on the buttocks, saying, "Enough is enough!", and subsequently disappearing as swiftly as she had entered. The girl was immediately silenced and fell asleep. The attendant reported this procedure and its results to the night shift. Indeed, when at 4.30 a.m. the child resumed her intense screaming, the same policy was adopted, once more with success.

The second evening and night were quite a different story. Until 01.30 a.m. she had short periods of alternately yelling, talking to herself, thumping on the door and being quiet. The rest of the night she slept straight through.

The third evening started again with crying and yelling; this time the staff's response came at 8 p.m., again with a sudden spank to the buttocks. The girl was instantly quiet and slept through the rest of the night.

During the following six nights the child yelled occasionally for only short periods and not all too fiercely, and intervention was no longer needed. From the tenth night onwards she was an excellent sleeper and those problems never recurred. At times she would even hum tunes to herself in the morning before getting up. Fortunately, this positive result had not been achieved at the cost of the loss of her good toileting habits: except for the third night, she did not wet her bed.

This girl stayed at the Eekwal home for six months on account of her other behavioural problems, which proved to be very resistant to correction. Her daytime screaming and temper tantrums could partly be curtailed by giving her the cold shoulder. However, not a day passed without situations arising which she was unable to handle: having to wait her turn, being thwarted in her wishes, having to miss the attendant for a very short while, and so on. She was first given thioridazine, but this only resulted in drowsiness. Subsequently, she received pimozide; this possibly eased her responses somewhat, but not enough to justify its continuation after her return home.

Her social competence improved significantly on the 5% level; she scored 8L on the SRZ-Total shortly before her discharge. In all, the only real success yielded by treatment was the improvement of the half-specific problem of sleep disturbance, although in her case this was indeed extremely exasperating. At least this gain made it possible for her to live at home, where she has lived for the past three years.

The next example concerns a partially successful treatment of a reactive - and possibly to some extent also structural - sleep disturbance.

Subject No. 001: boy; age 6 years; moderately retarded; PDD-AD

This boy was the fourth of five children. During the first three months of pregnancy his mother had 'periods', and during the last months she suffered from oedema and dizzy spells. She had a prompt delivery, the baby cried immediately and his colour was good. For the first two years of his life he was an easy infant who could amuse himself very well. His first laugh came in time, but he did not laugh for other people. At three he spoke a few words, but his vocabulary did not enlarge. At four he was toilet-trained. He had few interests, and used to sniff at things and to put them in his mouth. He often roamed about and walked into any house just as it

146

suited him. Gradually he began to display a growing number of stereotypies; he also had temper tantrums, sometimes hitting himself. Still at the age of four he went to a nursery school, where he remained a loner and nothing interested him. His trouble in getting to sleep was one of his major problems. He remained awake until about 11 p.m., keeping his father busy the whole evening.

The team at the observation home saw a boy with a very serious contact disorder. Tested with the Merrill-Palmer Scale, which is known to place too much emphasis on performance skills and to yield too flattering results, he rather surprisingly scored an IQ of 66. Regrettably, he rushed through each item, each time again trying to cut himself off from the other person. Tested with the (original) Cain-Levine Social Competency Scale, he only obtained a reasonable score on the subscale Self-Help. Detailed examination failed to reveal any clear indication regarding etiology.

He remained a very solitary child, easily frustrated, dysphoric, and harbouring latent tensions. A rather curious finding was that, after he had been prescribed trifluperidol, he threw himself into drawing (post hoc or propter hoc?). He mainly drew quite recognizable human figures and graceful, although somewhat stereotyped, plant-like shapes. Later he gave this up again; he had had a similar passing fad before his stay at the observation home.

As for the management of his sleep disturbance, he was put to bed at 7 p.m.; there was a potty in his room and the door was locked. Gradually, but unmistakably, the time at which he fell asleep shifted to an earlier hour. As time went by, he almost completely stopped making a racket, but he did get out of bed, walk to and fro, play with the curtains, etc. It would take him about an hour to fall asleep; moving his bedtime to a later time did not help him to settle earlier. A possible explanation is that he really needed a full hour to relax after all the stresses he experienced throughout the day, even in such a predictable environment as that at the Eekwal home. However, it is also not inconceivable that his behaviour had become structural. Anyhow, his troubles were felt to have been reduced to acceptable proportions.

After a four-month stay at the clinic, the boy returned home. However, as he remained a source of much concern in his rather large family, he was placed one year later in an institution for mentally retarded persons. On the PDD-MR Scale his score was 12 (classification: PDD) and he was diagnosed as PDD (determined on the basis of the data from his file). At follow-up - 22 years after his discharge - his score on the PDD-MRS was 14 (classification: PDD) and he was again diagnosed as PDD. He still lives in the same institute and his behavioural disorders are considered to be serious. He uses pimozide, levomepromazine and pipamperone.

The next example concerns an almost purely reactive sleep disturbance.

Subject No. 133: boy; age 2 years; moderately retarded; PDD-NOS

This boy was a second child. The mother's pregnancy and the delivery were normal. He was bottle-fed and drank well, and was a quiet baby who slept a lot. For a long time he did not respond to sounds. He used to look past people (which he still did on admission). His mother reported that he did not talk, but made only buzzing or humming sounds or imitated the sound of a siren. If he wanted something, he took a person by the hand. He could become angry just like that, crying, yelling, or biting people. He also bit himself and banged himself until he bled. He scratched with his nails and teeth across toys and furniture. He preferred to play by himself, was very restless and could not leave anything alone. He had a special fascination for glittering or luminous things and was scared of cuddly toys and of the sound of household appliances. He strongly refused to be washed and dressed, and was unwilling to sit in someone's lap. He never imitated other people and was not toilet-trained. For a short period he ate all sorts of food indiscriminately and insatiably. However, when admitted, he had for more than half a year lived exclusively on custard, which he drank from a feeding bottle. Of this he consumed some litres a day, becoming outraged when the bottle was filled less than half-full. At times he hardly slept at all; every evening and night he would be up and doing things constantly for at least a couple of hours, destroying whatever he found in his room. To prevent complaints from the neighbours and for the sake of his sister's rest, his parents were busy throughout the night with calming him down and checking on him.

On admission, the boy was found to have a serious anaemia due to inadequate diet. Detailed examination failed to reveal any etiological indications for the boy's mental retardation and his problems in contact-making. There is some evidence of hereditary influences, as three persons in the mother's family (a brother and two uncles) were 'not all there' (two of them had died at an early age from unknown causes).

On the Griffiths (generally yielding scores of approx. 10% above the actual level) he obtained a GQ of 48. Assessments were made by means of three autism scales. On the Childhood Autism Rating Scale (CARS) his score was 37.5, and he was classified as autistic; on the Autism Behavior Checklist his score was 50, and he was classified as non-autistic; his score on the AUTI-scale was 31 and he was classified as a borderline case of autistic/non-autistic. On the PDD-MR Scale his score was 11 (classification: PDD) and he was diagnosed as PDD (determined on the basis of the data from his file).

The management of his eating problems will be discussed in Section II.4.8.2.2. Not surprisingly, considering his early age, toilet-training was without result, although within four weeks of training he did accept being seated on the potty, even doing something now and then, as luck would have it. The temper tantrums became less frequent, less violent and less protracted, thanks to the structured environment offering him a high degree of regularity and security. His stereotypical ways of body-rocking and gnawing on things or scratching them with his teeth also subsided. Furthermore, he displayed less SIB, but this behaviour proved to be reactive, as it flared up again on weekends at home. On returning to the clinic after such weekends he continued for some days with banging his head, and occasionally also biting himself, which had actually disappeared; apparently this behaviour unsettled the boy himself.

On the whole, the quiet environment at the clinic unmistakably did bring his mind to rest. The hyperkinetic and restless elements of his behaviour clearly slackened off. He was not allowed to nap. Within two weeks of his admission he was sleeping both evening and night. Although occasionally he did awake in the early morning, this is not uncommon with small children. He was not fastened to his bed but the door of his room was locked.

While remaining an irritable child, a few months' use of pimozide helped him to open up and he began to take some pleasure in contact games. He hummed to the songs sung to him, even watching what singers did in the way of facial expressions and movements of the mouth, and noticing word variations made in the songs.

After medication was discontinued, this chap remained quite manageable in the clinical setting. Ultimately, he could even be described as being fairly debonair. Weekends at home, however, continued to cause troubles for both himself and his parents. Placement into residential care seemed therefore to be the best option. As a suitable facility was not yet available, he was - at the time of writing this, more than a year ago - placed in a transitional setting, where he is still living. He displays no sleep disturbance, his SIB has completely disappeared and his diet is normal.

Finally, I want to discuss briefly two cases of sleep disturbance in children who in fact did not belong to the present sample of 137 PDD children: firstly, a child with an instrumental sleep disturbance which was cured after an unusually long time; secondly, a child with a purely structural sleep disturbance.

Subject No. 1xx: boy; age almost 4 years; severely retarded; Angelman syndrome

This boy was an extremely shy child and displayed a serious separation anxiety. The team at the Eekwal observation home were undecided for quite some time whether to label him as a case of Separation Anxiety Disorder or to place him within the broader category of PDD. His extremely serious sleeping problems were part of the more general problem of being unable to bear being

148

left alone. He was one of four children, all of them very young. All members of the family, a very harmonious group, dearly wanted to have the child back at home, even though his problems had played havoc with them. Therefore, the team decided to treat his problems with the seemingly harsh extinction technique.

The case is an interesting one for two reasons:

- Generally, extinction techniques are a rapid and effective method for reducing instrumental sleep disturbances, with major gains made within four weeks. With this child, however, the team had to wait five months before really substantial improvement set in, although ultimately treatment did turn out to be a complete success. In the first six months of the boy's stay at the observation home, the number of nightly howling spells per month were successively: 28; 19; 8; 8; 5; and 1. It really was necessary to wait until the frequency had lowered to once a month; the boy's crying was so loud and protracted that in an ordinary family setting uncontrollable reactions would have to be anticipated as it was simply out of the question to ignore the crying. Incidentally, the team was unable to find any reason why there were, all the same, so many nights in the third to fifth months during which the boy did enjoy completely untroubled sleep. This brings me to the next point.
- The lad suffered no harmful psychological consequences from the policy followed. On the contrary, from an infant boy he grew into a toddler; gradually he learned to bear other people better, even those who were almost strangers to him, and to tolerate one of his parents or an attendant being for a moment out of sight. He seemed even to have been relieved of a harassing pressure and was now able to enjoy things. By nature a child who was quick to laugh as long as he was in familiar surroundings and in the company of familiar people, he now even became a bit of a mischief-maker.

Consequently, any thought of labelling him as PDD was given up in the end. For completeness' sake, I inform the reader that he successively scored 6 (classification N: No PDD) and 9 (classification D: presence of a PDD doubtful) on the PDD-MRS and was first diagnosed as Doubtful PDD/non-PDD; the final diagnosis was non-PDD.

Subject No. 1yy: boy; age 4 years; profoundly retarded; PDD (-Childhood Disintegrative Disorder?/-NOS?) and Organic Personality Syndrome

This boy was the elder of two children. The mother's pregnancy and delivery and the child's initial development were without problems. When the boy was ten months old, a herpes simplex encephalitis was ascertained; in the first stages of the illness, convulsions were predominantly on the right side and he had a hemiparesis on the right side. He did recover, but seemed to have lost memory of things which had been familiar to him, and his responses were much less alert. EEG abnormalities were clearly demonstrable. To check his epileptic traits, he was given a combination of three anti-convulsants. The most recent CT scan revealed a considerable atrophy on both sides.

The boy remained very unresponsive to other persons; he displayed much stereotyped behaviour, both with and without the use of objects; he bit himself and hurt himself also in other ways. He had gradually more screaming tantrums, both by day and by night. During such tantrums he appeared to feel sad, but was inapproachable and inconsolable. The dysphoric states lasted several months and seemed to have some periodicity. The situation at home became increasingly unbearable.

On the Griffiths (generally yielding scores of approx. 10% above the actual level) his GQ was as low as 15. Assessment of his social competence by means of the SRZ scale yielded minimal scores on all five subscales, i.e., five times a score of 3 (in standard marks based on the norm laid down for day-care centres). Assessment by means of the PDD-MR Scale yielded a score of 12 (classification: PDD), and he was diagnosed as PDD. The observation team felt that, on account of the major role played by his organic brain damage, he was most appropriately categorized as Other childhood disintegrative disorder (ICD-10: F84.3) or Childhood Disintegrative Disorder (DSM-IV: 299.10); see also II.3.2.7 and Appendix A. This child was totally unable to concentrate on anything whatsoever; he had frequent moments of diminution of consciousness and displayed many stereotypies. He used to roam about restlessly and aimlessly. He had regularly and for no apparent reason screaming tantrums which could not be quietened, no matter whether he was given attention or cherished or comforted; the tantrums just as suddenly stopped again. By day these tantrums occurred from four to seventeen times; they lasted 2-5 minutes and occasionally 10-15 minutes. The nightly tantrums were less frequent, but went on longer; they generally took place between 1 and 5 a.m. and were, as will be understood considering the serious condition of this boy, equally unmanageable. Other anticonvulsants prescribed to him also failed to bring about any relief. Here professional help reaches the point of being at the end of its resources.

II.4.8 Special educational intervention and treatment of mentally retarded children with PDD: non-specific problems

II.4.8.1 *Short-tempered, aggressive and destructive behaviours*

Short-tempered, aggressive and destructive behaviours in mentally retarded children with a PDD often occur concurrently. Frequently the children concerned also display hyperactive behaviour. Clinical practice shows that these three forms of destructive behaviour are mostly reactive or instrumental, less frequently structural. If structural, the behaviour may be taken in most cases to have been initially instrumental or reactive, developing later into a fixed pattern; however, brain dysfunction or organic brain damage may be the cause of the trouble in some cases, notably those showing heightened irritability.

Clinical experience at the Eekwal observation home has shown that reduction and simplification of stimuli, as well as lowering the demands made in the cognitive, social and emotional areas, will generally bring about an elimination of most of the problems, or will at least subdue them to some degree. This holds for mentally retarded PDD persons of all ages, children, adolescents and adults alike, and also for that matter for mentally retarded persons without a PDD. In fact, completely or partially successful treatment of these kinds of problems may indicate that the behaviour problem in question was indeed reactive or instrumental. As far as instrumental behaviour is concerned, extinction and time-out techniques proved often to be effective measures, administering drugs as a supplement to this treatment in some cases. In a small number of cases this approach resulted in a shift of symptoms, making treatment of the newly developed instrumental forms of disruptive behaviour necessary. As for the structural forms of behaviour, including those which later became structural, these proved hardly or not at all amenable to intervention. In some of these cases prescription of psychotropic drugs was found to have some beneficial effect.

Cases to illustrate the principles outlined above are to be found in the following sections: II.4.7.4.2 (Subject No. 133, representing the reactive form of the behaviour), II.4.6.2 and II.5.3.2.4 (Subject No. 045, representing the instrumental form) and II.4.7.4.2 (Subject No. 001, representing the structural form).

II.4.8.2 *Eating disorders*

II.4.8.2.1 Some general remarks
The DSM-III-R distinguishes the following eating disorders: Anorexia Nervosa, Bulimia Nervosa, Pica, Rumination Disorder of Infancy, and Eating Disorder NOS. In the present context, however, the term 'eating disorder' applies to children who for at least three months have eaten insufficient food or an insufficient variety of foods, in the absence of clear (predominantly) organic reasons, such as a motor disturbance of the muscles of the mouth which would prevent a child from chewing or swallowing food. If a child has difficulty with eating due to a mere delay in motor development of the muscles of his mouth, this is not considered to be an eating disorder for the present purpose.

Eating disorders of the kind discussed here are comparatively common in mentally retarded children with and without a PDD (see II.1.2.4 and II.2.2.4.4). The disorder may be a source of much irritation and concern for the whole family. Consequently the relationship between child and parents may suffer, if only because the matter often develops into a battle between the two parties. Many parents feel as if they have their backs to the wall, particularly when the child's health is at risk; even guidance agencies are often unable to help parents surmount the problem. In such cases clinical treatment may be helpful.

As far as mentally retarded children with a PDD are concerned, eating disorders are considered to have started as *a problem within the child*. It is the child's extreme rigidity which hampers him in switching over to unfamiliar foods. The problem manifests itself in particular when liquid food is replaced by solid food and, in a more or less analogous way, when mushy food is replaced by granular food. The child may react to these changes with irritability, temper tantrums, and stereotyped rituals or preferences. In the course of time, however, the problem, though originating within the child, is likely to become *a problem with the parents* as well. Out of concern for their child's welfare, parents feel urged to force their child to eat. As a result, the child may become distressed, wayward, short-tempered, aggressive or destructive; meal-times will become all the more disagreeable for him, as he not only dislikes the food now, but also suffers from the strained atmosphere. Giving in and accepting a child's deviant appetite, an approach adopted by some parents, is only possible if the child's food intake, while being generally sufficient, is lacking in variety, e.g., when he is only willing to take custard or porridge, or only highly sweetened foods and drinks.

II.4.8.2.2 Aspects of the treatment of eating disorders
At the Eekwal observation home, treatment of eating disorders is only considered when a child has a *mental age of at least one year* and shows a *funda-*

mental and vital need for food. As a matter of fact, over the past 25 years the Eekwal observation home received two exceptional cases in whom this vital need seemed absent; one was a very profoundly retarded child with doubtful PDD, and the other (admitted recently) a moderately retarded child with PDD. Both children had been extremely bad eaters from their early infancy on; when eventually their lives were at risk, hospitalization and a protracted period of gavage feedings became mandatory. In these two cases the troubles had decidedly nothing to do with either faulty child-rearing methods or stressful reactions to existing eating problems. The nutritional situation of children with such serious disorders is bound to remain a cause for extreme concern; in their case the treatment strategies to be discussed below will be ineffective.

As far as the more common eating disorders are concerned, the treatment used at the Eekwal observation home has the following elements:

- Treatment starts right from the child's very first meal at the observation home; the treatment plan must therefore be prepared in advance. Just as with treatment of sleep disturbances, the attendants must be familiar with the methods used, and be experienced in applying them. Again, advantage is taken of the fact that the child for his part is completely unfamiliar with the environment and is less preoccupied with his own deep-rooted habits and rituals.
- Food is considered to be a precious gift to be enjoyed (a rather outdated view in this glutted Western world). For a child who, perhaps for many years, has been ceaselessly battling about food, it may come as quite a novel experience and possibly even a relief to discover that eating is something which is allowed rather than ordered.
- During meals at the Eekwal home all children of a group are supposed to sit at the table together with the attendant. Depending on which meal is being served, the attendant supplies each child's dish with three pieces of diced bread or just three morsels from the hot meal. If a given child is able to eat unaided he is then left to himself. Children not used to eating alone are proffered a mouthful after the other children have had their first helpings; good care is taken not to touch a child's mouth with the fork or spoon to avoid any suggestion that food will be forced into his mouth; a child who does not respond to the food offered to him is also left to himself. At the end of the meal all the dishes are taken away and nothing is said about the fact that some of the children have eaten nothing or apparently did not want to be fed. If a child has not finished his dinner he is not given the dessert; if he makes a mess of his food or spills it or whatever, his plate is immediately taken away without comment. A child who has finished his helping may ask for more as often as he wants, but each time again he is given the same small amount. Another helping is given only when a child asks for it himself one way or another. When a child persists in refusing to eat for three meal-times or so, he is

no longer supposed to need a dish or cutlery, but during meal-times is still expected to sit at the table and is not allowed to play.

- On the first or second day after admission the child is weighed, and an assessment is made of his overall nutritional condition; essential blood tests are taken if helpful information can be expected therefrom.
- After breakfast and lunch, ample drinks are given to all children, including those who refused to eat. Some insistence may be necessary. During meal-times no drinks are offered in order to prevent food from being washed down without being chewed (which is rather common), and also to prevent children from drinking so much that it takes away their appetite. In principle, skipping a meal or two does little physical damage. As for drinking, however, rather more caution is required; for that reason children are also given drinks between meals, even sweetened with a little extra sugar if need be. From the first day of his stay at the observation home, the child's intake of liquids is carefully recorded by volume.
- A child has to eat what is cooked. Porridge is never given as a substitute for bread or for the hot meal; neither are dishes made more appetizing by adding apple sauce or the such. Of course a child may have a dislike for a particular dish; then he is simply served less of it.
- Bread is eaten with crusts and all; a child may choose any filling he wants for his sandwiches on the understanding that the first sandwich has a savoury filling.
- Only a limited number of snacks between meals are given and they consist mainly of fresh fruit.
- Lazy eaters and those who have arrived late are not allowed to stay longer at the table than the others; there is ample time during meal-times for every child to satisfy his appetite. Unfinished food is taken away at the end of the meal.
- Preferably children eat unaided; they are never fed with the aim of making them eat more, contrary to what is known to happen in many families.
- The atmosphere at the table has to be as relaxed and friendly as possible, no matter if there are children who happen to eat little or nothing at all. Such behaviour is simply accepted; it is just a pity for them that they are denied dessert.
- If a child has a motor deficiency in the muscles of his mouth which seems more serious than was initially thought, the advice of the speech therapist - and if need be also that of the physiotherapist - is sought in order to establish whether such measures as stimulating the child's muscles or improving his sitting posture may be apposite.

The policy outlined above, which mainly addresses vital feelings of hunger and thirst while leaving affective aspects largely unheeded, was found to yield promising results. Peers with good eating habits certainly contributed to that by setting a good example. It is always amazing to see when children with eating disorders knuckle under after only a few days stay at the home.

Many of them eventually become fairly good or even excellent eaters, some to such a degree that they need to be checked. It proved to be possible to consolidate the gains made at the clinic by inviting parents to attend meals at the observation home and talking things over with them in counselling interviews both before and after trial weekends at home. No cases were seen which would have benefitted from graded change, the method employed by Howlin and Rutter (1987) in dealing with eating disorders; at the Eekwal home such a roundabout method would have been a mere waste of time.

Two examples of successful treatments are to be found elsewhere in this book. The first one, in Section II.4.7.4.2, describes in detail a two-year-old moderately retarded boy (Subject No. 133). He was used to being bottle-fed with custard, his only food for more than six months. Initially he had in fact been a good eater; quite unexpectedly he developed an entirely unmanageable fad for drinking custard once this had been given to him as a snack between meal-times. The first three days after his admission into the observation home this boy gave many problems, displaying a lot of resistance and anger; on the fourth day, however, he ate his sandwiches at cold meal-times, and at the hot meal he had two bowls of pea soup. From then on all eating problems were over. This extraordinary and spectacular result was probably mainly to do with the fact that in this case the eating disorder had started quite recently. The second example is described in Section II.5.3.2.1 (Subject No. 108).

In what follows, two further examples of the principles outlined above will be presented. (Again, for the interpretation of test results on the SRZ, SGZ and SMZ scales presented in the examples, the reader is referred to Appendix C.)

Subject No. 077: boy; age 5 years; profoundly retarded; PDD-NOS, deaf, and motor handicapped

This boy was the elder of two children. The mother's pregnancy had been normal. Delivery was on time, but there were complications due to malpresentation of the baby. The boy seemed nevertheless to be in good health: he cried well, drank well and was active. However, he did not babble and his development was slow. When he was about 6 months, his parents began to suspect that he might be deaf. At eighteen months, he began to refuse food. At some stage between his second and third birthdays he suffered from protracted seizures during fevers. By then his development had almost come to a complete standstill, but he did walk. He would not leave anything alone, displayed stereotyped ways of handling objects and manipulating his own body; his contact-making was virtually restricted to being able to tell his parents from other persons.

He was unable to eat alone, and refused all food unless it was highly sweetened as well as semi-liquid; if not to his taste he expelled it from his mouth. Indeed, each meal-time was a lengthy ordeal. However, he did drink large quantities of cocoa, the only thing he really liked. He knew where to find it, and when he wanted it he tried to lead his mother to where it was kept, pulling at her hand or clothes, and becoming very angry when his wish was thwarted. Apart from the eating disorder he also had serious difficulties in falling asleep.

On examination the boy was found to have a flaccid tetraparesis (his legs being more affected than his arms, and his left side more seriously than his right side), a muscular atrophy, and intense pathologic reflexes. Brain-stem audiometry revealed that he was completely deaf. No EEG abnormalities were found. Apart from the perinatal problems, a congenital defect may also

154

have been an etiological factor. On the Griffiths (generally yielding scores of approx. 10% above the actual level) he obtained a GQ of about 14; excluding the results of subtest Language up-graded the score by only 3 points, yielding a GQ of 17. Tested for social competence with the SRZ scale, he obtained minimal scores on all four subtests and the Total, i.e., five times a score of 3 (in standard marks based on the norm laid down for day-care centres). On the PDD-MR Scale his score was 10 (classification: PDD) and he was diagnosed as PDD (determined on the basis of the data from his file). His stereotyped behaviour and lack of contact-making were felt to be alarming, even when due allowance was made for his deafness and profound mental retardation; only via tactile and haptic games could some interplay be established.

After a few weeks at the observation home his sleeping problems had almost completely disappeared. This behaviour had probably been mainly reactive.

After six months at the Eekwal observation home his eating problems improved consider-ably, although they were still quite worrying. The positive results proved to be lasting. Ultimate-ly, on average he ate a sandwich (crusts and all) with savoury filling twice a day, putting small pieces into his mouth himself (with his fingers); for dinner he ate a fair amount of the hot meal (not sweetened and only moderately mashed) plus the dessert. He learned to eat with a spoon, needing occasional help with scooping up and sometimes also with steering the spoon to his mouth. By then, like the other children, he drank milk, tea and rose-hip syrup between meals.

In spite of his progress he remained in general a very autistic and profoundly retarded child. On seeing that the boy was happy at the Eekwal observation home, his parents, who were actually living on the Dutch Antilles, felt that it would be better if he was placed into an institu-tion in the Netherlands. This could be realized. Over twelve years later he was still living there. As might be expected, hardly any further development has taken place. On follow-up assess-ment he obtained a PDD-MRS score of 14 (classification: PDD) and was once again diagnosed as PDD.

Subject No. 051: girl; age 5 years; severely retarded; PDD-NOS

The mother's pregnancy (her fifth) and delivery were normal. The retrospective impression of the parents was that from the start the child was inactive and showed little interest in the sur-rounding world. However, she did look into the eyes of other people. Her first laugh did not come until her ninth month, and then she only laughed to herself. Her motor development was very retarded and she was two years old before she could stand.

Breast feeding and bottle feeding gave no problems. However, the change from liquid to solid food was a complete failure; the girl was three times hospitalized for this problem, but gains made in the hospital were not maintained at home. Two months before being admitted to the Eekwal observation home she started to eat bread at the day-care centre, but needed 45 minutes to eat only some of it and completely refused to eat bread at home, throwing it away immediately when it was given to her. Consequently at home she continued to eat only porridge (which was fed to her) at the cold meal-time, while at dinner she refused all dishes except meat (with a strong preference for cheaper meat products such as sausages). On that account she was allowed to eat porridge for dinner as well.

This girl displayed much stereotyped behaviour. She was short-tempered; when having a tantrum she often banged her head, mostly against doors. There were signs, however, that this latter behaviour was tending to ease off. She was often uncooperative. Her father, who used to address her in an obtrusive and menacing tone, succeeded best in commanding her respect. She was totally incontinent.

No etiological explanation for the autism nor for the severe degree of retardation was found. The family history revealed only the occurrence of uncomplicated mild mental retardation.

On the Griffiths (generally yielding scores of approx. 10% above the actual level) the girl ob-tained a GQ of 35. The results of testing with the SRZ scale are given below (in standard marks based on the norm laid down for day-care centres).

(Sub)scale	
Self help	5L
Communication	4
Persistence	5L
Social skills	4
SRZ-Total	4

On the PDD-MR Scale her score was 9 (determined on the basis of the data from her file; classification D: presence of a PDD doubtful) and she was diagnosed as PDD. Clinical examination revealed a 'massive retraction syndrome' (Hoejenbos & Kronenberg, 1967).

Treatment of her eating problems was very successful. Two months after her admission she was able to eat alone (with her fingers) at a fair pace. She ate one to three sandwiches, crusts and all, twice a day. The hot meals passed somewhat less smoothly, but she always ate at least a morsel. The food was always mashed and she was given only a tiny helping, as she would otherwise play with it. She was able to use a spoon unaided.

She completely gave up head-banging. She was practically dry during the day after three months at the observation home, provided that she was regularly put on the potty. Returning home after her discharge, her conduct was generally tolerable. Her parents had only a mediocre talent for bringing up children, however, and had four other children to take care of, so she was certainly not in optimal shape. Two years later the girl was placed into an institution. Still living there now (at the moment of writing this sixteen years later), she is doing fairly well. On follow-up assessment she obtained a PDD-MRS score of 10 (classification: PDD) and was diagnosed as PDD.

II.4.8.3   Constipation

As clinical experience at the Eekwal observation home shows, constipation occurs rather frequently in mentally retarded children with a PDD. Generally, mild forms of constipation tend to disappear if these children are offered a relaxed atmosphere and an environment which does not demand more from them than they can cope with. However, serious cases of constipation, which are less common, prove to be more difficult to cure. The condition is regarded as serious when (a) the problem does not stem from an ill-balanced dietary pattern or from demonstrable specific abnormalities in physical constitution or motility; (b) the condition has persisted for at least one year; (c) the condition evokes reactions of extreme concern, e.g., purgatives are administered, or lots of fuss is made about the child's infrequent stools and possibly also about his regular soiling of pants (which is not uncommon with this condition). Clinical treatment of a PDD child who suffers from a serious form of constipation was generally found to achieve little more than minor changes in the deep-rooted habits, even if this treatment spanned six months. At discharge the condition had at best improved to some degree, but had certainly not been cured.

The focus of treatment of constipation at the Eekwal observation home is to achieve regular bowel movements once a day or every other day, preferably at a fixed time of the day. The guiding principles are:

- so far as is possible, there should be plenty of time for toileting; the approach is friendly and relaxed;
- toileting is done at fixed times (at any rate after getting up and after meals);
- the child is encouraged by rewards (or, if his developmental level permits, by a system of rewards, such as a card with squares on which stickers can be stuck);
- the diet contains plenty of roughage and sufficient fluid; if need be, household remedies such as rye bread with treacle or stewed plums can be added to this diet;
- purgatives are only given as a last resort, chiefly to ensure regular bowel movements and to prevent pain during defecation.

In what follows, two illustrative examples will be presented, both involving children whose constipation was one of the very reasons for their admission to the observation home. The first case is comparatively mild, the second is serious. (For the interpretation of test results on the SRZ, SGZ and SMZ scales presented in the examples, see Appendix C.)

Subject No. 127: girl; age 8 years; moderately retarded; PDD-AD

This girl was the last born of four children, and a latecomer at that, her mother being 42 at the time. Delivery was on time but difficult. After birth the child looked pale and subsequently became cyanotic; Apgar score after one minute: 8; after ten minutes: 10. The baby was flaccid and did not look right. By way of precaution she was kept in an incubator for the first four days. At twelve months, she had seizures lasting twenty minutes (without fever); a week later an EEG examination was carried out and no abnormalities were found. Other epileptic manifestations did not occur. From the outset, the girl's development was slow; she did not walk before her second birthday. When she was six, she underwent an operation for a congenital defect of the urinary passages, and subsequently three further operations were performed for the same defect.

At the age of four this girl went to a nursery school, initially for only part of the day. Regular contacts with the child psychiatrist of an agency for outpatient mental health-care started at the same time. After nursery school she went to a IOBK (a special class for children whose development is in jeopardy). Her developmental level was described as "somewhere between mildly and moderately mentally retarded." According to the reports she was echolalic, chaotic, unrestrained and impulsive, and her mind often seemed to meander. A brain dysfunction was suspected. After her placement at a special school for educable mentally retarded children her behavioural problems increased. When she was admitted to the Eekwal observation home, her parents described her as wayward, uncompliant, constantly calling for attention, rigid and easily upset. Bowel movements were difficult and made her fearful; she tried to delay defecation and to establish all sorts of rituals in connection with it. On the whole her behaviour was very babyish, but occasionally she had surprisingly bright moments; more often, however, she was unable to do even the simplest of things, such as colouring pictures. She could not bear changes. She used to sniff at food and to pluck at blankets. Frustrations prompted her to head-banging or biting herself. Eye-to-eye contact, however, was normal according to her parents.

Detailed physical examination revealed no clear indication as to the etiology of the girl's condition. The circumference of the skull was found to be reduced (P2) and neurologically her motility was not entirely flawless. On audiometric examinations subnormal thresholds were repeatedly found. Apart from the perinatal problems, a congenital disorder could not be ruled out as an etiological factor.

Testing with the WISC-R (in a Dutch version) yielded the following scores: Verbal IQ (VIQ) 50; Performance IQ (PIQ) 47 (extrapolated); IQ 47 (again extrapolated). The results of assessment by means of both the SRZ and SGZ scales are given below (in standard marks based on the norm laid down for institutions for mentally retarded persons).

(Sub)scale	
Self help	6H
Communication	>9
Persistence	7H
Social skills	7L
SRZ-Total	7H

(Sub)scale	
Aggressive maladaptive behaviour	4
Verbal maladaptive behaviour	5L
Miscellaneous maladaptive behaviour	8L
SGZ-Total	6L

Her score according to the PDD-MRS was 16 (classification: PDD) and she was diagnosed as PDD.

At the Eekwal observation home the girl was found to be fearful, overdemanding, muddle-headed, poorly concentrated and cheerless. She displayed immediate and delayed echolalia; often her shifts of mood and affective responses seemed unrelated to actual circumstances and incomprehensible; she was obsessively interested in specific objects such as fluff and decorative baubles on the Christmas tree (notably the balls); some sounds, such as whistling, prompted panicky and aggressive reactions from her. Her potential for contact-making was found to be clearly substandard.

Medication (successively thioridazine and pimozide) had no beneficial effect whatsoever. She stayed for well over five months at the clinic and gradually calmed down. The clearly organized and predictable day programme and the modest demands made upon her in the clinic's class (with a programme geared to the level of trainable mentally retarded children) seemed to stand her in good stead. However, even the slightest hitch could cause her to relapse, albeit temporarily.

She was given ample time for passing motions; at fixed times of the day she was sent to the toilet by herself, and good care was taken to ensure that no time pressure would interfere. The girl's constipation problem was approached in a matter-of-fact way; when she had not done anything, attendants never showed anger; previously established rituals surrounding passing motions were ignored, while fresh rituals were given no chance to develop. A combination of household remedies and a system of rewards for producing bowel movements (one stick of chewing gum for a large bowel movement and half a stick for a lesser amount) helped to overcome the defecation problems completely. The result was lasting.

In all other respects, however, the girl hardly improved. After her return home she attended a school for trainable mentally retarded children. She became almost as restless as she had been before admission. Well over eighteen months after her discharge she was registered for placement into an institution for mentally retarded persons.

Subject No. 125: girl; age 6 years; moderately retarded; PDD(-AD?/-NOS?)

The mother's pregnancy (her second) was normal, except for an anaemia. Delivery was on time and without complications. In early infancy this girl was strikingly slow and dull; quite soon it became clear that a psychomotor developmental delay was involved. The girl was less than a year old when specialists were consulted, but only a slight hemiparesis was found. On admission to the Eekwal home, her parents described her as an elusive child and a law unto herself; at times she was pushy, wayward and defiant, at other times cheerful and fairly manageable. She ate little, making slow work of it. She was obsessed by such things as long hair, jewellery and mirrors. She was completely incontinent for urine and bowel movements. Throughout the day she had only small bowel movements and about once a week a large one. She was given 30 ml of a laxative (lactulose) twice a day.

Detailed physical examination revealed no serious problems. Only a doubtful retinitis pigmentosa was found and two minor neurological abnormalities, i.e., flaws in motility and a mild but clinically observable reduction of consciousness.

This girl stayed for almost eleven months at the Eekwal observation home. Most of the tests were performed shortly before her discharge. On the Griffiths (generally yielding scores of approx. 10% above the actual level) her mental age was found to be 3-5 and she obtained a GQ of 51 (the same score as nine months before, from which may be inferred that she had not been able to catch up in spite of the individualized approach). The results of tests with the SRZ, SGZ and SMZ scales are given below (in standard marks based on the norm laid down for institutions for mentally retarded persons).

(Sub)scale	
Self help	8L
Communication	9*
Persistence	7H
Social skills	7L
SRZ-Total	8H

* ten months earlier she scored 7L, a significant improvement on the 5% level of significance

(Sub)scale	
Aggressive maladaptive behaviour	7L
Verbal maladaptive behaviour	6L
Miscellaneous maladaptive behaviour	5H
SGZ-Total	5L

SMZ-Total	8H

Her score according to the PDD-MR Scale was 8 (classification D: presence of a PDD doubtful) and she was diagnosed as PDD. On the Childhood Autism Rating Scale (CARS) her score was 31, which classified her as borderline non-autistic/mildly autistic. Her score on the AUTI-scale was 30, which classified her as probably non-autistic.

After a four-month operant training programme the girl was generally dry in the daytime. Nighttime training, however, took eight months; in the initial stages of the treatment she was dressed in a nappy after having been picked up. Her eating disorder, which had not actually been very serious, improved; she now ate more and faster, with unaccountable slight relapses now and then, which would only last a couple of days.

The girl remained strange and unapproachable. She regularly displayed stereotyped behaviours (hand-flapping and body-rocking) and frequently talked to herself, repeating previously heard phrases word for word. Weekends at home, which started during the second half of the observation period, had an adverse effect on her; both at home and at the clinic her temper and screaming tantrums (which, by the way, had never been fully absent) began again to increase in frequency. This was probably a sign that she was unable to bear environmental change.

To treat her very serious constipation problems, elements from the strategies described above were combined. Occasional successes did not lead to any noticeable lasting progress. To be absolutely safe, a detailed physical examination was carried out but, as expected, no abnormalities were found. Quite remarkably, the girl would occasionally defecate at will when promised a reward. Medication (successively pimozide, thioridazine and another minor tranquillizer) had virtually no effect on her constipation, nor for that matter on her behavioural problems. For a short period, depression was suspected. However, the use of a tricyclic antidepressant led only to a minor, short-lived and possibly coincidental change for the better, and not to any lasting improvement.

After discharge she returned home and attended first a day-care centre and subsequently a school for trainable mentally retarded children. Her problems persisted, although now they were on the whole somewhat less serious than they had been before admission. On follow-up assessment by means of the PDD-MRS carried out four years later by her teacher, she obtained a score of 12 (classification: PDD) and was diagnosed as PDD.

II.4.8.4   Incontinence

A large number of the children with PDD admitted to the Eekwal observation home were incontinent. Evidently it is far from easy to toilet-train these children. Nevertheless, training can often be successful, as long as circumstances are not too unfavourable. One has to remain aware of two important points.

- Toilet-training mentally retarded children with a PDD will generally require more stamina and professional experience than training those without a PDD, although as a matter of fact a small number of children with a PDD do learn to stay dry and clean in a surprisingly short time.
- Quite a few profoundly and severely mentally retarded children without a PDD cannot be toilet-trained. It follows that this holds all the more true for profoundly and severely mentally retarded children with a PDD.

At the Eekwal observation home different methods are used for daytime and nighttime training.

The principles of *daytime toilet-training* are:

- daytime toilet-training precedes nighttime toilet-training;
- a child is first trained to sit on the potty or toilet (which, if necessary, may be fitted with a baby seat) for not more than five minutes. In the initial stages of the training programme the attendant stays nearby; sometimes a little force may be necessary to keep the child there. For some children a special toilet trainer seat provided with a fastening device may be required;
- toileting is done in a friendly and relaxed manner: there is plenty of time, the room is quiet, and the child is able to see the attendant from where he is seated;

- toileting takes place at any rate immediately after waking up, after meals, and before going to bed; for the rest of the day a schedule of regular intervals of ninety minutes or less is used;
- the child wears no nappy; wet pants are replaced instantly;
- the child is shown what the other children have done in toilet or potty;
- if the child has urinated or defecated in the appropriate place, he is praised enthusiastically; the attendant helps him to empty the potty or to flush the toilet; rewards, such as raisins or a sticker, may be given;
- praise and disapproval are expressed simply and explicitly ('well done, big job!' or, 'pooh, wet pants!');
- once the child has learned to eliminate in the appropriate place, the time of sitting may, if necessary, be extended gradually to a maximum of ten minutes; by then, it may be helpful not to replace wet pants immediately, particularly when an accident seems to be only a matter of carelessness or laziness;
- during the whole training period the child is predominantly approached in a positive way; however, if a child's incontinence lasts longer than seems necessary he may well earn an angry look or even a spank on the buttocks (provided this is done consistently and is in keeping with the current treatment plan).

The principles of *nighttime toilet-training* are:

- nighttime training is not started before sufficient progress has been made with daytime training;
- in the hours preceding bedtime the child is given neither more nor less than the normal amount of fluid; before going to bed the child is given ample opportunity to urinate; he wears no nappy;
- it may be expedient to place a potty in the child's room and to bring this to his attention expressly;
- the child is picked up somewhere between 9.30 and 10 p.m., i.e., when he has been in bed for a few hours and when there is a fair chance that he will be able to urinate; older children may need a nappy for the rest of the night in the initial stages of training to prevent them from wetting their beds too much;
- when the child is picked up he is thoroughly awakened, so as to ensure that he is fully aware of passing urine (and possibly also a bowel movement);
- the more progress a child makes, the later is he picked up;
- rewards are given in the morning;
- children at or above the mental age of about 4-0 with a persistent incontinence may benefit from the use of a pants alarm; alarm systems based on the principle that urinating or defecating completes an electric circuit leading to a mild shock are no longer considered acceptable, although they were actually more effective, particularly with children of an even lower mental age.

In what follows, the principles outlined above will be illustrated by the detailed report of a treatment; the boy in question was not only incontinent but was also handicapped by his frequent and loose stools. For two other relevant examples the reader is referred to Sections II.4.7.1.2 and II.4.8.3 (Subjects No. 029 and No. 125).

Subject No. 045: boy; age 2 years; mildly retarded; PDD-AD

An earlier discussion of this case can by found in Section II.4.6.2 and will be dealt with again in detail in Section II.5.3.2.4.

This boy stayed for well over ten months at the observation home. On admission he was completely incontinent. He suffered chronically from very loose stools for which no cause could be found. A slight improvement was brought about by putting him on a low-fat diet.

Wet or soiled pants clearly did not bother him. He was regularly put on the potty, but was often unwilling to sit still. He let himself fall off the potty and carried it around, but never did anything in it. If he saw an opportunity, he would smear his stools.

However, a policy was soon adopted to train him together with one or more other children, as he was then more ready to stay seated on the potty. He was expressly shown what the other children had done in their potties. Less than three weeks after the switch-over to the new policy he was willing to urinate in the potty, and his interest in his own performance clearly grew. The learning process accelerated, as the increasing success rates listed below demonstrate:

week 4 after admission: urine caught 4x;   faeces caught 1x
week 9 after admission: urine caught 16x;   faeces caught 3x
week 13 after admission: urine caught 27x;   faeces caught 4x

The upward trend was maintained. One fine day, seven months after his admission, he went to the toilet of his own accord to urinate in the potty; three months later he had gained almost full control over his bladder. His stools, however, being so loose, were more difficult for him to control. In reaction to his initial habit of smearing his stools (he used to take off his pants quickly to defecate on the floor) two measures were taken; he was given a spanking on the buttocks there and then, and in class encouraged to play with clay. After a time he clearly began to feel uncomfortable when he had soiled his pants. Saying 'pooh' or 'caca', he would take off his pants by himself and pick them up with his thumb and forefinger; if he dirtied his fingers or hand in so doing, he wanted to have them washed immediately. By then smearing of stools had definitely become a thing of the past.

II.4.9   Psychotropic drugs as adjuncts to management and treatment

II.4.9.1   Some general remarks

In his apercu on treatment of autism, Rutter (1985) writes, "To date there has been little indication that drugs make any decisive difference although they are of some value in the treatment of overactivity, sleep disturbance and aggression." In another overview, Gillberg (1990a) writes, "The pharmacological treatment of autism is still far from satisfactory." My personal findings, reported in another study (Kraijer, 1988d), are mainly in line with these two statements.

It is a sound principle in the management and treatment of children and adults with a PDD not to go beyond their ability to cope with stimuli, impressions, expectations and social contacts; ideally, strict observance of this principle would make any prescription of psychotropic drugs unnecessary. However, it must be realized that *not* prescribing these drugs implies that a number of behavioural deviations, such as aloofness, preoccupations, stereo-typed behaviours and adherence to rigid patterns (so intrinsic to pervasive disorders) have to be accepted or - if so preferred - tolerated. Only when totally unacceptable behavioural deficits and behavioural problems persist in spite of optimal environmental conditions, medication can be an option in order to make a child more amenable to treatment. Psychotropic drugs should therefore fit in with the overall management strategy (Kraijer, 1981). There is no point in using medication as a sole remedy for behavioural prob-lems, let alone as an antidote to the effects of a faulty approach, as it will fail to bring about substantial improvements and is also objectionable on moral grounds.

Whenever medication is considered, the pros and cons have to be weighed against each other. Drugs may, for example, reduce aggression, destructive behaviour, unrest, strain, rigidity or aloofness, but they may also have unfavourable side effects such as dullness, inertia or tardive dyskinesia. It follows that not only medical experts, but also behavioural scientists, at-tendants and/or parents can give valuable hints regarding the necessity of the use of psychotropic drugs as well as their side effects.

II.4.9.2   *The observation-home policy*

The Eekwal observation-home policy with respect to prescribing psychotro-pic drugs is based on the following principles.

- In almost all cases, the psychotropic drugs used before admission are reduced and discontinued. Evidently a clearer picture of someone's behaviour will be obtained when the person in question uses no drugs. Another very plain reason for following this policy is that evidently med-ication had not been able to bring about substantial improvement, other-wise admission to the Eekwal home would not have been requested.
- Epilepsy (criteria: epileptic EEG abnormalities have been found and epi-leptic phenomena are clinically observable) must be brought under con-trol; this is of the utmost importance, as epilepsy may well have many direct and indirect effects on behaviour. Therefore, anti-convulsants are given to eliminate this factor and to reduce, as much as possible, cerebral-organic dysfunction.
- As indicated earlier, a fundamental principle is first to examine thorough-ly what special educational intervention, treatment, management and environmental adjustments may achieve. Only when these approaches have failed to produce satisfactory results is the necessity or usefulness of prescribing psychotropic drugs considered.

- Finally, I would like to state once more that the best benefit which can be expected from medication is that it may make children more receptive to their general day-to-day care and to forms of special treatment.

The Eekwal observation home prescribed psychotropic drugs for two inter-related reasons: (a) to diminish clearly handicapping behaviours and conditions, such as stress, unrest, aggression, and self-injurious and destructive behaviours; (b) to promote the development of more positive attitudes, in particular with regard to openness for contact-making and awareness of and interest in the surrounding world.

The figures to be presented concerning the prescription of psychotropic drugs at the Eekwal observation home cover the period from January 1978 onwards. One reason for choosing this date is to highlight relatively recent developments. What is more important, however, is the fact that before 1978 pimozide, nowadays still the most frequently prescribed drug, was not easily available in the Netherlands, not being an officially approved drug at the time. Nevertheless, the Eekwal observation home did administer pimozide before that date; on discharge the drug had then either to be discontinued or substituted by another drug (mostly by trifluperidol). As recommended continuation of a drug after discharge is used as an indication of its effectiveness (with one exception which will be discussed below), inclusion of data from before 1978 would yield an unacceptably gross distortion.

Between January 1973 and August 1988, the Eekwal observation home admitted 101 children with a PDD. Only 27 of these children were not administered psychotropic drugs. In the Eekwal setting 119 prescriptions were written out to 74 children. In 36 of these cases an improvement could be observed, four of these needing only temporary use of a drug (pimozide) to achieve a permanent improvement. Continuation of the drugs was recommended for the remaining 32 cases, but with some of them medication was advised to be discontinued on a tentative basis if behavioural gains were found to persist both at home and at school or day-care centre; the effects of discontinuation were to be evaluated subsequently in joint deliberation so as to decide whether permanent discontinuation of the drug or rather its resumption was called for.

Table II.4.1 presents a list of the most frequently used drugs, the number of times they were administered, and the number of times their continued use was recommended after discharge.

The findings demonstrate that with only one third of the PDD children the prescriptions were beneficial. Fenfluramine, nicotinamide and clonidine, then only recently developed, were administered occasionally during the period covered by the table (not only to children for that matter, but also to adolescent and adult persons admitted to the Eekwal observation home); as is clear from recent findings, these drugs are even less effective; positive results were reported in roughly less than a third of the prescriptions. Neither does pimozide yield spectacular results; yet it is regarded by the Eekwal-home

Table II.4.1 Evaluation of the psychotropic drugs between 1973 and 1988 prescribed to 74 PDD children (of a group of 101)

	Frequency of prescription	Succes rate
Pimozide	57	17*
Thioridazine	14	3
Carbamazepine**	11	4
Haloperidol	10	4
Levomepromazine	5	3
Methylfenidate	4	1
Fenfluramine	3	1
Other drugs	14	3
Total	119	36

*   Including four temporary prescriptions of about two months each
** In this case not used as an anti-convulsant, but as a psychoactive drug

team as the medication of choice when a child needs help in opening up for contact-making.

It must be concluded that psychotropic drugs have certainly not yet played a crucial role in the treatment of autism and related disorders. Nevertheless, neuroleptics may be very useful for counteracting stress, irritability, and bottled up tensions which may prompt sudden explosive reactions to minor events; notably when such problems are displayed by PDD persons above nine years of age, these drugs may be beneficial. Even with these problems, however, the only gain obtained is a *reduction of symptoms*. In a small number of cases medication (mostly pimozide) is able to bring about better responsiveness to other people (or less aloofness) and less stimulus overselectivity (see II.4.3.3). Unfortunately, however, there is no way of predicting which children will benefit; moreover, in some children drugs prove to have untoward side effects. Pimozide in particular may increase irritability and agitation. Incidentally, this drug, if beneficial at all, invariably achieves the best results when given in low doses, i.e., 0.5 to 1.5 mg a day.

To summarize, psychotropic drugs are of minor importance in the treatment of mentally retarded children with a PDD. Very often the answers to the extremely serious and complicated problems involved must be found exclusively in management strategies, whether carried out by professionals or non-professionals.

II.4.9.3   *Institutional policy*

In a research project carried out by Kraijer and Meijer (1995), the use of psychotropic drugs in institutionalized persons with a PDD was examined and compared with that of institutionalized persons without a PDD. The setting was the Hendrik van Boeijen-Oord, a large residential institution for mentally retarded persons in Assen, the Netherlands. The sample consisted of 661 residents. Non-ambulatory very profoundly mentally retarded persons were excluded from the sample; as a consequence, particularly as far as level of functioning is concerned, the sample may not be regarded as fully representative of the entire population of residents of Dutch institutions for mentally retarded persons.

The sample contained 252 cases which had been diagnosed as PDD. Persons labelled doubtful PDD/non-PDD, a group comprising 61 cases, were for the present purposes ignored. The sample contained 448 subjects diagnosed as non-PDD. In the context of the study, the term psychotropic drug covers the following types of medication: neuroleptics; anxiolytics; hypnotics/sedatives; anti-depressants; non-specific drugs used as psychotropic drugs, such as methylfenidate, fenfluramine and clonidine. For clarity's sake I would like to add that anti-convulsants have been completely ignored. Actually they were administered in a small number of cases to treat behavioural problems, whether or not only to that end. Psychotropic drugs were administered predominantly to treat such behavioural problems as unrest, irritability, and aggressive or destructive behaviour.

In this sample, 213 subjects (32.2%) used at least one psychotropic drug. However, if the sample is subdivided into the three categories: non-PDD, doubtful PDD/non-PDD, and PDD, remarkable differences emerge. Only 18.4% of the non-PDD subjects used psychotropic drugs; for the persons categorized as doubtful PDD/non-PDD, the percentage was 24.6%; for the PDD subjects this percentage was as high as 53.2%. Not surprisingly, the differences are significant (Chi-square = 82.76; df = 2; p = <.0001). To rule out possible effects of level of functioning, the differences between the two categories PDD and non-PDD were determined for the four levels of retardation. Numbers, percentages and the statistical test are presented in Table II.4.2.

Table II.4.2 Level of functioning and use of psychotropic drugs in non-PDD persons (n = 348) and PDD persons (n = 252); subjects were selected from an institution for mentally retarded persons

Level of retardation	n	Non-PDD		PDD		Chi-square	p
		Number	Perc.	Number	Perc.		
Profound	103	1	2.4	31	50.0	23.89	<.0001
Severe	224	26	25.7	64	52.0	14.87	<.0001
Moderate	194	25	17.9	32	59.3	30.23	<.0001
Mild	79	12	18.2	7	53.9	5.74	<.02

The table shows that the number of persons using psychotropic drugs was significantly higher amongst residents with a PDD than amongst non-PDD residents, irrespective of level of functioning.

Another possible effect, that of chronological age, must also be ruled out. To that end, the differences between the two categories PDD and non-PDD were determined for three age-ranges. Numbers, percentages and the statistical test are presented in Table II.4.3.

Table II.4.3 The use of psychotropic drugs in three age-categories of non-PDD persons (n = 348) and PDD persons (n = 252); subjects were selected from an institution for mentally retarded persons

Age-range	n	Non-PDD		PDD		Chi-square	p
		Number	Perc.	Number	Perc.		
0 - 19	33	0	0.0	8	36.4	-	.02*
20 - 39	260	20	15.5	67	51.1	35.50	<.0001
> 40	307	44	21.2	59	59.6	42.75	<.0001

* Fisher exact probability test

As the table shows, age differences have no effect on the difference between the use of psychotropic drugs in PDD and non-PDD persons either. Somewhat surprisingly, even with advancing years the use of drugs in PDD persons does not decrease. In fact, the table shows percentage increases from 36.4 to successively 51.1 and 59.6; however, the increase is not significant (Chi-square = 4.35; df = 2).

To complete the picture, the possible role of the sex factor was also examined. These results are presented in Table II.4.4.

Table II.4.4 Sex distribution and use of psychotropic drugs in non-PDD persons (n = 348) and PDD persons (n = 252); subjects were selected from an institution for mentally retarded persons

Sex	n	Non-PDD		PDD		Chi-square	p
		Number	Perc.	Number	Perc.		
Male	353	40	20.1	80	51.9	39.82	<.0001
Female	247	24	16.1	54	55.1	37.84	<.0001

As the table shows, the sex factor was also found to have no effect on the difference between the use of psychotropic drugs in PDD and non-PDD persons.

As a matter of fact, using a different approach I did demonstrate earlier that institutionalized persons with a PDD display many more behavioural problems than those without a PDD, and also that their behavioural problems are much more serious. In a 1991 investigation covering 655 institutionalized mentally retarded persons, 68 of these were described as having serious behavioural problems. A comparison between them and the 587 residents without serious problems with respect to the presence of PDD revealed that the first group comprised a significantly higher proportion of persons with PDD. The figures are presented in Table II.4.5 (two-tailed test).

Table II.4.5 Relation between serious behavioural problems and presence of PDD in mentally retarded persons living in residential care

Serious behavioural problems	PDD	Non-PDD	Total
Present	42	26	68
Not present	210	377	587
Total	252	403	655

Chi-square = 17.39; p <.0001

To summarize, the findings of both studies warrant the same conclusion: that it is due to the behavioural problems of mentally retarded PDD persons that the prescription of psychotropic drugs is quite often called for, which explains why the use of these drugs is significantly higher in persons belonging to this category. The factors level of functioning, chronological age and sex proved to be unrelated to the differences found between PDD and non-PDD residents.

We should have our reservations, however, before generalizing the findings of the study by Kraijer and Meijer, because, as indicated above, the sample was not representative of the entire population of residents of Dutch institutions for mentally retarded persons. This must also be realized when the findings of this study are compared with those reported in the study by Van Essen and Romein (1985), which will be discussed in more detail in Section II.5.3.5.3. These researchers found that 22.2% of the entire population of residents of Dutch institutions for mentally retarded persons (among them PDD residents!) used psychotropic drugs. Compared with this finding, the 53.2% drug users amongst PDD residents of the Hendrik van Boeijen-Oord, reported above, is extremely high indeed.

Clearly, the kinds of drugs prescribed have also to be considered. Kraijer and Meijer found that 213 subjects of their sample used in total 265 psychotropic drugs, an average of 1.24 drugs per person. This finding demonstrates that the Hendrik van Boeijen-Oord follows the policy which is generally recommended in the literature in the field, i.e., to try to limit the kinds of drugs used to one only. The frequencies of the drugs most commonly used by PDD residents of the Hendrik van Boeijen-Oord are presented in Table II.4.5.

Pimozide was found to be prescribed much less frequently for the predominantly adult residents of this institution than for the children staying at the Eekwal observation home. When administered to adults with a PDD, pimozide has been found likely to increase rather than to diminish behavioural problems due to its excitatory effect.

Table II.4.6 Distribution of the different psychotropic drugs used by 134 mentally retarded PDD persons (53.2% of a sample of 252 PDD residents of an institution for mentally retarded persons)

Pipamperone	56
Levomepromazine	30
Haloperidol	27
Pimozide	15
Clopenthixol	14
Thioridazine	7
Other drugs	25
Total	134*

* 32 residents used two drugs; four residents used three drugs

The policy of placing mentally retarded persons with extremely difficult behaviour into institutions is not likely to change very much in the near future (Sherman, 1988; Blacher & Hanneman, 1992). The management of these people leans heavily on the use of psychotropic drugs, and this applies especially to persons displaying pervasive developmental disorders. In many cases there is indeed no other option than to administer drugs. The familiar neuroleptics, which have been available for many years, are still the most frequently prescribed these days (Van Essen & Romein, 1985; see also II.5.3.5.3), with only pipamperone as a comparatively novel drug. As often as not, however, medication can do no more than to make life a little easier for the persons concerned and for those involved in their care.

II.4.10   Summary, conclusions and recommendations

In conclusion I would like to state in the first place that in order to diagnose mentally retarded persons with a PDD it is of crucial importance to remember that a disharmonious profile of functioning is an essential feature of the disorder, both in children and in adults. A meticulous diagnosis is necessary to provide insight into the nature of the disharmony. If management and treatment focus only on the brighter aspects of a given person, the chances are that he will feel unhappy and may even display serious behavioural problems. Demands have to be geared to the individual developmental level of the PDD person, whatever his or her age. Therefore, special attention has to be given to deficits and disorders in emotional development, notwithstanding the fact that these are the very areas in which objective diagnosis is most difficult to achieve.

The second important principle is to offer a clear-cut structure. A coherent treatment plan has to be drawn up, making stimuli conform to the five forms of structuring, i.e., reduction, selection, regularization, strengthening and extension, in all three aspects, i.e., the material, serial and relational aspects. Although all mentally retarded persons with a PDD need structure, persons with the rigid form of PDD and those with the erratic form of PDD differ somewhat in the kind of structure they need.

Both principles, i.e., appropriate demands and adequate structuring, are essential in the care and management of PDD children, adolescents and adults. Only if behavioural problems persist in spite of optimal conditions in these respects are special treatment approaches , such as behavioural therapy and medication, worth considering.

In this chapter the strategies of management, special educational intervention and treatment needed to help mentally retarded children with pervasive developmental disorders were discussed in detail. The distinction made by Rutter (1985) between specific and non-specific problems of autistic children proved to be very useful. Some of my own qualifications to this system were introduced.

The specific problems and the most appropriate approach to them were considered first. Four domains of functioning, i.e., cognition, language, social behaviour and emotional development, proved amenable to treatment and intervention to a limited degree only. Self help or Daily living skills constituted the only domain in which significant gains were made.

As for the semi-specific and non-specific problems, these were subdivided on the basis of their background or origin into instrumental, reactive, self-stimulatory, and structural or patterned problems.

The following semi-specific problems were dealt with: self-injurious behaviour, stereotyped behaviour, hyperactivity and sleep disturbances. Self-injurious behaviour in mentally retarded persons was found to be one of the most serious problems and was, moreover, highly resistant to treatment. A top priority is to prevent self-injurious behaviour from becoming structural or patterned. However, at least in children, fairly good to good results were obtainable. Sleep disturbances, even those which were very serious, were often found to be quite amenable to treatment, with the exception of structural sleep-disturbances stemming from fundamental restlessness.

The non-specific problems dealt with were: short-tempered, aggressive and destructive behaviours; eating disorders; constipation; incontinence. In general, good results could be obtained, notably with the reactive types of these problems. As far as incontinence is concerned, the level of functioning was found to be a critical factor.

The contribution of psychotropic drugs in the treatment of mentally retarded children with a PDD was found to be of minor importance. Adults with a PDD, notably residents of institutions, are more often given psychotropic drugs, but in their case medication serves only to prevent and suppress behavioural problems.

It is important to realize that parents and professional workers involved in the care of mentally retarded persons with a PDD have to cope with extremely serious problems of management and treatment. They deserve as much help as possible with this onerous task. Obviously, *prevention* of non-specific and semi-specific problems is of the utmost importance. Should such problems develop, priority should be given to tackling those which have the best chance of being successfully treated and are the easiest to treat. Four broad guidelines may be provided on the basis of these considerations.

- Early recognition of disorders and disabilities as well as an early start of apposite professional help and advice concerning managemental problems are of crucial importance.
- The targets of management, teaching and socialization should preferably be modest, whatever the age of the PDD person concerned. Only too often is the utmost asked, particularly with respect to demands in the social and emotional areas. This may have serious consequences. The combination of a lower level of functioning and a pervasive developmental disorder is in fact so disabling that it is best to tailor the approach to a level which is directly below the actual level of functioning of the person concerned (see II.4.5).
- Additional problems have to be tackled in the following sequence: first the non-specific non-inherent problems, subsequently the semi-specific problems, and finally the specific problems. Experience shows that improvements obtained in the non-specific and semi-specific problems may indirectly take the edge off the specific problems. However, in actual practice it may well occur that a strict differentiation between non-specific, semi-specific and specific problems is not possible and not even necessary when setting the targets for treatment.
- Considered in terms of background or origin, additional problems have to be tackled in the following sequence: first the self-stimulatory and subsequently the instrumental problems, followed by the reactive and then the structural problems.

The primary objective of this policy is, as a matter of course, to spare persons with a PDD needless suffering. However, it must be realised that those involved in their care and management, professional as well as non-professional people, need support too. Good care has to be taken to prevent these people from burning themselves out. Dedication is an invaluable good, and professional expertise is scarce. These human resources must be handled with care.

CHAPTER II.5

HOW DO MENTALLY RETARDED CHILDREN WITH A PDD FARE AFTER DISCHARGE FROM THE OBSERVATION HOME?

II.5.1   Introduction

II.5.1.1   *General remarks*

As is well known, even mentally retarded people without concurrent disabilities are mostly dependent on care for the whole of their lives, although not all to the same extent. However, if mental retardation is combined with a pervasive developmental disorder the situation is bound to be more serious. This can be examined by collecting data about the later careers of these dually afflicted people, notably the data concerning the kinds of facilities into which they have been placed. As demonstrated earlier in this book, mentally retarded people admitted to the Eekwal observation home are far from representative of the entire population of mentally retarded persons, because many of them have concurrent problems and disabilities. For that reason it serves no useful purpose to make a follow-up comparison between former Eekwal-home children with a PDD and those without a PDD. A comparison between former Eekwal-home children with a PDD and mentally retarded persons with no concurrent disorders is more likely to reveal interesting information.

The type of living facility into which a person is placed is a reasonably good indication of his level of functioning, behavioural comportment and social-emotional adaptability. Data about current behaviour, the use of psychotropic drugs and other details may also prove to be relevant.

Another important issue to consider is whether changes in external circumstances may have affected the lives of former Eekwal-home children. To that end two groups of PDD children were compared, i.e., those who stayed at the home between 1968 and 1978 and those who stayed between 1978 and 1988.

Finally, the later careers of PDD-AD and PDD-NOS children have been compared.

Detailed information about the results of the Eekwal follow-up study and the methods used will be presented in Sections II.5.2 and II.5.3. This will be preceded by a general overview of similar follow-up studies which are presented in Sections II.5.1.2 and II.5.1.3, so as to make a comparison possible between their findings and those obtained in the Eekwal follow-up study.

II.5.1.2   Introduction

Even a cursory survey of previous follow-up studies reveals that in actual practice such studies inevitably suffer from all sorts of shortcomings. There are several reasons for this.

To begin with, the methods and techniques of classification and diagnosis frequently change. Such changes make a reassessment of the subjects in the initial sample necessary. The study of Szatmari et al. (1989) is a good case in point. Many of the children in this follow-up study had been diagnosed long ago, some as long ago as 27 years. This time the reassessments needed were made by means of the DSM-III. As a matter of fact, the same procedure was used in the Eekwal-home follow-up study (see Section II.1.1.2).

Furthermore, the follow-up sample may no longer be representative. The number of subjects declines for all sorts of reasons; people die, their current whereabouts are unknown, and parents and current professional helpers may be unwilling to provide relevant information, etc.

A more general problem concerning representativeness is that no information is available about the number of cases not referred to institutions, clinics and other settings; what is known is only the number of cases which have been referred or admitted. Consequently, nothing is known as to how representative the referred cases are. To what extent may, for instance, a group of mentally retarded persons who have been investigated with respect to such aspects as level of functioning, gravity of the disorder, and help provided by other persons or agencies, be considered as a representative sample? As far as the present study is concerned, it would be particularly interesting to know at which age problem-children tend to receive special attention and help, and whether the help given is in accordance with their specific needs. Autistic children generally benefit most from professional hometraining given by a special autism team, or from placement into a setting which is familiar with autism, be that a day-care centre, school or treatment facility.

Another problem is that long-term comparisons are often difficult to make, as the amount, quality and types of professional help available tend to vary in time. In the Netherlands, for instance, the services provided for PDD children were found to have undergone considerable change over a period of about fifteen years (Snijders-Oomen, 1989). An investigation which covers a shorter period is not always a good alternative, as the number of cases may then become too small to allow for general conclusions. This holds notably for follow-up studies of PDD children, as PDD is a comparatively uncommon disorder.

Another issue concerns the comparison of two or more follow-up studies with the aim of drawing general conclusions. Again, several problems arise.

Szatmari et al. (1989), in their previously mentioned article, report that they were able to identify 28 articles containing follow-up data of autistic and schizophrenic children. Whether these studies deal with disorders of the same category is highly questionable, considering the diagnostic terms used, and whether the children concerned are comparable with respect to level of functioning and chronological age is another key question.

Often results of follow-up studies carried out the world over will not be fully comparable. The ways in which children are brought up, facilities and services provided, and attitudes towards deviant behaviour may diverge considerably.

Finally, the qualifications used to indicate level of social functioning are highly imprecise. Often the distinctions used by Rutter and Lockyer (1967), i.e., 'good', 'fair', 'poor', and 'very poor' outcome, are adopted, but they are actually ill-defined. In different parts of the world the terms may have different meanings.

As a matter of fact, many of these problems may be inevitable. Nevertheless, it seems a good exercise to explore systematically the major follow-up studies hitherto carried out before engaging upon the Eekwal-home follow-up study. In the next section a review will be presented of these earlier studies, and reference will be made to them later when we compare their approach with that adopted in the Eekwal-home study.

II.5.1.3   *Earlier follow-up studies*

There are ten crucial points on which approaches and methodologies used in follow-up studies may differ. It is with reference to these ten points that the earlier studies will be considered.

- *Psychological/psychiatric criteria on the basis of which subjects were included.*
  The psychological and psychiatric diagnostic or classificatory criteria on which subjects are selected in follow-up studies obviously affect the results obtained to a great extent. These criteria appear to differ considerably. The earliest follow-up studies in the field generally derived their criteria from the studies by Kanner and Creak, examples being Rutter and Lockyer (1967), Kanner (1971), DeMyer et al. (1973), Lotter (1974a,b) and Brown (1978). In some studies different terms are used to label the disorders, e.g., 'early childhood schizophrenia including autism' (Bender, 1973) and 'atypical children' (Brown, 1978). In later studies the criteria established by Rutter (1978) were partly or completely adopted, examples being Gillberg and Steffenburg (1987) and Chung et al. (1990). In the most recent studies international classificatory systems, predominantly the DSM-III or the DSM-III-R, are utilized; examples of these are Rumsey et al. (1985), Gillberg and Steffenburg (1987), Szatmari et al. (1989), and Kobayashi et al. (1992, published after the Eekwal follow-up study).

- *Somatic criteria on the basis of which subjects were excluded.*
  Somatic criteria on the basis of which subjects are excluded are used in the following studies: Frye (1968); Brown (1978) at least to some degree; Rumsey et al. (1985) to a great degree. On the other hand, in some studies, such as that by Gillberg and Steffenburg (1987), it is explicitly stated that somatic deficiencies or disabilities were no reason for excluding subjects.
- *Representativeness of the sample.*
  Two types of survey have been published:
  - *population-based surveys;* the sample is drawn after screening all inhabitants of a given geographical area for the characteristics to be investigated;
  - *clinic-based surveys;* the sample consists of individuals who have been referred to a clinic or other setting for observation and/or treatment.
  There are two examples of population-based follow-up studies, Lotter (1974a,b) and Gillberg and Steffenburg (1987). In all other follow-up studies in this field the original samples were based on referrals of children to some kind of specialized clinic. As noted earlier such a sample is very unlikely to be representative of the entire population. However, to what extent these samples are biased regarding such characteristics as gravity of disorders or socioeconomic position will never be known. If a sample contains only cases with successful outcomes, as is the case in the study by Kanner et al. (1972), its representativeness becomes highly questionable indeed.
- *Level of functioning of the subjects involved.*
  For simplicity's sake, any inconsistencies resulting from different methods of assessment are in the present context ignored, although there may well be some inconsistency between reported levels of functioning. Some investigators, such as Frye (1968), Kanner et al. (1972) and Brown (1978), have restricted themselves more or less to autistic persons in the average-normal ranges of intelligence. Others explicitly studied samples with subjects of all ranges of intelligence, examples being Lotter (1974a,b), Gillberg and Steffenburg (1987), Chung et al. (1990), and Kobayashi et al. (1992). As far as I know, no follow-up studies have been carried out to date focussing on mentally retarded autistic persons as a separate group.
- *Size of the sample.*
  The samples in follow-up studies differ widely with respect to the number of subjects involved. There are some which cover as few as a dozen persons or less, examples being Frye (1968) and Kanner (1971). In most studies about fifty persons are involved, examples being Bender (1973), Gillberg and Steffenburg (1987), and Szatmari et al. (1989). Comparatively large-scale follow-up studies are those by Brown (1978) which covered one hundred subjects, DeMyer et al. (1973) which covered 126 subjects, and Kobayashi et al. (1992) which covered 201 or 197 subjects (depending on which data are considered).

- *Proportion of lost cases.*
  Obviously the proportion of subjects who can be traced for follow-up information is also a very important aspect. In some studies a backward procedure was followed, implying that only those subjects were included about whom sufficient information was available for the entire period considered, the method employed by Brown (1978); the whole problem of lost cases is then insoluble. More often, however, the cause and number of lost cases are indicated more or less precisely. Sometimes losses are quite considerable. In the study by Kanner et al. (1972), which, as mentioned before, included only subjects for whom treatment had been successful, there was a loss of 81% of the cases in the follow-up study. The lost cases in the study by Szatmari et al. (1989) represented 64%. However, in the study by Kobayashi et al. (1992) the proportion of lost cases was only 13-15%, and in that by DeMyer et al. (1973) a mere 7%; moreover, in these latter studies the samples were very large. As will be clear, a low percentage of lost cases means that the results are more likely to be representative.
- *Length of the follow-up period.*
  Again, there are wide differences with regard to this aspect. In most studies, subjects were seen first in their early childhood and then followed until their puberty or at best early adolescence, an average period of 6-9 years. Examples of this type of follow-up study are DeMyer et al. (1973) and Chung et al. (1990). Attempts to follow children until their adulthood were made by Frye (1968), Kanner (1971), Bender (1973), Brown (1978), and Rumsey et al. (1985); these studies covered periods of up to 15-20 years and longer.
- *Differences regarding breadth and scope of findings.*
  The differences regarding these aspects are also very substantial. Some studies, such as that by Frye (1968), provide detailed reports of the subjects followed. In others, such as that by Kanner (1971), only overall descriptions are presented. Some studies present only quantified, matter-of-fact information regarding the group as a whole, as is found in Lotter (1974a,b) and Szatmari et al. (1989). As far as the latter study is concerned, the data refer to such things as IQ scores, speech attainments, severity of the autistic disorder, and what DeMyer and Barton (1973) have termed work-school status. For more informative reviews the reader is referred to Lotter (1978) and DeMyer et al. (1981).
- *Geographical area.*
  Most follow-up studies to date have been carried out in the USA, such as those by Kanner (1971), Bender (1973), DeMyer et al. (1973), Brown (1978), and Rumsey et al. (1985). The studies by Rutter and Lockyer (1967) and by Lotter (1974a,b) are British. Frye's study (1968) was carried out in the Netherlands, Beeckmans-Balle's (1973) in Belgium, and Gillberg and Steffenburg's (1978) in Sweden. Studies were carried out in Canada by Szatmari et al. (1989), in Hong Kong by Chung et al. (1990), and in Japan by Kobayashi et al. (1992). As was noted in the introduction to this

section, research findings may show substantial regional differences; various socio-cultural factors may - positively or negatively - influence the lives of the subjects investigated.

- *Changing circumstances.*
The time lapse between the earliest published study mentioned here, i.e., that by Rutter and Lockyer (1967), and the most recent one, that by Kobayashi et al. (1992), is 25 years. During this period important changes may have taken place. However, the first observations referred to in the study by Szatmari et al. (1989), for instance, date back to the late 1960s, those reported by Kanner (1971) as far back as 1935, representing an even greater lapse of time.

While devising the Eekwal follow-up study, the investigators profited by the work carried out by their predecessors, paying due attention to the points listed above.

II.5.2   The Eekwal follow-up study in broad outline

II.5.2.1   *The objectives of the study*

In what follows, the general design of the Eekwal follow-up study will be presented along the lines of the ten points listed in the foregoing section.

- *Psychological/psychiatric criteria on the basis of which subjects were included.*
Presence of PDD-AD or PDD-NOS, as defined by the DSM-III-R, was determined on the basis of file data, in keeping with the principles of long-term diagnostics.
- *Somatic criteria on the basis of which subjects were excluded.*
Somatic deficiencies or disabilities were no reason for excluding subjects.
- *Representativeness of the sample.*
The Eekwal follow-up study is clearly a clinic-based survey; it involves the entire group of children with a PDD admitted to the Eekwal observation home between August 1968 and August 1988, and not just a sample therefrom.
- *Level of functioning of the subjects involved.*
Fairly accurate data concerning the level of functioning of these children are available; all were mentally retarded and had been diagnosed or classified as such before their fifteenth birthdays. The criteria used for mental retardation were low levels of function in the areas of intelligence and social competence, in keeping with DSM-III-R principles. Their levels of retardation ranged from profound to mild.
- *Size of the sample.*
The initial sample contained 137 subjects, which is a comparatively large sample.

- *Proportion of lost cases.*
  The number of lost cases was kept to a minimum. Regarding some of the issues investigated this proportion is less than 2%; regarding a small number of issues, however, almost 17% of the cases are lost. In view of the long period covered by the project this may be regarded as a very satisfactory achievement.
- *Length of the follow-up period.*
  On average the follow-up period is 13.0 years; this means that about a half of the subjects were followed into adulthood.
- *Breadth and scope of the findings.*
  In the Eekwal follow-up study many quantitative data were collected. Analyses were made for the entire group and for subgroups. Individual case histories were available, some of which will be presented.
- *Geographical area.*
  The children in the study all live in the Netherlands; only six of these have a non-Dutch cultural background (Surinam, Dutch Antilles, Indonesia, Turkey), but in two of these cases the mother is Dutch. Four of the six non-Dutch children were born in the Netherlands.
- *Changing circumstances.*
  The Eekwal follow-up study covers the rather lengthy period of twenty years. As the group investigated is sufficiently large, it can be subdivided into two groups of recently and not so recently admitted subjects. This allows the evaluation of the effects of recent developments, such as the growth of and improvement in facilities and services for mentally retarded people. One might hypothesize, for instance, that children are nowadays better integrated as a result of the creation of more and better provisions over the past ten years.

II.5.2.2   *Comparing the results with those of other follow-up studies*

Can the findings from the Eekwal follow-up study be compared with those reported in other studies? The answer to this question will be discussed point by point.

- To date the entire spectrum (or continuum) of pervasive developmental disorders as defined by the DSM-III-R - i.e., embracing both PDD-AD and PDD-NOS - has never been the object of follow-up research. Even in the most recent study to date, that by Kobayashi et al. (1992), only persons with PDD-AD are investigated. The studies by Lotter (1974a,b) and by Gillberg and Steffenburg (1987) probably cover the widest range of cases, as not only are autistic children involved, but also, as far as the first study is concerned, children with 'similar but less marked signs', and in the second study, children with 'autistic-like conditions.'
- As the Eekwal follow-up study is clinic-based, to what extent the results may be regarded as representative is a crucial question. Comparison with population-based studies may therefore be very helpful. Fortunately the

aforementioned studies by Lotter and by Gillberg and Steffenburg are population-based.

- The Eekwal follow-up study involves only mentally retarded persons; therefore, its findings are only comparable with those of follow-up studies which include people of similar levels of functioning. In addition, the follow-up period should be of about the same length. Strictly speaking, on the basis of these two criteria, the Eekwal follow-up study is not comparable with any of the other follow-up studies. However, the studies by Lotter (1974a,b) and by Gillberg and Steffenburg (1987) do offer interesting material for comparison, at least concerning some of their findings. In these two studies children were followed until they were at least sixteen years old. As for level of functioning, 60% of the subjects in Lotter's sample had an IQ below 55, while in the study by Gillberg and Steffenburg 76% of the subjects investigated were below the normal/slightly subnormal range of intelligence. The study by Kobayashi et al. (1992) does not allow meaningful comparison with the Eekwal follow-up study in spite of the fact that 76% of the subjects were mentally retarded (according to their IQ scores), and that the children investigated were followed until they were at least eighteen; however, this study does concern only persons with PDD-AD.
- Almost all subjects involved in the Eekwal follow-up study are of Dutch origin. Consequently the findings of other West-European studies will offer the best material for comparison. For this reason too, Lotter's study (carried out in the United Kingdom) and the study by Gillberg and Steffenburg (carried out in Sweden) meet the present purposes better than the study by Kobayashi et al. (carried out in Japan). In particular, cultures may differ considerably in the way level of social functioning is assessed.

On the basis of the above considerations, the Eekwal follow-up study will be compared only with the studies carried out by Lotter and by Gillberg and Steffenburg, both in terms of the methods applied and the results obtained. To what extent the comparison contributed to a better insight will also be evaluated.

II.5.3 Results of the Eekwal follow-up study

II.5.3.1 *The sample*

The initial sample consists of 137 children born between 1955 and 1985 who were admitted to the Eekwal observation home between August 1968 and August 1988. The children stayed at the observation home for a comparatively short period. After diagnosis some tentative (occasionally successful) treatment was started, and prognoses and recommendations were formulated. Consequently the children's stay at the observation home is only one of the factors directly and indirectly influencing their later careers and development. Therefore, the Eekwal follow-up study should certainly not be regarded as an evaluation of what was done at this home.

Part of the follow-up information was readily available by making use of the routine contacts within the field of professional care. In case of incomplete or not immediately available data other sources of information were tapped, such as the agency by which the child concerned was referred at the time (usually a social guidance bureau for mentally retarded people or a regional agency for outpatient mental health-care), the home or facility where he or she was staying, and parents or other family members. A major and in some cases almost insurmountable barrier was that many agencies used to destroy files not long after a case had ceased to be under their guidance, for reasons of privacy. Schools and agencies for outpatient mental health-care in particular followed this policy; social guidance bureaus for mentally retarded people did so to a somewhat lesser degree.

Follow-up information was sought with respect to the following three questions:

1 Where did the child live in the period between his/her discharge from the Eekwal home and the follow-up date (i.e., the last quarter of 1989/ first half of 1990)?
2 Which day-care centre, school and/or workplace did the child attend?
3 Which prognoses (if available) have been made regarding the most appropriate future facilities for the child in question?

In the Netherlands, the type of daytime facility or living facility into which a mentally retarded person is placed is a fairly good indicator of his level of functioning and performance. (For an overview of Dutch mental retardation facilities the reader is referred to the end of this section.) One of the major advantages of this indicator is that it can be clearly defined by specifying a minimum duration of placement into a facility before it is counted. (In the Eekwal follow-up study, placements discontinued within six months and probationary placements were not included.)

To ascertain the presence of a pervasive developmental disorder in the subjects, the PDD-MRS (Kraijer, 1990; see also Chapter III.1 and Appendix B) had to be filled in, preferably by a psychologist or educational psychologist. Assessments made by people other than these specialists proved to yield less reliable results. I will come back to this later.

To obtain a general indication of the *subjects' behaviours and the amounts of attention they needed*, assessors were asked to circle the appropriate word in the following two statements:

- The staff spends a comparatively *large / normal / small* amount of time in discussing the behavioural problems of this person and how to tackle them.

181

- This person needs a *less than average / average / more than average* amount of tact and heedfulness to prevent behavioural problems from arising.

These questions could be answered by a psychologist, educational psychologist, teacher or attendant. In addition, *prognoses* were requested of the same professionals regarding the most appropriate future daytime and living facilities.

Finally, assessors were asked to indicate whether a subject used psychotropic drugs, and if so which drugs.

Of the initial 137 subjects only two could not be traced. Three children had died during the intervening years. They could be included in the follow-up sample regarding some issues; their life histories were available, but some essential details were lacking. Summarized case histories of the five children who had to be excluded from the follow-up sample (either completely or with respect to some issues) will be presented below. As in previous chapters, the basic personal data of each child are given, i.e., the number of the subject (allotted by the author and only known to him); sex; chronological age in completed years at the date of admission; level of mental retardation; PDD category (according to DSM-III-R criteria); concurrent disabilities if present.

Subject No. 052: boy; age 5 years; severely retarded; PDD-NOS

After discharge, this boy returned home and attended a day-care centre. Although he did present some managemental problems, his parents wanted to keep him at home for a little while longer. They had another mentally retarded child a few years his senior who had already been placed into an institution for mentally retarded persons. Ultimately, however, this boy was also placed into an institution; according to the referring agency he was then about eight years old. It seems most unlikely that he should have moved from there since; however, all attempts to find the boy's current whereabouts and his parents's address were to no avail.

Subject No. 120: boy; age 7 years; moderately retarded; PDD(-AD?)

The parents of this boy came from the Dutch Antilles. He displayed many behavioural problems, both at home and at the day-care centre. He had been referred to a children's psychiatric clinic for these problems prior to being admitted to the Eekwal observation home. Neither at this clinic nor at the Eekwal observation home did his behaviour improve sufficiently to make returning to his parents' home a realistic option; medication given at the Eekwal home (fenfluramine) did have some positive effect though. A short time after the boy's discharge the family returned to the Dutch Antilles.

Subject No. 004: boy; age 11 years; severely retarded; PDD-NOS and epilepsy

This boy did not go to any daytime facility. Instead, he would loiter around on his parents's farm. After discharge he returned home. By then his parents were aware that he must eventually be placed into an institution, but they preferred to keep him with them for a few years more, offering him a happy and very tolerant environment. At the age of fourteen he drowned having ventured onto thin ice.

Subject No. 005: girl; age 10 years; moderately retarded; PDD-AD

This girl lived at home and attended a school for the trainable mentally retarded. After discharge from the Eekwal observation home she remained a very problematic child, as had been anticipated. An attempt to treat her in a group home for autistic children failed. Subsequently she went to a short-stay home and from there, at the age of eleven, to an institution for mentally retarded persons. Here she died from a sarcoma at the age of fourteen.

Subject No. 063: boy; age 4 years; severely retarded; PDD-NOS and severely hard of hearing

Before his admission this boy attended a day school run by an institution for the deaf, but only for part of the day. He was found to suffer from a metabolic disorder (the Sanfilippo syndrome). Almost immediately after his discharge from the Eekwal observation home his condition grew rapidly worse and he was placed into an institution. The progressive deterioration of his condition reduced him to an essentially vegetative state; he died at the age of seventeen.

The first of the cases reviewed above, subject No. 052, was excluded from the follow-up sample on all issues except that of age of placement into an institution; the other cases were excluded on a range of different issues, because the answers provided were incomplete or because data had been lost or could not be retrieved for lack of time.

Table II.5.1 presents the number of years between first observation and follow-up assessment of the 132 subjects, i.e., 137 children of the initial sample minus five cases.

Table II.5.1 Length of time between initial clinical observation and follow-up assessment of 132 children

Number of years	Frequency	Number of years	Frequency	Number of years	Frequency
2	5	9	8	16	6
3	5	10	6	17	10
4	7	11	7	18	16
5	3	12	11	19	5
6	2	13	5	20	6
7	2	14	7	21	5
8	4	15	8	22	4

The period between first observation and follow-up assessment ranged from 2-22 years, with an average of 13.0 and a median of 14 years. The average age of the children at the end of the follow-up study was 19.2 years, standard deviation 3.63 years.

As noted before, the types of settings into which children were placed after discharge are a good indicator of their functioning, both in the cognitive area and in the area of (mal)adaptive behaviour. When, for example, a mildly retarded person is placed into an institution for mentally retarded persons, this is an indication that his behaviour is problematic or even very problematic. The same applies to a moderately retarded child who fails to move on from a day-care centre to a school for trainable mentally retarded children. Alternatively, placement history may also reveal positive developments.

Mental retardation care in the Netherlands offers the following day and residential services:

KDV: day-care centre for mentally retarded children. This facility was originally intended as a nursery school for young severely and moderately retarded children. However, these facilities now accept an age-range of 2-18 years, and over the past ten years a growing number of profoundly retarded children. Children believed to be capable of attending a special education school will generally leave the day-care centre between their sixth and eighth years.

DVO: day-care centre for mentally retarded adults. This facility is mainly attended by severely and moderately retarded persons aged eighteen and over; the day occupations offered by these centres are tailored to level of functioning and may also include simple tasks. People attending the centres live either with their parents or at a group home for mentally retarded persons.

SW: sheltered workshop. This type of facility offers a wide variety of tasks. Ideally those employed here should be able to achieve a minimal degree of productivity (about one third of standard productivity) after an initial training period. The setting is suitable for mildly retarded persons and for moderately retarded persons who are socially adapted and are able to cope with the demands of everyday life.

ZMLK: school for trainable mentally retarded children. This type of school is suitable for moderately mentally retarded children ('children with very serious learning problems') in the age-range of about six to a maximum of twenty years.

MLK: school for educable mentally retarded children. This type of school is suitable for mildly mentally retarded children ('children with serious learning problems') in the age-range of six to about fourteen years; if feasible, follow-up vocational training may be given at schools with individualized programmes (ITO, IHNO and others); if this is not feasible, the alternative is a special secondary education school (VSO-MLK).

KGVT: group home for mentally retarded children. This facility is intended for children who attend a school for trainable mentally retarded children but who, due to their behavioural or other problems, have to be placed outside the parental home. In principle, children leave this home before they are twenty; in practice, however, stretching the rule is far from uncommon, as group homes for mentally retarded adults and institutions tend to have long waiting lists.

GVT: group home for predominantly moderately and mildly retarded persons of eighteen years and over. This facility is intended to offer permanent accommodation; however, some persons may perform well enough to be considered capable of living in an annexe or in an apartment with some kind of supervision.

KVT: short-term residential facility. This facility was originally intended to accommodate young mentally retarded persons when their parents were ill or on holiday or whatever. Sadly, however, these facilities came to be used more and more as a temporary solution for people awaiting placement into an AZI (see below). Nowadays long-drawn-out stays of a few years are not uncommon.

AZI: general institution for mentally retarded persons. This facility offers both daytime activities and accommodation. Almost all profoundly and severely retarded persons are eventually placed into an institution. The same holds for moderately and mildly retarded persons who have serious additional disabilities, are mentally or socially very vulnerable and/or display much problem behaviour.

In the context of the Eekwal follow-up study, placement into a KVT (short-term residential facility) was counted as a placement into an institution when the explicit aim was to place the subject concerned as soon as possible into an AZI. Two placements into an institution for mentally retarded persons with visual impairments have been counted as placements into an AZI.

II.5.3.2   *Level of functioning and placement history of former Eekwal-home children with a PDD*

II.5.3.2.1   *Placement history of profoundly mentally retarded PDD children*
This involves a group of only eight children. Six of them attended a day-care centre for mentally retarded children for at least six months. Seven children currently live in an AZI; their age at placement ranged from six to nine years, their mean age at placement being slightly above seven years.

The findings, summarized in the table below, have only limited value, as the number of profoundly mentally retarded PDD subjects was small and they were, moreover, very young at the time of follow-up.

At home	At home + child care centre	General institution
0 years	3-4 years	7 years

By way of illustration a rather typical example of such a life history will be presented below.

Subject No. 111: girl; age 5 years; profoundly retarded; PDD(-AD?), OPS; epilepsy

The mother's pregnancy was normal and delivery was extremely rapid. In early infancy this girl was strikingly slow and dull, and she made no contact. She was bottled-fed and sucked well. Epilepsy was found to be present when she was three. It was at that age too that she was placed into a day-care centre. When admitted to the Eekwal observation home she had the following problems: much stereotyped behaviour; self-injurious behaviour; strong disinclination for toilet-training; difficulty in dressing and undressing her; strong adherence to routines; unpredictable shifts of mood and temper tantrums; insufficient contact-making (which did improve slightly once she began attending a day-care centre). Detailed examination failed to reveal any etiological indication.

On the Griffiths (generally yielding scores of approx. 10% above the actual level) the girl obtained a subtest-age of 1-5 and a GQ of 25. Assessment by means of the SRZ and SMZ scales at the end of the observation period yielded an SRZ-Total of 4 and an SMZ-Total of 5H. Determined on the basis of the data from her file, her score according to the PDD-MRS was 15; classification: PDD; diagnosis: PDD.

No positive results were obtained either with the highly individualized care that she was given at the observation home nor with fenfluramine, which was tried as an adjunct to her treatment. After discharge she returned home and resumed attending the day-care centre. At the age of seven, when a third child arrived in the family, it was decided to place the girl into an institution. She still lives there now (and at the moment of writing this is thirteen years old). She needs a more than average amount of care and uses levomepromazine and clomipramine. Her current score on the PDD-MRS is 13 (classification: PDD; assessment made by the institution's educational psychologist) and she has been diagnosed as PDD.

The next subject is a girl who still lives at home and at the time of writing is nineteen years old; the case is noteworthy because it is rather unique.

Subject No. 108: girl; age 10 years; profoundly retarded; PDD(-AD?), epilepsy and hard of hearing

This girl was the fifth and last arrival in the family. She was born two weeks earlier than expected; pregnancy and delivery had been normal. The child's development was very retarded in all respects. Her first smile came when she was about four months old and she could not walk before she was about four years old. Contact-making was generally insufficient. She had been suffering from convulsions from as early as about her fourth month.

She attended a day-care centre between the ages of five and eight years. According to her parents this was not of much benefit to her; moreover, the journey to and fro (taking more than one hour twice a day) tired her too much. On admission to the Eekwal observation home she was completely incontinent, had to be fed, ate only sweetened dishes and drank only custard. She was blind to danger. At home she had not really been considered a nuisance; chiefly, her parents and the referring agency wanted to be informed about her developmental prospects.

No etiological indications were found. On the Griffiths (generally yielding scores of approx. 10% above the actual level) this girl obtained a test age of 0-11 (the subtest Hearing & speech not administered) and a GQ of 8 (again Hearing & speech not administered). Assessment by means of the SRZ and SMZ scales at the end of her observation period yielded an SRZ-Total of <3 and an SMZ-Total of 6H. A hearing-aid was prescribed on a probationary basis, but did not noticeably improve her response to sounds. Toilet-training was ineffective, neither was any improvement seen in her contact-making or interest in the surrounding world, in spite of the individualized approach. Treatment of her eating habits, however, was very successful. At the end of the observation period she was able to eat her hot meals with a spoon and her cold meals with a fork; she ate her bread with crusts and all and in general whatever else she was served with. As long as she was well cared for and closely watched and everything around her was kept well-organised, she gave surprisingly little trouble.

After discharge the girl returned home. Her parents felt they could cope for the time being and accepted the fact that hardly any further progress was to be expected. The idea of sending their daughter to a day-care centre did not appeal to them. At the time of writing this, nine years later, things are still going quite pleasantly according to the information received from her parents. This undemanding family (which has for a long time been living on invalidity benefit, the father an unskilled labourer, the mother a housewife and probably mildly mentally retarded) lives in a very remote spot. The girl has reverted to being fed and is still incontinent.

II.5.3.2.2 Placement history of severely mentally retarded PDD children

The group consists of 42 children. Of these, 35 had been placed into a day-care centre for a period of at least six months, and six attended, at one time or another, a school for trainable mentally retarded children (some whilst living in an institution for mentally retarded persons). Currently 41 of these children (roughly 98%) live in an institution for mentally retarded persons. (A fifteen-year-old child who is considered a priority case and has been waiting for many years to be placed into an institution has also been included.) The age at admission ranges from four to fifteen years, with the average age lying somewhat above eight years (for the child on the waiting list the age of admission has been taken to be fifteen years). One child still lives at home and attends a day-care centre; she has a high-priority place on the waiting list, but her case does not seem to be that urgent.

The placement history of the severely mentally retarded PDD children is summarized in the table below.

At home	At home + day-care centre	Institution
0 years	3 years	8 years

Again, an example of such a career will be presented by way of illustration.

Subject No. 098: boy; age 9 years; severely retarded; PDD-AD

This boy was the third and last-but-one child in the family. His mother's pregnancy was without complications. At delivery the umbilical cord twisted and the boy was cyanotic. However, he did cry well and his condition improved soon enough. Although initially his development seemed normal, with hindsight the parents thought that his response to the surrounding world was probably inadequate. At about the age of two he became a cause for concern, mainly because he hardly spoke and sometimes gave the impression of being deaf (which could be ruled out on examination).

Shortly before his fourth birthday he was placed into a day-care centre. His development almost came to a standstill. His interests were rather unusual; he could be absorbed in such activities as balancing and manipulating things and spinning them around. He ate paint, sand, rinds of oranges and leaves. For some time he took to gnashing his teeth and banging. His lack of responsiveness, non-compliant behaviour, and determination to have things his own way increasingly worried both his parents and the staff of the day-care centre.

Detailed examination failed to reveal any etiological indication other than the perinatal complication, which is a questionable one. On the Griffiths (generally yielding scores of approx. 10% above the actual level) the boy obtained a subtest age of 2-0 and a GQ of 21. Assessment by means of the SRZ scale at the end of the observation period yielded an SRZ-Total of 5L. Determined on the basis of the data from his file, the boy's score on the PDD-MRS was 13; classification: PDD; diagnosis: PDD.

This boy's upbringing had clearly been good; he was toilet-trained, reasonably able to dress himself, and ate alone. In spite of intensive treatment and medication given as an adjunct (successively pimozide and trifluperidol), his behaviour at the Eekwal observation home remained exactly as it had been at home and at the day-care centre. After discharge he returned home. No medication was prescribed and the prognosis looked bad. Not long afterwards the boy was placed into an institution for mentally retarded persons. At the time of writing he is nineteen years old and still living there. He uses no psychotropic drugs and needs no more than the average amount of care and attention. His current score on the PDD-MRS is 12 (classification: PDD), and he has been diagnosed as PDD (assessment made by the educational psychologist of the institution).

II.5.3.2.3   Placement history of moderately mentally retarded PDD children
This group consists of 41 children. Well over half of these children attended a day-care centre for mentally retarded children for at least six months (although the actual number is probably higher, as some of the case histories are incomplete in this respect). Of the entire group, 27 children attended - or still attend - a school for trainable mentally retarded children; some of them were - or are - living in institutions, some of which have the expertise to provide this educational service. Six subjects attended - or still attend - a day-care centre for mentally retarded adults. As for living facilities, six subjects, who were unmanageable at home because of behavioural problems, were placed into a group home for mentally retarded children some years ago; 32 subjects (roughly 78%) live in an institution for mentally retarded persons, three of whom actually live at home and are on a waiting list for such a facility. (To be precise, the three subjects who are on a waiting list include a nineteen-year-old and a 22-year-old person currently attending a day-care centre for mentally retarded adults and urgently in need of placement into an institution, and an eleven-year-old girl attending a school for trainable mentally retarded children who was denied admission into a group home for mentally retarded children.) The age at admission ranges from 3-22 years, with the average age lying somewhat above eleven years.

There are nine subjects in this group who still live at home; they are aged 27, 23, 23, 21, 17, 12, 10, 8, and 6 years; they have the following daytime occupations: one person attends a day-care facility provided by an institution for mentally retarded persons, four attend a day-care centre for mentally retarded adults, one attends a secondary special-education school, one attends a school for trainable mentally retarded children, and two attend a day-care centre for mentally retarded children. Going by the judgement of current professional helpers, for four of these nine subjects placement into an institution for mentally retarded persons will be necessary in due time, for two persons such a placement will definitely not be necessary, and for three persons the kind of accommodation needed in future cannot yet be determined.

The placement history of the moderately mentally retarded PDD children is summarized in the table below.

At home	At home + KDV*	At home (group home) + KDV*/ZMLK**	General institution sometimes providing ZMLK**
0 years	3 years	6-8 years	11 years

Again, by way of illustration, a typical example of such a career will be presented.

Subject No. 030: girl; age 6 years; moderately retarded; PDD(-AD?)

This girl was born in a socially poorly adapted working-class family. She was the mother's fourth child. Pregnancy and delivery were without complications. The girl's early development did not strike her parents as out of the ordinary. However, she was well over four years old and already attending nursery school before she began to produce pre-speech sounds. The school's description of the child's behaviour makes clear that she was much more problematic than her parents had ever made known. The girl's only talent was for putting together jigsaw puzzles and all her other achievements were inferior; she screamed and shrieked quite a lot, was non-compliant and stubborn, did not make contact with her peers, kept putting things into her mouth, and stroked her cheeks with specific objects. When she was six she went to a school for trainable mentally retarded children where her problems were certainly not fewer. It was at the request of this school that she was extensively examined at the Eekwal observation home. No major physical abnormalities were found. It was noticed, however, that the girl was strikingly similar, both in appearance and behaviour, to her sister, two years her senior, who had also stayed at the Eekwal observation home at the same age and had since been placed into a group home for mentally retarded children. This fact suggests the presence of an as yet unknown syndrome in the family.

Tested with the Stanford-Binet she obtained a mental age of 2-2 and an IQ of 32. As the Stanford-Binet has a strong verbal-intelligence bias, she was also tested with the Merrill-Palmer Scale which mainly tests performance skills and is therefore known to give a flattering picture; on this test she scored a mental age of 4-10 and an IQ of 72. Assessment by means of the SRZ scale at the end of the observation period yielded an SRZ-Total of 7H (in standard marks based on the norm laid down for day-care centres for mentally retarded children). Determined on the basis of the data from her file, her score on the PDD-MRS was 11; classification: PDD; diagnosis: PDD.

At the Eekwal observation home we tried educational intervention, individual speech therapy and special educational treatment aimed at improving contact-making. Some progress was achieved in the areas of appropriate habits and routines, sense of duty, differentiation of play and other activities, and language development; her hyperactivity slightly diminished. Two drugs (successively carbamazepine and benperidol) proved to be ineffective.

Her parents urgently wanted to have the girl back home. However, eighteen months after her discharge she was placed into a group home for mentally retarded children; this home arranged placement into another school for trainable mentally retarded children. For many years she was given speech therapy and training in language skills, as indeed had been recommended by the Eekwal team.

At the age of ten, her re-admission into the Eekwal observation home was requested. She was displaying increased hyperactivity, aggressive behaviour towards peers, destructive behaviour, loss of interest in play, and purely imitative speech (although her language skills had improved).

Tested again with the Stanford-Binet, she now obtained a mental age of 3-7 and an IQ of 37. Assessment again by means of the SRZ scale at the end of this second observation period yielded an SRZ-Total of 8H (this time in standard marks based on the norm laid down for institutions for mentally retarded persons). Determined on the basis of the data from the file of this second observation period, her score on the PDD-MRS was 15 (classification: PDD) and she was again diagnosed as PDD.

The most striking change in the girl was her elusiveness. This made it much more difficult to correct her increased stereotypical behaviours, hyperactivity, and her unpredictable disruptive

189

behaviours (suddenly destroying things, hitting other people, and the like).

The psychotropic drugs tried this time (successively trifluperidol and levomepromazine) again proved to be ineffective. Placement into an institution for mentally retarded persons seemed therefore to be the best option. However, for the time being she had to return to the group home. At the age of twelve, she was placed into an institution. At the moment of writing this she is 24 years old and still lives there. The staff spends a comparatively large amount of time discussing her behavioural problems; a more than average amount of tact and heedfulness is needed to prevent behavioural problems from arising. She uses haloperidol and cisclopenthixol. Her current score on the PDD-MRS is 18; classification: PDD; diagnosis: PDD (assessment being made by the psychologist of the ward of the institution).

The next case represents an unusual career.

Subject No. 106: girl; age 3 years; moderately retarded; PDD-AD

This girl was the illegitimate child of a mentally disturbed mother and a Moroccan father. At delivery, which was four weeks early, the mother had a fever; her waters broke three days before delivery. The child was in good condition except for a herpes simplex on the cornea of the left eye. As the mother was found to be unable to take good care of her child, the girl was placed into a foster home when she was ten months old. By now the girl's contact problems and her developmental lag of several months were becoming apparent and the district branch of the Dutch Association for Autism and Related Developmental Disorders started to provide guidance. By the time the child was almost four her foster parents were at the end of their tether. At the Eekwal observation home the girl's problematic behaviour could only be traced back to the perinatal complications and the herpes simplex. The inadequate care which the child's natural mother had initially provided seemed to be a factor of only secondary importance, if any.

On the Griffiths (generally yielding scores of approx. 10% above the actual level) the girl obtained a subtest age of 1-10 and a GQ of 46. Assessment by means of the SRZ and SMZ scales at the end of the observation period yielded an SRZ-Total of 5H and an SMZ-Total of 6H. Determined on the basis of the data from her file, the girl's score on the PDD-MRS was 14; classification: PDD; diagnosis: PDD.

In spite of much personal attention the girl remained hyperactive, short-tempered, elusive and unmanageable. Medication (successively pimozide and trifluperidol) was ineffective. After discharge she was placed into an institution for mentally retarded persons. Two years later the institution's staff decided that she no longer needed this kind of care; she was then placed into a home for children with autism and other behavioural problems. There she was given speech therapy, kinesitherapy and some training in basic reading skills; she developed a special talent for memorizing dates and for calculating the day of the week for any date. However, she remained a loner; she had unpredictable temper tantrums and fits of rage, during which she used to bite her hand; at times she was grumpy or defiant. By then haloperidol had been prescribed. When at the age of nine she was above the age limit laid down for this setting she was placed into a foster home. At the time of writing she is eleven years old and still lives there. She gives many problems, both at home and at the school for trainable and educable mentally retarded children. She rebels against whatever she is requested to do, is defiant, and has violent temper tantrums. She has preoccupations such as using foul language and displays extreme panic reactions. Her contact-making is almost exclusively provocative. The school does not see a way out any more; at home handling and guiding her require endless tact, heedfulness and tolerance. The only hope still left is that next year the secondary school for special education will be able to find a more successful approach. Her current score on the PDD-MRS is 14 (classification: PDD).

Her foster parents, who are really doing an admirable job, indicate that the situation is definitely becoming unbearable and that placement into an institution may soon prove to be inevitable.

II.5.3.2.4 Placement history of mildly mentally retarded PDD children

This group consists of 44 children. Of these, 21 children had been at a day-care centre for at least six months; two children had been in a therapeutic nursery; the remaining 21 children had attended a mainstream nursery school. Four children attended a mainstream primary school for at least six months, two attended a remedial school, 25 attended a school for educable mentally retarded children, 28 attended a school for trainable mentally retarded children, and six attended a secondary school for special education. Some further information regarding the attendance figures for these two types of school seems pertinent. As for the schools for educable mentally retarded children, nineteen children began their primary school careers here, but only seven of them managed to complete the course; of the six children who joined the school in mid-course, four managed to complete the course. As for the schools for trainable mentally retarded children, again nineteen children began their primary school careers here; four children left a school for trainable mentally retarded children in mid-course in order to attend a school for educable mentally retarded children; two of them eventually returned to a school of the original type; eleven children joined a school for trainable mentally retarded children in mid-course after having left a school for educable mentally retarded children. To all appearances then, moving down a level benefitted these children.

As far as living facilities are concerned, twenty of the 44 children (roughly 45%) currently either live in an institution for mentally retarded persons or are on a waiting list for such a facility (three young adults who are considered high-priority cases find themselves in this position, i.e., two persons aged 22 who currently live in a group home and one person of nineteen who still lives at home). The age at admission ranges from 6-22 years, with an average age of 14 years (taking the present age of the three persons who are on waiting lists as the age of admission). Of the remaining 24 subjects, thirteen live with their parents (aged 27, 26, 23, 21, 20, 17, 17, 17, 14, 13, 10, 8 and 7 years); three (aged 24, 24 and 34 years) live more or less independently on their own; three (aged 22, 24 and 27 years) live in a group home; four (aged 20, 18, 17 and 15 years) live in a group home for children, and one person (aged sixteen) lives in a setting specialized in the training and socialization of autistic adolescents of normal or almost normal intelligence. Of the other daytime facilities should be mentioned day-care centres for mentally retarded adults (attended by six persons), sheltered workshops (attended by two persons) and individualized vocational training (attended by two persons).

Going by the judgement of current professional helpers, four of the 24 subjects will have to be placed into an institution for mentally retarded persons in due time; for fifteen subjects such a placement will definitely not be necessary; regarding four persons the kind of accommodation needed in future cannot yet be determined; regarding one person no answer was received regarding the question about future prospects.

191

The placement history of the mildly mentally retarded PDD children is summarized in the table below.

At home	At home + Nursery or KDV**	At home + MLK*** or ZMLK****	AZI* At home + Sec. special school or Vocational school	AZI* At home/group home + Day-care centre or Workshop
At: 0	3-4	6	14	18

*	AZI	=	General institution for mentally retarded persons
**	KDV	=	Day-care centre for mentally retarded children
***	MLK	=	School for educable mentally retarded children
****	ZMLK	=	School for trainable mentally retarded children

In what follows, three examples of placement histories will be presented by way of illustration.

Subject No. 003: boy; age 4 years; mildly retarded; PDD-AD

This boy displayed a developmental delay at an early stage; he could not sit before he was twelve months old, was unresponsive to other people, and only smiled to himself. No etiological explanation could be found in the mother's pregnancy or delivery or in the boy's extensively examined physical condition. The main reasons for his admittance to the Eekwal observation home were his extreme rigidity, panic, short-temperedness, absence of usual interests (while on the other hand he was obsessively interested in such things as twigs and leaves), and sudden shifts of mood. He had recently started going to a nursery school for part of the day, where he seemed to open up a little.

Tested with the Merrill-Palmer Scale, which mainly tests performance skills and is therefore known to give a flattering picture, he scored a mental age of 3-4 and an IQ of 73. Determined on the basis of the data from his file, his score on the PDD-MRS was 17; classification: PDD; diagnosis: PDD.

This boy had clearly been pushed too hard to behave in a normal way. When the demands made on him were drastically lowered his behaviour grew much better, though not changing fundamentally. In fact, he remained a very strange, highly irritable, rigid and inaccessible child. Medication did not seem appropriate.

The advice given on discharge was to let him remain at the nursery school. Overdemanding, especially in emotional respects, had to be avoided. He needed a safe and secure environment. Some measures concerning practical management were suggested. Follow-up observation was arranged to take place in one-and-a-half years so as to provide these very cooperative parents with further support and to help them in selecting a suitable primary school.

According to plan, the boy was readmitted when he was six-and-a-half years old. He had made quite some progress in language skills and was more adaptable, but was still a rigid and unresponsive loner and occasionally reacted with inexplicable panic to quite ordinary things.

Tested with the Stanford-Binet (which in fact is more suitable to assess academic skills) he obtained a mental age of 4-5 and an IQ of 67.

Re-observation at the Eekwal observation home resulted in the following recommendations: keep demands simple and understandable; avoid overdemanding; give the boy ample time to adapt to new situations; accept some of his unusual habits; place him into a school for educable mentally retarded children in the near future.

When the boy was almost nine-and-a-half years old, he was readmitted for a third time. By then he had attended a school for educable mentally retarded children for two years. Initially his behaviour had become less problematic and he had made some progress in academic skills;

subsequently, however, his behavioural problems started all over again and his school achievements came to a standstill. He now sought a great deal of attention from the people around him, time and again came up with new preoccupations (staircases and corridors; the concepts high, deep and faraway, etc.), and remained an absolute loner.

Retested with the Stanford-Binet he now obtained a mental age of 5-5 and an IQ of 56. On the WISC his IQ was 54 (verbal IQ 60, performance IQ 61). On the SRZ he obtained an SRZ-Total of 7H (standard mark based on the norm laid down for institutions for mentally retarded persons), a rather low score in view of his intelligence level (although this level was itself slightly declining). The boy was more restless, inaccessible and stranger than before. He now used pimozide and thioridazine, prescribed to him by a non-clinical medical practitioner in the intervening period; however, when these drugs were discontinued at the observation home his behaviour did not grow appreciably worse. Subsequently haloperidol was tried to no avail. He was discharged without medication. According to the Eekwal-home team, the boy urgently needed a well-organized and tranquil environment, such as that offered by an institution for mentally retarded persons. However, his parents, well-intentioned people, were not ready to make this decision yet, despite the fact that they themselves were almost overstressed. On the advice of the Eekwal observation home the boy was now sent to a school for trainable mentally retarded children, as the school for educable mentally retarded children was clearly aiming at too high a level. By the time he was placed into an institution he was already eleven years old. At the moment of writing he is 26 years old and still living there. He uses thioridazine and needs an average amount of care. His current score on the PDD-MRS is 12 (classification: PDD) and he has been diagnosed as PDD.

Subject No. 010: boy; age 14 years; mildly retarded; PDD-AD; epilepsy

During the last two months of her pregnancy this boy's mother suffered from oedema and was on a salt-free diet. Three hours after a satisfactory delivery she developed an eclampsia which made hospital treatment mandatory. There is a family history of mild mental retardation, both on the father's and mother's sides; in addition, three members of the family have epilepsy. The mother had attended a school for educable mentally retarded children. The serious toxaemia in the final months of pregnancy and the family history of retardation can be seen as etiological factors. From the boy's physical examination no useful pointers emerged. Developmental lags had been clearly apparent from the child's first year onwards, notably in the area of vocalization. He did not speak his first words until he was about three years old. His first convulsion occurred at about eighteen months, but it is not known at what age he started to use anticonvulsants. On admission he used fenobarbital and fenytoin. After attending a nursery school for a few years he was sent to a school for educable mentally retarded children. Because of his speech problems he was subsequently referred to a residential school run by an institute for the deaf, where he stayed for two-and-a-half years. His speech and language skills improved considerably, but he had a parrot-like way of talking and an abnormal intonation. His level of intelligence was also found to be inadequate. The institute did not seem to be the right place for him and his parental home offered him insufficient stimulation. He was therefore placed into an institution for mildly mentally retarded children and adolescents with behavioural problems. He attended a school for educable mentally retarded children. When he was thirteen he joined a secondary school for special education; although a slow learner, he could keep pace with the programme. However, his behaviour became increasingly embarrassing, notably his strange obsessions (clocks, alarm clocks and women's clothing), his aloofness, his rigidity, and most of all his sudden impulsive reactions. About a year later he was admitted to the Eekwal observation home. Here he reacted favourably to a very clearly organised and tolerant environment, with some medication (such as clopenthixol) as an adjuvant.

Tested with the Stanford-Binet, he obtained a mental age of 7-2 and an IQ of 52 (there is reason to believe that he remained for many years at the level of a seven-year-old). Assessed by means of the Cain-Levine Social Competency Scale he was found to function on a level somewhere between mild and moderate mental retardation, but clearly below that level in the domains of Social Skills and Initiative. Determined on the basis of the data from his file, his score on the PDD-MRS was 15; classification: PDD; diagnosis: PDD.

After his discharge the boy went to an institution for mentally retarded persons where he was placed in a well-structured high-level group. He attended a school on the grounds of the institute. Contrary to all expectations, he continued to make progress at school. At nineteen years of age he scored an IQ of 68 on the Wechsler Adult Intelligence Scale (verbal IQ 69, performance IQ 74) and an SRZ-Total of 9 (standard mark based on the norm laid down for institutions for mentally retarded persons). After leaving school at nineteen he was employed at the institute's own workshop. His performance here was good, and six years later he joined a sheltered workshop. By then, all medication, including the anticonvulsants, had gradually been phased out. At the age of 27, he went to a group home for mentally retarded adults, and from there moved on to an annexe. At the moment of writing he is 34 years old and lives alone with some supervision. He is still a loner. His monotonous way of speaking and curious metallic voice have remained; his main preoccupations are kilometre distances and young children (whose companionship he seeks while being at the same time extremely fearful of being fooled by them). He is still a very rigid person, adhering to fixed patterns, and is painstakingly house-proud. He needs an average amount of care. His current score on the PDD-MRS is 10 (classification: PDD).

Subject No. 045: boy; age 2 years; mildly retarded; PDD-AD

During her pregnancy this boy's mother frequently used sedatives. She had to follow a salt-free diet (just as she had during her four previous pregnancies). The baby was born by caesarian section. Initially the child looked normal, although he was extremely active; after a while, however, a visual impairment was suspected because he gave no normal eye-to-eye contact and did not smile at the people around him. His mother, being depressed, was seldom affectionate towards him and tended to leave him to his own devices.

On admission this boy was restless, short-tempered and impatient. His contact-making was highly insufficient and he displayed many stereotypies. He rarely practised his limited vocabulary of three words (dad, mum and hello). Detailed examination failed to reveal any etiological indication; the role of the far from ideal upbringing cannot be fully ignored.

The boy stayed at the Eekwal observation home for ten months. He received intensive treatment, both in the group and individually (including the operant language training programme developed by Lovaas). His behaviour improved considerably: he was dry by day, became less short-tempered and irritable, his play became more varied, and his verbal imitation and active vocabulary grew considerably. However, he remained extremely aloof and rigid, and had much difficulty in adapting to persons and circumstances.

On the advice of the Eekwal observation-home team he was placed into an institution for mentally retarded persons which had a special ward for autistic children where the most could be made of his developmental potential.

Tested on discharge with the Griffiths (generally yielding scores of approx. 10% above the actual level), he obtained a mental age of 2-4 and a GQ of 67, a slight improvement when compared with the results of nine months earlier. Determined on the basis of the data from his file, his score on the PDD-MRS was 10; classification: PDD; diagnosis: PDD.

After a two-year stay at the institution, his father, feeling that the boy was failing to make further progress, wanted to have him back at home. He went to a nursery school, but not a year had gone by before this turned out to be a failure. The therapeutic nursery which was subsequently tried could not take care of him for much longer. A school for educable mentally retarded children was similarly unsuccessful. As the boy became very short-tempered, violent and pushy, he was placed into a child psychiatric setting. After staying there for six years he was placed into a setting for autistic adolescents; three years later he had to return to a psychiatric hospital on account of his acute behavioural problems. At the moment of writing the boy is nineteen years old and is staying in a short-term residential facility, pending his placement into an institution for mentally retarded persons. Going by the information received from his father, he is still very short-tempered and cannot stand any interference in his affairs; he has acquired some reading and writing proficiency and has mastered the basic principles of counting with

194

money. In the current residential setting he is doing rather well. He needs an average amount of care and uses pipamperone. His current score on the PDD-MRS is 10 (classification: PDD) and he has been diagnosed as non-PDD.

II.5.3.2.5   Relationship between level of functioning and placement history
Table II.5.2 summarizes the findings discussed in the foregoing sections.

Table II.5.2 Distribution of follow-up placements into institutions of former Eekwal-home PDD children by level of functioning (with and without prospective placements)

Level of mental retardation	n	Persons currently living in institutions			Persons currently in residential care plus thos likely to be so in the near future	
		n	Perc.	Average age at placement	n	Perc.
Profound	8	7	88	7 years	8	100
Severe	42	41	98	8 years	42	100
Moderate	41	32	78	11 years	36	88
Mild	44	20	45	14 years	24	56
Total	135	100	74	11 years	110	81

As the table shows, a high proportion of all former Eekwal-home children is currently living in an institution for mentally retarded persons. Subdividing the entire group into four groups in terms of level of functioning reveals that this level affects the proportion of placements and the age at which placement occurred.

The statistical significance of the two relationships was tested. The two-tailed values (unless explicitly stated otherwise) are presented in Tables II.5.3 and II.5.4. Severely and profoundly mentally retarded children were lumped together because there was only a small proportion of profoundly mentally retarded persons in the sample.

Table II.5.3 Relationship between level of functioning of PDD children and the age at which residential placement takes place

Level of mental retardation	Age		
	0-11 years	12 years and older	
Profound + severe	41	7	
Moderate	19	13	
Mild	7	13	
Total	67	33	100

Chi-square = 17.47; df = 2; p = <.001

195

Evidently, the lower the level of functioning, the sooner a mentally retarded child with a PDD tends to be placed into residential care.

Table II.5.4 Relationship between level of functioning of PDD children and the proportion of placements into residential care

Level of mental retardation	Placement into residential care	At home or elsewhere	
Profound + severe	48	2	
Moderate	32	9	
Mild	20	24	
Total	100	35	135

Chi-square = 31.62; df = 2; p = <.0001

Evidently, the lower the level of functioning, the higher the chance that a mentally retarded PDD child lives in residential care.

As a matter of fact, *profoundly and severely mentally retarded* PDD persons ultimately have a 100% chance of being placed into an institution. However, this same percentage is also likely to apply to profoundly and severely mentally retarded persons without a PDD. The average ages at which residential placement took place, which in the Eekwal study were found to be seven and eight years respectively for the two categories, may be more indicative. In order to compare profoundly and severely mentally retarded persons with and without a PDD with respect to age of placement into residential care, the 1978 figures have been traced for all profoundly and severely mentally retarded Dutch persons. (The year 1978 was chosen because it lies exactly in the middle of the period covered by the Eekwal follow-up study.) In 1978 the average age at which profoundly retarded persons were placed into residential care was 13.6 years (standard deviation 14.43); for severely retarded persons this figure was 20.8 years (standard deviation 15.97). The national figures apply to mentally retarded persons with and without a PDD. As has been emphasized in Chapter II.2 and will be re-emphasized in Part III, mentally retarded persons with a PDD display many behavioural problems which themselves represent reason enough for placement into residential care, regardless of level of functioning. Moreover, a considerable proportion of the total population of mentally retarded persons is found to display pervasive developmental disorders, as will be demonstrated in Chapter III.2. There is therefore every reason to assume that the average age at which profoundly and severely mentally retarded children with a PDD are placed into residential care lies well below that of corresponding categories without a PDD.

In the Eekwal follow-up study a remarkably high percentage of *moderately* and *mildly* mentally retarded PDD children was found to live in residential care. The exact difference with the corresponding national percentages (covering both PDD and non-PDD persons) cannot be indicated. However, for the mild range of retardation a rough estimate can be made on the basis of a study by Verbraak (1979). The figures presented in his study are in fact estimates, but the period involved, while being slightly longer, is about the same as that covered by the Eekwal follow-up study. According to this study, there was then a total of about seventy thousand mildly retarded persons in the Netherlands, about two thousand or 3% of whom lived in residential care. In reality this percentage may be thrice as high, but even then the difference with the 45% mildly mentally retarded PDD persons currently living in residential care (prospective placements not included) found in the Eekwal follow-up study is enormous.

According to national statistics, in 1978 the mean age of moderately mentally retarded persons at institutionalization was 24.8 years (standard deviation 21.94) and the mean age at residential placement of mildly mentally retarded persons was 24.7 years (standard deviation 15.57). (Figures provided by the SIG, the Dutch register for mental-health care.) The difference with what was found in the Eekwal follow-up study is very great indeed, considering that in the moderate range of mental retardation the mean age at residential placement was about eleven years and in the mild range about fourteen years. (The fact that placement into a short-term facility was in some cases counted as placement into residential care carries little weight, as this concerns only a small number of persons in the study.) All in all, it seems fair to conclude that moderately and mildly mentally retarded PDD persons are also placed into residential care at a much earlier age than those without a PDD.

II.5.3.3   *Placement history of former Eekwal-home children of two different age-groups*

The follow-up data also allow us to compare the careers of adult and non-adult former Eekwal-home children, which may reveal changes in the care field. Nowadays, for instance, many PDD children and adolescents receive home-training from an autism team for a longer or shorter period, but such a service hardly existed twenty years ago. If more help is available and the professional level of help is also higher, one may expect a decline of residential placements and a rise in the age at which placements take place.

Moreover, the two age categories may also differ in terms of the gravity of their behavioural problems. As a matter of fact, some investigators, among them Gillberg and Steffenburg (1987), report that autistic children tend to show an aggravation of symptoms at puberty. If the same holds true for the present sample, this would be reflected in differences in placement history between, on the one hand, the group of non-adult subjects (many of whom have not yet reached puberty), and, on the other hand, adult subjects.

An overview of the facilities into which the two broad age-categories of the follow-up sample have been placed will be presented in Sections II.5.3.3.1 and II.5.3.3.2; in Section II.5.3.3.3 a comparison will be made between these two age-categories.

*II.5.3.3.1   Placement history of mentally retarded PDD adults who in their
            childhood were seen at the Eekwal observation home*

In the present section the term adult refers to persons above the age of twenty. Turning twenty marks some important changes in the social position of a
Dutch mentally retarded person. Beyond that age it is no longer possible to
attend a school for trainable mentally retarded children nor to live in a
group home for mentally retarded children (although in fact this latter rule is
often stretched due to the lack of suitable follow-up living facilities).

Of the initial Eekwal-home sample, 66 adult persons could be traced.
Data concerning follow-up intervals are presented in Table II.5.5.

Table II.5.5 Follow-up intervals of 66 adult mentally retarded PDD persons
who in childhood had been seen at the Eekwal observation home

Interval in years	Number of persons	Interval in years	Number of persons	Interval in years	Number of persons
9	2	15	5	19	5
12	4	16	5	20	6
13	1	17	9	21	5
14	4	18	16	22	4

The follow-up interval ranges from 9-22 years, with a mean of 17.3 and a
median of 18. At the end of the follow-up period the average age of these 66
subjects was 23.7 years, standard deviation 3.35.

Table II.5.6 presents the current places of living of these 66 adult subjects.

Table II.5.6 Level of functioning and current place of living of 66 adult mentally retarded PDD persons who in childhood had been seen at the Eekwal
observation home

Level of mental retardation	Current place of living					Percentage institu-tionalized	Total
	Independent	Supervised	Parental home	Group home	Institution		
Profound	-	-	-	-	2	100	2
Severe	-	-	-	-	15	100	15
Moderate	-	-	4	-	21	84	25
Mild	2	1	5	4	12	54	24
Total	2	1	9	4	50	75.7	66

One of the four persons who was in fact living in a group home for mentally
retarded children was nevertheless counted as living in a group home for
adults (as this person had been on a waiting list for such a facility for quite
some time). Three persons who at the time lived in group homes for mentally retarded persons have nevertheless been counted as living in an institu-

tion, as they, on account of their behavioural problems, occupied high-priority places on waiting lists for such a facility.

As the table shows, the proportion of subjects living in residential care is high at all levels of functioning and is bound to be even higher in the near future. Nevertheless, the figures may still be on the low side. In fact, institutional placement seems near at hand for another five subjects. Two of these subjects are still living at home but are very likely to be placed into residential care. Two others are also still living at home and will certainly be so placed. One person, a 22-year-old woman now at a psychiatric clinic for serious behavioural problems, was placed into a group home a year ago, which was probably not a suitable environment for her considering that she had had similar problems twice before. These five persons were not regarded as institutionalized because they had not yet been placed on a formal waiting list.

The fifty PDD adults who at follow-up lived in residential care were on average 11.3 years old when institutionalized. In Table II.5.7 the four levels of mental retardation are compared in terms of average age at placement.

Table II.5.7 Level of functioning and age at institutionalization of fifty adult PDD persons who in childhood had been seen at the Eekwal observation home

Level of mental retardation	Numbers	Age at placement into residential care	
		Average age in years	Standard deviation
Profound	2	6.0	0.0
Severe	15	8.3	2.99
Moderate	21	11.7	5.29
Mild	12	14.8	5.01
Total	50	11.3	4.37

The figures given above indicate that level of functioning plays an important role with respect to the age at which a person will be placed into residential care. (For a more general discussion of these findings see also Section II.5.3.2.5).

The different types of accommodation into which the 66 PDD adults, subdivided according to their level of functioning, are likely to be placed ultimately (for instance, when their parents are no longer able to take care of them) are presented in Table II.5.8. However, these figures, which are based on prognoses made by current professional helpers and - in some cases - parents, should be regarded with due reserve.

Table II.5.8 Level of functioning and type of accommodation into which 66 adult PDD persons, who in childhood had been seen at the Eekwal observation home, are expected to live ultimately

Level of mental retardation	Place of living					Percentage institutionalized	Total
	Independent	Supervised	Parental home	Group home	Institution		
Profound	-	-	-	-	2	100	2
Severe	-	-	-	-	15	100	15
Moderate	-	-	-	-	25	100	25
Mild	2	1	-	7	14	58	24
Total	2	1	-	7	56	84.9	66

As the table shows, the expectation is that only seven persons (10.6%) will ultimately live in a group home, whereas 56 persons (84.9%) will ultimately live in an institution. Only a small minority will be able to live more or less on their own.

II.5.3.3.2   *Placement history of young and adolescent mentally retarded PDD persons subsequent to their stay at the Eekwal observation home*

In the present section information will be provided about the placement history of 69 former Eekwal-home children who had not yet reached adulthood at follow-up. The data are arranged in the same way as those for adults in the previous section.

At follow-up the mean age of the 69 non-adult subjects was 14.8 years, standard deviation 3.87. In calculating these figures, two subjects of the initial sample who had died at the ages of fourteen and seventeen were regarded as having that same age at follow-up.

The current places of living of these 69 children are presented in Table II.5.9. The two children who had died in the intervening period were in the present context regarded as living in residential care, which was in fact the situation until their deaths; one child was moderately and the other mildly mentally retarded; it may be assumed that had they lived they would have remained in residential care. Four children (aged nineteen, nineteen, fifteen and eleven) who are currently living with their parents but have high-priority places on waiting lists for institutions have been counted as living in an institution for mentally retarded persons.

Table II.5.9 Relationship between level of functioning and current place of living of 69 non-adult former Eekwal-home children

Level of mental retardation	Current place of living			Percentage institu-tionalized	Total
	Parental home	Group home	Insti-tution		
Profound	1	-	5	83	6
Severe	1	-	26	96	27
Moderate	5	-	11	69	16
Mild	8	4	8	40	20
Total	15	4	50	72.5	69

Again, the number of subjects living in residential care is bound to increase in the future; to be more precise, about half of the subjects currently living at home must, according to the reports received, be placed into residential care sooner or later.

The fifty PDD children currently living in an institution were on average 9.5 years old when institutionalized. In Table II.5.10 the four levels of mental retardation are compared in terms of average age at placement.

Table II.5.10 Relationship between level of functioning and age at institutionalization of fifty non-adult PDD persons previously seen at the Eekwal observation home

Level of mental retardation	Numbers	Age at placement into residential care	
		Average age in years	Standard deviation
Profound	5	8.0	1.40
Severe	26	8.6	3.01
Moderate	11	9.1	4.09
Mild	8	14.1	3.94
Total	50	9.5	3.14

To summarize, again it has been found that the lower the level of functioning the greater the chance that a person will be placed into residential care and the younger this person will be when so placed.

II.5.3.3.3   *Comparison between adult and non-adult persons previously seen at the Eekwal observation home*

The findings presented in the foregoing two sections can now be compared.

In general, level of functioning clearly affects both placement into residential care and age at placement. This overall conclusion should be kept in mind whilst we compare the results in more detail.

It is found that in both the adult and non-adult groups the subgroups of *profoundly* and *severely* mentally retarded persons display hardly any difference with respect to the proportions of those in institutions and their average age of institutionalization, as can be seen by comparing Table II.5.6 with II.5.9 and Table II.5.7 with II.5.10. Consequently the profoundly and severely retarded subgroups may be lumped together in both age categories. The first fact which then emerges is that all adult profoundly and severely retarded persons live in institutions, their average age at placement being 8.0 years. Secondly, 93.9% of the non-adult profoundly and severely retarded persons are found to live in institutions, their average age of placement being 8.5 years. From this it seems that the proportion of placements into residential care has slightly declined and age at placement has slightly increased. These shifts may be related to various developments. Nowadays parents receive better guidance on management at home, day-care centres accept more children of low and very low levels of functioning and care for them for longer periods. The statistical significance of the differences was tested; the results are presented in Tables II.5.11 and II.5.12.

Table II.5.11 Type of accommodation of 17 adult and 33 non-adult profoundly and severely mentally retarded PDD persons

Place	Adults	Children	
Institution	17	31	
Elsewhere	0	2	
Total	17	33	50

Chi-square = 1.07; ns

In both age categories the number of subjects living elsewhere is too low to make testing sufficiently satisfactory (in spite of the fact that the number of cases lies above the stated minimum of 40). Be that as it may, statistical testing confirms what a cursory look causes one to suspect, namely that the difference is definitely not significant.

Table II.5.12 Age at institutionalization of 17 adult and 31 non-adult profoundly and severely mentally retarded PDD persons

Age at placement	Adults	Children	
7 years or under	9	13	
8 years and over	8	18	
Total	17	31	48

Chi-square = 0.54; ns

The difference with respect to age at placement between the two age categories is again not found to be significant.

To summarize, neither better counselling of parents nor the changed admission policy of day-care centres seem to have affected residential placements of profoundly and severely mentally retarded PDD persons, as about the same proportions are placed into residential care as in the past and at the same average age.

As for *moderately* and *mildly* mentally retarded PDD persons, for whom figures are presented in Tables II.5.6, II.5.9, II.5.7, and II.5.10, more reliable testing of the statistical significance of differences in proportions of persons living in institutions and their average age at institutionalization is possible when the two groups are lumped together, as we did for the profoundly and severely retarded groups. However, the differences emerging between the two age categories are more prominent, and obviously the procedure is only legitimate when the proportions of moderately and mildly retarded persons are similar for both age categories. As shown in Table II.5.13, this is indeed the case.

Table II.5.13 Number of former Eekwal-home children of two levels of mental retardation within two age categories

Level of mental retardation	Adults	Children	
Moderate	25	16	
Mild	24	20	
Total	49	36	85

Chi-square = 0.36; ns

Table II.5.14 presents figures and statistical tests concerning the proportions of higher functioning mentally retarded persons living in institutions and elsewhere.

Table II.5.14 Type of accommodation of 85 adult and non-adult higher functioning mentally retarded PDD persons

Place	Adults	Children	
Institution	33	19	
Elsewhere	16	17	
Total	49	36	85

Chi-square = 1.85; ns

As the Table shows, there is no significant difference between the two age categories with respect to proportions of institutionalized persons. This finding in itself already suggests that the two groups will also show no difference with respect to age at institutionalization. However, in view of the fact that the quality of care in the field of mental retardation has improved it seems likely that mentally retarded persons will need *special accommodation* at a later age. In Table II.5.15 the figures and statistical tests with respect to higher functioning mentally retarded PDD persons are presented.

Table II.5.15 Age at institutionalization of 52 adult and non-adult higher functioning mentally retarded PDD persons

Age at placement	Adults	Children	
11 years or under	14	12	
12 years and over	19	7	
Total	33	19	52

Chi-square = 2.07; ns

Again, age at placement is found not to differ significantly between the two age categories.

We must therefore conclude that the provision of better care facilities for mentally retarded PDD persons of all levels of functioning has not led to less frequent placements into residential care or to placements at a later age. This last finding is especially striking, as national figures show a general postponement of institutional placements. A comparison of the years 1978 and 1988 reveals that mildly retarded persons were placed into residential care 6.1 years later, moderately retarded persons 4.0 years later, severely retarded persons 6.0 years later, and profoundly retarded persons five months later. Only with profoundly retarded persons is this difference found to be non-significant when tested by means of the t-test; the values for t and p for the mild, severe, and moderate levels of mental retardation were respectively: t = 3.31, p <.001; t = 2.39, p <.02; t = 3.40, p <.001. In view of these figures it is all the more remarkable that with former Eekwal-home PDD children the age at institutional placement was found not to have risen.

Contrary to what is reported by Gillberg and Steffenburg (1987), the results of the Eekwal follow-up study show no increase in behavioural problems of mentally retarded PDD persons at puberty. Persons in the profound and severe ranges were generally placed into residential care before reaching puberty, in fact at such an early age that puberty could not possibly have had anything to do with it; in the moderate and mild ranges a considerable number of persons lives in residential care (61.2% for the two groups combined) and half of them were institutionalized before reaching the age of twelve (see Tables II.5.14 and II.5.15).

II.5.3.4   *Placement history: comparing former Eekwal-home children with PDD-AD and those with PDD-NOS*

As will be recalled, the DSM-III-R distinguishes two categories of pervasive developmental disorder: PDD-AD and PDD-NOS. In the preceding sections about residential facilities these two categories were considered together. As PDD-AD may be assumed to be a more severe pervasive developmental disorder than PDD-NOS, differences will presumably emerge when these two subgroups are compared with respect to their placement history. It may be expected that the proportion of persons with PDD-AD living in institutions is higher than that of persons with PDD-NOS and that they were younger when institutionalized. Differences in placement frequencies can only be tested in the moderate and mild ranges of retardation; in the severe and profound ranges, level of functioning alone is the paramount factor. As for differences with respect to average age at placement, however, these are theoretically testable for the entire range of mental retardation.

Table II.5.16 presents figures and statistical tests concerning the proportions of mildly and moderately retarded persons with PDD-AD and those with PDD-NOS living in institutions and elsewhere.

Table II.5.16 Type of accommodation of higher functioning mentally retarded PDD-AD and PDD-NOS persons

Place	PDD-NOS	PDD-AD	
Institution	5	47	
Elsewhere	16	17	
Total	21	64	85

Chi-square = 16.40; p <.0001

As the table shows, within the ranges of mild and moderate retardation the proportion of institutionalized persons with PDD-AD is very significantly higher than that of institutionalized persons with PDD-NOS.

The five higher functioning PDD-NOS persons were on average 19.4 years old when placed into residential care (standard deviation 1.82). As the number of cases is small, testing cannot be other than rather unsatisfactory. As may be computed on the basis of the figures in Tables II.5.7 and II.5.10 the 47 higher functioning PDD-AD persons were placed into residential care at an average age of 11.5 years (standard deviation 4.13). This difference is at any rate considerable.

All in all, we must conclude that persons with PDD-NOS in the Eekwal follow-up study were institutionalized less frequently and at a later age than those with PDD-AD. The findings also confirm the hypothesis that PDD-AD is a more severe disorder than PDD-NOS.

II.5.3.5   *Indicators of current problem behaviour in former Eekwal-home children*

Four indicators were used to establish the presence of problem behaviour in former Eekwal-home children.

- The amount of time which is devoted to a person during staff discussions is an indication for existing behavioural problems.

- The amount of tact and heedfulness needed in the management of a person is an indication for mental vulnerability and instability.
- The use of psychotropic drugs is an indication for behavioural problems which are not amenable to other forms of treatment.
- Current outcomes on the PDD-MRS indicate whether or not autistic features are present and to what degree.

Each of the four indicators will be discussed separately in the next sections.

II.5.3.5.1 Do former Eekwal-home children require more staff discussion time because of their behavioural problems?
Current professional helpers in day-time or residential facilities were asked to estimate roughly how much time was spent by staff in discussing ways of dealing with the managemental problems of former Eekwal-home children. The data for 114 former Eekwal-home children are available in this regard. They are presented in Table II.5.17.

Table II.5.17 Frequency distribution of former Eekwal-home children by the amount of time which the staff spent discussing their behavioural problems

More than average time	Average time	Less than average time	Total
35	57	22	114

Assuming that the average discussion time devoted at staff meetings to an individual equals the time devoted to all individual problems divided by the total number of persons under their care, and that respondents are able to make a fair assessment of this time, the number of persons requiring more than average discussion time is theoretically the same as the number of those requiring less than average discussion time, which would result in a quotient of 1.0 for the two values. However, the figures for former Eekwal-home children given in Table II.5.17 yield a quotient of 1.6. In other words, the managemental problems of mentally retarded people with a PDD are found to require a comparatively large amount of time at staff meetings.

When the group investigated is divided into PDD-AD and PDD-NOS subgroups, the quotients are respectively 1.8 and 0.8. Figures and statistical test are presented in Table II.5.18.

Table II.5.18 Frequency distribution of former Eekwal-home PDD-AD and PDD-NOS children by the amount of time spent discussing their behavioural problems at staff meetings

Category of PDD	More than average time	Average or less than average time	
PDD-AD	31	59	
PDD-NOS	4	20	
Total	35	79	114

Chi-square = 2.81; ns

The table shows that the behavioural problems of persons with PDD-AD take up more time than those of persons with PDD-NOS; however, the difference is not significant.

II.5.3.5.2   *Do the behavioural problems of former Eekwal-home children require extra tact and heedfulness?*

Current professional helpers in day-time and residential facilities were asked to estimate roughly the amount of tact and heedfulness needed in the management of former Eekwal-home children. Data for 114 former Eekwal-home children are available in this regard. They are presented in Table II.5.19.

Table II.5.19 Frequency distribution of former Eekwal-home children by the amount of tact and heedfulness they require

More than average	Average	Less than average	Total
55	50	9	114

Again, the numbers of persons calling for more than average and those calling for less than average tact and heedfulness are theoretically equal, resulting in a quotient of 1.0 for the two values. However, the figures given in Table II.5.19 for former Eekwal-home children yield a quotient as high as 6.1. It may therefore be concluded that a mentally retarded person who in infancy or childhood has been classified as PDD may be expected to require a disproportionately large amount of tact and heedfulness throughout his life.

When the group investigated is divided into PDD-AD and PDD-NOS subgroups, the quotients found are respectively 8.0 and 2.3. This suggests that persons with PDD-AD require more tact and heedfulness than those with PDD-NOS. Figures and statistical test are presented in Table II.5.20.

Table II.5.20 Frequency distribution of former Eekwal-home PDD-AD and PDD-NOS children by the amount of tact and heedfulness they require

PDD-category	Amount of tact and heedfulness required		
	More than average	Average or less than average	
PDD-AD	48	42	
PDD-NOS	7	17	
Total	55	59	114

Chi-square = 4.43; p <.04

As the table shows, the number of PDD-AD persons requiring extra tact and heedfulness is significantly higher than that of PDD-NOS persons.

II.5.3.5.3   The use of psychotropic drugs at discharge and at the end of the follow-up period

The next issue concerning which current professional helpers in day-time or residential facilities were requested to provide information was the use of psychotropic drugs by former Eekwal-home children. In the context of the present study, the term psychotropic drug refers to neuroleptics, anxiolytics, hypnotics/sedatives, and antidepressants; methylfenidate, fenfluramine and similar drugs were regarded as psychotropic drugs if used as such. Anticonvulsants are not included; in fact they were rarely prescribed for the sole purpose of checking behavioural disturbances.

Usable returns were obtained for 122 former Eekwal-home children in this regard. These follow-up data were compared with data regarding which psychotropic drugs, if any, were prescribed to them at discharge from the observation home. Medication which had proved to be ineffective during the observation period was ignored. (In fact, more than two-thirds of these 122 children were prescribed psychotropic drugs on a tentative basis during their stay at the observation home.) Almost all children to whom medication was prescribed at discharge received their medication to treat semi-specific and non-specific behavioural problems which persisted in spite of a reduction of stimuli and demands. However, trifluperidol and pimozide were also prescribed with the explicit aim of reducing stereotyped behaviours and promoting interest in the surrounding world and a willingness to make contact, on the basis of the experience gained with these drugs at the Eekwal home. (Pimozide had been tried in collaboration with the manufacturer before it was generally available; trifluperidol has now been out of production for a long time.)

In Table II.5.21 a list is presented of psychotropic drugs prescribed at discharge. Drugs prescribed to just one or two children are placed under the heading 'miscellaneous.' The table shows that 35 of the 122 children (22.9%) used medication at discharge. We may therefore conclude that psychotropic drugs play a minor role in the treatment of mentally retarded children with a PDD. Fenfluramine, nicotinamide and clonidine are not mentioned in the table; these were novel drugs in 1988, the year in which this study was completed; moreover, if applied at all, these drugs proved to be rather ineffective.

Table II.5.21 Psychotropic drugs used by 122 mentally retarded PDD children; drugs are listed in descending order of frequency

Drug	Frequency
Pimozide	13
Trifluperidol	8
Haloperidol	8
Thioridazine	3
Miscellaneous	11

Frequency of children using psychotropic drugs n = 35
(Frequency of children using two kinds of drugs n = 8)

Table II.5.22 Psychotropic drugs used by 122 mentally retarded PDD children at follow-up; drugs are listed in descending order of frequency

Drug	Frequency
Levomepromazine	12
Haloperidol	11
Pipamperone	11
Pimozide	10
Clopenthixol	5
Oxazepam	3
Miscellaneous	12

Frequency of children using psychotropic drugs n = 47
(Frequency of children using two kinds of drugs n = 13; frequency of children using three kinds of drug n = 2)

As Table II.5.22 shows, 47 of 122 former Eekwal-home children (38.5%) were found to use psychotropic drugs at follow-up. Fifteen children (31.9%) used two or three kinds of drugs. Only one person used a non-specific drug (clonidine) as a psychoactive agent; this person also used a psycho-pharmacon proper.

To find out whether the figures given above are normal, below average or above average compared with the figures in the mental retardation field in general, I consulted data provided by the study carried out by Van Essen and Romein (1985), which is based on a large random sample. These investigators found that 22.2% of the residents of Dutch institutions for mentally retarded persons used psychotropic drugs, and 31.4% of these used more than one kind of psychotropic drug. This is considerably less than the 38.5% found in the Eekwal follow-up study. However, the comparison falls short, as only a proportion of the Eekwal follow-up subjects live in institutions; others live at home or in a group home. On the highly plausible assumption that subjects displaying the most serious problem behaviours will by now have been placed into institutions and that it will rarely be the case that prescription of psychotropic drugs alone will be enough to avert institutionalization, it seems very unlikely that mentally retarded persons with a PDD who live at home can continue to do so as a result of a more extensive use of psychotropic drugs. The actual situation may therefore be even less favourable than that suggested by the 38.5% found in the Eekwal study. A more adequate comparison with the figures given by Van Essen and Romein might reveal a more serious state of affairs. To this end the 89 institutionalized subjects of the Eekwal follow-up sample were singled out. Of these, 42 persons (47.2%) used psychotropic drugs, and fifteen persons (37.5%) used more than one kind of drug. These are indeed substantially higher percentages. The figures found in the two studies concerning institutionalized persons can be reliably tested. The results are presented in Table II.5.23.

Table II.5.23 The use of psychotropic drugs among institutionalized mentally retarded persons: comparison of a general sample with a sample of persons with a PDD

Use of psychopharmaco-logical drugs	Mentally retarded residents in general	Mentally retarded PDD residents	
Using drugs	184	42	
Not using drugs	643	47	
Total	827	89	916

Chi-square = 26.90; p <.0001

The table shows that the proportion of institutionalized mentally retarded persons with a PDD using psychotropic drugs is much greater than that of the general population of institutionalized mentally retarded persons (which obviously includes PDD persons). Furthermore, Van Essen and Romein report that 61.2% of the persons in their sample known to display behavioural disorders used psychotropic drugs, which is approximately the same figure as that found in the Eekwal follow-up study.

The finding that 42 of the 47 users of psychotropic drugs live in institutions strongly suggests that drug treatment is associated with the kind of setting into which a person is placed. The relevant figures and statistical test are presented in Table II.5.24.

Table II.5.24 Relationship between type of setting and use of psychotropic drugs

Use of psychopharmaco- logical drugs	Living in institutions	Living elsewhere	
Using drugs	42	5	
Not using drugs	47	28	
Total	89	33	122

Chi-square = 10.43; p <.002

The table shows that using psychotropic drugs occurs very significantly more frequently in institutionalized mentally retarded PDD persons than in PDD persons living elsewhere.

If PDD-AD is a more serious disorder than PDD-NOS, subdividing the group into subgroups of those with PDD-AD and those with PDD-NOS is likely to yield a higher proportion of PDD-AD users of psychotropic drugs. The relevant figures and statistical test are presented in Table II.5.25.

Table II.5.25 Frequency distribution of former Eekwal-home PDD-AD and PDD-NOS children currently using psychotropic drugs

Use of psychopharmaco- logical drugs	PDD-AD	PDD-NOS	
Using drugs	41	6	
Not using drugs	52	23	
Total	93	29	122

Chi-square = 5.11; p <.03

In terms of percentages, psychotropic drugs are used by 20.7% of PDD-NOS persons against 44.1% of PDD-AD persons. This difference is statistically significant.

Van Essen and Romein found that the psychotropic drugs prescribed to persons in their sample were mainly neuroleptics, especially haloperidol and levomepromazine, less frequently periciazine, thioridazine and pipamperone. In the Eekwal follow-up study this general picture is confirmed, the only exception being pimozide, which was found to be the most frequent drug used at discharge and very frequently prescribed at follow-up (see Tables II.5.21 and II.5.22). As a matter of fact, pimozide continues to this day to be the drug of choice for the majority of persons with autism and autistic-like conditions.

The number of psychotropic drugs used per person was found to be 1.4 in the Eekwal follow-up study, and 1.5 in that by Van Essen and Romein, which represents a negligible difference.

Information about changing patterns in the use of psychotropic drugs beyond childhood is provided in Section II.5.4.3.

II.5.3.5.4   Results of assessment by means of the PDD-MRS at discharge and follow-up

II.5.3.5.4.a General remarks

The behavioural features all former Eekwal-home PDD children at discharge were assessed with the PDD-MRS on the basis of the data from their files. These same files had been used earlier to classify the same children in terms of the DSM-III-R system. An independent assessment of 108 former Eekwal-home children was made by Elly van der Horst, educational psychologist, again on the basis of their files, in order to check bias on the part of the present author. On average, the scores she arrived at were one point under those of the present author; the product moment correlation coefficient between these assessments was .86. The author's assessments may therefore be regarded as sufficiently objective to be used for further comparisons.

The member of staff (the psychologist, educational psychologist, doctor of medicine or psychiatrist) currently supervising the subjects of this sample, was asked to make assessments by means of the PDD-MRS for the follow-up. (The PDD-MRS, unlike many other scales in the mental retardation field such as the SRZ, SGZ and SMZ, is supposed to be administered by psychological or medical experts rather than by group attendants). Regrettably, however, either through necessity or out of sheer habit, the assessments of some subjects were partly or even completely made by teachers and - in the case of subjects who were more or less living independently - guardians. In retrospect, it must be concluded that the instructions given to the respondents participating in this follow-up study were not clear enough on this point. Consequently, the results of the two assessments are not fully comparable. To be more precise, scores in the follow-up assessments are likely to be lower than they would have been had they been determined by medical or psychological experts (Kraijer, 1990). However, although a meaningful comparison between the absolute values obtained at the two assessments is not possible, it is possible to compare the successive scores of subgroups.

A high score on the PDD-MRS indicates a large number of autistic features (i.e., highly autistic behaviour); a low score indicates a small number of autistic features (i.e., only mildly or no autistic behaviour).

Usable follow-up returns concerning PDD-MRS scores were obtained for 116 subjects. For these subjects the interval between the two assessments ranges from 2-22 years, with a median of fourteen years.

In what follows, only those persons for whom two sets of scores are available (i.e., those obtained at discharge and at follow-up) will be considered.

II.5.3.5.4.b General relationship between PDD-MRS scores at discharge and at follow-up

As stated above, no comparison of the absolute values obtained in the two assessments can be made, as these values were probably arrived at in rather different ways. However, since in all likelihood imperfections in rating were randomly spread over the various subgroups and subcategories, a comparison of relative values is possible. To establish the correlation between relative values, ignoring absolute values, the product moment correlation coefficient is often used. Comparing the two assessments made for 116 subjects on the PDD-MRS yields a coefficient of .37. (At discharge: M = 12.33, s.d. = 3.16; at follow-up: M = 10.66, s.d. = 4.75.) Given that the median interval between the two assessments is fourteen years and that the homogeneous group of exclusively PDD cases implies 'restriction of range', the correlation is in fact surprisingly significant (p <.001).

II.5.3.5.4.c Comparison of the PDD-MRS scores of PDD-AD and PDD-NOS children

At discharge, ninety of the 116 subjects compared had been classified as PDD-AD and 26 had been classified as PDD-NOS. Table II.5.26 presents the average scores for the two assessments, the standard deviations and the two-tailed t-test.

Table II.5.26 Comparison of successive PDD-MRS scores for PDD-AD and PDD-NOS children

Assessment made	PDD-AD (n = 90)	PDD-NOS (n = 26)	t-test	p
At discharge	M = 13.09 s.d. = 2.71	M = 9.69 s.d. = 3.26	5.53	<.001
At follow-up	M = 11.43 s.d. = 4.59	M = 8.00 s.d. = 4.75	3.30	<.002

Comparing the PDD-MRS scores at the moment of discharge, those of PDD-AD children are found to be very significantly higher than those of PDD-NOS children; the difference between their follow-up scores is also significant. In other words, persons with PDD-AD continue to display more autistic features than those with PDD-NOS.

II.5.3.5.4.d Relationship between the PDD-MRS score and institutionalization

For a statistical testing of the differences between persons living inside and outside institutions with respect to scores on the PDD-MRS, it is meaningful to subdivide the total group into subgroups according to level of functioning. As reported in Sections II.5.3.3.1 and II.5.3.3.2, only the moderate and mild ranges of mental retardation contain sufficiently large numbers of institutionalized and non-institutionalized persons at follow-up. Profoundly and severely mentally retarded persons were almost exclusively living in institutions at the moment of follow-up. Consequently, this latter category has no relevance for the present issue. Of the 116 subjects considered (i.e., those whose follow-up PDD-MRS scores are known), 69 persons belong to the mild or moderate range of retardation. Within this range 47 persons were found to live in institutions, 22 persons elsewhere.

Of these two groups Table II.5.27 presents the average PDD-MRS scores at the moment of discharge and at follow-up, the standard deviations and the two-tailed t-test.

Table II.5.27 Successive PDD-MRS scores of mildly and moderately retarded former Eekwal-home children with a PDD: comparison between groups according to accommodation

Assessment made	In institutions (n = 47)		Elsewhere (n = 22)		t-test	p
At discharge	M =	12.74	M =	11.41		
	s.d. =	3.00	s.d. =	3.78	1.55	ns
At follow-up	M =	11.04	M =	8.00		
	s.d. =	5.06	s.d. =	4.98	2.30	<.03

As the table shows, persons living in institutions invariably have slightly higher PDD-MRS scores, but the difference is only significant at follow-up. In other words, PDD persons living in institutions display more autistic features than those living elsewhere.

II.5.3.5.4.e Relationship between the PDD-MRS score and age at
              institutionalization

Again, the total group had to be divided into subgroups according to level of functioning to make statistical testing meaningful. As demonstrated in II.5.3.3.3, only the moderately and mildly mentally retarded subgroups display fairly substantial differences with respect to average age at institutionalization. Therefore, only these categories are suitable for comparison with respect to the relationship between the PDD-MRS score and age at institutionalization. The age at which the 47 former Eekwal-home children belonging to the mild and moderate ranges of retardation were placed into institutions was found to correlate slightly with their PDD-MRS scores at the moment of discharge from the Eekwal observation home (product moment correlation coefficient $r = -.32$; $p < .03$). In other words, the higher the PDD-MRS score (i.e., the larger the number of autistic features) the earlier institutionalization takes place. However, at follow-up, fourteen years later (median value), there is no such correlation ($r = .08$; ns).

II.5.3.5.4.f Relationship between the PDD-MRS score and managemental
              problems indicated by the amount of staff discussion time

The presence of managemental problems with the 116 former Eekwal-home children for whom follow-up PDD-MRS scores are available was established on the basis of the information provided concerning how long the staff spent discussing them. Reportedly, the problems of 35 persons needed comparatively much attention, and those of 79 persons could be routinely dealt with. (For two persons no usable data were available.) Table II.5.28 presents the average PDD-MRS scores of these two subgroups at the moment of discharge and at follow-up, the standard deviations and the two-tailed t-test.

Table II.5.28 Successive PDD-MRS scores: comparison between persons according to amount of attention needed due to managemental problems (indicated by staff discussion time)

Assessment made	Requiring much time (n = 35)	Requiring normal time or less (n = 79)	t-test	p
At discharge	M = 12.97 s.d. = 2.99	M = 12.09 s.d. = 3.24	1.36	ns
At follow-up	M = 12.80 s.d. = 4.54	M = 9.96 s.d. = 4.44	3.10	<.003

The presence of managemental problems (indicated by amount of staff discussion time) is found to correlate only slightly (not significantly) with high PDD-MRS scores at discharge, but strongly with high PDD-MRS scores at follow-up.

II.5.3.5.4.g Relationship between the PDD-MRS score and the amount of
tact and heedfulness required
Of the 116 former Eekwal-home children for whom follow-up PDD-MRS scores are available, 55 persons reportedly required a large amount of tact and heedfulness in their management and 58 persons required a normal amount (usable data were lacking for three persons). Table II.5.29 presents the average PDD-MRS scores of these two subgroups at the moment of discharge and at follow-up, the standard deviations and the two-tailed t-test.

Table II.5.29 Successive PDD-MRS scores: comparison between persons in terms of amount of tact and heedfulness required

Assessment made	Requiring much tact and heedfulness (n = 55)	Requiring normal tact and heedfulnes (n = 58)	t-test	p
At discharge	M = 12.85 s.d. = 3.26	M = 11.91 s.d. = 3.08	1.56	ns
At follow-up	M = 12.38 s.d. = 4.25	M = 9.14 s.d. = 4.58	3.68	<.001

The amount of tact and heedfulness required is found to correlate only slightly (not significantly) with high PDD-MRS scores at discharge, but strongly with high PDD-MRS scores at follow-up.

II.5.3.5.4.h Relationship between the PDD-MRS score and the use of
psychotropic drugs
Of the 116 former Eekwal-home children for whom follow-up PDD-MRS

scores are available, 44 were reported to use psychotropic drugs at follow-up, 72 did not. Table II.5.30 presents the average PDD-MRS scores for these two subgroups at the moment of discharge and at follow-up, the standard deviations and the two-tailed t-test.

Table II.5.30 Successive PDD-MRS scores: comparison between users and non-users of psychotropic drugs

Assessment made	Users (n = 44)		Non-users (n = 72)		t-test	p
At discharge	M = 13.43		M = 11.67			
	s.d. = 2.53		s.d. = 3.18		3.09	<.004
At follow-up	M = 13.14		M = 9.15			
	s.d. = 3.43		s.d. = 4.30		5.20	<.001

There is a strong correlation between the use of psychotropic drugs and high PDD-MRS scores; this applies equally to the scores obtained at discharge and at follow-up fourteen years (median value) later.

II.5.4 Comparison with other follow-up studies

The present section will first focus on follow-up data concerning language skills, and subsequently on follow-up data of a more general nature.

II.5.4.1 *Acquisition of speech as a prognostic indicator*

A number of experts have stated that acquisition of speech before a particular age is an important prognostic indicator. Quite a few follow-up studies have been carried out to find out to what extent acquisition of speech before a particular age - which is generally taken to be about five years - is instrumental in predicting later outcome (Lotter, 1974a,b, 1978; DeMyer et al., 1973; Gillberg & Steffenburg, 1987; Chung et al., 1990; Kobayashi et al., 1992). The general conclusion is that prognosis is more favourable if speech is acquired before the age of six.

In the Eekwal follow-up sample information about the presence of expressive language skills before the age of six was available for 132 subjects. Expressive language was, in accordance with the PDD-MRS, considered to be absent when fewer than eight recognizable (single) words were used spontaneously and regularly. The group examined for this feature does include subjects with hearing defects, as in most cases the defects did not prevent them from acquiring at least rudimentary speech skills.

In all studies mentioned above a correlation was found to exist between level of functioning and acquisition of language skills; the higher the level of functioning the greater the chance for a child to develop expressive language skills before his or her sixth birthday. Table II.5.31 presents the numbers and percentages of children with and without speech, subdivided into the four ranges of mental retardation.

Table II.5.31 Frequency distribution of PDD children with and without expressive language skills acquired before age six according to level of mental retardation

Expressive language skills	Level of mental retardation				
	Profound	Severe	Moderate	Mild	
Speech	0	9	26	34	
No speech	8	32	15	8	
Total	8	41	41	42	132
Perc. no speech	100 %	78 %	37 %	19 %	

The percentages presented above suggest a strong correlation between level of functioning and presence of expressive language skills. Table II.5.32 presents the statistical test of these findings; the subgroups Profound and Severe have been combined.

Table II.5.32 Correlation between development of expressive language skills before age six in PDD children and level of mental retardation

Expressive language skills	Level of mental retardation			
	Profound + Severe	Moderate	Mild	
Speech	9	26	34	
No speech	40	15	8	
Total	49	41	42	132

Chi-square = 38.47; p <.00001

The correlation between level of functioning and development of expressive language skills before a child's sixth birthday proves to be highly significant.

In addition, it is important to point out that the percentage of non-PDD mentally retarded children who have not developed expressive language skills before the age of six may be assumed to be much lower than the percentage found in the present study. In my experience, about 50% of the severely mentally retarded children without a PDD are at the age of five not able to speak, whereas in the present study 78% of PDD children are unable to speak at that age; moderately and mildly retarded children without concurrent disabilities are predominantly able to speak by the age of five; by contrast, the present study finds 37% of PDD persons in the moderate range and 19% of PDD persons in the mild range of mental retardation unable to speak before the age of six. In other words, in mentally retarded children too, the development of expressive language skills seems to be seriously hampered by the presence of a PDD.

Again, it seems relevant to compare the PDD-AD and PDD-NOS subgroups of mentally retarded children. If on the continuum (or spectrum, if so preferred) of pervasive developmental disorders PDD-AD represents the most serious disorder, a higher proportion of PDD-AD persons will presumably not have developed expressive language skills before their sixth birthday. In Table II.5.33 the two subgroups of PDD-AD and PDD-NOS persons are compared in this respect; however, only those belonging to the mild and moderate ranges of retardation are singled out, as persons belonging to these ranges are usually able to speak before the age of six.

Table II.5.33 Frequency distribution of speaking and non-speaking moderately and mildly mentally retarded children according to type of pervasive developmental disorder

Expressive language skills	Pervasive developmental disorder		
	PDD-NOS	PDD-AD	
Speech	18	42	
No speech	2	21	
Total	20	63	83

Chi-square = 4.13; p <.05

As the table shows, PDD-NOS children are more likely to have acquired language skills by the age of five than PDD-AD children.

In Table II.5.34 the relevant figures are presented concerning the relationship between the acquisition of expressive language skills before the age of six and prognosis for future development. Again, later development has been estimated in terms of the types of setting into which subjects had been placed.

Table II.5.34 Frequency distribution of speaking and non-speaking former Eekwal-home PDD children according where they were living at follow-up

	Institution	Elsewhere	
Speech	40	29	
No speech	58	5	
Total	98	34	132

Chi-square = 20.02; p <.00001

Acquisition of speech before the age of six and placement history are found to correlate highly significantly, i.e., most persons who did not speak by that age were living in an institution at follow-up. However, the decisive factor in the figures presented above may have been the level of mental retardation, since almost all profoundly and severely mentally retarded persons are known to be placed into institutions in due time. To rule out this factor, the figures found for moderately and mildly mentally retarded persons are presented separately in Table II.5.35.

Table II.5.35 Frequency distribution of speaking and non-speaking moderately and mildly retarded former Eekwal-home PDD children according to where they were living at follow-up

	Institution	Elsewhere	
Speech	32	27	
No speech	19	5	
Total	51	32	83

Chi-square = 4.48; p <.04

As the table shows, the correlation between acquisition of speech before the age of six and placement history also holds when only the figures for moderately and mildly mentally retarded persons are considered.

II.5.4.2   *Comparison with findings reported by Lotter*

The results obtained in the Eekwal follow-up study are, as noted in II.5.2.2, best comparable with those of the studies done by Lotter (1974a,b) and Gillberg and Steffenburg (1987). These will be considered in the present section and that which follows.

In the two studies carried out by Lotter (1974a,b) figures are presented for a group of subjects with IQs below 55, subdivided into 21 'autistic' subjects, i.e., those who have strong signs of autism, and nine subjects with similar but less marked signs. At follow-up, these subjects were aged sixteen or eighteen years (his report was based on data from a cohort of autistic children identified in an epidemiological survey). Table II.5.36 presents the frequencies in two classes of follow-up outcomes found by Lotter. In this study the indication Poor/Very Poor outcome (the percentages of which are presented separately in the table) almost invariably implies placement into what Lotter terms a subnormality hospital, which roughly corresponds to what in the Eekwal-home study is called an institution for mentally retarded persons. Within the follow-up period of eight years none of the children placed into such a setting were discharged.

Table II.5.36 Outcome of children with IQs <55: children with strong signs of autism compared with children with less marked sings of autism (figures based on Lotter, 1974a,b)

Outcome	Strong signs of autism	Less marked signs of autism	Total
Good/Fair	2	2	4
Poor/Very Poor	19	7	26
Total	21	9	30
Perc. Poor/Very Poor	90.5 %	77.8 %	86.7 %

As will be noticed, the high percentages Poor/Very Poor outcome for the two categories are rather close (chi-square test is not suitable; Fisher exact probability test: ns). A possible explanation is that the two categories do not differ very much with respect to the severity of the disorders. Or, to put it another way, if classification had been done according to DSM criteria, children labelled 'autistic' would all have been classified as PDD-AD, while of the group described as having 'similar features' some children would also have been classified as PDD-AD and the remaining children as serious cases of PDD-NOS.

A comparison between the findings of Lotter's study and the Eekwal follow-up study is difficult to make for two other, although less serious, reasons. In the first place, Lotter's lower IQ group covers a slightly broader range than that created by lumping together the profound, severe and moderate ranges of the Eekwal follow-up study. However, the difference is only five IQ points. Secondly, the average age of the 135 subjects in the Eekwal follow-up study is 19.2 years, which is slightly above the average age of the subjects in Lotter's study. If only the group of 49 children and adolescents of the Eekwal follow-up study are considered, the average age is 14.8, which is slightly below Lotter's figure. These two averages will in all likelihood remain about the same if only persons in the profound, severe and moderate ranges of the Eekwal-home sample are considered (in other words, if the mild range is ignored). This procedure makes a comparison of the findings of the two studies possible. The figures and statistical test are presented in Table II.5.37; in this table the designation Poor/Very Poor corresponds with what was termed living in institutions in Tables II.5.2 and II.5.9.

Table II.5.37 The outcomes of profoundly, severely and moderately mentally retarded persons with a PDD; comparison between two follow-up studies

Outcome	Eekwal follow-up all ages	Eekwal follow-up children/adolescents	Study by Lotter
Poor/Very Poor	80	42	26
Other outcomes	11	7	4
Total	91	49	30
Perc. Poor/Very Poor	87.9 %	85.7 %	86.7 %

Chi-square = 0.03 and 0.01 (respectively); ns

As the table shows, the findings concerning the outcomes of PDD children are remarkably in agreement when comparing the Eekwal follow-up study with Lotter's.

In other respects the Eekwal follow-up study also confirms Lotter's findings concerning mentally retarded people, despite 'restriction of range', which makes significant associations less likely to occur. One such finding concerns prognosis. Lotter concluded - as did Rutter and Lockyer (1967) - that the two most important prognostic indicators for later outcome are IQ level and acquisition of expressive language. For its part, the Eekwal follow-up study found a strong association between level of functioning and placement history, both in terms of age at institutional placement and the percentage of institutional placements (see Tables II.5.3 and II.5.4). The same holds true for acquisition of expressive language skills before the age of six (see Tables II.5.34 and III.5.35).

With respect to prognosis, Lotter (1974b) writes, "It seems that, whichever index is used, it remains easier to predict a poor outcome than a good outcome." As a matter of fact it is also my clinical experience that the prognoses of persons in the profound and severe ranges of mental retardation are invariably poor or very poor, and those of persons in the mild range more variable and for that reason less predictable.

For illustrative examples the reader is referred to three cases (Nos. 003, 010 and 045) presented in II.5.3.2.4. These three former Eekwal-home children were all mildly mentally retarded, and at the end of the observation period were classified as PDD-AD. As for outcomes, the first and last cases should be regarded as having a poor or very poor outcome, the second case as having a fair or even good outcome. In addition, four other mildly mentally retarded former Eekwal-home children are described in the following paragraphs. Two of them have been classified as PDD-AD and their outcomes are at least fair. The two other cases seemed to have a more favourable prognosis as they were classified as PDD-NOS, but their outcomes were poor or very poor. These four cases are presented in chronological order of admission into the observation home.

Subject No. 014 boy; age 4 years; mildly retarded; PDD-AD

The mother of this boy bled slightly for a short time during the fourth month of her pregnancy. Parturition was induced and was sixteen days overdue. The baby cried instantly and was not cyanotic. There were no postnatal complications. The boy's motor development was delayed (sitting at fourteen months, walking at 25 months). He learned to say mum and dad when he was a little older than one year old, but subsequently did not extend his vocabulary until he was about two years and six months old. On admission, he had about ten words at his command, using them mostly in an echolalic way and never for communicative purposes. From the record given by the boy's parents - warm-hearted and level-headed people - I extract the following observations. He's not really toilet-trained, but occasionally does want to go to the toilet with his mother, taking her by the hand. He teases his younger brother and often snatches things from him. He likes to play with sand and water. He can't properly draw but only scribbles. He's just started to play with building blocks. He's afraid of animals. In general his contact-making is inadequate. However, when playing ball games, which he truly enjoys, he rolls or kicks the ball back and makes good eye-to-eye contact. When he's tired and lays in bed, he's also open to contact. By day he's predominantly absorbed in his own play and is unresponsive; if interfered, he becomes angry and flies into a temper. He likes to tap at things, not only at objects but also at other people's faces. He has many fixed habits. He dislikes spilling food and screams when a morsel sticks to his mouth. He's over-precise and cannot bear things not to be normal. He's much attached to a red bucket; he takes it with him to the toilet and also insists on having it placed on the table at meal-times with a spoon laying across it. Although generally lively and in good spirits, sometimes he can't stop nagging.

In spite of a very detailed examination no etiological indications were found; neither the minor fluxus during the mother's pregnancy nor the late delivery seemed to offer a plausible explanation.

From the psychiatrist's report I extract the following observations. The boy is an appealing child of slender build. He has a curious way of perceiving and experiencing reality. Consequently objects and people do not mean to him what they mean to other people. He is able to ignore something completely if he prefers to. For example, when his eyes were examined with the ophthalmoscope he first reacted to the object with fear, as is normal, then looked into it with curiosity, and finally completely disregarded the whole thing as if it did not exist at all. He has the ability - disability in fact - to cut himself off from the surrounding world, either for just a moment or for quite a while, but he does so only partially and certainly less intensely than autistic persons do. He explores the face of another person by pinching it and tapping at the nose; this examination upsets him and seems almost to be an obsession. He also taps at many objects; the way he handles objects does not seem completely stereotyped although there is little variation in what he does with things. Apparently objects often have a strong emotional connotation for him; his mind seems to be captured by them and it is not possible for him to look at them in a more objective way. As a result he is very inflexible and unadaptive. His rigidity and strong attachment to his own anticipation of the way things will go make him difficult to manage. When events take a different turn he reacts with shifts of mood and screaming tantrums. However, he does not then arouse our compassion, as he does not look particularly sorrowful.

From my own psychological examination I extract the following observations. This boy, while certainly not being a case of autism proper, makes nevertheless insufficient contact. He seems hardly aware, for instance, that a human being should not be treated like a doll. In the observation play-room he constantly makes eye-to-eye contact and also communicates by smiling and by showing things. He is able to imitate actions and words. He puts on all sorts of looks which he might think appropriate, but this seems only to be for the sake of good form. It is as if he tries hard to show some emotional response to what is going on, but only displays decorum. He easily becomes dysphoric, but easily gets over it. The boy is clearly very vulnerable both in his social contacts and in his relation to the physical world. To compensate for his lack of personal identity he has created a very rigid set of visions of the world which enable him to carry on. He apparently has a very fundamental disorder which has led to what is possibly best described as a mild retraction syndrome (as defined by Hoejenbos; see I.2.1).

Tested with the Stanford-Binet, he obtained a mental age of 1-11 and an IQ of 47. His lowest score was for expressive language. This was confirmed by his results on the Merrill-Palmer Scale (even when a 10% correction was applied because of the test's heavy emphasis on performance skills); on this test he scored a mental age of 2-7 and an IQ of 63. Determined on the basis of the data from his file, his score according to the PDD-MRS was 11; classification: PDD; diagnosis: PDD.

An intensive treatment programme during the boy's four-month stay at the observation home had many positive results. He became much less choosy about what he ate. He slept better. He learned to remain completely dry by day. He responded somewhat better when other people interfered with what he was doing or found fault with him. He was given playful speech-therapy on a tentative basis and this enlivened his interest in speech; notably his pleasure in pointing out pictures and objects increased. However, his contact problems and lack of personal identity only slightly improved, although he did develop a more positive attitude towards other children and made more adequate contact with adults. Small doses of trifluperidol and haloperidol, which helped him to cope with unexpected situations, were given as adjuncts to the treatment.

His parents stayed several days at the observation home to acquaint themselves with the approach adopted there. At discharge a number of managemental guidelines were provided; further recommendations were placement into a day-care centre and continued medication for at least some time. Readmittance to the observation home for a shorter period after a couple of years was also suggested. As the boy subsequently made good intellectual progress at the day-care centre it was concluded that there was no need for readmission to the observation home. When the boy was seven he was placed into a school for educable mentally retarded children; the school's report for his eighth year describes him as emotionally chaotic and not easily drawn into group activities. Academically, however, he did so well that at the age of about ten he was placed into a remedial school and from there into a small school for lower secondary education, where he passed his finals. Subsequently he attended a school for higher general secondary education, but it is not known how long he stayed there (his parents would rather not provide information). Reportedly he also attended a school for intermediate business education which he did finish. At the time of writing he is 24 years old, lives alone and has no work. Socially he functions poorly. This is all that is known about his subsequent development.

Compared with the other subjects in the sample, this boy is a unique case as far as his school career is concerned; only two other mildly retarded subjects were able to follow secondary education, but they attended a school for individualized vocational training. Socially, however, this boy's performance is far less satisfying. Thus his intellectual and academic development seems to have been of little avail.

Subject No. 038: girl; age 4 years; mildly retarded; PDD-NOS

The mother's pregnancy - her fourth - was without complications, except for a moped accident in the fourth month, in which she turned a somersault and sustained a foot injury. Delivery was normal. Although the baby seemed quite an ordinary infant who rarely cried, with hindsight her response to contact-making was probably inadequate right from the start. She lived in her own world and laughed only to herself. Eventually doubts arose about her sight and hearing. She was bottle-fed and drank well, but never learned to eat bread or dinner. At nine months she could sit, at sixteen months she could stand alone, and just before her second birthday she was walking. She did not speak until she was three, and even then it was largely parroting.

From the report given by the girl's parents I extract the following observations. She doesn't eat bread but wants porridge instead; when there are lumps in it she retches and vomits. She's been able to eat alone for a few months, thanks to grandma's help. She needs help getting dressed, but she can do up her own buttons. She isn't toilet trained; she never lets us know when she needs to go and can't be kept dry. At night we don't pick her up. She copies some of our household chores, and copies the actions of other children whilst they're playing tag or just romping around. She likes to watch her father pottering about and imitates him handling the screwdriver. She can be absorbed in examining a wall socket. She enjoys playing with water, shovelling in sand and making mud pies. She's very fond of noisy music, clapping her hands and dancing to the beat; she's not interested in television except when there is music on. She builds towers from building blocks. She loves to be chased. She pores over picture books, holding them upside down. Occasionally she gnaws on toys, and she used to bite her nails. She can be aggressive when she's angry. She doesn't run away from home. She never breaks things at home and is very fussy about having things in the right place; when she can't have it her way she screams angrily and is vexed for some time (at a certain stage such a dysphoric state might last half an hour). She's a vulnerable child and the slightest thing can set her off whining or put her into a rage.

Detailed examination failed to reveal any indication why the girl should be like this. For some time an anaclitic depression or a cryptogenic hyperaesthetic-emotional syndrome was suspected.

Tested with the Stanford-Binet she obtained a mental age of 2-2 and an IQ of 44. She was twice assessed by means of the SRZ with a three-month interval between the assessments (the second time was two weeks before her discharge). The results are given below in standard marks based on the norm laid down for day-care centres.

(Sub)scale	I	II
Self help	6H	7L
Communication	6H	7H
Persistence	5L	5L
Social skills	5H	6H
SRZ-Total	5H	7L

Her scores for the subscale Communication improved significantly on the 5% level. Determined on the basis of the data from her file, the girl's score according to the PDD-MRS was 7; classification: Doubtful PDD/Non-PDD; diagnosis: PDD.

The girl presented as a rather listless, lonely and dispirited child. When approached with due circumspection she became more accessible and less dysphoric. To promote contact-making she was also given pimozide and a now obsolete anti-convulsant that seemed to take the edge off her irritability. Educational intervention and playful speech-therapy yielded positive results in a number of areas. Her eating problems completely disappeared, she talked more and also more on her own account, made cautious moves towards contact-making, and extended her play repertoire. However, the improvements were based on a very small potential.

She was discharged from the observation home after approximately five months, with the advice that she was to continue medication (pimozide and an anticonvulsant) for at least the time being, and to be placed into a day-care centre for mentally retarded children. In addition some managemental guidelines were provided. She attended a day-care centre until she was six, and was subsequently placed into a school for trainable mentally retarded children. When she was thirteen she was admitted to another observation clinic on account of her defiant behaviour at school, screaming tantrums, strain, and lack of concern for others. From the clinic's reports I quote some quite noteworthy test results. On the WISC she obtained a verbal IQ (VIQ) of 53, a performance IQ (PIQ) of 96, and a full-scale IQ of 71. The SRZ scores are presented below (in standard marks based on the norm laid down for institutions for mentally retarded persons).

(Sub)scale	
Self help	9
Communication	8L
Persistence	9
Social skills	5L
SRZ-Total	8H

The clinic advised placement into a group home for mentally retarded children and that she should carry on attending the same school.

At the age of 21 she was placed into a group home for mentally retarded adults and attended a day-care centre for adults (on account of being overage for the other facilities). About a year later (and just shortly before the follow-up date) an emergency admission into a psychiatric hospital was mandatory on account of serious and unmanageable problems, notably severe self-injurious behaviour and fits of destructive behaviour, initially only at the day-care centre but subsequently also at the group home. At the moment of writing she is still in this hospital; she uses psychotropic drugs, including clopenthixol and diazepam. There are strong doubts whether she is able to live in a group home, although her scores on the SRZ-P (a social functioning scale for the mentally handicapped of a higher level) are in fact slightly above average, as can be seen from the table presented below (in standard marks based on the norm laid down for group homes for mentally retarded persons of all ages).

(Sub)scale	
Basic self help	7
Advanced self help	6
Verbal-numerical	7
SRZ-P-Total	7L

The team at the group home reported that she needed more than average tact and heedfulness. Her current score according to the PDD-MRS is 15; classification: PDD; diagnosis: PDD.

All in all, this girl continued to develop quite remarkably both in the intellectual and social areas. On the other hand, the profiles emerging from both the WISC and the SRZ tests should be considered to be typically autistic, while the PDD-MRS results also suggest an increase in autistic features (the increase in PDD scores is fairly significant on the 1% level). Such a development is not to be found in the previous literature; on the contrary, autistic features reportedly tend to level off with advancing years. Behavioural problems, on the other hand, are reported to increase (see for instance Gillberg & Steffenburg, 1987). Indeed, my own experience is by and large in agreement with this finding; however, I have also seen a number of cases with decreasing behavioural problems.

Subject No. 060: girl; age 7 years; mildly retarded; PDD-NOS and epilepsy

This girl was a fifth child. For the whole of her fifth month of pregnancy her mother was troubled by dizzy spells and seeing black spots before her eyes. The complaints would disappear when she lay down. From the seventh month of pregnancy she was on a salt-free diet. It struck her that the child inside her womb kicked a lot and also very violently. Delivery was without complications; the child was born after just two contractions. The baby looked fine and her initial development gave no special cause for concern. The child's weight at birth was 3500 grams. At four months, she contracted German measles; she had a fever and cried a lot; nevertheless her illness was not taken too seriously. Motor development was smooth and normal. She was toilet-trained at a very early age, shortly before her second birthday. She was also an early talker. At the age of 2-9 she had an epileptic seizure: she fell from her mother's lap, stared abstractedly, had recurrent symmetric contractions, developed a cyanosis and passed urine. She picked up following an injection given by her G.P.; she proved to have a fever. No drugs were prescribed. Her speech development came to a virtual standstill. Fears arose that she might be

225

mentally retarded. An identical seizure took place half a year later and from then on regularly at six-month intervals. The seizures were preceded by increased restlessness and sometimes fever, and they were accompanied by vomiting; afterwards she would scream terribly and be very demanding. From her seventh year onwards the seizures became considerably more frequent.

The following observations are extracted from her parents' descriptions of her behaviour. Since developing the seizures she's stopped eating hot meals at home, but still eats them at the day-care centre. She eats and drinks alone, but sloppily, carelessly, and with her back turned to the table. She's not capable of putting on her shoes for herself. Although apparently perfectly able to wash herself we have to wash her ourselves. She can go to the toilet by herself, but often needs help to clean herself afterwards. She helps with the washing up, lays the table of her own accord and makes her own bed. She likes a romp with the other children in the family and joins in simple games. She's very fond of playing with water. She likes drawing without being particularly good at it. She sings, but doesn't know many songs. She's completely unable to play by herself and needs continuous support and stimulation. She indiscriminately copies what other children do without adding anything of her own invention. She relies much on a well-ordered existence; it takes quite some manoeuvring and above all pleasantry to coax her into new routines. She's only content when every situation is exactly as it was the time before, with the same things and even the same people. When, for instance, we visit the day-care centre, she panics and gets into a fuss, doing things like hiding herself; when an attendant comes around to see us she behaves just the same. She wants to sleep with a nightlight on, but otherwise her former sleep problems (i.e., separation anxiety, manifested by her loud screaming and extreme fears at the moment of falling asleep, which dated from her first seizure) are now over. She likes to suck on a piece of cloth and occasionally bites her nails. In the last six months before admittance her aggressive and destructive spells became less explosive. At times she doesn't stop nagging and she can also be pretty unruly. She has a sharp eye for our reactions to her behaviour. She has a lowered sensitivity to pain; an infected tooth or a splinter under her nail won't make her cry.

The following observations are extracted from the psychiatrist's report. Even after a number of sessions it proved not to be possible to obtain a complete picture of this child, mainly because she was rather inaccessible. She was above all standoffish; she maintained a negativistic facade, with sudden fits of primitive (unpleasant though not extremely violent) aggression. Even when there was no apparent reason for such behaviour she relapsed almost automatically into it as if habituated to this impersonal manner of communication. There are possibly psychodynamic and projective mechanisms at work which make her feel threatened, but it is not easy to sympathise with her. Even after a number of sessions an affective relationship failed to develop.

In spite of very detailed examinations no etiological indications were found. There was a family history of mental retardation; a brother, seven years the girl's senior, suffered from cryptogenic epilepsy, but was not mentally retarded. In appearance the girl was quite beautiful, with almost flawless features.

Tested with the Stanford-Binet she obtained a mental age of 4-8 and an IQ of 61. Her SRZ results are given below (in standard marks based on the norm laid down for institutions for mentally retarded persons).

(Sub)scale	
Self help	8H
Communication	9
Persistence	8L
Social skills	9
SRZ-Total	9

Her high score on the subscale Social skills was mainly due to contact with her peers at the observation home who happened to be very sociable and exerted a good influence upon her. Determined on the basis of the data from her file, the girl's score according to the PDD-MRS was 3; classification Non-PDD; diagnosis: PDD.

The girl was given intensive social training and treatment. The aim was to strengthen her identity, potential for contact-making and self-confidence by providing her with positive experiences. However, the Eekwal-home team hardly succeeded in getting to grips with her, and no real progress was made. She was discharged with a slightly higher dose of anti-convulsants than she had used on admission. A school for trainable mentally retarded children was judged to be more suitable for her than one for educable mentally retarded children because of her identity problems and the risk of overtaxing her which might have resulted in disintegration. In case her behavioural problems became unmanageable at home, placement into a group home for mentally retarded children seemed to be the best option, which is exactly what happened a few years later. She attended a school for trainable mentally retarded children until she was sixteen. Subsequently she attended a day-care centre for mentally retarded adults. At the time of writing she is 23 years old and lives in a group home for mentally retarded adults, into which she was placed at the age of seventeen. She needs much tact and heedfulness, and the staff at the group home feels unable to provide the structure she requires. Eighteen months ago she was put on a waiting list for an institution for mentally retarded persons as an urgent case, but as yet no vacancy has presented itself. Her current score according to the PDD-MRS is 1; classification: Non-PDD; diagnosis: PDD. Reportedly she still uses anti-convulsants.

This case history suggests that the girl's contact problems are still as serious as they were when she stayed at the observation home, and that her behaviour problems have even increased. She was an erratic and strange child, and above all difficult to manage. On the one hand she may be regarded as a mild case of PDD-NOS, but on the other hand she possibly does not fit too well into this category. However, to classify her as a case of OPS, of Oppositional Defiant Disorder or of Separation Anxiety Disorder would be even wider of the mark.

Subject No. 100: boy; age 4 years; mildly retarded; PDD-AD

This boy is the elder of two children. Their father comes from Morocco. Both children were born out of wedlock, out of choice according to the mother. In the file she is described as a strange and almost autistic woman. Pregnancy and delivery were reported to have been normal. The infant was easily upset and cried a lot. He was fifteen months old before he could sit up and two years before he was walking. He was also a late talker. At the age of three he went to a day-care centre.

The following observations are extracted from his mother's description of his behaviour. He's got an unsatiable appetite and eats everything but meat. He doesn't help me to dress him. He doesn't toilet independently; at the day-care centre he can be kept dry by sitting him on the potty regularly, but at home this isn't feasible. He lacks all sense of danger, putting everything into his mouth and walking right into oncoming traffic. Recently he's been imitating me after his own fashion. He's fond of playing with sand and water, playing with the wooden sorting box and doing similar tasks, arranging blocks into patterns, and listening to music. He can draw a man. He wants to go his own way. He is a sound sleeper. He sniffs at objects. Faeces repel him. He doesn't have temper tantrums. He's careful with objects but rough with his younger brother. He's attached to daily routines and fixed patterns; for instance, he always wants me to sit in the same place. He's afraid of new things and it takes him a long time to get used to them. He looks past people, but can still keep an eye on them. He's been making better contact this past year. He's not willing to sit on anyone's lap; however, when he's hurt himself he does come to you.

In spite of a detailed examination no etiological indications were found. The boy looked fairly content, but he was aloof and unimpressionable. He chattered a lot, but in a low voice and often only to himself, echoing phrases he had heard shortly before or even some time ago, or repeating stereotypical sayings. His drawings were remarkable considering his chronological age; his favourite subjects for drawing were cranes, cars, planes, etc.

Tested a couple of weeks after his admission with the Griffiths (generally yielding scores of approx. 10% above the actual level), he obtained a subtest of 3-4 and a GQ of 70. He presented a very disharmonious test profile; his quotients on the subtests Personal-social and Hearing & speech were respectively 54 and 59, whereas his quotients on the subtests Eye & hand coordination and Performance were respectively 84 and 91.

This lad stayed at the Eekwal observation home for nineteen months. The team's approach was geared to an early developmental level and primarily directed at his emotional potential, while his splinter skills in the performance area and the semblance of verbal proficiency were largely ignored. He began to respond in a more personal way, sometimes almost showing some warmth. He began to like some people in particular and to feel attached to them. However, there were just too many people around at the observation home and this seemed to prevent him from forming close ties. Pimozide, which was given as an adjunct to treatment, seemed only to have an adverse effect, as he became irritable.

Shortly before discharge this boy was retested with the Griffiths; he obtained again a GQ of 70, but the profile had become less disharmonious, the difference between the highest and the lowest quotients having decreased from 37 to 8 points. Determined on the basis of the data from his file, his score according to the PDD-MRS was 15; classification: PDD; diagnosis: PDD. The results of the assessments by means of the SRZ, the SMZ and the SGZ scales are given below (in standard marks based on the norm laid down for day-care centres).

(Sub)scale	
Self help	8L
Communication	8L
Persistence	7L
Social skills	6L
SRZ-Total	7H
SMZ-Total	7L
Aggressive maladaptive behaviour	7L
Verbal maladaptive behaviour	7L
Miscellaneous maladaptive behaviour	6H
SGZ-Total	7L

After discharge the boy was placed into a very good foster home with his mother's consent. An autism team provided home help. First the boy attended a special class for children with developmental problems. Two years later he was placed into a remedial school. This school proved to be beyond his capability. After two more years, at the age of ten, he was placed into a school for educable mentally retarded children. Both at school and at his foster home he was performing excellently, and at the age of twelve his condition was considered to have stabilized to such a degree that help from the autism team was no longer necessary. At the time of writing he is fourteen and has been attending a special secondary education school for a year; he is still doing well. He requires no more than average help and guidance and everybody considers him to be well placed. Individualized vocational training was in all probability not suitable for him, as indeed his results for the entrance test to this type of school had indicated. The boy uses no psychotropic drugs. His current score on the PDD-MRS is 10; classification: PDD; diagnosis: PDD.

This boy is a typical case of autism. Obviously his very fortunate outcome can be attributed to sound advice, his devoted foster parents and the good approach adopted by successive schools. However, the fact that the boy displayed virtually no concurrent behavioural problems from an early age possibly played a crucial role. Conversely, behavioural problems in early child-hood need not necessarily lead to a bad outcome, witness the case already discussed of a mildly retarded PDD-AD child (subject No. 010, Section II.5.3.2.4).

Thus, once again Lotter proves to be right in saying that with respect to PDD it is easier to predict a poor outcome than a good one, if only because the poor outcomes are far more frequent. Only a few isolated cases do surprisingly well; the majority of these function on the mild level of mental retardation.

II.5.4.3   Comparison with findings reported by Gillberg and Steffenburg

In the population-based follow-up study carried out in Sweden by Gillberg and Steffenburg (1987) follow-up data concerning 46 cases are presented. The group is subdivided by level of functioning into non-retarded (IQs $\geq$ 71), mildly retarded (IQs 50-70) and below mildly retarded (IQs <50). In the present section only the two retarded categories will be considered, as the Eekwal follow-up study involves only mentally retarded subjects. As far as psychopathology is concerned, the sample of the Swedish study is subdivided into a subgroup Infantile Autism and a subgroup Other Childhood Psychosis. Individuals of the first subgroup were identified on the basis of the criteria for Infantile Autism as defined in the DSM-III. This subgroup contained eight mildly mentally retarded individuals and nine individuals in the lower ranges of mental retardation. The second subgroup was rather vaguely described as containing "classical cases of disintegrative psychosis as well as autistic-like conditions in which age at onset was not definitely before thirty months of age." From this subgroup I ignore two subjects labelled schizophrenic (on the basis of DSM-III criteria). The remainder meet the DSM-III criteria for Atypical PDD. This procedure seems legitimate in view of the fact that the authors wrote in an earlier publication, "What we refer to as 'autistic-like conditions' have been referred to as 'other childhood psychoses' in previous publications" (Steffenburg & Gillberg, 1986). Moreover, the case histories of many subjects record medical conditions such as the fragile-X syndrome, tuberous sclerosis, and Rett's Disorder, which according to the literature are widely associated with autism and autistic-like conditions (see, for instance, Gillberg, 1990a, 1992b). In what follows the two subgroups will be referred to as Infantile Autism and Autistic-like Conditions.

All in all, there are good reasons to assume that the Swedish follow-up study covers the complete range of pervasive developmental disorders as defined by the DSM-III-R system, i.e., PDD-AD and PDD-NOS. On the basis of these considerations it seems justified to include thirteen subjects belonging to the lower ranges of mental retardation and four mildly retarded subjects from the subgroup Other Childhood Psychosis in the comparison group. This procedure brings the number of mentally retarded persons to a total of 34 out of 44, or 77.3%. At the moment of follow-up one subject of the initial sample (a person in the lower range of mental retardation) had died.

The comparison group therefore contains 33 subjects. At follow-up their ages ranged from 18-23 years. Like Lotter, the investigators classified outcome along the lines suggested by Rutter and Lockyer (1967) into good, fair, poor and very poor. Regrettably, however, they also added a fifth qualification to the list, indicated as (+) and lying between Fair and Poor; this qualification is defined as 'restricted but acceptable outcome' or - elsewhere in the article - 'expected in relation to intellectual level, usually restricted.' Poor or Very Poor outcome in the context of this study almost invariably implies that the persons in question have been placed into institutions for mentally retarded persons, which are indicated as MR institutions in this study; however, it must be realized that Swedish MR institutions are nowadays rather small-scale settings.

The Swedish follow-up findings which are relevant for a comparison with the Eekwal follow-up study are presented in Tables II.5.38 to II.5.42. In the first two of these tables the outcomes for two subgroups in the Swedish study are compared (the ratios between mildly mentally retarded subjects and those who fell into the lower ranges of mental retardation were the same for both subgroups; chi-square = 1.73; ns).

Table II.5.38 The outcomes of mentally retarded (IQ 0-70) subjects aged 16-23: comparison between persons with infantile autism and persons with autistic-like conditions (adapted from Gillberg & Steffenburg, 1987)

Outcome	Infantile autism	Autistic-like conditions	Total
Good/Fair/(+)	7	3	10
Poor/Very Poor	10	13	23
Total	17	16	33
Perc. Poor/Very Poor	58.8 %	81.3 %	69.7 %

Just as in the aforementioned study by Lotter both categories are found not to differ significantly so far as the outcomes are concerned (chi-square = 1.69). Again, the most obvious explanation seems to be that the subgroup of persons with autistic-like conditions consists exclusively of persons who, in DSM terminology, would be classified as serious cases of PDD-NOS; in terms of outcome their conditions were as bad as those with infantile autism.

In order to make the results of the Swedish follow-up study better comparable with those of the Eekwal follow-up study, some additional adaptations to its data must be made.

Of the 21 severely mentally retarded subjects (the person who had died is not included) nineteen subjects (90.5%) are reported to have Poor/Very Poor outcomes. The outcomes of the remaining two subjects were qualified as (+). On the assumption that the average outcome of these two subjects may be considered to have been between Good/Fair and Poor/Very Poor, one subject is listed as having had a Good/Fair outcome, and one as having had a Poor/Very Poor outcome. This procedure brings the number of subjects with Poor/Very Poor outcomes to twenty, or 95.2%. As far as place of living is concerned, of the 21 subjects below the mild level of mental retardation, fourteen, or 66.7%, lived at follow-up in a setting for mentally retarded persons. Their median age was eighteen. This group matches the groups of profoundly, severely and moderately mentally retarded former Eekwal-home children lumped together. Their average age at follow-up was 19.2 years. Thus, in order to make the figures of both studies mutually comparable, the percentages found in the Swedish study were averaged with the formula:

$$\frac{\% \text{ P/VP} + \frac{1}{2} \% (+) + \% \text{ MR-inst.}}{2} = \frac{90,5 + 4,7 + 66,7}{2} = 80,9$$

On the basis of this calculation the percentages Poor/Very Poor outcome in both studies turn out to be very close, as can be seen in Table II.5.39.

Table II.5.39 The outcomes of profoundly, severely and moderately mentally retarded persons with a PDD; comparison of two follow-up studies

Outcome	Eekwal home	Gillberg and Steffenburg (1987)
Poor/Very Poor	80	17
Other outcomes	11	4
Total	91	21
Perc. Poor/Very Poor	87.9 %	80.9 %

Chi-square = 0.71; ns

The difference between the percentages is clearly not significant at all. On the assumption that the manipulations applied to the figures from the Swedish study are acceptable, both studies may be said to have arrived at the same conclusion.

Twelve subjects followed in the Swedish study belong to the mild range of mental retardation. Four of them (33.3%) were found to have Poor/Very Poor outcomes. The outcomes of six of these people were qualified as (+). Again, assuming that the average outcome of these six subjects may be considered to be between Good/Fair and Poor/Very Poor, the percentage of subjects with Poor/Very Poor outcomes is taken to be 58.3%. Regarding place of living, four of the twelve mildly mentally retarded subjects (33.3%) lived at follow-up in a setting for mentally retarded persons. Applying again the formula used above to average out the percentages, the qualification Poor/Very Poor outcome is applicable to 45.8% of the mildly retarded persons. Converting this percentage back into a number suggests that five (41.7%) may be regarded to have Poor/Very Poor outcomes.

On the basis of these calculations the percentages of Poor/Very Poor outcome in mildly retarded persons found in the Swedish and Dutch follow-up studies also turn out to be very close, as can be seen in Table II.5.40; again the difference between the percentages is clearly not significant.

Table II.5.40 The outcomes of mildly mentally retarded persons with a PDD; comparison of two follow-up studies

Outcome	Eekwal home	Gillberg and Steffenburg (1987)
Poor/Very Poor	20	5
Other outcomes	24	7
Total	44	12
Perc. Poor/Very Poor	45.5 %	41.7 %

Chi-square = 0.05; ns

With respect to the entire sample in their study, Gillberg and Steffenburg found a positive correlation between IQ and outcome at follow-up. On the basis of their material it is possible to determine whether the correlation also holds good for the mentally retarded subjects in their sample as a separate group. There are two ways to find out. The first one is to compare outcomes of the two groups of mentally retarded persons on the basis of the qualifications used by the investigators; the figures are presented in Table II.5.41.

Table II.5.41 The outcomes of persons with a PDD; comparison of two ranges of mental retardation found in the study by Gillberg and Steffenburg (1987)

Outcome	Profound, severe and moderate mental retardation	Mild mental retardation
Poor/Very Poor	19	4
Good/Fair/(+)	2	8
Total	21	12
Perc. Poor/Very Poor	90.5 %	33.3 %

Fisher exact test; p = .001

The second way is again to average out the percentages of those whose outcomes were qualified as (+) and those who lived in institutions. These figures are presented in Table II.5.42.

Table II.5.42 The outcomes of persons with a PDD; comparison of two ranges of mental retardation found in the study by Gillberg and Steffenburg (1987)

Outcome	Profound, severe and moderate mental retardation	Mild mental retardation
Poor/Very Poor/[(+) + Inst.]: 2	17	5
Good/Fair/[(+) + Inst.]: 2	4	7
Total	21	12
Perc. Poor/Very Poor	80.9 %	41.7 %

Fisher exact test; p = .028

Both tables indicate that the findings in the Swedish follow-up study are in agreement with those of the Eekwal study; the correlation between IQ and later outcome also holds true for IQ's in the retarded range, i.e., the higher a person's IQ the smaller the chance of a Poor/Very Poor outcome and/or of eventual placement into a institution.

Further, the Swedish investigators found that at follow-up the use of medication had significantly increased (which they attribute to the fact that puberty had set in by then). Whereas initially 25% of the subjects used psychotropic drugs and anti-convulsants, at follow-up this was 75%. If users of anti-convulsants at follow-up are ignored (a procedure which is legitimate in view of information provided by the study itself) 56% of the subjects used psychotropic drugs. Admittedly the comparison can actually no longer pass scrutiny after this procedure; nevertheless, the increase is impressive when contrasted with the initial 25%. Moreover, a percentage of 56% for users of psychotropic drugs is in itself indeed quite large. The investigators have not calculated the increase in the use of psychotropic drugs for the mentally retarded subjects separately, but it seems unlikely that this group would have displayed a different picture.

The figures for the increase in the use psychotropic drugs in the 122 former Eekwal-home children for whom usable returns were obtained (see II.5.3.5.3) are presented in Table II.5.43. Testing has been done by means of the sign test for large samples (Siegel & Castellan, 1988).

Table II.5.43 Users and non-users of psychotropic drugs in the Eekwal follow-up sample at discharge and at follow-up

Medication used at follow-up but not at discharge	25
Medication used at discharge but not at follow-up	14
Situation similar at both moments	83
Total	122

z (sign test) = 1.60; ns

As the table shows, no significant changes have taken place in the use of psychotropic drugs. However, a better comparison with the Swedish study is possible by singling out the children who had been admitted to the Eekwal observation home before the age of twelve and who at follow-up were at least above the age of sixteen, assuming that twelve marks the start and sixteen the end of puberty (whatever this term may denote in the case of mentally retarded subjects). This procedure generates a group of 84 former Eekwal-home children. At discharge 23.8% of them used psychotropic drugs; the follow-up figure is 38.1%. Numbers and statistical test are presented in Table II.5.44.

Table II.5.44 Users and non-users of psychotropic drugs among young Eekwal-home children at discharge and at follow-up

Medication used at follow-up but not at discharge	21
Medication used at discharge but not at follow-up	10
Situation similar at both moments	53
Total	84

z (sign test) = 1.80; ns

There is a slight increase in the use of psychotropic drugs, but it is not significant. In other words, present findings do not confirm the results of the Swedish study.

II.5.5   Summary

The careers of mentally retarded PDD persons were followed in order to gain a better insight into the gravity of their dual disorder. The present chapter will be concluded with an overview of our major findings.

Many mentally retarded persons with a PDD are eventually placed into institutions (AZI). This is notably the case with those functioning on the lower levels of mental retardation. However, a substantial number of moderately and mildly retarded persons with a PDD have the same prospects, the percentages being 88% and 56%, respectively, which is far higher than the percentages found in the entire population of moderately and mildly retarded persons. Moreover, mentally retarded persons with a PDD are institutionalized at a much earlier age than the general population of mentally retarded persons. This finding holds good for all levels of functioning. The data from the Eekwal follow-up sample also demonstrate that mentally retarded persons who had been diagnosed as PDD at the observation home differ from other mentally retarded persons in the following respects:

- PDD persons tend to require more staff discussion time, and also a greater amount of tact and heedfulness to prevent and to deal with their behavioural problems.
- More institutionalized PDD persons use psychotropic drugs than the entire institutionalized population.

With respect to the number of institutionalized former Eekwal-home children and age of placement, no differences were found between the children observed in the period 1968-78 and those observed in the period 1978-88. Whatever benefits may have been produced by better provisions in outpatient mental-health care, both for mentally retarded persons in general and for those with a PDD in particular, the result has not been fewer placements into institutions or institutionalization at a later age.

With respect to the differences between PDD-AD and PDD-NOS children the follow-up study confirms that PDD-AD is a more serious disorder than PDD-NOS, on the basis of the following:

- Significantly more PDD-AD than PDD-NOS persons were placed into institutions, and institutionalization tended to take place at an earlier age.
- Significantly more PDD-AD than PDD-NOS persons displayed language problems, i.e., developed speech at a later age or no speech at all.
- Significantly more PDD-AD than PDD-NOS persons require a more than average amount of tact and heedfulness in their management.
- Significantly more PDD-AD than PDD-NOS persons use psychotropic drugs.
- PDD-AD persons had higher scores on the PDD-MRS than PDD-NOS persons, both at discharge and at follow-up.

All findings are consistent with the concept used in the DSM classification system, according to which the subcategories PDD-AD and PDD-NOS belong to a continuum of pervasive developmental disorders. On the other hand, the findings do not contradict the concept of pervasive developmental disorders as a spectrum.

With respect to the five aspects listed above, no differences were found in the follow-up study between children with the rigid form and those with the erratic form of PDD; while clearly having distinguishing features, the two forms of PDD were not found to differ in gravity.

Several findings of other follow-up studies were confirmed by the Eekwal study.

In the first place, both the Eekwal follow-up study and other studies demonstrated that the presence or absence of expressive language skills is a very important prognostic factor. More specifically, the Eekwal follow-up study found that a significantly higher number of persons who were known not to have acquired speech before their sixth birthdays were institutionalized at follow-up.

In the second place, the figures regarding the outcome of mentally retarded persons with a PDD show a large degree of correspondence. In the profound, severe and moderate ranges of mental retardation, the following percentages of Poor/Very Poor outcome have been reported: about 87% (Lotter, 1974a,b), about 81% (Gillberg & Steffenburg, 1987) and about 88% (Eekwal follow-up study); in the mild range of mental retardation the following percentages have been found: about 42% (Gillberg & Steffenburg, 1987) and about 46% (Eekwal follow-up study).

However, unlike Gillberg and Steffenburg, the Eekwal follow-up study found no indication that behavioural problems increased at puberty. Any behavioural problems existing at that age had generally become manifest at an earlier age, as may be concluded from such data as early institutionalization and use of psychotropic drugs.

The picture emerging from the literature is that institutions for mentally retarded persons play an important role in the care of PDD persons. This was the situation in 1974, the year in which Lotter's study was published, and it was still the case more than a decade later, going by what Gillberg and Steffenburg reported, in particular with respect to persons with a Poor/Very Poor outcome. Similarly, Sherman (1988), who gathered information about families having developmentally disabled family members, found that his sample contained three times more cases of autism as an associated disorder in the out-of-home group than in the at-home group (p <.05).

My feeling is that the Eekwal follow-up study has contributed to a better insight into the gravity of the dual disability of mental retardation and a pervasive developmental disorder.

PART III

DIAGNOSTICS, PREVALENCE AND SPECIAL PROBLEMS

DIAGNOSIS OF PERVASIVE DEVELOPMENTAL DISORDERS IN MENTALLY RETARDED PEOPLE

III.1.1 Introduction

The problems involved in classifying mentally retarded persons on the continuum of pervasive developmental disorders were dealt with in Chapter II.3. Although the focus was mainly on children, the problems are virtually the same for adolescents and adults. Classification, the first step in the diagnostic process, ideally implies two things: in the first place the use of clinical experience (based on observations, case histories, etc.), and in the second place the use of an internationally acknowledged classification system, which in the present context is the DSM. Alternatively, the ICD-10 may be used. However, the descriptions provided by these classification systems are rather general; they are also often hard to apply in practice, notably in the examination of mentally retarded persons.

As far as autism is concerned, an increasing number of observation schedules, checklists and scales have become available to facilitate the gathering of objective and quantifiable data. A small number of these instruments are based on the DSM or ICD, having converted the systems' relevant concepts into operational definitions. However, measuring devices do provide only a limited insight; further examination will always be necessary. As stated in the manual to the PDD-MRS, a score on a scale certainly does not equal a diagnosis; it is but a means by which we arrive at a diagnosis. Scores have to be seen in a broader context; if not consistent with the overall impression they should be regarded as a stimulus to further examination. Assessments made by means of scales may or may not confirm results from clinical observation. In fact, they are quite frequently found not to fit; in some cases a novel perspective may then emerge, but in other cases initial views must be specified or substantiated. Quite rightly Gillberg (1990a) writes, "The diagnosis of autism is clinical and should not be made purely on the basis of some rating scale."

Finally, diagnostic procedures may also be supplemented by the use of less specific scales, developmental tests, intelligence tests and projective techniques. Examples of the tests and scales which are used in current differential-diagnostic practice to find specific profiles have been presented in Chapter I.2.

Ideally then, the diagnostic process needed to verify the presence of a PDD in mentally retarded persons passes through three phases, and under certain conditions five phases:

Phase I: If after the initial general observation a PDD is vaguely or strongly suspected, more specific and systematic observations will be carried out, to be concluded with a clinical classification based on clinical knowledge and - if applicable - on the guidelines provided by the most recent versions of the DSM or ICD.

Phase II: A specific (reliable and valid) scale is administered which is devised to reveal the presence of pervasive developmental disorders (the entire spectrum) in mentally retarded persons.

Phase III: An individual diagnosis is made on the basis of the conclusions arrived at in Phases I and II. If this is not possible, Phase IV is necessary.

Phase IV: Tests and scales are administered to reveal profiles or singularities which are specific for a PDD. If such features prove to be clearly present or absent, it is possible to move on to the next and final phase.

Phase V: A diagnosis may still be made.

Alternatively, the results of tests and scales may also be used in making the clinical classification (indicated above as Phase I). The second phase will then still involve the administering of a specific scale, and making a diagnosis will still be the final phase. However, in my view the procedures should not be mixed.

In Scheme III.1.1 the proposed diagnostic process is summarized.

This scheme calls for some additional remarks:

- My experience indicates that there is always a residual group of mentally retarded people labelled doubtful. In the present context the term doubtful implies that the person in question can neither be classified nor diagnosed. Generally it is recommendable to re-examine such a person at a later date - which is a form of long-term diagnostics - in order to reach a final conclusion.
- Although Phases IV and V are not required if the clinical and instrumental classifications agree, the disharmonious functioning in the cognitive, social and emotional areas which is characteristic of PDD persons remains an important aspect in their treatment and management (see Chapter II.4). In drawing up an individual treatment plan, it is crucial to take into account the specific profiles and features which emerge from the results of tests and scales.

240

Scheme III.1.1 The successive phases of the diagnostic process

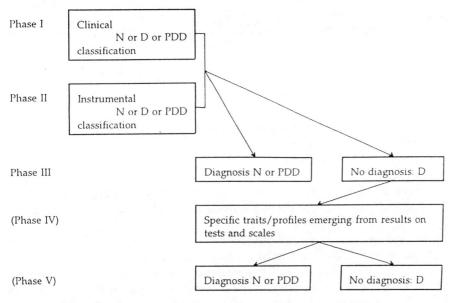

PDD = Pervasive Developmental Disorder; N = Non-PDD; D = Doubtful-PDD

In the following sections the most important instruments used for the identification and/or classification of autism or pervasive developmental disorders will be discussed. The focus will subsequently be on the PDD-MRS, which is devised to identify pervasive developmental disorders (of the entire spectrum) in mentally retarded persons in particular. The last sections of this chapter will deal with profiles and features emerging from the results of general tests and scales which prove to be typical of PDD persons.

III.1.2 Instruments for the identification of pervasive developmental disorders

III.1.2.1 *Introduction*

In what follows, three instruments used for the identification and/or classification of pervasive developmental disorders in general or of specific forms of autism in particular will be discussed, i.e., the ABC, the CARS and the AUTI(-R) scales. These instruments are used on a national or international basis, are known from the literature in the field, and have at least a reasonably sound psychometric basis. Standardized checklists such as the HBS or Handicaps, Behaviour and Skills Schedule (Wing & Gould, 1978) and the ADI or Autism Diagnostic Interview (Le Couteur et al., 1989) fall outside the present scope, as they provide primarily reliable and systematic guidelines for gathering relevant material when taking case histories. Each of the three

241

instruments to be discussed were used for some years at the Eekwal observation home; however, since 1989 the observation home has almost exclusively used the PDD-MRS.

For each of the three instruments the following information will be presented:

- Author(s) and year of publication.
- Format: arrangement and number of items and ways of scoring them.
- Period to be covered and - if indicated - sources needed.
- The problem area focussed upon and the intended target group.
- Principles used to order or classify the results.
- Composition of the sample.
- Validity.
- Critical evaluation, notably in terms of the test's applicability to mentally retarded people of all levels of functioning and maximum age-range.

As the reader may have noticed, only the tests' validity will be discussed and not their reliability (including internal consistency, test-retest reliability and interrater reliability). The first reason for this is that in my experience the validity of a test is much more difficult to realize than its reliability. Secondly and more importantly, high reliability tells nothing about validity, while, conversely, high validity presupposes high reliability.

III.1.2.2   *The Autism Behavior Checklist*

The first preliminary publication of this scale, commonly known as the ABC, dates from 1978. The authenticated manual was published a few years later (Krug et al., 1980). Actually the scale is the first part of the Autism Screening Instrument for Educational Planning (ASIEP), which is more general in scope. However, like a great many other reviews, the present discussion will be limited to the ABC, which is in fact an instrument in its own right, and the only ASIEP scale which is relevant here.

Format: there are five subscales, containing in total 57 items of different weight; scoring is dichotomic.

Assessment period: no explicit indications are given; the focus seems to be mainly on current behaviour, but clearly some items may in many cases refer to an earlier period (examples of which are, 'is (or was as a baby) stiff and hard to hold' and 'a developmental delay was identified at or before thirty months of age').

The problem area focussed upon: the scale aims at identifying (narrowly defined) autism in children, adolescents and young adults.

Classification: the scores have to be interpreted as follows:

≤53   : non-autistic
54-67 : difficulty in interpretation
≥68   : autistic

Norm group: 2002 subjects, predominantly aged 3-35 years, were examined; 1337 subjects were reportedly 'severely mentally retarded'; the group included deaf, blind and emotionally disturbed subjects.

Validity: According to the authors 90% of the more or less bona fide cases of autism and 95% of the non-autistic cases were correctly classified by means of the scale.

Critical remarks:

- Several authors have put forward fundamental criticisms of this scale. Wadden et al. (1991) found that the overall classification rate did not change when only the 34 items with the highest weight were used. A still more negative finding was reported by Oswald and Volkmar (1991), who found that only one single item (i.e., 'Looks through people') proved to have as much discriminating power as the total score of the 57 items.
- Wadden et al. (1991) evaluated by means of factor analysis the scale's division into five subscales which is based on subjective categorization of behaviours. Finding no empirical support for this subdivision they suggested that a three-factor model would be more meaningful.
- The ABC does not cover the autistic-like contactual disorders, at any rate not in its classificatory system.
- The norm group contains a large number of mentally retarded persons, but unfortunately it is not clearly demonstrated that the four levels of mental retardation are sufficiently represented.
- Teal and Wiebe (1986) found that the ABC achieved only a tolerable level of discrimination between autistic and non-autistic mentally retarded children if used in combination with the other parts of the ASIEP series. This would therefore necessitate the use of the entire instrument; it is, however, quite a voluminous instrument and moreover its application requires specific expertise. In an evaluation made by Volkmar et al. (1988) 120 children and adolescents were examined; even if the questionable cases with intermediate ABC total scores were ignored, the overall frequency of correct diagnosis was as low as 77.5%. Wadden et al. (1991) and Sevin et al. (1991) found that the cut-off scores recommended by the authors of the ABC were too strict when the more recent diagnostic criteria for autism were used. Wadden et al., using a sample of 67 autistic children (classified in the DSM-III-R category Autistic Disorder), found the correct classification rate of autism by means of the ABC to be as low as 49%, while Sevin et al. found a 50% correct classification rate in a sample of 24 similarly identified children.

III.1.2.3   The Childhood Autism Rating Scale

This scale, known as the CARS, was first published in the form of an article (Schopler et al., 1980). The companion manual, which appeared a few years later (Schopler et al., 1986), contains much information about the scale's application, but tells comparatively little about its construction.

Format: there are fifteen items (termed scales); scores are assigned according to a seven-point rating system (consisting of full points and half points ranging from 1-4).

Assessment period: no indications given; 'history records' are regarded as admissible sources of information; no precise limits are set as to the length of the assessment period, and no decrease in weight is suggested with respect to data from an earlier period.

The problem area focussed upon: 'objective classification of childhood autism', which corresponds with the classic concept of childhood autism, notably as defined by Kanner and Creak. The authors specify two objectives:

1 To identify children with autism and to distinguish them from developmentally handicapped children without autism.
2 To distinguish children with autism in the mild to moderate range from children with autism in the moderate to severe range.

Classification: the scores are interpreted as follows (according to the simplified 1986 system, which takes only the total score into account without adding the number of items with high scores):

    15-29.5 : non-autistic
    30-36.5 : mildly-moderately autistic
    37-60   : severely autistic

Norm group: 1520 infants and children, well over 88% being below the age of eleven; 71% of the children had an IQ <70.

Validity: the overall agreement rate with non-autistic children below thirteen years of age is 87.0%, and with severely autistic children in the same age category 88.8%. According to a study by Teal and Wiebe (1986), based on a sample of forty moderately mentally retarded children aged 3-13 years, half of them bona fide cases of autism, the scale had a 100% correct classification rate. In a study by Sevin et al. (1991), which is based on a small sample of 24 predominantly mentally retarded children with pervasive developmental disorders, average age eight years, the scale was found to have a 92% correct classification rate in discriminating mild and moderate autism from severe autism (cut-off score 30).

According to two studies carried out by Garfin et al. (1988) the scale is also applicable to young people up to the age of about twenty years. However, the authors do not present overall agreement rates to substantiate their view; they provide only indirect evidence by comparing the scores obtained in small groups of autistic adolescents and autistic children, and the scores obtained in small groups of autistic and non-autistic adolescents (the two matched groups containing 22 and 20 subjects, respectively).

244

Critical remarks:

- In practice the standard in terms of which behaviour has to be assessed, i.e., the behaviour of a normal child 'of the same age' (which apparently must be understood as the same mental age) presents quite some difficulty for each of the fifteen items, particularly when mentally retarded subjects are examined. At face value, behaviour must be evaluated as being either normal, mildly abnormal, moderately abnormal or severely abnormal.
- Teal and Wiebe (1986) found that the authors' original but later abandoned principle of taking not only the total score into account but also the number of items with high scores (i.e., scores ≥3) was in fact not such a bad idea; they even found that in their sample of forty subjects the number of high-scoring items discriminated more correctly than the total score.
- Garfin et al. (1988) found a negative correlation between the total score and item XIV which relates to 'Inconsistencies in Intelligence' (in the second version indicated as 'Level and Inconsistency of Intellectual Response'); they recommend elimination or modification of this item. However, Sturmey et al. (1992), in an attempt to check this finding, arrived at a positive correlation. My experience is that at least with mentally retarded people inconsistencies in intelligence are liable to escape superficial rating (although its measurement is possible by means of sophisticated techniques); for that reason elimination of item XIV seems indeed to be preferable.
- Item XV, 'General Impressions', seems to me altogether out of place in the scale. The examiner is supposed to make a subjective clinical assessment on the basis of the other fourteen items as to whether the subject under investigation is non-autistic, mildly autistic, moderately autistic or severely autistic. In the first place the scale is, as the authors themselves rightly state, designed to take behavioural and empirical data rather than clinical intuition as a basis for assessment. From this I conclude that item XV contradicts the authors' own objectives. However, there is another far more important reason for eliminating the item; the scores given for the foregoing items will no doubt affect the examiner's general impression. As a matter of fact, as indicated above, the examiner is more or less expressly instructed to score with foregoing scores in mind. It is therefore not surprising that Garfin et al. (1988) found item XV to have the highest correlation with the total score, while leaving this item out of account did reduce the coefficient alpha. As I have already argued in Section III.1.1, I for my part am convinced that the results of any scale have to be set alongside the clinical impression or, if so preferred, supplement it.
- It is not quite clear whether scores above 29.5 correspond to the entire spectrum of Pervasive Developmental Disorders.

- The norm group contains a substantial number of mentally retarded persons, but unfortunately it is not clearly demonstrated that the four levels of mental retardation are sufficiently represented. Precise information about age distribution is lacking, notably regarding infants.

III.1.2.4   The AUTI-R

The first version of this scale (Van Berckelaer-Onnes et al., 1981) was devised to identify autism in children in the age-range 4-7. The author converted the theoretical construct of early infantile autism (which she had developed in an earlier publication; see Van Berckelaer-Onnes, 1979, 1983) into operational definitions. The scale was intended to be used by professional workers; an adapted version was available which could be filled in by parents. Subsequently a radically revised version of the professional version was devised, and published as the AUTI-R (Van Berckelaer-Onnes & Hoekman, 1991). It has the same theoretical framework, but is based on a much larger norm group and suited to a wider age-range.

Format: there are 51 items; scores are assigned according to a six-point rating system. Items are weighted from 1-38; a number of arithmetical operations has to be carried out to compute the final score.

Assessment period: the items are formulated in such a way that they clearly focus on current behaviour.

The problem area focussed upon: early infantile autism in children belonging to two categories: non-talking children aged 10-155 months and talking children aged 36-155 months; the concept of early infantile autism is akin to and slightly extends the classical notion of autism (see Van Berckelaer-Onnes, 1983).

Classification: the final scores are interpreted as follows:
    <200   : autistic
    200-249 : not classifiable
    ≥250   : non-autistic

Norm group: the norm group consisted of 706 subjects aged under 156 months; 197 of them were labelled intellectually handicapped. The norm group was divided into four subgroups: talking subjects aged 36-83 months; non-talking subjects aged 10-83 months; talking subjects aged 72-155 months; non-talking subjects aged 72-155 months. The norms used to assess each subgroup are different. Only (clinically) unquestionably autistic and non-autistic cases were included in the norm group; doubtful cases were not included. In a later supplementary study another sample of 476 autistic and non-autistic mentally retarded subjects aged 12-25 years were examined (Hoekman, 1992).

Validity: in the manual to the scale the authors report that as far as the age category 10/36-155 months is concerned, 12% of the cases were not classifiable; of the remainder (88%) 92% were correctly classified as autistic and non-autistic cases. Hoekman (1992), examining mentally retarded subjects aged 12-25 years, reports that 16% of the talking subjects and as many as

52% of the non-talking subjects could not be classified. Hoekman and Van den Bergh (1992) carried out a kind of cross-validation using a sample of 523 children below the age of 156 months (330 of them mentally retarded); they found that 14% could not be classified, and, as far as the remaining 86% was concerned, a 93% correct discrimination between autistic and non-autistic cases was found. Thus, if the subgroup of non-classifiable subjects is included, the scale's sensitivity (= percentage cases correctly assessed) may be put at 70%, its specificity (= percentage non-cases correctly assessed) at 84%, and its overall misclassification rate at 20.0%. In 1993 Hoekman published another study, involving a sample of 556 autistic and non-autistic subjects, aged under 156 months, who had served as subjects in earlier investigations, and the majority of whom were mentally retarded. The author found that 18.3% could not be classified; as far as the remaining 81.7% is concerned he found a 96.7% correct discrimination between autistic and non-autistic cases.

Critical remarks:

- On closer examination the scale's content is found not to reflect the six elements which together constitute the construct 'early infantile autism' as developed by Van Berckelaer-Onnes (1979, 1983). Hoekman (1992) found a dichotomy running along quite different lines.
- For two reasons it would have been better if the lower limit of the norm table for the non-talking children had likewise been set at a chronological age of three years instead of ten months. In the first place the youngest subject is not ten but eighteen months old. In the second place the number of non-talking subjects is only five in the age group 10-23 months (four autistic, one non-autistic), and 23 in the age group 24-36 months (fifteen autistic, eight non-autistic), which taken together is a very low number on which to base a standardization, the more so because these norms constitute the scale's limit.
- Doubtful cases, i.e., subjects with autistic-like disorders (many of them presumably cases of PDD-NOS as defined by the DSM-III-R), were excluded. However, notably mentally retarded persons often belong to this category. By excluding this doubtful category the scale's sensitivity and specificity were raised artificially.
- No information is provided concerning the proportion of mentally retarded subjects in the norm group and their level of functioning.
- In practice the scale proves to be rather impracticable; filling it in is far from easy; processing the results per item is also a complicated affair. To begin with, there are many choices to be made, such as: the appropriate form in view of the subject's chronological age and potential for speech; which of three items has the lowest score; which scoring key out of four is appropriate; which of the four conversion tables is appropriate. Furthermore, the determination of the final score depends on a number of

rather complicated mathematical procedures. Not only are these procedures time-consuming, but, as experience teaches, somewhere along the line errors may occur.

III.1.2.5   *The scale of Pervasive Developmental Disorder in Mentally Retarded Persons*

This scale, known as the PDD-MRS, was originally published in Dutch as the AVZ (Kraijer, 1990). The norm group for the first Dutch version consisted of 578 mentally retarded subjects aged 3-50 years. After some experience was obtained with this scale, a slightly modified Dutch version was devised, based on a larger norm group. The revised scale was published as the AVZ-R (Kraijer, 1992). This revised version was translated into English and published as the PDD-MRS (Kraijer, 1997). In the present section the PDD-MRS will be reviewed along the same lines as the ABC, CARS and AUTI-R were considered above, and subsequently compared with these scales. A more detailed discussion of the PDD-MRS will be presented in Section III.1.3; directions for the use of the PDD-MRS along with a sample of the scale form will be presented in Appendix B.

Format: the scale has twelve items differently weighted; two items are divided into sub-items; scoring is dichotomic.

Assessment period: minimally the past two months and maximally the past six months. Sources of information: own observation; structured interviews with parents, professional workers, teachers, etc., taking the items of the scale as guidelines; reports written by the staffs of residential facilities, schools, clinical settings, day-care facilities, sheltered workshops, etc.

The problem area focussed upon: Pervasive Developmental Disorders (as defined by the DSM-III-R/DSM-IV and the ICD-10) occurring in mentally retarded people of all four levels of functioning, age-range 2-55 years. The entire spectrum of pervasive developmental disorders is covered, i.e., ranging from PDD-Autistic Disorder to PDD-NOS, or, in ICD-10 terminology, from Childhood Autism to (Other) Childhood disintegrative Disorder and Atypical Autism.

Classification: the scores are interpreted as follows:

    0 - 6   : Non-PDD
    7 - 9   : Doubtful
    10 - 19 : PDD

Norm group: 1096 mentally retarded subjects were examined, age-range 3-81 years. Distribution by level of functioning: 18% profoundly mentally retarded; 31% severely mentally retarded; 35% moderately mentally retarded; 17% mildly mentally retarded. No subjects were excluded for reasons of sensory handicaps, motor disorders, behavioural problems or psychiatric problems. Only a small group of non-ambulatory very profoundly mentally retarded persons who were virtually living a vegetable existence were at that time not included. (For two later additions to the sample, i.e., 56 non-ambulant, very profoundly mentally retarded subjects and 71 two-year-old mentally retarded children of all levels of mental retardation, see Appendix B.)

Validity: concerning the 376 PDD subjects the instrument's sensitivity (= percentage cases correctly assessed) was found to be 94.4%; concerning the 614 non-PDD subjects the instrument's specificity (= percentage non-cases correctly assessed) was found to be 92.7%. The overall misclassification rate was found to be 6.7% when the doubtful category was left out of account, and 9.4% when this category was included.

III.1.2.6 *Three instruments currently in the making*

This overview would be incomplete without at least mentioning the new instruments which are currently being developed.

Lord et al. (1989) devised the Autism Diagnostic Observation Schedule or ADOS, which is also intended to be a classification instrument. Standardized video recordings have to be evaluated by experienced and specially trained clinical observers. As yet the instrument's sensitivity and specificity have been determined only by means of a sample of forty autistic and non-autistic mentally retarded subjects, age-range 6-18. The overall rate of correct classification was found to be 80%.

DiLavore et al. (1995) devised the Pre-Linguistic Autism Diagnostic Observation Schedule or PL-ADOS. According to the authors this instrument is "a semistructured observation scale designed for use as a diagnostic tool for children below six years of age who are not yet using phrase speech and are suspected of having autism. The PL-ADOPS takes approximately thirty minutes to administer and is appropriate for use with this population because of its emphasis on playful interactions." To date, the scale has been administered to only a comparatively small number of children. Its reliability seems to be satisfactory. Its validity has only been tested on bona fide autistic or non-autistic subjects; the results were positive. As yet, the scale does not discriminate effectively between speaking autistic children on the one hand and non-speaking children with other developmental disorders on the other hand.

Barthélémy et al. (1990) devised the Behavioral Summarized Evaluation or BSE. The instrument has been tried out on two comparatively small samples. The largest and most recent sample consisted of 116 predominantly mentally retarded children, age-range 2-8 years; 58 of them had previously been diagnosed as cases of Infantile Autism according to the fairly strict criteria developed by the DSM-III; the other 58 children were all mentally retarded without associated disorders. Applying the scale to these two quite clearly distinguishable groups resulted in a 90.5% correct classification rate. Twelve of the twenty items were found to contribute hardly anything to this outcome. Some investigations have been carried out in preparation for an Infant Version of the BSE, extending the scale's applicability to children below two years of age (Adrien et al., 1992).

Lord et al. (1993, 1994) devised the Autism Diagnostic Interview-Revised or ADI-R, a revision of the ADI. The new version is intended for children and adults of a developmental age of eighteen months and above. In two respects the instrument shows a resemblance to the PDD-MRS. In the first place its content is largely based on the criteria for pervasive developmental disorders as developed by the ICD-10 and the DSM-IV. In the second place the scale's objective, according to the authors, is to make a discrimination between mentally handicapped autistic children and non-autistic severely mentally handicapped children. The scale contains 111 items in all; these have to be filled in on the basis of an interview with parents or professional helpers. The interview takes about ninety minutes if the child in question is very young, a little longer for an older child. Results are only known from assessments of children in the age-range 2-5. These results suggest that ADI-R discriminates reasonably well when applied to young children diagnosed according to strict criteria as being either autistic or non-autistic.

III.1.2.7   *Applicability of measuring instruments to mentally retarded subjects*

In the context of the present study the applicability of the instruments re-viewed above to mentally retarded persons in particular is of special interest.

- None of the instruments, with the exception of the PDD-MRS, makes a distinction between retarded and non-retarded subjects in the intended target group. This may be quite a drawback, especially when testing men-tally retarded persons in the lower levels of functioning. As mentioned in Chapter I.1, Bartak and Rutter (1976) found that there are considerable differences between mentally retarded autistic persons and autistic per-sons of normal intelligence. With respect to the AUTI-R in particular, the above mentioned studies which involved a fair number of mentally re-tarded persons of all ages found less than optimal classificatory power, sensitivity and specificity; this finding indicates that there may be notice-able differences between mentally retarded persons and persons in the normal range of intelligence.
- A related problem is that the norm groups on which the instruments are based were not composed in such a way that the four levels of mental retardation were proportionately represented, again with the exception of the PDD-MRS.
- The majority of the available scales has been devised more or less ex-pressly as instruments to assess children. However, the entire area of PDD diagnosis in mental retardation has been so grossly disregarded that it seems to me an absolute necessity that scales should be devised which are applicable to mentally retarded persons of all ages. The PDD-MRS fills a gap.

- The majority of the available scales is devised to identify classical infantile autism only. However, as is generally known, autistic-like disorders (or, in DSM-III-R terminology, PDD-NOS) are far from uncommon, and this holds also for the mentally retarded population; cases with these disorders are just as much in need of an early identification and diagnosis.

The PDD-MRS, devised especially for mentally retarded people, will be discussed in more detail in III.1.3. In devising this scale the weak points of earlier scales were avoided as much as possible.

III.1.3 The PDD-MRS in detail

In Sections III.1.3.1 to III.1.3.9 the constructional and psychometric principles used in devising the PDD-MRS are discussed elaborately. Useful information may also be found in the companion manual to the scale, appended to the present volume as Appendix B.

III.1.3.1 *Basic principles underlying the PDD-MRS*

In devising the PDD-MRS (PDD-MR Scale, in full: Scale of Pervasive Developmental Disorder in Mentally Retarded Persons) a number of principles have been kept in mind.

- Obviously the scale must measure what it claims to measure, or, in other words, its validity must be satisfactory.
- Just as obviously, the scale must yield the same results whenever it is applied by whichever expert, or, in other words, its reliability must be satisfactory.
- It is essential for a scale of this kind to comply with the concepts of and the criteria for Pervasive Developmental Disorders laid down by the DSM (and the ICD), which are increasingly adopted world-wide (a statement which was also made by Morgan, 1988). However, it must be realized that the application of DSM classification criteria in assessing severely and profoundly retarded subjects presupposes extensive clinical experience in many fields, viz., mental retardation, autism in all its manifestations and other disorders and mental defects.

    Another problem in this connection is that professional helpers, such as attendants and teachers, are generally rather unacquainted with autism as a clinical entity, for the simple reason that they have not seen many of these cases; moreover, due to their close familiarity with the mentally retarded persons under their care they are inclined to consider an autistic feature as a 'normal' personal characteristic. To my mind the first drawback may be remedied, but the second is less easily put right without damaging the original concepts. Therefore, the scale is devised to be administered by psychologists, educational psychologists, psychiatrists and medical doctors, as these experts have a more detached view. In fact, another instrument is still needed which would enable professional workers in the mental retardation field to identify not only autism and autistic-like disorders, but also a great many other behavioural and mental disorders known to occur in mentally retarded people, although in these people the disorders may manifest themselves in very specific ways. Such a scale should equally be based on DSM concepts and be devised to assess mentally retarded persons. The PDD-MRS may be seen as a first step towards such an enterprise, being an attempt to convert the DSM concept of Pervasive Developmental Disorders into operational definitions which are applicable in the mental retardation field. In this connection I would like to emphasize once more that the scale is not limited to autism, but covers the entire spectrum or continuum of pervasive developmental disorders; therein autism is the most serious disorder, while the related contactual and communicative disorders, labelled Atypical or Not Otherwise Specified, are the least serious. However, it seems unrealistic to expect a scale to be devised with the discriminating power to identify the various subtypes of pervasive developmental disorders, especially in the mental retardation field.

- The scale must be applicable to persons of all levels of functioning (i.e., profoundly, severely, moderately and mildly retarded people) and to persons with sensory defects, motor defects or other disabilities. However, the scale will presumably not be applicable to completely non-ambulatory profoundly retarded people (i.e., children with a DQ of 10 or less, and adolescents and adults with a mental age of twelve months or below). Due to their very narrow behavioural repertoire it generally will be very difficult to classify and diagnose these people; their contact skills can be assessed, but many other criteria usually have to be ignored. (See Appendix B.6.5.1.)
- The scale must cover mentally retarded persons in a very wide age-range, i.e., from very young to about fifty years of age.
- The scale must cover observations of current behaviour, i.e., that observed during the past two to six months.
- The scale must be easy to administer and must not require special preparatory training; to achieve this the following conditions have to be met: the number of items must be kept to a minimum; scoring must be an easy procedure; computation of the final score must not be too complicated an affair, so as to minimize possible errors; the behaviour to be scored must be readily observable at home, in the group home, school, day-care centre, etc.; clear instructions must be provided as to the sources from which additional information may be obtained.
- The scale must be devised primarily as an instrument which is able to categorize and screen; it is not intended as a diagnostic instrument, although it may be helpful in making diagnoses, especially with complicated cases.

III.1.3.2   *The pilot study*

The first thing to do was to develop a corpus of descriptions of behavioural patterns which are typical of autism and related disorders. These descriptions were mainly based on the criteria laid down by the DSM-III and DSM-III-R. Other sources used were the BRIAAC (Ruttenberg et al., 1977), the CARS, the ABC and the AUTI-R. Useful descriptions were also taken from the literature, such as Creak (1961) and a number of essays in the handbook of Cohen and Donnellan (1987); of special value at this stage were the articles written by Vela et al. (1983) and Adrien et al. (1987).

As the scale was intended to be used to assess mentally retarded persons, it seemed very apropos to make intensive use of the wealth of information to be found in the files of forty mentally retarded children in all four levels of functioning, aged 2-14 years, who had been observed and treated at the Eekwal observation home. On the basis of data from their files these children were classified by the present author as PDD. The selection was made from a random sample of 113 mentally retarded children observed and treated at the Eekwal home who were categorized as PDD, doubtful-PDD, and non-PDD. To prevent bias on the part of the author the help of a highly competent specialist in neuropsychiatry, Joke Weits-Binnerts, was called in to make a fresh additional classification. For the three categories we found 86.7% agreement; Cohen's kappa coefficient of agreement .78 (see Siegel & Castellan, 1988). This is 'excellent' according to the criteria given by Cicchetti and Sparrow (1981). The forty children classified as PDD fitted perfectly into the following DSM-III categories: IA, COPDD and Atypical.

The behavioural descriptions provided the material for a preliminary number of 37 scale items. These items had to do with either the presence of abnormal behaviour, such as echolalia or self-injury, or the absence of normal behaviour, such as eye-to-eye contact and expressive language skills. The scale was tried out on sixty PDD children, adolescents and adults, all living in institutions. The number of items was then reduced to 21, as some were eliminated because of overlapping items or difficulties in interpretation. Useful suggestions and commentaries, received from psychologists, educational psychologists and doctors after a second trial, led to a further reduction, bringing the final number of items down to nineteen. This inventory, having the form of a *behaviour-checklist* and used in the research phase, is presented below. (For the detailed instructions per item see Appendix B.)

BEHAVIOUR-CHECKLIST-19

Contact with adults:
1 Severely deficient contact with adults
2 Less severely deficient contact with adults
3 Generally giving response to contact initiative of adults, but without proper understanding of social cues

Contact with peers:
 4 Is a loner amongst peers
Language and speech:
 5 Expressive language absent or virtually absent
 6 Language and speech are present, but with deviances in form and content
 7 Language and speech are present, but with deviances in production
Other behaviours:
 8 Very restricted range of obsessive interests
 9 Stereotyped handling of objects
10 Stereotyped postures and/or motor behaviour
11 Strong dependence on fixed patterns, routines and/or rituals
12 Self-injurious behaviour
13 Defiant, teasing, obstructive behaviour
14 Seeking constant attention by verbal or physical means
15 Abrupt and extreme shifts of mood or turnabouts
16 Highly erratic, unpredictable behaviour
17 Excessive anxieties and/or panic reactions
18 Intense anxieties, fears or phobias in reaction to specific rather common-place situations
19 Obsessive preoccupations with strange thoughts and ideas

All items, with the exception of the first three, had to be marked with either a + or a - sign. This was done because a half-way category might offer too easy an excuse for potential users to evade the rigmarole of thinking and rethinking or checking and rechecking whether or not a given description actually applied to the subject under investigation. A similar decision had been made for previously developed scales: the SMZ (Gross Motor Skills Scale for the Mentally Retarded; see Kraijer & Kema, 1981/1994) and the SRZ-P (Social Functioning Scale for the Mentally Retarded of a Higher Level; see Kraijer & Kema, 1984/1994). The high interrater reliability and stability of both instruments (respectively .97; .97 and .92; .90) prove that a dichotomous system is in fact quite satisfactory.

In the pilot study the 19-item inventory was used. The aim of the study was to ascertain whether the inventory's discriminating power and reliability were satisfactory and whether any corrections or adaptations would be necessary. Two random samples were drawn, one from the population of an institution for mentally retarded people and the other from the non-adult population of the Eekwal home (an observation home for mentally retarded people with developmental disabilities). Both populations had been previously examined for the presence or absence of PDD (which, according to the DSM-III-R, includes both PDD-AD and PDD-NOS). The samples were composed in such a way that they contained:

- no subjects with severe motor or sensory handicaps;
- both male and female subjects;

- subjects performing reasonably well in the area of daily living skills, i.e., subjects whose Self-help subscale standard scores on the SRZ were ≥3 (Kraijer & Kema, 1972/1994; see also Appendix C); this area proves to be the least affected in mentally retarded people with autism and related disorders and seemed therefore to provide the best indicator for level of functioning (see I.2.3);
- about as many PDD subjects as non-PDD subjects;
- as much as possible equal proportions of persons within the PDD and non-PDD subgroups from each age category (chronological age) and from the four levels of functioning (indicated by their Self-help subscale standard scores on the SRZ).

The first sample thus composed consisted of 99 mentally retarded subjects. Of these, 44 had been classified as PDD (i.e., PDD-AD or PDD-NOS) and 42 had been classified as non-PDD. In what follows these two subgroups will be referred to respectively as P-INST-19 and N-INST-19 ('-19' referring to the nineteen items in the checklist).

Regrettably, the institutional sample could not simply be subdivided into a PDD-subgroup and a non-PDD subgroup, because of a number of divergent assessments and doubtful-PDD classifications.

The subgroup doubtful-PDD (D-INST-19) numbered thirteen subjects. The subgroups P-INST-19 and N-INST-19 were found to be similar with respect to distribution rates by age and level of functioning (t-test; ns). The mean chronological ages of the two subgroups were 29.4 years (s.d. 9.50) and 31.0 years (s.d. 10.29), respectively; the mean standard scores on the subscale Self help of the SRZ were 6.59 (s.d. 1.28) and 6.67 (s.d. 1.10), respectively. The checklist was completed by a psychologist or educational psychologist; in total eight of these experts were in charge of the subjects being assessed. Independently of these experts the checklist was also completed by one of the five medical specialists responsible for the subjects in question. Those who completed the list evidently knew the subjects concerned quite well and were free to gather information from the attendants in charge and to consult reports and files.

The second sample consisted of 76 subjects. All subjects were children with developmental disorders and additional problems; they were admitted to the Eekwal home for observation and for tentative treatment. The present author completed the checklist for the children on the basis of their files. These files provided very detailed reports regarding the condition of individual children during the observation period. To prevent bias on the part of the author from interfering, the same procedure was repeated by another expert at a later date. I will come back to this later. Again, there were three subgroups of subjects, classified as PDD, non-PDD and doubtful-PDD. In what follows these subgroups will be referred to as P-OBS-19 (n = 32), N-OBS-19 (n = 32) and D-OBS-19 (n = 12), respectively. Again, the sample was composed in such a way that the two subgroups P-OBS-19 and N-OBS-19 were similar with respect to distribution rates by age and level of functioning (t-test; ns). The mean chronological ages of these subgroups were 7.6. years (s.d. 3.41) and 7.9 years (s.d. 3.36), respectively; the age-range was 3-14 years; the mean standard scores on the subscale Self help of the SRZ were 6.41 (s.d. 1.19) and 6.75 (s.d. 1.39), respectively.

The results of the investigation will be presented separately for the two samples and in the same order as above.

Table III.1.1 presents the general results of the institutional sample; the figures for the first three items that are relevant to the contact area, the area which is of special interest here, are presented both separately and combined.

Table III.1.1 The Behaviour-checklist-19 administered by psychological and medical experts assessing institutionalized people categorized as PDD, Doubtful-PDD and Non-PDD: percentages of items which received plus scores

Item	P-INST (n = 44)			D-INST (n = 13)			N-INST (n = 42)		
	Psy-chol. ex-perts	Medi-cal ex-perts	M	Psy-chol. ex-perts	Medi-cal ex-perts	M	Psy-chol. ex-perts	Medi-cal ex-perts	M
1	52.3	40.9	46.6	7.7	0.0	3.8	0.0	0.0	0.0
2	34.1	43.2	38.6	42.6	7.7	26.9	9.5	14.3	11.9
3	13.6	15.9	14.8	23.1	46.2	34.6	11.9	11.9	11.9
1+2+3	100.0	100.0	100.0	76.9	53.8	65.4	21.4	26.2	23.8
4	84.1	88.6	86.4	46.2	23.1	34.6	16.7	21.4	19.0
5	47.7	40.9	44.3	23.1	23.1	23.1	31.0	22.7	27.4
6	38.6	38.6	38.6	15.4	7.7	11.5	7.1	11.9	9.5
7	36.4	38.6	37.5	15.4	7.7	11.5	9.5	19.0	14.3
8	56.8	38.6	47.7	15.4	7.7	11.5	7.1	7.1	7.1
9	45.5	31.8	38.6	23.1	30.8	26.9	4.8	9.5	7.1
10	81.8	61.4	71.6	42.2	15.4	30.8	16.7	19.0	17.9
11	86.4	90.9	88.6	30.8	46.2	38.5	33.3	40.5	36.9
12	47.7	40.9	44.3	30.8	23.1	26.9	14.3	9.5	11.9
13	15.9	9.1	12.5	38.5	38.5	38.5	14.3	4.8	9.5
14	31.8	18.2	25.0	53.8	53.8	53.8	35.7	33.3	22.6
15	38.6	38.6	38.6	38.5	38.5	38.5	9.5	14.3	11.9
16	20.5	22.7	21.6	23.1	15.4	19.2	2.4	2.4	2.4
17	36.4	20.5	28.4	15.4	0.0	7.7	2.4	7.1	4.7
18	15.9	11.4	13.6	7.7	7.7	7.7	9.5	7.1	8.3
19	22.7	18.2	20.5	7.7	15.4	11.5	7.1	7.1	7.1

On the face of it, the percentages given above indicate in the first place that the judgements of both groups of experts hardly differ from one another, and in the second place that the percentages of plus scores are predominantly in line with what one may expect, i.e., highest in the PDD-group, lower in the doubtful-PDD group and lowest in the non-PDD group. In Tables III.1.2 and III.1.3 the results of the verification of these impressions are presented.

Table III.1.2 Correspondence between judgments of psychological experts and medical experts when administering the Behaviour-checklist-19, in percentages and in terms of coefficient Kappa

Item	Behaviour assessed	Percentage agreement	Coefficient Kappa	p
1	Severely deficient contact	80	.47	<.001
2	Less severely deficient contact	72	.31	<.01
3	Misunderstanding of social cues	82	.29	<.05
4	Loner amongst peers	80	.59	<.001
5	Expressive language absent	87	.73	<.001
6	Language deviant in content	81	.49	<.001
7	Language deviant in production	81	.42	<.001
8	Obsessions/preoccupations	76	.41	<.001
9	Stereotyped handling of objects	76	.43	<.001
10	Stereotyped motor behaviour	72	.44	<.001
11	Fixed routines/rituals	84	.67	<.001
12	Self-injurious behaviour	81	.55	<.001
13	Defiant/teasing behaviour	80	.17	ns
14	Seeking constant attention	76	.44	<.001
15	Shifts of mood	66	.16	ns
16	Erratic/unpredictable behaviour	87	.48	<.01
17	Extreme anxieties/panic	79	.18	ns
18	Anxieties/fears	90	.44	<.05
19	Strange thoughts and ideas	86	.42	<.01

As the table shows, for most items the percentage of agreement is quite high. However, due to a comparatively high number of minus scores the results are in fact somewhat less convincing, at least for some items. The p-values, though generally good, carry comparatively little weight here (just as with the product moment correlation coefficients). Only significance values corresponding to $p \leq .001$ are taken into account. Conforming to stated norms (Cicchetti & Sparrow, 1981; Siegel & Castellan, 1988) two of the coefficient's values which were found to correspond to kappa >.60 may be qualified as 'good'; twelve which were found to correspond to kappa >.40 may be qualified as 'fair' or 'moderate.' For the sake of completeness, it should be noted that the coefficients of items 1, 2 and 3, supposedly referring to declining levels of contact skills, have been calculated separately and these values are therefore not weighted.

Table III.1.2 shows that the assessments diverge clearly or even considerably for items 2, 3, 13, 15, 17, 18 and 19, and the interrater reliability of these items is therefore not up to par. The results of the examination of their discriminating power are presented in Table III.1.3. The significance values have been established by means of the chi-square test.

Table III.1.3 Significance values p for the difference between the number of plus scores assigned in the Behaviour-checklist-19 to the subgroups P-INST-19 and N-INST-19 presented separately for assessments made by psychological experts and by medical experts

Item	Behaviour assessed	Psychol. experts	Medical experts
1	Severely deficient contact	<.001	<.001
2	Less severely deficient contact	<.01	<.01
3	Misunderstanding of social cues	ns	ns
4	Loner amongst peers	<.001	<.001
5	Expressive language absent	ns	ns
6	Language deviant in content	<.001	<.01
7	Language deviant in production	<.01	<.05
8	Obsessions/preoccupations	<.001	<.001
9	Stereotyped handling of objects	<.001	<.05
10	Stereotyped motor behaviour	<.001	<.001
11	Fixed routines/rituals	<.001	<.001
12	Self-injurious behaviour	<.001	<.001
13	Defiant/teasing behaviour	ns	ns
14	Seeking constant attention	ns	ns
15	Shifts of mood	<.01	<.05
16	Erratic/unpredictable behaviour	<.01	<.01
17	Extreme anxieties/panic	<.01	<.01
18	Anxieties/fears	ns	ns
19	Strange thoughts and ideas	<.05	ns

Table III.1.3 shows that the discriminating power of items 3, 5, 13, 14, and 18 is definitely not up to par, and that of item 19 is not quite satisfactory. This result is in fact not so disappointing, as the significance values have been calculated for the items separately, whereas ultimately the scale is intended to be an entity of interrelated items.

Before presenting further adaptations to the body of items, the findings of the second sample, consisting of observation-home children, will be considered. In Table III.1.4 the general results are presented; again the percentages of the three items which are relevant to the contact area are presented both separately and combined.

Table III.1.4 The Behaviour-checklist-19 administered to observation-home children categorized as PDD, Doubtful-PDD and Non-PDD: percentages of items which received plus scores

Item	P-OBS (n = 32)	D-OBS (n = 12)	N-OBS (n = 32)	p
1	25.0	0.0	0.0	<.01
2	56.3	66.7	6.3	<.001
3	18.8	8.3	6.3	ns
1+2+3	100.0	75.0	12.5	-
4	84.4	66.7	18.8	<.001
5	21.9	25.0	9.4	ns
6	75.0	33.3	28.1	<.001
7	62.5	41.7	25.0	<.01
8	78.1	16.7	9.4	<.001
9	65.6	33.3	15.6	<.001
10	68.8	41.7	34.4	<.01
11	78.1	50.0	37.5	<.001
12	53.1	41.7	25.0	<.05
13	25.0	16.7	31.3	ns
14	31.3	33.3	28.1	ns
15	56.3	25.0	12.5	<.001
16	34.4	16.7	0.0	<.001
17	28.1	0.0	3.1	<.01
18	12.5	16.7	6.3	ns
19	21.9	0.0	9.4	ns

The subjects of this sample differ from those of the institutional sample in many respects, the most important being that they are much younger. Moreover, in this sample the assessments were made by one single person. Nevertheless, the percentages found correspond to a fair degree, while the correspondence between the significance values concerning differences is considerable. In this sample the discriminating powers of item 3 (misunderstanding of social cues), item 5 (no expressive language), item 13 (defiant/teasing behaviour), item 14 (seeking constant attention), item 18 (anxieties/fears), and item 19 (strange thoughts and ideas) were found not to be quite so satisfactory.

On the basis of the findings presented in the previous four tables a reorganisation of the corpus of items was possible. However, it was important to prevent a loss of potential sources of valuable information as a result of the elimination of items. Bearing this in mind and making use of recommendations and critical remarks received from those who had made assessments by means of the checklist, the following adaptations were made: items 2 and 3 were combined; item 5 (which could not be left out as a minus score for this item necessitates the assessment of items 6 and 7) was reformulated; items 13 and 14 were combined so as to enhance their discriminating power; item 15, which proved to be less satisfactory, was combined with the highly satisfactory item 16; items 17 and 18, which for various reasons were less satisfactory, were combined; imprecise behavioural descriptions, in particular for item 19, were put right; two sub-items were added to the two items bearing on the contact area (i.e., response to contact initiative of adults/social interaction with peers is consonant with level of functioning), the intention being to promote conscious and careful scoring in an area which is very liable to subjective impressions; on the basis of findings obtained in three studies (Roosendaal & Van Grunsven, 1985; Kraijer, 1991) it was decided to include rumination in the behaviours listed for the item bearing on stereotyped manipulation of own body.

III.1.3.3   *Further rechecks*

The revised checklist, called Behaviour-checklist-15, was subsequently submitted to raters, again psychological and medical professionals. Its completion was in fact an entirely fresh undertaking, as the standard procedure had been to request the immediate return of the 19-item version on completion, and the revised version was not made available until six months later. The institutional sample contained again 99 persons. The only mutation made to the sample was the substitution of two doubtful-PDD subjects by one PDD-subject and one non-PDD subject. This change did not alter the distribution rates by age and level of functioning. The sample of observation-home children was exactly the same as that used in the pilot study, and again the assessments were made by the present author.

In what follows the main results will be presented in two tables. In Table III.1.5 the significance values of the difference between the number of plus scores assigned to the two PDD and non-PDD subgroups of both samples (designated as: P-INST-15; N-INST-15; P-OBS-15; N-OBS-15) are presented separately for comparison with the assessments made by experts from the two different disciplines. This time the level of significance does include values up to and including p <.00001 (chi-square test), so as to allow weighting of items if necessary.

Table III.1.5 Significance values p for the differences between the number of plus scores assigned in the Behaviour-checklist-15 in assessing the subgroups P-INST-15 and N-INST-15; P-OBS-15 and N-OBS-15

Item	Behaviour assessed	P-INST-15 ↔ N-INST-15		P-OBS-15 ↔ N-OBS-15
		Psychol. experts	Medical experts	Present author
1	Severely deficient contact	<.00001	<.00001	<.01
2	Less severely deficient contact	<.01	<.0001	<.00001
3	Loner amongst peers	<.00001	<.00001	<.00001
4	Expressive language absent	<.00001	<.02	ns
5	Language deviant in content	<.00001	<.01	<.001
6	Language deviant in production	<.00001	<.05	<.01
7	Obsessions/preoccupations	<.01	<.01	<.00001
8	Stereotyped handling of objects	<.0001	<.00001	<.0001
9	Stereotyped motor behaviour	<.001	<.00001	<.01
10	Fixed routines/rituals	<.0001	<.0001	=.001
11	Self-injurious behaviour	<.00001	<.01	<.05
12	Defiant/claiming behaviour	ns	ns	ns
13	Erratic/unpredictable behaviour	<.02	<.0001	<.0001
14	Anxieties/panic reactions	ns	<.001	<.02
15	Strange notions	ns	ns	ns

As the table shows, the levels of significance of ratings per item clearly agree. This holds just as true when comparing the ratings made by psychological and medical experts as when comparing the ratings made of the two widely diverging groups of mentally retarded persons. There are therefore sufficient grounds for lumping the two groups together (175 subjects in total) and comparing the ratings per item for the three combined subgroups P-15 (n = 77), D-15 (n = 23), and N-15 (n = 75). To calculate the weighted means for the ratings of both samples, the ratings made by the psychological and medical experts in the first sample were averaged beforehand.

Table III.1.6 The Behaviour-checklist-15 applied to the combined groups of mentally retarded subjects (n = 175) categorized as PDD, Doubtful-PDD and Non-PDD: weighted mean percentages of items which received plus scores

Item	Behaviour assessed	P-15	T-15	N-15
1	Severely deficient contact	49.7	5.8	0.7
2	Less severely deficient contact	50.3	61.7	10.1
3	Loner amongst peers	92.1	65.1	14.6
4	Expressive language absent	37.5	26.3	16.3
5	Language deviant in content	54.0	41.0	16.8
6	Language deviant in production	46.8	33.9	17.8
7	Obsessions/preoccupations	56.2	36.3	9.0
8	Stereotyped handling of objects	61.6	43.7	6.9
9	Stereotyped motor behaviour	68.7	40.0	6.9
10	Fixed routines/rituals	78.0	42.1	22.0
11	Self-injurious behaviour	52.6	32.2	15.9
12	Defiant/claiming behaviour	25.5	53.0	27.2
13	Erratic/unpredictable behaviour	45.3	55.7	10.5
14	Anxieties/panic reactions	30.3	17.8	7.5
15	Strange notions	20.5	22.3	7.5

The foregoing two tables allow us to draw the following conclusions:

- For most items the distribution of percentages of plus scores over the three groups is clearly in line with what one would expect, i.e., highest in the PDD-group, lower in the doubtful-PDD group and lowest in the non-PDD group.
- Thanks to a more precise wording of item 4 (concerning the absence of expressive language) the percentage of plus scores now shows a gradual decline, and the item's discriminating power has become significant (see Table III.1.5). Obviously this does not apply to infants and young children who in view of their developmental age are still in the prelinguistic stage. However, as noted earlier, a minus score for this item necessitates the assessment of items 6 and 7; this was the main reason why item 4 had to be retained. In fact, the combined figures for the two samples provide further proof that the item is an important one. Subgroup P-15 numbers 27 subjects without expressive language, subgroup N-15 only 11. This difference is significant on the 1% level (chi-square test). In conclusion, it was clear that item 4 had to be maintained.
- Item 12 (defiant/claiming behaviour) had to be eliminated as it proved again to lack discriminating power, even though it now combined behaviours first examined separately.
- To a lesser extent, the same holds true for item 15 (strange notions). The combined figures for the two samples yielded not more than a 5% level of significance. Therefore, it was decided that this item also had to be eliminated.

We are now approaching the final version of the list, which was eventually to become the PDD-MRS. The modifications successively made to the corpus of items have been summarized in Table III.1.7. Auxiliary items have been left out. The wording is now consistently modelled on that used in the final version.

Table III.1.7 Modifications made to the numbering system of the corpus of items

Behaviour checklist		PDD-MRS	Behaviour assessed
Version-19	Version-15		
1	1	1a	Severely deficient contact with adults
2	2	1b	Less severely deficient contact with adults
3			
4	3	2a	Deficient contact with peers
5	4	3	Expressive language absent
6	5	4	Language/speech deviant in content
7	6	5	Language/speech deviant in production
8	7	6	Obsessive interests
9	8	7	Stereotyped handling of objects
10	9	8	Stereotyped manipulation of own body
11	10	9	Fixed patterns, routines and/or rituals
12	11	10	Self-injurious behaviour
13	12		
14			
15	13	11	Erratic/unpredictable behaviour
16			
17	14	12	Unusual anxiety or panic
18			
19	15		

In the shortened version further amendments have been made to the wording of some items. In its definitive form, the PDD-MRS consists of no more than twelve items, one of which is subdivided. In point of fact, the auxiliary items are not counted. For the complete wording of all items the reader is referred to the manual (which is also presented in Appendix B, along with a sample of the scale form).

The interrater reliability per item was not retested, as the pilot study with the 19-item inventory had established sufficient proof in this respect. However, the overall reliability of the total score obviously carries much more weight and will receive ample treatment in Section 3.6.2 of the present chapter.

The next step was to maximize the discriminating power of the scale's total of plus scores, henceforth briefly termed the PDD-MRS score. To begin with, the final scores of the 175 subjects were computed by simply adding up their plus scores. For the 99 subjects of the institutional sample only assessments made by psychological experts were taken into account, on the assumption that eventually the main users of the scale would be persons in this field. The PDD-MRS scores of the P-, D- and N-subgroups, theoretically ranging from 0 to 13 points, were without a doubt asymmetrically distributed. Nevertheless, even sharper discrimination and a further reduction of overlapping proved to be feasible. On the basis of the significance levels presented in Table III.1.5, a weighting system was developed. The following system was found to yield the best results: weight factor 1 was assigned to items 3, 5, 6, 10, 11 and 12; weight factor 2 was assigned to items 1b, 4, 7, 8 and 9; weight factor 3 was assigned to items 1a and 2a. By this procedure the final scores could now range from 0-19 points; composite item 1 could score up to 3 points, as could item cluster 3, 4, and 5.

Table III.1.8 presents the mean PDD-MRS scores (and standard deviations) of the 175 subjects, divided into six subgroups. As will be noted, there is a close correspondence between the figures of the three subgroups of the two samples (t-test; ns). Furthermore, the differences between the mean PDD-MRS scores of the combined N-, D- and P-subgroups are highly significant (t-test, $p < .0001$; application to subgroup N is in fact not fully justified as the distribution of PDD-MRS scores is far from normal; however, the significance value may be regarded as sufficient in view of the very high t-value).

Table III.1.8 Mean PDD-MRS scores and standard deviations of the sub-groups N, D and P in both samples, separately and combined

Subgroups	INST			OBS			Total		
N	mean =	2.88		mean =	4.13		mean =	3.41	
	s.d. =	2.96		s.d. =	3.27		s.d. =	3.14	
	n	= 43		n	= 32		n	= 75	
D	mean =	7.27		mean =	8.50		mean =	7.91	
	s.d. =	4.31		s.d. =	3.00		s.d. =	3.71	
	n	= 11		n	= 12		n	= 23	
P	mean =	13.44		mean =	13.81		mean =	13.59	
	s.d. =	3.00		s.d. =	2.64		s.d. =	2.81	
	n	= 45		n	= 32		n	= 77	
n_{total}	99			76			175		

The results demonstrate that the PDD-MRS, applied to mentally retarded persons, effectively differentiates clear cases of PDD from clear cases of non-PDD. The two samples taken together represent a very heterogeneous group. As has been stated earlier, scale scores should be independent of chronological age and level of functioning. Sadly, however, not all scales meet this requirement, as the study by Wiegersma et al. (1978) concerning the BRIAAC demonstrates. To test the PDD-MRS in this respect, the mean scores of the following categories of PDD and non-PDD subjects were compared:

- children in the age-range 3-7 and those in the age-range 8-14;
- children in the age-range 3-14 and adolescents and adults in the age-range 15-50;
- subjects in the profound and severe ranges of mental retardation and subjects in the moderate and mild ranges of mental retardation.

The results are presented in Tables III.1.9, III.1.10, and III.1.11. For the sake of completeness, I should mention that for this inquiry sixteen fresh subjects were included in the age category 3-14 years.

Table III.1.9 Comparison of mean PDD-MRS scores and standard deviations: children of two age categories

Subgroups	Age 3-7			Age 8-14			t-test
N	mean =	4.33		mean =	4.00		
	s.d. =	3.18		s.d. =	3.48		ns
	n	= 18		n	= 17		
P	mean =	13.60		mean =	14.50		
	s.d. =	2.91		s.d. =	2.06		ns
	n	= 20		n	= 16		

Table III.1.10 Comparison of mean PDD-MRS scores and standard deviations: subjects of two age categories

Subgroups	Age 3-14		Age 15-50		t-test
N	mean =	4.17	mean =	2.75	
	s.d. =	3.29	s.d. =	2.88	ns
	n =	35	n =	40	
P	mean =	12.92	mean =	13.24	
	s.d. =	2.79	s.d. =	3.05	ns
	n =	52	n =	41	

Table III.1.11 Comparison of mean PDD-MRS scores and standard deviations: subjects of two ranges of mental retardation

Subgroups	Profound*-severe		Moderate-mild		t-test
N	mean =	4.25	mean =	3.02	
	s.d. =	3.77	s.d. =	2.87	ns
	n =	20	n =	55	
P	mean =	13.90	mean =	13.39	
	s.d. =	2.21	s.d. =	3.21	ns
	n =	31	n =	46	

* completely non-ambulatory very profoundly retarded persons excluded

The mean PDD-MRS scores of the parallel subgroups show a close to very close correspondence. The scale may therefore be said to differentiate between mentally retarded PDD persons and mentally retarded non-PDD persons within a wide age-range and within a virtually full range of mental retardation, in spite of the fact that only one single weighting system of items was used. There was, however, one worrisome question remaining, viz., possible bias in the assessments for the observation-home sample, as these had been made by the author. Therefore a completely independent assessment of the 76 files was made by Elly van der Horst, educational psychologist. The product moment correlation coefficient between both assessments (.86) proved to be very satisfactory. (The mean PDD-MRS scores successively arrived at were 8.89 and 7.29, the standard deviations being 5.36 and 5.91.)

III.1.3.4   *First steps towards validation*

Before a final decision could be taken regarding the scale's norms, it was crucial to obtain data from a larger number of subjects. At this stage, no mentally retarded persons would be excluded from the sample on account of their sensory or motor disabilities, or, indeed, for any sort of psychological or behavioural problem. Moreover, the norm group had to be more representative of the entire mentally retarded population than the sample used in the pilot study, which was, as will be recalled, drawn from one single institution and an observation home. This sample inevitably contained people who, apart from being mentally retarded, exhibited a miscellany of additional disorders and handicaps (see Chapters II.1, II.2 and II.3). Indeed, profoundly and severely mentally retarded people are overrepresented in institutions (Sherman, 1988), as are mentally retarded people with problem behaviour (this holds mainly for people in the mild and moderate ranges of retardation; see Sherman, 1988, and Blacher et al., 1992), while observation homes are populated almost exclusively by mentally retarded people with psychological and behavioural problems and people whose cases are poorly understood. It may well be expected that the scale will primarily be used with such complicated cases. If its discriminating power is satisfactory with these cases, we can already be quite assured of its efficacy. Nevertheless it seems useful to examine whether the scale would also yield good results when applied to a less anomalous group of mentally retarded people. The range of mental states of the mentally retarded population is, as far as the Dutch situation is concerned, well represented in the population of day-care centres for young mentally retarded children (Kraijer, 1991). For that reason children of this category were added to the norm group. This was also done to comply with a third requirement, namely that the norm group should not be made up exclusively of subjects from the Hendrik van Boeijen-Oord and the Eekwal observation home, two closely connected settings. This was also the reason for including a number of subjects from a similar institution in the north of the Netherlands (Huize Maartenswouden, Drachten). The psychologists and educational psychologists who acted as raters were asked to classify the subjects in their respective facilities as PDD, non-PDD and doubtful-PDD, according to the DSM-III-R criteria. Subsequently a random sample was drawn from these subjects to be added to the norm group. The raters were asked to assess these subjects by means of the scale (which we still purposely referred to as a 'behaviour-checklist'). Raters were not informed of the fact that a weighting system was going to be applied to the items of this scale. Generally, the assessments were carried out a couple of months after the classification procedure. Eventually, the norm group contained 578 subjects aged 3-50 years, including 214 institutionalized persons, 139 observation-home children, and 225 children attending day-care centres. In what follows this sample will be referred to as Sample-1990.

Table III.1.12 presents the PDD-MRS scores obtained in Sample-1990, subdivided into the subgroups N (n = 272), D (n = 77) and P (n = 229). The table also provides the cumulative and 100-minus cumulative percentages in order to allow the calculation of the scale's sensitivity (= percentage cases correctly assessed) and specificity (= percentage non-cases correctly assessed).

Table III.1.12 PDD-MRS scores of the subgroups N, D and P in Sample-1990, their mean scores and the standard deviations

PDD-MRS scores	N		D			P	
	n	cumul.%	n	cumul.%	100-cumul.	n	100-cumul.
0	81	29.8	1	1.3	98.7	-	-
1	67	54.4	-	1.3	98.7	-	-
2	28	64.7	1	2.6	97.4	-	100.0
3	22	72.8	7	11.7	88.3	1	99.6
4	19	79.8	1	13.0	87.0	2	98.7
5	14	85.0	6	20.8	79.2	6	96.1
6	8	87.9	6	28.6	71.4	1	95.7
7	8	90.8	6	36.4	63.6	3	94.4
8	9	94.1	14	54.6	45.4	6	91.8
9	3	95.2	5	61.1	38.9	6	89.2
10	6	97.4	6	68.9	31.1	16	82.2
11	4	98.9	10	81.9	18.1	18	74.3
12	1	99.3	6	89.7	10.3	25	63.4
13	1	99.7	2	92.3	7.7	30	50.3
14	-	99.7	3	96.2	3.8	27	38.5
15	1	100.0	1	97.5	2.5	32	24.5
16	-	-	1	98.8	1.2	25	13.6
17	-	-	-	98.8	1.2	19	5.3
18	-	-	-	98.8	1.2	8	1.8
19	-	-	1	100.0	0.0	4	0.0
n total	n = 272		n = 77			n = 229	
M	M = 2.51		M = 8.47			M = 13.18	
s.d.	s.d. = 3.00		s.d. = 3.56			s.d. = 3.18	

The relative values of mean scores and the standard deviations of the three subgroups come very close to the combined figures of the two pilot samples presented in Table III.1.8. If the mean scores of the three subgroups are compared per subgroup, the mean score of subgroup N is slightly lower, but the mean scores of subgroups D and P are virtually the same as those found in the pilot samples. It may therefore be concluded that the enlarged group (the norm group) presents practically the same picture as the small group (the two pilot samples). The differences between the mean PDD-MRS scores of the N-, D- and P-subgroups are again highly significant (t-test, $p < .0001$; again, application to subgroup N is in fact not fully justified as the distribution of PDD-MRS scores is far from normal; however, again in view of the high t-value, the significance value may be regarded as sufficient).

As mentioned in Section III.1.2, in devising and evaluating scales, doubtful cases, which in any classification system are bound to occur, are often excluded. Had this method been applied to the PDD-MRS, the scale would have had an excellent discriminating power, with a sensitivity of 91.8 (i.e., 8.2% of cases wrongly assessed as non-PDD), and a specificity of 94.1 (i.e., 5.9% of cases wrongly assessed as PDD), using 8 as the cut-off score. The weighted overall misclassification rate would then be as low as 7.0%. However, in reality things are much more complicated. In the first place, when classifying people, notably mentally retarded people, on the basis of behavioural features, some cases will inevitably have to be labelled doubtful. A second problem, which will hopefully be remedied in due course, is that many raters prove to have little experience in identifying autism and related disorders in mentally retarded people, and quite understandably so, as the criteria for PDD-AD and PDD-NOS are often less easily applicable in the field of mental retardation. This shortcoming is especially conspicuous when assessing cases occupying positions somewhere between PDD and doubtful-PDD. It is too often the case that symptomatic behaviours, such as contact problems, stereotypies and self-injury, are considered as inherent to mental retardation and consequently not identified as manifestations of a separate disorder. In a series of investigations aimed at listing the main disorders met with in a large institution (the latest in this series using the PDD-MRS), it was found that the number of doubtful cases declined with each new investigation, and that the number of PDD cases increased to a rate which, according to my experience, better reflected the actual situation (see III.2.2.1). On the other hand, profoundly and severely mentally retarded persons who display fearful aloofness and stereotyped behaviour are especially liable to be incorrectly categorized as PDD; instead of being indicative of a contact disorder their behaviour may be due to vulnerability to environmental factors. In this connection I would like to mention that as early as 1967 Hoejenbos made an attempt to differentiate between what he called 'purely idiotic behaviour' and the 'psychotic behaviour displayed by an idiot' (see II.3.2.2).

We must conclude that in making assessments one has to be aware of two possible pitfalls: that of attaching too little importance to additional behavioural problems and that of attaching too much importance to them. This dilemma also explains the wide range of prevalence rates found. Wing and Gould (1979,1981), for instance, report a 40% prevalence rate of autism and related disorders in moderately mentally retarded persons (IQ 35-49), whereas the present study arrived at a 20% rate in the same range of mental retardation (see Chapter III.2).

As a matter of fact, the PDD and non-PDD categories both overlap the doubtful category. Using 4 as the cut-off score between the doubtful category and the non-PDD category, the false positive classification rate is 20.2%, while the false negative classification rate is 13.0%, i.e., a weighted overall misclassification rate of 18.6%. Using 11 as the cut-off score between the doubtful category and the PDD category, the false positive classification rate is 18.1%, while the false negative classification rate is 25.7%, i.e., a weighted overall misclassification rate of 23.8%. The highest percentage misclassifications are made in the border area between PDD and doubtful-PDD; plainly, it is more difficult to decide that a person is PDD than it is to decide that he is non-PDD. The explicit aim in devising the PDD-MRS was, however, *to provide diagnosticians with a useful instrument for discriminating PDD from non-PDD cases, and thus to reduce the number of doubtful cases.* A scale has to establish clear standards and guidelines in order to be of any use. In short, the norms should be based as far as possible on the *discriminating features of the subjects themselves.* Doubts due to *lack of insight among raters* should be eliminated as far as possible.

For two reasons the category doubtful carries too much weight. Firstly, it does not seem right that the doubtful category, although covering such a small proportion of subjects (in the PDD-MRS norm group the N-D-PDD ratio was found to be 47:13:40) carries as much weight in the calculation of the values for sensitivity and specificity as the other two categories, as adherence to the prevailing statistical method would demand. Secondly, on the basis of my clinical experience the doubtful category nevertheless contains too many cases. It may be assumed that no more than 20% of the entire range of the mentally retarded population should be classified as PDD (see Chapter III.2). The N-D-PDD ratio in the entire mentally retarded population would probably be 7:1:2, which would imply an inconveniently high proportion of doubtful cases. Hopefully the proportion of doubtful cases will decline considerably as clinical insight grows and more proficiency is acquired in applying the scale. Nevertheless, no scale, *however helpful it may be in providing objective data, will ever be a substitute for clinical insight.* Likewise, no hard and fast criteria can be derived from the PDD-MRS. Notably cases classified by the PDD-MRS as doubtful-PDD are in need of clinical reassessment. Earlier, Volkmar et al. (1988) arrived at a similar conclusion, reporting, "... such diagnoses, made by experienced clinicians, offer a reasonable point of comparison for the evaluation of more specific diagnostic schemes, which in turn, present other potential risks and benefits."

In Table III.1.13 the eventual overall misclassification rates at different cut-off scores, computed by means of the standard statistical method, are set alongside two series of values computed by means of methods involving a weighted overall misclassification rate. The table also allows comparison with the clinical impression of the present author, based on data from his trial of the scale; in the present context this impression should be considered decisive.

Table III.1.13 Overall misclassification rates in Sample-1990 computed by three different methods and compared to the the present author's clinical impression

Cut-off scores		Unweighted o.m.r.	Weighted o.m.r. in terms of number of subjects (1)	Weighted o.m.r. in terms of the entire retarded population (2)	Clinical impression
	4	**16.6 %**	18.6 %	19.3 %	N
	5	*17.9 %*	16.3 %	15.7 %	N
N ↔ D	6	20.4 %	15.7 %	14.2 %	N/D
	7	22.8 %	**15.2 %**	12.6 %	D
	8	30.3 %	16.6 %	**12.0 %**	D
	8	26.8 %	**17.6 %**	20.6 %	D
	9	24.9 %	17.9 %	**20.2 %**	D
D ↔ P	10	24.5 %	21.2 %	22.2 %	P
	11	*21.9 %*	23.8 %	23.2 %	P
	12	23.5 %	30.0 %	27.8 %	P
		Unweighted optimal	Weighted optimal (1)	Weighted optimal (2)	Final (1990)
Cut-off scores for:	N	0 - 4	0 - 7	0 - 8	0 - 5
	D	5 - 11	8	9	6 - 9
	P	12 - 19	9 - 19	10 - 19	10 - 19

The table shows that the cut-off scores arrived at by means of standard statistical methods come very close to the cut-off scores eventually decided upon. As expected, the overall misclassification rate did increase compared with the figures computed by means of the standard statistical method (see the figures in boldface and italics in the table's left-hand column), but the increase is only a slight one. It may therefore be concluded that the modifications made have hardly lessened the scale's validity, which remains - compared with that of similar instruments - quite satisfactory. Much more importantly, however, both the users of the scale and the persons to be diagnosed will benefit from the fact that the doubtful area has been reduced.

III.1.3.5   Final Standardization

III.1.3.5.1   General remarks
The year following the publication of the PDD-MRS brought a wealth of response from users of the scale. Notably it was reported to be easily administered, to settle clinical doubts, and to furnish explanations for behavioural problems.

It seemed about time for a revision of the standardization. This time the gauge was to be the *final diagnosis*, i.e., the third (or fifth) phase in the diagnostic process (see III.1.1), instead of *the clinical classification*, i.e., the first phase.

Anyone involved in the pioneering work of devising an instrument aimed at measuring a phenomenon which is as yet insufficiently explored faces an enormous difficulty: how can the instrument's validity be established without having reference to set norms? In the present context this difficulty manifested itself in the following ways:

- The mental retardation field is poorly acquainted with the concept of pervasive developmental disorders, even with that of narrowly defined autism.
- The mentally retarded population is an extremely difficult one in which to explore this matter.
- There is no possibility of determining the scale's 'concurrent validity', as there are no analogous scales available. (In fact, if such a scale already existed, there would be little point in developing a new scale.)

In the preliminary stage of the standardization process the last problem had been tackled (a) by demanding that the raters (psychological and medical experts) observe strict adherence to the DSM-III-R criteria for PDD, and (b) by involving only facilities which offer more or less specialized professional care to mentally retarded PDD persons. This latter provision was to become a key element in the final stage of the standardization process. In devising a scale it is indeed of crucial importance that ratings are made by experts. In the mental retardation field, at any rate in the Netherlands, ignorance about pervasive developmental disorders is still widespread, and the disorders may even fail to be recognized (see I.1). Had the facilities from which the subjects of the pilot samples were taken been randomly selected, ratings might have been made without the expertise needed to make the scale into a useful classificatory instrument.

Since only clinical classifications were available and there were no diagnoses on which to base the standardization of the scale, the norms derived from my own clinical experience (see III.1.3.4) were used to make (minor) adaptations to the cut-off scores. The score-ranges covering the three categories were set as follows:

    0 - 5 : Non-PDD
    6 - 9 : Doubtful
  10 - 19 : PDD

Once the subjects had been classified according to these ranges, the most crucial step in the standardization process could be taken: establishing norms on the basis of *the final diagnoses* made by the clinicians themselves. Of those subjects for whom the clinical classification did not agree with the PDD-MRS classification, a final diagnosis had to be made on the basis of both clinical and instrumental classifications. The procedure was then as follows. The raters were provided with the PDD-MRS scores and the resulting PDD-MRS classifications of the subjects concerned, and were asked to reconsider these cases in order to make final diagnoses. These diagnoses were subsequently entered under the headings Diagnosis non-PDD, doubtful-PDD or PDD; the initial clinical classifications could now be disregarded.

Meanwhile a large number of subjects were added to the original pilot sample. Raters of new subjects were again first asked to make a clinical classification and subsequently to make an assessment on the basis of the PDD-MRS, and finally, if the classifications did not match, to make a final decision or diagnosis.

How were the two classification systems appraised by the raters themselves? They were in fact explicitly encouraged in the accompanying instructions to use their own judgement in order to prevent them from attaching too much importance to the results of the scale, which might otherwise have impressed them as being more objective. As can be seen in Table III.1.14 (a compilation of Tables III.2.2 and III.2.9 which will be presented in the next chapter), a number of raters did change their minds in the course of time.

Table III.1.14 Comparison of distribution of N, D and PDD identified in institutionalized adults and in children attending day-care centres in three successive diagnostic phases (n $_{total}$ = 1015)

Phase in the diagnostic process	N		D		PDD	
	Number	Perc.	Number	Perc.	Number	Perc.
I Clinical classification	652	64.2	138	13.6	225	22.2
II Classification by means of the PDD-MRS	517	50.9	152	15.0	346	34.1
III Diagnosis on the basis of I and II	566	55.8	107	10.5	342	33.7

From the figures presented above, two conclusions may be drawn. In the first place, raters obviously did not always base their diagnoses on the PDD-MRS classifications. In the second place, the number of subjects classified as PDD increases in the three successive phases, while the number of subjects placed into the other two categories declines. I consider it a positive result that the number of subjects diagnosed as doubtful-PDD became comparatively small in the end; apparently the scale has helped raters to reach a final conclusion.

The important question still to be considered is whether the kind of validation employed here, this time based on the third phase of the diagnostic process, affects the PDD-MRS norms, and if so, in which way. This issue will be dealt with in Section III.1.3.5.2. First, however, the most relevant features of the new norm group, henceforth indicated as Sample-1992, have to be reviewed.

- As noted before, the subjects were taken exclusively from facilities which were known to devote more or less specialized professional care to mentally retarded PDD persons. In this way there was a minimal risk of the received classifications and diagnoses containing errors. It follows that the group of subjects thus investigated represents a *paradigmatic sample* rather than a representative one.

- Again, completely non-ambulatory profoundly retarded people (i.e., children with a DQ of 10 or less and adolescents and adults with a mental age below twelve months) were not included.

- Intentionally, no subjects were excluded who displayed sensory disabilities, motor disorders, behavioural problems or psychiatric problems; as a matter of fact, in clinical practice mentally retarded persons are found who have a PDD in addition to these problems. Moreover, in the preliminary phase the PDD-MRS proved to be quite applicable to this category of mentally retarded persons.

- To prevent the interference of bias on the part of the author, the Eekwal-home subjects of Sample-1990 who had been assessed and classified by means of the PDD-MRS on the basis of the data from their files were excluded from Sample-1992. A smaller number of more recently admitted Eekwal-home subjects, classified by means of the PDD-MRS on the basis of direct observation and subsequently diagnosed by at least two members of the observation team, served as substitute subjects in the new sample. In fact, this made the sample more balanced, as the observation-home subjects represent a rather anomalous group in the mental retardation field. However, one might question whether indeed measures aimed at enhancing representativeness are meaningful interventions. It may be argued that the disorders of a mentally retarded person with a PDD are the same, regardless of what type of facility or accommodation he or she has been placed into - be this an institution, observation clinic, day-care centre, special school, or whatever. Nevertheless, all possible measures were taken to avoid biased sampling, as will hopefully be clear from this point as well as from the one which follows.

- The sample contains a disproportionately high number of children attending day-care centres when compared with the number of institutionalized subjects (that is, more than we find to be the case in reality). This has been done to compensate for the fact that the sample did not contain subjects from the following facilities: special schools, day-care centres for adults, and group homes for adults. The cooperation of these facilities had not been requested on the assumption that they lacked the expertise needed to make the clinical classifications for this study. (The fact that PDD does occur less frequently in persons placed into these facilities may be one of the reasons for this.)

- The four levels of mental retardation are represented in the same proportions as in the three subgroups in the sample: the institutionalized persons, the children attending day-care centres and the Eekwal-home subjects.

- My preliminary clinical experience with the first version of the scale suggested that it was also sufficiently able to discriminate between PDD and non-PDD when applied to persons above the age of 50. A comparison made between the data available concerning 56 elderly mentally retarded

persons (43 non-PDD, two doubtful-PDD and eleven PDD) and the data of 982 subjects in the age-range 3-50 (Kraijer, 1991) produced the following results:
- the discriminating power of the scale was found to be exactly the same for both age categories;
- there was a fair to good correspondence between the mean PDD-MRS scores in the subgroups N, D and PDD of both age categories (t-test);
- a high agreement was found between the three mean scores of the elderly group when subdivided into the age groups 51-55 and 56-81 (t-test).

On the basis of these findings it was decided to increase the scale's age-range to 55 years. With respect to persons above the age of 55 it seemed safer to maintain the caveat that the scale was possibly less valid and reliable, as the age distribution within the age-range 55-81 years was very uneven. Nevertheless, the entire group of 56 elderly subjects was added to the norm group.
- Eventually Sample-1992 contained 1096 subjects; of these not more than 41.0% (449 persons) had also served as subjects for Sample-1990.

III.1.3.5.2 Validation on the basis of Sample-1992
Sample-1992 contains 1096 subjects, all from the north-eastern provinces of the Netherlands, 444 of whom are female and 652 male. Of these subjects, 718 persons (age-range 5-81) were taken from two institutions, 305 children (age-range 3-15) from day-care centres, and 73 persons (age-range 3-55) from the Eekwal observation home. In terms of their level of functioning, 18% were profoundly mentally retarded, 31% severely mentally retarded, 35% moderately mentally retarded, and 17% mildly mentally retarded. In terms of age, 28% of the subjects were aged 3-9 years, 8% 10-19 years, 38% 20-39 years, and 26% >40 years. Special care was taken to ensure that the extremes of the entire age-range were represented in sufficient numbers; there were 59 subjects above the age of fifty (45 non-PDD, three doubtful-PDD, eleven PDD), and 68 three-year-olds (42 non-PDD, nine doubtful-PDD, eighteen PDD).

With an N-D-PDD ratio of 56:10:34, the present sample is in this respect more in agreement with the actual situation than Sample-1990 (the ratio in that sample being roughly 47:13:40).

The numbers and percentages of plus scores per item assigned to subjects of Sample-1992 are presented in Table III.1.15 for each of the three subgroups N, D and PDD. The table consists of three parts, the second of which presents the combined figures for items 1a (severely deficient contact with adults) and 1b (less severely deficient contact with adults). Actually, only by taking these items together will it be clear how many subjects with social-interaction problems are contained in the group. The third part concerns only speaking subjects, presenting separately their results for the two language-area items.

Table III.1.15 PDD-MRS items receiving plus scores in subgroups PDD, Doubtful-PDD and Non-PDD of Sample 1992 (n = 1096)

Behaviour assessed	N (n = 614)		D (n= 106)		PDD (n = 376)	
	Num.	Perc.	Num.	Perc.	Num.	Perc.
1a Severely deficient contact with adults	3	0.5	11	10.4	162	43.1
1b Less severely deficient contact with adults	70	11.4	70	66.0	200	53.2
2a Deficient contact with peers	60	9.8	67	63.2	351	93.4
3 Expressive language absent	195	31.8	56	52.8	208	55.3
4 Language/speech deviant in content	62	10.1	26	24.5	146	38.8
5 Language/speech deviant in production	69	11.2	27	25.5	114	30.3
6 Obsessive interests	69	11.2	34	32.1	246	65.4
7 Stereotyped handling of objects	48	7.8	28	26.4	254	67.6
8 Stereotyped manipulation of own body	95	15.5	59	55.7	298	79.3
9 Fixed patterns, routines and/or rituals	103	16.8	43	40.6	272	72.3
10 Self-injurious behaviour	73	11.9	31	29.2	174	46.3
11 Erratic/unpredictable behaviour	78	12.7	30	28.3	207	55.1
12 Unusual anxiety or panic	37	6.0	23	21.7	132	35.1

Items receiving plus scores in the area contact with adults; combined figures

	Num.	Perc.	Num.	Perc.	Num.	Perc.
1a + 1b Deficient contact with adults	73	11.9	81	76.4	362	96.3

Items receiving plus scores in the area deficient language with speaking persons

	Num.	Perc.	Num.	Perc.	Num.	Perc.
4 Language/speech deviant in content	62	14.8	26	52.0	146	86.9
5 Language/speech deviant in production	69	16.5	27	54.0	114	67.9
	N (n = 419)		D (n = 50)		PDD (n = 168)	

As the table shows, the percentages of plus scores received by the PDD subgroup are clearly and consistently above thóse received by the non-PDD subgroup, with the doubtful subgroup taking up a middle position throughout.

For all items the differences between the numbers of plus scores obtained by the PDD and non-PDD subgroups were found to be highly significant, as Table III.1.16 shows. The chi-square values given in the table indicate whether the use of the previously applied weighting per item procedure is still justifiable. This is another three-part table. In the second part the values obtained for sub-items 1a and 2b are taken together; the third part concerns only speaking subjects, presenting separately the figures they obtained for the two language-area items.

Table III.1.16 Chi-square values and significance values p for the difference between the number of plus scores assigned in the PDD-MRS to the subgroups PDD and Non-PDD of Sample-1992 (n = 1096)

Behaviour assessed	Chi-square	p	Weighting
1a Severely deficient contact with adults	304.65	<.00001	3
1b Less severely deficient contact with adults	205.33	<.00001	2
2a Deficient contact with peers	670.91	<.00001	3
3 Expressive language absent	53.63	<.00001	1
4 Language/speech deviant in content	116.00	<.00001	2
5 Language/speech deviant in production	56.35	<.00001	1
6 Obsessive interests	315.63	<.00001	1
7 Stereotyped handling of objects	392.52	<.00001	2
8 Stereotyped manipulation of own body	396.31	<.00001	2
9 Fixed patterns, routines and/or rituals	305.98	<.00001	2
10 Self-injurious behaviour	147.27	<.00001	1
11 Erratic/unpredictable behaviour	204.01	<.00001	1
12 Unusual anxiety or panic	139.30	<.00001	1

Items receiving plus scores in the area contact with adults; combined figures			
1a + 1b Deficient contact with adults	674.16	<.00001	3/2

Items receiving plus scores in the area deficient language with speaking persons			
4 Language/speech deviant in content	272.53	<.00001	2
5 Language/speech deviant in production	147.60	<.00001	1

Once more the chi-square test consistently yielded highly significant values; in other words, it has been demonstrated that each and every item in the PDD-MRS contributes considerably to the final score. Comparing weight factors previously given to items in connection with the chi-square values reveals that only one item (i.e., item 6: obsessive interests) is possibly insufficiently served with its weighting factor 1. However, introducing a weighting factor 2 to this item was found to result in negligible shifts in classification and would therefore contribute little to the scale's sensitivity and specificity. In fact, this finding is not so surprising in view of the very high significance values found for all items. In addition, it is not recommendable to introduce changes to a scale's weighting system after its first issue, unless these changes are to represent genuine improvements and the benefits are to outweigh the inconvenience of running two different systems side-by-side.

The next step in the validation process is a comparison of the final PDD-MRS scores of the three subgroups of Sample-1992. The figures are presented in Table III.1.17, together with the cumulative and 100-minus cumulative percentages in order to allow the calculation of the scale's sensitivity (= percentage cases correctly assessed) and specificity (= percentage non-cases correctly assessed).

Table III.1.17 PDD-MRS scores of the subgroups N, D and PDD (diagnoses) in Sample-1992, their mean scores and standard deviations

PDD-MRS scores	N		D			PDD	
	n	cumul.%	n	cumul.%	100-cumul.	n	100-cumul.
0	173	28.2	-	-	-	-	-
1	125	48.5	1	0.9	99.1	-	-
2	73	60.4	0	0.9	99.1	-	-
3	79	73.3	2	2.8	97.2	2	99.5
4	48	81.1	1	3.8	96.2	0	99.5
5	44	88.3	3	6.6	93.4	3	98.7
6	27	92.7	9	15.1	84.9	1	98.4
7	17	95.4	11	25.5	74.5	3	97.6
8	12	97.4	33	56.6	43.4	5	96.3
9	7	98.5	25	80.2	19.8	7	94.4
10	3	99.0	7	86.8	13.2	39	84.0
11	2	99.3	7	93.4	6.4	36	74.5
12	2	99.7	3	96.2	3.8	50	61.2
13	1	99.8	2	98.1	1.9	52	47.3
14	0	99.8	0	98.1	1.9	58	31.9
15	0	99.8	1	99.1	0.9	43	20.5
16	1	100.0	0	99.1	0.9	38	10.4
17	-	-	1	100.0	0.0	26	3.5
18	-	-	-	-	-	8	1.3
19	-	-	-	-	-	5	0.0
n		614		106			376
M		2.39		8.37			13.19
s.d.		2.52		2.22			2.68
n total = 1096				M = 6.67			s.d. = 2.54

As shown in Table III.1.17, there is a striking agreement between the mean scores of the subgroups in this sample and those of Sample-1990; in Sample-1990 the following figures had been found: for subgroup N: M = 2.51, s.d. 3.00; for subgroup D: M = 8.47, s.d. = 3.56; for subgroup PDD: M = 13.18, s.d. = 3.18. This agreement is all the more remarkable considering that Sample-1992 contains a much larger number of institutionalized persons and that the majority of the 139 former observation-home children was excluded from this sample, partly to be substituted by fresh observation-home subjects. In fact, the present investigation almost deserves to be called a cross-validation study, as 59.0% of the subjects had not been incorporated into the original sample, but were newly selected.

As could hardly be otherwise, again the differences between the mean scores of the three subgroups are found to be highly significant (t-test, p <.0001; as far as subgroup N is concerned, application is in fact not fully justified, the distribution of PDD-MRS scores being far from normal; however, the significance value may be regarded as amply sufficient in view of the high t-value).

Finally, the table shows that the most optimal percentages for sensitivity and specificity (in boldface in the table) prove to refer to exactly the same ranges as those given two years earlier as the 'final ranges' (see Table III.1.13): for subgroup N, 0-5; for subgroup D, 6-9; for subgroup PDD, 10-19. The cut-off point for N-PDD lies, just as with Sample-1990, between 8 and 9 (see Table III.1.12). As has been argued in Section III.1.3.4, computation of a weighted overall misclassification rate should be preferred to an unweighted one; this weighting should preferably be done on the basis of the actual distribution of N, D and PDD in the entire retarded population. Accordingly, both the weighted and unweighted overall misclassification rates are presented in Table III.1.18. There are good reasons for assuming that the proportions of N, D and PDD subjects in the sample correspond fairly with those in the entire population, as intended. This table also presents the optimal ranges earlier presented in Table III.1.13 under the heading 'Clinical impression.'

Table III.1.18 Unweighted and weighted overall misclassification rates in Sample-1992 compared with the clinical impression of the present author

Cut-off scores		Unweighted o.m.r.	Weighted o.m.r. in terms of the entire population	Clinical impression (1990)
	4	11.4 %	16.7 %	N
	5	9.2 %	11.0 %	N
N ↔ D	6	11.2 %	8.5 %	N/D
	7	15.1 %	7.7 %	D
	8	29.6 %	10.6 %	D
	8	23.6 %	12.4 %	D
	9	12.7 %	8.7 %	D
D ↔ P	10	14.6 %	15.4 %	P
	11	16.1 %	21.3 %	P
	12	21.3 %	31.1 %	P
		Unweighted optimal	Weighted optimal	Final (1992)
Cut-off scores for:	N	0 - 5	0 - 7	0 - 6
	D	6 - 9	8 - 9	7 - 9
	P	10 - 19	10 - 19	10 - 19

- There is no doubt regarding where the cut-off score between the two diagnostic categories D and PDD must be set. Once again a close correspondence has been found between classification in the PDD-subgroup and assignment of PDD-MRS scores of 10 and higher. The respective 12.7 and 8.7 percentages for the unweighted and weighted means may be considered highly satisfactory.

- There is still room for uncertainty, however, concerning the right cut-off score between the diagnostic categories D and Non-PDD. My feeling is that there are good reasons for shifting the cut-off score from 5 to 6, and possibly even to 7.
- In everyday use the scale has to yield the lowest possible number of classification errors. Therefore the N:D:PDD ratio as found in the entire population is an important criterion. It follows that the weighted overall misclassification rate constitutes an essential value.
- When the weighted overall misclassification rate of non-PDD versus doubtful-PDD, presented in Table III.1.18, is considered, it is clear that from the *diagnoses* made by psychological experts it can be inferred that the cut-off score should actually be set higher than 5, although their *classifications* made on the basis of the PDD-MRS produced a non-PDD category corresponding with scores 0-5, and a doubtful-PDD category corresponding with scores 6-9.
- In fact, I had already had my clinical doubts regarding whether even subjects scoring as low as 6 on the PDD-MRS should still be placed into the doubtful category, although I myself had followed this procedure for the 1990 study (see Table III.1.13, right-hand column).

Table III.1.19 shows which effects would be produced on the overall misclassification rates by shifting the cut-off score for N ↔ D.

Table III.1.19 The effects of shifting the N ↔ D cut-off score on the overall misclassifications rates

Cut-off shifted	Unweighted o.m.r.	Weighted o.m.r.
from 4 to 5	- 2.2 *	- 5.7
from 5 to 6	+ 2.0	- 2.5
from 6 to 7	+ 3.9	- 0.8

* a minus sign indicates a reduction, a plus sign a rise in the percentage of incorrect classifications

Balancing the pros and cons in considering the weighted overall misclassification rate, a shift from 5 to 6 proves to yield a substantial reduction (2.5) in the weighted overall misclassification rate, and comparatively the least substantial increase (2.0) in the unweighted overall misclassification rate. The gain can also be expressed in terms of numbers of subjects. As Table III.1.17 shows, using 6 as a cut-off score results in 27 subjects being correctly classified as non-PDD, nine subjects being incorrectly classified as doubtful-PDD, while the number of subjects incorrectly classified as PDD has increased by only one single subject.

On the other hand, a shift from 6 to 7 results in only a minor reduction in the weighted overall misclassification rate, whereas the rise in the unweighted misclassification rate is substantial. All in all, we can only conclude that the cut-off score is better set at 6.

The definitive norm table on the basis of PDD-MRS scores is now:

   0 - 6   : Non-PDD
   7 - 9   : Doubtful
   10 - 19 : PDD

III.1.3.6 *Reliability*

III.1.3.6.1 *Internal consistency*

A first and foremost index of a scale's reliability is its own internal consistency. Internal consistency was measured by means of the coefficient alpha computed for the results obtained in Sample-1992 (n = 1096). This figure was found to be .80, indicating good internal consistency.

III.1.2.6.2 *Interrater reliability*

To determine the interrater reliability of the PDD-MRS, the Behaviour-checklist-15 ratings made by psychological experts were compared with those made by medical experts. These ratings had been made independently. This time 99 institutionalized mentally retarded persons were assessed. In computing the mean scores from the two sets of ratings, items 12 and 15 were ignored. The means computed in this way were 8.12 (s.d. = 5.95) and 7.27 (s.d. = 5.63), respectively. These means are clearly not very far apart and both lie within the area of doubtful-PDD. The product moment correlation coefficient is .83, which is high, particularly in view of the fact that the ratings were made by representatives of quite different disciplines.

As reported in III.1.3.2, the interrater reliability was also measured for the pilot sample of 76 observation-home children. These ratings were made on the basis of detailed files. One of the raters was the present author. A happy (or possibly not so happy) coincidence was that the subjects concerned were quite familiar to him as he had personally observed and monitored them for several months. For these ratings, the product moment correlation coefficient was found to be .85.

In the context of a follow-up study involving 42 former observation-home children, two independent ratings were made by means of the scale. The ratings were successively made by the present author and Elly van der Horst, educational psychologist. The product moment correlation coefficient was found to be .89, again a very satisfactory result.

The three assessments made of the scale's interrater reliability are summarized in Table III.1.20.

Table III.1.20 Interrater reliability of the PDD-MRS

n	Raters	Mean (s.d.)		r
99	Psychol. experts ↔ Medical experts	8.12 (5.95)	7.27 (5.63)	.83
76	Present author ↔ Van der Horst	8.89 (5.36)	7.29 (5.91)	.85
42	Present author ↔ Van der Horst	9.33 (5.08)	8.12 (6.33)	.89

III.1.3.6.3   Test-retest reliability
The ratings made by psychological and medical experts by means of the two successive versions of the Behaviour-checklist (the 19- and 15-item versions) were about six months apart. The two versions are reasonably comparable after adapting them to the final version of the PDD-MRS, as shown in Table III.1.7. To compute the test-retest reliability, again our standard weighting system was used. The product moment correlation coefficients for the ratings made by the medical and psychological experts were found to be .81 and .86, respectively. These results may be considered to be excellent, the more so in view of the fact that the wording of the two versions differed for many of the items, in some cases quite substantially so. The means and standard deviations obtained in these ratings are presented in Table III.1.21.

The follow-up study, discussed in the foregoing chapter, also included a comparison between two ratings of 42 persons who had been observed at the Eekwal observation home and were ultimately placed into the Hendrik van Boeijen Oord (an institution for mentally retarded persons); the ratings involved were based on the Eekwal-home files and on behavioural observations carried out by psychological experts who were at the time responsible for the persons concerned. The sample contained 21 persons who were diagnosed as non-PDD and 21 persons who were diagnosed as PDD, the diagnoses being determined on the basis of the data from the available files. The average age of the children during their stay at the observation home was 6.21 years (s.d. 2.25); their current average age is 20.05 years (s.d. 5.87); the average interval between the two ratings is nearly fourteen years. As for the ratings made on the basis of the files, these were carried out independently by two experts, as previously mentioned.

The scale's test-retest reliability results are summarized in Table III.1.21.

Table III.1.21 Test-retest reliability of the PDD-MRS

n	Raters	Follow-up interval	Mean (s.d.)		r
99	Medical experts (2x)	6 months	7.65 (4.85)	7.09 (5.65)	.81
99	Psychol. experts (2x)	6 months	8.48 (5.81)	8.11 (5.76)	.86
42	File (author) ↔ Psychol. expert	14 years	9.33 (5.08)	8.45 (5.61)	.70
42	File (V.d.H.) ↔ Psychol. expert	14 years	8.12 (6.33)	8.45 (5.61)	.72

The coefficients presented in the table all indicate that the test-retest reliability of the PDD-MRS is good.

III.1.3.7   Validity

As noted in III.1.3.5.1, the final version of the PDD-MRS was validated against the diagnoses made by experienced psychological and medical experts. The diagnoses were primarily based on their own clinical classification (as much as possible by means of DSM-III-R criteria, and additionally going on their own clinical experience with mental retardation and autism); however, these diagnoses could subsequently be altered if the experts came to the conclusion that an incompatible PDD-MRS score, arrived at later, should be given more weight.

Classification by means of the PDD-MRS of previously diagnosed non-PDD and PDD persons yielded the following results: of the 614 non-PDD subjects 92.7% were correctly classified as non-PDD (5.9% as doubtful-PDD and 1.4% as PDD); of the 376 PDD subjects 94.4% were correctly classified as PDD (4.0% as doubtful-PDD, 1.6% as non-PDD). Ignoring subjects classified as doubtful-PDD yields an overall misclassification rate of 6.7%, whereas inclusion of these subjects yields an overall misclassification rate of 9.4%.

There is hardly any difference between the mean scores and standard deviations found in Sample-1990 and Sample-1992 (see Tables III.1.12 and III.1.17), in spite of the fact that 59.0% of the subjects in the second sample were newly selected. As noted before, the two studies are in fact not far from constituting a cross-validation.

In Section III.1.3.9 the discriminant validity of the PDD-MRS is explored by comparing the PDD-MRS scores with the scores on the non-related SRZ, SGZ and SMZ. It was found that the PDD-MRS measures something other than these three scales do. A few subscale scores do in fact correspond with the PDD-MRS score, but this correspondence is invariably far below the $r = .80$ value (the minimum value at which two instruments are considered to be interchangeable) and in all cases there are obvious and valid reasons for the correspondence.

Additional information concerning the internal structure of the PDD-MRS

In Table III.1.22 a correlation matrix is presented of all PDD-MRS items, with the exception of sub-items 1c and 2b.

Table III.1.22 The internal correlation between PDD-MRS items and the correlation between these same items and the PDD-MRS score (unweighted; n = 1096)

Item	1a	1b	2a	3	4	5	6	7	8	9	10	11
1a	*											
1b	-.29	*										
2a	.47	.42	*									
3	.28		.25	*								
4	**	.26	.22	-.44	*							
5		.22	.17	-.41	.48	*						
6	.32	.24	.44		.21	.18	*					
7	.42	.15	.50	.25			.52	*				
8	.36	.26	.52	.22	.22		.39	.48	*			
9	.25	.26	.40		.21	.18	.31	.30	.35	*		
10	.21	.15	.29				.21	.29	.33	.23	*	
11	.21	.22	.33		.22		.26	.27	.30	.29	.32	*
12	.17	.19	.24		.21	.17	.25	.25	.21	.31	.17	.27

** Only correlations of .15 and above are included

The following conclusions may be drawn:

- The matrix shows a correlation between most of the items, suggesting that the scale is internally consistent. However, none of the correlations are so high as to allow the omission of items.
- The three negative correlations are in line with our expectations; in fact, these three items are included in the scale for that very reason. These items are:
  - items 1a and 1b, which are mutually exclusive;
  - item 3, which excludes items 4 and 5 in the sense that a plus score for item 3 preempts a plus score for items 4 and 5.
- In spite of the three negative internal correlations, all items correlate positively with the total score, the correlations ranging between .22 and .83; the median correlation is .50.

In Table III.1.23 a factor analysis is presented for the data of Sample-1992. Only those factors with eigenvalues greater than 1.00 were retained.

Table III.1.23 Factor analysis of PDD-MRS items (n = 1096; varimax rotation with Kaiser normalisation)

Item	Factor		
	I	II	III
1a Severely deficient contact with adults	.55 *	- .07	- .73
1b Less severely deficient contact with adults	.40	.10	.84
2a Deficient contact with peers	.79	- .01	.06
3 Expressive language absent	.33	- .80	- .03
4 Language/speech deviant in content	.26	.77	.10
5 Language/speech deviant in production	.17	.77	.03
6 Obsessive interests	.66	.12	- .07
7 Stereotyped handling of objects	.73	- .06	- .19
8 Stereotyped manipulation of own body	.73	- .01	- .00
9 Fixed patterns, routines and/or rituals	.59	.17	.08
10 Self-injurious behaviour	.51	- .05	.05
11 Erratic/unpredictable behaviour	.54	.13	.11
12 Unusual anxiety or panic	.44	.25	.04

Factor	Eigenvalue	Perc. explained variance	Cum. perc.
I	3.95	30.4	30.4
II	2.05	15.8	46.1
III	1.19	9.1	55.3

* Italics indicate loadings >.40 and loading differences >.20

The table shows that Factor I covers severely autistic persons. Their contact potential with adults and peers is poor and they display many other features which are typical of a PDD, with the exception of item 3 (expressive language absent), which applies only to a limited number of cases. These people would have met the rather stringent criteria for Infantile Autism of the DSM-III (1980), and they certainly meet the criteria for Autistic Disorder as set by the DSM-III-R (1987) and the DSM-IV (1994). Factor II covers persons who have mainly problems in the language area. Factor III covers persons to whom item 1b (less severely deficient contact with adults) almost exclusively applies, but this single feature is very strongly present in them. A clear picture emerges from Factor I, but not from Factors II and III.

Possibly a better insight into the subdivision of this body of items may be gained by consideration of the following variables: PDD-MRS score, diagnosis, sex, level of functioning, and chronological age. This procedure is also the first part of the final testing intended to determine whether the PDD-MRS scores are independent of sex, level of functioning and chronological age. The results of this factor analysis are presented in Table III.1.24.

Table III.1.24 Factor analysis of PDD-MRS items in terms of PDD-MRS score, diagnosis, sex, level of functioning, and chronological age (n = 1096; varimax rotation with Kaiser normalisation)

Item	Factor				
	I	II	III	IV	V
1a Severely deficient contact with adults	.61	-	- .68	-	-
1b Less severely deficient contact with adults	- *	-	.87	-	-
2a Deficient contact with peers	.82	-	-	-	-
3 Expressive language absent	-	- .84	-	-	-
4 Language/speech deviant in content	-	.67	-	-	-
5 Language/speech deviant in production	-	.69	-	-	-
6 Obsessive interests	.68	-	-	-	-
7 Stereotyped handling of objects	.72	-	-	-	-
8 Stereotyped manipulation of own body	.71	-	-	-	-
9 Fixed patterns, routines and/or rituals	.59	-	-	-	-
10 Self-injurious behaviour	-	-	-	-	-
11 Erratic/unpredictable behaviour	-	-	-	-	-
12 Unusual anxiety or panic	-	-	-	-	-
(PDD-MRS score	.97	-	-	-	-)
(Diagnosis	.90	-	-	-	-)
Sex	-	-	-	- .78	-
Level of functioning	-	.67	-	-	-
Chronological age	-	-	-	-	.92

Factor	Eigenvalue	Perc. explained variance	Cum. perc.
I	5.81	32.3	32.3
II	2.33	13.0	45.2
III	1.25	7.0	52.2
IV	1.15	6.4	58.6
V	1.05	5.8	64.4

* Figures are only included if the loading is >.40 and the loading difference is >.20

In the table presented above the three factors which were presented in Table III.1.23 re-emerge in about the same way. Again, Factor I covers persons with the most severe pervasive developmental disorders.

The table also shows that the variable Sex is almost totally independent of the item scores and of the total score; in fact, it constitutes a separate factor (Factor IV). This applies even more to the variable Chronological age (Factor V). For both factors the percentage explained variance is to all intents and purposes negligible. Not surprisingly, the variable Level of functioning is linked with the item bearing on expressive language. The absence of expressive language may be indicative of a low level of functioning, but also (as demonstrated in Tables III.1.15 and III.1.16 and in Section II.5.4.1) of a pervasive developmental disorder.

The relationship between the variables Sex, Chronological age and Level of functioning, on the one hand, and the PDD-MRS score on the other hand, may also be explored by computing the correlation per item. The results are presented in Table III.1.25.

Table III.1.25 The correlations of item scores and total scores on the PDD-MRS with the variables Sex, Level of functioning and Chronological age (n = 1096)

Item		Variable		
		Sex	Level of funct.	Chronol. age
1a	Severely deficient contact with adults	.04	-.20	-.02
1b	Less severely deficient contact with adults	.02	-.08	.01
2a	Deficient contact with peers	.08	-.26	.08
3	Expressive language absent	.03	-.56	-.09
4	Language/speech deviant in content	-.02	.15	-.02
5	Language/speech deviant in production	-.03	.20	.02
6	Obsessive interests	.13	-.09	-.01
7	Stereotyped handling of objects	.06	-.24	-.04
8	Stereotyped manipulation of own body	.05	-.28	.03
9	Fixed patterns, routines and/or rituals	.05	-.04	.15
10	Self-injurious behaviour	.06	-.16	.05
11	Erratic/unpredictable behaviour	-.03	-.07	-.01
12	Unusual anxiety or panic	.02	.04	-.06
	PDD-MRS score	.06	-.25	.03

The figures presented above further substantiate the claim that the PDD-MRS is fully applicable to all mentally retarded persons of either sex, between the ages of 3 and 55 years; a uniform weighting system and norm scale can be maintained throughout. Again, the variable Level of functioning is found to be closely correlated with item 3, i.e., the lower the level of functioning, the higher the number of cases without expressive language. The correlation of -.25 between Level of functioning and PDD-MRS score might raise some doubts. When the sample is large, as in the present study, the likelihood that a given product moment correlation coefficient is statistically significant is rather high. However, Fleiss (1973) states in his handbook that in actual practice correlations lying below .30 to .35 may be taken to indicate no more than a trivial association. We may therefore also be confident that the PDD-MRS is suitable for the entire range of mental retardation.

As indicated above, the two factor analyses failed to yield clear pictures concerning either closely associated behavioural symptoms of pervasive developmental disorders, or concerning specific subtypes within the category of mentally retarded people with a PDD. By way of a trial, a cluster analysis of the PDD-MRS items has been carried out. The results, plus a trial weighting of items, are presented in Table III.1.26. However, I wish to remind the reader that the PDD-MRS is not devised to discriminate subtypes within the domain of pervasive developmental disorders.

Table III.1.26 Results of cluster analysis of PDD-MRS items (n = 1096; SPSS - Quickcluster)

Item		Cluster A	Cluster B	Cluster C	Weighting of item
1a	Severely deficient contact with adults	- *	.44	-	3
1b	Less severely deficient contact with adults	.54	.50	-	2
2a	Deficient contact with peers	.71	.93	-	3
3	Expressive language absent	.85	-	-	1
4	Language/speech deviant in content	-	.55	-	2
5	Language/speech deviant in production	-	.42	-	1
6	Obsessive interests	.69	.69	-	1
7	Stereotyped handling of objects	.74	.68	-	2
8	Stereotyped manipulation of own body	.77	.85	-	2
9	Fixed patterns, routines and/or rituals	-	.82	-	2
10	Self-injurious behaviour	-	.60	-	1
11	Erratic/unpredictable behaviour	.58	.56	-	1
12	Unusual anxiety or panic	.40	-	-	1
Summed weighting of items		13	17/18**	0	19

* Loadings <.40 are omitted
** This figure is 17 when item 1b is applicable, and 18 when item 1a is applicable

The clusters emerging in the table presented above are best considered in relation to the way the three subgroups of Sample-1992 are distributed over the three clusters. This distribution is shown in Table III.1.27.

Table III.1.27 Distribution of the subgroups N, D and PDD (diagnosed) in Sample-1992 over the three clusters

Subgroup	Cluster A	Cluster B	Cluster C	Total
N	34	7	573	614
D	30	16	60	106
PDD	99	239	38	376
Total	163	262	671	1096

The chi-square of this distribution is 730.14, for df = 4, p <.001. This warrants the conclusion that the distribution cannot reasonably be attributed to chance.

Clearly, a very substantial proportion of subjects diagnosed as non-PDD falls into Cluster C, which implies that none of the behaviours characteristic of a PDD are noticeably displayed by these subjects.

About two-thirds of subjects in the sample displaying the most central features of a PDD fall into Cluster B, which implies that they have the following characteristics: their contact-making is more or less seriously deficient both with adults and with peers; generally, expressive language skill is present, but deviances both in content and production are common; almost all other behavioural symptoms of a pervasive developmental disorder are also present, by and large outstandingly so.

Into Cluster A fall PDD persons with less marked PDD features, which implies that they share the following characteristics: their contact-making with adults is less severely deficient; their contact-making with peers is deficient; in addition, many do not speak; other forms of autistic behaviour may also be present.

Well over half of the subjects who belong to the subgroup doubtful-PDD fall into Cluster C, which implies that they display behaviour which is not characteristic of a pervasive developmental disorder. Each of the other two clusters contains a fair share of this subgroup, which may therefore be considered a good example of an intermediate category.

As is becoming widely accepted, autistic features are hard to categorize. Wadden et al. (1991), for instance, found no empirical support for subdividing the Autism Behavior Checklist into five subscales. In this study it is stated that searching for a single common factor for autism may be fruitless (see also III.1.2.2). However, neither does the three-factor solution proposed by the authors seem crystal-clear; moreover, it was found to account for only 31% of the variance in the ABC, which is a rather poor foundation. The construct 'early childhood autism', consisting of six elements, together constituting the basis for the AUTI-R, was examined by Hoekman (1992) by means of a factor analysis, which likewise failed to demonstrate the existence of the construct; two factors were found to remain, and they proved not to run parallel to the three sets of features which, according to the DSM-III-R, together constitute the criteria for Autistic Disorder. If autism is hard to subcategorize by means of autism scales, then it surely comes as no surprise that the PDD-MRS is unable to subcategorize the spectrum of pervasive developmental disorders.

The only subdivision the PDD-MRS has more or less been able to confirm is that between PDD-AD and PDD-NOS. It was found that the PDD-MRS scores of the first group were significantly higher than those of the second group (see II.5.3.5.4.c). For a brief discussion of the practical implications of this difference the reader is referred to the companion manual to the PDD-MRS (see Appendix B).

III.1.3.9   *The PDD-MRS score and the scores on the SRZ, SGZ, and SMZ*

Sample-1992 included 114 institutionalized male and female mentally retarded persons in the severe and moderate ranges of retardation (standard scores on the SRZ subscale Self help 5L-8H) for whom the results of three other scales were available. The ages of the subjects were in the range of 10-55 years; 57 of the subjects had been *diagnosed* as PDD, 57 as non-PDD. The scales concerned are: the SRZ (Kraijer & Kema, 1972/1994), the SGZ (Kraijer & Kema, 1976/1994), and the SMZ (Kraijer & Kema, 1994). Currently, the standard scores on the SRZ and SMZ scales constitute the most specific measures of level of functioning, regardless of whether or not a PDD is present (see also I.2.3). The scores obtained on these two scales by the 114 subjects may therefore be used to examine whether there is a sound basis for claiming that in applying the PDD-MRS a uniform weighting system may be used to assess mentally retarded people of whatever sex, chronological age or level of functioning.

The PDD and non-PDD subgroups in the sample had been matched on two variables, i.e., mean standard scores on the subscale Self help and mean chronological age (see III.3.3.2). In Table III.1.28 the product moment correlation coefficients are presented together with significance values. For the sake of completeness, the figures are also presented for the correlation between PDD-MRS scores and the presence of a PDD.

Table III.1.28 The relationship between PDD-MRS score and the variables: presence of a PDD, sex, chronological age, and SRZ Self Help/SMZ standard scores (n = 114)

Variable	r	p
PDD	.85	.000
Sex	.00	ns
Chronological age	- .18	ns
SRZ Self Help	- .11	ns
SMZ-Total	- .01	ns

Clearly, the results come up to expectation. The PDD-MRS score proves to be very significantly associated with the presence/absence of a PDD, and is independent of sex, chronological age, and level of functioning.

Subsequently, the association between a PDD and the SRZ-Total and the scores on the remaining SRZ subscales, and between a PDD and the SGZ-Total and the scores on the SGZ subscales were considered. In this connection the findings of other studies in the field were also taken into account. Four hypotheses regarding the differences between PDD subjects and non-PDD subjects were tested (the criterion for PDD being a high PDD-MRS score as well as diagnosis PDD).

- Severely and moderately mentally retarded subjects with a PDD will yield significantly lower scores on the two subscales Communication and Social Skills of the SRZ than those without a PDD.
- There will be no significant difference between the scores of PDD and non-PDD subjects on the subscale Persistence.
- If the foregoing two hypotheses are confirmed, PDD subjects will be found to yield significantly lower standard scores on the SRZ-Total than non-PDD subjects, due to the combined effect of corresponding scores on the subscales Self help and Persistence on the one hand and, on the other hand, lower scores on the subscales Communication and Social Skills.

- PDD subjects will yield significantly higher scores on the SGZ subscale Verbal maladaptive behaviour (indicating less verbal maladaptive behaviour) than non-PDD subjects, and will yield significantly lower scores on the subscale Miscellaneous maladaptive behaviour of the SGZ; due to the fact that the latter subscale carries more weight, the PDD subjects will yield significantly lower scores on the SGZ-Total.

The results are presented in Table III.1.29. Product moment correlation coefficients between the scores on the SRZ and SGZ scales and subscales on the one hand and, on the other hand, both the scores on the PDD-MRS and the diagnosis PDD have been computed. Again, significance values are also presented.

Table III.1.29 Correspondence between PDD-MRS score/presence of a PDD and SRZ/SGZ standard scores (n = 114)

Scale/subscale		r		p
		PDD-MRS score	Diagnosis PDD	
	Communication	-.35	-.34	.000 / id
SRZ	Persistence	-.19	-.23	.04 / .01
	Social skills	-.43	-.42	.000 / id
	SRZ-Total	-.40	-.36	.000 / id
	Agressive maladaptive behaviour	-.16	-.16	ns / id
SGZ	Verbal maladaptive behaviour	.46	.36	.000 / id
	Miscellaneous maladaptive behaviour	-.49	-.47	.000 / id
	SGZ-Total	-.36	-.35	.000 / id

The three hypotheses concerning the SRZ scores are confirmed: mentally retarded persons with high PDD-MRS scores/diagnosed as PDD have significantly lower scores on the subscales Communication and Social skills, and are, generally speaking, socially less competent than mentally retarded persons with low PDD-MRS scores/without a PDD. The mentally retarded persons with a PDD proved also to lag slightly behind in Persistence. However, again it must be realized that in actual practice a product moment correlation coefficient below the range of .30 to .35 may not have much real import.

The hypotheses concerning the SGZ scores are also confirmed: mentally retarded persons with a PDD display significantly less Verbal maladaptive behaviour and significantly more Miscellaneous maladaptive behaviour; they are, generally speaking, more maladapted. In accordance with what is known from the literature in the field, the two subgroups are found not to differ with respect to Aggressive behaviour.

The findings reported above may also be said to provide additional support for the validity of the PDD-MRS, as the correlation figures and significance values found with respect to mentally retarded persons diagnosed as

PDD hardly diverge from those found with respect to mentally retarded persons with high PDD-MRS scores.

III.1.4 Specific profiles and singularities emerging from the results obtained by PDD persons on tests and scales

III.1.4.1 *Introduction*

The discussion of the problems encountered in determining the presence of a PDD in mentally retarded persons now brings us to Phase IV of the diagnostic process as defined in III.1.1. In this phase the results of PDD persons on more general tests and scales are considered. Many earlier studies in the field have already presented data concerning this. Useful references to such studies may be found in Chapter 6 of Cohen and Donnellan (1987), and in Sections I.2.2, I.2.3, and III.1.3.9 of the present volume. In the following sections these research findings as well as those which the reader may find in Chapter III.3 will be drawn upon; my own clinical observations will certainly also play a role.

Some general points must be presented before the subject can be dealt with any further.

The first point concerns the measuring devices to be considered. In the present context the results of three types of instruments are relevant.

- Standardized tests devised to assess developmental and intelligence levels in the entire adult or non-adult population, with special emphasis on tests in which a distinction between verbal and performal skills is made.
- Standardized scales chiefly devised to assess social functioning in mentally retarded populations; however, only those scales are considered in which the various domains of social competence have been established upon a sound basis (as should be expected from any scale designed to discriminate mentally retarded people with a PDD from those without a PDD).
- Two less standardized projection techniques, i.e., the Rorschach technique (introduced by Rorschach in 1921), and the House-Tree-Person Projective Technique or HTP technique (Buck, 1981). Although these techniques have been widely documented in general, studies focussing on their application in the mental retardation field are comparatively scarce. Of these I would like to mention my own study on the use of the Rorschach technique in assessing uncomplicated mildly and moderately mentally retarded persons aged 11-46 years (Kraijer, 1987b); some of the findings of this study could be quantified and may provide at least some insight. Predominantly, however, I have used my own clinical experience in evaluating the results of projective techniques, especially as far as the HTP technique is concerned. A fair measure of subjectivity is therefore inevitable.

To my knowledge, no research has been carried out to date concerning the application of projective techniques in the domain of pervasive developmental disorders in particular.

As a matter of fact, many investigators have been able to identify specific profiles and singularities in the test results of retarded as well as non-retarded persons with (narrowly defined) autism. The results of a set of investigations carried out at the Hendrik van Boeijen-Oord (see I.2.3 and III.1.3.9) strongly suggest that the test and scale results of mentally retarded persons with *all* forms of pervasive developmental disorders (in these studies designated as contact-disordered persons, a category virtually covering the two DSM-III-R categories PDD-AD and PDD-NOS) will equally tend to display specific profiles and singularities. More research to confirm this impression would be welcome.

Differences found in the results of tests and scales are generally expressed as a central tendency measure per group. Individually the scores will display some deviation from the central tendency. As far as PDD is concerned, individual subjects whose scores display the specific profiles and singularities characteristic of a PDD are likely to have a PDD; however, this does not imply that individual subjects whose scores do not display these specific profiles and singularities can be automatically categorized as non-PDD. Notably the test results of persons with the erratic form of PDD are hard to anticipate. I will come back to this point in III.1.4.2 and III.1.4.3.

The next issue is closely related to the above. A comparatively large number of PDD persons cannot easily be categorized as belonging either to the rigid or to the erratic subgroup (see III.1.4.4). This is yet another reason why specific features will not be found in their pure forms in each and every case.

Moreover, some of the specific profiles and singularities found in the test results might also be characteristic of disorders other than a PDD. This possibility has as yet received little attention, but it must certainly not be ignored.

The following sections concern merely the specific singularities and profiles emerging from the tests and scales. Nothing will be said regarding underlying cognitive disorders or defects because little is known about these matters.

As for profoundly mentally retarded persons - in fact constituting a very small minority within the entire retarded population (about 1-2%) - their behavioural repertoire is so narrow and their general level of functioning so low that from their results on tests and scales no profiles can possibly emerge; their very low level of overall performance simply precludes the possibility that they might perform exceedingly badly on specific items or in specific domains.

III.1.4.2   *Specific profiles emerging from developmental and intelligence tests*

In this section the test results on the Griffiths and three Wechsler tests

(WPPSI, WISC-R and WAIS) are considered. In the present context only reports will be considered which concern the results of subjects on tests which were suitable for their level of functioning and age (generally referring to chronological age, occasionally to mental age).

Scheme III.1.2 presents the specific profiles emerging from the total scores and from the scores in the subtests and test domains obtained by PDD persons. For a proper appraisal of the findings the following considerations may be helpful.

- As argued in II.4.2.2, Griffiths' division into five domains does not stand up to scrutiny. Notably the comparatively low scores of PDD children on the subtest Eye and Hand Coordination have to be regarded with some caution; as the battery of items in this domain is ill-founded, this finding may be indicative of a test-artifact rather than of a genuine lack of competence. Sandberg et al. (1993) state that lower scores can probably be accounted for by the fact that this subtest, particularly when compared with the subtest Performance, demands 'some imitative and creative skills.'
- The findings regarding the WISC-R and WAIS show that the scores of PDD persons on the subtest Digit Span are rather high, at least when compared with their scores in the other verbal subtests. On the other hand, as Happé (1994), among others, has demonstrated, the high scores of many PDD persons on Object Assembly and their even higher scores on Block Design are not relatively but absolutely high. The performance of some PDD persons on Block Design may even be called a splinter skill.
- PDD persons who can clearly be categorized as erratic PDD (fairly comparable with what Wing and Gould call the active-but-odd type) and whose mental retardation lies in the mild or mild-to-moderate range are found to have lower scores on the Full scale IQ of the three Wechsler scales, but their scores on the VIQ are equal to or even slightly above their PIQ scores.

Scheme III.1.2 Profile deviations in the results of mentally retarded PDD persons assessed by means of four developmental/intelligence tests

(Sub)test		Severely retarded	Moderately retarded	Mildly retarded
Griffiths:	Locomotor	-	-	-
	Personal-Social	↓↓	↓↓	↓↓
	Hearing & Speech	↓↓	↗↓↓	↓↓
	Eye & Hand Co-ordination	↓	↓	↓
	Performance	-	-	-
	General Quotient	↓	↓	↓
WPPSI:	VIQ compared with PIQ		↓↓	↓↓
	Comprehension		↓	↓
	Block Design		↑↑	↑↑
	Full scale IQ		↓	↓
WISC-R:	VIQ compared with PIQ		↓↓	↓↓
	Digit Span		↑	↑
	Comprehension		↓	↓
	Object Assembly		↑	↑
	Block Design		↑↑	↑↑
	Full scale IQ		↓	↓
WAIS:	VIQ compared with PIQ		↓↓	↓↓
	Digit Span		↑	↑
	Comprehension		↓	↓
	Object Assembly		↑	↑
	Block Design		↑↑	↑↑
	Full scale IQ		↓	↓

- = mentally retarded persons with a PDD do not differ from those without a PDD

↑/↑↑ = mentally retarded persons with a PDD score on average higher/much higher than those without a PDD

↓/↓↓ = mentally retarded persons with a PDD score on average lower/much lower than those without a PDD

III.1.4.3   *Specific profiles emerging from the results on scales devised to assess social competence and temperament*

The scales considered in this section comprise two standardized scales on adaptive functioning and one scale on temperament. To be precise, results on the following scales are summarized: the Vineland Adaptive Behaviour Scales; the SRZ, SMZ and SGZ scales considered together; and the TVZ. The TVZ was devised by Blok et al. (1990) and is a Dutch adaptation of the Parent and teacher questionnaire on temperament (Thomas & Chess, 1977). The norm group used for the Dutch version consisted of mentally retarded people in the severe and moderate ranges of retardation. Results yielded by mentally retarded PDD persons on the TVZ were compared to those yielded by a control group of non-PDD persons. More details about this study and about the TVZ itself are presented in Chapter III.3.

The deviations emerging from the results of PDD persons on the scales are summarized in Scheme III.1.3. For a proper appraisal of the findings two considerations may be helpful.

- My clinical experience indicates that persons with erratic PDD whose mental retardation lies in the mild or mild-to-moderate range do not yield exceptionally low scores on the SRZ subscale Communication, which actually tests the more technical rather than the denotative aspects of verbal skills. PDD persons of this subgroup may even perform comparatively well on this subscale. The same holds true for their results on the SGZ subscale Verbal Maladaptive Behaviour. It would seem likely that similar findings may emerge with respect to the domain Communication of the VABS. As for the TVZ profile, this aspect is currently being investigated.
- The SMZ scores of mildly mentally retarded PDD persons tend to be comparatively low. When assessing profoundly, severely and moderately mentally retarded persons, the SMZ actually measures gross motor skills, such as being able to walk, to use the stairs, to make walks of a given length, to pick things up from the floor, to ride on a tricycle, etc. When assessing higher functioning persons, the items also measure an additional social aspect, such as the ability to join in a game of shuttlecock or a bicycle ride, for example.

Scheme III.1.3 Profile deviations in the results of PDD persons assessed by means of two social competence scales and a temperament scale

(Sub)scale		Severely retarded	Moderately retarded	Mildly retarded
VABS:	Communication	-	↓	↓
	Daily Living Skills	-	-	-
	Socialization	↓↓	↓↓	↓↓
	Motor Skills	-	-	-
	Maladaptive Behaviour	↑	↑	↑
	Adaptive Behaviour Composite	↓	↓	↓
SRZ:	Self Help	-	-	
	Communication	↓	↓↓	
	Persistence	-	-	
	Social Skills	↓↓	↓↓	
	Total Adaptive Functioning	↓	↓	
SMZ:	Gross Motor Skills	-	-	↓
SGZ:	Agressive Maladaptive Behaviour	-	-	
	Verbal Maladaptive Behaviour	↓	↓↓	
	Miscellaneous Maladaptive Behaviour	↑↑	↑↑	
	Total Maladaptive Behaviour	↑	↑	
TVZ:	Adaptibility	↓↓	↓	
	Intensity	-	-	
	Responsiveness	↓	-	
	Mood	↓	-	
	Persistence	↓	↓	
	Distractibility	↓↓	↓	
	Approach/Withdrawal	↓↓	↓↓	
	Easy/Difficult Temperament	↓↓	-	
	Communicativeness	↓	↓↓	

- = mentally retarded persons with a PDD do not differ from those without a PDD

↑/↑↑ = mentally retarded persons with a PDD score on average higher/much higher than those without a PDD

↓/↓↓ = mentally retarded persons with a PDD score on average lower/much lower than those without a PDD

III.1.4.4   *Singularities emerging from results on the Rorschach technique and the HTP technique*

III.1.4.4.1   Introduction

Mentally retarded people pose many problems for psycho-diagnosis. The most appropriate way of assessing them is by means of scales, as these do not require the cooperation of the subjects concerned. Good or at least reasonably good results may often be obtained with many of the commonly used performance tests, notably those measuring level of intelligence and functioning, although even such tests may present their own thorny problems. However, a variety of formidable obstacles may be expected when tests are used which are devised to assess feelings, emotional response, social involvement and personality traits. In the first place, many mentally retarded persons, even those in the mild range of retardation, are hardly able to talk about their own feelings, due to their poor skills in language and abstraction. They tend to express themselves rather superficially or in black-and-white phrases. Secondly, their reading difficulties prevent them from properly understanding items in personality inventories. The examiner may solve this problem by reading the items to the subject, but this goes against procedure. Thirdly, sentence completion tests are not suitable for those subjects with insufficient skills in comprehending written language and/or writing. Finally, the picture cards used in some tests - such as the Thematic Apperception Test (Murray, 1943), Children's Apperception Test (Bellak & Bellak, 1943), and the Columbus (Langeveld, 1969) - too often fail to elicit self-expressive stories. Mentally retarded subjects tend to restrict themselves to recognizing and describing the things depicted, offering no further meaning, reason or intention to them.

On the basis of my own clinical experience I have come to the conclusion that, as far as mentally retarded persons are concerned, the best tests currently available for personality assessment are the Rorschach and HTP techniques (the latter without its verbal part, i.e., the Post-Drawing-Interrogation). These techniques have been found to be suitable for persons of a mental age of about four years and onwards. Both techniques have been used by the present author since 1964, always bearing in mind that the findings obtained from these tests cannot be other than qualitative and that their interpretation is necessarily highly subjective. Nevertheless, if used with caution, qualitative findings certainly are valuable as they may provide a wealth of personal details; for this reason the team at the Eekwal home considers the results from these tests to be useful supplements to the highly valuable quantitative results (i.e., scores from tests and scales) and to the observations made of a subject in face-to-face contacts, in the observation playroom or amongst his or her peers.

The results obtained by assessing PDD persons by means of the Rorschach and HTP techniques proved not be quantifiable. To begin with, the results of these techniques are by virtue of their special character hard to quantify. In the present context quantification was even less feasible, as the sample was very heterogeneous with respect to age and level of functioning, and both techniques yielded widely divergent results. The presence or absence of a number of singularities seemed to be rather a matter of mere chance; moreover, they manifested themselves in various ways and in varying combinations. However, some singularities were found quite frequently; these will be discussed below.

III.1.4.4.2 The Rorschach technique
Before moving on to the application of the Rorschach technique to mentally retarded persons with a PDD, some consideration of its use in the mental retardation field in general seems apposite.

The Rorschach consists of ten white cards, each one displaying a bilaterally symmetrical, meaningless ink blot. The subject is invited to tell what he thinks might be represented on each card. What makes this test suitable for mentally retarded persons is that a very short reply, be it only one word or even just a syllable, may count. One of its drawbacks is that the test allows much more freedom than performance tests. This means that subjects are supposed to have some originality or even creativity, which for many mentally retarded persons is expecting too much. As demonstrated in a study involving a sample of adolescent and adult persons with uncomplicated mild and moderate mental retardation (Kraijer, 1987b), the Rorschach results of mentally retarded persons deviate from those of non-retarded persons, the main reason for this being, undoubtedly, lower intelligence. The findings of this study are summarized in Scheme III.1.4.

Scheme III.1.4 Rorschach results of moderately and mildly retarded persons (n = 80); differences from scores obtained by intellectually average-normal subjects are indicated in the right-hand column (Kraijer, 1987b)

Formal element	Mean score	s.d.	Difference from average-normal
Total number of responses	14.3	5.3	Lower
Correct Form per cent, F+ %	54.2 %	17.1	Lower
Animal per cent, A %	67.6 %	23.4	Higher
Number Populars, P	2.8	1.8	Lower
Correct Original per cent, O+ %	0.08		Lower
Number Movement responses, M	0.3		Lower
Number of rejections	0.7	1.2	Higher

All differences presented in Scheme III.1.4 mirror not only the low intellectual level of the mentally retarded subjects, but certainly also their lack of imagination and playfulness. It is therefore far from surprising that projective tests tend to be extremely puzzling for mentally retarded persons with a PDD, who often display rigid, stereotyped, obsessive and ritualistic behaviours.

Clinical experience teaches that the Rorschach results obtained by mentally retarded persons with the rigid type of PDD differ somewhat from those obtained by persons with the erratic type. As was argued in II.3.2, the rigid and erratic types of PDD correspond closely to the aloof group and active-but-odd group as distinguished by Wing and Gould (1979). As for persons belonging to the passive group (the third category distinguished by these authors), their Rorschach results come close to those obtained by persons displaying the rigid type; for this reason the rigid and passive groups may be lumped together when considering projective techniques. However, I would like to add that a considerable proportion of mentally retarded PDD persons, possibly even about 40%, is not easily categorized as belonging to either of the three subgroups; consequently their Rorschach results are not likely to display a specific picture.

In what follows the specific features emerging from the Rorschach results of mentally retarded PDD persons from each of our two subgroups will be presented. Subsequently their results will be compared with those of mentally retarded non-PDD persons of the same level of functioning.

- The test results of persons belonging to the rigid and passive subgroup have the following characteristics:
  - a lower total number of responses, not infrequently fewer then 10;
  - accordingly, a higher number of rejections;
  - a lower number of good answers, some subjects getting lost in details or trivialities, others repeating the same answer over and over again, which may even yield a 'monotypical record';
  - a tendency towards a very low number of Populars;
  - almost complete absence of O+ responses;
  - a very low number Human responses or none at all;
  - virtually no Movement responses.
- The test results of persons belonging to the erratic subgroup show the following characteristics:
  - a sufficient or even high total number of responses, occasionally a very low total number of responses;
  - however, also a comparatively high number of rejections;
  - a highly variable quality of responses; many subjects, having made a good start, go off the rails at every new card, many others doing rather well with the first cards but subsequently producing only poor responses; in either case the poor responses are wild, uncontrolled or purely associative, implying that there are only Colour responses, that a few details are haphazardly emphasized, or that the answers given are indiscriminately anatomical, geographical, or bizarre;
  - from the foregoing point it follows that the F+ % may be low or very low, and that there will be a large number of O- responses.

The observations presented above are summarized in Scheme III.1.5.

Scheme III.1.5 Deviations found in the Rorschach results of mentally retarded PDD persons belonging to the rigid/passive and erratic subgroups, when contrasted with those of mentally retarded non-PDD persons of the same level of functioning

Formal element	Rigid/passive PDD	Erratic PDD
Total number of responses	↓	↓ / - / ↑
Correct Form per cent, F+ %	↓	↓
Animal per cent, A %	-	-
Number Populars, P	↓	- / ↓
Correct Original per cent, O+ %	↓	↓
Number Movement responses, M	↓	- / ↓
Number of rejections	↑	- / ↑
Number Human responses	↓	- / ↓
Number O- responses	- / ↑	↑

- = mentally retarded persons with a PDD do not differ from those without a PDD

300

↑ = mentally retarded persons with a PDD yield a higher number or percentage than those without a PDD

↓ = mentally retarded persons with a PDD yield a lower number or percentage than those without a PDD

The scheme above demonstrates that the Rorschach results of mentally retarded PDD persons belonging to the rigid (plus passive) subgroup are much more consistent than those of mentally retarded persons belonging to the erratic subgroup; as the right-hand column shows, the latter group yields widely diverging results in many aspects of the test.

III.1.4.4.3 The HTP technique

It is well known that the HTP technique involves the drawing of pictures. In this context it is therefore relevant to highlight the fact that the assessment of mentally retarded persons on the basis of their drawing skills is rather a unique enterprise. Very young children and profoundly mentally retarded persons may reveal a great deal about themselves when faced with such a simple task as having to sit down at a table and do something with pencil and paper. Apart from requiring motor and visual-motor skills, the activity also involves a certain degree of familiarity with the equipment and situation, which may imply the following problems:

- What is a pencil for? (Some subjects prefer to balance a pencil, to throw it away, to tap with it, or to gnaw on it.)
- What is drawing paper for? (Some subjects prefer to tear it up, to crumple it up into a ball, or to put it into their mouth.)
- The drawing is supposed to be made only on the paper and not on the table or wall. It may be quite difficult to limit the drawing to within the borders of the sheet of paper. (How does the subject behave should he discover that he has failed to do so?)
- Is the subject indifferent towards his own performance, or is he proud of his own drawing, and if so, how does he show it?
- What level of functioning does the drawing itself indicate? Does it consist of lines, dots or scribbles, and have they been made in a more or less differentiated way? Has the subject been able to draw more or less closed figures, or is there even something vaguely recognizable in his drawing?
- Is the subject interested when the tester makes a drawing? Does he like to join in then, or does he even imitate what the tester has drawn?

Thus, even when the HTP technique proves not to be suitable for its intended purposes, the activity itself and its results may provide useful information about a subject's mental level and adaptive behaviour.

Generally, the HTP results of mentally retarded PDD persons prove, not surprisingly, to lag behind those of non-PDD persons of the same level of functioning. As usual, more precise ratings may be provided by means of the available scoring systems (e.g., Buck, 1981; Harris, 1963).

In what follows, the group of PDD persons will again be subdivided into two groups, i.e., those belonging to the erratic subgroup and those belonging to the combined rigid and passive subgroup. First, the total results will be examined for discriminating features. Subsequently, drawings of houses, trees and human figures will be considered in more detail. The test results of the two subgroups will be compared with those of mentally retarded non-PDD persons of the same level of functioning. Of necessity, observations are limited to general trends.

- The test results of persons belonging to the combined rigid/passive subgroup have the following characteristics:
  - generally, the performance level is low; however, a small number of exceptional subjects perform surprisingly well, although the field of interests tends to be limited to themes such as cranes, electric wiring systems including switches and sockets, maps, geometrical figures and similar things;
  - essential details are often lacking;
  - occasionally there seems to be a more or less obsessive urge for overprecision, driving subjects to draw meticulously each and every brick and tile of a house, for instance, which actually spoils the final result;
  - drawings are often rather small;
  - occasionally, exactly identical pictures are made again and again, notably of human figures or trees; a piece of paper may be so filled up with such a motif that there is no empty space left; in some cases details (such as windows, branches or hair) conceal the representation itself;
  - on the whole, the drawings are characterized by frigidity, formalism and lack of warmth.
  As for rendering the three specific objects involved in the HTP, the following features tend to emerge:
  - the *houses* have no doors or have very small doors, have no windows at all or very few, and walls are conceived to be transparent;
  - the *trees* have very rudimentary forms, often drawn in sharp outline with massive trunks, while the treetops are simple and disproportionately small;
  - the *human figures* are rather frequently shown in profile, notably the heads; however, occasionally they are also rendered from behind; essential details are absent, e.g., a face is often drawn with no ears, nose or mouth to it, arms have sometimes no hands, legs no feet; the heads are often drawn last.
- The test results of persons belonging to the erratic subgroup share the following characteristics:
  - generally, the performance level is low, although occasionally a single drawing or part of a drawing may be up to scratch; only a very small

proportion of persons display a special talent for drawing specific objects;
- the drawing technique is rash and slovenly and indicates a lack of fine motor skills;
- in proportion to the size of the paper, the dimensions of the drawings are normal, large, or even too large; 'paper chopping' and 'paper-topping' occur rather frequently;
- an overabundance of non-essential additions such as bizarre details and queer captions; some subjects comment on them elaborately of their own accord;
- on the whole, the drawings are wild, sloppy and unpleasant.

As for rendering the three specific objects involved in the HTP, the following features tend to emerge:
- the *houses* have too many windows and the proportions are not right (e.g., the roof is disproportionately large);
- the *trees* are more poorly drawn than the other objects;
- the *human figures* lack essential details; notably ears, nose or mouth are omitted or drawn in a perfunctory way; on the other hand, internal organs and systems, such as the intestines, heart and blood-vessels, are rather frequently extensively portrayed.

To sum up, again the results of mentally retarded PDD persons belonging to the rigid/passive subgroup are much more consistent than those of mentally retarded PDD persons from the erratic subgroup; the drawings of some persons belonging to the latter subgroup are highly singular and grotesque.

III.1.5 Summary

Diagnosing mentally retarded children, adolescents and adults with a suspected PDD or other additional disorders may be brought to a successful conclusion, but certainly a large amount of meticulousness, precision and clinical experience is required. With complicated cases, the entire diagnostic process may in fact last three months or even longer.

To the present day I have always considered clinical experience, in the broadest sense of the term, to be crucially important to the entire diagnostic process, right from the first phase.

This first phase of the diagnostic process involves the application of a classificatory system, such as the DSM. From the data provided by observations and case histories patterns may be discovered which are symptomatic of certain disorders. (See also Chapter II.3.)

In the second phase, examination involves the application of a scale which is suitable for the identification of pervasive developmental disorders in the entire spectrum of mental retardation. Several available scales were reviewed. Special attention was given to the PDD-MRS. The validation methods employed in devising this scale have been treated in detail. The PDD-

MRS is based on the DSM (and ICD) concept of Pervasive Developmental Disorders; more particularly, the DSM-III-R criteria have been converted into operational definitions and adapted for application to mentally retarded persons. The PDD-MRS proves to be able to identify a PDD in mentally retarded people in the profound, severe, moderate, and mild ranges of retardation, age-range 2-55 years.

The third phase, the individual diagnosis, will generally yield a final diagnosis. However, at this stage a number of cases will be categorized as doubtful-PDD.

In the fourth and fifth phases of the diagnostic process the number of doubtful cases can be narrowed down by examining whether PDD features emerge from the results of more general tests and scales, viz., tests devised to assess developmental and intelligence levels, and scales devised to assess social competence and temperamental features. If need be, the Rorschach and HTP projection techniques may also be applied.

PREVALENCE OF PERVASIVE DEVELOPMENTAL DISORDERS IN MENTALLY RETARDED PEOPLE

III.2.1   Introduction

As noted in Chapter I.1, pervasive developmental disorders tend to be overlooked in the mental retardation field. Nevertheless, some studies concerning prevalence rates are available.

In an investigation carried out by Hoejenbos in 1963, 15% of the subjects in a sample of mentally retarded institutional residents were found to meet the criteria for 'retraction syndrome' (see Section I.2.1). Another remarkably early study is that carried out by Assink in 1976. In a sample of four hundred institutionalized mentally retarded persons, Assink found that - depending on level of functioning - 25.0-60.5% of the subjects could be classified as 'decidedly autistic.' Sadly, however, the questionnaire used in this study lacked a sound quantitative basis. Studies by Wing and Gould (1979) and Wing (1981a) report findings of a survey carried out among mentally retarded children living in a London borough. Again depending on level of functioning, 1.8-82.2% of the children involved were found to display impairments in social interaction, verbal and nonverbal communication, and imaginative activities, and 0.4-14.0% were found to display features of 'typical autism.' A Swedish study, carried out by Gillberg et al. (1986), found that 48.5% of the severely mentally retarded children and 13.3% of the mildly mentally retarded children displayed 'psychotic behaviour' - in later publications labelled 'autistic and autistic-like disorders.' (For the studies by Assink, Wing and Gould, and Gillberg et al., the reader is also referred to Section I.2.4.) Finally, in my own investigation carried out in 1988 and reviewed in Part II of the present volume, 34.9% of subjects in a sample of 393 observation-clinic children, aged 0-14 years, were found to meet the DSM criteria for PDD (see Section II.1.2.8).

However, none of the studies mentioned above provides us with reliable figures concerning the prevalence of pervasive developmental disorders - as defined by the DSM - in the entire mentally retarded population. The studies by Hoejenbos and Assink covered only institutionalized persons, and the conditions investigated in these two studies - retraction syndrome and autism, respectively - do not clearly correspond with DSM categories. The English and Swedish studies, while being population based, are questionable with respect to their representativeness, notably because the numbers of profoundly, severely and moderately mentally retarded subjects are rather low. Moreover, the criteria used in these studies are not unequivocal. Nevertheless, the studies by Wing and Gould and that by Gillberg et al. may be instrumental in making comparisons.

In the survey carried out by Wing and Gould a small number of children belongs to the category 'history of typical autism'; a much larger number belongs to a broader category, 'aloof at interview'; both categories are embraced by a still broader one, 'all with triad.' In the DSM system this triad concept corresponds to the category PDD; therefore the findings concerning the group 'all with triad' are best comparable with those obtained in my study.

The concept 'autism and autistic-like conditions', eventually used by Gillberg et al., covers the following disorders: schizophrenia, infantile autism, the triad of language and social impairment (according to the definition given by Wing and Gould), severe social impairment (of which no clear definition is provided) and Asperger's syndrome (represented by only one case, a mildly mentally retarded child). For reasons of comparison, the cases with schizophrenia (as defined by the DSM-III) are ignored in the present context.

My own clinic-based study (Kraijer, 1988c) involved an observation home for children. However, most mentally retarded children admitted to a clinic have concurrent problems and disabilities; it follows that the children investigated definitely do not constitute a random sample and from the results of this study little can be derived concerning the prevalence of PDD in the entire mentally retarded population. The samples used in a set of two facility-based studies, the results of which will be reported in Sections III.2.2 and III.2.3, may be regarded as more representative. The first sample was taken from a large institution for mentally retarded people, the second from a number of day-care centres for mentally retarded children.

In the Netherlands many mentally retarded people ultimately come to live in an institution; the group of institutionalized people is therefore quite large. Currently the Dutch institutional population numbers about 28000 persons. This population covers a large proportion of mentally retarded people with problem behaviour and virtually *all adolescent and adult profoundly and severely mentally retarded persons* (see III.1.3.4 of the present book; see also Sherman, 1988, and Blacher et al., 1992). Consequently, the sample may be regarded as quite representative of the severe and profound ranges of mental retardation, but the moderate range is not sufficiently represented and the mild range even less so. Therefore, a second sample had to be involved, covering persons belonging to the moderate range of mental retardation and mentally retarded children of all levels of mental retardation (the number of children living in institutions being also comparatively low). In the Netherlands the total population of day-care centres for mentally retarded children is about 4000. This population covers a substantial majority of children in the profound, severe and moderate ranges of mental retardation. The population of Dutch day-care centres for children may be said to be quite representative of *young mentally retarded children functioning below the mild level of retardation.*

The category of *mildly mentally retarded persons* is hard to investigate. In the Netherlands many mildly mentally retarded adults are no longer registered as such. Between three and seven years of age (the prevailing age-range of the population of day-care centres, see Table III.2.7), children of this level of functioning are often not yet recognized as problematic, or they manage to keep up in the regular classroom; as for mildly mentally retarded adolescents and adults, they are generally not placed into institutions unless they have serious behavioural problems and/or additional disabilities.

The prevalence study discussed in the next sections differs from the aforementioned studies by Assink, Wing and Gould, and Gillberg et al. in some important respects:

- Cross-validation is possible, as two samples have been used.
- The entire sample contains a larger number of subjects (n = 1015) and larger subgroups in terms of the four levels of functioning.
- Diagnoses have been backed up by means of a standardized, reliable and valid measuring device, the PDD-MRS (for detailed information about this scale see Chapter III.1).

The main questions posed in this study are:

- What is the prevalence rate of pervasive developmental disorders in mentally retarded people?
- Is the prevalence rate of pervasive developmental disorders correlated with level of retardation?
- Is the prevalence rate of pervasive developmental disorders correlated with sex? (See also Section II.2.2.3.)

III.2.2 The prevalence of PDD in institutionalized mentally retarded persons

III.2.2.1 *Introduction*

To find out more about the prevalence rate of PDD in institutionalized mentally retarded persons the entire population of the Hendrik van Boeijen-Oord, a large residential institution in Assen, the Netherlands, was examined. This population consisted of 718 mentally retarded persons of all levels of retardation (many of the very profoundly mentally retarded persons were multiply disabled); the numbers of persons below the age of ten and those above the age of sixty were comparatively small; the number of persons belonging to the age-range 25-45 years was comparatively large. In many respects this population is typical of the entire institutionalized population in the Netherlands. The population is neither extremely young, nor extremely old, and all levels of mental retardation are fairly well represented. The population contains a fair number of mentally retarded people with behavioural problems and very profoundly mentally retarded people, as the Hendrik van Boeijen-Oord was a pioneer in the North of this country in admitting these people. (Currently, however, all Dutch institutions follow this admission policy, as more facilities have been created for people in the more favourable ranges of mental retardation and for mentally retarded people with less serious behavioural problems.)

The sample of 718 institutionalized persons represents 2.6% of the entire population of all Dutch institutions for mentally retarded people. The group contains 423 males and 295 females (58.9% and 41.1%, respectively), i.e., a sex ratio of 1.50:1.00, which corresponds with the sex ratio found in most mental retardation facilities.

The distribution of subjects over the four levels of retardation in this sample is presented in Table III.2.1.

Table III.2.1 Frequencies of profoundly, severely, moderately and mildly retarded subjects in the Hendrik van Boeijen-Oord sample (n = 718) indicated by standard scores on the SRZ subscale Self Help

| | Level of retardation/SH-standard score | | | |
	Profound <3-4	Severe 5L-6H	Moderate 7L-8H	Mild ≥9
Number	192	250	198	78
Percentage	26.7	34.8	27.6	10.9

The reason for using the standard scores on the SRZ subscale Self Help as an indication of level of mental retardation was that this domain has been found to be the least affected by the presence of a pervasive developmental disorder (see I.2.2, I.2.3 and III.1.3.9). However, only an estimate could be made of the level of mental retardation of 27 seriously motor-disabled subjects in the sample who cognitively functioned better than those of the profound level; the estimate yielded the following frequencies: five subjects severely mentally retarded, fifteen subjects moderately mentally retarded, and seven subjects mildly mentally retarded. In the DSM-IV the percentage distribution within the mentally retarded population is as follows: 1-2% profoundly mentally retarded, 3-4% severely mentally retarded, 10% moderately mentally retarded, and 85% mildly mentally retarded. As the table shows, compared with these percentages the profound and severe ranges are greatly overrepresented in the present sample, and the mild range is greatly underrepresented.

The population of the Hendrik van Boeijen-Oord was twice examined, with a ten-month interval between the surveys. The first step was to request the staff's eight psychological experts to examine the persons currently living in the institution for the presence or absence of PDD-AD or PDD-NOS, according to DSM-III definitions. Assessments had to be made on the basis of the files and personal clinical observations (preferably in collaboration with the medical expert involved with the case). The ratings involved 650 persons (this time not the entire population), of whom 141 subjects (21.7%) were categorized as PDD. However, in spite of the fact that the Hendrik van Boeijen-Oord has gained a great deal of experience in identifying contact disorders in mentally retarded persons, some seven subjects were reportedly very hard to classify. Moreover, the psychological experts reported that the DSM definitions were often hard to apply, notably when assessing lower-functioning subjects. In the second part of the investigation, therefore, the category doubtful-PDD was introduced. This time the ratings yielded 457 subjects without a PDD, 158 with a PDD and as many as 103 doubtful subjects (14.4% of all subjects examined). In what follows, the ratings thus obtained will be indicated as the *clinical classification* of the sample.

The first version of the PDD-MRS had been completed by this time. The scale could now be used by the psychological experts to make fresh ratings, leading to a *PDD-MRS classification* of the sample. Subsequently the experts were asked to make a *final diagnosis* on the basis of two previous classifications, i.e., the more subjective clinical classification and the more objective PDD-MRS classification. An 'evasive' diagnosis of doubtful-PDD was this time accepted as such (i.e., experts were not asked to engage in Phases IV and V as discussed in III.1.1 and III.1.4). The results of both classifications and of the final diagnoses are presented in Table III.2.2.

Table III.2.2 PDD prevalence rates found in the population of a large institution for mentally retarded people; presence of a PDD determined in three successive phases of the diagnostic process

Phase of the diagnostic process	Non-PDD	Doubtful-PDD		PDD	
	Number	Number	Perc.	Number	Perc.
I Clinical classification	457	103	14.4	158	22.0
II PDD-MRS classification*	328	118	16.4	272	37.9
III Diagnosis	368	75	10.5	275	38.3

* Classification on the basis of Normtable-1990

The psychological experts reported that the use of the PDD-MRS helped them to identify the presence of a PDD in a number of subjects previously labelled doubtful-PDD or non-PDD. As a matter of fact the table shows that the final diagnoses yielded far more cases with a PDD and far fewer doubtful cases.

III.2.2.2 Sex and prevalence of PDD

The next question to be examined is whether the sex ratio of PDD persons is the same as that of the entire sample. Numbers, percentages, ratios and the statistical test are presented in Table III.2.3.

Table III.2.3 Frequency and percentage distribution of PDD by sex in the population of a large institution for mentally retarded people

Diagnosis	Number Male	Female	Percentage Male	Female	Ratio	Chi-square	p
PDD	170	105	61.8	38.2	1.62:1.00	1.55	ns
Doubtful-PDD	45	30	60.0	40.0	1.50:1.00	0.04	ns
Entire sample	423	295	58.9	41.4	1.43:1.00		

As the table shows, the sex ratios of subjects diagnosed as PDD and of subjects in the doubtful-PDD and non-PDD categories taken together do not differ significantly, although the percentage of male PDD persons is slightly above that of the entire sample (1.62:1.00 versus 1.43:1.00). A slight and not quite significant male PDD preponderance of mentally retarded persons was also found in earlier studies (Wing & Gould, 1979; Gillberg et al., 1986; Kraijer, 1988c). However, a very closely corresponding sex ratio emerges when doubtful-PDD subjects are compared with PDD and non-PDD subjects taken together (again classification according to final diagnosis).

III.2.2.3 Level of functioning and prevalence of PDD

In the clinic-based study carried out in 1988 I found no association between the presence of a PDD and level of functioning. However, such an association was found to exist in two population-based studies (Wing & Gould, 1979; Gillberg et al., 1986) and in one institution-based study (Assink, 1976). The same association was also found in the sample of the 1991 study under review, as the figures and statistical tests in the next two tables demonstrate.

Table III.2.4 Numbers and percentages of PDD persons according to level of functioning in the population of a large institution for mentally retarded people

Diagnosis	Level of retardation Profound	Severe	Moderate	Mild	Total
PDD	85	121	55	14	
Others	107	129	143	64	
Total	192	250	198	78	718

Perc. PDD	44.3	48.4	27.8	18.0

Chi-square 36.64; df = 3; p <.001

Table III.2.5 Numbers and percentages of Doubtful-PDD persons according to level of functioning in the population of a large institution for mentally retarded people

Diagnosis	Level of retardation				
	Profound	Severe	Moderate	Mild	Total
Doubtful	34	22	16	3	
Others	158	228	182	75	
Total	192	250	198	78	718
Perc. Doubtful-PDD	17.7	8.8	8.1	3.9	

Chi-square 16.37; df = 3; p <.001

In Table III.2.6 the findings of four studies (i.e., Assink, 1976; Wing & Gould, 1979, 1981a; Gillberg et al., 1986; Kraijer, 1991) are summarized. To make findings comparable, PDD is assumed to correspond with the conditions which Wing and Gould indicate as 'triad', with those which in the terminology of Gillberg et al. range from 'infantile autism' to 'severe social impairment', and with those which are labelled 'autistic behaviour' by Assink. Also on that account were the profound, severe and moderate levels of retardation combined (as was done in the study by Gillberg et al.).

Table III.2.6 Comparison of frequency and percentage distributions of PDD persons according to two broad categories of mental retardation found in four prevalence studies

Study by:	Below mildly retarded			Mildly retarded		
		PDD			PDD	
	n_{total}	Number	Perc.	n_{total}	Number	Perc.
Assink (1976)	350	145	41.4	24	6	25.0
Wing & Gould (1979, 1981a)	133	75	56.4	± 700	± 13	1.8
Gillberg et al. (1986)	66	32	48.5	83	11	13.3
Kraijer (1991)	640	261	40.8	78	14	18.0

As in my sample the categories of profoundly and severely mentally retarded persons may be assumed to be fairly representative of those found in the entire Dutch mentally retarded population, the proportions of PDD persons found in this sample for these levels will in all likelihood closely correspond to the proportions found in the entire population. In the higher-functioning

311

categories, however, the proportions found are probably higher than the general figure, as higher-functioning persons are generally not institutionalized unless they have additional problems; this holds true for the mildly retarded even more than for the moderately retarded range. The figures found by Assink come very close to mine, show the same distribution, and are subject to the same qualifications. Be this as it may, the finding (which was presented in Table III.2.2) that PDD is found in 275 (261 + 14) individuals of a fairly representative institutional population, or 38.3%, deserves to be taken seriously.

The percentages of PDD cases in the lower ranges of mental retardation found in the two institutional studies are lower than those found in the two population-based studies. Nevertheless, PDD may be assumed to occur more frequently in institutionalized moderately mentally retarded persons, as these persons are known to display problem behaviour more frequently. On the other hand, as already argued in II.3.2.2, notably persons below the level of moderate mental retardation may display forms of behaviour which are apt to be mistaken for symptoms of a contact disorder. This also explains why the proportion of doubtful-PDD is comparatively high in the profounder ranges of mental retardation, as Table III.2.5 shows. In fact, their behaviour may often find its origin in a serious lack of coping abilities, which is indeed an inherent and almost irreversible feature of this level of functioning. Clinicians who want to identify pervasive developmental disorders in individuals in the profounder ranges of mental retardation should have a thorough knowledge of both conditions, i.e., of autism and related disorders as well as of profound mental retardation in all its manifestations. It is unknown to me to what extent the raters in the three studies other than mine meet this condition. At least some information regarding this is provided in the study by Gillberg et al. The subjects in their sample were assessed by doctors "who all had a minimum of six months' training in child psychiatry" and the assessments made were supervised by Gillberg. I am not convinced that such assessments may be regarded as fully reliable. It must be realized that even experienced clinicians may encounter considerable difficulties when diagnosing profoundly mentally retarded persons.

III.2.3 The prevalence of PDD in mentally retarded children attending day-care centres

III.2.3.1 *Introduction*

The second part of the prevalence survey concerns the population of ten day-care centres. In principle, a mentally retarded child may enter a day-care centre after his or her second birthday. In practice, however, children are generally not admitted before their third birthday. For that reason children below the age of three have been excluded from the sample. Children who seem able to benefit from school education are generally placed into a school (usually a school for trainable mentally retarded children) when they are about six years old (see also Table III.2.7). Children of lesser capabilities remain longer at the day-care centre, some until their eighteenth year. At the age of eighteen placement into a day-care centre for mentally retarded adults is possible. Placement into an institution is possible at an earlier age. It follows that the age distribution in the day-care centres is heavily skewed towards the younger ages. As I wanted my sample to be reasonably homogeneous I excluded children of fifteen years and older.

Eventually, the sample contained 297 subjects in the age-range 3-14 years. This number represents 9% of all children in this age-range attending Dutch day-care centres for mentally retarded children. The sample consisted of 180 boys (60.6%) and 117 girls (39.4%), which, again, corresponds closely to the proportions found in the entire population of facilities for mentally retarded people. The distributions by age and by level of functioning are presented in Tables III.2.7 and III.2.8.

Table III.2.7 Frequency distribution of children aged 3-14 years attending ten day-care centres, according to chronological age (n = 297)

Chronological age	3	4	5	6	7	8	9-11	12-14
Number of subjects	61	62	57	38	31	20	19	9

Table III.2.8 Frequency and percentage distribution of children aged 3-14 years attending ten day-care centres, according to level of mental retardation (n = 297)

	Level of retardation			
	Profound	Severe	Moderate	Mild
Number	59	83	100	55
Percentage	19.9	27.9	33.7	18.5

As Table III.2.8 shows, again the percentages of profoundly and severely mentally retarded persons are much higher than those given in the DSM-IV, whereas notably that of the mildly mentally retarded category is lower (see III.2.2.1).

Staff members of the day-care centres involved were asked to determine, on the basis of DSM-III-R definitions, the presence or absence of PDD-AD or PDD-NOS in the children under their care. As had been the case in the institutional survey, raters reported that the application of DSM definitions presented difficulties. However, in their case the difficulties seemed less serious, which can probably be explained by the fact that behavioural and psychological problems are less common in people attending day-care centres than in institutionalized persons. In a second stage, ratings were made by means of the PDD-MRS. Final diagnoses were subsequently made on the basis of clinical and PDD-MRS classifications. The results of the three stages of the diagnostic process are presented in Table III.2.9.

Table III.2.9 Prevalence rates of PDD found in children aged 3-14 years successively determined in three phases of the diagnostic process (sample taken from ten day-care centres for mentally retarded children; n = 297)

Phase of the diagnostic process	Non-PDD	Doubtful-PDD		PDD	
	Number	Number	Perc.	Number	Perc.
I Clinical classification	195	35	11.8	67	22.6
II PDD-MRS classification*	189	34	11.5	74	24.9
III Diagnosis	198	32	10.8	67	22.6

* Classification on the basis of Normtable-1990

According to the final diagnoses, well over 20% of this sample, which is fairly representative of the entire population of Dutch day-care centres, has been categorized as PDD. As the table shows, again the number of doubtful cases is comparatively large, in spite of the fact that raters could use the broad category PDD-NOS. This suggests that the staffs of day-care centres have considerable difficulty in identifying autism and related disorders in mentally retarded children. As was the case in the institutional survey, in the successive stages of the diagnostic process the choice between either PDD or non-PDD seems to become easier, resulting in a decreasing number of cases regarded as doubtful. However, the tendency is much weaker in this sample; in other words, clinical classification and final diagnosis do not widely diverge.

III.2.3.2   *Sex and prevalence of PDD*

Our next question regards whether the sex ratio of PDD persons is the same as that in the entire sample. Numbers, percentages, ratios and the statistical test are presented in Table III.2.10.

Table III.2.10 Frequency and percentage distribution of mentally retarded PDD children aged 3-14 years attending ten day-care centres, according to sex

Diagnosis	Number		Percentage		Ratio	Chi-square	p
	Male	Female	Male	Female			
PDD	48	19	71.6	28.4	2.53:1.00	4.41	<.05
Doubtful-PDD	23	9	71.9	28.1	2.56:1.00	1.91	ns
Entire sample	180	117	60.6	39.4	1.54:1.00		

As the table shows, the sex ratio of subjects diagnosed as PDD does differ from that of non-PDD and doubtful-PDD cases taken together, but only at the 0.05 level of significance.

III.2.3.3 *Level of functioning and prevalence of PDD*

The next question regards whether there is an association between the presence of a PDD and level of functioning. Figures and statistical tests are presented in Tables III.2.11 and III.2.12.

Table III.2.11 Proportions of mentally retarded PDD children aged 3-14 years attending ten day-care centres, according to level of functioning (n = 297)

	Level of retardation			
Diagnosis	Profound	Severe	Moderate	Mild
PDD	10	27	21	9
Others	49	56	79	46
Total	59	83	100	55
Perc. PDD	17.0	32.5	21.0	16.4

Chi-square 7.13; df = 3; ns

Table III.2.12 Proportions of mentally retarded Doubtful-PDD children aged 3-14 years attending ten day-care centres, according to level of functioning (n = 297)

	Level of retardation	
Diagnosis	Profound/Severe	Moderate/Mild
Doubtful	23	9
Others	119	146
Total	142	155
Perc. Doubtful	16.2	5.8

Chi-square 8.32; p <.01

As can be seen in Table III.2.11, the lower the range of mental retardation the higher the number of subjects diagnosed as PDD tends to be. However, the differences are just below the 0.05 level of significance. Neither does combining the profound and severe categories on the one hand and the moderate and mild categories on the other hand yield a significant difference. The explanation is probably to be found in the fact that persons in the profound range of mental retardation are comparatively seldom diagnosed as PDD. Table III.2.12 shows that the number of doubtful cases is significantly higher in the two lower ranges of mental retardation. This demonstrates once more that in the profounder ranges of mental retardation in particular, pervasive developmental disorders are extremely difficult to pigeonhole. Possibly, the high proportion of doubtful cases in the profounder ranges accounts for the comparatively low proportion of PDD cases in these ranges, shown in Table III.2.11.

The population of day-care centres is subject to a number of fluctuations. Children with a fair developmental level and a fair level of adaptive behaviour (in other words, those who display some sociability, some sense of duty, and not too much disturbing behaviour) are placed into school at a rather early age, thus sharply reducing the number of children in age-ranges above six years. On the other hand, very seriously disabled or disordered children (i.e., those with a very low level of functioning and/or many behavioural problems) tend to be placed into institutions at a very early age. Both factors account for the fact that in the two broad age-ranges the proportions of subjects in the four levels of retardation differ very significantly; there is a much larger number of higher-functioning children in the younger group and a much larger number of lower-functioning children in the older group, as shown in Table III.2.13.

Table III.2.13 Frequency distribution of mentally retarded children in two broad age categories within the age-range 3-14 years, according to level of functioning (sample taken from ten day-care centres; n = 297)

Level of retardation	Age 3-6	Age 7-14
Profound	38	21
Severe	49	34
Moderate	80	20
Mild	51	4
Total	218	79

Chi-square 23.79; df = 3; p <.001

Presumably in this sample the main reason why the moderately and mildly mentally retarded children in the age-range 7-14 years are still in a day-care centre is that they have behavioural problems. As has been demonstrated in the present volume and will be demonstrated again, behavioural problems are very often found in PDD persons. It might therefore be anticipated that the proportion of PDD children in the age-range 7-14 is higher than in the age-range 3-6 years. However, very young PDD children of, let us say, three or four years of age are often still reasonably tractable at home as well as at a day-care centre; above that age, placement into an institution generally proves to be necessary, especially with lower-functioning PDD children (see III.5.3.3.2). The distribution of PDD cases over the two age-ranges in the day-care sample is therefore hard to predict. The figures and two-tailed statistical test are presented in Table III.2.14.

Table III.2.14 Numbers of mentally retarded PDD children in two broad age categories within the age-range 3-14 years (sample taken from ten day-care centres; n = 297)

Diagnosis	Age 3-6	Age 7-14
PDD	36(16.5 %)	31(39.2 %)
Others	182	48
Total	218	79

Chi-square 17.14; p <.001

As the table shows, a significantly larger number of PDD children is found in the age-range 7-14 than in the age-range 3-6 years. In all likelihood this may be explained by the fact that in the age-range 7-14 years a substantial proportion of children without a PDD move from a day-care centre to a school for trainable mentally retarded children. On the other hand, many PDD children in that same age-range are not yet placed into institutions. The figures presented in Tables III.2.13 and III.2.14 confirm the general impression that both a low level of functioning and the presence of a PDD prevent children from being placed into a (special) school.

As far as PDD prevalence is concerned, neither the institutional sample nor that taken from day-care centres may be regarded as representative of the entire population of mentally retarded people. The institutional sample contains a higher proportion of PDD persons, the day-care sample a lower proportion. However, both samples may be assumed to be fairly representative of the populations of the two corresponding types of facilities.

III.2.4   Summary and discussion

In what follows the main findings of this chapter will be summarized and discussed separately.

Table III.2.15 summarizes the figures found in both prevalence surveys for each of the four levels of functioning.

Table III.2.15 Percentage distribution of PDD persons in an institutional sample (n = 718) and a day-care sample (n = 297), according to level of functioning

Level of retardation	Institutional sample Age 5-81	Day-care sample Age 3-14	n total
Profound	44.3	17.0	251
Severe	48.4	32.5	333
Moderate	27.8	21.0	298
Mild	18.0	16.4	133

Table III.2.16 presents the figures found in three other studies, so as to compare them with the figures found in my two prevalence surveys.

Table III.2.16 Percentage distribution of mentally retarded PDD persons found in four prevalence studies, according to level of functioning

Study by:	Below mildly retarded		Mildly retarded	
	n	Perc. PDD	n	Perc. PDD
Assink (1976)	350	41.4	24	25.0
Wing & Gould (1979, 1981a)	133	56.4	± 700	1.8
Gillberg et al. (1986)	66	48.5	83	13.3
Kraijer (1991)	882	36.2	133	17.3

In what follows the mildly mentally retarded category will be left out of consideration. Only a very small proportion of persons belonging to this category is placed into an institution or day-care centre for mentally retarded children. Persons so placed are predominantly those with behavioural disorders such as a PDD, and to a lesser degree those bordering on the moderate range of mental retardation. Therefore in all likelihood PDD will be much more common in the mildly mentally retarded subjects of Assink's institutional study and in the mildly mentally retarded subjects in my set of studies (which was based on samples taken from two types of facilities) than in the mildly mentally retarded population in general. Of the two population-based studies included in Table III.2.16, which report lower percentages of PDD cases in mildly mentally retarded people, those carried out by Wing and Gould seem to provide the best estimate, as their studies involve the largest number of subjects. Moreover, the mildly mentally retarded subjects in their studies represent 84% of the entire mentally retarded group involved, a percentage which comes very close to that given in the DSM-IV.

As Table III.2.15 shows, the percentages of PDD cases in the profound, severe and moderate ranges of mental retardation differ widely in the two samples of my study. As indicated earlier, the institutional sample is likely to contain a comparatively high percentage of PDD cases in these categories, while the day-care sample is likely to contain a comparatively low percentage of PDD cases. It may be assumed that almost all profoundly and severely mentally retarded persons will be placed into institutions at a rather early age. As the institutional sample covers a much broader age-range than the day-care sample, the percentages found in the former sample should carry more weight. To estimate the percentage of PDD persons in the ranges below mildly mentally retarded, those who have been classified as doubtful-PDD are better left out of consideration altogether, except for the profound range of mental retardation, as this category contains a comparatively high proportion of doubtful cases (see Tables III.2.5 and III.2.12). In view of the above considerations, *about 40% of the entire profoundly and severely mentally retarded population will presumably display a PDD*. As far as moderately mentally retarded persons are concerned, predominantly only those displaying behavioural problems are placed into institutions. Ignoring for the moment the rather small number of moderately mentally retarded persons with such conditions as severe motor disorder or severe epilepsy, and again taking into account the above considerations, *about 20% of the entire moderately mentally retarded population will presumably display a PDD*.

If the PDD percentage found by Wing and Gould for the mildly mentally retarded range and the estimated PDD percentages presented above for the profound, severe and moderate ranges are assumed to be representative, the Eekwal observation home should, considering the distribution of its population over the four levels of functioning (see Table II.1.2), contain about 22.5% PDD cases. In actual fact, however, this figure is as high as 34.9%. This is in line with the statement made earlier that children admitted to observation homes display behavioural problems comparatively frequently.

The percentages of PDD cases in the profound, severe and moderate ranges of mental retardation which I found in my prevalence surveys are substantially lower than those found in the population-based studies by Wing and Gould and by Gillberg et al. However, to my mind my results are better grounded, as a larger number of subjects was assessed and the methods of diagnosis were more sophisticated.

The lower percentages of PDD cases I found in the profound, severe and moderate ranges of mental retardation have to be viewed in their proper perspective. Nothing can be found concerning the prevalence of the entire spectrum of pervasive developmental disorders in the DSM-IV; however, the older DSM-III-R does estimate the overall PDD prevalence in children - mentally retarded children included - to be 0.1 to 0.15%. The highest estimates made thus far are 0.21% (Gillberg, 1990a) and 0.26% (Wing, 1981a). (Wing's estimate is in fact based on a re-appraisal of the findings of an earlier study by Wing and Gould, 1979.) These two estimates are the highest known to me, but still lie far below the 36.2% PDD prevalence rate for persons functioning below the mild level of retardation given in Table III.2.16. Nevertheless, even this percentage may be a conservative figure. It may be concluded that *the prevalence rate of pervasive developmental disorders in profoundly, severely*

and moderately mentally retarded persons is many times higher than in the intellec-
tually average-normal population.

Taking the findings of my two prevalence surveys together reveals a slightly higher number of male than female subjects displaying a PDD (chi-square 4.02; p <.05). A male-female ratio of 1.76:1 is found, representing a very slight male preponderance compared to the 4:1 ratio given in the DSM-IV, and to the ratio presented by Gillberg (1990a) which ranges from 2:1 to 5.7:1. However, to my mind PDD is rather equally distributed between male and female mentally retarded persons. In this I am in agreement with many oth-er authors (Wing, 1981b; Tsai & Beisler, 1983; Steffenburg & Gillberg, 1986; Bryson et al., 1988). This may therefore be taken as an established fact.

A significantly larger number of profoundly mentally retarded persons is categorized as doubtful-PDD, in both of my (institutional and day-care) sam-ples. This demonstrates again that even experienced clinicians find it espe-cially difficult to classify and diagnose profoundly mentally retarded people, and notably those displaying problem behaviour. However, this should not be interpreted as a sign that pervasive developmental disorders occur less frequently in profoundly mentally retarded people. As has been argued in several studies (e.g., Došen, 1993), mental disorders manifest themselves dif-ferently in mentally retarded people below the mildly retarded range due to their very narrow behavioural repertoire. Mental disorders, including a PDD, can only be identified by observing behaviour. When behavioural variation is limited, as is the case with profoundly mentally retarded people, clinicians have to find ways of making a well-founded judgement in spite of a smaller range of data. Nevertheless, as was argued in Section II.3.2.2 and will be demonstrated in Appendices A and B, the task can be brought to a fairly successful conclusion.

PERVASIVE DEVELOPMENTAL DISORDERS AND TEMPERAMENT

III.3.1   Introduction

For many decades characterology and temperamental theories were regarded as outworn. The writings of once famous pioneers associated with this approach - those of the German psychiatrist Kretschmer (1921), the German philosopher and psychologist Klages (1910, 1926), and the Dutch psychologist Heymans (1906-1918) - were long forgotten. Recently, however, when these theories were stripped of their static aspect, i.e., with the growing realisation that character, personality traits and temperament are not purely inborn and immutable, this approach received renewed attention. Kouwer (1951), one of the pioneers of this revival, states that the distinctive features of the behaviour of a given individual, in other words his 'lifestyle', are the result of an interaction between his character and the specific situation in which he lives. The German philosopher and psychologist Helwig (1951) states that the structure of character develops as a response to what a person undergoes in actual situations; in course of time this response grows into a more or less constant attitude, a basic frame of mind.

In his characterological treatise, Klages distinguishes the following main constituent parts of the concept character:

1 *Substance*, i.e., individual disposition, covering intellect, emotion and volition; the properties of substance are *quantifiable*.
2 *Quality*, i.e., the sum total of personal drives which are *directive* (in present-day terminology this would be called motivation).
3 *Structure*, i.e., that which determines how mental processes tend to run, or briefly, behavioural style. It will be clear that this element comes very close to temperament proper. This concept can be traced back to Hippocrates, who advanced a theory of a neurohumoral basis for temperament. In a far more recent past Heymans distinguished eight main personality types differing from each other in three basic aspects.

In current psychological literature the designation *character* is hardly used

321

any more except as a normative concept. However, the notions *personality* and *temperament* are winning ground. Strelau (1984) defines these two notions by contrasting them.

(1) Temperament is a result of biological evolution, whereas personality should be regarded as the results of sociohistorical conditions; (2) Temperament can be attributed to both man and animals, whereas personality can be attributed to man only; (3) From the fact that temperament is determined by inborn physiological mechanisms, it follows that the individual has a temperament from the moment he is born. On the other hand, personality does not exist from the very beginning of the individual's life. It is moulded through human activity and interaction with the social environment; (4) Temperament is constituted by formal dimensions of behavior, independent of content. In contrast, personality comprises primarily the content of behavior in which the individual's relationship with the world is expressed.

In the present chapter I will focus on studies concerning temperamental traits in mentally retarded persons in general and on my own study concerning temperamental traits in mentally retarded PDD persons in particular. Theoretically, my approach adheres to the definitions given by two comparatively recent pioneers in the field, Thomas and Chess (1977). These authors write:

Temperament may best be viewed as a general term referring to the *how* of behavior. It differs from *ability*, which is concerned with the *what* and *how well* of behaving, and from *motivation*, which accounts for *why* a persons does what he is doing. *Temperament*, by contrast, concerns the *way* in which an individual behaves.

The differentiation made here between ability, motivation and temperament is especially important when examining mentally retarded persons, as will be made clear in Section III.3.3. In fact, this division has its roots in the system developed by Klages.

III.3.2 Studies focussing on temperamental traits in mentally retarded persons

Temperament seems to be an interesting subject in the mental retardation field (as was noted earlier in studies by Blok, 1989). Mentally retarded persons clearly display serious impairments to their cognitive functioning, and in addition (possibly as a result), impairments to their emotional and social functioning. In this respect, to use Klages' terminology, they are wanting in *substance*. Regarding what Klages termed *quality* - in modern terminology, motivation - to me mentally retarded people seem to be less differentiated than intellectually normal people. In all likelihood this is related to insufficient substance. However, the domains of affectivity, mental processes, character and personality are rather inaccessible when examining mentally retarded people. Many verbal measuring techniques, whether assessing active or passive language skills or both, prove to be poorly applicable (Flynn et al., 1985; Kraijer, 1987a). There are two aspects to this problem:

a in mentally retarded people there are fewer things to be measured and the things that might be measured are less differentiated;

b things which in principle are measurable are in mentally retarded people difficult to measure due to a lack of understanding between rater and subject.

Clinical experience shows that mentally retarded people, no less than intellectually normal people, do have individual temperamental traits, at any rate in the narrowly defined meaning employed by Thomas and Chess. Therefore it may be useful to investigate this issue in greater detail. As has been demonstrated in several studies (e.g., Thomas & Chess, 1977), temperamental traits are *observable in behaviour*, and are also measurable. It follows that active (verbal) cooperation of the subjects investigated is not necessary. There are reasons to assume that problem behaviour is often associated with temperamental properties (Chess & Korn, 1970; Kohnstamm, 1989). If this proves to be the case, a better insight into the temperamental traits of mentally retarded people might also provide a better insight into their often observed behavioural problems, and might even be helpful in preventing at least some of them. Behavioural problems are, as is repeatedly emphasized in this present volume, very common in mentally retarded persons with autism and autistic-like disorders. In this respect, the recently developed Scale of Temperament in Mentally Retarded Persons, or TVZ (Blok, 1989; Blok et al., 1990), is very welcome indeed.

The TVZ is based on the theories developed in a study by Thomas and Chess (1977) and on the scale presented therein, i.e., *the Parent and teacher questionnaire for children 3-7 years of age*. The Dutch version is a five-point rating scale consisting of seven subscales which together contain 56 items. From these seven subscales two clusters may be formed, called combined scales. Subscales and combined scales cover the following areas:

- *Adaptability*, indicating at which rate a person is able to adapt to new situations or modified circumstances.
- *Intensity*, indicating whether reactions to outward stimuli are strong or weak (while ignoring the quality of these reactions).
- *Responsiveness*, indicating whether outward stimuli are quickly or slowly perceived and quickly or slowly responded to.
- *Mood*, indicating such things as happiness or unhappiness, content or discontent, sadness or cheerfulness.
- *Persistence*, indicating good or poor concentration on activities, whether involving listening, watching, playing, self-help activities, or working.
- *Distractibility*, indicating poor or good amenability to intervention in case of agitated, disturbed or disturbing behaviour, etc.
- *Approachability*, indicating interest in or avoidance of new stimuli or constellations of stimuli, whether of human or non-human origin.

- *Easy/difficult temperament*, involving a combination of the four subscales Adaptability, Intensity, Mood, and Distractibility; a combination of low scores on Adaptability, Mood and Distractibility and a high score on Intensity is interpreted as a difficult temperament; a combination of high scores on Adaptability, Mood and Distractibility and a low score on Intensity is interpreted as an easy temperament.
- *Communicativeness*, involving a combination of the three subscales Approachability, Responsiveness, and Persistence; high scores on these three subscales are interpreted as indicating a high degree of communicativeness; low scores on these three subscales are interpreted as indicating a low degree of communicativeness.

III.3.3 Pervasive developmental disorders and temperament

III.3.3.1 *Hypotheses*

In the context of the present study the main question is obviously whether mentally retarded PDD persons differ temperamentally from those without a PDD. Temperamental studies are not very likely to provide more insight into the basic pathology underlying pervasive developmental disorders. As the subscales in the TVZ refer to broad areas of behaviour and the given definitions are rather general, an investigation by means of this scale will do little more than to register and pigeonhole behaviours which are objectively observable. Consequently, data thus obtained will not go beyond the symptomatologic level. However, should the results of PDD persons on the TVZ display a specific profile, this may benefit differential diagnosis.

As noted before, clinical experience and research findings indicate that mentally retarded PDD persons tend to display more non-specific and semi-specific behavioural problems (see I.2.3; II.2.2.4 ff.; II.4.9.3; III.4.2). Mentally retarded as well as intellectually normal persons with autism and autistic-like disorders also tend to display such idiosyncratic behaviours as aloofness and insistence on sameness. It seems likely, therefore, that they will have common temperamental characteristics. In what follows these general ideas are converted into a set of nine hypotheses referring to the nine areas covered by the seven subscales and the two combined scales of the TVZ.

Adaptability. Mentally retarded PDD persons will display a lower degree of adaptability than persons without a PDD, as one of the key features of PDD persons is their inability to conform to the vibrating social life and its numerous and complicated codes and conventions.

Intensity. No significant differences will be found between persons with and without a PDD with respect to the area Intensity. As a matter of fact, extreme (and even pathologic) irritability is frequently found in PDD persons, as well as extreme passiveness; in some PDD persons the two reactions alternate. My impression is that persons with the rigid form of PDD tend to display a lower degree of Intensity, while persons with the erratic form of

PDD and, to a lesser extent, those with PDD-NOS tend to display a higher degree of Intensity. (For definitions of these subgroups and categories, see II.3.2.1.) However, as the sample is not subdivided according to these categories, such differences are not demonstrable.

Responsiveness. For the same reasons as those aforementioned, no significant differences will be found between persons with and without a PDD with respect to the area Responsiveness. Not only pathologic irritability, but also systematic ignoring, as well as alternating ways of reacting, are all found in mentally retarded PDD persons. Overselectivity is also found. For instance, the interest is exclusively directed towards the glitter of an object or the sounds which can be made with it, while its other aspects are almost completely ignored. Exclusive interests may also give rise to strong reactions (see Intensity). In all likelihood, a high degree of Responsiveness is predominantly to be found in persons with the erratic form of PDD.

Mood. Mentally retarded PDD persons will display a lower degree of Mood than those without a PDD; clinical experience indicates that a very large number of PDD persons show dysphoria and moodiness (liability to become disconcerted by minor events); only a small minority of these people seem content.

Persistence. No hypothesis can be formulated. Clinical experience indicates that both extreme concentration and extreme inattention may occur in the same person, depending on whether the occupation or task is found interesting.

Distractibility. Mentally retarded persons with a PDD will display a lower degree of Distractibility than those without a PDD; clinical experience indicates that it is often very difficult to comfort or distract a PDD person once disturbing or disturbed behaviour has set in.

Approachability. Mentally retarded PDD persons will display a lower degree of Approachability than those without a PDD; after all, avoidance of contact is a key feature of PDD; however, a small minority, mainly persons with the erratic form of PDD and, to a lesser extent, those with PDD-NOS, tends to be claiming, defying, unreserved or intrusive, especially towards adults and staff members.

Easy/difficult temperament. Mentally retarded PDD persons will display a higher degree of difficult temperament than those without a PDD. This is indeed what clinical experience indicates. This hypothesis is in keeping with the hypotheses concerning the areas Adaptability, Mood and Distractibility (provided that persons with similar levels of Intensity are compared).

Communicativeness. Mentally retarded PDD persons will display a lower degree of Communicativeness than those without a PDD. After all, communication is a key problem in persons with a PDD. This hypothesis is in keeping with that concerning the area Approachability (while the areas Responsiveness and Persistence will, according to my hypothesis, contribute virtually nothing to the combined score).

III.3.3.2   *The sample*

The sample consists of 114 severely and moderately mentally retarded subjects, all residents of the Hendrik van Boeijen-Oord, an institution for mentally retarded persons. In the context of an earlier project the entire population of the Hendrik van Boeijen-Oord had been diagnosed - according to clinical observation as well as by means of the PDD-MRS - as PDD, non-PDD or doubtful-PDD. The TVZ was administered to a number of these persons as a separate exercise. The subjects were randomly chosen in such a way that the sample contained equal numbers of persons with and without a PDD (ignoring doubtful cases). Only persons belonging to the age-range 10-55 years, and only persons with Self Help scores on the SRZ within the range 5L-8H were included. Moreover, the PDD and non-PDD groups also had to contain equal numbers of male and female subjects. The sample thus composed had the following characteristics:

> Non-PDD: 57 institutionalized subjects; 36 males and 21 females; mean standard score on subscale Self Help of the SRZ 6.42 (s.d. 0.73); mean chronological age 32.3 years (s.d. 11.62);
>
> PDD: 57 institutionalized subjects; 36 males and 21 females; mean standard score on subscale Self Help of the SRZ 6.23 (s.d. 0.96); mean chronological age 29.0 years (s.d. 10.05).

The differences between the mean standard scores and mean chronological ages are too small to be significant. (On the t-test with df = 112, the values are t = 1.20 and t = 1.60, respectively.)

III.3.3.3   *The subscale results*

In what follows, the figures for the scores on each of the subscales, i.e., their mean (decile) values and standard deviations, the t-values, and significance values (if present) will be presented separately. (The tests are two-tailed.)

III.3.3.3.1   Adaptability

Table III.3.1 Mean scores and standard deviations obtained by 57 PDD and 57 Non-PDD persons on the TVZ subscale Adaptability

Non-PDD	PDD	t-test	p
M = 6.00	M = 3.93	t = 4.35	.000
s.d. = 2.92	s.d. = 2.10		

As the table shows, the hypothesis that mentally retarded PDD people display significantly less Adaptability than those without a PDD is confirmed. According to Blok (1989), this means that the impact of changes on PDD persons is very strong. If new changes are introduced before old ones have been digested and no possibility has been provided to talk things over, a PDD person will feel congested. This will only do more damage to a person's receptivity, and create discomfort and strain, possibly leading to violent reactions. Such a harmful situation has to be prevented by reducing the amount and scope of change, and by introducing changes gradually (see also III.4.3).

III.3.3.3.2 Intensity

Table III.3.2 Mean scores and standard deviations obtained by 57 PDD and 57 Non-PDD persons on the TVZ subscale Intensity

Non-PDD	PDD	t-test	p
M = 5.09	M = 5.42	t = 0.61	ns
s.d. = 2.91	s.d. = 2.89		

As the table shows, the hypothesis that there are no differences between PDD and non-PDD persons on the subscale Intensity is confirmed. There is even a strikingly close agreement between the two statistical values found for both groups. In analyzing the individual results it is found that in both groups a considerable number of subjects obtained extremely high decile scores and also a considerable number of subjects obtained extremely low decile scores, i.e., in the non-PDD group a decile score of 9 or 10 was achieved nine times and a score of 1 or 2, thirteen times; in the PDD group a decile score of 9 or 10 was achieved nine times and a score of 1 or 2, sixteen times. At any rate, neither of the groups is homogeneous with respect to the area Intensity. Differences in scores on Intensity are possibly associated with subtypes, and if this proves to be the case, these subtypes may be associated with scores for other areas of temperament. To answer these questions more research covering a larger number of subjects is required, as this would allow the creation of at least some PDD sub-categories.

III.3.3.3.3 Responsiveness

Table III.3.3 Mean scores and standard deviations obtained by 57 PDD and 57 Non-PDD persons on the TVZ subscale Responsiveness

Non-PDD	PDD	t-test	p
M = 5.67	M = 4.32	t = 2.79	.006
s.d. = 2.69	s.d. = 2.47		

No hypothesis was formulated regarding the area Responsiveness. Nevertheless, the table shows that PDD persons obtain lower scores on the subscale Responsiveness than persons without a PDD. Mentally retarded PDD persons notice fewer things, possibly due to a lack of openness towards the surrounding world or even self-isolation. Only a minor role in this area seems to be played by overselectivity and the presence of an Attention-Deficit/

Hyperactivity Disorder (which is rather common in PDD).

I find that many mentally retarded PDD persons seem to be tense. Although such a condition may increase responsiveness, the results presented above suggest that ignoring stimuli occurs more frequently. However, it is also possible that this finding is due to a sample-artifact (subclassification would then clear matters up), or that many non-PDD persons in the sample were institutionalized precisely because of their high responsiveness, i.e., because of an Attention-Deficit/Hyperactivity Disorder. The next section will discuss this problem in further detail.

III.3.3.3.4   Mood

Table III.3.4 Mean scores and standard deviations obtained by 57 PDD and 57 Non-PDD persons on the TVZ subscale Mood

Non-PDD	PDD	t-test	p
M = 5.25 s.d. = 2.38	M = 4.07 s.d. = 2.71	t = 2.46	.02

As the table shows, the hypothesis that mentally retarded people with a PDD obtain significantly lower scores on the subscale Mood than those without a PDD is confirmed. For the sake of completeness, I should remind the reader that the two groups compared in this project are all *institutionalized* mentally retarded persons. The difference between the two groups is comparatively small, probably because non-PDD persons, too, are frequently institutionalized on account of their behavioural problems, amongst which we find extreme sensitivity and dysphoria. In all likelihood larger differences between the two groups will be found in samples taken from other facilities, such as group homes.

III.3.3.3.5   Persistence

Table III.3.5 Mean scores and standard deviations obtained by 57 PDD and 57 Non-PDD persons on the TVZ subscale Persistence

Non-PDD	PDD	t-test	p
M = 5.70 s.d. = 2.74	M = 3.95 s.d. = 2.64	t = 3.49	<.001

No hypothesis was formulated regarding the area Persistence. Nevertheless, the table shows that mentally retarded PDD people obtain significantly lower scores on the subscale Persistence than those without a PDD. I tend to agree with Blok (1989), who recommends that PDD persons who are not trainable in persistence should be protected from too many stimuli and offered a quiet and peaceful existence. Indeed, a relaxed and orderly programme may help to prevent capricious and chaotic behaviour; in such a situation outer order and control offset the effects of a lack of order within the person.

III.3.3.3.6 Distractibility

Table III.3.6 Mean scores and standard deviations obtained by 57 PDD and 57 Non-PDD persons on the TVZ subscale Distractibility

Non-PDD	PDD	t-test	p
M = 6.07 s.d. = 2.63	M = 3.98 s.d. = 2.53	t = 4.32	.000

As the table shows, the hypothesis that mentally retarded PDD people obtain lower scores on the subscale Distractibility than those without a PDD is confirmed at a very significant level. These findings are also in keeping with those found by Blok (1989). In dealing with PDD persons it is therefore very important to create conditions in which this vulnerable area may be spared. To achieve this, Blok recommends a simple environment, familiar staff, and a consistent approach. Considerable inventiveness is required to find the proper means by which to distract these people. Sadly, such measures will offer too little too late in any case.

III.3.3.3.7 Approachability

Table III.3.7 Mean scores and standard deviations obtained by 57 PDD and 57 Non-PDD persons on the TVZ subscale Approachability

Non-PDD	PDD	t-test	p
M = 6.32 s.d. = 2.87	M = 3.39 s.d. = 2.20	t = 6.11	.000

As the table shows, the hypothesis that mentally retarded PDD persons obtain significantly lower scores on the subscale Approachability than those without a PDD is clearly confirmed; the t-value is comparatively high. These findings are also in keeping with those found by Blok (1989), who characterizes these people as self-centred. He regards a low score on the subscale Approachability as indicative of a contact disorder or even autism. On the basis of my clinical experience I would go as far as to say that poor approachability is one of the key features of autism and autistic-like disorders. Due to their cognitive deficits, PDD people are unable to cope with what to them must be an excessive amount of incoherent information; as a result they cannot do other than simply withdraw. Blok reports that people with low scores for Approachability who in addition have low scores for Adaptability tend to remain very withdrawn. As a matter of fact, the PDD persons in the present sample were found to have low scores on both subscales.

III.3.3.4 The results on the two combined scales

III.3.3.4.1 Easy/difficult temperament

Table III.3.8 Mean scores and standard deviations obtained by 57 PDD and 57 Non-PDD persons on the combined TVZ scale Easy/difficult temperament

Non-PDD	PDD	t-test	p
M = 5.95 s.d. = 2.62	M = 4.21 s.d. = 2.58	t = 3.57	<.001

The hypothesis that mentally retarded persons with a PDD are temperamentally more difficult than those without a PDD is clearly confirmed (as might also have been expected in view of the subscale results); the level of significance is very high. The substantial problems displayed by persons with difficult temperament may, according to Blok (1989), be tackled by providing ample professional personnel and roomy living accommodation; the demands and expectations of the environment have to be geared to the capacities and temperamental characteristics of the persons involved so as to achieve 'goodness of fit' (see also Thomas & Chess, 1977). These measures may help *to prevent temperamental problems from developing into behavioural problems.*

III.3.3.4.2 Communicativeness

Table III.3.9 Mean scores and standard deviations obtained by 57 PDD and 57 Non-PDD persons on the combined TVZ scale Communicativeness

Non-PDD	PDD	t-test	p
M = 5.91 s.d. = 2.88	M = 3.21 s.d. = 2.28	t = 5.50	.000

The hypothesis that mentally retarded PDD persons display a lower degree of Communicativeness than those without a PDD is confirmed. Indeed, the t-value is second only to that found for the subscale Approachability, which is included in this combined scale. However, the scores on the other two subscales, Responsiveness and Persistence, also contribute to the high level of significance. The very low mean score on Communicativeness found in the PDD group of this sample, in which all forms of pervasive developmental disorders covered by the PDD spectrum are represented, demonstrates that this spectrum clearly constitutes a distinctive entity with distinctive features, in spite of the diversity therein. This may serve as yet another proof of the legitimacy of the PDD concept introduced by the DSM system.

III.3.3.5   *Associations between TVZ results and level of functioning in the PDD and non-PDD groups*

The subgroup of severely mentally retarded people in the sample numbers 44 subjects, eighteen of them non-PDD, 26 PDD; the subgroup of moderately mentally retarded people in the sample numbers seventy subjects, 39 of them non-PDD and 31 PDD. Table III.3.10 presents the p-values for the differences between the mean scores on the subscales and combined scales for the PDD and non-PDD members of the two subgroups.

Table III.3.10 p-values for the differences between the mean scores on the subscales and combined scales obtained by PDD and non-PDD subjects for two levels of mental retardation

(Sub)scale	Level of retardation		
	Severe	Moderate	Severe + Moderate
Intensity	ns	ns	ns
Distractibility	.000	.04	.000
Mood	.008	ns	.02
Adaptibility	.000	.04	.000
Easy/difficult temperament	.000	ns	<.001
Responsiveness	<.01	ns	.006
Approachability	<.001	.000	.000
Persistence	.03	.02	<.001
Communicativeness	<.001	.000	.000

Although the general trend of the results on the subscales and combined scales is similar for the two subgroups, there are differences between them with respect to level of significance. The subscales Distractibility, Adaptability and Approachability are found to have a strong and consistent discriminatory power; the same holds true for the combined scale Communicativeness. The scale's validation is based on an institutional population. It seems likely that our findings will be more prominent when the scale is applied to the populations of schools for trainable mentally retarded children and group homes. After all, the present sample contains exclusively institutionalized persons, which means that behavioural problems may be assumed also to occur in a fair proportion of the non-PDD subjects.

For easy reference, the differences found in the sample between PDD and non-PDD subjects concerning the seven subscales and two combined scales are summarized in Scheme III.3.1.

Scheme III.3.1 Divergence of scores obtained by PDD subjects on TVZ sub-scales and combined scales from those obtained by non-PDD subjects[*]

Easy/difficult temperament					Communicativeness		
Intensity	Distractibility	Mood	Adaptability		Responsiveness	Approachability	Persistence
=	↓↓	↓	↓↓		↓	↓↓	↓

Easy/difficult temperament		Communicativeness
↓		↓↓

* =   indicates no difference
↓   indicates a significantly lower mean score in the entire PDD category
↓↓   indicates consistently significantly lower mean scores in the two subgroups of severely and moderately mentally retarded PDD persons

III.3.3.6 *Association between the TVZ results and the different forms of PDD*

Finally, in a first attempt to discover whether characteristic TVZ profiles emerge for the three main forms of PDD within the general PDD group, I carried out a small-scale pilot study. This study involved a small number of comparatively young institutionalized moderately and severely mentally retarded persons of the rigid and erratic types of PDD, and of the passive group (see Wing & Attwood, 1987) of PDD. The conclusions represent only vague impressions, as the number of subjects in each of the three subgroups is small. Moreover, subjects with the passive form of PDD are possibly poorly represented, because they are liable to be overlooked. The findings are presented in Scheme III.3.2.

Scheme III.3.2 First attempt to find TVZ profiles in institutionalized severely and moderately mentally retarded persons with rigid, erratic and passive PDDs

(Sub)scale	Form of PDD		
	Rigid	Erratic	Passive
Intensity	-	↑	↓
Distractibility	↓	↓	-
Mood	↓	↓↓	-
Adaptability	↓↓	↓↓	-
Easy/difficult temperament	↓	↓↓	↑
Responsiveness	↓	-	↓
Approachability	↓↓	↓	↓↓
Persistence	↑	↓	↑
Communicativeness	↓↓	↓↓	↓↓

The scheme calls for some comment:

- It should be stressed once more that the data by no means permit definite conclusions.
- Many persons with a PDD are hard to categorize into the appropriate type/group of PDD; with adult mentally retarded persons in the lower ranges of retardation this may apply to as many as half of the cases; it follows that for this reason alone the division is of limited use.
- In all forms of PDD the low scores on the combined scale Communicativeness emerge as a distinctive feature; the low scores on the subscale Adaptability seem to contribute the most to this outcome.

III.3.4   Summary and conclusion

As argued in Chapter II.4, prevention of problem behaviour is especially important when dealing with mentally retarded persons with a PDD. Hopefully I have been able to make it clear that these persons are in fact predisposed to such behaviour not only because of their difficult temperament and lack of communicativeness, but also because of insufficient 'substance' due to their mental retardation. As Moor (1951) put it, their lack of inner steadiness should be compensated by external stability. Mentally retarded children with a PDD in particular may suffer heavily from discrepancies between, on the one hand, the demands made by their environment and, on the other hand, their poor mental and temperamental equipment; this may result in what Thomas and Chess (1977) describe as poorness of fit between child and environment. As mentally retarded persons with a PDD are characterized in the first place by limited cognitive, emotional and social skills (or lack of substance), and in the second place by difficult temperament and lack of communicativeness, it is of the utmost importance to promote consonance between individual features and environmental properties. To this end both suitable educational programmes and situational measures have to be considered.

The findings of the present chapter may be summarized by the following points:

- Mentally retarded PDD persons have distinctive temperamental features when compared with mentally retarded persons without a PDD; even when the passive group and the rigid and erratic types of PDD are considered separately this observation possibly still holds true. It may therefore be concluded that the TVZ is a helpful differential-diagnostic instrument.
- Mentally retarded PDD persons constitute a group with special problems; the temperamental factors responsible for this are the generally low out-

comes in the areas Adaptability, Responsiveness, Persistence, Distractibility, Approachability and Mood, which in many cases result in Difficult temperament and insufficient Communicativeness.

- Findings concerning distinctive temperamental features in mentally retarded persons with a pervasive developmental disorder may help us to understand the disorder itself, and may be used to shore up treatment procedures. The findings are in line with what was stated in Chapter II.4.

- Sadly, my temperamental study concerning mentally retarded people with a PDD has contributed little to a better understanding of the basic pathology underlying pervasive developmental disorders. The behaviour assessed in order to obtain scores in such areas as Mood, Distractibility and Approachability may be regarded as resulting from a certain condition rather than representing a fundamental condition in itself. More sophisticated research will be needed to reveal the underlying disorder. What the study did yield was that a number of problems in mentally retarded PDD persons are now more clearly earmarked and quantitatively demonstrated, but the findings do not reach further than the outer layer of directly observable behaviour.

- The scope of the present study does not permit far-reaching conclusions concerning different temperamental profiles of mentally retarded PDD persons subdivided by form of PDD, i.e., the passive group and the rigid and erratic types. However, should TVZ results suggest that such distinctive profiles do exist, the difficulty would remain that, as far as I can see, pure representatives of these three forms of PDD are rather uncommon, particularly in the mentally retarded adult population and in the lower ranges of mental retardation.

SELF-ENCLOSED BEHAVIOUR IN PERVASIVE DEVELOPMENTAL DISORDERS

III.4.1   Self-enclosed behaviour

Self-enclosed behaviour, known more commonly in the literature as self-stimulatory behaviour, implies that both action and reaction, or stimulation and being stimulated, take place exclusively within the individual. People displaying this behaviour are insufficiently outwardly directed; they hardly seek to communicate, ask questions, or try to elicit reactions. Their behaviour is, as it were, locked within its own system. Examples of such behaviour are: stereotyped behaviour, masturbation, self-injurious behaviour, and rumination. The instrumental, reactive and patterned aspects of these behaviours have been extensively discussed in Section II.4.7.1.1. The present chapter concerns itself mainly with the self-enclosed aspect of this behaviour.

III.4.2   PDD and the occurrence of self-enclosed behaviour

As mentally retarded persons with a PDD are characterized by contact problems and a lack of communicativeness, it seems likely that self-enclosed behaviour will more often be found in these persons than in those without a PDD. Studies involving the use of SGZ scores (Brakenhoff-Splinter et al., 1977; Altena et al., 1980) provide additional support for this view. In what follows, the hypothesized association between PDD and self-enclosed behaviour will be explored separately for each type of behaviour.

III.4.2.1   *Stereotyped behaviour*

Bartak and Rutter (1976) demonstrated that stereotyped behaviour occurs more frequently in mentally retarded autistic children than in intellectually normal autistic children. However, the authors did not compare autistic and non-autistic mentally retarded children. In the two aforementioned SGZ-based studies, significantly more mentally retarded children with a PDD were found to display *Stereotyped motor behaviour*, which is a pure form of self-enclosed behaviour, than those without a PDD. The same association was found regarding *Stereotyped handling of objects*. Although this is a less pure form of self-enclosed behaviour, it may certainly be regarded as such; persons engaged in this behaviour are very absorbed in the activity, are hardly able to disengage themselves from it, and seem to experience the object as if it represents a part of their body. When devising the PDD-MRS, I arrived at similar conclusions. In Item 8 of this scale, concerning stereotyped manipulation of own body, the following activities are presented by way of examples: teeth-grinding, forced breathing, ruminating, masturbating, walking on tiptoe, rocking oneself, pacing up and down, assuming unusual postures, staring at own hands, hand-flapping, finger-flicking, head-rolling, grimacing, and covering the ears. In Item 7, concerning stereotyped unusual handling of objects, the following activities are presented by way of examples: tapping, scratching, rubbing, bouncing, tearing up, gnawing, licking, biting, sniffing, waving, balancing, spinning, taking off own clothes, lining things up in rows, sorting things by colour, and building identical structures. The two items seem fit to be combined into the broader concept of stereotyped behaviour, as they were found to have a product moment correlation coefficient of .48 (one of the highest interrelation figures found for PDD-MRS items; see Table III.1.22).

In the entire sample of 1096 subjects (see Table III.1.15), the item Stereotyped manipulation of own body received a plus score in 15.5% of the non-PDD subjects, 55.7% of the doubtful-PDD subjects, and 79.3% of the PDD subjects. Plus scores on the item Stereotyped, unusual handling of objects were assigned to 7.8% of the non-PDD, 26.4% of the doubtful-PDD and 67.6% of the PDD subjects. Absolute numbers and statistical tests are presented in Tables III.4.1 and III.4.2.

Table III.4.1 Scores on the PDD-MRS item Stereotyped manipulation of own body assigned to PDD, Doubtful-PDD and Non-PDD subjects of Sample-1992 ($n_{total} = 1096$)

Score	Diagnosis		
	N	D	PDD
+	95	59	298
-	519	47	78
Total	614	106	376

Chi-square 396.31; df = 2; p <.0001

336

Table III.4.2 Scores on the PDD-MRS item Stereotyped, unusual handling of objects assigned to PDD, Doubtful-PDD and Non-PDD subjects of Sample-1992 (n_{total} = 1096)

Score	Diagnosis		
	N	D	PDD
+	48	28	254
−	566	78	122
Total	614	106	376

Chi-square 392.52; df = 2; p <.0001

As anticipated, stereotyped behaviours are very significantly more prevalent in mentally retarded persons with a PDD than in those without a PDD, the doubtful category occupying an intermediary position.

Jacobson and Ackerman (1990), who used a very large sample of mentally retarded persons, also report that stereotypies occur significantly more in PDD persons than in non-PDD persons.

III.4.2.2 *Masturbation*

Masturbation is one of the self-enclosed activities listed in the PDD-MRS item Stereotyped manipulation of own body. As noted in Section I.2.3, in two SGZ-based studies this activity was found to occur significantly more frequently in mentally retarded people with a PDD than in those without a PDD. For the sake of completeness, I should remind the reader that the SGZ ratings of masturbation, unlike those of the PDD-MRS, apply to adult as well as non-adult subjects.

III.4.2.3 *Self-injurious behaviour*

III.4.2.3.1 *Introduction*
Self-injurious behaviour deserves to be discussed at length, as it may have serious consequences. To my knowledge, only a small number of investigations have been carried out concerning the association between PDD (or autism) and self-injurious behaviour. Bartak and Rutter (1976) report that a higher number of mentally retarded children with autism display self-injurious behaviour than intellectually normal children with autism. Possibly this difference is due to level of functioning. Both Schroeder et al. (1978) and Jacobson and Ackerman (1990) did pioneering work demonstrating a clear association between autism (as an additional disorder to mental retardation) and self-injurious behaviour. Further confirmation of the association is to be found in Hyman et al. (1990); in the sample of their study, covering 97 predominantly mentally retarded adult and non-adult subjects, 22.7% of the autistic subjects were found to display self-injurious behaviour.

In devising the PDD-MRS, I found a very significantly higher prevalence of self-injurious behaviour in PDD than in non-PDD subjects of the norm group. In the item concerning self-injurious behaviour, the following acts are presented by way of examples: scratching/rubbing self; hitting/biting/pinching parts of the body; pulling hair; eye-poking; head-banging on walls, floor, furniture, etc; keeping sores open. A plus score is only given when the observer considers the act in question to be painful. When a person is protected against himself by restraints such as arm tubes intended to prevent self-injurious behaviour, he or she is also given a plus score. In casting such a wide net, incipient self-injurious behaviour is also taken into account. If we were to include only unmistakably self-injurious behaviour, I think that we would be seeing only the tip of the iceberg. The gravity of self-injurious behaviour often tends to fluctuate more or less periodically or even cyclically. This is also reported by other authors, amongst them Lewis et al. (1994). These authors describe the cyclical patterns in a small number of profoundly and severely retarded persons; the cycles were found to last between two and five months. A very rigid circumscription of self-injurious behaviour might result in not counting persons who at the time of the inquiry happened to be in a favourable period.

As for the sample of 1096 subjects, self-injurious behaviour (as defined above) was found to occur in 11.9% of the non-PDD subjects, 29.2% of the doubtful-PDD subjects and 46.3% of the PDD subjects. Table III.4.3 presents absolute numbers and the statistical test.

Table III.4.3 Scores on the PDD-MRS item Self-injurious behaviour assigned to the PDD, Doubtful-PDD and Non-PDD subjects of Sample-1992 (n = 1096)

Score	Diagnosis		
	N	D	PDD
+	73	31	174
-	541	75	202
Total	614	106	376

Chi-square 147.27; df = 2; p <.0001

The table shows that the prevalence of self-injurious behaviour is very significantly higher in mentally retarded persons with a PDD than in those without a PDD; again, the doubtful category occupies an intermediary position.

The above reported results may be said to be highly convincing and consistent. An additional inquiry was carried out further to confirm the findings. This inquiry was based on two samples. The first sample consisted of 874 male and female institutionalized subjects living in six institutions, aged 3-81 years; their level of functioning ranged from very profoundly to mildly retarded. The second sample consisted of 485 male and female mentally retarded children attending day-care centres, 22 facilities in all, age-range 3-14 years; their level of functioning ranged from very profoundly to mildly retarded. The use of two separate samples allows cross-validation. The two respective samples, covering a total of 1259 subjects, are fairly representative of the populations of Dutch institutions and of Dutch day-care centres for mentally retarded children. There are, however, two restrictions therein. The first one concerns the rather high percentage of persons with Down syndrome (DS) in the samples, which is 20.1% (253 persons). By comparison, Down syndrome was found in an earlier study (Kraijer, 1991) to be present in 16.9% of mentally retarded children attending day-care centres, while a nation-wide registration in 1995 yielded a 15.0% DS figure for institutionalized mentally retarded persons. In the second place it may be assumed, on the basis of what has already been stated in III.2.1, that the mildly retarded range is insufficiently represented, both in the institutional and day-care samples. Most mildly mentally retarded young children are not identified as such and are not served by the facilities in question. Mildly mentally retarded persons who do attend these facilities predominantly border on the moderate range of mental retardation and/or display behavioural problems. Consequently, the present inquiry will tend to yield a comparatively high frequency of self-injurious behaviour in the mildly mentally retarded category. I nevertheless decided to include the results for this category, although they must be regarded with due caution.

The subjects were assessed in terms of level of functioning (on the basis of cognitive skills and social competence) and categorized as PDD, non-PDD or doubtful-PDD (on the basis of clinical judgement) by the psychological experts attached to the facilities involved. Subsequently the subjects were assessed by means of the PDD-MRS. Finally, the diagnoses (PDD, non-PDD or doubtful-PDD) were made both on the basis of clinical judgement and on that of the PDD-MRS scores.

In what follows, the most important results are discussed for the entire group of 1259 subjects. The results for the two samples show a close resemblance to those found for the entire group and are generally also significant. Level of functioning, type of facility, sex, chronological age, and the presence of two concurrent syndromes (i.e., Down syndrome and fragile X syndrome) were considered to be independent variables. The two-tailed test was used throughout. For easy comparison the results are presented in percentages.

III.4.2.3.2 Association between self-injurious behaviour and PDD according to level of functioning

Table III.4.4 Percentages of self-injurious Non-PDD, Doubtful-PDD and PDD subjects of the combined day-care and institutional samples, according to level of functioning

Level of functioning	n	Diagnosis N	Diagnosis D	Diagnosis PDD	Chi-square (df = 2)	p
Profound	268	16.4	32.0	50.0	28.15	<.0001
Severe	403	11.4	22.7	50.6	67.79	<.0001
Moderate	433	9.5	29.3	35.2	39.37	<.0001
Mild	155	5.0	60.0 *	34.2	21.40 **	<.0001

*   3 subjects out of only 5
** df = 1; category doubtful-PDD ignored because of a too low expected frequency

As the table shows, the association between PDD and self-injurious behaviour is highly significant at all levels of functioning. The doubtful category occupies an intermediary position. Self-injurious behaviour occurs very frequently in profoundly and severely mentally retarded PDD persons; the percentages for these two categories are about the same. Self-injurious behaviour occurs much less frequently in the mild and moderate ranges than in the severe and profound ranges. Ignoring the mild range, the following statistical values are found for the difference between the profound and severe ranges on the one hand and the moderate range on the other: chi-square 7.15; df = 1; p <.01. Including the mild range, the values for the difference between the profound and severe ranges on the one hand and the moderate and mild ranges on the other hand are: chi-square 8.61; df = 1; p <.01.

III.4.2.3.3. Association between self-injurious behaviour and PDD according to type of facility

Table III.4.5 Percentages of self-injurious Non-PDD, Doubtful-PDD and PDD subjects of a day-care sample and an institutional sample, according to type of facility (n = 1259)

Facility	n	Diagnosis N	Diagnosis D	Diagnosis PDD	Chi-square (df = 2)	p
Day-care centres	485	4.6	13.6	27.3	34.49	<.0001
Institutions	874	13.8	36.5	49.4	117.80	<.0001

As the table shows, in both types of facilities the association between PDD and self-injurious behaviour is highly significant. The doubtful category occupies an intermediary position. More than one quarter of PDD children attending day-care centres and as much as a half of institutionalized PDD persons display self-injurious behaviour.

III.4.2.3.4 Association between self-injurious behaviour and PDD according to sex

Table III.4.6 Percentages of self-injurious Non-PDD, Doubtful-PDD and PDD subjects of the combined day-care and institutional samples, according to sex (n = 1259)

Sex	n	Diagnosis			Chi-square (df = 2)	p
		N	D	PDD		
Female	494	12.1	32.7	55.9	95.21	<.0001
Male	765	9.1	27.3	39.2	88.26	<.0001

As the table shows, the association between PDD and self-injurious behaviour is highly significant, both in male and in female persons. Strikingly, the percentages of self-injurious behaviour in female subjects are for all subgroups higher than in male subjects, but the difference is only significant for the PDD subgroup (p = .001). Maisto et al. (1978), who carried out an investigation involving the population of a large institution, report a similar finding. As suggested by Rutter and Schopler (1987), this difference might be related to the fact that female persons tend to display the more serious forms of autism, although autism in general occurs less frequently in females than in males.

III.4.2.3.5 Association between self-injurious behaviour and PDD according to chronological age

In the present section the sample is subdivided into three age categories. The first reason for this is that these categories correspond with broad developmental phases, and the second is that the numbers of subjects in these three age categories are about the same.

Table III.4.7 Percentages of self-injurious Non-PDD, Doubtful-PDD and PDD subjects of the combined day-care and institutional samples, according to chronological age (n = 1259)

Chronol. age	n	Diagnosis			Chi-square (df = 2)	p
		N	D	PDD		
0-19	452	7.6	18.4	35.7	48.71	<.0001
20-39	472	15.0	28.9	52.1	67.40	<.0001
40 and older	335	8.9	39.1	42.9	50.04	<.0001

As the table shows, the association between PDD and self-injurious behaviour is highly significant in all of the three age categories.

III.4.2.3.6 Association between self-injurious behaviour and PDD according to the presence of two syndromes

The sample contained 253 subjects with Down syndrome, and 54 male persons with fragile X syndrome (or fra(X)).

Table III.4.8 Percentages of self-injurious Non-PDD, Doubtful-PDD and PDD subjects with DS or fra(X) from the combined day-care and institutional samples (n $_{total}$ = 307)

Syndrome	n	Diagnosis			Chi-square (df = 2)	p
		N	D	PDD		
DS	253	3.7	43.5 *	31.0	48.56	<.0001
Fra(X)	54	7.1	26.1	52.9	7.96	<.05

* 10 subjects out of only 23

The significance values are, as the table shows, highly significant and just significant, respectively, for the association between PDD and self-injurious behaviour in persons with the two syndromes.

III.4.2.3.7 Association between the gravity of self-injurious behaviour and the presence of a PDD

It has now been demonstrated that more mentally retarded people with a PDD display self-injurious behaviour than those without a PDD, but what about the gravity of this behaviour? To investigate this, I asked some of the medical and psychological experts involved to rate the gravity of the self-injurious behaviour of sixty non-PDD and 149 PDD cases (predominantly institutionalized subjects). This behaviour was to be rated as mild, moderate or severe.

Table III.4.9 Percentage distribution of self-injurious Non-PDD and PDD predominantly institutionalized subjects according to degree of gravity (n $_{total}$ = 209; n $_{non-PDD}$ = 60, n $_{PDD}$ = 149)

Diagnosis	Degree of gravity		
	Mild	Moderate	Severe
Non-PDD	51.7	33.0	13.3
PDD	41.0	38.9	20.1

Chi-square 2.38; df = 2; ns

As the table shows, regarding the gravity of self-injurious behaviour, non-PDD and PDD cases were not found to differ significantly.

III.4.2.3.8 Level of functioning and PDD as risk factors for the emergence of self-injurious behaviour

Many investigators have been able to demonstrate that self-injurious behaviour occurs more frequently in the lower levels of functioning (see for instance Maisto et al., 1978; Rojahn, 1986; Oliver et al., 1987; Hyman et al., 1990). However, as the preceding sections have made clear, PDD is also an important factor. To explore the relative weights of these two factors, an investigation by means of an analysis of variance (ANOVA) was carried out (Kraijer, 1996). The occurrence of self-injurious behaviour was regarded as the dependent variable, and level of functioning and the diagnostic category were regarded as independent variables. Only the results obtained for the entire sample of 1259 subjects are presented here. Level of functioning was found to have a significance value of $p = .010$ (df = 3; F = 3.79); the diagnostic category was found to have a significance value of $p = <.000$ (df = 2; F = 88.03). Within the context of the present section the following findings are relevant:

- The association between level of functioning and prevalence of self-injurious behaviour, widely documented in the literature in the field, is clearly confirmed. The lower the level of functioning of a given person the more likely he is to display self-injurious behaviour. The association is found to be especially strong in profoundly and severely mentally retarded persons.
- The association between the presence of a PDD and the prevalence of self-injurious behaviour, comparatively rarely documented, is clearly confirmed. In persons categorized as doubtful-PDD, which may suggest a very mild form of PDD, a weaker association is found.
- Comparing low level of functioning and PDD as predisposing factors, PDD is consistently found to play a more important role.

These three conclusions also demonstrate that early intervention in cases of self-injurious behaviour is imperative, particularly in order to prevent such behaviour from becoming structural (see II.4.7.1.1). The following three strategies are recommended:

- Mentally retarded young children with a PDD, of all levels of functioning, should be closely monitored, so that the signs of self-injurious behaviour can be spotted at the earliest, given that such behaviour was found to occur in some 45% of the mentally retarded PDD persons investigated.
- The same strategy must be followed with respect to the comparatively small category of doubtful-PDD children, bearing in mind that about 30% of doubtful-PDD persons were found to display self-injurious behaviour.
- Special vigilance is also needed with respect to profoundly and severely mentally retarded non-PDD children, as in these lower levels of functioning the prevalence rate of self-injurious behaviour was found to be 14%.

The recommendations given above also constitute a strong argument in favour of an early psycho-social diagnosis regarding children with developmental problems. It is especially important to determine whether or not a pervasive developmental disorder is involved, as this allows us to take appropriate measures at an early stage. As a matter of fact, this applies not only to self-injurious behaviour.

III.4.2.4 Rumination

Rumination may also be regarded as self-enclosed behaviour. Persons engaged in this behaviour regurgitate food after it has been swallowed. Just as with self-injurious behaviour, an organic factor may be involved. However, at least as far as mentally retarded PDD persons are concerned, such a factor serves only to prompt this behaviour; it subsequently develops into a more or less permanent behavioural pattern. In the two previously mentioned SGZ-based studies (Brakenhoff-Splinter, et al., 1977; Altena, et al., 1980), rumination was not frequently found. However, both studies report a slightly higher frequency of this behaviour in contact-disordered mentally retarded persons than in those without a contact disorder. The differences found were not significant, but this may be due to the overall low prevalence figure. In addition, it is questionable whether the prevalence was indeed as low as that reported. Roosendaal and Van Grunsven (1985) draw attention to the fact that the questionnaires in the SGZ-based studies had to be filled in by attendants; these workers tend to ignore or fail to report rumination, being unaware of the fact that this behaviour may cause serious damage to teeth, gullet, or (indirectly) to haemoglobin content. By instructing and questioning attendants more systematically, Roosendaal and Van Grunsven were able to verify more reliably the occurrence of rumination in a number of institutionalized mentally retarded persons. Frequencies were further confirmed by 24-hour pH measurements (see Roosendaal & Bijleveld, 1994). On the basis of the data from this investigation it is also possible to explore the association between rumination and PDD. To this end, the data of 196 male and female mentally retarded persons in the profound, severe and moderate ranges of retardation, aged 8-66 years, were inspected. Reportedly, 34 of these subjects displayed rumination, as defined by the DSM-IV (under 307.53, Rumination Disorder). Data concerning the presence of a PDD in the 196 persons of the sample were also available. The diagnoses PDD, doubtful-PDD and non-PDD had been made by psychological experts, on the basis of both clinical evaluation and PDD-MRS scores. These findings are presented in Table III.4.10.

Table III.4.10 Frequency distribution of ruminating and non-ruminating persons according to the presence of a PDD (n = 196)

Diagnosis	Rumination	Non-Rumination
Non-PDD	8 (9.2 %)	79
Doubtful-PDD	5 (16.1 %)	26
PDD	21 (26.9 %)	57
Total	34	162

Chi-square 9.05; df = 2; p <.02

As the table shows, there is a significant association between rumination and PDD. Ignoring the category doubtful-PDD yields an even more convincing significance value (chi-square 8.92; df = 1; p <.01). In other words, rumination also occurs significantly more frequently in mentally retarded persons with a PDD than in those without a PDD.

III.4.3   Summary

The findings presented in this section demonstrate clearly that self-enclosed behaviours, including stereotyped motor behaviour, masturbation, self-injury, rumination and stereotyped handling of objects, occur significantly more frequently in mentally retarded persons with a PDD than in those without a PDD.

As far a self-injurious behaviour is concerned, the figures presented in the preceding paragraphs leave us with no doubt that mentally retarded PDD persons are much more predisposed to this type of behaviour than those without a PDD, irrespective of level of functioning, chronological age, sex, or type of facility into which these people are placed. As self-injurious behaviour constitutes a severe problem in the mental retardation field, this finding clearly demonstrates the urgent need for the following measures. In the first place, early identification of a pervasive developmental disorder must be promoted; this may be achieved by examining all children with developmental disorders for the presence of a PDD. Secondly, all children predisposed to self-injurious behaviour should be closely monitored so as to enable us to intervene as soon as such behaviour, for whatever reason, emerges.

Mental retardation alone tends to cut people off socially and to hamper communication. As a consequence, self-enclosed behaviour is far from uncommon in mentally retarded people. The presence of a concurrent PDD, which by its very nature is a communication disorder, aggravates the situation still further. The unfavourable results found in mentally retarded PDD people can be explained by the serious problems they have in entering into a relationship with the surrounding world, which may even imply that they react negatively to contact-making by others. Thus disabled, these people often fail, on the one hand, to understand others and, on the other hand, to make themselves understood by others. As a result, they tend to be deprived of stimuli and responses by others. This may induce them to stimulate themselves. Thus they remain lonely and trapped in their own world.

PERVASIVE DEVELOPMENTAL DISORDERS IN PEOPLE WITH DOWN SYNDROME

III.5.1   Introduction

Down syndrome, or DS (in the past referred to as mongolism or Down's syndrome), is still the most widely known mental retardation syndrome. The condition is comparatively common (approximate birthrate 1-2 per 1000). The underlying chromosomal anomaly usually leads to permanent developmental disability. Down syndrome is particularly frequently found to be the etiology for moderate and severe mental retardation (8-15%). However, it occurs also in profoundly and mildly mentally retarded people.

Some DS people are found to be not only mentally retarded but also autistic. Regarding frequencies, opinions are much divided and even opposed. Up until now investigations have produced incongruous results. They have also proven to have various shortcomings, such as:

- Failure to mention the level of functioning (profound, severe, moderate or mild retardation) of the subjects investigated.
- Failure to indicate whether the investigation is limited to autism proper, or focussed on the entire spectrum of pervasive developmental disorders, and/or failure to use a classification system such as the DSM.
- Biased samples. Cocchi (1991), for instance, bases his conclusions exclusively on examinations he carried out on DS people referred to him for psychiatric consultation. Kraijer (1991) bases his conclusions almost exclusively on results obtained from institutionalized people. (Problematic cases are probably overrepresented in both samples.)
- Insufficient size of samples. This may be a hindrance to a generalization of the findings. There even exist n=1 studies; although such studies may be useful, they do not permit any generalization.
- Exclusive reliance upon clinical observations for making the diagnoses, without checking them against the results of standardized screening devices.
- Failure to use a control group matched, individual for individual, for possibly relevant features.

It seems therefore quite expedient to reconsider this issue, while avoiding the aforementioned pitfalls. Findings should have enough reliability and validity to allow a reasonable amount of generalization regarding the entire DS population. To this end, the following strategies were decided upon:

- To investigate two separate categories of mentally retarded people, i.e., children attending day-care centres and institutionalized persons. Obviously, these two groups differ in chronological age; in all likelihood they also differ regarding the presence of behavioural problems. Collecting data from two different groups which are sufficiently large makes cross-validation possible.
- To use diagnoses made by qualified specialists (psychologists and educational psychologists), according to the three phases of the diagnostic process described in III.1.1, and utilizing assessments by means of the standardized, valid and reliable PDD-MRS.
- To use the figures for PDD prevalence in mentally retarded persons (presented in Chapter III.2) as a rather broad gauge.
- To use control groups, matched (individual for individual) on the variables placement history, chronological age, level of functioning, and sex, with the aim of making more discriminating comparisons.

III.5.2   Results from earlier investigations

Today it is generally acknowledged that autism and autistic-like disorders are not exceptional in mentally retarded people. However, the idea that autism occurs only rarely in DS people, put forward by Wing and Gould (1979) and Rutter (1987), amongst others, is still in wide circulation (see for instance Fombonne & Du Mazaubrun, 1992). Nevertheless, reports of such cases do exist in the literature, but they are generally presented as incidental occurrences. An overview of these reports is presented below.

To my knowledge, the first to mention explicitly the occurrence of autism in association with DS was Rossi (1977). In his study, two such dually disabled children are described in detail.

Wakabayashi (1979) presents a case history of one person with this dual disability.

Wing and Gould (1979) found in their epidemiological survey that one of the 28 DS children investigated displayed severe social impairment, which in the context of that study amounted to autism.

In the population-based study by Gillberg et al. (1986), twenty mentally retarded DS children were identified, only one of whom (i.e., 5%) was also autistic.

Gath and Gumley (1986), studying a sample of 193 DS children, found that nineteen (9.8%) of them fitted the criteria for psychosis with origin specific to childhood, or for infantile autism.

Lund (1988) found that in a group of 44 severely mentally retarded DS persons, five should be labelled autistic on account of their deviant interaction with others.

Bregman and Volkmar (1988) described a severely mentally retarded girl with DS and autism.

Cocchi (1991), the first among the authors mentioned here to base his study on a large sample of DS subjects and to use the DSM-III-R classification system, found that 42 of the 413 DS children investigated, or 10.2%, also displayed pervasive developmental disorders (probably including both PDD-AD and PDD-NOS).

Kraijer (1991), also using a fairly large sample, found that twenty of the 77 DS adults, or 26.0%, displayed a pervasive developmental disorder (including both PDD-AD and PDD-NOS). In this study the disorders were identified not only by means of clinical observation but also by means of the PDD-MRS. All but a few subjects in this investigation lived in institutions for mentally retarded persons. Subsequently, the number of DS subjects was increased to 120, mainly by adding DS children attending day-care centres; the new sample contained 24 DS persons with a concurrent pervasive developmental disorder, or 20.0%.

Of the studies reviewed above, my investigations clearly yielded by far the highest PDD percentage in DS persons. One of the reasons may be that these investigations focussed on the entire spectrum of pervasive developmental disorders, i.e., both PDD-AD and PDD-NOS. Moreover, the samples used in these two studies contained a large number of institutionalized subjects; as is well-known, problem behaviour is rather common in the institutional population, while problem behaviour is also one of the concomitants of pervasive developmental disorders.

Ghaziuddin et al. (1992) estimate that about 4-5% of the DS population will also display PDD-AD. Their study presents a description of three persons with both DS and PDD-AD (according to the DSM-III-R criteria).

III.5.3   Two pilot studies

III.5.3.1   *A pilot study of DS children attending day-care centres*

The first pilot study of a pair (Kraijer, 1994) involved a sample of 103 DS children, 67 boys and 36 girls, aged 3-14 years. Twenty day-care centres, with a total population of some six hundred children, were involved in this study. All children who had been diagnosed as DS were included in the sample; in other words, 16.9% of the children placed in these day-care centres belonged to the DS category.

Of the 103 DS children investigated, eight were profoundly mentally retarded, 36 severely mentally retarded, 47 moderately mentally retarded and twelve mildly mentally retarded. Examination for the presence of a PDD in these children yielded the following results: eight children (7.8%) doubtful-

PDD (average score on the PDD-MRS 9.75, s.d. 1.49), and six children (5.8%) PDD (average score on the PDD-MRS 10.67, s.d. 3.01).

The following details may prove to be relevant:

- A comparatively small number of DS children attended a regular primary school rather than a day-care centre. Consequently, the percentage of DS children in the sample may be slightly lower than in the mentally retarded population in general, and better-functioning children may be under-represented. However, this could not be verified.
- In view of the figures reported in the literature, the percentage of DS children in the sample is decidedly not low. In other words, mainstreaming seems to have played a minor role, if any. Other factors which may have affected the percentage of DS children in the sample are the higher average age at which women in the Netherlands tend to have children on the one hand, and the increased possibilities of prenatal diagnosis and elective abortion on the other hand. The role of these factors is as yet unclear.
- The expected frequency of PDD children in the sample can be computed on the basis of what is known about the prevalence of PDD in the entire mentally retarded population. In Section III.2.4 the following percentages for the four levels of mental retardation were reported: 40% in profoundly and severely mentally retarded persons, 20% in moderately mentally retarded persons, and 1.8% in mildly mentally retarded persons. Applied to the present sample, the expected frequencies are 17.6, 9.4 and 0.2 persons, respectively. For the entire sample this would amount to 27.2 persons. However, as reported above, the sample contained only six PDD persons, which is a considerably lower number.
- The six Down-syndrome children with concurrent PDD (diagnosed) obtained a mean PDD-MRS score of 10.67; this is comparatively low, but does lie within the range of the PDD domain. In this connection it may be helpful to remind the reader that in the norm group the mean PDD-MRS score of PDD persons is 13.19 (see Table III.1.17). In fact, in my earlier studies (Kraijer, 1991), DS people with a pervasive developmental disorder also obtained a low mean PDD-MRS score.
- The eight DS children who were 'diagnosed' as doubtful-PDD obtained a mean PDD-MRS score of 9.75, which is comparatively high. In fact, this average lies within the range of the PDD domain, but only just.
- In the combined group of the eight doubtful-PDD and six PDD persons, five belong to the profound range of mental retardation, seven to the severe range, only two to the moderate range, and not a single one to the mild range.

III.5.3.2   *A pilot study of institutionalized DS persons*

The sample in the second pilot study (Kraijer, 1994) contained 145 DS persons of whom 79 were male and 66 female, aged 18-55 years. (For various reasons persons above the age of 55 were excluded.) Of these, eighty subjects were taken from the Hendrik van Boeijen-Oord. In selecting them, non-ambulatory very profoundly mentally retarded residents and those aged 56 years or above were ignored. Of the remaining 591 persons, all those diagnosed as DS (i.e., eighty subjects, or 13.4%) were included. The other 65 subjects in the sample were the DS residents of five other institutions for mentally retarded persons and were randomly chosen.

In this sample of 145 persons, 26 are profoundly mentally retarded, 65 severely mentally retarded, 51 moderately mentally retarded, and three mildly mentally retarded. Examination for the presence of a PDD in these persons yielded the following results: fifteen persons (10.3%) doubtful-PDD (mean PDD-MRS score 10.00; s.d. 2.73), and 31 persons (21.4%) PDD (mean PDD-MRS score 11.16; s.d. 2.30).

Again, some further details may be useful.

- The reported DS prevalence rates confirm the findings of other studies.
- Again, the expected frequency of PDD persons can be computed on the basis of what is known about the prevalence of PDD in the mentally retarded population. Following the same procedure as was used in the foregoing paragraphs, the expected distribution in the present group is 36.4 persons (40%) in the profound and severe range, 10.2 persons (20%) in the moderate range, and virtually none (1.8%) in the mild range of mental retardation; this is 46.6 persons in all. As reported above, the sample contained in actual fact only 31 PDD persons, again a considerably lower number.
- The 31 DS persons with a concurrent PDD (diagnosed) obtained a mean PDD-MRS score of 11.16, which lies within the range of the PDD domain. However, the mean score is again comparatively low for PDD persons (as was also found in 1991), as the mean PDD-MRS score of PDD persons in the norm group is 13.19 (see Table III.1.17).
- The fifteen DS persons 'diagnosed' as doubtful-PDD obtained a mean PDD-MRS score of 10.0, which again is comparatively high. In fact, the average lies within the range of the PDD domain.
- In the combined group of the fifteen doubtful-PDD and 31 PDD persons, seventeen belonged to the profound range of mental retardation, 23 to the severe range, only six to the moderate range, and not a single one to the mild range.

III.5.3.3 *Implications of the findings of the two pilot studies*

The prevalence rates of PDD found in Down-syndrome persons in the day-care and institutional samples allow some preliminary inferences and conclusions.

- Down syndrome is still found to play a very important role in the etiology of mental retardation, more specifically in the severe and moderate ranges. The prevalence rates found in the two samples (16.9% and 13.4%) are high, if compared with findings from the research literature, but certainly not unique. As the prevalence of DS was especially high in the day-care sample, it must be concluded that, as far as the Netherlands is concerned, the increased possibilities of prenatal diagnosis and elective abortion do not seem to have brought about a substantial decrease in DS. Moreover, it is not unlikely that the second pilot study would have yielded a higher percentage of DS persons if the maximum age limit for eligible subjects had been set lower than 55 years, as the mortality rate of DS children has decreased considerably since the 1950s (Eyman et al., 1991; Carr, 1994).
- In both samples the PDD prevalence in DS people lies below the expected frequency. This finding strongly suggests that PDD occurs less frequently in people with Down syndrome than in those with other etiologies for mental retardation; nevertheless, PDD is certainly not uncommon in DS people. The prevalence rates also suggest that there is some correlation with level of functioning; PDD was more often found in lower-functioning DS people.
- However, in neither sample has the low number of PDD cases in DS persons entailed a high number of doubtful-PDD cases. The percentages found in the two samples (7.8 and 10.3%, respectively) hardly differ from the general prevalence percentages (10.8 and 10.5%, respectively; see Tables III.2.9 and III.2.2).
- The PDD prevalence rates for DS people differ considerably in the two samples: 5.8% of the DS children of the day-care sample compared with 21.4% of the DS persons in the institutional sample. This seems to be at least partly due to the fact that the percentage of DS people functioning on the profound and severe levels of mental retardation was significantly higher in the institutional sample than in the day-care sample (the percentages were 62.8% and 42.7%, respectively; chi-square 16.79; df = 3; p <.001). Whether the populations of the two types of facilities also differ in terms of problem behaviour is unknown. In any case, the institutional sample did not include persons below the age of eighteen (although actually the minimum age had been set at a chronological age of three years). The 10.2% PDD prevalence in DS people which was found by Cocchi (1991) lies half-way between the percentages found in the two pilot studies. His study resembles my first pilot study in that it involved children below fifteen years of age who were living at home. Possibly his sample contains a disproportionate number of children displaying behavioural problems and problems with contact-making, as the subjects of his study are children who had been referred to him from all parts of Italy for psychiatric examination.

- Remarkably, in the two pilot studies the mean PDD-MRS scores are low for PDD and high for non-PDD persons, when compared with those of the norm group. It follows that the mean PDD-MRS scores obtained by doubtful-PDD persons come very close to those obtained by persons with a PDD.

- In two earlier studies (carried out in 1991; see III.5.2) involving 77 and 120 subjects, I found that DS people diagnosed as non-PDD obtained a comparatively high mean PDD-MRS score. Only in the institutional sample of the two pilot studies under consideration did the DS persons diagnosed as non-PDD obtain a mean PDD-MRS score which was higher than that obtained by non-PDD persons in the norm group. (For the sake of completeness, I should mention that comparisons were always made with the results of corresponding categories in the norm group, which include scores obtained by a number of DS people. It follows that the differences in the scores may have additional significance.)

III.5.4   An investigation using matched control groups

III.5.4.1   *General design of the investigation*

Two non-DS control groups were composed. These covered 103 non-DS subjects attending day-care centres and 145 non-DS subjects living in institutions for mentally retarded persons (Kraijer, 1995). These numbers correspond with those of the two DS groups discussed in Sections III.5.3.1 and III.5.3.2. In what follows, the two control groups will be referred to as Non-DS-CDC and Non-DS-INST; the two experimental groups investigated in the pilot studies will be referred to as DS-CDC and DS-INST. The two groups were matched, individual for individual, on the following criteria: sex; chronological age (for children this was done as precisely as possible; for adults a maximum difference of nine years was used and the sample was to contain neither persons below the age of eighteen nor those above the age of 55 years); level of functioning (four levels of functioning, i.e., profound, severe, moderate and mild; the assessments were made by the behavioural scientist involved on the basis of available data regarding intelligence as well as social competence). The matching procedure regarding chronological age could be ·evaluated by computing and comparing the average ages of the four groups; the results are: average age DS-CDC 6.2 years (s.d. 2.95), average age Non-DS-CDC 5.9 years (s.d. 2.89), difference ns; average age DS-INST 34.1 years (s.d. 8.74), average age Non-DS-INST 34.8 years (s.d. 8.94), difference ns.

The following questions were posed:

- Is it correct that pervasive developmental disorders occur less frequently in people with DS than in those without DS?

- How is the presence of pervasive developmental disorders distributed over DS people within the four ranges of mental retardation?
- Are there differences in type and/or severity of pervasive developmental disorders (in terms of total PDD-MRS scores and PDD-MRS item scores) when comparing DS and non-DS persons?

Statistical testing was by means of the t-test and the chi-square test (or, if the latter was not suitable, the Fisher exact probability test). If possible, tests were two-tailed. Moreover, as far as the total PDD-MRS scores are concerned, an analysis of variance (ANOVA) was applied with respect to each of the three diagnostic categories (PDD, non-PDD and doubtful-PDD); in this analysis etiology (DS/Non-DS), sex, and level of functioning were considered to be independent variables.

III.5.4.2   *Down syndrome and the prevalence of PDD: synopsis*

A comparison of PDD prevalence in the experimental and control groups from the two types of facilities is presented in Tables III.5.1 and III.5.2.

Table III.5.1 Frequency distribution of PDD, Non-PDD and Doubtful-PDD children attending day-care centres, age-range 3-14 years, according to the presence or absence of DS

Diagnosis	DS	Non-DS	
Non-PDD	89	62	
Doubtful-PDD	8	11	
PDD	6	30	
Total	103	103	206

Chi-square 21.30; df = 2; p <.0001

As the table shows, about as many DS as non-DS children were found to fall into the category doubtful-PDD; however, PDD was significantly less frequently found in DS than in non-DS children.

Table III.5.2 Frequency distribution of institutionalized PDD, Non-PDD and Doubtful-PDD persons, according to the presence or absence of DS

Diagnosis	DS	Non-DS	
Non-PDD	99	63	
Doubtful-PDD	15	17	
PDD	31	65	
Total	145	145	290

Chi-square 20.17; df = 2; p <.0001

The figures presented in this table show exactly the same trend as those of the previous table.

To summarize, the results thus far demonstrate that pervasive developmental disorders decidedly do occur in DS persons, but significantly less frequently so than in persons without DS. The application of an analysis of variance revealed that a further exploration of the figures was necessary, as level of functioning was found to play a significant role in the differences in prevalence rates. In the next section these relationships will be presented in detail.

III.5.4.3 *The effect of level of functioning on the occurrence of PDD in persons with Down syndrome*

Table III.5.3 shows the prevalence rates of PDD in the experimental and control groups, subdivided by level of functioning. Separate statistical testings have been performed concerning the four levels of retardation for each of the two types of facilities.

Table III.5.3 Comparison of the proportions of persons with PDD in DS and Non-DS persons of different levels of retardation, subdivided by type of facility

| Level of retardation | Children in day-care centres | | | |
	n	More/Less/Equal		p
Profound	2x 8	=	*	ns
Severe	2x 36	↓	**	<.001
Moderate	2x 47	↓		<.01
Mild	2x 12	=		ns
Total	2x 103			

Level of retardation	Institutionalized adults		
Profound	2x 26	=	ns
Severe	2x 65	↓	<.001
Moderate	2x 51	↓	=.001
Mild	2x 3	=	ns
Total	2x 145		

* = indicates that PDD occurs in about equal numbers in DS and non-DS persons
** ↓ indicates that PDD occurs significantly less in DS than in non-DS persons

The table shows that both types of facilities present a strikingly similar picture, i.e., in the profound and mild ranges of mental retardation the proportions of PDD persons are about the same in DS persons and non-DS persons, whereas in the severe and moderate ranges the proportions of PDD persons are significantly lower in DS persons than in non-DS persons.

Although the number of subjects in the profound range is small and very small in the mild range, statistical testing is still possible. In both types of facilities the two groups present a similar picture; this allows us to combine the numbers and to test them statistically once more. Again, in both ranges of mental retardation a non-significant difference was found.

III.5.4.4   *Type and severity of pervasive developmental disorders in persons with Down syndrome*

III.5.4.4.1   *Type and severity of PDD expressed in terms of the PDD-MRS score*
As indicated in Sections III.5.3.1 and III.5.3.2, the mean PDD-MRS score of DS persons with a PDD was found to be comparatively low, and that of DS persons with doubtful-PDD comparatively high. In two earlier studies I found that DS people diagnosed as non-PDD showed a tendency to obtain comparatively high PDD-MRS scores. In order to know whether this relationship has a more general validity, we will now examine the figures in more detail. In this context comparisons with non-PDD Down-syndrome people may also prove to be relevant.

In Table III.5.4 the PDD-MRS scores of non-PDD persons with DS are compared with those of non-PDD persons without DS, according to the type of facility into which these people were placed.

Table III.5.4 Comparison of the mean PDD-MRS scores of non-PDD persons with and without DS, according to type of facility

	DS			Non-DS			
Facility	n	Mean	(s.d.)	n	Mean	(s.d.)	p*
Day-care centres	89	2.18	(2.89)	62	1.61	(2.01)	ns
Institutions	99	3.45	(2.76)	63	2.44	(2.84)	<.03
Combined	188	2.85	(2.84)	125	2.03	(2.60)	<.01

* t-test

The table shows that in both types of facilities the mean PDD-MRS scores of non-PDD persons with DS are higher than those of non-PDD people without DS. However, the difference is only significant for institutionalized subjects. As the differences lay in the same direction in the two types of facilities, the figures may be combined to be statistically retested. This procedure results in a slightly more significant difference between the DS and non-DS categories (p <.01).

As day-care centres have been found to contain a significantly larger proportion of higher-functioning persons than institutions (see III.5.3.3), and, moreover, analysis of variance has revealed that the PDD-MRS scores of DS people diagnosed as non-PDD co-vary with level of mental retardation, a better insight is likely to be obtained by subdividing the non-PDD subgroup according to level of functioning. The following results were found: in the profound and severe levels of functioning the PDD-MRS scores of non-PDD persons with DS are significantly higher than those of non-PDD persons without DS; the respective mean scores are 4.28 (s.d. 2.80) and 2.02 (s.d. 2.00); p <.001; no differences were found for the moderate and mild levels of functioning. The findings apply both to male and female persons, as is also the case with other findings which will be presented shortly.

In the subgroup doubtful-PDD the only finding of note is that the combined mean PDD-MRS score of DS subjects from the two types of facilities is 9.91, which lies above the arithmetical 9.50 cut-off score for PDD (which is set at 10). Further analysis of the findings is not feasible due to the small number of subjects. However, as only a comparatively small number of DS persons belongs to the doubtful-PDD subgroup, this does not seem to present a serious omission.

Finally, in Table III.5.5 the PDD-MRS scores of PDD persons with and without DS are compared, again according to the type of facility into which they were placed.

Table III.5.5 Comparison of the mean PDD-MRS scores of DS and Non-DS PDD persons, according to type of facility

| Facility | DS | | | Non-DS | | | |
	n	Mean	(s.d.)	n	Mean	(s.d.)	p*
Day-care centres	6	10.67	(3.01)	30	13.27	(3.58)	ns
Institutions	31	11.16	(2.30)	65	13.11	(2.43)	<.001
Combined	37	11.08	(2.81)	95	13.16	(3.22)	<.001

* t-test

The table shows that the combined average PDD-MRS scores of PDD persons with DS differ significantly from those of PDD persons without DS. This also holds true for institutionalized persons considered separately. The difference between the figures for the day-care groups is not significant, but this is in all likelihood due to the small number of DS children diagnosed as PDD. However, the mean scores of the DS and non-DS children are very close to those of the institutionalized adults; the two groups in both types of facilities clearly present the same trend. Separate statistical testing of the combined figures revealed that this finding holds true for the profound, severe and moderate levels of functioning (i.e., the levels containing sufficient numbers of DS and non-DS PDD subjects).

III.5.4.4.2   Type and severity of PDD, expressed in terms of PDD-MRS item scores

Thus far no explanation has been offered for two findings:

- the comparatively high PDD-MRS scores of DS people diagnosed as non-PDD (in the profound and severe ranges of mental retardation);
- the comparatively low PDD-MRS scores of DS people diagnosed as PDD (in the profound, severe and moderate ranges of mental retardation).

Item analysis yielded the following results:

- Comparing non-PDD people with and without Down syndrome, a significantly higher number of profoundly and severely mentally retarded DS people received a plus score for item 8 (Stereotyped manipulation of own body; $p < .0001$), and (to a slightly lesser extent) for item 7 (Stereotyped, unusual handling of objects; $p = .002$).
- Comparing PDD people with and without Down syndrome, a significantly lower number of profoundly, severely and moderately mentally retarded DS people received a plus score for item 1a (Severely deficient response to contact initiative of adults/in social interaction; $p = .004$) and for item 10 (Self-injurious behaviour; $p = .02$). For the sake of completeness, I should also mention that a slightly significantly higher number of DS persons received a plus score for item 1b (Less severely deficient response or fluctuating response to contact initiative of adults/in social interaction); as the reader will remember, this item contributes less to the raw score than item 1a, being of less importance in the behaviour area concerned.

III.5.4.5   Overall prevalence rates of PDD in people with Down syndrome

On the whole, the findings recorded in the present chapter permit only very preliminary conclusions to be made regarding the occurrence of PDD in DS people, as will be clear from the absolute numbers and percentages presented in Table III.5.6.

Table III.5.6 Prevalence rates of PDD in DS persons of different levels of functioning, subdivided by type of facility

Level of retardation	Children in day-care centres		
	n	PDD	Perc. PDD
Profound	8	1	12.5
Severe	36	3	8.3
Moderate	47	2	4.3
Mild	12	-	0.0
Total	103	6	5.8

Level of retardation	Institutionalized adults		
	n	PDD	Perc. PDD
Profound	26	12	46.2
Severe	65	18	27.2
Moderate	51	1	2.0
Mild	3	-	0.0
Total	145	31	21.4

As the table shows, in both samples the numbers of mildly mentally retarded persons with DS are too low to enable us to draw a general conclusion regarding the prevalence of PDD.

Concerning the three other ranges of mental retardation, I may only present very provisional conclusions concerning the prevalence of PDD in persons with Down syndrome. (For information about the relative weights of the figures concerning day-care centres and those of the institutions, the reader is referred to Section III.2.4.) In the profound level of functioning the percentage of PDD persons is possibly about the same as in the entire profoundly mentally retarded population, i.e., around 40%. In the severe range the percentage of PDD persons will presumably be much lower in DS people, i.e., around 20%, compared with 40% for the entire severely mentally retarded population. In the moderate range this percentage will presumably also be much lower in DS persons, i.e., around 4%, compared with 20% for the entire moderately mentally retarded population. The estimated figures are summarized in Table III.5.7.

Table III.5.7 Estimated percentages of PDD in mentally retarded persons in the four ranges of retardation: percentages for the entire population and percentages for Down-syndrome people

Level of retardation	PDD prevalence	
	Entire population	Exclusively Down syndrome
Profound	40 %	40 %
Severe	40 %	20 %
Moderate	20 %	4 %
Mild	1.8 %	?

III.5.5 Discussion and summary

From the findings obtained by comparing experimental and control groups the following conclusions may be drawn:

- Pervasive developmental disorders are found in a substantial number of persons with Down syndrome, albeit less frequently than in mentally retarded people without Down syndrome.

- In comparing mentally retarded DS and non-DS persons according to level of functioning, the following conclusions may be drawn concerning PDD prevalence:
  - in the profound range of mental retardation the percentages of PDD will possibly be about the same in DS and non-DS persons, i.e. around 40%;
  - in the severe range of mental retardation the percentage of PDD persons will possibly be around 20%, which is about a half of the figure for non-DS persons;
  - in the moderate range of mental retardation the PDD percentage will possibly be around 4%, which is one fifth of the figure for non-DS persons;
  - in the mild range of mental retardation the PDD percentage will possibly hardly deviate from that of non-DS persons, i.e., around 1.8%.
- Down-syndrome people who are diagnosed as PDD are generally found to display a comparatively mild form of this disorder, as is evident from their comparatively low PDD-MRS scores; their low total scores are due to the fact that they often receive minus scores for the items bearing on severely deficient response to contact initiative of adults/in social interaction, and on self-injurious behaviour. Clinical observation suggests that a comparatively high number of these persons belongs to the passive group of PDD.
- Profoundly and severely mentally retarded persons with Down syndrome who are diagnosed as non-PDD are generally found to receive comparatively high PDD-MRS scores; their comparatively high total scores are due to the fact that they often receive a plus score for the items bearing on stereotyped manipulation of own body and on stereotyped and unusual handling of objects.
- The conclusions listed above apply to both male and female persons.

My findings confirm that Down syndrome is a very important cause of mental retardation. To be more precise, it constitutes the most common somatic (and clearly demonstrable) cause of severe and moderate mental retardation in both males and females.

Although pervasive developmental disorders occur less frequently in mentally retarded persons with Down syndrome than in those without Down syndrome, the percentages found in the profound, severe and moderate ranges of mental retardation are nevertheless many times higher than those of the entire population, which is, according to the highest estimate made thus far (Wing, 1981a), about 0.26%. Any statement which suggests that pervasive developmental disorders are rare in DS people must therefore be said to lack a factual basis.

Two further issues are important:

- The strong correlation found for DS people between the presence of a PDD and profound and severe mental retardation (see Table III.5.7) is possibly due to a second etiological factor which further aggravates mental retardation in the unborn child and additionally carries the risk of a PDD developing (which holds true for the entire mentally retarded population). Perinatal problems may constitute such a factor. After all, it has been known for quite a long time that DS children are liable to suffer perinatal problems at birth (see, for instance, McIntire et al., 1965; Pueschel et al., 1976). Gibson (1978) holds an even more pronounced viewpoint on this matter. He writes that DS is not only 'a *primary* mental deficiency', but also important as 'a *secondary* disorder' responsible for pregnancy and delivery complications.
- Although DS people with a pervasive developmental disorder are often found to have this disorder in a mild form (notably displaying less self-injurious behaviour), problem behaviours are quite common. Even self-injurious behaviour proves to occur more frequently in DS people with a PDD than in DS people without a PDD (see III.4.2.3.5).

Finally, the finding that in the profound and severe ranges of mental retardation a larger number of DS people without a PDD than those with a PDD displays stereotyped behaviour is worthy of note. It seems to indicate that, within these ranges of retardation, this behaviour is more associated with Down syndrome than with a pervasive developmental disorder.

My clinical experience indicates that mentally retarded PDD people with Down syndrome hardly differ from those without Down syndrome with respect to the sorts of problems they have and to the persistence of these problems. It follows that an early identification of pervasive developmental disorders is just as important in Down-syndrome people as it is in people without Down syndrome, and that treatment and management should be geared to this diagnosis.

PERVASIVE DEVELOPMENTAL DISORDERS IN MALE PERSONS WITH FRAGILE X SYNDROME

III.6.1   Introduction

Just like Down syndrome, fragile X syndrome, or fra(X), is due to a chromosome abnormality; however, the abnormality in fra(X) is hereditary. The retardation involved is, at least when mutation is complete, permanent.

The first studies regarding an association between fra(X) and mental retardation appeared in the 1980s. According to some estimates the syndrome contributed to as much as 20% of mental retardation cases. However, a growing number of more recent publications have produced evidence that mental retardation is far less frequently due to fra(X) than was initially thought. According to Rutter et al. (1990), mental retardation in male persons is in 5-10% of the cases due to fra(X); Maes (1993), summarizing data from an extensive amount of literature, concludes that on average 3.1% of mentally retarded male persons have fra(X) (and 0.9% of mentally retarded female persons).

Many investigators regard fra(X) as a specific etiological factor for autism. However, studies giving high percentages for autism as a concurrent disorder in fra(X) - some with estimates as high as 50% or more - are, as was argued by Rutter et al. (1990) and Bailey et al. (1993) - based on incorrect cytogenetic criteria and unclear criteria for autistic behaviour, and samples which were too small.

In the aforementioned study by Maes, the results of fourteen investigations published between 1985 and 1992 were used. The author concludes that the prevalence rate of 'autism' and PDD-AD (as defined by the DSM-III-R) in persons with fra(X) is about 20.5%. An excellent study, which somehow seems to have escaped Maes' notice, is that of Einfeld et al. (1989). These authors compared 44 mentally retarded male persons with fra(X) and 45 mentally retarded male persons without fra(X), matched for level of functioning. They found that each group contained four persons with PDD-AD (or about 9% on average) and concluded that the specific association between autism and fra(X) was not confirmed. A similar conclusion (but on a less solid basis) was reached by Payton et al. (1989). Likewise, Maes (1993) compared a fra(X) and matched non-fra(X) group, each consisting of 58 male persons. She found that the two groups did not differ significantly regarding the numbers of subjects belonging to the category Autistic, according to the very strict criterion provided by the Autism Behavior Checklist (see III.1.2.2); four fra(X) subjects (6.9%) and one non-fra(X) subject (1.7%) were found to be autistic.

Kerby and Dawson (1994) compared nine male fra(X) persons with a non-fra(X) male control group, matched for chronological age and level of functioning. They found that the fra(X) subjects displayed more autistic features (i.e., the sixteen criteria for PDD-AD established by the DSM-III-R) than the subjects without fra(X). However, for the sake of completeness, I remind the reader that the presence of autistic features is not tantamount to autism or a pervasive developmental disorder.

As will be clear, investigations in the field to date have employed rather diverging definitions of autism. A narrowly defined concept was most often used; autistic-like conditions were rarely considered. However, it seems highly important to consider the entire spectrum of pervasive developmental disorders, PDD-NOS included, when exploring the association with fra(X). People with fra(X) often display behaviours which are more or less typical of autism or autistic-like conditions. Although the behavioural descriptions provided in the literature vary somewhat - as was also pointed out by Maes (1993) - they do agree by and large with what I have clinically observed. To my mind, the following behavioural features are typical. In personal contacts, fra(X) persons may be rather kind and interested, which implies that they certainly do not ignore other people; however, when approached too enthusiastically they tend to shy away, avoiding eye-to-eye contact, becoming withdrawn or aloof, or even breaking off all contact. Maes regards this as an inner conflict between *attractive* and *repulsive* agents. Towards less familiar people fra(X) persons remain shy and reserved for a rather long time. Their ability to bear frustrations is limited and they are oversensitive. Being irritable and easily over-agitated, they are liable to become unsettled; they may then be hyper-active, chaotic or even self-injurious. Stereotyped manipulation of own body, stereotyped language and obsessive interests also occur. Fra(X) people generally rely strongly on predictability and routines, and are much embarrassed by changes and uncertainty.

When exploring the association between PDD and fra(X) there are quite a few pitfalls to be avoided, as was found to be the case with Down syndrome (see III.5.1). In my investigation I have used the same strategies to enhance validity and reliability as I did when investigating PDD in Down-syndrome persons, i.e.:

- To investigate two separate categories of mentally retarded people, i.e., children attending day-care centres and institutionalized persons.
- To use the PDD-MRS.
- To use the figures for PDD prevalence in mentally retarded persons (presented in Chapter III.2) as a rather broad gauge.

364

- To use control groups, matched (individual for individual) for the factors placement history, chronological age, level of functioning, and sex.

A general (but hitherto neglected) problem concerns the selection of subjects for the experimental and control groups. To date children attending day-care centres and institutionalized persons are comparatively rarely examined for the presence of fra(X); such examinations, if carried out at all, are probably only carried out when there are strong indications for the disorder, i.e., marked external characteristics and/or marked behavioural characteristics. If this assumption is correct - but unfortunately it cannot be verified - the experimental group is likely to be biased. However, for its part, the control group may contain not only subjects without fra(X) (reliably diagnosed or not), but also undetected fra(X) cases, and this may to some extent reduce any disproportionate difference between the control and experimental groups. In sum, the data are not optimally reliable. Little can be done about this, as even the selection of diagnosed non-fra(X) subjects for a control group will not solve the problem. Ideally, all persons of a given population of mentally retarded people should be examined for the presence of fra(X), even those for whom a clear etiology for their mental retardation has been previously established (see R.J. Hagerman, Invited Paper 10th World Congress IASSID, Helsinki, 1996).

III.6.2 Two pilot studies

III.6.2.1 *A pilot study of fra(X) children attending day-care centres*

As fra(X) is not very common, it is rather difficult to find a sufficient number of cases to serve as subjects in an experimental group. Inquiries involving 21 day-care centres with a total population of well over six hundred children (19% of the Dutch day-care centre population) were carried out (Kraijer, 1994). In this way sixteen fra(X) boys in the age-range 3-14 years could be traced; this represents 2.5% of the entire population and 4.2% of the male population of these facilities. Five of these sixteen boys are severely, ten moderately and one is mildly mentally retarded. According to their diagnoses, eight boys (50.0%) belong to the group doubtful-PDD (their mean PDD-MRS score was 8.50; s.d. 2.27) and four boys (25.0%) belong to the PDD group (their mean PDD-MRS score was 12.00; s.d. 1.41); two of the PDD boys are severely mentally retarded, one is moderately and one mildly mentally retarded.

Two conclusions may be drawn from these figures:

- The proportion of doubtful-PDD children is extremely high compared with both the 10.8% found in the day-care population in general (see Table III.2.9) and the 9.7% found in the PDD-MRS norm group (in which

106 of the 1096 subjects were doubtful-PDD; see Table III.1.17).

- The proportion of PDD children is entirely in agreement with the expected figure (i.e., 40% of five subjects plus 20% of ten subjects, which amounts to 4.0 subjects; see III.2.4).

III.6.2.2 *A pilot study of institutionalized fra(x) persons*

According to the data available from seven institutions for mentally retarded persons with a population of 3400 persons (which is about 13% of the entire Dutch institutionalized population), 38 persons (35 males and 3 females), or 1.1%, had been diagnosed as fra(X) (Kraijer, 1994). All were adults, except for one eleven-year-old boy. To preclude the interference of complicating factors, the three female persons were ignored in the present context. The remaining 35 fra(X) males represented 1.7% of the male population of the seven institutions involved; one of these persons is profoundly mentally retarded, fourteen are severely, seventeen moderately and three mildly mentally retarded. According to diagnoses made by the supervising psychological experts, thirteen persons (37.1%) belonged to the group doubtful-PDD (mean PDD-MRS score 7.31; s.d. 2.21), and twelve persons (34.3%) belonged to the PDD group (mean PDD-MRS score 12.33; s.d. 2.84).

Two conclusions may be drawn from the figures given above:

- The proportion of doubtful-PDD persons is extremely high, both when compared with the 10.5% found in the institutionalized population in general (see Table III.2.2) and with the 9.7% found in the PDD-MRS norm group (in which 106 of the 1096 subjects were doubtful-PDD; see Table III.1.17).
- The proportion of PDD persons is in fair agreement with the expected figure (i.e., 40% of 15 (1 + 14) plus 20% of 17 plus - for the sake of completeness - 1.8% of 3, which amounts to 9.4 persons; see III.2.4).

III.6.2.3 *Discussion of the results*

The results of the two pilot studies concerning PDD prevalence in fra(X) persons may give rise to some speculation and preliminary conclusions:

- In the two pilot studies the prevalence rates of fra(X) in male persons are found to be very low, 4.2% and 1.7%, respectively; the figures come close to the 3.1% average of the figures reported in the literature (see Maes, 1993). (In the present context the negligibly small number of female fra(X) persons is ignored.) Further confirmation that the figures I found for fra(X) as an etiological factor in mental retardation were hardly or not below the actual figures may be found in the following reports:
  - Systematic examinations carried out at the Eekwal observation home from 1985 until 1992; initially, only suspected cases were examined for

the presence of fra(X), but in the course of time all persons admitted were examined. These examinations revealed that of the two hundred adult and non-adult cases examined, six male persons (i.e., about 3% of all persons examined and about 4% of all male adult and non-adult persons admitted to the Eekwal home) displayed fra(X); the prevalence rate did not rise when the examinations were extended to all persons admitted, nor when advanced DNA techniques were introduced.

- Similar examinations were carried out at an institution for mentally retarded persons, the Hendrik Van Boeijen-Oord, predominantly involving cases in which outward appearances suggested the presence of fra(X). Recently DNA techniques were introduced. These examinations revealed, according to the information received from the head of the medical staff (J.J. Roosendaal), that in the cases examined for the presence of fra(X) over the years (almost two hundred cases), seven male persons and one female person (i.e., about 4% of all persons examined and about 1.8% of all male inhabitants of the institution) were positively identified as fra(X).

All findings indicate that, compared with the far more familiar Down syndrome, fra(X) must be viewed as a minor contributor to mental retardation, but certainly not as a negligible one. Moreover, fra(X) as a cause of mental retardation is found to occur almost exclusively in male persons.

■ The number of fra(X) subjects examined for the presence of a PDD is very small. In both pilot studies a comparatively large proportion of them belonged to the group doubtful-PDD. Statistical testing is needed to ascertain whether this finding has a more general significance. This also applies to findings concerning the proportion of PDD persons in the two experimental groups, which were found to diverge. Compared with the PDD prevalence rate in the entire mentally retarded population, the figures for the institutional sample were slightly higher than expected, but in line with expectation in the day-care sample. Therefore, the findings will be compared with those of non-fra(X) control groups.

■ Conclusions concerning behavioural characteristics of persons with fra(X), expressed as total PDD-MRS scores and PDD-MRS item scores, likewise require comparison with control groups.

III.6.3   Comparison with matched control groups

III.6.3.1   *Study design*

Non-fra(X) subjects were selected from day-care centres and institutions for comparison with the subjects of the two experimental groups (described in Sections III.6.2.1 and III.6.2.2). The subjects of the control groups were matched individual for individual. In addition to the variables *type of facility* and the exclusively *male sex*, the groups were matched for *chronological age* (i.e., children matched in terms of completed years; adults matched in terms of a maximum difference of twenty years and this category was to contain no persons below the age of eighteen), and for *level of functioning* (ratings being made by the psychological experts involved on the basis of available data concerning intelligence as well as social competence). In view of the fact that PDD is less common in persons with Down syndrome (see Chapter III.5), the control groups had to contain maximally 15.0% DS subjects. (The eventual proportions were 12.5% and 14.3%, respectively, for the two groups.)

The main questions posed were:

- Are fra(X) persons more often placed into the 'evasive' diagnostic category doubtful-PDD than non-fra(X) persons?
- Are the same numbers of fra(X) and non-fra(X) persons diagnosed as PDD?
- Do the PDD-MRS total scores and PDD-MRS item scores suggest the existence of behavioural differences between fra(X) and non-fra(X) persons, within the diagnostic categories PDD, non-PDD and doubtful-PDD?

Statistical testing was by means of the t-test and the chi-square test (or, if the latter was not suitable, the Fisher exact probability test). If possible, tests were two-tailed. Moreover, as far as PDD-MRS scores were concerned, analyses of variance (ANOVA) were carried out with respect to each of the three diagnostic categories (PDD, non-PDD and doubtful-PDD); etiology (fra(X)/non-fra(X)) and level of functioning served as independent variables in these analyses (Kraijer, 1996a).

III.6.3.2   *Fragile X syndrome and the prevalence of PDD*

A comparison of PDD cases in the day-care experimental and control groups is presented in Table III.6.1.

Table III.6.1 Frequency distribution of children attending day-care centres, with diagnoses PDD, Doubtful-PDD and Non-PDD, according to the presence of fra(X)

Diagnosis	Fra(X)	Non-fra(X)	
Non-PDD	4	10	
Doubtful-PDD	8	0	
PDD	4	6	
Total	16	16	32

Fisher exact probability test for:
(Non-PDD + PDD) ↔ Doubtful-PDD: p =.001
Non-PDD   ↔ Doubtful-PDD: p =.002
PDD   ↔ Doubtful-PDD: p =.01

Testing within a 2x3 table is not possible because of the low frequencies. Comparing combinations yields only significant differences when the doubtful category is isolated. A significantly higher number of fra(X) than non-fra(X) children is placed into the diagnostic category doubtful-PDD.

As far as the institutional groups are concerned, two tendencies found in the fra(X) group have to be tested statistically: (a) is the higher number of institutionalized fra(X) persons categorized as doubtful-PDD a chance finding, or may it hold true for the entire institutionalized fra(X) population? (b) is the slightly higher number of fra(X) persons categorized as PDD a chance finding, or may it hold true for the entire institutionalized fra(X) population? The prevalence figures for PDD in the institutional experimental and control groups and the statistical tests are presented in Table III.6.2.

Table III.6.2 Frequency distribution of institutionalized persons with diagnoses PDD, Doubtful-PDD and Non-PDD, according to the presence of fra(X)

Diagnosis	Fra(X)	Non-fra(X)	
Non-PDD	10	16	
Doubtful-PDD	13	3	
PDD	12	16	
Total	35	35	70

Chi-square 8.21; df = 2; p <.02
Chi-square for:
(Non-PDD + PDD) ↔ Doubtful-PDD: 8.10; df = 1; p <.01
Non-PDD   ↔ Doubtful-PDD: 7.32; df = 1; p <.01
PDD   ↔ Doubtful-PDD: 6.12; df = 1; p <.02

Only the three 2x2 table testings in which the doubtful category is isolated yield significant differences. Consequently, only one conclusion may be legitimately drawn, viz., that a significantly higher number of institutionalized fra(X) than non-fra(X) persons is categorized as doubtful-PDD.

As the results found for the day-care and institutional groups are very similar, the figures of the two fra(X) and non-fra(X) groups may be combined. Statistical testing then yields the following values: chi-square 18.05; df = 2; p <.001. By carrying out the same statistical procedures as above, it could once again be confirmed that the high level of significance was due to differences between the numbers of persons categorized as doubtful-PDD. The results were as follows: non-PDD ↔ PDD: ns; (non-PDD + doubtful-PDD) ↔ PDD: ns. It may therefore be concluded that a significantly higher number of male persons with fra(X) is categorized as doubtful-PDD. In fact, we may be more specific in our conclusions, because 90.2% of the subjects of

369

the two combined experimental groups belong to the severe and moderate ranges of mental retardation, and analyses of variance carried out on these figures revealed that level of functioning was unrelated to the PDD-MRS score in each of the three diagnostic categories. Taking these facts into account, we may conclude as follows: a significantly higher number of moderately and severely mentally retarded adult and non-adult male persons with fra(X) than those without fra(X) is categorized as doubtful-PDD within the same age ranges and the same levels of functioning, while the two groups do not differ with respect to the numbers categorized as PDD.

III.6.3.3 PDD in fra(X) males: form and severity

A comparison between doubtful-PDD subjects with fra(X) and doubtful-PDD subjects without fra(X), with respect to their PDD-MRS scores and PDD-MRS item scores, revealed that there were no differences for either age category. Similarly, no differences were found when PDD subjects with fra(X) were compared with PDD subjects without fra(X). However, differences do emerge when non-PDD fra(X) subjects are compared with non-PDD non-fra(X) subjects, as shown in Table III.6.3.

Table III.6.3 Comparison of the mean PDD-MRS scores obtained by Non-PDD persons with fra(X) and Non-PDD persons without fra(X) in two types of facilities

Facility	Fra(X)			Non-fra(X)			
	n	Mean	(s.d.)	n	Mean	(s.d.)	p*
Day-care centres	4	4.25	(2.99)	10	0.90	(0.99)	= .007
Institutions	10	3.20	(1.99)	16	1.75	(2.21)	ns
Combined	14	3.50	(2.50)	26	1.42	(1.30)	<.002

* t-test

In both facilities, fra(X) persons are found to obtain higher mean PDD-MRS scores than non-fra(X) persons, but only in the day-care group is the difference significant. As the tendencies within the two groups are the same, they may be combined. The significance value found for the combined groups is even slightly higher than that found for the day-care group considered separately.

Analysis of variance reveals that, within the same age range and the same level of retardation, severely and moderately mentally retarded non-PDD males with fra(X) obtain higher PDD-MRS scores than non-PDD males without fra(X). For the sake of completeness, I would like to inform the reader that the higher PDD-MRS scores of the non-PDD persons with fra(X) are nevertheless clearly within the non-PDD range (i.e., within the range 0-6).

Item analysis revealed the origin of the found difference. A significantly higher number of severely and moderately mentally retarded non-PDD males with fra(X) than those without fra(X) (within the same age-range and the same level of functioning) obtained plus scores for two PDD-MRS items, i.e.,

1b Less severely deficient response or fluctuating response to contact initiative of adults in social interaction (p =.03);
 9 Strong dependence on fixed patterns, routines and/or rituals (p =.01).

III.6.4   Discussion and summary

From the comparisons made between the experimental and control groups regarding the presence of a PDD (diagnoses based on clinical evaluations and PDD-MRS scores), the following conclusions may be drawn:

- Pervasive developmental disorders are found in about equal numbers amongst - predominantly severely and profoundly - mentally retarded male persons with fra(X) as amongst those without fra(X).
- A very significantly higher number of male persons with fra(X) than those without fra(X) is categorized as doubtful-PDD.
- Non-PDD male persons with fra(X) obtain comparatively high PDD-MRS scores due to their poor contact-making and strong attachment to patterns and routines.

Regarding the first conclusion, an interesting recent finding reported in the literature is that narrowly defined autism does not occur more frequently in fra(X) male persons than in comparable groups of non-fra(X) male persons. The results of my study suggest that this finding probably holds true for the entire spectrum of pervasive developmental disorders.

The second and third conclusions call for further discussion. The number of doubtful-PDD cases amongst persons with fra(X) is extremely high in comparison with those found amongst non-fra(X) persons and with those of the PDD-MRS norm group, i.e., 41.2% against 5.9% and 9.7%, respectively. Apparently, a great many fra(X) persons are difficult to diagnose with respect to the presence of a PDD; even the residual category PDD-NOS is not felt to be applicable to them, nor can they be categorized as non-PDD. The behavioural features of persons with fra(X) even result in some discrepancy between clinical classification and PDD-MRS classification. Examination of the PDD-MRS scores obtained by fra(X) persons who, according to their final 'evasive' diagnoses, belonged to the group doubtful-PDD presented in Table III.6.4, will make this clear.

Table III.6.4 PDD-MRS scores obtained by fra(X) persons with a doubtful-PDD 'diagnosis' in two different kinds of facilities, according to the PDD-MRS classification

Facility	PDD-MRS classification			Total
	Non-PDD	Doubtful-PDD	PDD	
Day-care centres	6;6	7;8;8	10;11;12	8
Institutions	4;4;6;6;6	7;7;8;8;9;9;9	12	13
Total number	7	10	4	21

As the table shows, eleven of the 21 fra(X) persons with the 'evasive' diagnosis doubtful-PDD obtain scores which fall outside of the range for classification as doubtful-PDD; this amounts to 52.4%, a very high percentage. The number of doubtful-PDD persons obtaining scores which, in a PDD-MRS classification would classify them as non-PDD, is higher than those obtaining scores which would classify them as PDD. For the sake of completeness, I would like to inform the reader that, of the sixteen fra(X) persons diagnosed as PDD, only one person scored below the PDD cut-off figure of 10 (with a PDD-MRS score of 7), while of the fourteen fra(X) persons diagnosed as non-PDD, only two persons scored above the PDD cut-off figure of 6 (with PDD-MRS scores of 7 and 8).

How does a diagnostician arrive at the 'diagnosis' doubtful-PDD? When the score on a comparatively objective measuring tool, such as the PDD-MRS, is used as a supplement to other information, there are three possibilities:

1 Clinical observation suggests a PDD, but the impression is not sufficiently convincing, while, on the basis of the PDD-MRS score, the case should be categorized as non-PDD (score lying in the 0-6 range).
2 Clinical observation suggests a PDD, but the impression is far from convincing, while, on the basis of the PDD-MRS score, the case should be categorized as doubtful-PDD (score lying in the 7-9 range).
3 Clinical observation does not clearly suggest a PDD, but, on the basis of the PDD-MRS score, the case should be categorized as PDD (score lying in the 10-19 range).

As far as fra(X) persons are concerned, each of the three ambiguities listed are found to occur quite frequently.

Must we go as far as to say that fra(X) is an important and specific cause of autism and autistic-like conditions in male persons? It should be realized that even the entire spectrum of pervasive developmental disorders is displayed by about the same numbers of fra(X) and non-fra(X) mentally retarded persons. However, the behaviour displayed by fra(X) persons undeniably suggests the presence of a PDD. This applies notably to their ambivalent ways of seeking and avoiding human contact. On the other hand, this behaviour is also very idiosyncratic. The result is that diagnosticians often hesitate to categorize these persons as cases of PDD, preferring the safer option of doubtful-PDD. In the investigation discussed above, the ambiguous situation is reflected in two complementary findings: a high number of cases was diagnosed as either PDD or doubtful-PDD (37 of the 51 fra(X) subjects, or 72.5%, were thus categorized), and non-PDD fra(X) persons obtained comparatively high PDD-MRS scores.

Maes (1993) also gave some consideration to the diagnostic problems involved. Comparing scale scores obtained by fra(X) and matched non-fra(X) mentally retarded persons on the one hand, and those obtained by PDD and non-PDD persons on the other hand, she reports striking differences. (See also the findings presented in III.1.4.3). Maes found that fra(X) persons differed from non-fra(X) persons in the following respects:

- As far as the SRZ is concerned, they obtain slightly higher scores on the subscale Self Help; they do not obtain lower scores on the subscales Communication and Social skills, nor a lower SRZ-total score.
- As far as the TVZ is concerned, they do not obtain lower scores on the subscales Approachability, Adaptability and Distractibility, nor on the combined scale Communicativeness; they even have higher scores on the subscale Mood and on the combined scale Easy/difficult temperament!
- As far as the SGZ is concerned, they do not display less Verbal maladaptive behaviour, nor more Miscellaneous maladaptive behaviour, and their SGZ-total scores for maladaptive behaviour in general are not higher. However, the SGZ findings are at variance with those reported by Gielen et al. (1988). These investigators found that 22 institutionalized fra(X) persons (twenty males and two females) obtained higher scores for Miscellaneous maladaptive behaviour and higher SGZ-total scores for maladaptive behaviour in general. (However, the subjects in this investigation also obtained higher scores on the subscales Aggressive maladaptive behaviour and Verbal maladaptive behaviour, which does not suggest a pervasive developmental disorder.)

Other relevant data are provided by Cohen et al. (1988,1989,1991). Using sophisticated methods, these authors were able to demonstrate that the mechanisms responsible for poor eye-to-eye contact in male fra(X) persons and male autistic non-fra(X) persons probably differ. When displayed by autistic persons, poor eye contact seems to be a reflection of a more generalized attentional or associative learning deficit; this deficit may account for a lack of interest in or even avoidance of social contact. When displayed by male fra(X) persons, however, the behaviour seems rather to be related to 'gaze aversion', which may even stem from a greater sensitivity to social contact. Strikingly, the authors found that the same difference emerged when autistic fra(X) persons and autistic non-fra(X) persons were compared. From this it may be concluded that the same behavioural phenotype in male PDD and non-PDD persons with fra(X) and in male PDD persons without fra(X) may result from different mechanisms.

In view of these considerations, it is actually not surprising to find that in the present investigation such a large number of fra(X) subjects was categorized as doubtful-PDD. Their behaviour is very similar to that of PDD persons, but in some respects rather different indeed.

Some important questions remain.

Firstly, do fra(X) persons need the same approach as PDD persons, or do they need a specific approach? Although my clinical experience with fra(X) persons is limited, I am nevertheless under the impression that they may benefit from the approach which is found to be suitable for persons with the erratic form of PDD.

Secondly, do the specific behavioural features of male fra(X) persons call for the creation of a separate sub-category within the already broad category of PDD? This is probably the best solution. It was adopted with respect to Rett's Disorder, both in the DSM and ICD systems, mainly because of the disorder's characteristic picture and course. Regarding fra(X) persons, it may be argued that they are very similar to PDD persons both in behavioural respects and in the kind of treatment they need, and that their condition is clearly an infantile developmental disorder. If fra(X) is incorporated into the PDD category, this would at any rate settle the long-drawn-out controversy about the extent to which the behavioural features of fra(X) male persons may be regarded as autistic; as a result of this controversy the place of fra(X) in the major classification systems to date remains unclear. In the DSM system, fra(X) would then be regarded behaviourally as a reasonably distinct sub-category within the spectrum of pervasive developmental disorders, clearly separate from the PDD category Autistic Disorder. This would make it clear that fra(X) is, like the far less frequent Rett's Disorder, a cause of both mental retardation and a very specific form of pervasive developmental disorder. The equally important somatic aspect of fra(X) may be emphasized by placing it on Axis III of the DSM, General Medical Conditions.

AN OVERVIEW AND A LOOK INTO THE FUTURE

In the opening chapter of the present volume I expressed my intention of dealing with the qualitative and quantitative problems involved in autism and autistic-like disorders in mentally retarded people, which to date is a neglected field of inquiry.

I think that I have clearly demonstrated that even in mentally retarded people it is generally possible to establish the presence or absence of autism and autistic-like disorders, and to classify these people on the basis of existing systems and scales. In these respects, notably the concept Pervasive Developmental Disorder as developed by the DSM, and the Scale of Pervasive Developmental Disorders in Mentally Retarded Persons (PDD-MRS), which is based on the DSM concept, proved to be very helpful.

A number of pilot studies were undertaken in preparation for a fact-finding survey. It was quite reliably established that pervasive developmental disorders occur in about 40% of profoundly and severely mentally retarded people, and in about 20% of moderately mentally retarded people, which implies a PDD ratio of approx. 27:100 in the ranges below mild mental retardation. The prevalence rate for mild retardation is about 1.8% (Wing & Gould, 1979). These percentages must strike us as disconcerting when compared with figures reported in studies published only a few years ago (see Chapter I.1).

Whether narrowly defined autism (in ICD-10 terminology Childhood autism, and in DSM-IV terminology PDD-Autistic Disorder) occurs in equal or higher proportions in mentally retarded people, notably those in the ranges below mild mental retardation, is hard to know. The pioneering studies of Menolascino (1983, 1990) revealed that mentally retarded people may be afflicted by the same psychiatric disorders as intellectually normal persons. However, the lower the level of functioning, the more difficult it is to recognise these disorders, as the inability to display differentiated behaviour also affects the ways in which psychiatric disorders may manifest themselves. On that account genuine cases of autism in lower-functioning persons are liable to be diagnosed as atypical autism (in ICD terminology) or PDD-NOS (in DSM terminology). The PDD concept, introduced by the DSM, proves to be very useful in the mental retardation field; it enables us to pronounce upon the mere presence or absence of a pervasive developmental disorder, even when a severely or profoundly mentally retarded person is examined. In addition, the severity of the disorder can sometimes be ascertained, for instance by means of the PDD-MRS. However, further differentiations are still hard to make.

The high PDD prevalence rate is also an important issue when considering how serious the problems are for persons with the dual diagnosis of mental retardation and PDD. Ample evidence may be found in the present study that these people are very vulnerable and easily become prey to a variety of often serious problem behaviours. The fact that behavioural problems are hard to treat in persons with pervasive developmental disorders only aggravates the situation. From this it must be clear that the prevention of problems is of crucial importance when dealing with mentally retarded PDD persons.

Because of their very special features and extreme vulnerability, mentally retarded PDD persons require special educational intervention and specific treatment regimens. Although these people do frequently benefit from an appropriate strategy, their specific disorders are not curable by treatment or training. Virtually all mentally retarded PDD persons are, sooner or later, destined to be placed into facilities which offer accommodation and day-time activities.

Hopefully, my book will help to improve the care of mentally retarded PDD people. Much is needed: better understanding of the problems involved, identification at the earliest possible stage, well-thought-out plans for treatment and care, and systematic evaluation of the effects of the chosen strategy. Last but not least, society has to provide the finances and organisational means to secure highly professional care for these people.

With respect to mentally retarded PDD *children* in particular, they are in principle best cared for at home. To fulfil this task parents do need adequate practical support from specialized guidance and home-training agencies, which should closely collaborate with the schools and day-care centres involved. In case of serious problems, supplementary advice may be given in a clinical setting, such as the Eekwal observation home, on the basis of detailed examinations.

In the Netherlands, virtually all profoundly and severely mentally retarded children with a PDD are placed into institutions at a fairly early age, the majority before they have even reached the age of ten. As far as PDD persons functioning on moderate and mild levels of retardation are concerned, institutionalization is less frequent, and also tends to take place at a later stage. Many mildly retarded adults are able to live in a group home. *Adult* or *nearly adult* PDD persons, including those with normal intellectual abilities, have only recently been receiving more professional attention. It is becoming increasingly clear that many of these persons require lifelong care, which - and this is also highly important - should be provided by specially trained helpers.

For a number of adults in the moderate and mild levels of functioning, group-home placements may end in failure. Once they have gone off the rails these people tend to become entirely unmanageable in these facilities (Kraijer, 1993). In a number of instances institutional placement is then the only alternative available at present. In the Dutch residential-care field the rate of institutionalization is much higher than in the rest of the world (Hatton et al., 1995). Typically, Dutch institutions are set in rather remote areas. They consist of bungalows, generally dating back to the 1970s or later, which are surrounded by parkland. The grounds usually offer a shop, a restaurant, a hairdresser's salon, a pedicurist's parlour, buildings with recreational and workshop facilities, a centre for indoor swimming and sports, a place for religious meetings, and consultation rooms for the doctor and dentist. In fact, it is a village-type community in which everybody knows everybody else and nobody would pass another person without say-ing hello. Fixed rhythms help to make life predictable; demands and stimuli are geared to the capacities of the members of the community. Nevertheless, even these institutions may not fully comply with the special care needs of mentally retarded people with a PDD. Before elaborating on these needs, I first want to dispel five fallacies regarding the care of the mentally retarded which seem to me to be rooted in preconceived and still widely acclaimed notions;

- The first fallacy is that normalization and integration are intrinsically good.

  Too often have I seen in my clinical work mentally retarded adults who were victims of the normalization principle and had developed behavioural disorders or even become seriously unsettled (Kraijer, 1988b). Other studies confirm this observation. Mesibov (1990), for instance, warning that the normalization principle tends to become an end in itself, states that, "A theoretical system is needed that accepts and values handicapped people for what they *are* instead of for what a small group would like them to *become*" (italics mine, DWK). Another cautio-nary note is sounded by Schopler and Hennike (1990) who write, "When concepts like 'integration' and 'normalisation' are used as single-minded ideologies, they can soon become counter productive."

- The second fallacy is that institutions are by their very nature inferior to facilities which are more integrated into social life, such as group homes, and certainly inferior to the home situation.

  In fact, however, clinical experience shows that many people who were unmanageable at home or in the group home may pick up after institutional placement; this, of course, is not to say that institutionalization is the answer to each and every problem.

- The third fallacy is that small-scale provisions are invariably better than large-scale provisions.

Schopler and Hennike (1990) state that, "Small community-based group homes [...] have the same potential for sterility, isolation and neglect found in the largest institutions." Van Bourgondien and Schopler (1990) argue that, "The assumption is frequently made that fewer numbers of handicapped clients in one setting leads to higher quality care and more social interactions with others." However, the authors add that, "Unfortunately, the available data do not support this simplified approach to assuring a quality program." A literature study carried out by Van Gennep (1989b) confirms these conclusions.

- The fourth fallacy is that de-institutionalisation invariably has a positive effect.

In fact, various investigators found that de-institutionalisation had neither positive nor negative effects. Burd et al. (1991), for instance, found no decline in the use of psychoactive medication in persons who had moved from institutions to community-based group homes. Emerson et al. (1992) describe a project in which institutionalized mentally retarded persons with serious behavioural problems were placed into detached homes, which measure coincided with an increase in the number of caregivers. The inhabitants seemed neither better nor worse off. These investigators conclude that environmental re-modelling and more personnel apparently do not suffice to bring about real improvement.

Some investigators, however, found that both positive and negative behavioural changes are effected by de-institutionalization. This is reported by Landesman (1987), for instance. This author studied the behaviour of autistic-like institutional residents who were placed into a small unit within the grounds of the institution. However, the effect was difficult to measure as the move coincided with a reduction in group size. Lowe et al. (1993) found that a de-institutionalized group of mentally retarded people improved in their social skills but displayed more problem behaviour. The new facility seemed insufficiently structured and the authors conclude, "Philosophy, no matter how sound in principle, is clearly insufficient to effect positive change in problem behaviours..."

It may be concluded that de-institutionalization clearly carries a risk, notably for dually disabled mentally retarded people with behavioural problems. Specific measures should be taken to reduce this risk (Galligan, 1990; Causby & York, 1991). The presence of behavioural problems is, as Van Gennep (1992) rightly argues, even a strong counter-indication for placement into a socially more integrated facility. To put it mildly, de-institutionalization should not be regarded as exclusively beneficial for the mentally retarded population as a whole. Prudence is especially needed when dealing with complicated cases. I have elaborated on this issue with the special aim of safeguarding people with pervasive developmental disorders against ill-considered measures which merely comply with a prevailing ideology.

- The fifth fallacy is that institutional care is invariably more expensive than that given in community-based services.

There is nothing wrong with taking financial aspects into account; it is even necessary. When making a matter-of-fact efficiency evaluation, the cost per person per day for comprehensive care in Dutch institutions has been for many years just as high (perhaps even less high) as that for community-based group homes and day-care centres combined. Van Bourgondien and Schopler (1990) arrive at a similar conclusion; they state that the cost of providing care in group homes for mentally retarded people with concurrent disorders is significantly higher than it was first thought to be and that care in large institutions is hardly more expensive or not at all.

By reviewing these fallacies I have hopefully cleared the way for a more rational consideration of the specific and fundamental conditions which are essential for the care of mentally retarded PDD people in day-care and residential facilities. Van Gennep (1989a) rightfully argues that mentally retarded people represent the most vulnerable group in our society. This being the case, mentally retarded people with a PDD must be considered to be the most vulnerable persons within this most vulnerable group. Consequently, if, according to Van Gennep, mentally retarded people are entitled to *special help* when *regular help* proves not to suffice, mentally retarded people with a PDD are entitled to an even greater amount of special help.

Which special help is needed by mentally retarded PDD people? In the first place, whatever their level of functioning, they have to be protected against overstimulation. As nothing in the world is so unstable and rousing as a human being, a primary requisite is that *groups must be small;* a group size of *no more than six persons* is crucial for PDD children, adolescents and adults alike. It must be realized that genuine group interaction is beyond PDD persons, even those in the mild range of mental retardation. As will be clear, groups must be composed in such a way that poor skills in the areas of interaction, social-emotional discrimination and adaptability (typical of PDD persons) are taken into account; again, this also applies to mildly mentally retarded persons. Some mildly mentally retarded persons are better off when living independently, provided that they are carefully monitored.

In the second place, as was also put forward by Schopler and Hennike (1990), a well-balanced day programme is absolutely essential. (This applies even to mentally retarded persons without additional disorders; see Van Gennep, 1989a,b). I agree with Van Bourgondien and Elgar (1990) that mentally retarded people with autism need extra time, effort and expertise from the staff to provide the structure necessary for their behavioural problems; agitation, confusion and disorientation have to be prevented, as these may lead to aggression, self-injury and other adverse reactions. Consequently, both attendants and supervising psychological and medical experts need special competence for the creation of a tolerant, relaxed and supportive milieu. (For more details, see Chapter II.4.) I want to underline, moreover, that in dealing with mentally retarded PDD persons one has to be cautious in making demands and offering stimuli. Too often have I seen adult and non-adult persons with pervasive developmental disorders being expected to perform to the best of their abilities; although things may run fairly well for some time, the day will come that the last straw breaks the camel's back. A more or less serious event - let's say, an attendant is leaving, or there is a change within the group or family - may be unsettling or even trigger off disintegration. Not infrequently the harmful effects are very hard to remedy. Such situations must therefore be prevented at all costs. To preserve and promote competence, all professional helpers, whatever their specialty, should follow special training and refresher courses, and keep abreast of the literature in their fields. Occasionally they even have to make a radical mental switchover, in order to admit, for instance, that ordinary kindness alone is of little use when dealing with persons who primarily need a specific and professional approach because of their highly uncommon features and problems.

In the third place, people with pervasive developmental disorders must be given opportunities to withdraw. This means that they should have at any rate *a private bedroom* with sufficient space for some leisure activities. The institutional unit or group home must have a quiet workroom; the communal living room must have separate *nooks* which can be screened off. At fixed moments of the day and also under clearly defined circumstances withdrawal must be possible. However, *withdrawal must not be allowed to become loneliness.*

The three conditions mentioned above constitute together a *comprehensive strategy*, which for adults in particular is mainly focussed on *providing a home* rather than on treatment. The guiding principles are continuity and safety. Work and leisure facilities must be in the immediate vicinity of the living accommodation or indeed be an integral part thereof. Personally I am not an advocate of groups exclusively consisting of PDD people on principle. Group attendants for their part clearly find work within mixed groups emotionally more satisfying. However, if group members are selected with an eye to similar or possibly supplementary needs and dispositions, in practice this will generally mean that units of mentally retarded persons are predominantly composed of either PDD or non-PDD persons (Kraijer, 1991).

The problems of PDD in mental retardation need to be addressed more systematically. Primarily, the existing provision of services has to be evaluated in terms of available knowledge and expertise. In the Dutch situation, PDD persons in the profound and severe ranges of retardation, and a substantial proportion of those belonging to the moderate range, decidedly benefit best from the care which institutions are able to provide. Still, professional competence in these facilities needs further promotion. As far as PDD persons of the mild and moderate-to-mild ranges of retardation and those of borderline intellectual functioning (IQ between about 71 and 84) are concerned, there is a need in the Netherlands for intermediary facilities, such as special work facilities and special group homes with annexed private apartments, both of which must be amply provided with specially trained personnel. Hopefully such provisions will come about by the combined efforts of the autism teams and institutional and group-home staffs. These facilities may on the one hand be socially more integrated than institutions, but on the other hand offer close and competent supervision which is indispensable.

More specialized professional care is urgently needed to create acceptable living conditions for the seriously disabled group of mentally retarded PDD persons. As will be understood, new insights and approaches alone will not suffice to help them. Many of the measures advocated above are indeed costly affairs. Not much can be achieved unless central government and local authorities recognize the necessity of better care, and are willing to provide more financial support to this end. The present book has been written to demonstrate the legitimacy of this demand.

CLASSIFYING PDD IN MENTALLY RETARDED PEOPLE ON THE BASIS OF THE DSM-IV; PROBLEMS OF DIFFERENTIATION

In some respects the issues to be dealt with in the present appendix are similar to those discussed in Chapter II.3, which concerns the classification of children on the basis of the DSM-III-R. For the sake of coherence, no further reference to that chapter will be made. As the DSM-IV and ICD-10 systems are fairly uniform by now, references to the clinical conditions discussed will use the code numbers of both systems (with those of the ICD-10 in parentheses).

Two subgroups within the general category of pervasive developmental disorders are of major importance in the mental retardation field: *Autistic Disorder* or PDD-AD, *299.00 (F84.0)*, and *Pervasive Developmental Disorder NOS, 299.80 (F84.9)*. The first subgroup is, according to the DSM-IV system (and for that matter also according to the DSM-III-R system), characterized by qualitative impairment in three areas: social interaction, communication, and the range of interests and activities. In the DSM-IV each of the three areas contains four items. In order to be placed into subgroup PDD-AD, subjects must present the behaviour indicated in at least six of the items in a specified combination.

In the mental retardation field, the criteria for PDD-AD stipulated by the DSM-IV often prove not to be applicable, as many mentally retarded people have a low level of functioning and an extremely limited behavioural repertoire. If a mentally retarded person does not meet the criteria for PDD-AD and nevertheless clearly has a pervasive developmental disorder, placement into the residual category PDD-NOS is possible, as the number of criteria involved in this category is rather small. As will be clear, people with a higher level of functioning may also be categorized as PDD-NOS; however, these are cases with a *partial or atypical pervasive developmental disorder*. Moreover it should be realised that people with PDD-NOS may need the same amount of professional care as those with PDD-AD.

Two other subgroups of pervasive developmental disorders are *Rett's Disorder, 299.80 (F84.2)*, and *Childhood Disintegrative Disorder, 299.10 (F84.3)*. They are comparatively uncommon and therefore much less important.

Rett's Disorder is only found in girls. Communication and interaction skills show a serious decline; some cases, however, slightly improve after puberty. The syndrome may be considered as a special case of Childhood Disintegrative Disorder. One of the criteria for this latter disorder is that the child did show *normal* development for at least his first two years, but subsequently lost previously acquired skills. However, in the mental retardation field, this criterion cannot be rigidly applied. In my clinical practice I have seen some children who met all the criteria for Childhood Disintegrative Disorder except for this one, as more or less serious developmental lags - in terms of mental retardation - might be supposed to have been present before the age of two. Another problem: one specific case, whose regression was really dramatic, had in all likelihood started to deteriorate at the age of just eighteen months.

As will be understood, *Asperger's Disorder, 299.80 (F84.5)*, is outside the scope of the present book, as the normal or nearly normal development of cognitive and language skills is one of the criteria for this condition.

In some respects there is overlap between PDD and other DSM (or ICD) categories, which may create classificatory problems. In the remainder of the present appendix, four schemes will be presented to facilitate the discussion of the various types of problems involved. The relationships between the relevant DSM-IV categories are also indicated.

Scheme A.1 summarizes the problems encountered when classifying *children* and *adolescents* on the basis of their behavioural symptoms.

309.21 (F93.0) Separation Anxiety Disorder
As the name implies, this disorder involves primarily an intense anxiety for being separated from the home or from those to whom the person is attached. Quite a few children with pervasive developmental disorders, particularly those with the *erratic* type of PDD (or, in the terminology of Wing & Attwood, those belonging to the *active-but-odd* group) are found to display this anxiety, which can even be an overriding feature in many cases. However, the manual to the DSM-IV specifies that the presence of a PDD excludes Separation Anxiety Disorder. Consequently, children who seem to be afflicted by this disorder must be carefully examined for the presence of other PDD features. In other words, placement into category 309.21 (F93.0) should only be considered when separation anxiety occurs as a rather isolated problem.

312.8 (F91.8) Conduct Disorder
Fairly clear cases of this disorder are quite often found amongst children and adolescents with problem behaviour belonging to the mild range of mental retardation. The principal criteria for this disorder are *aggressive-physical cruel behaviour* towards human beings and animals, *destruction of property*, and

Scheme A.1 Differentiation between PDD and other DSM-IV disorders in children and adolescents

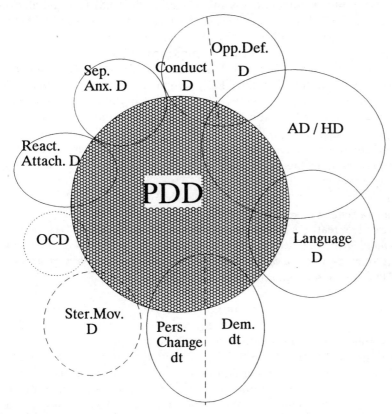

Sep. anx. D	= 309.21	(F93.0)	Separation Anxiety Disorder
Conduct D	= 312.8	(F91.8)	Conduct Disorder
Opp. Def. D	= 313.81	(F91.3)	Oppositional Defiant Disorder
AD/HD	= 314.01	(F90.0)	Attention-Deficit/Hyperactivity Disorder, Combined Type
Language D	= 315.31	(F80.1)	Expressive Language Disorder
	315.31	(F80.2)	Mixed Receptive-Expressive Language Disorder
Dem. dt ...	= 294.1	(F02.8)	Dementia Due to ...
Pers. Change dt ...	= 310.1	(F07.0)	Personality Change Due to ...
Ster. Mov. D	= 307.3	(F98.4)	Stereotypic Movement Disorder
OCD	= 300.3	(F42.8)	Obsessive-Compulsive Disorder
React. Attach. D	= 313.89	(F94.x)	Reactive Attachment Disorder of Infancy or Early Childhood

lying or *stealing*. PDD children, even of school age, may also behave quite 'unfeelingly' by, for instance, pulling hard at other children's hair, or squeezing the goldfish or hamster to death for no apparent reason. Breaking things is also far from uncommon. What matters when observing such behaviour is to look for special features, such as whether only certain objects are obsessively chosen as targets. For instance, there may be an urge to destroy faulty objects completely, even if the flaws are very minor. Making off with objects also occurs. A complicating factor may be the presence of *poor communicativeness*, which is not explicitly mentioned in the DSM-IV as a criterion for Conduct Disorder, but is, in my experience, not only found in PDD children but also in children with this disorder. However, poor communicativeness manifests itself differently in the two groups. A PDD child or adolescent will never flatly deny things or tell bald-faced lies, as may youngsters with a Conduct Disorder. Actually, PDD people are completely unable to distort facts; many are even too naive and frank. Children and adolescents with a Conduct Disorder, on the other hand, may be quite sophisticated in exploiting their social skills to their own advantage. Again, when classifying persons with features of a Conduct Disorder, we have to be very alert to the presence of specific PDD features, such as stereotyped behaviour and characteristic speech and language anomalies.

Oppositional Defiant Disorder, 313.81 (F91.3)
This disorder has features in common with the erratic type of PDD, notably *incessant claiming/eliciting reactions/trying out* (liable to be regarded as challenging behaviour), and *poor communicativeness*. Again, the presence or absence of other PDD features is the crucial point.

314.01 (F90.0) Attention-Deficit/Hyperactivity Disorder, Combined Type
AD/HD has features which are very frequently also found in PDD children and adolescents. In fact, the manual to the DSM-IV explicitly states that the two conditions cannot be attributed to one and the same person. Persons who present features of both conditions must be categorized as PDD. In Section II.4.1 of the present volume, hyperactivity was considered to be one of the semi-specific problems of PDD persons. Gillberg (1993), taking a different stance, suggests the introduction of a broader category, *Deficits in Attention, Motor control and Perception (DAMP)*, which he says will be applicable to many PDD persons. In my experience, differentiation is especially difficult with respect to poor attention skills, which may occur in association with unproductive activity and, more frequently, with *fleeting contact*. Fleeting contact may either be the result of simply taking insufficient time over everything, or reflect a fundamental incapacity to establish genuine personal contact. It is therefore crucial to ascertain which of the two possibilities applies.
    The AD/HD disorder may also be hard to differentiate from *Conduct Disorder, 312.8 (F91.8)*, and from *Oppositional Defiant Disorder, 313.81 (F91.3)*, especially as far as messy, impulsive and unmanageable behaviour is involved.

315.31 (F80.1) Expressive Language Disorder/Mixed Receptive-Expressive Language Disorder
Both mental retardation and a pervasive developmental disorder usually entail insufficient or poor language skills. The PDD-MRS norm group - which consisted of PDD persons of all levels of functioning, most of whom were

above five years of age - was found to include 55% of persons who spoke only a few words or none at all. In my follow-up study of former Eekwalhome subjects (see II.5.4.1), I found that 37% of those in the moderate range of mental retardation and 19% of those in the mild range were still unable to speak at the age of five. Insufficient language skills may indicate retarded speech development as a separate defect, which, as a matter of fact, does occur in mentally retarded people (to be categorized, for instance, as Mildly mentally retarded and Expressive language disordered). What makes matters still more complicated is that there is overlap between Language Disorder and AD/HD; in other words, many mentally retarded children with a language disorder show poor concentration, are hyperactive, and make only fleeting contact. According to the DSM system, the presence of a PDD excludes Language Disorders. It follows that we have to be very alert to the presence of speech and language anomalies which are typical of a PDD.

310.1(F07.0) Personality Change Due to ... /294.1 (F02.8) Dementia Due to ...
[medical condition to be indicated]
These disorders are frequently found in profoundly and severely mentally retarded people; in those who are very profoundly mentally retarded, the prevalence rate even exceeds the 50% level (Kraijer, 1997). Occasionally, the disorders are also found in moderately and mildly mentally retarded people.

The most common cause of the first disorder of the two is brain damage, often occurring in association with severe epilepsy. Not uncommonly, cases display a more or less low level of consciousness or constant fluctuations thereof; in some cases the condition is further aggravated by frequent absences. *Slow thinking and acting, perseveration, and lack of initiative* are comparatively frequently found. In the DSM-IV, five types of personality change are distinguished. In the lower levels of functioning the *Apathetic Type* is most common; people with this type of disorder have the features described above; however, they may also display aspects of the Labile Type, mainly emotional instability - easily breaking into laughter or tears - and/or hypersensitivity. The *Disinhibited Type*, mainly characterized by impulsivity, is frequently found in persons with problem behaviours in the severe, moderate and mild ranges of mental retardation. Incidentally, I would like to remark that I find the word 'disinhibited' rather unfortunate, as the word inhibited also denotes an undesirable state.

The second disorder, which is caused by progressive conditions, such as Sanfilippo disease (a metabolic disorder), eventually produces the same personality changes as described above under Personality Change. Isolated aspects of a higher level of functioning displayed earlier may remain, or reappear on occasion.

Both disorders are generally marked by insufficient contact skills either due to a varying or to a poor level of consciousness. However, some people with one of these disorders are, during their bright moments, capable of contact-making on a level which is consonant with their level of functioning. Both disorders may occur in association with PDD-NOS or Childhood Disintegrative Disorder; these cases display not only insufficient contact skills, but also other PDD symptoms.

In an earlier study (Kraijer, 1997) I found that the presence of PDD features may be observed in non-ambulatory very profoundly mentally retarded people (Developmental Quotient <10; mental age <1-0), if clinical observation is carried out at a time when these people happen to be optimally aware and alert. These features are:

- lack of initiative to contact-making, even towards familiar attendants;
- constant and intentional ignoring of others by looking the other way or turning away;
- resistance to contact initiatives (demonstrated by putting hands over eyes or over ears or showing discontent), or a complete absence of response;
- no eye-to-eye contact (looking past or through people, gazing from a safe distance, looking out of the corner of the eye);
- greater interest in *things* (a person's watch, spectacles, or jewellery, toys, a favourite object) than in *people*;
- a *comparatively high level of dexterity* in playing with objects, performing stereotyped tricks such as playing with own fingers, etc.;
- stereotyped manipulation of own body, either involving a *broad range* of activities (of which some may be practised *eagerly*) or a *limited range* of activities (all practised very *eagerly*).

Clear counter-indications for the presence of a PDD are initiative to contact-making and positive and amiable response to the contact-making initiative of others.

307.3 (F98.4) Stereotypic Movement Disorder

This disorder is rather ill-defined, as was also pointed out by Rutter (1989) in his analysis of the draft version of the ICD-10. In fact, the only criterion for the disorder is stereotyped behaviour, either combined or not with self-injurious behaviour. Thus, the category is not instrumental in spotting new aspects and is liable to be used in a makeshift manner. In addition, the item 'Markedly interferes with normal activities' may be difficult to apply in assessing low-functioning persons; for many of these persons the only option left besides stereotyped activities is doing nothing at all, which generally produces the same amount or even a greater amount of displeasure. To summarize, my advice is to ignore this category. Accordingly, in Scheme A.1 the area is indicated by a dashed line.

As will be understood, the choice of either PDD, Tic Disorder, or *300.3 (F42.8) Obsessive-Compulsive Disorder* (to be discussed in the next paragraph) excludes the category Stereotypic Movement Disorder.

300.3 (F42.8) Obsessive-Compulsive Disorder

Unlike obsessions, and habits and routines of an apparently compulsive nature, all of which are typical of a PDD, the behaviour covered by the category Obsessive-Compulsive Disorder is ego-dystonic, i.e., the behaviour causes distress or even marked distress and is experienced by the person as if it were not a part of the self; nevertheless, there is an inability to check this behaviour. PDD persons, on the other hand, may be indifferent to their own fixed patterns and rituals, or may even enjoy them. Moreover, the contact skills of persons with an Obsessive-Compulsive Disorder are normal in principle. Although PDD and Obsessive-Compulsive Disorder are mutually exclusive, there are cases nevertheless which seem to fit into either category.

Analyses of case histories and of the results of tests and scales, such as the PDD-MRS, may then be required in order to make a final diagnosis.
    Two qualifying notes made in the DSM-IV manual are relevant here. Firstly, as far as *children* are concerned, the category Obsessive-Compulsive Disorder has a limited applicability. In Scheme A.1 this area is therefore indicated by a dotted line. Secondly, again as far as *children* are concerned, their obsessive and compulsive behaviours are not necessarily felt to be beyond rhyme or reason. However, it is not clear whether this implies that the ego-dystonic criterion is not crucial or less crucial when classifying children, nor whether this qualification also applies to mentally retarded persons.

313.89 (F94.x) Reactive Attachment Disorder of Infancy or Early Childhood
This disorder may present itself in two ways, either by *extreme aloofness* (being hypervigilant and showing resistance to comfort) or by *diffuse, indiscriminate sociability* (lack of selectivity in the choice of attachment figures). Obviously, these two types may be hard to discriminate from the *rigid* and *erratic* types of PDD, respectively. To differentiate between the two disorders, a careful examination of the case history is crucial. Serious and prolonged emotional-social neglect, possibly combined with physical neglect, is a criterion for Reactive Attachment Disorder; PDD does not stem from neglect, as everyone agrees by now. Thus, the presence of a PDD excludes a Reactive Attachment Disorder.

307.22 (F95.1) Chronic Motor or Vocal Tic Disorder
This disorder is comparatively rarely applicable in the mental retardation field, because in the lower levels of functioning in particular it is very difficult to tell tics from stereotyped behaviours. Moreover, the manual to the DSM-IV does not clearly indicate whether or not the disorder may be classified in association with a PDD, while the ICD-10 completely ignores this issue, which possibly implies that according to this system the two disorders may be classified as concurrent disorders. Thus, the category is of little use in respect to differentiation, and I saw no reason for including the disorder in Scheme A.2.

Scheme A.2 summarizes the problems encountered when classifying *adults* on the basis of behavioural symptoms.

389

Scheme A.2 Differentiation between PDD and other DSM-IV disorders in adults

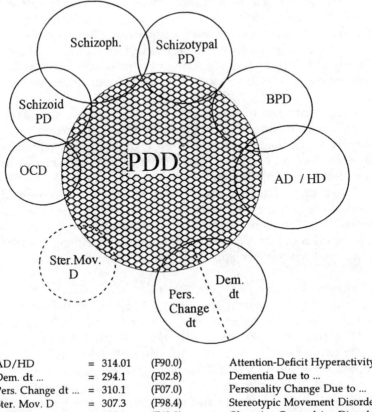

AD/HD	= 314.01	(F90.0)	Attention-Deficit Hyperactivity
Dem. dt ...	= 294.1	(F02.8)	Dementia Due to ...
Pers. Change dt ...	= 310.1	(F07.0)	Personality Change Due to ...
Ster. Mov. D	= 307.3	(F98.4)	Stereotypic Movement Disorder
OCD	= 300.3	(F42.8)	Obsessive-Compulsive Disorder
Schizoid PD	= 301.20	(F60.1)	Schizoid Personality Disorder
Schizoph.	= 295.xx	(F20.xx)	Schizophrenia
Schizotypal PD	= 301.22	(F21)	Schizotypal Personality Disorder
BPD	= 301.83	(F60.31)	Borderline Personality Disorder

In what follows only those DSM-IV categories will be discussed which have not yet been considered.

295.xx (F20.xx) Schizophrenia
Even today PDD persons are often misdiagnosed as schizophrenic, particularly in adult psychiatry. As a matter of fact, the two conditions are quite hard to distinguish, notably when *295.60 (F20.5x) Residual Type*, a chronic form of schizophrenia, is involved. A mentally retarded person with acute schizophrenia may seem to be afflicted by *erratic* PDD; however, when the delusions, hallucinations, confused behaviour and catatonic symptoms have subsided, the general picture has a strong resemblance to that of the *aloof* group (Wing & Attwood, 1987) or to that of the *rigid* type of PDD. In two respects schizophrenic persons are clearly distinguishable from those with a

PDD. In the first place, schizophrenia is characterized by either a gradual or abrupt deterioration in functioning subsequent to a state without any or hardly any symptoms, which generally extends into early adolescence. It follows that for the final diagnosis an analysis of the case history is crucial. In the second place, recurrent and intractable delusions and hallucinations strongly suggest a schizophrenia. As will be understood, the two conditions have to be carefully differentiated, as not only the prognoses differ but also the kind of care and treatment needed.

A further complicating factor is that mentally retarded PDD persons may develop a psychosis in addition to their dual disability. In such cases, *marked behavioural changes* will generally be observed, which must therefore be taken seriously.

Notably with severely and profoundly mentally retarded persons it may be hard or even impossible to establish the presence of delusions and hallucinations, as these persons typically have severe speech and language deficiencies and restricted expressive faculties. Again, *behavioural changes* are a telltale sign. Unfortunately, however, only more or less acute changes are perceived in time, and even these may be overlooked. Moreover, even experienced professional workers often find it difficult to appraise this kind of behavioural change properly; after all, not only schizophrenia may effect such changes, but also depression, reactive disturbances due to overstimulation or overloading, and physical-somatic factors. In a substantial number of cases, classification and diagnosis is indeed rather like crystal gazing.

301.20 (F60.1) Schizoid Personality Disorder/301.22 (F21) Schizotypal Personality Disorder

To begin with, these two conditions are hard to discriminate from one another, at any rate in mentally retarded people. In addition, each condition is hard to discriminate from a PDD, in particular from PDD-NOS. In fact, one might question whether there are good reasons at all for discriminating these two personality conditions as separate entities. Hopefully, this issue will be clarified in the future by detailed analyses of similarities and dissimilarities in early developmental histories.

In my experience, *Schizoid Personality Disorder* is hardly distinguishable or even indistinguishable from the *rigid* type of PDD, as may also be evident from some of the discriminating features indicated by the DSM-IV, such as detachment from social relationships, little interest in having sexual experiences with another person, an inability to form close friendships, and a constricted affect. According to the manual, the presence of a PDD excludes Schizoid Personality Disorder.

Similarly, *Schizotypal Personality Disorder* is hardly distinguishable or even indistinguishable from the *erratic* type of PDD. Both conditions are characterized by speech and language idiosyncrasies, inappropriate or constricted affect, odd and eccentric behaviour, and the reduced capacity for close relationships. Again, the presence of a PDD excludes Schizotypal Personality Disorder.

Both personality disorders share some criteria with *295.xx (F20.xx) Schi-zophrenia,* notably with the mild forms of schizophrenia and with the picture it presents in convalescence. In the ICD-10, schizotypal personality is even incorporated into the schizophrenia concept.

Finally, *301.20 (F60.1) Schizoid Personality Disorder* shares some criteria with *300.3 (F42.8) Obsessive-Compulsive Disorder* and with the hitherto unmen-tioned *301.4 (F60.5) Obsessive-Compulsive Personality Disorder.* This latter disor-der is more complex than the former, which rather involves separate behavi-oural disturbances. With mentally retarded people these two disorders are hard to tell apart. When in doubt, it would seem safer to categorize a person as a case of Obsessive-Compulsive Disorder, which is the less ambiguous and extensive category. If a case fits into one of these categories as well as into the PDD category, again analyses of case histories and of the results of tests and scales, such as the PDD-MRS, may be required to make a final dia-gnosis (as was recommended in parallel situations with respect to *300.3 (F42.8) Obsessive-Compulsive Disorder*).

301.83 (F60.31) Borderline Personality Disorder
Just as with the nine other personality disorders, it will not be certain that a case has been correctly placed into this category until late adolescence. Con-sequently, when both BPD and PDD seem applicable, the decision must of-ten be postponed. Case histories should be examined carefully. The follow-ing considerations must be kept in mind:

- Identification of personality disorders is very difficult in people below the mild range of mental retardation.
- Only the *erratic* type of PDD may be confused with a BPD.
- A person with a BPD displays more psychodynamics than a person with a PDD; he seeks to establish a relationship with other people but is una-ble to do so because of an 'emptiness of mind'.
- In my experience, the distinction between a BPD and a PDD may be rat-her questionable; I have seen some mildly and moderately mentally retar-ded persons who in early adulthood completely met the criteria for a BPD, but who, judging by their case histories, might well have been clas-sified as cases of PDD-NOS in their childhood. Both conditions may have a common background in at least a few cases.
- Nothing is said in the DSM-IV manual concerning the mutual exclusion of BPD and PDD. Theoretically, both disorders may therefore be assigned to one and the same person. However, to my mind such a dual classifica-tion seems not to be very satisfactory or helpful. My feeling is that a single PDD classification is the best option if the case history contains any suggestion of a PDD.

More than once in the foregoing discussion the rigid and erratic types of PDD were considered separately. It may therefore be convenient to present two schemes which show the overlapping of the two PDDs by the major disorders discussed in this appendix. I trust that Schemes A.3 and A.4 will be self-explanatory.

Scheme A.3 Differentiation between the rigid type of PDD and other DSM-IV disorders

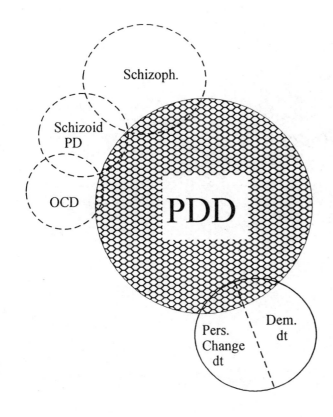

Scheme A.4 Differentiation between the erratic type of PDD and other DSM-IV disorders

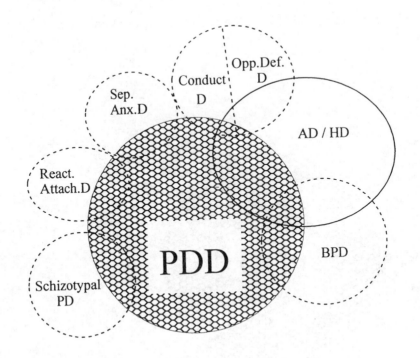

DIRECTIONS FOR THE USE OF THE PDD-MRS

B.1   Introduction

The PDD-MRS is a simple classification and screening instrument designed for the identification of Pervasive Developmental Disorders in mentally retarded persons of all four levels of functioning, age-range 2-55 years. The scale is based on the definitions of Pervasive Developmental Disorder given in the DSM-III-R, ICD-10, and DSM-IV; the entire spectrum of autism and autistic-like conditions is covered. The norms of the scale are based on the research protocols of 1096 Dutch mentally retarded persons (children, adolescents and adults) in the profound, severe, moderate and mild ranges of mental retardation. The psychometric qualities of the PDD-MRS are discussed in Sections III.1.3.1 to III.1.3.9 of the present volume.

To my mind the use of scales such as the PDD-MRS is indispensable in day-to-day clinical practice (as well as in research), although I also fully agree with Gillberg (1990a) that, "The diagnosis of autism is clinical and should not be made purely on the basis of some rating scale."

Diagnoses involving the use of the PDD-MRS follow several phases. The first phase is a clinical classification. Once this has been made, the diagnostician is referred to the table in the middle of the front page of the scale form. After the words *Clinical classification* the diagnostician must circle either N, D or PDD; in this table,

N   stands for no Pervasive Developmental Disorder
D   stands for doubtful whether a Pervasive Developmental Order is present or not, and
PDD   stands for Pervasive Developmental Disorder.

In the second phase of the diagnostic process the PDD-MRS is administered; the results are specified in the *PDD-MRS classification*, which is to be found on the second line of the same table. Again the appropriate abbreviation, N, D or PDD, must be circled.

The PDD-MRS classification is based on scores assigned to twelve scale items. These items refer to forms of:

a *normal behaviour* (making contact, using expressive (verbal) language) and
b *unusual or deviant behaviour* (stereotyped handling of objects, self-injurious behaviour, etc.).

Mentally retarded people with a PDD display fewer forms of normal behaviour and more forms of unusual or deviant behaviour than do those without a PDD.

Each item consists of several distinguishable features of behaviour, clearly described to facilitate assessment. For each item there is only the choice of either a plus or a minus score. *Only current behaviour*, i.e., behaviour observed during the last two- to six-month period, and *only spontaneous behaviour*, i.e., behaviour taking place in normal, day-to-day situations, should be considered. No willingness on the part of the subject to cooperate is required.

The scale should be completed only by raters who can satisfy the following requirements:

a familiarity with autism and autistic-like disorders;
b familiarity with mental retardation, notably profound and severe mental retardation;
c emotional detachment with respect to the subject being assessed; personal involvement may make assessments less objective and accurate, notably when considering contact items 1 and 2; accordingly, a child should not be rated by his or her parents, for instance;
d ability to make personal observations (in fact the best way to gain insight) and to interview parents, teachers, caregivers, etc., and possibility of consulting written reports concerning the subjects in question.

In general, these qualities are present in psychological experts, psychiatrists, and senior staff members of special wards and institutions. In addition, these professionals should be prepared to make a careful study of the manual to the scale, which provides general guidelines and specific directions per item. The PDD-MRS form contains a summary of the general and specific instructions.

Ratings take about 10-25 minutes, including interviews, report-reading and the like; assessments of uncomplicated cases as well as those of extremely disturbed cases tend to take the least time (i.e., ten minutes), while those of difficult cases take more time (i.e., 25 minutes).

The PDD-MRS items are printed on the two inside pages of the form. Item scores must be marked in the right-hand margins; the positions of the plus and minus signs in the margins indicate how the scores must be added in order to arrive at the five raw scores to be entered into the five boxes at the bottom of the inside pages. These raw scores are subsequently transferred to the table on the front page and then multiplied by the indicated weights. The results are added to produce the PDD-MRS score (range 0-19), which determines the PDD-MRS classification. Again, there are three categories: N, D and PDD. Score-ranges determining each of the three categories are as follows:

N   : 0 - 6
D   : 7 - 9
PDD : 10 - 19

Finally, in the third phase of the diagnostic process, a *diagnosis* is made on the basis of both the clinical and PDD-MRS classifications.

B.2   General principles

- *Only **current** behaviour, i.e., that observed during the past two- to six-month period, should be considered.*
  As the PDD-MRS is specifically devised to record current behaviour, information concerning earlier periods, early infancy included, must be ignored.
- *If the type of behaviour indicated in the item has not or has hardly been displayed during this period, circle* + / ⊖ .
- *If the behaviour indicated in the item has been displayed during this period, circle* ⊕ / − .
- *Score all items.*
  There are three reasons for this stipulation:
  - to ensure that the choice between 1a/1b/1c and that between 2a/2b are carefully considered;
  - to ensure that the connection between items 3, 4 and 5 is taken into account;
  - to ensure that all other items are checked for the presence or absence of the listed symptoms.
- *In scale items which are marked +, **underline** one or more of the specific manifestations of the behaviour listed, or, if necessary, specify on the dotted line.*
  These specifications highlight individual aspects of the behaviours concerned; in addition, they enable us to discover changes therein when reassessments are made.
- In devising the PDD-MRS, efforts were made to prevent developmental level from affecting the outcome of the assessment; this was achieved by utilizing items which are, as much as possible, also applicable to subjects with poor levels of adaptive behaviour and intelligence, i.e., those with quotients roughly below 75. This target proved hardest to achieve with the two interaction-items 1 and 2, which made the addition of ample explanatory notes to these two items unavoidable.
- Scoring must be carried out according to the directions provided in the manual. Regular re-reading of this part of the manual is strongly recommended to maintain a reasonable level of accuracy.

Social interaction with adults.
(Before scoring, scan all items (1a, 1b, and 1c); then select the most appropriate item to be marked with a + score; subsequently mark the remaining two items with a − score)

1a SEVERELY DEFICIENT RESPONSE TO CONTACT INITIATIVE OF ADULTS/IN SOCIAL INTERACTION
inadequate interaction, possibly limited to isolated and more or less specific and recurrent situations, such as finger-games, frolicking, tickling; a standard kiss/ smile/chat; frequent disregard, rejection, avoidance of eye-to-eye contact, and/or virtually no or only mechanical imitation

This sub-item covers only response to contact initiative, as mentally retarded persons may be too handicapped to initiate contact themselves. A plus score implies a serious impairment of response which cannot be ascribed to low level of functioning.

The phrase 'contact initiative' should be broadly understood to cover not only the overt forms of drawing attention (such as making sounds, saying things, smiling, or touching) but also potential contact-making (such as coming into or staying in the same room).

1b LESS SEVERELY DEFICIENT RESPONSE OR FLUCTUATING RESPONSE TO CONTACT INITIATIVE OF ADULTS/IN SOCIAL INTERACTION
Manifestation(s) of behaviour leading to a + score:
a) contact is made, but is too fleeting;
b) some incipient contact-making is present (possibly only in everyday situations), but shows insufficient continuity (let alone growth);
c) extreme and persistent shrinking from contact with unfamiliar people and/or exclusive involvement with a very small number of familiar people;
d) the contact-making is bizarre;
e) the contact-making is extremely defiant and/or provocative;
f) the contact-making is overdemanding and/or extremely clinging;
g) the contact-making with strangers lacks due reserve

The term 'contact initiative' is used as defined above for 1a.

The types of behaviour mentioned under a, b, and c imply a *deficit*, i.e., contact-making is too infrequent.

The behaviour mentioned under d implies *odd or bizarre aspects*, i.e., contact-making is inadequate (some examples of which are: exaggerated, formal politeness; approaching people too closely when talking to them; gazing at other persons long and penetratingly in the eye; grimacing or fidgeting when approached too closely).

The types of behaviour mentioned under e, f and g refer to *excessive* contact, which may even imply obtrusiveness. The behaviour is not only intemperate, but also stereotyped and devoid of content. It does not involve real contact-making; subjects may constantly ask questions or ask the same questions again and again, while being indifferent to the answers provided; some are endlessly claiming attention and eliciting reactions, while further development of the contact itself fails to take place; some accost strangers and may even enter upon very private matters (e.g., 'Do you have a willy?').

In some of the deviant behaviours listed above, level of functioning should be taken into account in accordance with the following guidelines:

- There are deficiencies in response which at any level of functioning must be regarded as deficiencies, such as never or scarcely looking someone in the eye (in spite of normal eyesight).
- There are also deficiencies in response which must only be regarded as deficiencies if they are *grossly out of keeping with the general level of functioning*. It is not uncommon, for instance, for a three-year-old child to chat with an utter stranger, but by the age of five a child should have developed some restraint; thus, this behaviour must be regarded as deviant when displayed regularly by a person of a developmental age of five.

Accordingly, in identifying deficient response to contact initiative in mentally retarded people, the following considerations should be borne in mind:

- A mentally retarded person may, just as an intellectually normal person, display genuinely deviant behaviour. Especially experienced workers in the mental retardation field, such as attendants, are liable to see such deviant behaviour as more or less inherent to the mental retardation itself; specific problems - such as poor contact, fleeting contact, persistent annoying or defying behaviour, repetitive asking of the same questions, etc. - may then be misinterpreted. This may result in *underrating* the occurrence of PDD in mentally retarded people.
- Obviously, the chief difference between mentally retarded and intellectually normal people concerns their level of mental development. However, notably with mentally retarded adults it is often very difficult to make a reasonably accurate estimate of this level. Nevertheless, this information is of crucial importance when deciding whether or not a given kind of behaviour should be regarded as deviant. To give an example, a twenty-year-old man with a mental age of 2-0 who follows the attendant like a toddler tied to his mother's apron strings, may be said to display perfectly normal behaviour as he can hardly be expected to have learned to stand on his own two feet. For a proper assessment of the situation the general developmental level must therefore be taken into account, otherwise *overrating* the prevalence of PDD in mentally retarded people may result.

As we have already established, classification and diagnosis may be very difficult when assessing profoundly and severely mentally retarded persons.

A sufficiently reliable and valid measuring device which is also fairly easy to apply would be very helpful when examining persons of these levels of functioning. It has been demonstrated in several studies that the two domains of functioning which are least affected by the presence of a PDD are *self help/daily living skills* and *elementary gross motor skills*; PDD people are found to display neither peaks nor lows in these two domains (see, for instance, Brakenhoff-Splinter et al., 1977; Altena et al., 1980; Volkmar et al., 1987; Loveland & Kelly, 1988; Kraijer, 1987a, 1990, 1991). Level of functioning in these two domains is therefore a good indication of level of functioning in general, and may be used as a norm when evaluating a subject's level of social interaction.

The milestones in normal development regarding the domains of daily living skills, motor skills and *social interaction* are presented below in three separate schemes. At least 80% of all persons of the indicated ages have passed the milestones. The criteria for developmental age are based on the items of the following scales: Bayley Scales of Infant Development - Dutch version (1983); Denver Developmental Screening Test, American version (second edition, 1975) and Dutch version (third edition, 1979); The Griffiths Mental Development Scales (1954); the Vineland Social Maturity Scale-Dutch version (1966); the Vineland Adaptive Behavior Scales (1984). Descriptions of behaviours correspond as much as possible to the ones used in these scales. On the basis of the developmental criteria it is possible to compare the level of social-interaction skills with the levels of motor and daily-living skills. However, the method can do no more than indicate whether or not a developmental delay is involved; it is not feasible to work out a system of fixed or relative intervals between the various milestones so as to make a more exact estimate of the amount of delay/deficiency in social interaction. It must be realised that ultimately assessments cannot be other than qualitative. In my experience, this is not a serious drawback with the PDD-MRS.

Daily living skills

0;8	Eats a cracker alone

1;8	Manages (half-full) cup well

2;0	Eats with a spoon
2;6	Takes off most clothing, unzips (but does not unbutton)
2;10	Eats with a fork

3;0	Puts on most clothing; zips (but does not button)
3;2	Remains dry by day and night
3;6	Washes own hands and face with some help
3;8	Unbuttons

4;0	Sets the table, properly arranging dishes, glasses and cutlery
4;2	Puts on most clothing, buttons (but does not tie shoelaces)
4;8	Clears dishes and glasses away without breaking them

Gross motor skills

0;4	Holds head steady in upright posture
0;10	Sits alone for at least three minutes
0;11	Stands holding furniture or wall

1;1	Walks at least ten steps when led
1;3	Stands alone for at least ten seconds
1;6	Walks alone at least ten steps

2;0	Ascends stairs holding banisters
2;2	Kicks a ball
2;5	Turns a doorknob to open a door

| 3;0 | Pedals a three- or four-wheeled vehicle for at least ten metres |

| 4;6 | Rides a bicycle for at least one hundred metres |

Social interaction

0;1	Looks caregiver in the face
0;2	Smiles in response when caregiver smiles and talks
0;4	Smiles spontaneously (social smile)
0;5	Uses vocalizations when spoken to
0;7	Initially shy with strangers
0;9	Shows interest in other children besides siblings
0;10	Enjoys playing peek-a-boo and joins in

1;1	Waves 'bye bye'
1;3	Clasps hands, plays pat-a-cake, etc.
1:5	Seeks comfort when hurt
1;7	Rolls ball back

| 2;10 | Understands notion of turn-taking |

| 3;3 | Starts playing with other children in a co-operative way |

1c *RESPONSE TO CONTACT INITIATIVE OF ADULTS AND/OR SOCIAL INTERACTION IS CONSONANT WITH LEVELS OF FUNCTIONING IN THE TWO CRUCIAL SKILL AREAS (i.e., daily-living and motor skills)*

The sole aim of this sub-item is to force the rater to make comparisons with the levels of functioning in the other domains, to help him to discover major lags.

Social interaction with peers
(Before scoring, scan both items; select then the most appropriate item to be marked with a + score; mark subsequently the other item with a − score)

2a IS A LONER AMONGST PEERS
   presence of any one of the five possibilities given below must yield a + score for item 2a
   a) *does not notice or hardly notices peers;*
   b) *does not usually join in, stands aloof;*
   c) *very regularly disturbs play or occupation of peers by thwarting/teasing;*
   d) *is exclusively oriented towards adults and/or staff;*
   e) *ability to consider others, participate in joint activities and make friends is not consonant with general level of functioning*

Especially when deciding whether or not option e is applicable, the level of functioning has to be taken into account. However, as the three schemes for developmental age presented above do not stretch beyond the age of 4-6 years, decisions concerning option e are in many cases bound to be based on the personal judgement of the rater.

2b SOCIAL INTERACTION WITH PEERS IS CONSONANT WITH LEVELS OF FUNCTIONING IN THE TWO CRUCIAL SKILL AREAS *(i.e., daily-living and motor skills)*

Again, the sole aim of this sub-item is to force the rater to make comparisons with levels of functioning in the other domains, to help him to discover major lags.

Language and speech
(If item 3 is marked with a + score, items 4 and 5 must receive a − score)

3 EXPRESSIVE LANGUAGE IS ABSENT/VIRTUALLY ABSENT
   fewer than eight recognizable (single) words are produced spontaneously and regularly

Only spontaneous and more or less appropriate use of word combinations or single words must be considered. The conditions for a plus score are the same for subjects with limited expressive language skills because they are hard of hearing or deaf, and for subjects with expressive language disorders and motor disabilities; the rater is not supposed to assess to what extent the additional disabilities have impaired the subject's language and speech skills.

4 LANGUAGE AND SPEECH ARE PRESENT, BUT WITH DEVIANCES IN CONTENT
stereotyped repetition; extreme literalness; neologisms; idiosyncratic language; senseless language; bookish language; immediate/delayed echolalia; no/limited/incorrect use of the pronouns I, me, etc. ....

When scoring this item, level of functioning must be disregarded. Anomalies, such as echolalia and omission of first pronouns, *must always be scored plus*, even when the feature is normal in view of the subject's chronological age.

As an illustration of concrete language may serve 'purple cabbage' when red cabbage is meant.

Unusual language implies coining words or phrases such as 'a sweep-the-floor' for a broom, as well as idiosyncratic language, such as 'I wish to extract a biscuit from the tin' (quoted by Wing, 1976).

Delayed echolalia implies copying previously heard words and phrases from other people, television advertisements and the like. (To give an example, at the observation home Bart told an attendant, 'Bart, you're really making Mummy a bit tired.')

5 LANGUAGE AND SPEECH ARE PRESENT, BUT WITH DEVIANCES IN PRODUCTION
the voice is either too loud, or extremely soft; unusual voice quality, such as harsh or metallic; unusual rate, possibly either drawled or hurried; un-usual use of pitch, such as monotonous intonation or with idiosyncratic inflectional patterns or stresses; articulation problems (not associated with developmental level), such as stuttering and lisps ....

All forms of disturbed articulation *(excluding developmentally determined mispronunciations)*, deviances in voice production, etc., must receive a plus score, with two exceptions:

- the coarse voice of subjects with Down syndrome;
- unusual articulation or pronunciation originating from dialects and/or foreign languages spoken by subjects.

Other behaviours
(The items may be scored individually)

6 OUTSTANDING AND OBSESSIVE INTERESTS
in: push-buttons; taps; twigs; running water; lamps; specific types of toys; glittering ornaments; spectacles; parts of the body (sometimes with sexual overtones); fur; hair; an object to twiddle with; making sounds with objects; shadows; exhaustpipes; eating or drinking; specific foods or drinks; looking forward to special events such as visiting or being visited by the family; holes; jig-saw puzzles;

distances in miles; the calender; maps; electronics; drawing the same thing again and again; broken/intact; the workings of the human body; illness/death; etc.

The list presented above contains some typical examples of objects or events by which persons may be disproportionately preoccupied. The presence of one single obsessive interest suffices to make the item eligible for a plus score. The rater is supposed to be well acquainted with the wide range of obsessive interests found in persons with autism and autistic-like disorders.

7 STEREOTYPED, UNUSUAL HANDLING OF OBJECTS
tapping; scratching; rubbing; bouncing; tearing up; gnawing; licking; biting; sniffing (also at people); waving; balancing; spinning; taking off own clothes; lining things up in rows; sorting things by colour; building identical structures; etc. . . . .

Again, the list presented above contains some typical examples of the behaviour in question. The presence of one single manifestation suffices to make the item eligible for a plus score. The rater is supposed to be well acquainted with the wide range of manifestations of this behaviour found in persons with autism and autistic-like disorders.

Scoring of this item is *irrespective of level of functioning;* in other words, the behaviour must receive a plus score whenever a subject displays such behaviour.

8 STEREOTYPED MANIPULATION OF OWN BODY *(no objects involved)*
teeth-grinding; forced breathing; ruminating; masturbating (in children below age 12); walking on tiptoe; rocking oneself; pacing up and down; assuming unusual postures; staring at own hands; hand-flapping; finger-flicking; head-rolling; grimacing; covering the ears; etc. . . . .

Again, the list presented above contains some typical examples of the behaviour in question. The presence of one single manifestation suffices to make the item eligible for a plus score. The rater is supposed to be well acquainted with the wide range of manifestations of this behaviour found in persons with autism and autistic-like disorders.

Note that masturbating is only regarded as a manifestation of this behaviour when displayed by persons below the age of twelve, as masturbating is found not to discriminate between PDD and non-PDD mentally retarded adolescents and adults.

Again, scoring of this item is *irrespective of level of functioning;* in other words, the behaviours, such as hand-flapping, etc., are marked plus whenever they are displayed by a subject.

'Covering the ears' may be accompanied by excessive anxiety or panic reactions due to fear for specific sounds; in such cases item 12 must also receive a plus score.

9 *STRONG DEPENDENCE ON FIXED PATTERNS, ROUTINES AND/OR RITUALS*
fixed routines; fixed position of household objects; resistance to change and disorderliness; strong preferences for a limited number of dishes/drinks/kinds of clothes/a private nook and the like; extreme rigidity; over-precision or 'compulsiveness' . . . .

Again, the list presented above contains some typical examples of the behaviour in question. The presence of one single manifestation suffices to make the item eligible for a plus score. The rater is supposed to be well acquainted with the wide range of manifestations of this behaviour found in persons with autism and autistic-like disorders.

Again, scoring of this item is *irrespective of level of functioning;* in other words, the behaviour is marked plus whenever displayed by a subject.

So-called 'compulsive' behaviours, such as constantly washing hands, closing all doors, etc., must also be scored plus.

10 *SELF-INJURIOUS BEHAVIOUR (acts which are painful according to the observer)*
scratching/rubbing self; hitting/biting/pinching parts of the body; pulling hair; eye-poking; head-banging on walls, floor, furniture, etc.; keeping sores open .

Again, the list presented above contains some typical examples of the behaviour in question. The presence of one single manifestation suffices to make the item eligible for a plus score. The rater is supposed to be well acquainted with the wide range of manifestations of this behaviour found in persons with autism and autistic-like disorders.

Again, scoring of this item is *irrespective of level of functioning;* in other words, the behaviour is marked plus whenever displayed by a subject.

The crucial point in scoring is the observer's judgement as to the painfulness of the act, not whether it produces real injuries.

A plus score must also be assigned when measures proved to be necessary to prevent self-injury (restraints, arm tubes, etc.).

11 *HIGHLY ERRATIC/UNPREDICTABLE BEHAVIOUR (minor/no noticeable reasons for shifts)*
marked and abrupt shifts of mood; fits of rage; aggressive outbursts; very fluctuating levels of performance; capriciousness; being alternately overactive and apathetic; strange whims; constantly new problems; etc. . . . .

Again, the list presented above contains some typical examples of the behaviour in question. The presence of one manifestation suffices to make the item eligible for a plus score. The rater is supposed to be well acquainted with the wide range of manifestations of this behaviour found in persons with autism and autistic-like disorders.

12 *UNUSUAL, UNREASONABLE AND EXCESSIVE ANXIETY OR PANIC*
  anxiety/panic: when going to bed; for certain animals; for traffic; for sounds of machines/appliances/musical instruments; for flash-light; for the hairdresser/doctor/dentist; for cutting nails; etc. . . . .

Again, the list presented above contains some typical examples of the behaviour in question. The presence of one manifestation suffices to make the item eligible for a plus score. The rater is supposed to be well acquainted with the wide range of manifestations of this behaviour found in persons with autism and autistic-like disorders.

B.4   Further handling of the item scores

When all fifteen items have been marked plus or minus, the five boxes at the bottom of item pages 1 and 2 can be filled by adding the appropriate scores. Subsequently, the totals have to be copied into the corresponding boxes of the table in the right-hand lower corner of the front page. These totals have to be added up again; the new totals must then be multiplied by the weights 1, 2 and 3. Finally, the PDD-MRS score can be computed by adding up the three products and entering the total in the box at the bottom of the page. Subsequently, this PDD-MRS score must be circled in the left-hand column of the front page. The cut-off scores N ↔ D and D ↔ PDD apply to male and female subjects of all four levels of mental retardation in the age-range 2-55 years. The scale may be less valid and reliable when applied to subjects who are a) aged 0-1, b) aged 56 and above, c) of normal or almost normal intelligence. The appropriate category N, D or PDD is determined by the position of the circled score in the column. The appropriate category must be circled after *PDD-MRS classification* in the second box of the table in the middle of the front page.

When the results of clinical and PDD-MRS classifications (entered in the first and second box of the table in the middle of the page) agree, the diagnosis can be simply derived from these two classifications. When, however, the two classifications do not agree, the PDD-MRS results should be a stimulus to reconsider a subject; if possible, further examinations (including administering psychological tests and behaviour scales) should be carried out. In some cases prolonged observation and new assessments may be deemed necessary. As readers of my study will understand, a PDD-MRS classification is by no means a substitute for a clinical classification and should never replace it.

To allow a comparison of an individual PDD-MRS score with general results, the summarized results of the scores and corresponding classifications of 1096 research subjects are presented on the last page of the record form. Again, the score assigned to the subject concerned has to be circled.

To illustrate the scale's application, a completed form is presented below.

PDD-MRS

SCALE OF PERVASIVE DEVELOPMENTAL DISORDER IN MENTALLY RETARDED PERSONS

D.W. Kraijer

Name	Aria B.
Birth date	14-04-1978 (M)F
Date of assessment	17-02-1992
Chronological age	13 years

Assessed by:
Eekwal
S. Fokkema /
H. Gevnaat

PDD-MRS classification

0
1
N
2
3
4
5
6
7
D
8
9
10
11
12
(13)
PDD
14
15
16
17
18
19

Clinical classification	N	(D)		PDD
PDD-MRS classification	N	D		(PDD)
Diagnosis	N	D		(PDD)

Chronological age > 55 years	(no)/yes*
Chronological age < 2 years	(no)/yes*
Intelligence normal or near to normal	(no)/yes*

* Scale possibly less valid/reliable

Results according to prior assessments

Date(s)	04-12-91	
Score(s)	10	
Diagnosed as	PDD	

	A	B	C	D
Raw scores page 1	O		1	1
Raw scores page 2		4	2	
Totals		4	3	1
Weighting		x1	x2	x3
Weighted totals		4	6	3

PDD-MRS score	13

Social interaction with adults.
(Before scoring, scan all items (1a, 1b, and 1c); then select the most appropriate item to be marked with a + score; subsequently mark the remaining two items with a − score)

1a. SEVERELY DEFICIENT RESPONSE TO CONTACT INITIATIVE OF ADULTS/IN SOCIAL INTERACTION
inadequate interaction, possibly limited to isolated and more or less specific and recurrent situations, such as finger-games, frolicking, tickling; a standard kiss/smile/chat; frequent disregard, rejection, avoidance of eye-to-eye contact, and/or virtually no or only mechanical imitation .... $+$ / $\ominus$

1b. LESS SEVERELY DEFICIENT RESPONSE OR FLUCTUATING RESPONSE TO CONTACT INITIATIVE OF ADULTS/IN SOCIAL INTERACTION
Manifestation(s) of behaviour leading to a + score:
a)   contact is made, but is too fleeting;
b)   some incipient contact-making is present (possibly only in everyday situations), but shows insufficient continuity (let alone growth);
c)   extreme and persistent shrinking from contact with unfamiliar people and/or exclusive involvement with a very small number of familiar people;
d)   the contact-making is bizarre;
e)   the contact-making is extremely defiant and/or provocative;
f)   the contact-making is overdemanding and/or extremely clinging;
g)   the contact-making with strangers lacks due reserve .... $\oplus$ / $-$

1c. RESPONSE TO CONTACT INITIATIVE OF ADULTS AND/OR SOCIAL INTERACTION IS CONSONANT WITH LEVELS OF FUNCTIONING IN THE TWO CRUCIAL SKILL AREAS (i.e., daily-living and motor skills) .... $+$ / $\ominus$

Social interaction with peers.
(Before scoring, scan both items; select then the most appropriate item to be marked with a + score; mark subsequently the other item with a − score)

2a. IS A LONER AMONGST PEERS
presence of any one of the five possibilities given below must yield a + score for item 2a
a)   does not notice or hardly notices peers;
b)   does not usually join in, stands aloof;
c)   very regularly disturbs play or occupation of peers by thwarting/teasing;
d)   is exclusively oriented towards adults and/or staff;
e)   ability to consider others, participate in joint activities and make friends is not consonant with general level of functioning .... $\oplus$ / $-$

2b. SOCIAL INTERACTION WITH PEERS IS CONSONANT WITH LEVELS OF FUNCTIONING IN THE TWO CRUCIAL SKILL AREAS (i.e., daily-living and motor skills) .... $+$ / $\ominus$

raw scores page 1

O	/	/
A	C	D

408

Language and speech.
(If item 3 is marked with a + score, items 4 and 5 must receive a – score)

3. EXPRESSIVE LANGUAGE IS ABSENT/VIRTUALLY ABSENT
    fewer than eight recognizable (single) words are produced spontaneously and regularly ...... + /⊖

4. LANGUAGE AND SPEECH ARE PRESENT, BUT WITH DEVIANCES IN CONTENT
    stereotyped repetition; extreme literalness; neologisms; idiosyncratic language; senseless
    language; bookish language; immediate/delayed echolalia; no/limited/incorrect use of the
    pronouns I, me, etc. .... ⊕/ –

5. LANGUAGE AND SPEECH ARE PRESENT, BUT WITH DEVIANCES IN PRODUCTION
    the voice is either too loud, or extremely soft; unusual voice quality, such as harsh or
    metallic; unusual rate, possibly either drawled or hurried; unusual use of pitch, such as
    monotone intonation or with idiosyncratic inflectional patterns or stresses; articulation
    problems (not associated with developmental level), such as stuttering and lisps .... ⊕/ –

Other behaviours.
(The items may be scored individually)

6. OUTSTANDING AND OBSESSIVE INTERESTS
    in: push-buttons; taps; twigs; running water; lamps; specific types of toys; glittering
    ornaments; spectacles; parts of the body (sometimes with sexual overtones); fur; hair; an
    object to twiddle with; making sounds with objects; shadows; exhaust-pipes; eating or
    drinking; specific foods or drinks; looking forward to special events such as visiting or being
    visited by the family; holes; jig-saw puzzles; distances in miles; the calender; maps;
    electronics; drawing the same thing again and again; broken/intact; the workings of the
    human body; illness/death; etc. ....*breasts*..................... ⊕/ –

7. STEREOTYPED, UNUSUAL HANDLING OF OBJECTS
    tapping; scratching; rubbing; bouncing; tearing up; gnawing; licking; biting; sniffing (also at
    people); waving; balancing; spinning; taking off own clothes; lining things up in rows;
    sorting things by colour; building identical structures; etc. .... + /⊖

8. STEREOTYPED MANIPULATION OF OWN BODY (no objects involved)
    teeth-grinding; forced breathing; ruminating; masturbating (in children below age 12);
    walking on tiptoe; rocking oneself; pacing up and down; assuming unusual postures; staring
    at own hands; hand-flapping; finger-flicking; head-rolling; grimacing; covering the ears; etc. + /⊖

9. STRONG DEPENDENCE ON FIXED PATTERNS, ROUTINES AND/OR RITUALS
    fixed routines; fixed position of household objects; resistance to change and disorderliness;
    strong preferences for a limited number of dishes/drinks/kinds of clothes/a private nook and
    the like; extreme rigidity; over-precision or 'compulsiveness' *(knives and forks; table-cover)* ⊕/ –

10. SELF-INJURIOUS BEHAVIOUR (acts which are painful according to the observer)
    scratching/rubbing self; hitting/biting/pinching parts of the body; pulling hair; eye-poking;
    head-banging on walls, floor, furniture, etc.; keeping sores open .... ⊕/ –

11. HIGHLY ERRATIC/UNPREDICTABLE BEHAVIOUR (minor/no noticeable reasons for shifts)
    marked and abrupt shifts of mood; fits of rage; aggressive outbursts; very fluctuating levels
    of performance; capriciousness; being alternately overactive and apathetic; strange whims;
    constantly new problems; etc. .... ⊕/ –

12. UNUSUAL, UNREASONABLE AND EXCESSIVE ANXIETY OR PANIC
    anxiety/panic: when going to bed; for certain animals; for traffic; for sounds of
    machines/appliances/musical instruments; for flash-light; for the hairdresser/doctor/dentist;
    for cutting nails; etc. .... + /⊖

raw scores page 2

4	2
B	C

409

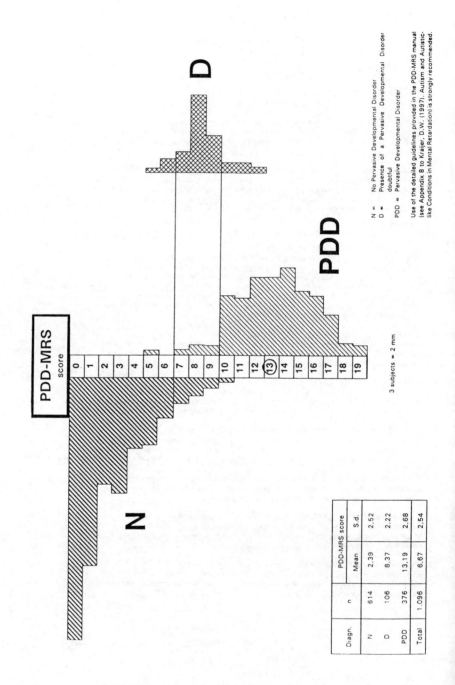

Diagn.	n	PDD-MRS score	
		Mean	S.d.
N	614	2,39	2,52
D	106	8,37	2,22
PDD	376	13,19	2,68
Total	1.096	6,67	2,54

3 subjects = 2 mm

N = No Pervasive Developmental Disorder
D = Presence of a Pervasive Developmental Disorder doubtful
PDD = Pervasive Developmental Disorder

Use of the detailed guidelines provided in the PDD-MRS manual (see Appendix B to Kraijer, D.W. (1997). Autism and Autistic-like Conditions in Mental Retardation) is strongly recommended.

B.5   The PDD-MRS score itself

The standard error of measurement is 2.2. This figure is derived from the following norm-group values: the mean PDD-MRS score (6.67), the corresponding standard deviation (2.54), and Cronbach's alpha (.80).

The following two questions can now be answered with respect to the PDD-MRS score:

- Which value for the difference between PDD-MRS scores of the same person obtained at different assessments may be regarded as significant?
- Which value for the difference between PDD-MRS scores of different persons (for instance residents living in the same ward) may be regarded as significant?

The values and corresponding levels of significance are presented in Table B.1.

Table B.1 Critical intervals between PDD-MRS scores and the corresponding levels of significance with intra- and inter-individual comparisons

Siginificance level	Score difference
.05	≥ 4 [*]
.01	≥ 5

* Score differences rounded up to integers

B.6   Practicalities and impracticalities in administering the PDD-MRS to special categories of persons

B.6.1   *The discriminating potential of the PDD-MRS with respect to the diagnoses PDD-AD and PDD-NOS*

The PDD-MRS is designed for use in the identification of a PDD in mentally retarded persons. No claim is made that the scale discriminates between the DSM-III-R categories PDD-Autistic Disorder and PDD-Not Otherwise Specified, although the scale may still have some use in this respect. It is conceivable that people diagnosed as PDD-AD generally have higher PDD-MRS scores that those diagnosed as PDD-NOS. PDD-NOS is in fact a rather vaguely determined residual category, and persons placed into this category share some features with persons diagnosed as doubtful-PDD. To explore this matter, the distribution of PDD-MRS scores of 83 PDD children of the PDD-MRS norm group (serving as subjects in the observation-home and day-care samples), who additionally had been clinically classified as either PDD-AD or PDD-NOS, is presented below in Table B.2, along with the corresponding cumulative and 100-minus cumulative percentages.

Table B.2 Comparison of the PDD-MRS scores obtained by persons with diagnosis PDD-NOS and those with diagnosis PDD-AD

PDD-MRS score	PDD-NOS			PDD-AD		
	n	cumul.%		n	cumul.%	100—cumul.%
0	-	-		-	-	-
1	-	-		-	-	-
2	-	-		-	-	-
3	1	3.5		-	-	-
4	-	3.5		-	-	-
5	2	10.3		-	-	-
6	1	13.8		-	-	-
7	-	13.8		-	-	-
8	-	13.8		-	-	-
9	1	17.2		1	1.9	98.1
10	8	44.8		2	5.6	94.4
11	1	48.3		3	11.1	88.9
12	4	62.1		7	24.1	75.9
13	4	75.9		8	38.9	61.1
14	4	89.7		7	51.9	48.1
15	2	96.6		7	64.1	35.9
16	1	100.0		11	85.2	14.8
17	-	-		4	92.6	7.4
18	-	-		3	98.2	1.8
19	-	-		1	100.0	0.0
n		29			54	
Mean		11.07			14.26	
s.d.		3.20			2.28	

Total: $n_{(NOS + AD)}$ = 83; Mean PDD-MRS score = 13.15; s.d. = 2.91

As the table shows, the mean PDD-MRS scores of the persons in the two PDD categories fall within the PDD domain of the scale. However, the difference between the means of the two categories is significant (t-test, p <.001). The general expectation that mentally retarded people with PDD-AD should obtain higher PDD-MRS scores than those with PDD-NOS is confirmed. With respect to the overlap between the PDD-NOS and doubtful-PDD categories it should be noted that 82.8% of the scores of persons diagnosed as PDD-NOS fall within the PDD domain of the scale, while the remaining 17.2% fall partly within the non-PDD and partly within the doubtful-PDD domain. By comparison, 98.1% of the PDD-AD scores fall within the PDD domain of the scale, the bulk lying in the 12-16 range.

In Table B.3 the PDD-MRS item scores of PDD-NOS and PDD-AD persons are compared. The significance values for the differences between the numbers of plus scores obtained are presented per item (two-tailed testing by means of the chi-square test).

412

As Table B.3 shows, for six PDD-MRS items PDD-AD persons receive significantly more frequently a plus score than PDD-NOS persons. To be precise, significantly more PDD-AD persons display contact deficiencies (1a and 2a), absence of expressive language (item 3), stereotyped behaviour (7 and 8) and self-injurious behaviour (10). In terms of item profile, PDD-AD shows the closest correspondence to - but certainly not complete conformity with - Factor I (Table III.1.23) and Cluster B (Table III.1.26). For two PDD-MRS

Table B.3 Comparison of separate PDD-MRS item scores assigned to PDD-NOS and PDD-AD persons

Sub-category	PDD-MRS-item												
	1a	1b	2a	3	4	5	6	7	8	9	10	11	12
PDD-NOS	5	23	18	7	19	13	18	15	18	14	6	20	11
PDD-AD	34	20	52	36	19	14	44	52	45	37	25	31	18
p	<.0001	<.001	<.0001	<.001	<.01	ns	ns	<.0001	<.05	ns	<.05	ns	ns

* Numbers printed in boldface indicate a significantly higher number of plus scores

items PDD-NOS persons receive significantly more frequently a plus score than PDD-AD persons. To be precise, significantly more PDD-NOS persons display less seriously deficient contact skills (1b) and deviances in speech and language (4).

These findings allow two conclusions to be made:

- While the idea, put forward in the DSM manuals, that PDD-AD and PDD-NOS lay on a *continuum* is indeed confirmed, the idea that both conditions are part of a *spectrum* apparently has also some legitimacy, as both conditions are found to differ qualitatively.
- The distribution of PDD-MRS scores suggests that, at least as far as the mentally retarded population is concerned, the two sub-categories not only merge into each other, but to some extent also into areas outside of the PDD domain.

The practical consequences of these findings are:

- No cut-off point can be indicated to discriminate between PDD-NOS and PDD-AD. However, it may be safely stated that a PDD-MRS score of 15 or more strongly suggests a PDD-AD and strongly contra-indicates a PDD-NOS.
- A small, but not negligible, minority of people with PDD-NOS yield PDD-MRS scores outside the PDD area, i.e., below score 10.
- The PDD-MRS score seems to be a more suitable indication of PDD-AD than specific patterns of separate item scores, and is certainly easier to use.
- Mentally retarded people who reasonably meet the DSM-IV criteria for 299.10 Childhood Disintegrative Disorder must, in my experience, invariably be classified as PDD-NOS; in most cases their PDD-MRS scores lie in the 9-12 range. As far as the DSM-IV sub-category 299.80 Rett's Disorder is concerned, I am not in a position to say anything, being not sufficiently acquainted with this disorder.

B.6.2   *The discriminating potential of the PDD-MRS regarding the rigid type, the passive group and the erratic type of PDD*

Again, no claim is made that the PDD-MRS discriminates between the aloof, passive and active-but-odd PDDs distinguished by Wing and Attwood (1987), or between the rigid and erratic types of PDD (see II.3.2.1). However, it would be helpful if the PDD-MRS had a discriminating potential in this respect, as persons belonging to these groups need different types of approaches (see II.4).

As far as the rigid and erratic types of PDD are concerned, an attempt was made to confirm this typology by means of the scores obtained on separate PDD-MRS items (see II.3). The following - rather general - conclusions may be drawn on the basis of the (significant) differences found:

414

- A comparatively large number of people with the *rigid* type of PDD obtain plus scores on the following items:
  1a Severely deficient response to contact initiative of adults;
  3   Expressive language is absent/virtually absent.
- A comparatively large number of people with the *erratic* type of PDD obtain plus scores on the following items:
  1b Less severely deficient response to contact initiative of adults, notably displaying bizarre contact-making, defiant and/or provocative contact-making, overdemanding and/or extremely clinging contact-making, and lack of due reserve in contact-making (options d to g);
  11 Highly erratic/unpredictable behaviour.
  A slightly smaller number of people with the erratic type of PDD obtain plus scores on the following items:
  4/5 Deviancies in content and production of speech and language;
  10 Self-injurious behaviour;
  12 Unusual, unreasonable and excessive anxiety or panic.
- The scores obtained by people belonging to the *passive* group of PDD correspond closely to those obtained by people with the rigid type of PDD; however, they less frequently obtain a plus score on item 1a; in addition, when they obtain a plus score on item 1b, this is predominantly on account of insufficient continuity in contact-making and extreme and persistent shrinking from contact with unfamiliar people (options b and c).

No difference was found to emerge between the total PDD-MRS scores of people with the rigid and erratic types of PDD. People belonging to the passive group of PDD tend to obtain lower PDD-MRS scores.

In sum, the PDD-MRS has only a very modest contribution to make in discriminating between the rigid, passive and erratic PDDs found in mentally retarded people.

B.6.3 *Using the scale to assess persons with Down syndrome*

Assessments of *Down-syndrome people* by means of the PDD-MRS may be expected to proceed somewhat differently, considering the findings reported in Chapter III.5. The following points are relevant:

- The PDD-MRS is reasonably able to discriminate DS people diagnosed (on the basis of the entire diagnostic process) in terms of non-PDD, doubtful-PDD or PDD; the differences between two of the three categories were found to be significant;
  N↔D $p < .0001$
  D↔PDD ns
  N↔PDD $p < .0001$
- Compared with the mean PDD-MRS score yielded by non-PDD persons in the norm group (M = 2.39), the mean score of non-PDD persons in the profound and severe ranges of mental retardation of the DS group is

rather high (M = 4.28); level of significance p <.001. This high mean score is due to a significantly higher number of plus scores on the following items:

7   Stereotyped, unusual handling of objects;
8   Stereotyped manipulation of own body.

- Compared with the mean PDD-MRS score yielded by doubtful-PDD persons in the norm group (M = 8.37), the mean score of doubtful-PDD persons of the DS group is rather high (M = 9.91); actually the mean score is just above the upper limit (9.50) of the PDD domain. Level of significance p <.01. An item analysis was not feasible because of the low number of doubtful-PDD Down-syndrome subjects.
- Compared with the mean PDD-MRS score yielded by PDD persons in the norm group (M = 13.19), the mean score of persons of the DS group is rather low (M = 11.08); level of significance p <.001. The low mean score is due to a significantly lower number of plus scores on the following items:

1a   Severely deficient response to contact initiative of adults;
10   Self-injurious behaviour.

The non-significant difference between the mean PDD-MRS scores of the doubtful-PDD and PDD categories is obviously produced by a comparatively high mean of DS persons with doubtful-PDD and a comparatively low mean of those with a PDD. However, this finding has no consequence for the cut-off scores used in the scale, as the determination of the scale's sensitivity and specificity for the DS group has demonstrated. It may therefore be concluded that the PDD-MRS is also a useful tool for identifying a PDD in persons with Down syndrome.

B.6.4   *Using the scale to assess male persons with fragile X syndrome*

In view of the findings concerning *fra(X) adult and non-adult males* (see Chapter III.6), the following points are relevant:

- The PDD-MRS is able to discriminate fra(X) persons diagnosed (on the basis of the entire diagnostic process) in terms of non-PDD, doubtful-PDD or PDD; the differences between the three categories were found to be very significant:
  N↔D   p <.0001
  D↔PDD p <.0001
  N↔PDD p <.0001
- The mean PDD-MRS scores yielded by non-PDD, doubtful-PDD and PDD persons with fra(X) were 3.50, 7.76 and 12.25; these figures do not deviate from the corresponding scores yielded in the norm group.
- It is noteworthy that adult and non-adult males with fra(X) are very often diagnosed as doubtful-PDD. In the study referred to above - involving mainly severely and moderately mentally retarded persons with fra(X) -

the proportion of persons diagnosed as doubtful-PDD was as high as 41%. As a matter of fact, the behaviour of these persons has much in common with that of PDD persons. My suggestion was therefore to include fra(X) as a separate sub-category in the PDD spectrum, just as was done with 299.80 (F84.2) Rett's Disorder.

B.6.5   *The PDD-MRS administered to persons belonging to categories which were not included in the norm group*

By now, the PDD-MRS has been administered for validation purposes to persons belonging to categories which had not been included in norm-group-1992. In what follows the results obtained with specific samples will be discussed. They involved non-ambulatory very profoundly mentally retarded persons, two-year-old children, and intellectually borderline-functioning individuals.

B.6.5.1 *Using the scale to assess completely non-ambulatory, very profoundly mentally retarded persons*

A group of 56 *completely non-ambulatory, very profoundly mentally retarded* institutionalized persons has been investigated for the presence of a PDD. The entire diagnostic process was carried out, including the application of the PDD-MRS (Kraijer, 1997; see also Appendix A). The distribution of PDD-MRS scores over the three subgroups diagnosed as non-PDD, doubtful-PDD and PDD was found to be as follows:

- N   M 4.58 s.d. 2.27 (n = 26)
- D   M 6.83 s.d. 2.17 (n = 12)
- PDD M 9.61 s.d. 2.85 (n = 18)

The following additional information with respect to these figures is relevant:

- The differences between the three mean PDD-MRS scores are significant:
  N↔D $p < .01$
  D↔PDD $p < .01$
  N↔PDD $p < .0001$
- Compared with the mean PDD-MRS score yielded by non-PDD persons in the norm group (2.39), the mean score of the non-PDD persons in this group is rather high, but is still sufficiently below the cut-off score. Their high mean score is due to a significantly higher number of plus scores obtained for the following items:
  1b   Less severely deficient response or fluctuating response to contact initiative;
  3   Expressive language is absent/virtually absent;
  8   Stereotyped manipulation of own body.

- Compared with the mean PDD-MRS score yielded by doubtful-PDD persons in the norm group (8.37), the mean score of the doubtful-PDD persons in this group is rather low; it is only marginally above the lower limit (6.50) of the doubtful-PDD range. This low figure is mainly the result of a significantly lower frequency of plus scores obtained by these subjects on one item, i.e.,
2a   Deficient contact with peers.
The score is obviously due to the very low level of functioning of these subjects, their mental age being twelve months or lower; any performance at all in this field may simply not be expected.
- Compared with the mean score of the PDD subgroup in the norm group (13.19), the PDD subgroup in this sample is found to have a fairly low mean PDD-MRS score, which is just above the upper limit of the doubtful-PDD range (9.50). This low figure is the result of a significantly lower frequency of plus scores obtained by these subjects on four items:
2a   Deficient contact with peers;
4   Language/speech deviant in content;
5   Language/speech deviant in production;
6   Obsessive interests.

However, not surprisingly in view of the very low level of functioning, the subgroup obtained a significantly higher frequency of plus scores on item 3, Expressive language absent.

From these findings we may conclude that the scale may also be regarded as a suitable instrument for assessing people with highly restricted capacities, provided that due account is taken of the distinctive group characteristics listed above. However, a comparatively high proportion will be categorized as doubtful-PDD (well over 21% in the present study). As has been demonstrated in Sections III.2.2.3 and III.2.3.3, this has to do with the very restricted behavioural repertoire of these people.

B.6.5.2   Using the scale to assess two-year-old mentally retarded children
Until recently, reliable and valid results with the PDD-MRS could only be guaranteed when the scale was administered to persons above two years of age. However, reliable assessments of *two-year-old children* by means of the PDD-MRS were still urgently needed in the care field. For that reason an additional investigation was initiated in 1996. The clinical classifications, PDD-MRS classifications and final diagnoses of a sample of 71 two-year-old children (34 boys and 37 girls) were recorded. The subjects were taken from 25 day-care centres and one clinical observation setting; seven children were profoundly, thirty severely, 22 moderately and twelve mildly mentally retarded. No subjects were excluded from the sample for reasons of sensory handicaps or motor disorders.

Table B.4 presents the PDD-MRS scores obtained in this sample, subdivided into the subgroups non-PDD, doubtful-PDD and PDD. The table also provides the cumulative and 100-minus cumulative percentages in order to allow the calculation of the scale's sensitivity (= percentage cases correctly assessed) and specificity (= percentage non-cases correctly assessed).

Table B.4 PDD-MRS scores of the subgroups N, D and PDD (diagnoses) in a sample of two-year-old children, their mean scores and standard deviations

PDD-MRS scores	N		D			PDD	
	n	cumul.%	n	cumul.%	100-cumul.	n	100-cumul.
0	13	23.2	-	-	-	-	-
1	21	60.7	-	-	-	-	-
2	4	67.9	-	-	-	-	-
3	7	80.4	-	-	-	-	-
4	4	87.5	-	-	-	-	-
5	2	91.1	-	-	-	-	-
6	2	**94.6**	-	0.0	**100.0**	-	-
7	0	94.6	-	0.0	100.0	-	-
8	1	96.4	3	42.9	57.1	-	-
9	2	100.0	2	71.4	28.6	-	-
10	-	-	2	**100.0**	0.0	-	**100.0**
11	-	-	-	-	-	3	62.5
12	-	-	-	-	-	1	50.0
13	-	-	-	-	-	2	25.0
14	-	-	-	-	-	1	12.5
15	-	-	-	-	-	1	0.0
16	-	-	-	-	-	-	-
17	-	-	-	-	-	-	-
18	-	-	-	-	-	-	-
19	-	-	-	-	-	-	-
n	56		7			8	
M	2.04		8.86			12.50	
s.d.	2.27		0.90			1.51	

From the table three conclusions may be drawn. The first concerns the similarity of the results with those of the norm group. The mean scores in the three subgroups hardly differ from those found in the PDD-MRS norm group (n = 1096), which were for the non-PDD subgroup M = 2.93 (s.d. = 2.52), for the doubtful-PDD subgroup M = 8.37 (s.d. = 2.22), and for the PDD subgroup M = 13.19 (s.d. = 2.68). Statistical testing confirms this impression (two-tailed t-test, thrice ns).

The second conclusion concerns the differences between the three subgroups. The mean scores of the three subgroups are found to be significant (two-tailed t-tests; N↔D: p <.0001; D↔PDD: p <.0001; N↔PDD: p <.0001).

The third conclusion concerns the values for sensitivity and specificity for N versus D, and for D versus PDD. The most optimal percentages are indicated in boldface in the table; the corresponding ranges for subgroup N are 0-6, for subgroup D 7-10, and for subgroup PDD 11-19. These ranges hardly differ from those of the norm group. As the sample was comparatively small - the numbers of subjects were notably small in the doubtful-PDD and PDD subgroups - there seems to be little objection to applying the normally used cut-off scores when assessing two-year-olds, i.e., for subgroup N, 0-5; for subgroup D, 6-9; for subgroup PDD, 10-19. Adhering to this principle yields in this sample an overall misclassification rate of only 7.0% (five of the 71 children).

B.6.5.3 Using the scale to assess intellectually borderline-functioning persons
With respect to intellectually borderline-functioning persons of all ages, the available evidence suggests that the PDD-MRS is also a satisfactory instrument of assessment. However, only preliminary conclusions may be drawn from the results obtained with the sample involving subjects of this category, as the number of persons involved was rather small. Nevertheless, there are signs that the scale is reasonably able to discriminate PDD persons from non-PDD persons when assessing *intellectually borderline-functioning individuals* (IQ range approx. 71-84).

ASSESSMENT OF SOCIAL FUNCTIONING BY MEANS OF THE SRZ, SGZ AND SMZ

In the present study repeated references have been made to the SRZ, SGZ and SMZ. These scales are widely used in the Dutch mental retardation field. In what follows the scales will be briefly discussed. In addition, the use of the standard marks for scoring will be explained.

SRZ, Social Functioning Scale for the Mentally Retarded

The SRZ is a modified version of the Cain-Levine Social Competency Scale (Cain et al., 1963), adapted to Dutch norms (Kraijer & Kema, 1972, 1994). The scale has 31 items. Each item presents four statements corresponding with four levels of the skill concerned; for each item the most appropriate statement has to be singled out.

The scale is divided into four subscales on the basis of factor analysis. The subscales are:

SH	Self Help	12 items
C	Communication	9 items
P	Persistence	5 items
SS	Social Skills	5 items

By way of illustration, four items from each of the four subscales are presented below (using the wording of the Cain-Levine Social Competency Scale).

SH
  7 Toileting
      1 Does not wipe self
      2 Occasionally wipes self
      3 Frequently wipes self
      4 Nearly always wipes self

C

   26 Understandable speech
     1 Cannot be understood by anyone
     2 Can be understood by immediate family only
     3 Can be understood by neighbours and friends
     4 Can be understood by most people

P

   10 Attending to tasks
     Will pay attention to tasks (e.g., cleaning up, putting things away):
     1 If time does not exceed five minutes
     2 If time does not exceed ten minutes
     3 If time does not exceed fifteen minutes
     4 Even if time exceeds fifteen minutes

SS

   21 Offering assistance
     1 Does not offer assistance to others
     2 Occasionally offers assistance to others
     3 Frequently offers assistance to others
     4 Nearly always offers assistance to others

The SRZ is a reliable and valid scale; 4312 Dutch mentally retarded persons, aged four years and over, served as subjects for the determination of the scale's norms.

SGZ, Maladaptive Behaviour Scale for the Mentally Retarded

The SGZ was developed in the Netherlands (Kraijer & Kema, 1977, 1994). The scale has 32 items. To arrive at the final score, both severity and frequency of the assessed behaviour are taken into account. The scale is divided into three subscales on the basis of factor analysis. The subscales are:

    A   Aggressive Maladaptive Behaviour   8 items
    V   Verbal Maladaptive Behaviour   5 items
    M   Mixed Maladaptive Behaviour   19 items

By way of illustration, items of the three subscales are presented below.

A

   2 Scratches and/or pinches parents, teachers, attendants

V

   9 Abuses brothers, sisters, fellow group members

M

19 Tears clothes
22 Has screaming tantrums
27 Masturbates
29 Has sleeping disorders

The SGZ is a reliable and valid scale; 4218 Dutch mentally retarded persons, aged three years and over, served as subjects to determine the scale's norms.

SMZ, Gross Motor Skills Scale for the Mentally Retarded

The SMZ was developed in the Netherlands (Kraijer & Kema, 1981, 1994). The scale has 22 items. Scoring is dichotomic. By way of illustration, three items are presented below:

2 Holds head steady in upright posture
14 Pedals a three- or four-wheeled vehicle for at least ten metres
19 Swims well (without swimming belt or water wings)

The SMZ is a reliable and valid scale; 4538 Dutch mentally retarded persons, aged three years and over, served as subjects to determine the scale's norms.

The standard marks

The raw scores obtained with the SRZ, SGZ and SMZ have to be converted into 'standard marks'. The system of standard marks is adopted from that of Dutch schools, which use a scale of 1 to 10. In the Dutch evaluation system of academic performance, marks of 1 and 2 (indicating very poor performance) and a mark of 10 (indicating excellent performance) are in practice seldom awarded. A computing programme, developed on the basis of the distribution of the more frequently occurring marks 3-9, was utilized by the authors of the scale to establish what they have termed standard marks; a further subdivision into H (high) and L (low) was added (indicating an amply and a narrowly obtained score, respectively). By way of illustration, the score distribution for the SRZ is presented below in Scheme C.1.

Scheme C.1 Percentage distribution, per standard mark, of lower/equal/ higher functioning persons of similar age

Standard mark	Percentages			Standard mark
9	5% persons with the highest level of social functioning			9
	Lower level	Same level	Higher level	
8H	88	7	5	8H
8L	81	7	12	8L
7H	68	13	19	7H
7L	55	13	32	7L
6H	41	14	45	6H
6L	27	14	59	6L
5H	18	9	73	5H
5L	9	9	82	5L
4	2	7	91	4
3	2% persons with the lowest level of social functioning			3

By way of an hypothetical example, let us say that a person yields a standard mark of 7L on the SRZ. This implies that 55% of persons belonging to the same age category have a lower level of social functioning, 13% the same level, and 32% a higher level. In the SGZ the phrase '5% persons with the highest level of social functioning' has to be replaced by '5% persons with the least amount of problem behaviour', in the SMZ by '5% persons with the highest level of gross motor skills.'

REFERENCES

Adrien, J.L., Ornitz, E., Barthelemy, C., et al. (1987). The presence or absence of certain behaviors associated with infantile autism in severely retarded autistic and nonautistic retarded children and very young normal children. *J. of Autism and Developmental Disorders, 17,* 407-416.

Adrien, J.L., Barthélémy, C., Perrot, A. et al. (1992). Validity and Reliability of the Infant Behavioral Summarized Evaluation (IBSE): A Rating Scale for the Assessment of Young Children with Autism and Developmental Disorders. *J. of Autism and Developmental Disorders, 22,* 375-394.

Altena, H.W., Bolt, D., Bosscher, H. et al. (1980). *Projectverslag ontwikkeling van het contactgedrag bij zwakzinnigen.* Groningen: scriptie Rijksuniversiteit.

American Association on Mental Retardation (1992). *Mental Retardation. Definition, Classification and Systems of Supports.* Washington: AAMR.

American Psychiatric Association (1980). *Diagnostic and Statistical Manual of Mental Disorders. Third Edition, DSM-III.* Washington: APA.

American Psychiatric Association (1987). *Diagnostic and Statistical Manual of Mental Disorders. Third Edition - Revised, DSM-III-R.* Washington: APA.

American Psychiatric Association (1994). *Diagnostic and Statistical Manual of Mental Disorders. Fourth Edition. DSM-IV.* Washington: APA.

Ando, H. & Yoshimura, I. (1979). Effects of Age on Communication Skill Levels and Prevalence of Maladaptive Behaviors in Autistic and Mentally Retarded Children. *J. of Autism and Developmental Disorders, 9,* 83-93.

Ando, H., Yoshimura, I. & Wakabayashi, S. (1980). Effects of Age on Adaptive Behavior Levels and Academic Skill Levels in Autistic and Mentally Retarded Children. *J. of Autism and Developmental Disorders, 10,* 173-183.

Asperger, H. (1944). Die "Autistischen Psychopathen" im Kindesalter. *Archives of Psychiatry, 117,* 76-136.

Asperger, H. (1968). Zur Differentialdiagnose des Kindlichen Autismus. *Acta Paedopsychiatrica, 35,* 136-145.

Assink, A.W. (1976). *Autisties gedrag bij zwakzinnigen. Verslag van een onderzoek in drie inrichtingen voor zwakzinnigen naar het verschijnsel autisties gedrag.* Doctoraal scriptie IKIP, Rijksuniversiteit Utrecht.

Baartman, H. (1982). Autisme in het gezin: verbijster(en)de kinderen en perplexe ouders. *Ts. Orthoped. Kinderpsych., VII,* 22-34.

Bailey, A., Bolton, P., Butler, L. et al. (1993). Prevalence of the Fragile X anomaly amongst autistic twins and singletons. *J. Child Psychol. Psychiatr.*, *34*,
673-688.

Baker, H.J. (1959). *Exceptional Children.* New York: The Macmillan Cy.

Baron-Cohen, S. (1992). Debate and Argument: On Mòdularity and Development in Autism: a Reply to Burack. *J. Child Psychol. Psychiatr.*, *33*, 623-629.

Baron-Cohen, S., Tager-Flusberg, H. & Cohen, D. (Eds). (1993). *Understanding
other minds: perspectives from autism.* Oxford: Oxford University Press.

Bartak, L. & Rutter, M. (1973a, 1973b). Special educational treatment of autistic children: a comparative study, I en II. *J. Child Psychol. Psychiatr.*, *14*,
161-180 en 241-270.

Bartak, L. & Rutter, M. (1976). Differences Between Mentally Retarded and
Normaly Intelligent Autistic Children. *J. of Autism and Childhood Schizophrenia*, *6*, 109-120.

Barthélémy, C., Adrien, J.L., Tanguay, P. et al. (1990). The Behavioral Summarized Evaluation: Validity and Reliability of a Scale for the Assessment
of Autistic Behaviors. *J. of Autism and Developmental Disorders*, *20*, 189-204.

Barthélémy, C., Adrien, J.L., Roux, S. et al. (1992). Sensitivity and Specificity
of the Behavioral Summarized Evaluation (BSE) for the Assessment of
Autistic Behaviors. *J. of Autism and Developmental Disorders*, *22*, 23-31.

Beeckmans-Balle, M. (1973). Le syndrome d'autisme infantile. *Acta Psychiatrica Belgica*, *73*, 537-555.

Bellak, L. & Bellak, S.S. (1949). *Children's Apperception Test (CAT).* New York.

Bender, L. (1973). The Life Course of Children with Schizophrenia. *Am. J.
Psychiatry*, *7*, 783-786.

Berkson, G. & Mason, W.A. (1963). Stereotyped movements of mental defec-
tives III. Situation Effects. *Am. J. of Mental Deficiency*, *68*, 409-412.

Blacher, J.B., Hanneman, R.A. & Rousey, A.B. (1992). Out-of-home placement
of children with severe handicaps: a comparison of approaches. *Am. J. on
Mental Retardation*, *96*, 607-616.

Blok, J.B. (1989). *Temperament bij zwakzinnigen. Constructie van een meetinstru-
ment.* Amsterdam: Vrije Universiteit.

Blok, J.B., Berg, P.Th. van den & Feij, J.A. (1990). *Temperamentsschaal voor
zwakzinnigen, TVZ. Handleiding.* Lisse: Swets & Zeitlinger.

Brakenhoff-Splinter, J., Krist-Heideveld, Th. & Stoetman, A. (1977). *Kontaktstoornissen bij zwakzinnigen, enkele beschouwingen en een onderzoek.* Groningen: skriptie Rijksuniversiteit.

Branford, D. & Collacott, R.A. (1994). Comparison of community and institutional prescription of antiepileptic drugs for individuals with learning
disabilities. *J. of Intellectual Disability Research*, *38*, 561-566.

Bregman, J.D. & Volkmar, F.R. (1988). Autistic social dysfunction and Down
syndrome. *J. of the Am. Academy of Child and Adolescent Psychiatry*, *27*, 440-
441.

Brown, J.L. (1978). Long-Term Follow-Up of 100 "Atypical" Children of Normal Intelligence. In: Rutter, M. & Schopler, E. (Eds.) *Autism. A reappraisal
of concepts and treatment.* New York/London: Plenum Press.

Bryson, S.E., Clark, B.S. & Smith, I.M. (1988). First report of a Canadian epidemiological study of autistic syndromes. *J. of Child Psychology and Psychiatry, 29,* 433-445.

Buck, J.N. (1981, sixth edition). *The House-Tree-Person technique. Revised manual.* Beverly Hills, California: Western Psychological Services.

Burd, L., Fisher, W., Vesely, B.N. et al. (1991). Prevalence of psychoactive drug use among North Dakota group home residents. *Am. J. on Mental Retardation, 96,* 119-126.

Cain, L.F., Levine, S. & Elzey, F.F. (1963). *Cain-Levine Social Competency Scale.* Palo Alto: Consulting Psychologists Press.

Cantor, S. (1988). *Childhood Schizophrenia.* New York: Guildford Press.

Causby, V.D. & York, R.O. (1991). Prediction of succes in community placement of persons with mental retardation. *Brit. J. of Mental Subnormality, XXXVII,* 25-34.

Carr, E. (1989). Childhood Schizophrenia. S. Cantor. *Schizophrenia Bulletin,* 688-690.

Carr, J. (1994). Annotation: Long Term Outcome for People with Down's Syndrome. *J. Child Psychol. Psychiatr., 35,* 425-439.

Chess, S. & Korn, S. (1970). Temperament and Behavior Disorders in mentally retarded children. *Archives of General Psychiatry, 23,* 122-130.

Chung, S.Y., Luk, S.L. & Lee, P.W.H. (1990). A Follow-Up Study of Infantile Autism in Hong Kong. *J. of Autism and Developmental Disorder, 20,* 221-232.

Cicchetti, D.V. & Sparrow, S.S. (1981). Developing criteria for establishing interrater reliability of specific items in a given inventory. *Am. J. of Mental Deficiency, 86,* 127-137.

Clements, J., Wing, L. & Dunn, G. (1986). Sleep problems in handicapped children: a preliminary study. *J. Child. Psychol. Psychiatr., 27,* 399-407.

Cocchi, R. (1991). Psychosis in Down children: an epidemiological and clinical survey on 413 subjects. In: Cocchi, R. & Došen, A. (Eds.): Comparing theories and therapies in childhood psychoses. *Italian J. of Intellective Impairment, 4,* 83-88.

Cohen, D.J., Paul, R. & Volkmar, F.R. (1987). Issues in the Classification of Pervasive Developmental Disorders and Associated Conditions. In: Cohen, D.J. & Donnellan, A.M. (Eds.). *Handbook of Autism and Pervasive Developmental Disorders.* New York: Wiley & Sons.

Cohen, D.J. & Donellan, A.M. (Eds.), (1987). *Handbook of Autism and Pervasive Developmental Disorders.* New York: Wiley & Sons.

Cohen, I.L., Fisch, G.S., Sudhalter, V. et al. (1988). Social gaze, social avoidance and repetitive behavior in fragile X males: a controlled study. *Am. J. of Mental Retardation, 92,* 436-446.

Cohen, I.L., Vietze, P.M., Sudhalter, V. et al. (1989). Parent-child dyadic gaze patterns in fragile X males and in non-fragile X males with autistic disorder. *J. Child Psychol. Psychiatr., 30,* 845-856.

Cohen, I.L., Vietze, P.M., Sudhalter, V. et al. (1991). Effects of age and communication level on eye contact in fragile X males and non-fragile X autistic males. *Am. J. of Medical Genetics, 38,* 494-502.

Corbett, J. (1987). Development, disintegration and dementia. *J. of Mental Deficiency Research, 31,* 349-356.

Couteur, A. le, Rutter, M., Lord, C. et al. (1989). Autism Diagnostic Interview: A Standardized Investigator-Based Instrument. *J. of Autism and Developmental Disorders, 19,* 363-387.

Creak, M. (1961). Schizophrenic Syndrome in Childhood: Progress report of a working party. *Cer. Palsy Bulletin, 3,* 501-504.

Crews, W.D., Bonaventura, S. & Rowe, F. (1994). Dual Diagnosis: Prevalence of Psychiatric Disorders in a Large State Residential Facility for Individuals With Mental Retardation. *Am. J. on Mental Retardation, 98,* 688-731.

De Boer, J.E., Minderaa, R.B., Verhey, F. et al. (Eds.), (1989). *Aan autisme verwante contactstoornissen.* Dr Paul Janssen Stichting.

De Vriendt, A. & Vandenbussche, I. (1990). Autisme, kinderpsychose, ontwikkelingsstoornissen: één begrip? *Ts. Orthoped. Kinderpsych., 15,* 110-122.

De Vriendt, A. (1990). Specifieke accenten in de opvoeding en de behandeling van kinderen met een pervasieve ontwikkelingsstoornis. *Ts. Orthoped. Kinderpsych., 15,* 123-139.

DeMyer, M.K., Barton, S. & Norton, J.A. (1972). A comparison of adaptive, verbal and motor profiles of psychotic and non-psychotic subnormal children. *J. of Autism and Childhood Schizophrenia, 2,* 359-377.

DeMyer, M.K., Barton, S., DeMyer, W.E. et al. (1973). Prognosis in Autism: A follow-up study. *J. of Autism and Childhood Schizophrenia, 3,* 199-246.

DeMyer, M.K., Barton, S., Alpern, G.D. et al. (1974). The measured intelligence of autistic children. *J. of Autism and Childhood Schizophrenia, 4,* 42-60.

DeMyer, M.K. (1976). The Nature of the Neuropsychological Disability in Autistic Children. In: Schopler, E. & Reichler, R.J. (Eds.) *Psychopathology and Child Development.* New York: Plenum Press.

DeMyer, M.K. (1979). *Parents and children in autism.* Washington: Winston & Sons.

DeMyer, M.K., Hingten, J.N. & Jackson, R.K. (1981). Infantile Autism Reviewed: A Decade of Research. *Schizophrenia Bulletin,* 388-451.

DiLavore, P.C., Lord, C. & Rutter, M. (1995). The Pre-Linguistic Autism Diagnostic Observation Schedule. *J. of Autism and Developmental Disorders, 25,* 355-379.

Doll, E.A. (1953). *Measurement of Social Competence.* USA: Educational Publishers, Inc.

Došen, A. (1993). Diagnosis and treatment of psychiatric and behavioural disorders in mentally retarded individuals: the state of the art. *J. of Intellectual Disability Research, 37,* Supplement 1, 1-7.

Duker, P.C. & Seys, D. (1977). *Behandeling van probleemgedrag bij zwakzinnigen 2.* Rotterdam: Lemniscaat.

Duker, P.C. (1989). *Teaching the developmentally handicapped communicative gesturing.* Lisse: Swets & Zeitlinger.

Einfeld, S.L., Molony, H. & Hall, W. (1989). Autism is not associated with the fragile X syndrome. *Am. J. of Medical Genetics, 34,* 187-193.

Emerson, E., Beasley, F., Offord, G. & Mansell, J. (1992). An evaluation of hospital-based specialized staffed housing for people with seriously challenging behaviours. *J. of Intellectual Disability Research, 36*, 291-307.

Eyman, R.K., Call, T.L. & White, J.F. (1991). Life Expectancy of Persons with Down Syndrome. *Am. J. on Mental Retardation, 95*, 603-612.

Factor, D.C., Freeman, N.L. & Kardash, A. (1989). Brief Report: A Comparison of DSM-III and DSM-III-R Criteria for Autism. *J. of Autism and Developmental Disorders, 19*, 637-640.

Fleiss, J.L. (1973). *Statistical methods for rates and proportions*. New York: Wiley & Sons.

Flynn, M.C., Whelan, E. & Speake, B. (1985). The mentally handicapped adult's concepts of good and bad acts. *J. of Mental Deficiency Research, 29*, 55-62.

Fombonne, E. (1992). Diagnostic Assessment in a Sample of Autistic and Developmentally Impaired Adolescents. *J. of Autism and Developmental Disorders, 22*, 563-581.

Fombonne, E. & Mazaubrun, C. du (1992). Prevalence of infantile autism in four French regions. *Social Psychiatry and Psychiatric Epidemiology, 27*, 203-210.

Frye, I.B.M. (1968). *Fremde unter uns. Autisten, ihre Erziehung, ihr Lebenslauf*. Meppel: Boom.

Galligan, B. (1990). Serving people who are dually diagnosed: A program evaluation. *Mental Retardation, 28*, 353-358.

Garfin, D.G., McCallon, D. & Cox, R. (1988). Validity and Reliability of the Childhood Autism Rating Scale with Autistic Adolescents. *J. of Autism and Developmental Disorders, 18*, 367-378.

Gath, A. & Gumley, D. (1986a). Behaviour problems in retarded children with special reference to Down's syndrome. *Brit. J. of Psychiatry, 149*, 156-161.

Gath, A. & Gumley, D. (1986b). Family background of children with Down's syndrome and of children with a similar degree of mental retardation. *Brit. J. of Psychiatry, 149*, 161-167.

Ghaziuddin, M., Tsai, L.Y. & Ghaziuddin, N. (1992). Autism in Down's syndrome: presentation and diagnoses. *J. of Intellectual Disability Research, 36*, 449-456.

Gibson, D. (1978). *Down's Syndrome. The Psychology of Mongolism*. Cambridge: Cambridge University Press.

Gielen, J., Smits, A., Janssens, J. & Jonge, I. de (1988). Storend gedrag bij het fragiele-X syndroom. Een fenotypisch gedragsrepertoire. *De Psycholoog*, 629-633.

Gillberg, C., Persson, E., Grufman, M. & Themner, U. (1986). Psychiatric Disorders in Mildly and Severely Mentally Retarded Urban Children and Adolescents: Epidemiological Aspects. *Brit. J. of Psychiatry, 149*, 68-74.

Gillberg, C. & Steffenburg, S. (1987). Outcome and Prognostic Factors in Infantile Autism and Similar Conditions: A Population-Based Study of 46 Cases Followed Through Puberty. *J. of Autism and Developmental Disorder*, 17, 273-287.

Gillberg, C. & Steffenburg, S. (1989). Autistic Behaviour in Moebius Syndrome. *Acta Paediatrica Scandinavica*, 78, 314-316.

Gillberg, C. (1990a). Autism and Pervasive Developmental Disorders. *J. Child Psychol. Psychiatr.*, 31, 99-119.

Gillberg, C. (1990b). Infantile autism: diagnosis and treatment. *Acta Psychiatrica Scandinavica*, 81, 209-215.

Gillberg, C., Ehlers, S., Schaumann, H. et al. (1990). Autism under age 3 years: a clinical study of 28 cases referred for autistic symptoms in infancy. *J. Child Psychol. Psychiatr.*, 31, 921-934.

Gillberg, C. (1991). Debate and Argument: Is Autism a Pervasive Developmental Disorder? *J. Child Psychol. Psychiatr.*, 32, 1169-1170.

Gillberg, C. (1992b). Subgroups in autism: are there behavioural phenotypes typical of underlying medical conditions? *J. of Intellectual Disability Research*, 36, 201-214.

Gillberg, C. & Coleman, M. (1992). *The biology of the autistic syndromes. Second edition.* Londen: Mac Keith Press.

Gillberg, C. (1993). Autism and related behaviours. *J. of Intellectual Disability Research*, 37, 343-372.

Goldfarb, W. (1961). The mutual impact of mother and child in childhood schizophrenia. *Am. J. of Orthopsychiatry*, 31, 738- 747.

Gould, J. (1977). The use of the Vineland Social Maturity Scale, the Merrill-Palmer Scale of Mental Tests (non-verbal items) and the Reynell Developmental Language Scales with Children in contact with the services for severe mental retardation. *J. of Mental Deficiency Research*, 21, 213-226.

Gresnigt, H.A.A. & Gresnigt-Strengers, A.M.C. (1973). *Ouders en gezinnen met een diepzwakzinnig kind.* Amsterdam: Swets & Zeitlinger.

Groen, K. & Houwink, R.H. (1966). *De Dolderse Schaal, een methode ter bepaling van de sociale redzaamheid en de sociale informatie.* Groningen: J.B. Wolters/ Lisse: Swets & Zeitlinger.

Grossman, H.J. (Ed.), (1973), (1977), (1983). *Manual on terminology and classification in mental retardation.* Washington: AAMD.

Gunning, W.B. (1989). *Het Borderline Child Syndrome: de grenzen met de Pervasive Developmental Disorders en met de atypische persoonlijkheidsontwikkeling.* Voordracht NIP-Winterconferentie "Borderline bij kinderen en volwassenen", 18 maart 1989.

Hamers, J.H.M., Castelijns, J.H.M. & Pennings, A.P. (1989). De ontwikkeling van leertests: Ontstaan, onderzoek en toekomstbeeld. *Ned. Ts. voor Opvoeding, Vorming en Onderwijs*, 5 (2), 66-75.

Happé, F. & Frith, U. (1991). Is Autism a Pervasive Developmental Disorder? Debate and Argument: How useful is the "PDD" label. *J. Child Psychol. Psychiatr.*, 32, 1167-1168.

Happé, F. (1994). *Autism: an introduction to psychological theory.* London: UCL Press.

Happé, F.G.E. (1994). Wechsler IQ profile and theory of mind in autism: a research note. *J. Child Psychol. Psychiat., 8,* 1461-1471.

Harris, D.B. (1963). *Children's drawings as measures of intellectual maturity.* New York: Harcourt, Brace & World.

Hatton, C., Emerson, E. & Kieman, C. (1995). People in institutions in Europe. *Mental Retardation, 33,* 135.

Helwig, P. (1951). *Charakterologie.* Stuttgart: Ernst Klett Verlag.

Herderschêe, D. (1956, third edition). *Achterlijke kinderen.* Groningen: Wolters.

Heymans, G. & Wiersma, E.D. (1906-1918). Beiträge zur speziellen Psychology auf Grund einer Massenutersuchung. *Zeitschrift fur Psychologie, Band 42, 43, 45, 46, 51, 62, 80.*

Hoejenbos, E. (1960). *De imbecil als patiënt.* In: Uitgave ter gelegenheid van de Conferentie Imbecillenonderwijs. Zeist: Christelijk Paedagogisch Studiecentrum.

Hoejenbos, E. (1963). Enkele facetten van de zwakzinnigheid. In: Hart de Ruyter, Th. (Ed.). *Capita Selecta uit de Kinder- en Jeugdpsychiatrie.* Zeist: De Haan.

Hoejenbos, E. (1967). *Psychotic Traits in Mental Deficiency.* Concilium Psychiatricum. Wiesbaden: Proceedings 3rd Europ. Congr. Pedopsychiatr.

Hoejenbos, E. & Kronenberg, J.W. (1967). Symposium on the autistiform profoundly retarded mentally subnormal child. Sensation and retraction. *J. of Mental Subnormality, XIII/2,* 53-57.

Hoekman, J. (1992). *Onderkenning van autisme. De ontwikkeling van de AUTI-R-schaal.* Amsterdam: proefschrift.

Hoekman, J. & Bergh, P.M. van den (1992). De trefzekerheid van de AUTI-R-schaal bij de onderkenning van autisme. *Ned. Ts. voor Opvoeding, Vorming en Onderwijs, 8,* 377-387.

Hoekman, J. (1993). Autisme en verstandelijke handicap: het gebruik van de AUTI-R-schaal bij differentiaaldiagnostiek. *Ts. Orthopedagogiek Kinderpsychiatrie 18,* 12-23.

Howlin, P. (1996). *Autism in adolescents and adults.* London: Routledge.

Hyman, S.L., Fisher, W., Mercugliano, M. & Cataldo, M.F. (1990). Children with Self-Injurious Behavior. *Pediatrics Supplement,* 437-441.

Jacobson, J.W. & Ackerman, L.J. (1990). Differences in Adaptive Functioning Among People With Autism or Mental Retardation. *J. of Autism and Developmental Disorders, 20,* 205-219.

Jol, K.W.Th. & Duker, P.C. (1984). Het gebruik van non-aversieve middelen bij de behandeling van ernstig probleemgedrag: vier gevalsstudies. *RUIT, 37,* 11-22.

Jordan, R. & Powell, S. (1995). *Understanding and teaching children with autism.* Chicester: Wiley and Sons.

Kanner, L. (1943). Autistic Disturbances of Affective Contact. Reprint in: *Acta Paedopsychiatrica, 35 (1968),* 98-136.

Kanner, L. (1971). Follow-up Study of Eleven Autistic Children Originally Reported in 1943. *J. of Autism and Childhood Schizophrenia, 1,* 119-145.

Kanner, L., Rodriguez, A. & Ashenden, B. (1972). How far can Autistic Children go in Matters of Social Adapation? *J. of Autism and Childhood Schizophrenia, 2,* 9-33.

Kerby, D.S. & Dawson, B.L. (1994). Autistic features, personality, and adaptive behavior in males with the Fragile X syndrome and no autism. *Am. J. on Mental Retardation, 98,* 455-462.

Klages, L. (1910). *Prinzipien der Charakterlogie.* Leipzig: Barth.

Klages, L. (1926). *Die Grundlagen der Charakterkunde.* Leipzig: Barth.

Klijn, W. (1978). Autisme bij laag funktionerende kinderen (theorie en behandeling). *Ts. voor Orthopedagogiek, 10,* 483-502.

Kobayashi, R., Murata, T. & Yoshinaga, K. (1992). A Follow-Up Study of 201 Children with Autism in Kyushu and Yamaguchi Areas, Japan. *J. of Autism and Developmental Disorders, 22,* 395-411.

Kobi, E.E. (1975). *Grundfragen der Heilpädagogik und der Heilerziehung.* Bern: Verlag Paul Haupt.

Kohnstamm, G.A. (1989). Temperamentsverschillen bij kinderen II. *Ts. voor Orthopedagogiek, 28,* 34-53.

Kok, J.F.W. (1987). Orthopedagogische theorie: vraagstelling als centrale categorie. In: Groot, R. de et al. (Eds.). *Handboek Orthopedagogiek.* Groningen: Wolters-Noordhoff.

Konstantareas, M. (1986). *Sign language.* Amsterdam: PAOS-Autisme, 30-31 oktober.

Kouwer, B.J. & Linschoten, J. (1951). *Inleiding tot de psychologie.* Assen: Born.

Kraijer, D.W. (1971). Bijkomende handicaps - speciale methoden. In: Hoejenbos, E. & Hoeing, J. (Eds.). *Leergang Opleiding Zwakzinnigenzorg. Tweede leerjaar.* Lochem: De Tijdstroom.

Kraijer, D.W. & Kema, G.N. (1972, 1994). *SRZ, Sociale Redzaamheidsschaal voor Zwakzinnigen. Handleiding.* Lisse: Swets & Zeitlinger.

Kraijer, D.W. & Kema, G.N. (1977, 1994). *SGZ, Storend Gedragsschaal voor Zwakzinnigen. Handleiding.* Lisse: Swets & Zeitlinger.

Kraijer, D.W. (1978). *Test- en schaalgebruik in de zwakzinnigenzorg.* Amsterdam/Lisse: Swets & Zeitlinger.

Kraijer, D.W. & Kema, G.N. (1981, 1994). *SMZ, Schaal voor Motoriek bij Zwakzinnigen. Handleiding.* Lisse: Swets & Zeitlinger.

Kraijer, D.W. (1981, second edition). Opvoeding/begeleiding en het gebruik van psychofarmaca. In: Kraijer, D.W. (Ed.). *Leerstof voor de Opleiding tot Z-verpleegkundige, derde leerjaar.* Lochem: De Tijdstroom.

Kraijer, D.W. (1983). Testen en inschalen in de zwakzinnigenzorg. Wat moet ik ermee? *RUIT, 36,* 21-32.

Kraijer, D.W. & Kema, G.N. (1984, 1994). *Sociale Redzaamheidsschaal voor Zwakzinnigen van hoger nivo, SRZ-P. Handleiding.* Lisse: Swets & Zeitlinger.

Kraijer, D.W. (1985). Volwassen zwakzinnigen van hoger niveau met gedragsstoornissen. Om welke mensen gaat het? *RUIT, 43,* 5-15.

Kraijer, D.W. (1986). Het gebruik van de ontwikkelingstest van Griffiths in de zwakzinnigenzorg. *RUIT, 47,* 14-22.

Kraijer, D.W. (1987a). Autisme en zwakzinnigheid. Een bijdrage tot de differentiaaldiagnostiek. *RUIT, 51,* 15-28.

Kraijer, D.W. (1987b). De Rorschach bij zwakzinnigen. *De Psycholoog, XXII,* 390-395.

Kraijer, D.W. (1988a). De pas verschenen DSM-III-revisie, naast verbeteringen ook nieuwe vragen. *RUIT, 54,* 25-30.

Kraijer, D.W. (1988b). Twintig jaar klinische observatie door de "Eekwal". Ontwikkelingen en knelpunten. In: Kraijer, D.W. (Ed). *Klinische en poliklinische hulpverlening in de zwakzinnigenzorg.* Assen: Hendrik van Boeijen-Oord.

Kraijer, D.W. (1988c). Autisme en aanverwante algemene ontwikkelingsstoornissen bij zwakzinnige kinderen. In: Kraijer, D.W. (Ed). *Klinische en poliklinische hulpverlening in de zwakzinnigenzorg.* Assen: Hendrik van Boeijen-Oord.

Kraijer, D.W. (1988d). Gebruik van psychofarmaca bij autisme en verwante contactstoornissen. *Engagement, 15,* 12-13/27.

Kraijer, D.W. & Nelck, G.F. (1989). Zwakzinnigheid, pervasieve ontwikkelingsstoornissen en aetiologie. *Ned. Ts. voor Zwakzinnigenzorg, 15,* 4, 171-192.

Kraijer, D.W. (1990). *AVZ, Autisme- en Verwante kontaktstoornissenschaal voor Zwakzinnigen. Handleiding.* Lisse: Swets & Zeitlinger.

Kraijer, D.W. (1991). *Zwakzinnigheid, autisme en aan autisme verwante contactstoornissen. Aspecten van classificatie, diagnostiek, prevalentie, specifieke problematiek, opvoeding en behandeling.* Amsterdam/Lisse: Swets & Zeitlinger.

Kraijer, D.W. (1992). *AVZ-R, Autisme- en Verwante stoornissenschaal voor Zwakzinnigen-revisie. Instruktiesupplement.* Lisse: Swets & Zeitlinger.

Kraijer, D.W. (1993). De populatie van het observatiehuis, spiegel van de zorg. In: *Dertig jaar klinische observatie en behandeling, 25 jaar Eekwal.* Assen: Hendrik van Boeijen-Oord.

Kraijer, D.W. (1994). *Zwakzinnigheid, autisme en aan autisme verwante stoornissen. Classificatie, diagnostiek, prevalentie, specifieke problematiek, opvoeding en behandeling.* Lisse: Swets & Zeitlinger.

Kraijer, D.W. (1995). Pervasieve ontwikkelingsstoornissen bij mensen met het syndroom van Down. *Ned. Ts voor de Zorg aan verstandelijk gehandicapten, 21,* 164-178.

Kraijer, D.W. & Meijer, H. (1995). *Gebruik van psychofarmaca bij inrichtingsbewoners.* Assen: St. Hendrik van Boeijen.

Kraijer, D.W. (1996). Risicofactoren voor het vertonen van automutilatie. *Ned. Ts. voor de Zorg aan verstandelijk gehandicapten, 22,* 248-263.

Kraijer, D.W. (1996a). Pervasieve ontwikkelingsstoornissen bij mannen met het fragiele-X syndroom. *Ts Orthopedagogiek, Kinderpsychiatrie en Klinische Kinderpsychologie, 21,* 73-81.

Kraijer, D.W., Meijer, H., Nelck, G.F. (1996). Autistische stoornissen, somatische zwakzinnigheidsoorzaken en epilepsie. *Ned. Ts. voor de Zorg aan verstandelijk gehandicapten, 22*, 91-105.

Kraijer, D.W. (1997). Pervasieve ontwikkelingsstoornissen bij niet-ambulante, zeer diep zwakzinnige mensen. *Ts. Orthopedagogiek, Kinderpsychiatrie en Klinische Kinderpsychologie, 22*, 48-61.

Kretschmer, E. (1921). *Körperbau und Charakter.* Berlin: Springer.

Krug, D., Arick, J.R. & Almond, P.J. (1980). *Autism screening instrument for educational planning.* Portland, Oregon: ASIEP Ed. Co.

Langeveld, M.J. (1955, fifth edition). *Beknopte theoretische Paedagogiek.* Groningen: Wolters.

Langeveld, M.J. (1969). *The Columbus. Picture Analysis of Growth Towards Maturity.* Basel: S. Karger.

Leslie, A.M. & Frith, U. (1990). Prospects for a Cognitive Neuro-psychology of Autism: Hobson's Choice. *Psychological Review, 97*, 122-131.

Lewis, M.H., Silva, J.R. & Silva, S.G. (1994). Cyclicity of agression and self-injurious behavior in individuals with mental retardation. *Am. J. on Mental Retardation, 99*, 436-444.

Lord, C., Rutter, M., Goode, S. et al. (1989). Autism Diagnostic Observation Schedule: A standardized Observation of Communicative and Social Behavior. *J. of Autism and Developmental Disorders, 19*, 185-212.

Lord, C., Storoschuk, S., Rutter, M. & Pickles, A. (1993). Using the ADI-R to diagnose autism in preschool children. *Infant Mental Health Journal, 14*, 234-252.

Lord, C., Rutter, M. & Couteur, A. Le (1994). Autism Diagnostic Interview-Revised: A revised version of a diagnostic interview for care givers of individuals with possible Pervasive Developmental Disorders. *J. of Autism and Developmental Disorders, 24*, 659-685.

Lotter, V. (1966-1967). Epidemiology of autistic conditions in young children. *Social Psychiatry, 1*, 124-137 en 163-173.

Lotter, V. (1974a). Social Adjustment and Placement of Autistic Children in Middlesex: A Follow-up Study. *J. of Autism and Childhood Schizophrenia, 4*, 11-32.

Lotter, V. (1974b). Factors related to Outcome in Autistic Children. *J. of Autism and Childhood Schizophrenia, 4*, 263-277.

Lotter, V. (1978). Follow-up Studies. In: Rutter, M. & Schopler, E. (Eds.) *Autism. A reappraisal of concepts and treatment.* New York/London: Plenum Press.

Lovaas, O.I. (1987). Behavioral Treatment and Normal Educational and Intellectual Functioning in Young Autistic Children. *J. of Consulting and Clinical Psychology, 55*, 3-9.

Lovaas, O.I., Koegel, R.L. & Schreibman, L. (1979). Stimulus over-selectivity in autism: a review of research. *Psychol. Bulletin, 86*, 1236-1254.

Loveland, K.A. & Kelley, M.L. (1988). Development of Adaptive Behavior in Adolescents and Young Adults With Autism and Down Syndrome. *Am. J. on Mental Retardation, 93*, 84-92.

Loveland, K.A. & Kelley, M.L. (1991). Development of Adaptive Behavior in Preschoolers with Autism or Down Syndrome. *Am. J. on Mental Retardation, 96,* 13-20.

Lowe, K., Paiva, S. de & Felce, D. (1993). Effects of a community-based service on adaptive and maladaptive behaviours: a longitudinal study. *J. of Intellectual Disability Research, 37,* 3-22.

LRZ (1995). *Jaarboek verstandelijk gehandicaptenzorg.* Utrecht: NVGz/NZi.

Luckasson, R., Coulter, D.L., Polloway, E.A. et al. (1992). *Mental Retardation: definition, classification and systems of supports.* Washington DC: AAMR.

Lund, J. (1988). Psychiatric aspects of Down's syndrome. *Acta Psychiatrica Scandinavica, 78,* 369-374.

Maes, B. (1993). *Het psychosociaal functioneren van volwassen mentaal gehandicapte mannen met het fragiele-X syndroom.* Dissertatie Katholieke Universiteit Leuven.

Maisto, C.R., Baumeister, A.A. & Maisto, A.A. (1978). An analysis of variables related to self-injurious behaviour among institutionalised retarded persons. *J. of Mental Deficiency Research, 22,* 27-36.

McGee, J.J., Menolascino, F.J., Hobbs, D.C. & Menousek, P.E. (1987). *Gentle teaching.* New York: Human Sciences Press, Inc.

McIntire, M.S., Menolascino, F.J. & Wiley, J.H. (1965). Mongolism, some clinical aspects. *Am. J. of Mental Definciency, 69,* 794-800.

Menolascino, F.J. & McCann, B.M. (1983). *Mental health and mental retardation: Bridging the gap.* Baltimore: University Park Press.

Menolascino, F.J. (1990). Mental illness in the mentally retarded: diagnostic and treatment considerations. In: Dosen, A., Gennep, A. van & Zwanikken, G.J. (Eds.). *Treatment of mental illness and behavioral disorder in the mentally retarded.* Leiden: Logon Publications.

Mesibov, G.B., Schopler, E., Schaffer, B. & Landrus, R. (1988). *Individualized assessment and treatment for autistic and developmentally disordered children. Vol. 4. Adolescent and Adult Psychoeducational Profile (AAPEP).* Austin, Texas: Pro-Ed.

Mesibov, G.B. (1990). Normalization and its relevance today. *J. of Autism and Developmental Disorder, 20,* 379-390.

Minderaa, R.B. (1989). Het stellen van de diagnose bij kinderen met autisme en verwante contactstoornissen. *Ned. Ts. Geneeskunde, 133,* 222-225.

Minderaa, R.B. & Uleman-Vleeschdrager, M. (1989). Diagnostiek en afgrenzing van pervasieve ontwikkelingsstoornissen. In: Boer, J.E. de, Minderaa, R.B., Verheij, F. & Wielink P.S. van (Eds.). *Aan autisme verwante contactstoornissen.* Dr Paul Janssen Stichting.

Minderaa, R.B. (1990). Kinderen met autisme en aan autisme verwante contact- en communicatiestoornissen. In: Gemert, G.H. van, Minderaa, R.B. & Peet, R.A.M. van der (Red.). *Consultatie bij geestelijk gehandicapten met een ernstige gedragsstoornis.* Groningen: St. Kinderstudies.

Moor, P. (1951, 1958). *Heilpedagogische Psychologie, Band 1. und 2.* Bern: Hans Huber.

Morgan, S. (1988). Diagnostic Assessment of Autism: A Review of Objective Scales. *J. of Psychoeducational Assessment, 6,* 139-151.

Mulder, S., Ronde, W. & Schaddenhorst, M. (1979). *Kontaktstoornissen bij zwakzinnigen, een vervolgonderzoek.* Groningen: skriptie Rijksuniversiteit.

Munro, J.A. (1968). Early abilities and their later development. *Advancement of Science, 24,* 464-468.

Murray, H.A. (1943). *Thematic Apperception Test.* Cambridge (Massachusetts): Harvard University Press.

Newson, E. (1986). *The treatment of autistic children.* Amsterdam: PAOS-Autisme, 30-31 oktober.

Oliver, C., Murphy, G.H. & Corbett, J.A. (1987). Self-injurious behavior in people with mental handicap: a total population study. *J. of Mental Deficiency Research, 31,* 147-162.

Olsson, I., Steffenburg, S. & Gillberg, C. (1988). Epilepsy in autism and autisticlike conditions. *Arch. Neurol., 45,* 666-668.

Oswald, D.P. & Volkmar, F.R. (1991). Brief Report: Signal Detection Analysis of Items from the Autism Behavior Checklist. *J. of Autism and Developmental Disorders, 21,* 543-549.

Payton, J.B., Steele, M.W., Wenger, S.L. & Minshew, N.J. (1989). The fragile X marker and autism in perspective. *J. of the Am. Academy of Child and Adolescent psychiatry, 28,* 417-421.

Pueschel, S.M., Rothman, K.J. & Ogilby, J.D. (1976). Birth weights of children with Down's syndrome. *Am. J. of Mental Deficiency, 80,* 442-445.

Quine, L. (1991). Sleep problems in children with mental handicap. *J. of Mental Deficiency Research, 35,* 269-290.

Repp, A.C., Singh, N.N., Olinger, E. & Olson, D.R. (1990). The use of functional analyses to test causes of self-injurious behavior: rationale, current status and future directions. *J. of Mental Deficiency Research, 34,* 95-105.

Repp, A.C., Karsh, K.G., Deitz, D.E.D. & Singh, N.N. (1992). A study of the homeostatic level of stereotypy and other motor movements of persons with mental handicaps. *J. of Intellectual Disability Research, 36,* 61-75.

Rescorla, L. (1988). Cluster Analytic Identification of Autistic Preschoolers. *J. of Autism and Developmental Disorder, 18,* 475-492.

Reynolds, W. & Reynolds, S. (1979). Prevalence of speech and hearing impairment of noninstitutionalized mentally retarded adults. *Am. J. of Mental Deficiency, 84,* 62-68.

Rimland, B. (1964). *Infantile autism. The syndrome and its implications for a neural theory of behavior.* Englewood Cliffs, N.J.: Prentice-Hall.

Rispens, J. (1988). Diagnostische modellen en het opzetten van een behandelingsplan. In: Gemert, G.H. van & Noorda, W.K. (Eds.) *Leerboek Zwakzinnigenzorg.* Assen: Van Gorcum.

Rispens, J. (1989). Over het problematische van het begrip Problematische Opvoedings Situatie. *Ts. voor Orthopedagogiek, XXVIII,* 411-427.

Robinson, N.M. & Robinson, H.B. (1976). *The mentally retarded child. Second Edition.* New York: McGraw-Hill.

Rodrigue, J.R., Morgan, S.B. & Geffken, G.R. (1991). A Comparative Evaluation of Adaptive Behavior in Children and Adolescents with Autism, Down Syndrome and Normal Development. *J. of Autism and Developmental Disorders, 21*, 187-196.

Rojahn, J. (1986). Self-injurious and stereotypic behavior of non-institutionalized mentally retarded people: prevalence and classification. *Am. J. of Mental Deficiency, 91*, 268-276.

Roosendaal, J.J. & Grunsven, M.F. van (1985). Rumineren en zijn gevolgen. *RUIT, 43*, 21-25.

Roosendaal, J.J. & Bijleveld, Ch.M.A. (1994). Toepassing vierentwintiguurs pH-meting bij verstandelijk gehandicapten. *Ned. Ts. Zorg aan verstandelijk gehandicapten, 4*, 239-248.

Rorschach, H. (1926, 1954, seventh printing). *Psychodiagnostik. Methodik und Ergebnisse eines Wahrnehmungsdiagnostischen Experiments.* Bern: Huber.

Rossi, G. (1977). Autismo precoce e mongoloidismo. *Rivista Sper. Freniat., 101*, 430-442.

Rumsey, J.M., Rapaport, J.L. & Sceery, W.R. (1985). Autistic Children as Adults: Psychiatric, Social and Behavioural Outcomes. *J. of the Am. Ac. of Child Psychiatry, 24*, 465-473.

Ruttenberg, B.A., Kalish, B.I., Wener, Ch. et al. (1977). *BRIAAC, Behavior Rating instrument for Autistic and other Atypical Children.* Lisse: Swets & Zeitlinger.

Rutter, M. & Lockyer, L. (1967). A Five to Fifteen Year Follow-up Study of Infantile Psychosis. I. Description of Sample. *Brit. J. Psychiatr., 113*, 1169-1182.

Rutter, M. (1978). Diagnosis and definition of childhood autism. *J. of Autism and Childhood Schizophrenia, 8*, 139-161.

Rutter, M. (1985). The treatment of autistic children. *J. Child Psychol. Psychiatr., 26*, 193-214.

Rutter, M. & Schopler, E. (1987). Autism and Pervasive Developmental Disorders: Concepts and Diagnostic Issues. *J. of Autism and Developmental Disorder, 17*, 159-186.

Rutter, M. (1989). Child psychiatric Disorders in ICD-10. *J. Child Psychol. Psychiatr., 30*, 499-513.

Rutter, M., Macdonald, H., Couteur, A. le et al. (1990). Genetic factors in child psychiatric disorders-II. Empirical findings. *J. Child Psychol. Psychiatr., 31*, 39-83.

Rutter, M. & Schopler, E. (1992). Classification of Pervasive Developmental Disorders: Some Concepts and Practical Considerations. *J. of Autism and Developmental Disorders, 22*, 459-482.

Sandberg, A.D., Nydèn, A., Gillberg, C. & Hjelmquist, E. (1993). The cognitive profile in infantile autism. A study of 70 children and adolescents using the Griffiths Mental Development Scale. *Brit. J. of Psychology, 84*, 365-373.

Sarason, S.B. (1953, second edition). *Psychological Problems in Mental Deficiency.* New York: Harper & Brothers.

Schoonbeek, H.R. & Boer, J.E. de (1989). Poliklinisch psychologisch onderzoek van kinderen met een aan autisme verwante contactstoornis. In: Boer, J.E. de, Minderaa, R.B., Verheij, F. et al. (Eds.). *Aan autisme verwante contactstoornissen.* Dr Paul Janssen Stichting.

Schopler, E. & Reichler, R.J. (1976). *Psychopathology and Child Development. Research and Treatment.* New York: Plenum Press.

Schopler, E. & Reichler, R.J. (1979). *Individualized Assessment and Treatment for Autistic and Developmentally Disabled Children. Volume I Psychoeducational Profile.* Baltimore: University Park Press.

Schopler, E., Andrews, C.E. & Strupp, K. (1979b). Do Autistic Children come from Upper-Middle-Class Parents? *J. of Autism and Developmental Disorder,* 9, 139-152.

Schopler, E., Reichler, R.J., Vellis, R.F. de & Daly, K. (1980). Toward objective classification of childhood autism: Childhood Autism Rating Scale (CARS). *J. of Autism and Developmental Disorders,* 10, 91-103.

Schopler, E. & Mesibov, G.B. (1983). *Autism in Adolescents and Adults.* New York: Plenum Press.

Schopler, E., Reichler, R.J. & Renner, B.R. (1986). *The Childhood Autism Rating Scale (CARS) for diagnostic screening and classification of autism.* New York: Irvington Publishers INC.

Schopler, E., Reichler, R.J., Bashford, A. et al. (1990). *Individualized assessment for autistic and developmentally disabled children. Volume I Psychoeducational Profile Revised (PEP-R).* Austin, Texas: Pro-Ed.

Schopler, E. & Hennike, J.M. (1990). Past and present trends in residential treatment. *J. of Autism and Developmental Disorder,* 20, 291-298.

Schopler, E. & Mesibov, G.B. (Eds.) (1995). *Learning and cognition in autism.* New York: Plenum.

Schroeder, S.R., Schroeder, C.S., Smith, B. & Dalldorf, J. (1978). Prevalence of Self-injurious behaviors in a large state facility for the retarded: a three year follow-up study. *J. of Autism and Childhood Schizophrenia,* 8, 261-269.

Schuring, G., Barnhard, I., Kardaun, H. et al. (1990). *Ernstig probleemgedrag. Een inventarisatie van probleemsituaties rond bewoners in de intramurale zwakzinnigenzorg.* Utrecht: NZI/NZR.

Scriver, C.R., Beaudet, A.L., Sly, W.S. & Valle, D. (Eds.) (1989). *Metabolic basis of inherited disease.* New York: McGraw Hill.

Sevin, J.A., Matson, J.L., Coe, D.A. et al. (1991). A Comparison and Evaluation of Three Commonly Used Autism Scales. *J. of Autism and Developmental Disorders,* 21, 417-432.

Sherman, B.R. (1988). Predictors of the decision to place developmentally disabled family members in residential care. *Am. J. on Mental Retardation,* 92, 344-351.

Siegel, B., Anders, Th.F., Ciaranello, R.D. et al. (1986). Empirically Derived Subclassification of the Autistic Syndrome. *J. of Autism and Developmental Disorder,* 16, 275-293.

Siegel, B. (1991). Toward DSM-IV: A Developmental Approach to Autistic Disorder. In: Konstantareas, M.M. & Beitchman, J.H. (Eds.). Pervasive Developmental Disorders. *Psychiatric Clinics of North America, 14.*

Siegel, B. (1996). *The world of the autistic child. Understanding and treating autistic spectrum disorders.* Oxford: Oxford Press.

Siegel, S. & Castellan, N.J. (1988). *Nonparametric Statistics for the Behavioral Sciences.* New York: McGraw-Hill.

Snijders, J.Th. & Snijders-Oomen, N. (1975). *Snijders-Oomen niet-verbale intelligentieschaal. SON 2½-7.* Groningen: Wolters-Tjeenk Willink.

Snijders-Oomen, A.W.M. (1989). Autisme 1989. *Ned. Ts. voor Zwakzinnigenzorg, 15,* 28-39.

Sparrow, S.S., Balla, D. & Cicchetti, D. (1984). *The Vineland Adaptive Behavior Scales: Interview edition, Survey Form.* Circle Pines, M.N.: American Guidance Service.

Spelberg, H.C. lutje (1987). *Grenzentesten.* Groningen: Stichting Kinderstudies.

Steffenburg, S. & Gillberg, C. (1986). Autism and autistic-like conditions in Swedish rural and urban areas: a population study. *Brit. J. of Psychiatry, 149,* 81-87.

Strauss, A.A. & Lehtinen, L.E. (1960, ninth edition). *Psychopathology and education of the brain-injured child.* New York: Grune & Stratton.

Strelau, J. (1984). The understanding of temperament and personality. In: Bonarius, H., Heck, G. van & Smid, N. (Eds.). *Personality psychology in Europe.* Lisse: Swets & Zeitlinger.

Sturmey, P., Matson, J.L. & Sevin, J.A. (1992). Brief Report: Analysis of the Internal Consistency of Three Autism Scales. *J. of Autism and Developmental Disorders, 22,* 321-328.

Sturmey, P. & Sevin, J.A. (1993). Dual diagnosis: an annotated bibliography of recent research. *J. of Intellectual Disability Research, 37,* 437-448.

Swaak, A.J. (1977). Een oriënterend onderzoek naar het slaapgedrag van zwakzinnige kinderen van 4-6 jaar. *Ts. voor Zwakzinnigheid en Zwakzinnigenzorg,* 199-214.

Szatmari, P., Bartolucci, G., Bremner, R. et al. (1989). A follow-up Study of High-Functioning Autistic Children. *J. of Autism and Developmental Disorder, 19,* 213-225.

Teal, M.B. & Wiebe, M.J. (1986). A Validity Analysis of Selected Instruments Used to Assess Autism. *J. of Autism and Developmental Disorders, 16,* 485-494.

Thomas, A. & Chess, S. (1977). *Temperament and Development.* New York: Brunner/Mazel.

Tredgold, A.F. (1952, eighth edition). *A Text-Book of Mental Deficiency.* London: Baillière, Tindall and Cox.

Tsai, L.Y. & Beisler, J.M. (1983). The development of sex differences in infantile autism. *Brit. J. Psychiatry, 142,* 373-378.

Van Berckelaer-Onnes, I.A., Harinck, F.J.H. & Smit, M. (1981). *AUTI-schaal. Handleiding en verantwoording.* Lisse: Swets & Zeitlinger.

Van Berckelaer-Onnes, I.A. & Snijders-Oomen, A.W.M. (1982). *Autisme in ontwikkeling*. Lisse: Swets & Zeitlinger.

Van Berckelaer-Onnes, I.A. (1983; Dutch version 1979). *Early childhood autism: a child-rearing problem*. Lisse: Swets & Zeitlinger.

Van Berckelaer-Onnes, I.A. & Kwakkel-Scheffer, J.J.C. (1988). *Autisme en thuisbehandeling: hometraining in gezinnen met een autistisch kind*. Meppel: Boom.

Van Berckelaer-Onnes, I.A. & Hoekman, J. (1991). *AUTI-R-schaal. Handleiding en verantwoording*. Lisse: Swets & Zeitlinger.

Van Berckelaer-Onnes, I.A. & Duijn, G. van (1993). A Comparison Between the Handicaps Behaviour and Skills Schedule and the Psychoeducational Profile. *J. of Autism and Developmental Disorders, 23,* 263-272.

Van Bourgondien, M.E. & Elgar, S. (1990). The relationship between existing residential services and the needs of autistic adults. *J. of Autism and Developmental Disorder, 20,* 299-308.

Van Bourgondien, M.E. & Schopler, E. (1990). Critical issues in the residential care of people with autisme. *J. of Autism and Developmental Disorder, 20,* 391-399.

Van Essen, Ch. & Romein, Th. (1985). Geneesmiddelen in de zwakzinnigenzorg. *Medisch Contact, 1,* 17-20.

Van Gennep, A.Th.G. (1989). *De kwaliteit van het bestaan van de zwaksten in de samenleving*. Meppel: Boom.

Van Gennep, A.Th.G. (1992). Integratie van personen met een verstandelijke handicap. *Pedagogisch Tijdschrift, 17,* 17-25.

Van Grunsven, M.F. (1977). *Tandheelkundige zorg voor dieper-zwakzinnigen. Tandheelkundige monografieën XXI*. Leiden: Stafleu-Tholen.

Van Krevelen, D.A. (1959). Autismus Infantum. *Ned. Ts. voor Geneeskunde, 103,* 2194-2198.

Van Krevelen, D.A. (1963). On the relationship between Early Infantile Autism and Autistic Psychopathy. *Acta Paedopsychiatrica, 30,* 303-323.

Van Krevelen, D.A. (1972). Problems of differential diagnosis between mental retardation and autismus infantum. *Acta Paedopsychiatrica, 39,* 199-203.

Van Osch, G.J.M. (1968). *Mogelijkheden en beperkingen van de Griffiths als diagnosticum bij zwakzinnigen*. Doctoraal scriptie Katholieke Universiteit, Nijmegen.

Van Osch, G.J.M. (1981). Dwangverschijnselen bij zwakzinnigen: een bezinning op theorie en behandeling. *Gedragstherapeutisch Bulletin, 14,* 13-18.

Van Soest, M.H.G. (1989). *Autisme als gevolg van een dysfunctionele zintuigenhiërarchie*. Leuven: Acco.

Vandenbussche, I. (1990). Kinderen met een pervasieve ontwikkelingsstoornis en hun invloed op ouders en opvoeders. *Ts. Orthoped. Kinderpsych., 15,* 140-150.

Vela, M.D., Gottlieb, E.H. & Gottlieb, H.P. (1983). Borderline Syndromes in Childhood. A critical review. In: Robson, K.S. (Ed.). *Borderline Child*. New York: McGraw-Hill.

Velthausz, F.J.M. (1987). *Sociaal gedrag, sociale interaktie en kommunikatie bij diepzwakzinnigen*. Dissertatie Rijksuniversiteit Utrecht.

Verbraak, P. (1979). Planning in de zwakzinnigenzorg I. Het aantal geestelijk gehandicapten in Nederland. *Ts. Soc. Geneesk., 57*, 801-806.

Verhoeven, W.M.A. (Ed.), (1992). *Diagnostiek en behandeling van automutilatie bij mentaal geretardeerden*. Venray: Vincent van Gogh Instituut.

Volkmar, F.R., Sparrow, S.S., Goudreau, D. et al. (1987). Social deficits in autism: An operational using the Vineland Adaptive Behavior Scales. *J. of Am. Ac. of Child and Adolescence Psychiatry, 26*, 156-161.

Volkmar, F.R., Cicchetti, D.V., Dykens, E. et al. (1988). An Evaluation of the Autism Behavior Checklist. *J. of Autism and Developmental Disorder, 18*, 81-97.

Volkmar, F.R., Bregman, J., Cohen, D.J. & Cicchetti, D.V. (1988). DSM-III and DSM-III-R Diagnoses of Autism. *Am. J. Psychiatry, 145*, 1404-1408.

Volkmar, F.R. (1989). Childhood Schizophrenia. S. Cantor. *J. of Autism and Developmental Disorders, 19*, 355-357.

Volkmar, F.R. & Nelson, D.S. (1990). Seizure disorders in autism. *J. Am. Acad. Child Adolesc. Psychiatry, 29*, 127-129.

Volkmar, F.R. & Cohen, D.J. (1991). Debate and Argument: The Utility of the Term Pervasive Developmental Disorder. *J. Child Psychol. Psychiatr., 32*, 1171-1172.

Volkmar, F.R. (1992). Childhood Disintegrative Disorder: Issues for DSM-IV. *J. of Autism and Developmental Disorders, 22*, 625-642.

Volkmar, F.R., Carter, A., Sparrow, S.S. & Chicchetti, D.V. (1993). Quantifying social development in autism. *J. Am. Acad. Child Adolesc. Psychiatry, 32*, 627-632.

Wadden, N.P.K., Bryson, S.E. & Rodger, R.S. (1991). A Closer Look at the Autism Behavior Checklist: Discriminant Validity and Factor Structure. *J. of Autism and Developmental Disorders, 21*, 529-541.

Wakabayashi, S. (1979). A case of infantile autism with Down's syndrome. *J. of Autism and Developmental Disorders, 9*, 31-36.

Wassing, H.E. & Krevelen, D.A. van (1968). Zur Frage der Intelligence zeichen begabter autistische Kinder. *Acta Paedopsychiatrica, 35*, 215-227.

Watkins, J.M., Asarnow, R.F. & Tanguay, P.E. (1988). Symptom Development in childhood onset schizophrenia. *J. Child Psychol. Psychiatr., 29*, 865-878.

Wiegersma, P.H., Velde, A. van der & Koops, W. (1978). *Een onderzoek naar de mogelijkheden van de BRIAAC als screeningsinstrument voor geestelijk geretardeerden*. Groningen: Instituut Persoonlijkheids- en Ontwikkelingspsychologie, Rijksuniversiteit.

Wing, J.K. (1966). *Early Childhood Autism*. Oxford: Pergamon Press.

Wing, L. (1976, second edition). *Early childhood autism. Clinical, educational and social aspects*. London: Pergamom Press.

Wing, L. (1977). Vroeg-kinderlijk autisme: definiëring en theorieën betreffende de aetiologie. *Ts. voor Psychiatrie, 19*, 516-533.

Wing, L. & Gould, J. (1978). Systematic Recording of Behaviours and Skills of Retarded and Psychotic Children. *J. of Autism and Childhood Schizophrenia, 8,* 79-97.

Wing, L. & Gould, J. (1979). Severe Impairments of social Interactions and Associated Abnormalities in Children: Epidemiology and Classification. *J. of Autism and Developmental Disorder, 9,* 11-29.

Wing, L. (1981a). Language, Social, and Cognitive Impairments in Autism and Severe Mental Retardation. *J. of Autism and Developmental Disorder, 11,* 31-44.

Wing, L. (1981b). Sex ratios in early childhood autism and related conditions. *Psychiatry Research, 5,* 129-137.

Wing, L. & Attwood, A. (1987). Syndromes of Autism and Atypical Development. In: Cohen, D.J. & Donnellan, A.M. (Eds.). *Handbook of Autism and Pervasive Developmental Disorders.* New York: Wiley & Sons.

World Health Organization (1980). ICIDH. *International Classification of Impairments, Disabilities and Handicaps.* Geneva: WHO.

World Health Organization (1992). *The ICD-10 Classification of Mental and Behavioural Disorders. Clinical descriptions and diagnostic guidelines.* Geneva: WHO.

INDEX

DR. DIRK W. KRAIJER graduated in clinical and developmental psychology, and subsequently in educational psychology, at the University of Utrecht, the Netherlands. He has worked at the Hendrik Van Boeijen Foundation, Assen, the Netherlands, since 1964. Until 1968 he served as general psychologist at this newly established institution, which has the capacity for 730 residents. From 1968 until 1993 he headed a team of experts in a subdepartment of this institution, The Eekwal Observation Home. In this clinical setting mentally retarded persons (children, adolescents and adults) with additional mental and behavioural problems are diagnosed and treated. Dirk also served for some time as lecturer in the Departments of Educational Psychology and Child and Adolescent Psychiatry at the University of Groningen, the Netherlands. Since 1993 he has been involved in research under the auspices of the Hendrik Van Boeijen Foundation.

Over the years he has written studies on various subjects in the mental retardation field. Together with the psychologist Gerard Kema he developed four scales for the assessment of adaptive behaviour, much in use nowadays in the Netherlands and Dutch-speaking regions of Belgium. From 1986 onwards his main focus of interest was the prevalence of autism and related disorders in mentally retarded persons. This resulted in the Scale of Pervasive Developmental Disorder in Mentally Retarded Persons (PDD-MRS) and in the present study which also presents detailed information about the scale.

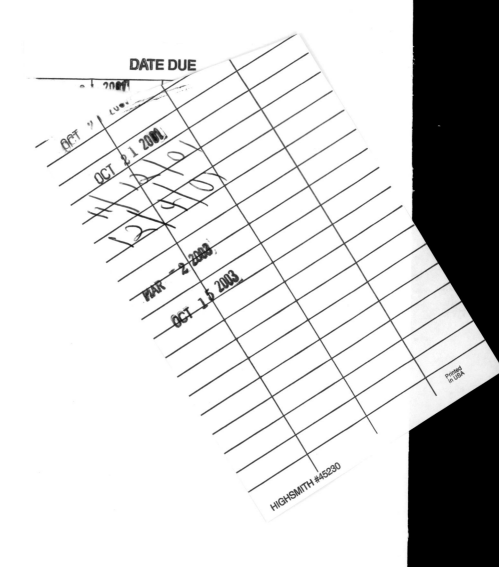

DATE DUE

OCT 2 1 2001

OCT 2 1 2001

MAR 2 2003

OCT 1 5 2003